MANAGEMENT AND ORGANISATIONAL BEHAVIOUR

(TEXT & CASES)

P. SUBBA RAO
Currently: Professor of Business Administration
School of Business Administration
University of Papua New Guinea
Papua New Guinea (Australia)
and
Formerly: Professor & Dean (On-leave)
Faculty of Commerce and Management
SK Institute of Management
Sri Krishnadevaraya University
Anantapur-515 003 (AP), India
E-mail: pulapas@rediffmail.com

Assisted By

VENKATRAM TEJ KUMAR
MS (USA)

ISO 9001:2015 CERTIFIED

First Edition : 2004
Reprint : 2005 to 2008
Second Edition : 2012
Reprint : 2017, 2019, 2021
Reprint : 2023

Published by : Mrs. Meena Pandey for **Himalaya Publishing House Pvt. Ltd.,**
"Ramdoot", Dr. Bhalerao Marg, Girgaon, Mumbai - 400 004.
Phone: 022-23860170/23863863, Fax: 022-23877178
E-mail: himpub@bharatmail.co.in; **Website:** www.himpub.com

Branch Offices :

New Delhi : "Pooja Apartments", 4-B, Murari Lal Street, Ansari Road, Darya Ganj, New Delhi - 110 002.
Phone: 011-23270392, 23278631; Fax: 011-23256286

Nagpur : Kundanlal Chandak Industrial Estate, Ghat Road, Nagpur - 440 018.
Phone: 0712-2738731, 2721216

Bengaluru : Plot No. 91-33, 2nd Main Road Seshadripuram, Behind Nataraja Theatre,
Bengaluru - 560 020. Phone: 080-41138821, Mobile: 09379847017, 09379847005.

Hyderabad : No. 3-4-184, Lingampally, Besides Raghavendra Swamy Matham, Kachiguda,
Hyderabad - 500 027. Phone: 040-27560041, 27550139

Chennai : No. 34/44, Motilal Street, T. Nagar, Chennai - 600 017. Mobile: 09380460419

Pune : First Floor, "Laksha" Apartment, No. 527, Mehunpura, Shaniwarpeth
(Near Prabhat Theatre), Pune - 411 030. Phone: 020-24496323/24496333; Mobile: 09370579333

Cuttack : Plot No 5F-755/4, Sector-9, CDA Market Nagar, Cuttack - 753 014,
Odisha. Mobile: 09338746007

Kolkata : 3, S.M. Bose Road, Near Gate No. 5, Agarpara Railway Station, North 24 Parganas,
West Bengal - 700109. Mobile: 09674536325

Printed at : **Mudrashilpa Offset Printers, Nagpur. On behalf of HPH.**

PREFACE

Intensified competition among domestic private and public sector companies and multinational companies consequent upon globalisation, economic boom and recessionary conditions along with the changed demographic factors like increase in women employees, aging populations, shortage of talented employees and adapted mindset and attitude of the people brought paradigm shifts in organisational and competitive strategies. Different competitive strategies need distinctive management practices and behaviours of employees. In fact, effective strategy implementation depends on the appropriate management concept and employee bahaviour. Thus appropriate management concept and employee behaviour assume greater significance after globalisation and consequent economic boom and recession. Now, most of the organisations recognized the emerging vitality of appropriate management concept and employee behaviour based on organisational strategies and placed organisational behavioural issues at strategic level in the organisational hierarchy.

The overwhelming response from the students, Lecturers, Professors and heads of various Business Schools and Human Resource Management Departments/Divisions of various universities in India, Papua New Guinea and other countries to the first and second editions of my book on *"Management and Organisational Behaviour"*, inspired me and my publishers to bring the revised edition.

This book is endowed with latest information, developments and data on various management concepts, job design and alternate work arrangements, strategic organisational behaviour, counseling, mentoring and empowerment and decision-making in multiple modes like updated text, boxes, figures, tables, exhibits and cases.

Many students particularly from SKIM, SK University, Anantapur, India, Executive MBA students and HRM students of the School of Business Administration, UPNG, Papua New Guinea and students from other universities across the developing countries provided online feedback as well as persuaded me to bring this edition. I, immensely thank them for their support and encouragement. I am grateful to the teachers who provided to me the comments for upgrading the book. Particularly, I would like to express my gratitude to Prof. Albert C. Mellam, Executive Dean, School of Business Administration and Mr. P. Manohar, Head, Business Management Division, School of Business Administration, University of Papua New Guinea, Papua New Guinea and Prof. M. Gangadhara Rao, my teacher and the Vice-Chancellor, GITAM University.

Mr. Niraj Pandey, Mrs. Ujjwala Pandey, Mr. Anuj Pandey, Mr. Vijay Pandey, and Mrs. Nimisha of Himalaya Publishing House have provided immense support in bringing this revised edition. I thank all of them immensely.

My wife Mrs. Pulapa Rama Devi, was put in inconvenience during the period of writing this book. I express my gratitude to her.

I request the students, teachers and other readers to write to me with their comments and suggestions via e-mail.

Port Moresby, Papua New Guinea
12th April, 2011

Pulapa Subba Rao
pulapas@rediffmail.com

CONTENTS

Part - A: Principles of Management

Part - B: Organisational Behaviour

DETAILED CONTENTS

Part - A: Principles of Management

Part - B: Organisational Behaviour

PART - A

PRINCIPLES OF MANAGEMENT

CHAPTER **1**

NATURE AND FUNCTIONS OF MANAGEMENT

☛ Chapter outline

(A) Introduction
(B) Definition of Management
(C) Management: A Science or an Art?
(D) Management: A Profession?
(E) Management vs. Administration
(F) Management Functions
(G) Managerial Skills
(H) Managerial Roles
(I) Management Levels
(J) Functional Areas of Management
(K) Universality of Management Principles
(L) International Management
- Key Terms
- Questions
- References

☛ Learning Objectives

After studying this Chapter, you should be able to:

- ✓ Analyse the causes for similarities and dissimilarities among individuals;
- ✓ Discuss various models of man like economic man, social man organisational man, self-actualisation man and complex man;
- ✓ Understand the need for study of organisational behaviour;
- ✓ Know the meaning and features of organisational behaviour;
- ✓ Know the factors responsible for increase in diversity of human resources;
- ✓ Analyse the contributions of various disciplines to organisational behaviour; and
- ✓ Understand the model of organisational behaviour.

(A) INTRODUCTION

Some companies like Reliance Industries, Procter and Gamble, Hindustan Lever, ITC, Dr.Reddy's Labs, HDFC Bank, Tata Iron and Steel Company (TISCO) Limited etc. are most successful and on the other side some companies like Kolleru Paper Mills Ltd., Agrifural Chemicals Ltd., Binny Mills and Panyam Cements belong to the unsuccessful category. Similarly, we find some outperforming companies like Infosys Technologies and WIPRO. While other companies like Nava Bharat Ferro Alloys Ltd., Hindustan Machine Tools (HMT) Ltd. and Hindustan Cables Limited are low on the performance graph. Some companies like Tata, the Birla Group and Gujarat Gas Company expand and diversify their activities whereas the activities of other companies shrink day by day, subsequently recording low performance rates.

Companies of the same industry are being affected by the same environmental factors. Some companies attract a number of customers while some other companies repel them. Employees prefer to be identified with some companies while they prefer to be unemployed in case of some other companies. Why do companies perform differently when they operate under the same environmental conditions, serve the same customer, use the same raw material and technology and employ the people with similar skills? The answer for this question, invariably, is management practices. Thus 'Management' makes remarkable difference between the companies regarding their performance in terms of productivity, products, sales, profitability, service to the customer, employee welfare etc. Management plays a vital role in deciding the destiny of business as well as non-business organisations.

This background urges us to know what management is? Now, we shall discuss the meaning of the term 'management.'

(B) DEFINITION OF MANAGEMENT

Management: Art of getting things done through others

Mary Parker defines the term management as *"the art of getting things done through others."*[1] But research studies concluded that management is a field of endeavour that combines art and science.[2]

Ivancerich, Donnelly and Gibson, define the term management as "*the process undertaken by one or more persons to coordinate the activities of other persons to achieve results not attainable by any one person acting alone.*"[3] Managers perform a number of activities, in addition to coordination. Further, this definition covers only one resource *i.e.,* human resources and does not focus on material resources and financial resources.

John A.Pearce and Richard B.Robinson included all kinds of resources in their definition on management. According to them, "*Management is the process of optimizing human, material and financial contributions for the achievement of organizational goals.*"[4] This definition ignores the integrated aspect of the contribution of all resources towards the attainment of organizational goals.

According to Harold Koontz and Heinz and Weihrich, Management is "*the process of designing and maintaining an environment in which individuals, working together in groups, efficiently accomplish selected aims.*"[5] This definition ignores the external environment through which most of the stakeholders interact with the company.

Now, we shall define the term management as designing, providing and maintaining a conducive internal environment in tune with the opportunities and challenges of the external environment through planning, organizing, directing and controlling all resources and operations in order to achieve effective organizational strategies efficiently.

The analysis of the above definitions provide the following aspects of management:

- The purpose of management is to formulate effective (right) organizational strategies and to achieve them efficiently (productively) based on the mission's objectives and goals.
- Management deals with both internal and external environment.
- Management is concerned with all kinds of resources viz., human, financial, material, machines, technology and technical know-how.
- Management functions include: planning, organizing, directing and controlling.
- Managers should possess varied skills in order to play a variety of roles.
- It applies to managers at all levels in an organisation.
- Management is applicable to all kinds of organisations i.e., both profit and non-profit oriented organisations.
- Management vs. Administration.
- Management is both an art and a science in order to create a surplus.
- Management needs to be a profession to achieve goals continuously with an incremental efficiency.

Now we shall discuss each of these aspects of management.

Purpose of Management: To Achieve MOST

Managers basically formulate Mission, Objectives, Strategies and Tactics (MOST). Management is essential to achieve the MOST. The organisational mission is the basic reason for its existence. Mission provides a statement of what the company stands for, i.e. its purpose for existence. For example, the mission statement of a commercial bank is: "A vibrant bank committed to excellence in performance through customer satisfaction."

Managers formulate objectives based on this mission. Objectives are the ends towards which the activity is aimed. This goal is precise and is expressed in clear and specific terms. For example, the objective of a company is to earn profits whereas the goal is to earn certain percentage of profit on capital employed.

Managers formulate objectives based on mission

Management formulates strategies in order to achieve the goals. Strategy is a unified, comprehensive and integrated plan that relates the strategic advantages of the firm with the opportunities of the environment. For example, entering the car financing business in order to enhance the sales is a strategy to achieve the goal of earning profit on capital employed. Tactics is an action programme through which strategies are executed. Thus the purpose of management is to achieve the company's mission, objectives and strategies.

Management Deals with Internal and External Environment

Management while formulating strategies, studies and analyses both internal and external environment. Internal environment consists of organisational structure, finances, marketing, production and human resources. External environment consists of STEPIN *viz.*, Social and Cultural, Technical, Economic, Political, International and Natural (see Fig.1.1).

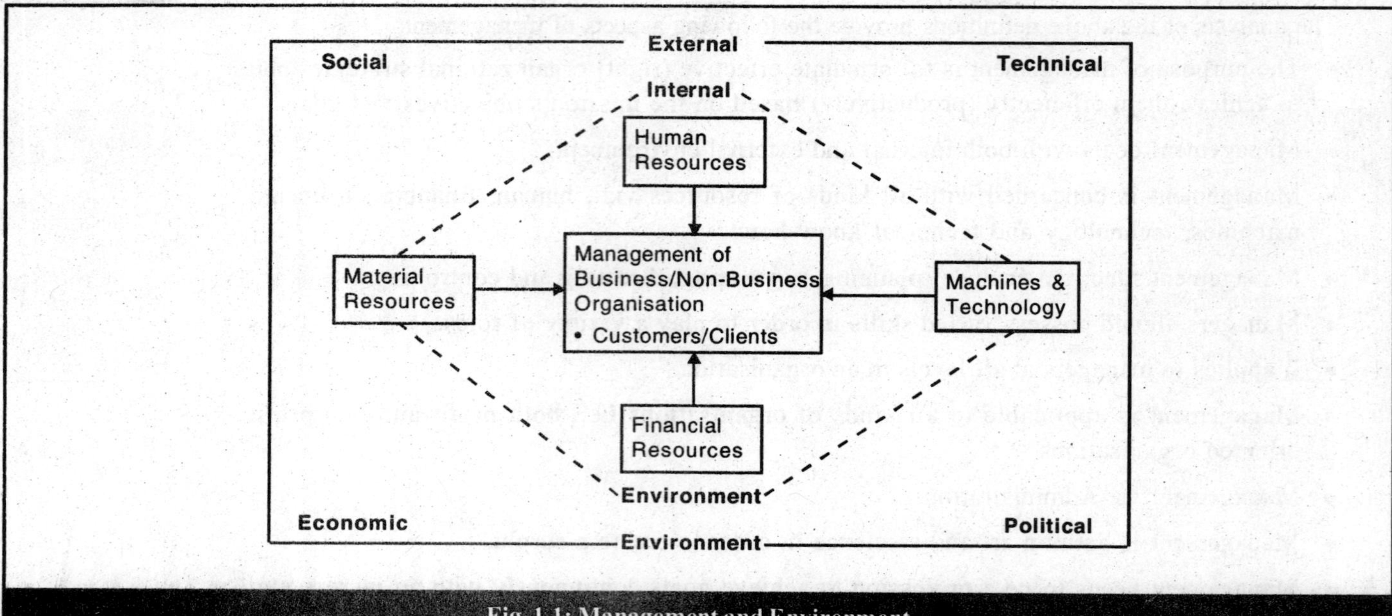

Fig. 1.1: Management and Environment

Management is Concerned with All Kinds of Resources

Managers manage and utilise all kinds of resources like financial resources, human resources, materials resources etc., in the process of achieving their strategies and goals.

(C) MANAGEMENT: A SCIENCE OR AN ART?

We should know what is science and what is an art before discussing whether management is a science or an art?

What is a Science?: Science is a body of knowledge developed systematically, based on observation, measurement, experimentation and drawing inferences based on data. The knowledge can be verified through cause-effect relationship. The knowledge provides principles, theory and laws. Management satisfies the characteristics of science like:

- Body of knowledge is developed systematically. Management knowledge is developed through a number of systems like input-output system, organisational system, functional system etc.
- Management knowledge is developed through observation, measurement and experimentation.
- Inferences are drawn based on data analysis.

Management is a developing science. However, management cannot be equated with exact sciences like physics and chemistry. Most of the managerial activities like decision-making, planning, organizing and directing cannot be an exact science.

Management: both science and art

What is an Art?: Art is understanding how a particular activity can be done. Art can be acquired by conscious effort and practice. Management is getting things done by and through other people. They have to continuously analyse the environment and formulate the plans and strategies. They have to modify the strategies based on environmental changes. The principles of management and theories of management cannot be implemented as learnt, in the real world. They are to be applied after making necessary modifications based on the real life situations.

Thus, management is both a science and an art as it acquires the characteristics of both. (See Box 1.1).

Box 1.1: Dhirubhai Ambanis's Management: Blend of Science and Art

Dhirubhai never followed the textbook style of management. Instead, he evolved a unique style, which combined the American style of entrepreneurship, with the Japanese focus on the latest technology. And to this, he added the innate shrewdness of a Gujarati businessman. Analysts feel that he was a perfect manager of time, money and men and exhibited a passion to find solutions to problems. Dhirubhai started Reliance at a time when most companies in India were owned by the government, and the private players were given step-motherly treatment by the government while offering licenses and permits. Similarly, when most Indian business houses depended on government – owned financial institutions for funds, Dhirubhai raised capital from the public by offering shares of his companies.

(**Source**: http://www.icmrindia.org/free%20resources/casestudies/Dhirubhai-Leadership%20Case%20Studies.htm)

The next question to be answered: Is management a profession?

(D) MANAGEMENT: A PROFESSION?

Any occupation to be called a profession should satisfy the following:

(i) **Body of knowledge:** Management knowledge is developed systematically and scientifically based on research studies, experiments, experiences and observations. Further, management literature is continuously developed by researchers and practitioners.

(ii) **Development and updating the knowledge:** Management knowledge has been developing continuously. Managers should update their knowledge by learning and acquiring the latest developments through training, executive development and formal study.

(iii) **Professional Journals:** There should be professional journals to publish the findings of research studies. There are a number of professional journals all over the world to publish the findings of research studies and latest developments in management: Harvard Business Review, Vikalpa, Decision, Indian Management and Indian Journal of Industrial Relations.

(iv) **Professional Associations:** There should be professional associations in order to monitor and enable professional development. Further, they implement the code of conduct. Management professional associations in India include: All India Management Association (AIMA), National Institute of Personnel Management, Institute of Chartered Accountants of India etc.

(v) **Code of Conduct:** The professionals should behave ethically while discharging their duties. AIMA, National Institute of Personnel Management, Institute of Chartered Accountants of India and other professional organisations formulate the code of conduct.

(vi) **Specialised Educational Qualifications:** There should be specialised educational qualifications for employment for professional jobs. Specialised educational institutions are established to impart specialized education. Indian Institutes of Management and Departments of Management in the Universities are established to provide specialized management education leading to Post-graduate Diploma in Management (PGDM) and Master of Business Management (MBA) degree.

Management satisfies all the characteristics of a profession. Therefore, management is a profession like medicine and law.

(E) MANAGEMENT VS. ADMINISTRATION

Management involves executing plans and strategies

Different writers and management thinkers view management and administration differently.

There is no unanimity among the writers regarding these two concepts. According to one section of writers, administration involves policy making, formulation of vision, mission, objectives and strategies. As such, administration is the function of the top level management. Further, administration decides the organisational structure and prepares the organizational plans.

Management involves executing the plans and strategies and carrying out various activities determined by the administration. It directs and controls the subordinates. Thus, management is the function of lower level people in the company.

The second view has been advocated by E.F.L. Brech.[6] According to E.F.L.Brech, management is a comprehensive and integrated term. Management includes planning, organizing, directing and controlling. According to him, management can be classified into two categories *viz.*, administrative management and operative management.

Administrative Management: Administrative management represents the top level management pertaining thinking and planning functions. Administrative management performs the functions of formulation of vision, mission and strategies. It includes board of directors, managing director, general managers and chief managers.

Operative Management: Operative management represents the lower level management covering execution and implementation functions. It performs the functions of execution, directing and controlling which involves the contribution of middle level managers and lower level managers.

The third view has been advocated by Peter F. Drucker. According to him, the term *administration* is applicable to non-profit organisations like government organisations, service-oriented hospitals and educational institutions, military, churches, temples etc. The main activity of administration is planning, organizing, directing controlling and rendering services. Thus, governance of non-profit organisations is called administration. Governance of business organisations is referred to as management. Thus, management is concerned with business organisations and profit-oriented organisations. It is measured by the efficiency in profit-making and administration is measured by efficiency in rendering services.

(F) MANAGEMENT FUNCTIONS

As indicated earlier, management is the process of planning, organizing, staffing, directing and controlling the efforts of organisation members in utilising all resources to achieve organizational goals, objectives and mission. Management is a process as it operates the activities systematically. Fig.1.2 presents the management process.

Functions of management include planning, organising, staffing, directing and controlling.

Planning

Plan: What should be achieved?

Planning consists of the activities involved in choosing courses of action to achieve organisational objectives. It is deciding in advance what to do, when to do, how to do and who will do it, in order to achieve these objectives. Both long-term and short-term plans are necessary to achieve goals. It is necessary for the management to adopt certain assumptions or premises with regard to external factors that serve as a background for the planning function. Some companies have adopted the practice of contingency planning in view of growing difficulty of predicting future environmental conditions. Planning is a part of the activities of all managers.

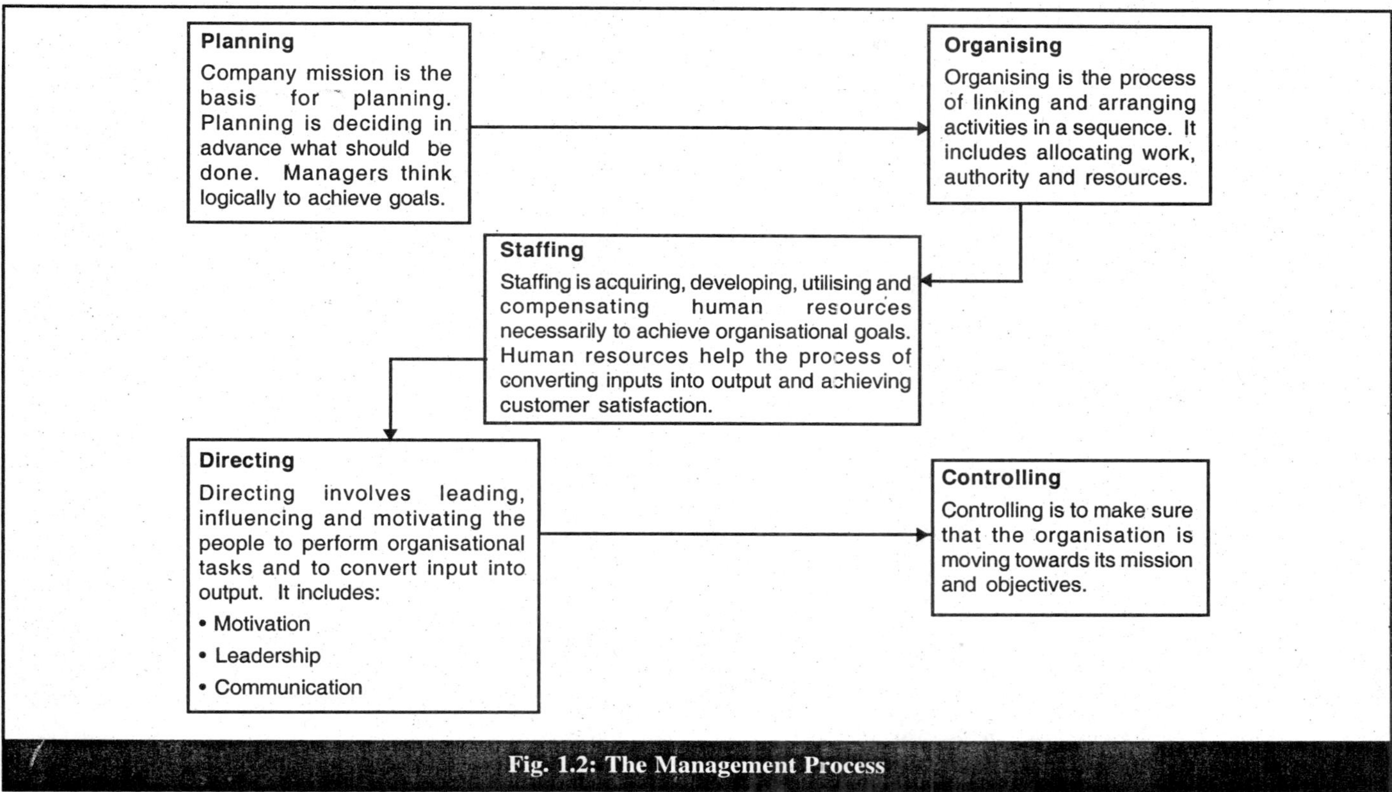

Fig. 1.2: The Management Process

Organising

Organisations: Grouping of jobs

Organising involves the grouping of jobs into a framework for coordination and direction. Formal organisations may be portrayed by use of an organisation chart. Careful structuring of an organisation is beneficial in terms of clarifying lines of command and eliminating gaps and overlaps. However, extremely detailed organisation structures may be dysfunctional.

Once job content is determined, jobs and activities must be grouped to devise an overall structure. Decisions affecting organisational structure involve values and goals for both enterprises and individuals.

Organisations are structured based on product, function, geography, customer and project. The matrix structure has evolved as a result of complex environments, markets and technology. It combines both functions and projects. Organisational culture reflects not only social values and expectations, but also the unique set of values, beliefs and behaviours that characterise each organisation.

Staffing

Staffing is planning, organising, directing and controlling of procurement, development, compensation, integration and maintenance of people for the purpose of contributing to individual, organisational and social goals. Thus, building an effective organisational team requires planning and control of human resources. This process requires the performance of the functions like job analysis, human resources planning, recruitment, selection, induction, placement, training, executive development, wage and salary administration, leadership, teamwork, motivation, grievance procedure, disciplinary procedure etc.

Once the employee is employed, his development needs are identified through performance appraisal. Once these needs are identified, the employee will be trained/developed with the application of on-the-job and off-the-job methods. Staffing function is also known as human resource management.

Directing

The next logical function after completing planning, organising and staffing is the execution of plan. The important function of management at any level is directing the people by motivating, commanding, leading and activating them. The willing and effective cooperation of employees for the attainment of organisational goals is possible through direction. Tapping the maximum potentialities of the people is possible through motivation and command. Thus, direction is an important managerial function in securing employee's contribution. Coordination deals with the task of blending efforts in order to ensure successful attainment of organisational objectives.

Controlling

After planning, organising, staffing and directing the various activities, the performance is to be verified in order to know whether the activities are performed in conformity with the plans and objectives or not. Controlling also involves checking, verifying and comparing of actual performance with the plans, identification of deviations, if any and correcting of identified deviations. Thus actions and operations are adjusted to predetermined plans and standards through control.

The purpose of control is to ensure the effective operation of an organisation by focusing on all resources — human, material, finance and machines. Financial control is attained through a number of means *viz.,* financial statements interpreted through ratio analysis and budgets.

Managers should have required skills in order to perform the functions discussed above. Now, we shall discuss managerial skills.

(G) MANAGERIAL SKILLS

According to Robert L.Katz[7], there are three types of managerial skills *viz.*, technical skills, human skills and conceptual skills. Fig.1.3 presents the managerial skills.

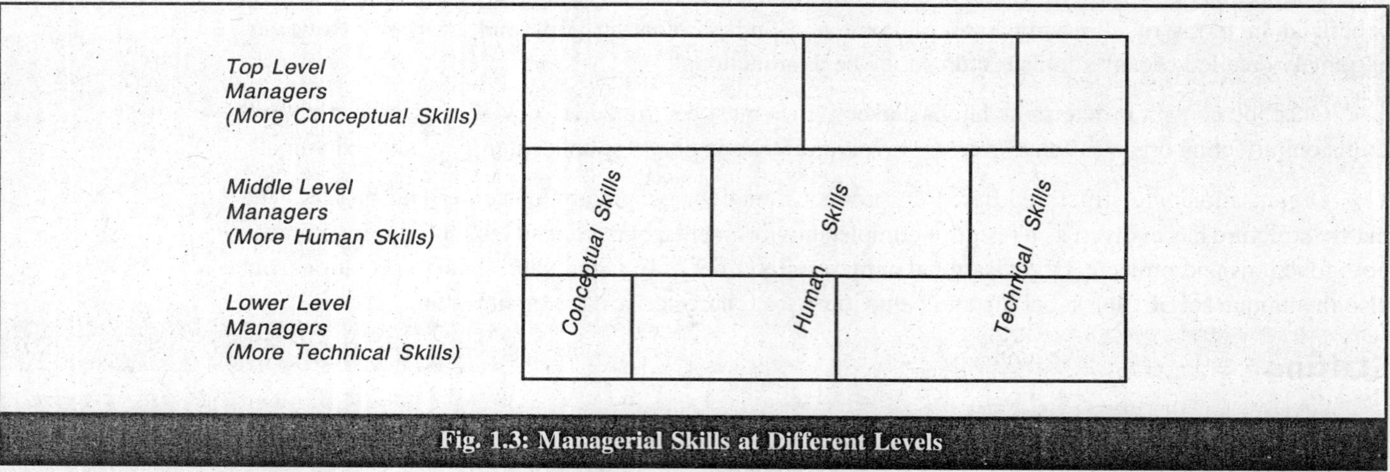

Fig. 1.3: Managerial Skills at Different Levels

Technical Skills

Technical Skills: Proficiency in Performaning the content of the job

Technical skills are the proficiency in working with machines, tools and techniques in human resource management, financial management, marketing management and production management. Managers at all levels should possess technical skills. Those at the lower level should possess more of technical skills whereas managers at the top level possess less technical skills compared to those at middle and lower levels.

Human Skills

Human skills include the ability to work with people tactfully, interpersonal proficiency, ability to build, maintain and work in teams and create an open environment. Managers at all levels should possess these skills.

Conceptual Skills

Conceptual skills include the ability to draw the total, integrated, comprehensive and the macro view of the company, situations and the ability to develop solutions for the probable problems and challenges. Top level managers should possess more of conceptual skills compared to those of lower level managers.

(H) MANAGERIAL ROLES

Managers perform different roles as shown in Fig. 1.4. As can be seen from the figure, formal authority gives rise to three inter-personal roles and three informational roles. The two sets of roles enable the manager to play the four decisional roles.

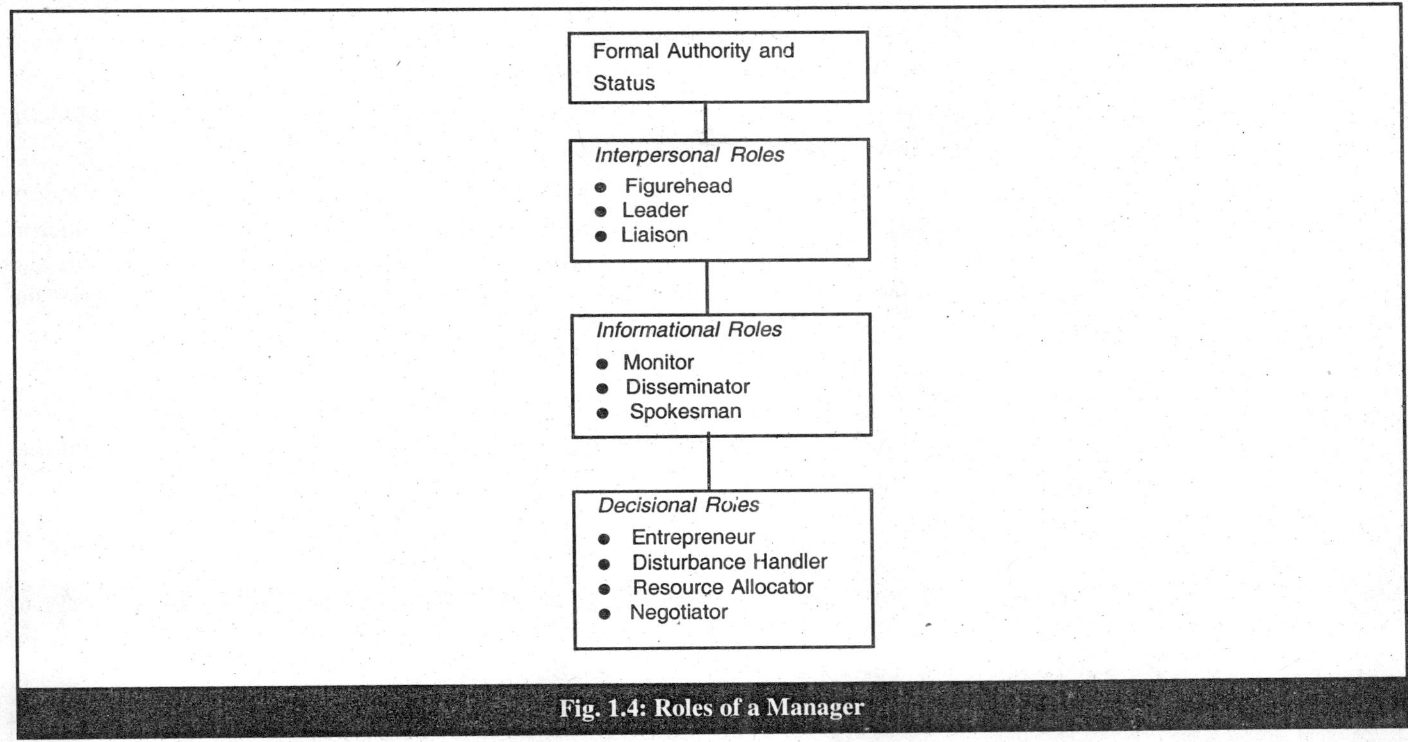

Fig. 1.4: Roles of a Manager

(**Source:** Henry Mintzberg, "The Manager's Job", in James Brain Quinn, Henry Mintzberg and Robert M. James, "The Strategy Process," Prentice-Hall, New Jersey, 1988, p. 27).

Interpersonal Roles

The important interpersonal roles of managers are:

Figurehead Role: Managers perform the duties of a ceremonial nature as head of the organisation, a strategic business unit or department. Duties of interpersonal roles include routine, involving little serious communication and less important decisions. However, they are important for the smooth functioning of an organisation or department.

Leader Role: The manager, in charge of the organisation/department, coordinates the work of others and leads his subordinates. Formal authority provides greater potential power to exercise and get the things done.

Liaison Role: As the leader of the organisation or unit, the manager has to perform the functions of motivation, communication, encouraging team spirit and the like. Further, he has to coordinate the activities of all his subordinates, which involves the activity of liaison.

Informational Roles

Manager emerges as the nerve centre of his organisation/department in view of his interpersonal links with his subordinates, peers, superiors and outsiders. Therefore, the manager has to play the informational role effectively to let the information flow continuously from one corner of the organisation to other corner.

The information roles of a manager include:

Monitor's Role: As a result of the network of contacts, the manager gets the information by scanning his environment, subordinates, peers and superiors. Managers mostly collect information in verbal form often as gossip, hearsay, speculation and through grapevine channels.

Disseminator's Role: The manager disseminates the information which he collects from different sources and through various means. He passes some of the privileged information directly to his subordinates, who otherwise have no access to it. The manager plays an important role in disseminating the information to his subordinates, when they don't have contact with one another.

Spokesman's Role: Some insiders and/or outsiders control the unit/department or the organisation. The manager has to keep them informed about the developments in his unit. He has to keep his superior informed of every development in his unit, who in turn inform the insiders and outsiders. Directors and shareholders must be informed about financial performance. Customers must be informed about the new product developments, quality maintenance, government officials about implementation of law etc.

Decisional Roles

Information is an important and basic input to decision-making. The managers play a crucial role in decision-making system of the unit. Only the manager can commit the department to new courses of action and he has full and current information to initiate and implement the decisions that determine the department's or organisational strategy. The decisional roles of the manager are:

Entrepreneurial Role: As an entrepreneur, the manager is a creator and innovator. He seeks to improve his department, adapt to the changing environmental factors. The manager appreciates new ideas and initiates new developmental projects. (See Box 1.2).

According to Peter F. Drucker, "*the manager has the task of creating a true whole that is larger than the sum of its parts, a productive entity that turns out more than the sum of the resources put into it.*"

Disturbance Handler Role: Entrepreneurial role describes the manager as the voluntary initiator of change, the disturbance handler role presents the manager as the involuntarily responding to pressures. Pressures of the situation are severe and highly demand the attention of the manager and as such the manager cannot ignore the situation. For example, workers' strike, declining sales, bankruptcy of a major customer etc.

Box 1.2: The Fishing Story: An Entrepreneurial and Challenging Role

The Japanese love fresh fish. However, the waters close to Japan have not held many fish for decades. So to feed the Japanese population, fishing boats got bigger and went farther than ever.

The farther the fishermen went, the longer it took to bring in the fish. If the return trip took more than a few days, the fish were not fresh. The Japanese did not like the taste. To solve this problem, fishing companies installed freezers on their boats. They would catch the fish and freeze them at sea. Freezers allowed the boats to go farther and stay longer.

However, the Japanese could taste the difference between fresh and frozen and they did not like frozen fish. The frozen fish brought a lower price. So fishing companies installed fish tanks. They would catch the fish and stuff them in the tanks, fin to fin. After a little thrashing around, the fish stopped moving. They were tired and dull, but alive.

Unfortunately, the Japanese could still taste the difference. Because the fish did not move for days, they lost their fresh-fish taste. The Japanese preferred the lively taste of fresh fish, not sluggish fish. So how did Japanese fishing companies solve this problem? How do they get fresh-tasting fish to Japan? If you were consulting the fish industry, what would you recommend?

Too Much Money

As soon as you reach your goals, such as finding a wonderful mate, starting a successful company, becoming independently wealthy or whatever, you might lose your passion. You don't need to work so hard so you relax. You experience the same problem as lottery winners who waste their money, wealthy heirs who never grow up and bored homemakers who get addicted to prescription drugs.

Like the Japanese fish problem, the best solution is simple. It was observed by L. Ron Hubbard in the early 1950's.

"Man thrives, oddly enough, only in the presence of a challenging environment."— L. Ron Hubbard

The Benefits of a Challenge

The more intelligent, persistent and competent you are, the more you enjoy a good problem. If your challenges are the correct size, and if you are steadily conquering those challenges, you are happy. You think of your challenges and get energized. You are excited to try new solutions. You have fun.

You are alive!

How Japanese Fish Stay Fresh

To keep the fish tasting fresh, the Japanese fishing companies still put the fish in the tanks. But now they add a small shark to each tank. The shark eats a few fish, but most of the fish arrive in a very lively state.

The fish are challenged.

Recommendations

Instead of avoiding challenges, jump into them. Beat the heck out of them. Enjoy the game. If your challenges are too large or too numerous, do not give up. Failing makes you tired. Instead, reorganize. Find more determination, more knowledge, more help. If you have met your goals, set some bigger goals. Once you meet your personal or family needs, move onto goals for your group, the society, even mankind.

(**Source**: BeMobile <stella.bita@bemobile.com.pg>)

The manager should have enough time in handling disturbances carefully, skilfully and effectively.

Resource Allocator's Role: The most important resource that a manager allocates to his subordinates is his time. He should have an open-door policy and allow the subordinates to express their opinions and share their experiences. This process helps both the manager and his subordinates in making effective decisions. In addition, the manager should empower his subordinates by delegating his authority and power.

Negotiator's Role: Managers spend considerable time in the task of negotiations. He negotiates with the subordinates for improved commitment and loyalty, with the peers for cooperation, coordination and integration, with workers and their unions regarding conditions of employment, commitment, productivity and with the government about providing facilities for business expansion etc.

These negotiations are an integral part of the manager's job for only he has authority to commit organisational resources and is the nerve centre of information.

Though the different roles of a manager are discussed separately for convenience, they are, in fact inseparable. The manager has to perform these roles simultaneously by integrating one with the another. Thus, the major role of the manager is integrating all the roles while playing the managerial role or performing his tasks. Infact, the manager cannot play any one role isolating the other roles. As a strategist, the manager has to integrate all the roles in decision-making and performing his tasks. (See Exhibit 1.1).

Exhibit 1.1 Key Roles of Managers

Henry Mintzberg concluded that the job of a top manager contains ten interrelated roles. The importance of each role and the amount of time demanded by each probably varies from one job to another. These roles are as follows:

Figurehead : Acts as legal and symbolic head; performs obligatory social, ceremonial or legal duties (hosts retirement dinners, luncheons for employees, and plant dedications; attends civic affairs; signs contracts on behalf of firm).

Leader : Motivates, develops and guides subordinates; oversees staffing, training, and associated activities (introduces Management By Objectives [MBO], develops a challenging work climate, provides a sense of direction, acts as a role model).

Liaison : Maintains a network of contacts and information sources outside the top management in order to obtain information and assistance (meets with key people from the task environment, meets formally and informally with corporate division managers and the CEOs of other firms).

Monitor : Seeks and obtains information in order to understand the corporation and its environments; acts as the nerve centre for the corporation (reviews status reports from vice-presidents, reviews key indicators of corporate performance, scans *Wall Street Journal* and key trade journals, joins select clubs and societies).

Disseminator : Transmits information to the rest of the top management team and other key people in the corporation (chairs staff meetings, transmits policy letters, communicates five-year plans).

Spokesman : Transmits information to key groups and people in the task environment (prepares annual report to stockholders, talks to the Chamber of Commerce, states corporate policy to the media, participates in advertising campaigns, speaks before congressional committees).

Entrepreneur : Searches the corporation and its environment for projects to improve products, processes, procedures, and structures; then supervises the design and implementation of these projects (introduces cost reduction programmes, makes plant trips to divisions, changes forecasting system, brings in subcontract work to level the workload, reorganises the corporation).

Disturbance Handler : Takes corrective action in times of disturbance or crisis (personally talks with key creditors, interest groups, congressional committees, union leaders; establishes investigative committees; revises objectives, strategies, and policies).

Resource Allocator : Allocates corporate resources by making and/or approving decisions (reviews budgets, revises programme, scheduling, initiates strategic planning, plans personnel load, sets objectives.)

Negotiator : Represents the corporation in negotiating important agreements; may speak directly with key representatives of groups in the task environment or work through a negotiator; negotiates disagreements within the corporation by working with conflicting division heads (works with labour as negotiator; resolves disputes, negotiates with creditors, suppliers and creditors).

(**Source**: H. Mintzberg, *The Nature of Managerial Work*, Harper & Row, New York, 1973, pp. 54-94).

Now, we shall study another aspect of management *i.e.*, management levels.

(I) MANAGEMENT LEVELS

Management includes all the managers of a company. Management is classified as managers at different levels *viz.*, top level managers, middle level managers and lower level managers.

Top Level Managers

Top level managers are the senior level executives of the company including the Managing Director or President Vice-Presidents, General Managers, Chief Managers of the company, etc. Top level management particularly the Managing Director or President of the company is responsible for the overall management and performance of the company.

Top level managers: Senior executives

Top level management formulates objectives, policies and corporate level strategies of the company. Top level managers lead and motivate the middle level managers. They coordinate the activities of middle level managers.

Middle Level Managers

Middle level managers are responsible for coordination of the activities of various departments. Middle level managers include managers of various departments like Production department, Marketing department, Finance department, Human Resource Department and Research and Development department. These managers are responsible for the success or failure of their departments.

Middle level managers formulate the objectives, goals and strategies of their departments based on those of the organisation. In addition, middle level managers lead, motivate and coordinate the activities of the lower-level managers.

Lower Level Managers

Lower level managers are responsible for the work of the operating staff working with them. Lower level managers are also called First-Line or First-Level or Junior Managers. They direct, lead, motivate and coordinate the activities of the operating employees. These managers mostly supervise the operating employees while they perform their work. As such, the lower level managers are also called 'Supervisors.' Fig.1.5 presents management levels.

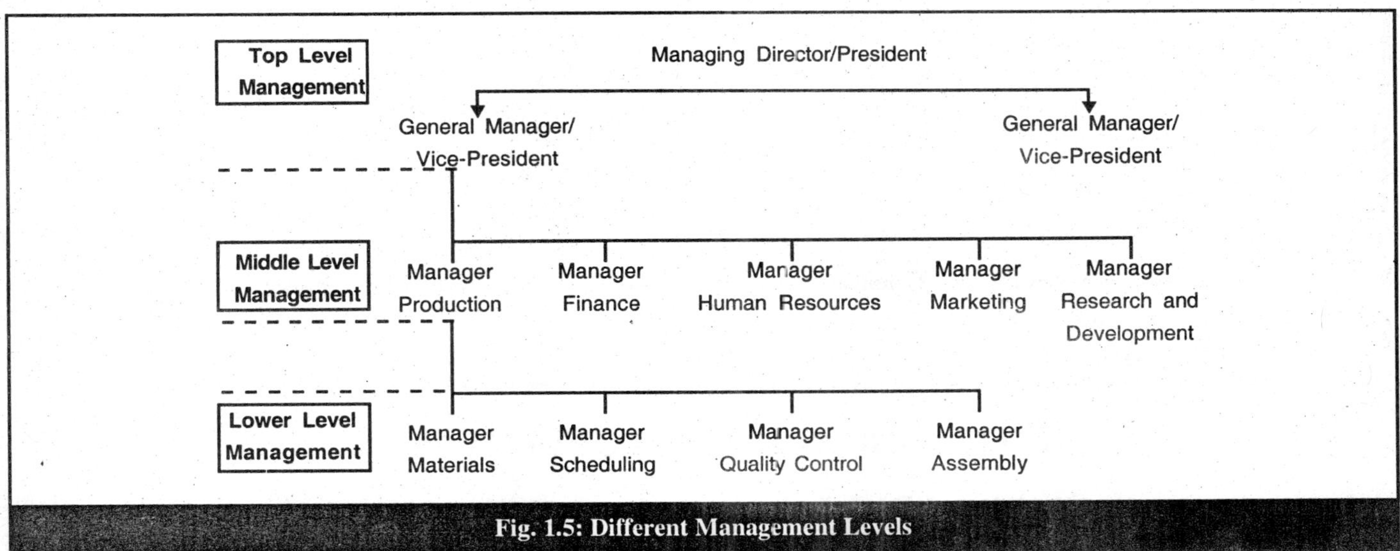

Fig. 1.5: Different Management Levels

(J) FUNCTIONAL AREAS OF MANAGEMENT

Managers are also classified based on the functional areas of management. The functional areas of management include: production, marketing, human resource, finance, research and development. The functional managers include: production manager, marketing manager, finance manager, human

Functional areas of management: Production, marketing, finance and human resource

resource manager and manager-research and development. Functional managers mostly perform the activities of their respective functional area. As such, they fail to see the total company.

General managers view the total company in an integrated and comprehensive approach. They also see the total of the sub-units and subsidiary companies besides integrating and coordinating the activities of the production department, marketing department, finance department and human resources department. General managers formulate strategies at the corporate and the business unit level.

(K) UNIVERSALITY OF MANAGEMENT PRINCIPLES

Organisations are basically of two types *viz.*, profit-oriented organisations and non-profit oriented organisations. Business organisations are also called profit-oriented organisations. Non-business organisations belong to the second type. They are also called social organisations.

Non-profit organisations include colleges, universities, churches, temples, government hospitals, clubs, service societies etc. Management principles and functions are applicable to both profit-oriented and non-profit organisations.

There are varied differences among different types of non-profit organisations. The differences may be both to do with the different expectations of influencing bodies and also the special nature of revenue generation in terms of resources. Exhibit 1.2 presents the characteristics and difficulties of the management in non-profit organisations. However, it can be stated that the concepts, techniques and principles of management are applicable to both profit and non-profit organisations. As such, it is said that management principles are applicable universally.

Exhibit 1.2 Characteristics and Likely Difficulties of Management in Non-Profit Organisations

Characteristics	*Likely Difficulties*
Objectives and Expectations:	• Complicates planning
• Multiple service objectives and expectations	• High incidence of political lobbying.
• Expectations of funding bodies' influence.	• Difficulties in delegating/decentralizing responsibilities and decision-making.
Market and Users:	
• Beneficiaries of services not necessarily contributors of revenue/resources.	• Service satisfaction cannot be measured in financial terms
	• Influence from funding bodies maybe high.
Resources:	• Emphasis may be on finance rather than service.
• High proportion from Government/ Sponsors.	• Objectives may be addressed to sponsors as much as clients.
• Received in advance of services.	
• May be multiple sources of funding	

(L) INTERNATIONAL MANAGEMENT

Management styles and practices vary from country to country based on the cultures. However, there may be similar styles and practices in countries with more or less similar cultures. In addition, the levels of economic development and structure of the economy also determine the management styles. There is broad distinction between the Japanese management and American management. Exhibit 1.3 provides the characteristics of Japanese management and American management

Exhibit 1.3 Characteristics of Japanese Management and American Management

Japanese Managment	*American Management*
• **Life Time Employment:** Japanese companies used to provide life time employment to the people. Now this concept is changed to life time employability. In other words the companies continue the employment of those employes who continuously acquire new skills required by the company from time to time.	• Short-term employment
• Slow evaluation and promotion	• Rapid evaluation and promotion
• Non specified career paths	• **Specialised career paths:** Software industry in USA encourages multicareer paths
• Implicit control mechanisms	• Explicit control mechanism
• Collective decision-mechanisms particularly software companies have been practicising group decision-making	• **Individual decision making:** American companies
• Collective responsibility	• Individual responsibility
• Holistic concern	• Segmented concern

Management styles and approaches vary widely between the western countries and the eastern countries.

- Individualistic approach is more predominant in the west particularly in the USA while the group approach is more predominant in the east particularly in Japan.
- Decisions are mostly made by the top management in USA and are pushed downwards. Decisions in Japan are mostly made by the interaction and participation of both top level management and lower level employees.
- Employees volunteer to assist the management in the eastern countries whereas in western countries employees do not take up the work unless otherwise the work is formally assigned to them.
- Information flows freely through all directions in eastern countries, whereas it flows with a direction though a particular channel in the western countries.
- Employees in USA strive for individual achievements and rewards whereas the employees in Japan strive for group achievements and rewards.
- Team work is the culture of the Japanese firms and individual work is the culture of American firms.
- Employees in Japan are mostly prefer empowerment while their counterparts in the USA prefer close supervision.
- Japanese organisations used to employ the people throughout the life time. But, the globalisation and information technology made the Japanese organisation to develop the human resources of their employees, enhance their employability and provide employment. As such the employee turnover is almost nil in Japanese firms.
- Employment in USA is for a short run. The USA companies fire the employees quite often as they follow 'hire-and-fire' policy. As such the employee turnover is high in the USA.

- Japanese organisations follow humanistic approach in employing and managing people while the American companies follow mechanistic approach or 'use and throw' policy in managing people.
- Japanese organisations follow long run and relationship-oriented approach whereas American companies follow short-run and pure-business oriented approach in managing business.

Approaches to Management

Different approaches to management include systems approach, the contingency approach, human resources management approach and management science approach. Different approaches to management have been discussed in detail in the next chapter *i.e.,* Development of Management Thought.

KEY TERMS

- Management
- Objectives
- Art
- Organising
- Directing
- Mission
- Science
- Planning
- Human Skills
- Interpersonal Role
- Decisional Roles
- Resources
- Technical Skills
- Staffing
- Controlling
- Administration
- Strategies
- Profession
- Conceptual Skills
- Information Role

QUESTIONS

1. What is management? Critically comment on various definitions on management.
2. What are the functions of management? Explain each of them.
3. What are the managerial skills? Who should have more of conceptual skills?
4. Comment on different managerial roles.
5. Is management Science or Art? Defend your answer with examples.
6. What are the features of a profession? Does management satisfy these features?
7. Comment on different levels of managers. Explain their functions.
8. Discuss the differences between management and administration.

REFERENCES

1. James A.F.Stoner, *Management*, Prentice Hall of India (P) Ltd., New Delhi, 1984, p.7.
2. John A.Pearce and Richard B.Robinson, *Management*, McGraw Hill, 1989, p.4.
3. Ivancerich, Donnelly and Gibson, *Management:Principles and Functions*, Richard D.Irwin Inc., Homewood, 1991, p.5.
4. John A.Pearce and Richard B.Robinson, op.cit., p.4.
5. Harold Koontz and Heinz Weilinch, *Essentials of Management*, McGraw Hill, New York, 1990, p.4.
6. E.F.L.Brech, *Principles and Practice of Management*, Pitman, London, 1971.
7. Robert L.Katz, *Skills of an Effective Administrator*, Harvard Business Review, January-February 1955, pp.33-42 and Robert L.Katz., *Retrospective commentary*, Harvard Business Review, September-October 1974, pp.101-102.

CHAPTER **2**

DEVELOPMENT OF MANAGEMENT THOUGHT

Chapter Outline

(A) Introduction
(B) Scientific Management
(C) Administrative Management
(D) Towards Human Relations Approach
(E) Human Relations Approach
(F) Systems Approach to Management
(G) Contingency Approach
(H) Human Resource Management Approach
(I) Management Science Approach
(J) Conclusion
- Key Terms
- Questions
- References

Learning Objectives

After studying this Chapter, you should be able to:

- ✓ Know the contributions of Robert Owen, Charles Babbage, F.W.Taylor, Henry Gnatt and The Gilbreths to Scientific Management.
- ✓ Understand the Principles of Scientific Management and also criticisms leveled against them.
- ✓ Analyse the contributions made by Henry Fayol and Max Weber to Administrative Management.
- ✓ Appraise the Fayol's Principles of Management and criticism leveled against them particularly due to globalisation and information technology.
- ✓ Comment on the contributions of Mary Parker Follett, Chester I Barnard and Elton Mayo to Human Relations School.
- ✓ Evaluate the contributions of human relations approach to management thought.
- ✓ Understand the contributions of Systems Approach to management, Contingency approach to management, HRM approach and Management Science Approach to management.

(A) INTRODUCTION

The principles of management as in the case of other disciplines, have their impact on the practice of management. The nature of management principles include: universal applicability, dynamism, relative but not absolute limits due to human behaviour and the like. A number of practitioners, thinkers and academicians of management have contributed to the formation and development of management principles, thought and approaches.

The importance of organisation and administration in the bureaucratic states of antiquity was manifest in the interpretations of early Egyptian papyri, extending as far back as 1300 B.C.[1] The same kind of records exist for ancient China. Practical suggestions for proper public administration and admonitions to choose honest, unselfish and capable public officers were included in Confucius' parables.[2]

Even though the records of early Greece and Rome do not offer much insight into the principles of management, existence of Athenian Commonwealth and the Roman Catholic Church indicates a consideration of management principles and functions.

In military organisations too, principles of management have been considered. Although certain important principles have been applied in recent times, several others were considered long back in military organisations.

Public administrators also considered several management principles for administering the people properly.

The study of theories is more important as they guide management decisions, they shape our organisation, make us aware of the business environment and are a source of new ideas.

Now, we shall study these theories in order to know how the management thought is developed, principles of management are evolved and different approaches to management are designed. The first among the management theories is scientific management.

(B) SCIENTIFIC MANAGEMENT

The forerunners of Scientific Management theory are Robert Owen, Charles Babbage and Henry Robinson Towne.

Robert Owen

Robert Owen, who was the manager of different cotton textile mills between 1800 and 1828, was the first person to pay attention to labour welfare. He suggested a change in the attitude of industrialists towards workers. He worked up to his maximum possible extent for the amelioration of working conditions of workers and thereby tried to win over their confidence. He stated that men should not be treated as secondary and inferior to machines.

Charles Babbage

Besides Robert Owen, there were some scientists who thought of making improvements in the management by observing the scientific techniques. Prominent among them was Charles Babbage, a leading British mathematician at Cambridge University from 1828-1839. He studied the working conditions of factories in England and France and observed that most of the factory class used to work on the basis of estimates and imagination. They were tradition-oriented rather than scientific-minded. Two pioneering works of Babbage are *The Differential Engine and On the Economy of Machinery and*

Manufacturers. He stated that the methods of science and mathematics could be applied to the solution of the factory's problems.

Contribution of Babbage

Babage advocated: division of labour and time study

- Babbage stressed that good machines and efficient workers do not inevitably ensure success in business. Good management that directs and controls machines and workers is the most crucial element in successful business.
- He advocated, like Adam Smith, the principle of division of labour.[3] He also suggested the use of time study techniques.[4]
- Babbage conceived an analytical machine as far back as 1833 which was a forerunner of today's digital computer. So he was a visionary much ahead of time.
- He considered all aspects of contemporary management thinking-mutuality of interest between employees and employer, production control, incentive pay, quality control, wage and salary administration, profit sharing, operations research, preventive maintenance and research and development.

It is rightly stated "*He wrote a premiere of management before the world is able to read it and he invented the computer before its time.*"

McFarland indicates: "To Babbage goes the credit for advocating in relation to industrial problems in fundamental thinking which preceded the formulation of a science of management." Hence the background for the formulation of the science of management was provided initially by Charles Babbage. Afterwards, credit has been given to F.W.Taylor for enunciating the area of scientific management.

Frederick Winslow Taylor

F. W. Taylor: father of scientific management

Frederick Winslow Taylor, known popularly as the father of scientific management and a classicist in management theory, was the first person who insisted on the introduction of scientific methods in management. He made for the first time a systematic study of management and evolved an orderly set of principles to replace the trial and error methods then in vogue.

F.W.Taylor made a humble beginning by joining as an apprentice in a small machine-making shop in Philadelphia in the 1870s. Later he became a machinist in 1878 at the Midvale Steel Works in Philadelphia (USA). Afterwards he rose to the position of a machinist foreman.

He observed that workers were not enthusiastic and were doing as little as possible, just adequate to maintain their job. Instead of becoming angry at the outlook of workers, Taylor sympathized with them. He wrote "When a naturally energetic man works for a few days besides a lazy one, the logic of the situation is unanswerable: Why should I work hard when that lazy fellow gets the same pay that I do and does only half as much work?"[5]

Taylor formed opinions on the basis of his observations. There was an uncompromising nature on his part and he never tried to satisfy his opponents. He was a man of firm convictions. After leaving the Midvale Factory, he joined Bethleham Steel Company: wherein he introduced scientific management. But there was strong opposition from all the managers because of his uncompromising nature and this led to the termination of his services unceremoniously. After leaving Bethleham in 1901, he wrote his pioneering work '*Shop Management*.' Besides this, he wrote several other books and among them the pioneering work was *Principles and Methods of Scientific Management* (1911).

Principles of Scientific Management

Principles of scientific management: Time and motion study, differential payment, group harmony, standardisation etc.

The contributions to scientific management evolve into principles. These principles are called principles of scientific management. They include:

***(i)* Time and Motion Study:** Workers were performing their work haphazardly before the era of scientific management. F.W.Taylor observed that a number of movements of the workers at the work place were unnecessary and consequently they were taking more time to do the job than necessary.

Hence, he proposed time and motion study. This study involves the following aspects:

- Observing the various motions (movements) of the worker at the work place.
- Identifying the necessary and unnecessary movements in carrying out the work
- Elimination of unnecessary movements.
- Observing the time required for each of the necessary movements with the help of a stop watch.
- Developing shorter and fewer motions and
- Standardising the motions and time.

Thus, this study developed the best way of doing the job, replacing the old rule of thumb knowledge of the workers.

***(ii)* Science, but not Rule of the Thumb:** Scientific management suggests doing the work systematically, determining the work clearly and sequentially, standardisation of motions and time for each motion and allotment of fair work to each worker. Thus, scientific management eliminated the rule of the thumb at the workplace.

***(iii)* Differential Payment:** F.W.Taylor suggested differential piece rate system. He fixed the standard level of production. Those employees who produce less than the standard production received low piece rate and employees produced above the standard production received higher piece rate. Differential piece rates are introduced in order to motivate the employees to produce more than the standard level and enhance productivity.

***(iv)* Group Harmony:** F.W.Taylor emphasised upon group harmony which can be achieved through satisfying the needs of the group members, eliminating the dissatisfaction and frustration of group members, maintaining the sound interpersonal relations among the group members and involving them in various group activities.

***(v)* Cooperation Between Workers and Management:** He also advocated sound employee-employer relations which should result in cooperation between workers and the management. Sound employee-employer relations can be achieved in the following ways:

- Management should understand the workers' needs and take steps to satisfy them.
- Workers should understand the organisational requirements like increasing productivity, sales, profitability etc. and maximising their contribution.

***(vi)* Methods Study:** F.W.Taylor believed that a methodological and systematic movement of materials ensure fast movement of materials in the factory, avoidance of unnecessary transportation of material from one stage to another stage of production, reduction of distance from one machine to another machine, reduction of the transportation time etc.

***(vii)* Scientific Selection and Training:** He suggested the scientific selection of employees based on job analysis and using various selection tests. He also suggested providing training and development facilities to all the employees based on training needs. This process helps the organisation to exploit the employers' potentialities and faculties for organisational success.

***(viii)* Standardisation:** Taylor advocated the importance of standardisation tools, instruments, working hours, working conditions, quality of work, cost of production etc.

***(ix)* Separation of Planning from Execution:** He advocated separation of the planning function from the execution function. He advocated that supervisors perform planning function whereas workers perform execution functions.[6]

Taylor got an excellent opportunity in 1912 to explain his scientific management philosophy when he was invited to give a testimony before the house of Representatives Committee. Some of the extracts from his testimony are as follows:

- Scientific management involves a complete mental revolution on the part of the working men engaged in any particular establishment or industry – a complete mental revolution on the part of these men as to their duties towards their work, towards their fellowmen and towards their employers.
- Employer and employees both realise that when they substitute friendly co-operation and mutual helpfulness for antagonism and strife, they are together able to make surplus so enormously greater than it was in the past that there is ample room for a large increase in wages for the workmen and an equally great increase in profits for the manufacturer.[7]

Thus, Taylor advocated a total mental revolution on the part of management and workers. Even though his scientific management was confined to management at the shop level, he indicated the possibility and significance of the scientific analysis of the various aspects of management. To sum up, he stressed the following:

(i) Replacement of rule-of-thumb by science.

(ii) Achieving harmony in group action rather than discord.

(iii) Attaining maximum output in place of restricted output.

(iv) Scientific selection, training and placement of workers and

(v) Development of all workers to the fullest extent possible for their own and their enterprise's highest priority.

Criticism of Taylor's Contributions

F.W.Taylor's contribution was criticised on the following grounds:

(i) The consideration of the word 'Scientific' before 'Management' was criticised since what actually is meant by scientific management is nothing but an approach to management.

(ii) His principles were mostly confined to production management. He ignored other functional areas of management like finance, marketing, personnel and accounting.

(iii) His functional foremanship violates the principle of unity of command.

(iv) Trade unionists criticised Taylor's principles as the means to exploit workers due to the reason that wages of the workers were not increased in direct proportion to the increase in productivity.

Despite the criticism leveled against Taylor's scientific management, the techniques advocated by him were further refined by his followers like Henry L.Gantt, Frank B.Lillian and M.Gilbreth.

Henry L.Gnatt

Henry L.Gnatt (1861-1919) had worked on several projects jointly with F.W.Taylor. He had modified Taylor's incentive system when he worked independently. He abandoned the differential rate system as having too little motivational impact, introduced 50% bonus to those workers who could complete a day's work. He also introduced bonus to the supervisors for each worker who could complete a day's work and additional bonus, if all the workers reached it, with a view to enable the supervisors to train their workers to do a better job. Gnatt also built upon Owen's idea of rating an employee's work publicly.

The Gilbreths

Frank B.Gilbreth (1868-1924) and Lillian M.Gilbreth (1878-1972) made their contributions to the scientific management movement as a husband and wife team. Although both of them collaborated on fatigue and motion studies, Lillian also focused on ways of promoting the individual workers' welfare. According to her, the ultimate aim of scientific management was to help workers reach their full potential as human beings. According to them, a worker would do his/her present job, prepare for the next highest job and train his/her successor, all at the same time. Thus every worker would always be a doer, a learner and a teacher.[8]

The developments in the scientific management approach and principles led to the development of administrative management. Now, we shall discuss the contributions to administrative management.

(C) ADMINISTRATIVE MANAGEMENT

Henry Fayol was a major contributor to administrative management approach.

Henry Fayol

Henry Fayol started his career as a mining engineer in 1860 in a colliery company in France. In 1866, he was appointed as the manager of the collieries and remained in this position for 22 years. In 1888, when the company's financial position was critical, he was appointed as the General Manager. He held this position with his expertise for 30 years and retired in 1918, at a time when the company had become one of the biggest coal companies in France. His observations on the principles of general management first appeared in 1916 in French under the title *Administration Industriella et Generale*, and this was translated into English in 1949 under the title *General and Industrial Administration*.[9]

Faylol: Division of business activities into six groups

This book contains two parts: the first part is concerned with the theory of administration and the second part with the discussion on training for administration.

Fayol felt that the activities of business could be divided into six groups: *(i)* Technical; *(ii)* Commercial; *(iii)* Financial; *(iv)* Security; *(v)* Accounting; and *(vi)* Managerial.

Fayol felt that the first five were well known and as a result, devoted most of his book to an analysis of the sixth. He classified the managerial group into six sub-groups, *viz*., forecasting, planning, organising, coordinating, commanding and controlling. Fayol stated the qualities required by managers to be physical, mental, moral, educational and technical. As a matter of fact, he emphasised that as one goes higher up in the levels of management, the administrative knowledge and skills become relatively more and more important, and technical knowledge and skill less important.

Fayol's Principles of Management

In addition, Fayol listed out fourteen principles of management. They are:

***(i)* Division of Labour:** The more people specialise, the more efficiently they can perform their work. This principle is epitomised by the modern assembly line.

***(ii)* Authority:** Managers must give orders so that they can get things done. While their formal authority gives them the right to command, managers will not always compel obedience unless they have personal authority (such as relevant expertise) as well.

***(iii)* Discipline:** Members in an organisation need to respect the rules and agreements that govern the organisation. To Fayol, discipline results from good leadership at all levels of the organisation, fair agreements (such as provisions for rewarding superior performance) and judiciously enforced penalties for infractions.

***(iv)* Unity of Command:** Each employee must receive instructions from only one person. Fayol believed that when an employee reported to more than one manager, conflicts in instructions and confusion of authority would ultimately result.

***(v)* Unity of Direction:** Those operations within the organisation that have the same objective should be directed by only one manager using one plan. For example, the personnel department in a company should not have two directors, each with a different hiring policy.

***(vi)* Subordination of Individual Interest to the Common Goal:** In any undertaking, the interests of employees should not take precedence over the interests of the organisation as a whole.

***(vii)* Remuneration:** Compensation for work done should be fair to both employees and employers.

***(viii)* Centralisation:** Decreasing the role of subordinates in decision making is centralisation, increasing their role is decentralisation. Fayol believed that managers should retain final responsibility, but should at the same time give their subordinates enough authority to do their jobs properly. The problem is to find the proper degree of centralisation in each case.

***(ix)* The Hierarchy:** The lines of authority in an organisation are often represented today by the neat boxes and lines of the organisation chart that runs in order of rank from the top management to the lowest level of the enterprise.

***(x)* Order:** Materials and people should be in the right place at the right time. People in particular, should be in the jobs or positions in which they are most suited.

***(xi)* Equity:** Managers should be both friendly and fair to their subordinates.

***(xii)* Stability of Staff:** A high employee turnover rate undermines the efficient functioning of an organisation.

***(xiii)* Initiative:** Subordinates should be given the freedom to conceive and carry out their plans, even though some mistakes may result.

***(xiv)* Esprit de Corps:** Promoting team spirit will give the organisation a sense of unity. To Fayol, even small factors could help to develop the spirit. He suggested, for example, the use of verbal communication instead of formal, written communication whenever possible.[10]

It may be stated that F.W.Taylor and Henry Fayol together gave an almost complete theory of management. Taylor studied with utmost care the lowest level of industrial hierarchy whereas Fayol, on the other hand, worked from the top of the industrial hierarchy downward.

The universality of the principles of management could be understood throughout the treatise of Fayol. He should be regarded as the father of modern management theory since he was first to emphasise that better management is not merely a question of improving the output of labour, but of planning of the subordinate units of an organisation.

Criticism of Fayol's Principles

The contributions of Henry Fayol were criticised as hereunder.

- The principles of unity of command and unity of direction are redundant in modern private organisations. Most of the private organisations after the announcement of liberalisation, privatisation and globalisation are dynamic in order to meet the customer's needs before the customers identify or realise them.
- The dynamic organisations are team-based, loosely structured, flat organisations and they change their structures based on strategy (structure follows the strategy principle) etc. Orders and commands flow through different directions in teams and loosely structured organisations. Similarly, direction also flows through various directions in modern organisations. Thus, these two principles are not applicable in modern organisations.
- The principle of scalar chain is also not applicable in modern organisations as the information requests for carrying out the work flow in different lines.
- Many modern organisations implemented business process reengineering (BPRE) and enterprise resource planning (ERP). These two techniques are based on team work and need the employees with multiple skill sets as the team members are required to carry out multiple activities. As such, the principles of division of labour and specialisation are not applicable to those organisations which implemented BPRE and ERP.
- Fayol's principles indicate that organisations are a closed system. But most of the organisations today are open systems. As such, Fayol's principles are not applicable to the organisations based on open systems.
- Fayol's principles like unity of command, unity of direction, division of labour, specialisation and span of management are applicable to tall and mechanistic organisations. Mechanistic organisations are insensitive to employees' social and psychological needs. Further, they do not use the employees skills and potentialities to the maximum extent.

Max Weber

Max Weber (1864-1920) felt the need for controlled regulations particularly in large organisations where thousands of people are employed and developed a theory of bureaucratic management, which emphasizes on a strictly defined hierarchy governed by clearly defined regulations and lines of authority.[11] For Weber, the ideal organisation was a bureaucracy. Today, we view bureaucracies as vast, impersonal organisations that put impersonal efficiency ahead of human needs. But Weber sought to improve the performance of socially significant organisations by making their operations productive.[12]

Improve the performance of socially significant organisations

(D) TOWARDS HUMAN RELATIONS APPROACH

Mary Parker and Chester I Barnard developed the theories on the basic framework of classical school, but they introduced many new elements in the area of human relations and organisational structure.

Mary Parker Follett

Mary Parker Follett (1868-1933) was convinced that labour and management shared a common purpose as members of the same organisation. But she believed that the distinction between superiors (order givers) and subordinates (order takers) hindered natural partnership.[13] She developed a behavioural model of organisational control. In her model, control was sponsored by and oriented towards the group. Self control was exercised by both individuals and groups, with the result being shared control or power.

Chester I Barnard

According to Barnard (1886-1961), people work together to achieve organisational goals as individually they are not able to accomplish and at the same time they must also satisfy their individual goals. The central thesis of Barnard is that an organisation should balance its goals with the needs and aims of employees for its efficient functioning and survival. He also stressed the use of informal groups effectively, even when they work at cross-purposes to achieve management objectives, sometimes, in order to ensure organisational survival. He believed that executives had a duty to install a sense of moral purpose in their employees. He also stressed considerable attention on the role of individual worker as "as the basic strategic factor in an organisation."[14]

(E) HUMAN RELATIONS APPROACH

The human element was recognised even in the Scientific Management School. The human relations approach is the outcome of reactions of classical theorists like Mary Parker and Chester I Barnard. Elton Mayo[15] and his associates pointed out that the techniques of scientific management are not adequate and they do not contribute to individual and organisational goals.

The essence of human relations approach is that workers should be treated as human beings but not as mere factors of production. Workers' needs, feelings, attitudes, values and desires are extremely important. The theme of human relations approach is that (i) organisational situation should be viewed in social terms as well as in economic and technical terms and (ii) the social process of group behaviour can be understood in terms of the clinical method analogous to the doctor's diagnosis of the human organism.[16]

Hawthorne Experiments

An intensive and systematic analysis of human factor was made in the form of Hawthorne Experiments. Elton Mayo is generally recognised as the father of human relations approach although a number of professors of the Harvard Business School and managers of Hawthorne Plant of Western Electric Company USA where the experiments were conducted between 1924 and 1933 had been associated with him. The series of experiments conducted may be classified as:

(i) Phase 1. Illumination Experiments

This experiment was conducted to know the impact of illumination on productivity. The experiment involved the prolonged observation of two groups of employees making telephone relays. The intensity of light under which one group worked (*test group*) systematically varied while the light was held constant for the second group (*control group*). The productivity of the test group and control group increased. The researchers concluded that some other variables were contaminating the effects of the light changes.

(ii) Phase 2. Relay Assembly Test Group

A small group of workers was placed in a separate room and a number of variables were altered - like wages were increased, rest periods of varying lengths were introduced, the workday and work week were shortened. The supervisors, who acted as observers, also allowed the groups to choose their own rest periods and members of their own groups and to involve in decision making regarding suggested changes. Performance tended to increase over the period but it also increased and decreased erratically.

(iii) Phase 3. Interviewing Programme

Mayo initiated a three year long interviewing programme in 1828, covering more than 21,000 employees to find out the causes for increased productivity. The emphasis of this phase was on human relations rather than on working conditions. This programme initially proved to be useless as employees often gave stereotyped responses. This led the interviewers towards asking indirect questions. Then the employees began to air their feelings freely. The point demonstrated by this interviewing programme is central to the human relations approach. And for the first time, the importance of the informal work group is recognised. Then, the bank wiring room experiment was set up in order to find out how informal work groups operate.

(iv) Phase 4. The Bank Wiring Observation Room Experiment (1931-32)

In this experiment, 14 male workers were formed into a work group and intensively observed for seven months in the bank wiring room, engaged in the assembly of terminal banks for the use in telephone exchanges. The employees were paid individual wages and a bonus based on group effort. It was expected that highly efficient workers would bring pressure on others for increased output and high bonus. However, the expected results did not come about and indeed the group developed specific mechanisms to protect themselves based on certain sentiments:

The rate buster sentiment : don't turn out too much work.

The chiseler sentiment : don't turn out too little work.

The squealer sentiment : don't tell superiors anything that would harm an associate.

The officious sentiment : don't act too officious in performing duties, conform rather to work group norms.

Work group norms, beliefs, sentiments had a greater impact in influencing individual behaviour than did the monetary incentives offered by the management. Thus, the Hawthorne Experiments indicated that employees were not only economic beings but social and psychological beings as well.

The researchers concluded that employees would work better had they believed that the management was concerned about their welfare and supervisors paid special attention to them. This phenomenon (subsequently labelled the Hawthorne effect), has remained quite controversial to this day.

The concept *social man*, according to Mayo, motivated by social needs, wanting, rewarding, on-the-job relationships and responding more to work-group pressures than to management control – was necessary to complement the old concept of rational man motivated by personal economic needs.[17]

Human relations approach: democratic leadership, training, group dynamics and motivation

Contributions of the Human Relations Approach

There is a departure from the scientific management approach regarding the influence of engineering factors for increase in productivity. Mayo had rediscovered Robert Owen's century-old dictum that a true concern for workers, 'those vital machines', paid dividends.

- This approach suggested that the democratic style of supervision yields more benefits than task-centred leadership by informal organisation than by formal organisation.
- In addition, the researchers recognized the significance of a manager's style and thereby stressed on management training.
- More attention was paid on teaching management skills rather than technical skills to people. (See Box 2.1)
- Finally their work led to a new interest in group dynamics, group process and group reward rather than individual worker.
- Another contribution of human relations approach was that business organisation is more than the logical arrangement of work functions and social factors should also be considered in designing an organisation structure. This school is characterised by a genuine interest in organic (humanistic) structure rather than mechanistic structure.
- Workers' output is determined by the group norms but not by the time study and motion study.
- Workers are motivated not only by the money but also by non-financial rewards.

Box 2.1: Azim Premji: People are Capable of Extraordinary Things

Premji firmly believes that ordinary people are capable of extraordinary things. The key to this is creating highly charged teams. He takes a personal interest in developing teams and leaders and invests personal time in his managers. Managers agree that Premji is happy to work alongside them, making sales calls with the marketing team, and is said to welcome criticism. A just boss, if a stern master. "I demand of others only what I demand of myself," he says.

That's fine if you also happen to enjoy working fifteen hours a day. Mistakes are not penalized but deception is akin to waving a red flag in front of a raging bull. There's a legend (true!) that Premji once preferred to face a tough, three-month strike rather than rehire an employee who had submitted fraudulent expense accounts. "The person said he was traveling in first class, when in fact he was traveling in second class and pocketing the difference," he recalls, "that was unacceptable.

To be able to predict the future and rightly predict it is what differentiates smart managers from managers. And Premji has proved himself as a manager with a finger on the pulse of the world. The future, according to him,

will see significant changes in technology, economy and society. "But what will remain unchanged is the need of the customer for an organization with a human face."

(**Source**: http://www.moneycontrol.com/news/management/azim-premji-his-strategy-for-wipro_189075.html)

Human Relations: Definition

Human relations pertains to motivating people in organisations in order to develop teamwork which effectively fulfils their needs and leads to achieving organisational goals. Thus human relations:

- strive to create a positive and conducive work environment, focuses on people,
- has the ultimate goal of increase in productivity and
- seeks to build human cooperation towards achievement of organisational goals.

Major Concepts in Human Relations: According to experts in human relations, organisations should be viewed as a social system with economic and social dimensions. The work environment should be conducive for the restoration of man's dignity.

Sound human relations encourage people to work together. It is determined by the nature of the leader, the work environment and the work (Fig.2.1).

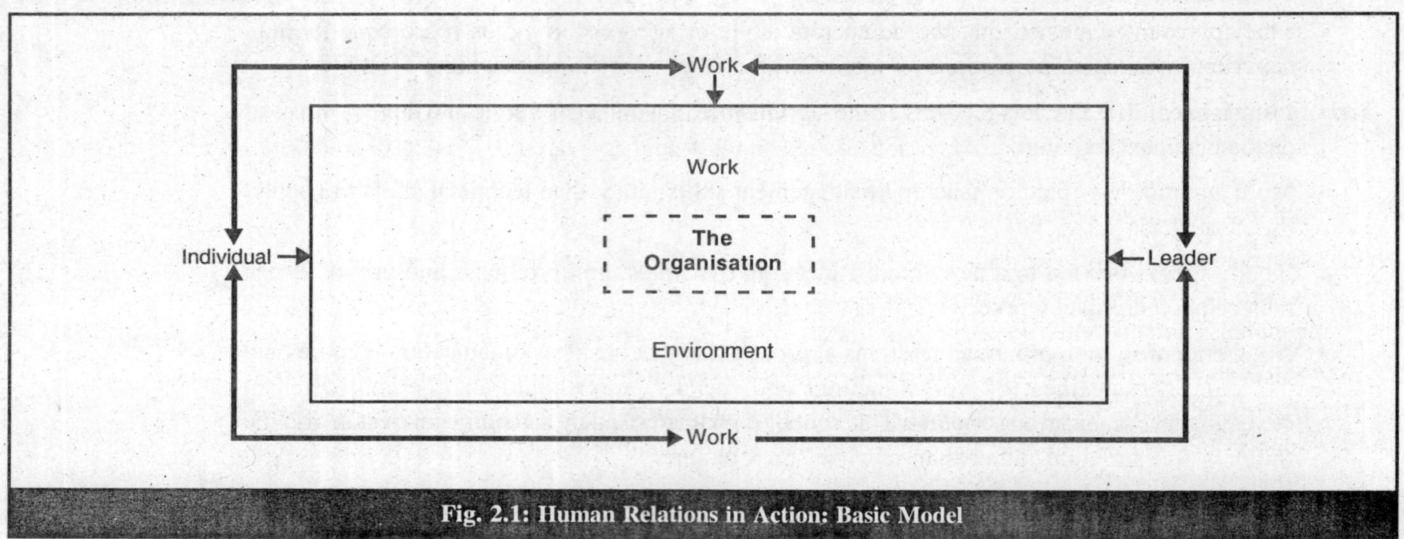

Fig. 2.1: Human Relations in Action: Basic Model

Basic Model

The humanistic approach is based on two assumptions *viz.* *(i)* the organisation is a system designed to produce or distribute a product or a service at a reasonable price and *(ii)* the organisation is a social system through which individuals try to find expression for their needs, goals and aspirations. The basic model for this approach should be employer participation, job satisfaction and increased productivity.

The Individual: According to the neoclassical theory, individual behaviour is affected by feelings, sentiments and attitudes. An individual is motivated not only by economic factors but also by social factors. Due consideration should be given to economic and social factors in motivating employees.

The Work Group: The social group is the centre of focus of human relations studies. The Hawthorne studies proved that the informal work groups exert tremendous influence over workers' behaviour patterns. Work is a social interaction, where workers are more satisfied as members in a social group.

The Organisation and the Work Environment: An industrial organisation is a techno-economic and social system. Hence it is necessary to understand rational as well as non-rational and formal as well as informal aspects and the work environment of an organisation. Positive work environments are characterized by factors like: clearly stated goals, incentives to improve performance, performance feedback, employee involvement in decision making, rules to the minimum extent, interesting and challenging work and the like.

The Leader: The leader has to use all types of resources including human resources in the process of attaining organisational goals. Proper utilisation of human resources enables the leader to achieve these goals effectively. A leader can contribute significantly for high productivity by creating a conducive and free-work environment.

Criticisms of the Human Relations Approach

(i) **Scientific Validity:** Although the Hawthorne Experiments profoundly influenced the managers in managing their employees, the studies had many weaknesses of design, analysis and interpretation. Whether Mayo and his colleagues' conclusions are consistent with their data is still the subject of lively debate and considerable confusion.[18] These studies had a clinical bias

as they discounted theory and stressed on radical empiricism. Most of the conclusions are not supported by adequate scientific evidence.

(ii) **Shortsighted:** The following points confirm the shortsightedness of this approach: *(i)* it lacks adequate focus on the work; *(ii)* human relations tend to neglect economic dimensions of work satisfaction and *(iii)* human relations research is concerned with only operative employees but not managerial and supervisory personnel.

(iii) **Over-concern with happiness:** The Hawthorne studies suggested that happy employees would be productive employees. But studies have failed to establish a positive correlation between happiness and productivity.

(iv) **Misunderstanding of Participation:** Many of the post Hawthorne human relationists expected that participation would reduce resistance to formal authority and would ensure worker's support for organisational goals. But recent studies indicate that employees want to be utilised properly.

(v) **The Mystery surrounding group decision-making:** Research evidence on the superiority of group decision-making to individual decision-making is conflicting and inconclusive. The entire thinking of group decision-making is mystical.

(vi) **Conflict:** The human relationists failed to recognise positive aspects of conflict like creative force in society. They believed that conflict is always bad and should be minimised.

(vii) **Anti-Individualist:** The human relations movement is anti-individualist. The concept of individualism and individual behaviour which is predominant in an organisational setting is overridden by the concept of group decision-making and group behaviour. Human relations approach failed to describe completely individuals in the work place.

(viii) **Total Work Environment is not considered:** Work environment comprises of organisational structure, its culture and climate, labour-management relations, social environment etc. But the human relations approach considered only social environment as the total work environment.

The next approach developed towards management is systems approach. Now, we shall study the system approach to management.

(F) SYSTEMS APPROACH TO MANAGEMENT

A system is a set of interrelated but separate parts working towards a common purpose. The arrangement of elements must be orderly and there must be proper communication facilitating interaction between the elements and finally this interaction should lead to achieve a common goal.

Organisation: Unified, proposeful system composed of interrelated parts.

Thus, systems approach to management views the organisation as a unified, purposeful system composed of interrelated parts. Hence, managers have to deal with the organisation as a whole rather than dealing separately with various segments of an organisation. This approach also gives the managers to see the organisation as a whole and as a part of the larger external environment. Systems theory reveals to us that the activity of any segment of an organisation, affects in different degrees, the activity of every other segment.[19]

Systems-oriented managers would make decisions only after they have identified impact of these decisions on all other departments and the entire organisation. The essence of the systems approach is that each manager cannot function in isolation and within his organisational boundary of authority and responsibility of the traditional organisational chart. They must intertwine their departments with the total organisation and communicate with all other departments and employees and also with other organisations.[20]

Key Concepts of Systems Approach

***(i)* Subsystem:** Subsystems are those parts which make up the whole system. Each system in turn may be a subsystem of a still larger system. Thus, a department is a subsystem of a factory, which is a subsystem of a firm, which is a subsystem of an industry, which is a subsystem of a national economy, which is a subsystem of the world economic system.

***(ii)* Synergy:** Synergy is the situation in which the whole is greater than the sum of its parts. In organisational terms, synergy means that departments that interact co-operatively are more productive than they would be, if they operated in isolation.

***(iii)* Open System:** It is a system that interacts with its environment. All organisations interact with their environment, but the extent to which they do so varies.

***(iv)* Closed system:** It is a system that does not interact with its environment.

***(v)* System Boundary:** It is the boundary that separates each system from its environment. It is rigid in a closed system while flexible in an open system.

***(vi)* Flows:** A system has flows of information, materials and energy. These enter the system from the environment as inputs (like raw materials), undergo transformation process within the system (like production process) and exist in the system as outputs (like products/services). (Fig.2.2 shows the flows and feedback in an open system).

***(vii)* Feedback:** It is the part of system control in which the results of actions are returned to the individual, allowing work procedures to be analysed and corrected.

Systems approach helps the dynamic and interrelated nature of organisations to plan for actions and anticipate consequences and mutual effects. It helps the general managers to maintain balance among various subsystems and the organisation. Thus a major contribution of the systems approach results from its strong emphasis on the interrelatedness or mutuality of various subsystems of the organisation. Treatment of the organisation as an open system is another contribution of systems approach.

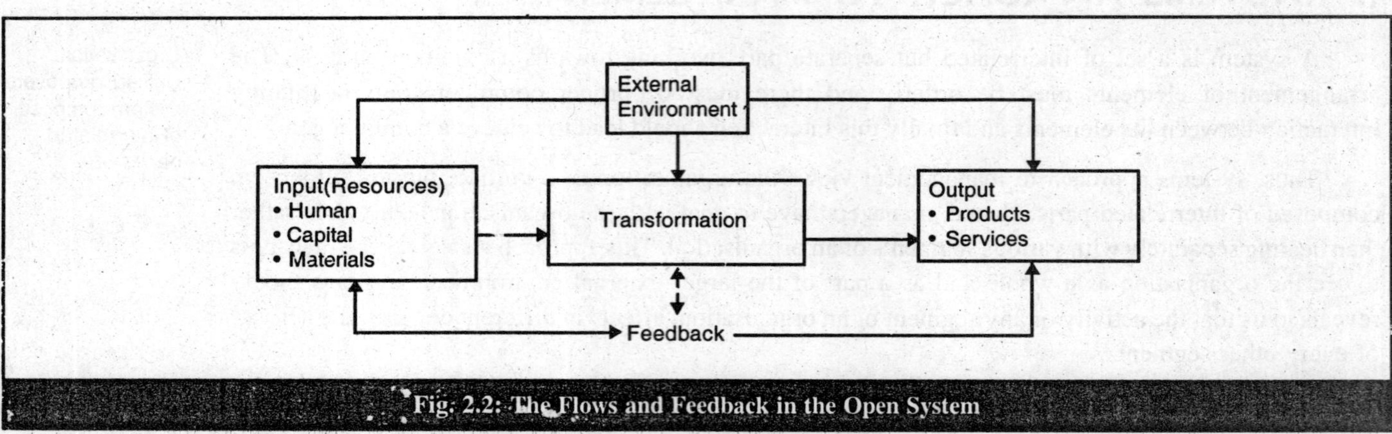

Fig: 2.2: The Flows and Feedback in the Open System

Features of Systems Approach to Management

According to Herbert B.Hicks and C.Ray Gullett,[21] the characteristics of systems approach to management are:

(i) **Dynamic:** The process between subsystems within an organisation is dynamic.

(ii) **Multilevel and multidimensional:** An organisation can interact with other organisations and the economy at various levels and in multifarious ways.

(iii) **Multimotivated:** Since the organisation is dynamic and has multiple goals, an act in the organisation may be motivated by several motives.

(iv) **Probabilistic:** Management would be mostly probabilistic as it is operated under a highly turbulent and dynamic environment.

(v) **Multidisciplinary:** Systems theory of management is contributed by various disciplines.

(vi) **Descriptive:** Instead of providing certain prescriptions, this theory describes the features of organisation and management.

(vii) **Adaptive:** All the subsystems should be adaptable and accommodate to the changes in other subsystems.

(G) CONTINGENCY APPROACH

Contingency approach is also called *situational approach*. This approach was developed by managers, consultants and researchers who tried to apply the concepts of the major schools to real life situations. They sought to know the causes for the success of methods in one situation and failure in another situation. Advocates of this approach answered that results differ because situations differ, as such a technique that works effectively in one situation will not necessarily work in all cases. Hence managers have to identify the technique which will best contribute to the attainment of the management's goal in a particular situation, under particular circumstances and at a particular time. Classical theorists suggest work implication for increase in productivity whereas behavioural scientists suggest job enrichment. But the manager under contingency approach should find out which method will work better in that particular situation. This approach builds upon systems approach. The composition of a particular situation or system will help to know the technique best suited to that particular situation or system. (See Box 2.2).

Box 2.2: Ratan Tata: Genius who is India's Gift to World - Contingency Management

When Ratan Tata visited the home of the designer Ralph Lauren last year, the two car enthusiasts spent much of the time in the garage admiring Lauren's car collection, including the classic 1955 Jaguar XKD. Now Tata is poised to take over Jaguar. Tata Motors said on Thursday it was beginning detailed talks with Ford Motor about buying the Jaguar and Land Rover brands, confirming what investors and analysts in India, Detroit and Britain have expected for months. Tata said it wanted to reach an agreement over the next few weeks.

For Ratan Tata, 70, the takeover will cap 16 years of transforming one of the world's most diverse and unusual conglomerates, the Tata Group. Through 98 companies, Tata creates and sells products ranging from steel to tea to watches, making the company's name ubiquitous in India. Under Ratan Tata the name has started to reverberate around the globe as well. A string of international deals has diversified Tata to the point where more than half its revenue this year will come from outside India.

Tata's increasingly global outlook is also bolstering the overseas ambitions of other Indian companies. Going overseas was necessary, Ratan Tata said. In the late 1990s the group's truck unit recorded a loss that was the biggest in Indian history, he said in a recent interview in Tata's headquarters in the leafy Colaba district of Mumbai. "We were so dependent on one economy. I decided we needed a broader view."

Since then Tata has done dozens of deals, buying businesses as diverse as the Tyco Global Network, Daewoo Commercial Vehicles, the Moroccan chemical company Imacid, Tetley Teas and, most audaciously, the $US11.3 billion ($12.8 billion) takeover of the British steel maker Corus last year, a company several times the size of Tata Steel. The group's 27 listed companies have a market capital of more than $US70 billion, and the group reported after-tax profit of $US2.8 billion the last financial year, a 33 per cent increase from the year before, in part because of the Corus acquisition.

The Corus deal garnered Ratan Tata rare criticism, analysts wondering whether he had taken on too much. Corus "came to us; we didn't seek them out", he said, and it was a deal he could not pass up. In "one swoop we were in Europe, where we weren't before. That opportunity was going to happen once."

The Tata Group is an unusual corporate enterprise. Started in 1868 by Jamsetji Tata, one of India's dwindling group of Parsis, the group has often seemed to value employees as much as profits (paying laid-off Tata Steel employees for the rest of their lives when the company made cuts, for example), and has prided itself on fair practices, rather than cut-throat manoeuvring or paying bribes, a practice still prevalent in some of corporate India.

Indeed, Ratan Tata seems the most unlikely of corporate titans - almost preternaturally humble, unabashedly open about the company's mistakes and about the fact that he never really wanted to be an industrialist. He studied architecture at Cornell University. After decades of working for the family business, he says he is considering opening a small architecture firm when he retires.

He is a distant relative of the founder - his father was adopted by the wife of one of Jamsetji's sons. Never married, he lavishes attention on his dogs, writes thank-you notes to employees who do him favours, and is often spied on Sundays driving alone Marine Drive in Mumbai in one of the several cars he owns.

"None of us observers of the Tatas could have predicted that he would grow and blossom the way he has and be in total charge of the company the way he has," said R.M. Lala, the author of several books about the family and companies, and a one-time director of the Tata Trust, a charity that finances health care and education projects in India. Other executives and companies may have made more money in India, Mr Lala said, "but Tata is still the most respected name in Indian industry".

As company chairman, Ratan Tata has been instrumental in carrying on the family legacy and turning what was a loosely aligned group of companies that shared one name into a group with seven business lines and centralised management. It is a business plan he developed in the most unlikely of settings: he spent three months at his mother's bedside at Memorial Sloan-Kettering Cancer Centre in Manhattan in 1981. At the time he was chairman of Tata Industries, then a small part of the group responsible for new ventures.

When he was named chairman in 1991 he started reining in some of the company's independently minded managers and giving the parent company sizable equity stakes in its offspring.

The process was not easy, he wrote in a 2003 epilogue to The Creation of Wealth, a book about the Tatas.

"If I reflect on what these 10 years have been for me personally, they have been a mixed bag," he wrote. "There is some satisfaction that I've seen the group come together in many ways ... [but] at the same time there is a sense of frustration at the resistance to change from many of my colleagues that I have seen through this period of time."

All in all, he wrote, "it has been a hard and sometimes unrewarding experience". Outsiders do not see it that way. The Tata family has been "all about building businesses and being farsighted about it", said Tarun Jotwani, the chief executive of Lehman Brothers in India.

What Ratan Tata has done very well is be the strategic and ethical head, while providing a "culture of integrity", Mr Jotwani said. Ratan Tata's reign may come to an end soon. He said he was considering retiring after one of his pet projects, the $US2500 People's Car, hits showrooms this year. Tata has no heirs, and there is no likely family member to take over his role, meaning the man who brought the Tata Group to the rest of the world may be the last Tata to run the company.

(**Source:** http://www.smh.com.au/business/ratan-tata-genius-who-is-indias-gift-to-world-20080106-1kg8.html)

(H) HUMAN RESOURCE MANAGEMENT APPROACH

Human resource is a principal and central sub-system and resource of an organisation. Both the human resource system and the entire organisation operate under the same environmental factors. Greater the effectiveness and productivity of human resources, the more will be the effectiveness of the organisation. Most of the managers say, our greatest asset is people. Human resource management approach is developmental. It is concerned with the growth and development of people toward higher levels of competency, creativity and fulfilment.

The human resource management approach is supportive.[22] It helps employees to develop through training and development and other techniques of human development. It also develops more responsible and committed persons through the creation of conducive organizational climate, strong culture, attractive reward system, free and challenging work environment, team spirit and the like.

This approach assumes that increased capabilities and expanded opportunities for people will lead directly to the improvement of the organizational effectiveness and efficiency. Employee job satisfaction will also be a direct result when employees make use of their resources to the fullest extent. Thus, the human resource management approach reveals that sound management of human resources through proper training and development, judicious salary administration, creating conducive work environment, providing challenging job and maintaining sound industrial relations result in the employee contribution for achievement of organizational goals.

(I) MANAGEMENT SCIENCE APPROACH

Science is a systematically organized body of knowledge based on proper findings and exact principles and is capable of verification and general application. Science is systematic in the sense that certain relationships between variables have been ascertained, principles and their limitations have been discovered, tested and established. Facts are determined based on events or things observed initially with the help of scientific methods. The accuracy of the facts are verified through observations on a continuous basis. Thus, the knowledge obtained must be verifiable in scientific method. Any subject to be called science must have the following characteristics:

(i) Systematic body of knowledge

(ii) Method of scientific enquiry

(iii) Should establish cause and effect relationship

(iv) Principles should be verifiable

(v) Should ensure predictable results

(vi) Should have universal application.

Management has a systematized body of knowledge pertaining to its field. The scientific character of management is well supported by mathematical models and operations research. A manager can also take appropriate decisions based on decision science like any scientist.

The principles underlying time and motion studies, market research, morale, motivation, job satisfaction etc. are developed based on scientific enquiry. Many management principles like planning, direction, organisation, motivation, morale etc., establish cause and effect relationship. Management principles like unity of command, span of control and unity of direction can be verifiable. Those in the category of job satisfaction, morale and job enrichment ensure predicable results. Almost all the management principles are universally applicable.

(J) CONCLUSION

However, it must be pointed out that management cannot be an exact science like physics, chemistry and natural science. According to Peter F.Drucker, management can never be an exact science. Further, management cannot be an exact science as business is highly dynamic and business conditions change continuously. Management can be a social science as it mostly deals with human beings.

KEY TERMS

- Group Harmony
- Management Science Approach
- Motion Study
- Functional Foremanship
- Standardisation
- Division of Labour
- Authority
- Time Study
- Human Relations
- Work Group
- Systems Approach
- Contingency Approach
- HRM Approach
- Unity of Command
- Synergy
- Open System
- Closed System
- Differential Payment

QUESTIONS

1. What is scientific management? Discuss the contributions made to scientific management.
2. Discuss the principles of scientific management in detail.
3. Why and how the principles of scientific management have been criticised?
4. Explain the contributions made to the Administrative Management.
5. Discuss in detail Fayol's principles of management and their relevance to the modern companies.
6. Comment on the Hawthorne Experiments and their outcome.
7. What is human relations? Discuss the contributions to and major concepts in human relations.
8. Appraise the systems approach to management. What are its features?
9. Write short notes on : *(i)* Contingency approach to management *(ii)* HRM approach to management *(iii)* Management Science Approach to management.

REFERENCES

1. A.Lepawsky, *Administration,* Alfred A.Kropt. Inc., 1949, pp.78-81.
2. L.S.Msu, *The Political Philosophy of Confucianism,* E.P.Dutton & Co.Inc., New York, 1932, p.124.
3. Charles Babbage, *On the Economy of Machinery and Manufacturers*, London, 1832, p.v.
4. *Ibid.*, p.132.
5. F.W.Taylor, *Shop Management in Scientific Management*, Harper & Row, New York, 1947, p.31.
6. *Ibid.*, pp.36-37.
7. *Ibid.*, pp.26-30.
8. James A.F.Stoner and R.Edward Freeman, *Management*, Prentice Hall of India (P) Ltd., New Delhi, 1992, p.33.
9. Henri Fayol, *General Administrtion*, Sir Issac Pitman and Sons Ltd., London, p.3.
10. Henri Fayol, *Industrial and General Administration*, J.A.Coubrough. trans.International Management Institute, Geneva, 1930.
11. Max Weber, *The Theory of Social and Economic Organisations*, Free Press, New York, 1947.
12. James A.F.Stover and R.Edward Freeman, *Op.Cit.*, p.36.
13. Mary P.Follett, *The New State*, Glowcester Mass, Peter Smith, 1918.
14. James A.F.Stoner and R.Edward Freeman, *Op.Cit.*, p.40.
15. Elton Mayo, *The Human Problems of an Industrial Civilisation*, The MacMillan Company, New York, 1933, p.29.
16. *Ibid*.
17. *Ibid*.

18. Gary Yunker, *The Hawthorne Studies : Facts and Myths*, Faculty Working Papers, Department of Psychology, Jacksouville State University, Summer, 1985.

19. Kenneth E.Bowlding, *General Systems Theory-A Skeleton of Science*, Management Science, April 1956, pp.197-208.

20. Seymour Tilles, *The Manager's Job - A System's Approach*, Harward Business Review, January-February 1963, pp.73-81.

21. Herbert G.Hicks and C.Ray Gullett, *Organisation Theory and Behaviour*, McGraw Hill Book Company, New York, 1975, pp.209-221.

22. Keith Davis, *Human Behaviour at Work*, McGraw Hill Publishing Co., New York, 1990.

CHAPTER **3**

SOCIAL RESPONSIBILITIES OF BUSINESS

Chapter Outline

(A) Introduction : Traditional View, Modern View

(B) Social Responsibilities of Business

(C) Influence of Environment

- Key Terms
- Questions
- References

Learning Objectives

After studying this Chapter, you should be able to:

✓ Understand the rationale behind the traditional view of social responsibility of business.

✓ Evaluate why the modern view of social responsibility of business has emerged.

✓ Discuss the arguments for and against social responsibilities of business.

✓ Discuss the social responsibilities of business towards consumers/customers, employees, shareholders/stockholders, Government, other business firms and community.

✓ Scan the external environment and analyse its impact on business.

(A) INTRODUCTION

From the above case incident, it creates a curiosity in our cognition to know what is social responsibility? Now, shall we discuss the concept of social responsibility?

Traditional View of Social Responsibility

Friedman: Business's business is business

In traditional societies, the prime purpose of business was profit maximisation. Even as late as 1970, Milton Friedman stated that '*the business of business is business*'. In other words, the only objective of business is the making of profits. Friedman argues that the profit earned by business belongs exclusively to the shareholders of the business and these profits cannot be diverted to any other social purpose. He defended his argument by saying that "if the executive uses corporate resources for social ends, he is using the money for the purposes for which it was not intended... "[1] He further states that "there is one and only one social responsibility of business-to use its resources and engage in activities designed to increase its profits..."[2] John Lodd expressed a similar opinion in 1970, saying "it is improper to expect organisational conduct to conform to the ordinary principles of morality..."[3]

However, most academicians, economists, socialists, philosophers, politicians and even businessmen and bankers do not compromise with these opinions. It is doubtful whether these opinions hold good today, especially during the post liberalisation era. T.A.Mathias felt that "moral behaviour pays....at least in the long run."[4] An enlightened approach aims at long-run objectives and not mere short-run gains.The days of traditional views are gone. Now, we shall study the modern view towards social responsibilities.

Modern View of Social Responsibility

It is now being increasingly recognised that business is not an end in itself. It is only a means to an end. That end is man, be it a worker, customer, consumer or any member of society. It is also recognized that business is a social and economic institution which cannot live in isolation.

The establishment and development of business is dependent on the contributions made by society. Society has to bear the cost and consequences of the establishment and operation of business. It has to allot land, supply water and other materials, provide infrastructural facilities and develop and provide human resources. In addition to this, consumers who are members of society, allow the business to continue its operations by creating effective demand for the goods and services produced/ rendered or distributed by the business.

Modern view: Not as the be-all and end-all of the business's operations

Thus, business is mostly dependent upon society. Realising this, most of the businessmen today feel that their objective is not merely profit maximisation but it also consists of contributing something towards solving the problems of their employees, consumers and society at large. Here it is appropriate to state that, "a socially and ethically conscious firm and its managers should, therefore, look upon profits not as the be-all and end-all of their operations.."[5] '*Social Audit*' is one such technique used to measure performance.

Table 3.1: Summary of Major Agruments for and against Social Responsibility for Business

For Social Responsibility
• It is in the best interest of a business to promote and improve the communities where it doesbusiness.
• Social action can be profitable.
• It is an ethical thing to do.
• It improves the public image of the firm.

- It increases the viability of the business system. Business exists because it gives society benefits. Society can amend or take away its charter. This is the 'iron law of responsibility.'
- It is necessary to avoid government regulation.
- Sociocultural norms require it.
- Laws cannot be passed for all circumstances. Thus, business must assume responsibility to maintain an orderly legal society.
- It is in the stockholders' best interest. It will improve the price of stock in the long run as the stock market will view the company as less risky and open to public attack.
- Society should give business a chance to solve social problems that the government has failed to solve.
- Business is considered by some groups to be the institution with the financial and human resources to solve social problems.
- Prevention of problems is better than cure-so let business solve problems before they become critical.

Against Social Responsibility

- It might be illegal.
- Business plus government equal monolith.
- Social actions cannot be measured.
- It violates profit maximisation.
- The cost of social responsibility is too great and would increase prices too much.
- Business lacks social skills to solve societal problems.
- It would weaken the balance of payments because price of goods will have to go up to pay for social programs.
- Business already has too much power. Such involvement would make business too powerful.
- Business lacks accountability to the public.
- Such business involvement lacks broad public support.

(**Source:** Adapted from R.Joseph Monsen, Jr., *The Social Attitudes of Management*, in Joseph W.McQuire, ed., Contemporary Management (Englewood Cliffs,N.):Prentice Hall, 1974), p.616, Quoted in Certo and Peter, p.222.)

Thus, it is accepted today that the business has to discharge its responsibility towards society. The concept of 'Social Responsibility of Business' includes responsibilities towards itself, shareholders, employees, other business firms, government, customers/consumers, creditors and the society.

This declaration also emphasised certain main features of Social Responsibility of Business, viz.

- In addition to making a fair and adequate return on capital, business must be just and humane, as well as efficient and dynamic.
- The social responsibilities of business can best be assumed in an atmosphere of freedom with the least possible restraint on healthy competition.
- Every business has an overriding responsibility to make the fullest possible use of its resources, both human and capital.
- It highlights the respective roles of the enterprises, the shareholders, the workers, the customers, the management and the community.
- It laid emphasis on the reciprocal duties between business and the community.

(B) SOCIAL RESPONSIBILITIES OF BUSINESS

Now, we shall study the social responsibilities of business towards different stakeholders *viz.*, consumers/customers, employees, shareholders/ stockholders, other business firms, state and community. The social responsibilities of Business, in the Indian context are presented in Fig. 3.1.

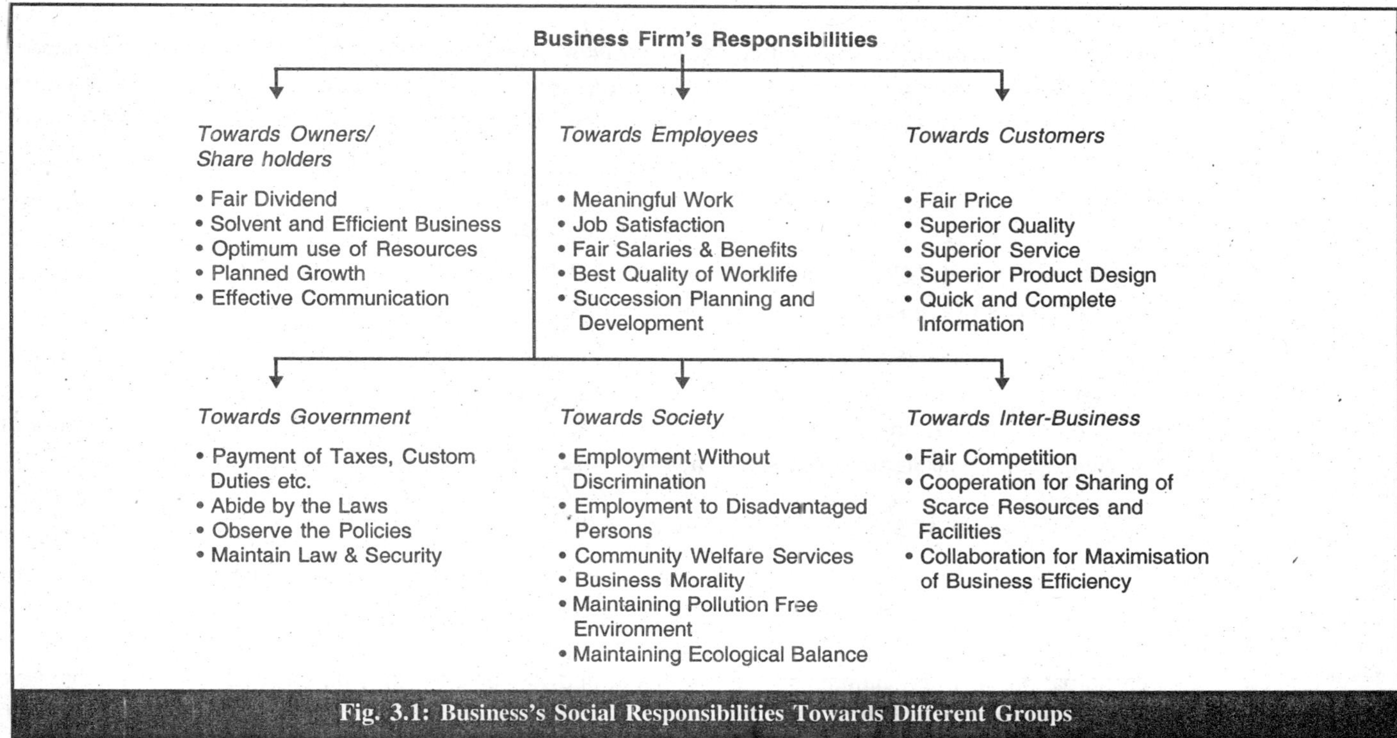

Fig. 3.1: Business's Social Responsibilities Towards Different Groups

Responsibilities Towards Consumers/Customers

Responsibilities towards consumers: Meet the needs of the consumers

Consumer satisfaction is the ultimate aim of all economic activity. This includes:

- the goods must meet the needs of the consumers of different classes, tastes and the purchasing power;
- they must be reasonably priced, be of a dependable quality and of sufficient variety;
- the sale of such goods must be followed by after sales service to ensure advice, guidance and maintenance;
- there should be a fair and wide spread distribution of goods and services among all the sections of consumers and community and
- there should be prevention of concentration of goods in the hands of a limited number of producers, purchasers or groups.

In other words, business owes to itself the primary obligation to give a fair and square deal to its customers and consumers. They should be charged a fair and reasonable price which should be well within their reach. The supply of goods should be of uniform standard and of reasonably good quality. Their distribution must be widespread as to be within the easy reach of the consumer. No business should directly or indirectly indulge in profiteering, hoarding or creating artificial scarcity. Business should not mislead the consumer and community by false, misleading and exaggerated advertisements, because obscene advertisements are demoralizing the society and a danger to public morals.

Consumer satisfaction is the ultimate aim of all economic activity. But adulteration of goods, poor quality, failure to give fair measure, lack of service and courtesy to the customer, misleading and dishonest advertising, are all examples of violation of its obligations by a business enterprise towards the consumers.

Therefore, free competition must be allowed to operate and should be encouraged by anti-monopoly legislation. Where certain monopolies are accepted as unavoidable or in public interest, the price of their toleration has to include the government's right to impose any controls that may be needed to check undue monopoly power. Legislation is required to prevent deception and fraud being practiced on consumers, and where essential goods are in short supply, their fair distribution should be ensured.

Moreover, internal accountability to consumers should be extended. The Memorandum of Association (MoA) of public limited companies and state enterprises should embody a specific declaration of these wider responsibilities of management. The management should encourage the establishment of the Consumers' Advisory Councils/Committees so that these bodies could represent the grievances of consumers to the management.

The consumers themselves have social responsibilities to their fellow-consumers. If they passively submit to exploitation, they help to lower the standards of service. Equally, they are a support to consumers' associations which, by investigation and reporting on the comparative prices and quality of products, can assist them in making a more informed choice of their purchases.

Responsibilities Towards Employees

Responsibilities towards employees: Fair wage, conductive work environment and protection of human rights.

It is the basic responsibility of the enterprise to produce wealth and also to provide opportunities for meaningful work. The management should develop its administration in such a way so as to promote a spirit of cooperative endeavour between employers and employees. There should be a sense of participation between capital, on the one hand, and labour and skill, on the other, in their objective towards prosperity and progress. The cooperation of workers can be won by creating conditions in which workers are enabled to put forward their best efforts in the common task as free men. This means recognition:

- of the workers' right to a fair wage;
- of the right to participate in decisions affecting their working life;
- to membership of the trade union;
- to collective bargaining and
- to the right to strike.

Management should give workers opportunity to develop their capabilities through training, education and enjoyment of freedom to the greatest possible extent. Management should develop among workers a sense of belonging to the business and provide them with healthy living conditions, cheap houses, leisure and amenities, profit-sharing and an efficient system of communication.

The business or a plant is a community and justice should be its rule. This means there should be a company code of conduct with a recognized procedure for settling grievances which result in improved performance. The code should guarantee religious, political and social independence of the workers and make reasonable provisions for them to take part in civic activities which benefit the community.

The image of business should be improved in the eyes of the workers so that persons of high calibre and capacity could be drawn to it. Routine monotony and boredom should be broken by job enrichment and job enlargement programmes. Finally, industrial peace and new techniques of professional management must be ensured within the precincts of the industry itself.

Likewise, workers should realise their moral duty to do a good day's job for a good day's salary, to cooperate in increasing productivity, to come forward with suggestions and to participate in discharging their responsibility to the life of the plant and the community.

Responsibilities Towards Owners/Shareholders

Management's first duty is to see that enterprise is stable, enterprising and actively engaged in accomplishing its objectives. It would then be capable of providing those who commit their capital to it with such a fair and adequate reward for risk taken. It permits the company to attract the necessary capital from the market. This capital is raised by the owners (proprietors, retailers, wholesalers, sole-traders) owning business, its property and looking after its management; the share of stockholders who contribute to the shares and debentures of the company or the partners (if there are any).

The expectations of these types of owners are:

- a fair and reasonable return on the capital invested by them;
- a part in profit, if the Memorandum so specifies, in the shape of profit-sharing or bonus payment schemes;
- political and economic security for investment through a stable government, good law and order situation and stable tax policies and fiscal measures;
- knowledge about the working of the enterprise, its periodical progress report, so that they may be satisfied that their capital has been faithfully and usefully employed;
- a fair amount of dividend or retained earnings and
- profiteering, black-marketing, cornering of supplies, unfair trade practices are curbed and legally prohibited.

Responsibilities towards owners: Fair return on capital, stable dividend and growth of the company

The shareholders also have their obligations. Shareholders in the General Meetings should question the Directors on the accounts and discuss policy matters and make their representation more effective through their associations. They can thus ensure that the company is pursuing a dynamic policy and that sufficient profit is laid aside for innovation and expansion. They should play a constructive role in encouraging the directors to pursue a responsible policy towards the company, its obligations to the community, employees and customers, upon which in the long run, the company's reputation and future prospects depend.

Responsibilities Towards Inter-Business

The social responsibilities of business include a healthy co-operative business relationship between different businesses. Businessmen must resist unfair and unethical competition and avoid unfair interference in their rival's business such as price-rigging, undercutting, patronage, unfair canvassing, supply of substandard goods, application of undue financial, legal and political pressure; spreading false rumours/statements about the rival's products, creating labour troubles for the competitors' industry or launching a boycott campaign of their products, employing unethical advertisements and controlling the supply of particular goods/services produced by them only so that an artificial scarcity is created in the market, giving rise to monopolistic conditions, artificial high prices as per quality of goods etc.

Destructive competition is always harmful, as it destroys confidence in business and introduces chaos instead of order and discipline. Therefore, the correct solution is not retaliation but the development of true ideas among the business community and to secure such legal regulation as is necessary to protect businessmen. A good businessman should adopt fair means to meet his rival's competition. This may be by adopting better designs, good advertisements, quick and safe delivery with after-sales service, reasonable price etc.

It is needless to say that unfair competition enters with extortion, bribery, kick backs and granting of discriminatory advertising allowances or brokerage fees and these should be avoided at all costs.

Responsibilities Towards the State

Responsibilities towards state: tax payments, environmental protection, ecological balance, good corporate citizen

The social responsibilities of business towards the state (government) demands that:

- it will be a law-abiding citizen;
- it will pay its dues and taxes to the state fully and honestly;
- it will not corrupt public servants and the democratic process for his selfish ends;
- it will not purchase political support by unfair means;
- it will strive fairly and honestly to stimulate economic growth even by making reasonable sacrifices on occasions of national need;
- it will participate in the public life of the country in helping to make policies, fair legislation and working on advisory bodies;
- it will sell his goods, commodities and services without adulteration at fair and reasonable prices and
- it will maintain fair trade practices and refrain from activities like restraint of trade and will not take recourse to hoarding, cornering and profiteering and other such unfair practices.

The government has also some obligations towards business, such as to provide:

- a clean, prompt and efficient administration;
- intelligent, practical laws, easily understood and easily applied;
- reasonable political and social stability without frequent changes in legislative, administrative and fiscal policies;
- law and order ensuring safety of life, property and continuing business;
- a dynamic framework for rapid economic growth (infrastructure, legal aid);
- rule of law;
- holding of scales evenly between groups and sections in society;
- political and social stability where business can grow and develop;
- reasonable legislation for protecting units of business against monopoly and
- healthy atmosphere to industrial peace.

Unfortunately, both have failed to fulfil their reciprocal obligations because of the following causes:

- **Economic-Political and Organisational Factors**
  - breach of law by employers;
  - monopolism/groupism among all sectors;
  - business's apathy to change for lack of time and unwillingness;

- ideological and methodical conflicts and differences between different states;
- existence of price-cutting, malpractices and unfair trade practices;
- division of management and labour into two warring groups, one endeavouring to win over the other and
- technological changes, rationalisation, modernisation, leading to false notions of mass employment among labour.

- **Government Administrative Factors**
  - breach of law by employers;
  - discriminatory authority vested in government officials;
  - excessive political bias in the formulation of targets, policies and procedures without regard to basic economic laws;
  - loose, short-lived uncoordinated administrative structure;
  - multiplicity and complexity of laws;
  - frequent changes in laws and policies;
  - absence of integrated economy linking the private-public, large-medium, small and tiny sectors;
  - administrative delays and red-tapism and
  - unstable law and order situation.

What is, therefore, needed is that the government should adopt progressive legal tax policies, and to ensure their strict observance; reduction in tax burden; careful planning, keeping in view the economic principle; strict supervision of and penalty for defaulters; easily understandable laws which are not frequently changed.

Responsibilities Towards the Community

Responsibilities towards community: Infrastructure development, communal harmony.

The business owes great responsibility to the community in various directions. Some of the major areas where business can and does contribute towards community welfare as part of its social responsibility are:

(i) **In the field of Industry:** Industry/business can help rural areas by introducing 'self- help' and 'earn-while-you-learn' programmes. Initially, such programmes may be labour-intensive in areas like carpentry, pottery, spinning, weaving, agro-based industry, farming, dairy farming, poultry and pig rearing, storage etc., so that increasing employment could be provided in rural areas. For this purpose, identification of areas needing improvement, facilities, skill requirements and financial assistance may be surveyed by business experts.

(ii) **In the field of Agriculture:** As a social responsibility, a large business house can play an important role in agricultural development, to provide full-time employment to the vast unemployed rural labour force. For this purpose, the business should get the survey done by its experts in the field of climate, soil conditions, breeding of livestock facilities for irrigation, water supply and actual supply of fertilizers, seeds, pesticides, expertise, and finances. Non-agricultural activities seeking linkage with the agricultural sector and the industrialised sector can also be developed.

(iii) **Housing Facilities:** The social responsibility of business in this sphere is great, specially because a major proportion of the rural population is doomed to illnesses, squalid existence in techniques

ill-planned and filthy houses. Business can, therefore, play its role in changing house-building, extending loans and financial-aid facilities, providing material and manpower support. In the urban areas, slum clearance schemes, one or two room tenements with facilities for sanitation should be provided in labour colonies.

(iv) **Transportation:** Business and other agencies can help the government by undertaking studies and programmes of technical and financial assistance for the development of cheap public transport and distribution systems through improved journey planning and traffic regulation, increased operational efficiency and utilisation of road capacity, improved systems and procedures of granting licenses, more rational and scientific estimates for vehicle fleet size and manpower for different modes of transport, improved maintenance and replacement policy for the spares and structural changes in urban and rural layouts.

(v) **Health and Education:** Business organisations also hold a responsibility towards improvement of the quality of life the people in the community. They can and should be engaged in works like providing water sources for drinking and bathing, improving sewage disposal system, cleaning dirty areas of the solid waste, reducing pollution (caused by soot of chimneys, and crowded industrial units, disposal of waste water and other residues; noise, etc.), improving sanitary facilities (through construction of underground drains, cleaning of existing foul water and waste-carrying open drains, improving roads by filling pits and giving them a regular slope, provision of public toilets and bathrooms and maintaining their cleanliness). Such measures would reduce preventable and water-borne diseases. They can also distribute free medicines, nutritious food to school-going children and pregnant mothers, the aged and the sick. Holding of open camps for operation of minor ailments, eye diseases, family planning (vasectomy or tubectomy) can also be arranged by them. The explosion in population can be held in check by making available cheap contraceptives and advice for their use.

The problems responsible for ill-health in the rural areas need solution, for they result from no proper health education, unhealthy environment, unclean habits of living, poverty, poor diet and the social culture. These problems can be solved through medical help, and the help of social workers. Besides, rural education could provide individuals with knowledge and skills to enable them to manage their families, to participate in cultural and economic life and to sharpen problem-solving capabilities.

(vi) **Industrial Aid to Education in Urban Areas:** Progressive individual businessmen and individual business houses (such as Birlas, Tatas, Modis, Ruias, Lalbhais, Shreerams and others) are running and supporting schools, colleges and technical/professional educational institutions. In fact, it is a part of modern social responsibility of business that it should support educational programmes, more particularly technical education. In some cases, they help by lending the services of their specialists (as visiting experts) and giving financial help.

The National Industrial Conference Board of America in its Report on *'Industrial Aid to Education'* has suggested five different forms of educational aid which business can render to the community.

- cash contribution to educational institutions;
- scholarship and loans to undergraduate students;
- contribution of material and equipments to educational institutions;
- teaching aids for students and teachers and
- contribution of company manpower.

(vii) **Social Audit on Factual Assessment:** This should be done by trained and professional personnel to show the social performance of business. The team 'social audit' generally means a comprehensive evaluation of the way a company discharges all its responsibilities to shareholders, customers, employees, community and the government. A social audit should generally adopt a four-step process, viz.

- firm must itemise all the activities that have a potential social impact;
- the circumstances leading to these actions or activities must be explained;
- some evaluation of the performance must be conducted and
- the company must examine the relationship between the goals of the firm and those of society to see how the programmes relate to one another.

In brief, it may be said that "business must accept responsibility to the society and its various constituents as a trustee for the goods and services that it produces, consumes, saves and reinvests." Such responsibilities extend beyond the business to the lives of the people and the community and as such they should endeavour to:

- play a proper role in civil affairs within the goals of the business;
- promote amenities and help, create better living conditions;
- help in making people law-abiding and improving legislation and administration in municipal and industrial affairs and
- set up socially desirable standards of living, themselves avoiding ostentatious, wasteful expenditure and improvident display in weddings, festivities and parties.

Towards Input Suppliers: The business owes responsibility towards input suppliers and ancillary industries. They include:

(i) Providing technical know-how and assistance

(ii) Providing fair price

(iii) Assuring continuous purchase of inputs

(iv) Helping them in expansion and development

Towards Bankers and Financial Institutions: Responsibilities towards bankers and financial institution include:

(i) Providing correct data and information for project appraisal.

(ii) Prompt payment of interest.

(iii) Clearance of the principal amount on or before due date.

Towards Market Intermediaries: Business should render its responsibilities towards wholesalers, retailers and franchises. They include:

(i) Providing products quiet in advance.

(ii) Providing freedom to have price margins

(iii) Taking back poor quality products.

(iv) Providing technical managerial know-how.

(v) Training the personnel.

(vi) Providing freedom in promotional programmes.

Business is continuously influenced by the environment. In fact, business also influences and manipulates the environment.Now, we shall study the business environment.

(C) INFLUENCE OF ENVIRONMENT

Environmental influence includes: Social, technical, economic, political, intenational and natural

Manager can't perform his job in a vacuum as a number of environmental factors affect the business. The environment furnishes the macro context and the organisation is the micro unit. The external environment comprises those factors which affect an organisation from outside the organisation. Environmental factors include social, technical, economic, political, international and natural (STEPIN).

(i) **Social Factors:** Social factors that influence business include society, culture, religion, family, attitude of people towards work, wealth, family, marriage, education, ethics, human relations etc. Culture is mostly derived from climatic conditions, geographical regions, demographic factors, norms, customs and traditions. These factors affect both the business and management.

(ii) **Technological Factors:** Just as necessity is the mother of invention, competition and a host of other reasons are responsible for the rapid technological changes and innovations. As a consequence of these changes, business has to adapt latest technology in addition to employing new technical personnel and providing training to the existing employees.

(iii) **Governmental and Legal Factors:** Government influences business through its legislations and policies.Government takes care of customers and society at large while influencing the business.

(iv) **Economic Factors:** A number of economic factors affect business. Significant among them are, economic system, economic policies, national income, per capita income, industrial policies,wage level and structure, distribution of income and wealth etc.

(v) **Political Factors:** Political stability, political parties and their ideologies and political gimmicks, formations of new political parties, splits in and amalgamation of existing parties naturally affect the business.

(vi) **International Factors:** After the globalisation of Indian economy, the influence of international factors on management increased significantly. The important among them are:

- Changes in the organisation structure. The modern organisations have acquired the characteristics of flat structure, team structure and virtual structure.
- Increase in outsourcing.
- Certain principles of Henry Fayol, F.W.Taylor and Adam Smith Division of Labour of have become redundant particularly in MNCs and Private Sector business organisations.
- Global organisational culture has been emerging due to the joint ventures, mergers and amalgamations between the domestic companies and foreign companies.
- Increase in the competition from the foreign companies.

(vii) **Natural Factors:** Natural factors particularly control of pollution, maintenance of ecological balance, protecting the consumers' health influences the business and management. For example, managements of Coca-Cola and Pepsi in India have been in uncertain conditions due to the news of the effect of these soft drinks on the consumers' health. Similarly, ITC could not expand its cigarette operations. Management of some companies receives the treats from the public and government regarding pollution. Union Carbide is the best example here. Managements of such companies have to adopt crisis management principles and styles rather than using normal management principles and styles.

KEY TERMS

- Social Responsibility
- Customers
- Consumers
- Shareholders
- Stockholders
- Employees
- Inter-Business
- Government
- Fair Wage
- Fair Prices
- Transportation
- Health
- Education
- Community
- Social Audit

QUESTIONS

1. What is social responsibility of business? Explain the arguments for and against responsibilities of business towards the society.
2. Compare and contrast the traditional view and modern view of social responsibility of business.
3. "The business of business is business." Critically comment.
4. List out the responsibilities of business towards various stakeholders.
5. What is external environment? State the impact of external environment on business.

REFERENCES

1. Milton Friedman, *The Social Responsibility of Business to Increase Profits*, New York Time Magazine, September 13, 1970, p.32.
2. Milton Friedman, *The Social Responsibility of Business*, in Tom,L:. and Norman (Eds.), *Ethical Theory and Business*, Prentice Hall Inc., New Jersery, 1979, p.136.
3. John Lodd, *Morality and the Ideal Rationality in Formal Organisations*, October 1970, p.499.
4. T.A.Mathias, *Profits or People-Business and Society*, Indian Management, June 1984, p.4.
5. *Ibid.*

CHAPTER **4**

THE PLANNING PROCESS

"Fail to Plan is Plan to Fail"

☛ Chapter Outline

(A) Introduction
(B) Nature of Planning
(C) Need for Planning
(D) Types/Hierarchy of Plans
(E) Steps in the Process of Planning
(F) Advantages and Limitations of Planning
(G) Planning practices in Japan, USA and China
- Key Terms
- Questions
- References

☛ Learning Objectives

After studying this Chapter, you should be able to:

✓ Know the meaning of planning and the difference between planning and forecasting
✓ Understand the need for and importance of planning
✓ Evaluate the different types of hierarchy of plans and the difference among them
✓ Judge how the planning process begins and also know why the planning is a never ending process
✓ Explain the limitations of planning

(A) INTRODUCTION

Peter F. Drucker has proposed two criteria to judge manager's performance *viz.*, *effectiveness* – the ability to do the right things and efficiency – the ability to do the things right. These two criteria are parallel to two aspects of planning *viz.* setting the right goals and choosing the right means for achieving these goals.

Planning is a primary function of corporate management. It is a bridge between the present and the future. It gives managers some purpose, objectives, programme and direction towards the goals. Further it helps in the process of motivation and provides a framework for decision-making. It also provides standards for control of performance of overall corporations. First, we discuss the meaning before we study the *process* of planning.

Definitions

According to Harold Koontz and O'Donnell, planning is deciding in advance what is to be done in future. Plan bridges the gap between where we are and where we want to go.[1]

Planning: Deciding in advance what is to be done in future

Alfred and Beatly defined the term planning as "the thinking process, the organized foresight, the vision based on fact and experience that is required for intelligent action."[2]

Stoner and Freeman defined planning as "the process of establishing goals and suitable action for achieving these goals."[3]

Planning is selecting information and making assumptions regarding the future to formulate activities necessary to achieve organisational goals. It is composed of numerous decisions oriented to the future.[4] Planning is deciding in advance what is to be done. It involves the selection of objectives, policies, procedures and programmes from among alternatives.[5] Thus, planning is primarily concerned with looking into the future and involving the selection of the best alternative.

Forecasting Vs. Planning

We generally tend to confuse forecasting with planning. Forecasts are predictions or estimates of the future changes. In other words, forecast is an attempt to probe the future by inferences from known facts. For example, the sales of baby soaps of Johnson and Johnson were 5 lakh pieces in 2009. The population growth rate is 5 per cent and it is assumed that all other factors will remain constant in 2009-10. It is forecasted that the sales of baby soaps of Johnson and Johnson would be 5.25 lakhs in 2010-11. Thus, forecast is estimating what will happen in future. But planning is deciding in advance what is to be done in future. For example, recall the Johnson and Johnson example. If the company decides to achieve sales of 6 lakh pieces of soaps in 2010-11, it is called *planning*. The derivative plans include planning for attractive product design and substantially investing in more promotional programmes. Thus, planning is what is to be done in the future while forecasting is what will happen in the future. The implementation of planning needs extra effort. Planning is a wider aspect whereas forecasting has a narrow dimension and so forecasting is a technique of planning.

Forecasts are predictions or estimates of the future changes.

It is clear to us that planning is broader and it is different from forecasting. Now, we study the need for planning.

(B) NATURE OF PLANNING

Planning decides the objectives, goals and course of action in advance and the method of implementing and achieving the plans. Planning aims at achieving the goals more economically and accurately. It is the basic management function. The nature of planning includes:

(i) **Primary Planning:** Planning is the primary and basic function among the management functions *viz.*, planning, organising, staffing, directing and controlling. In fact, all other functions follow the function of planning. Managers first perform the planning function and then perform all other functions.

(ii) **Contributes to Objectives:** Organisational objectives specify the purpose for which the organisations are established. These objectives are converted into goals. Managers perform the planning function in order to achieve the goals and objectives. Thus planning contributes to the achievement of objectives.

(iii) **Intellectual Activity:** Planning includes foreseeing the future environmental opportunities and threats. Further, it includes acquiring organisational strengths and eliminating weaknesses in order to match these strengths and environmental opportunities. It also includes strengthening the organisation to face the environmental challenges and threats.

Managers develop alternative courses, evaluate these alternatives and select the best course. Managers should have intellectual ability and multiple skills to perform planning effectively. Thus, planning is an intellectual activity.

(iv) **Higher Efficiency:** Efficiency is the ratio between input and output. Achieving more output with the same input and/or reducing the input to achieve the same output is referred to as *efficiency*. Planning minimises the input and maximises output. Thus, planning maximises organisational efficiency.

(v) **Flexibility:** Planning should proact and react to the environmental changes. Liberalisation, privatisation and globalisation make the external environment more dynamic. This in turn results in high competitiveness and customer-centred production and marketing. In addition, customer tastes and preferences have been changing at a fast rate. All these factors made the business firms to introduce total quality management (TQM) and business process reengineering (BPRE). Planning function has acquired the character of flexibility in view of these developments.

(vi) **Consistency:** Managers at different levels formulate plans based on the internal and external environmental factors. Therefore, planning should be in consistence with the strengths of the firm and opportunities provided by the external environment. Similarly, planning at the departmental level should be in consistence with the corporate level plans.

(C) NEED FOR PLANNING

The need for planning arises mostly due to the fact that modern organisations have to survive, operate and grow in highly competitive market economies where change is the order of the day. The change may be either revolutionary (sudden) or evolutionary (slow). The different areas of change include: change in technology, change in population, change in taste preference of consumers, changes in income levels, structures and distribution, changes in competition and in economic structures and systems, changes in policies of home government or foreign government, changes in employee attitudes, behaviour etc. These changes create problems for the management through threats and challenges. Managers have to bear the problems caused due to the changes and act upon them tactfully in order to avoid or reduce the effects of these problems on the survival, operation and growth of the organisation.

Efficient managers try to foresee the problems before they actually occur and prevent them. As pointed by Terry,[6] successful managers deal with foreseen problems and unsuccessful managers struggle with unforeseen problems. The difference lies in planning. Managers have to foresee and make the future favourable to the organisation in order to achieve the goals effectively. They introduce action, overcome current problems, prevent future uncertainties, adjust the goals with the unforeseen environmental conditions and exert all their resources to achieve their goals.

Efficient managers try to foresee the problems before they actually occur and prevent them.

According to Megginson et al., "to have an organisation that looks forward to the future and tries to stay alive and prosper in a changing world, there must be active, vigorous, continuous and creative planning."[7]

Thus, there is a greater need for planning in order to keep the organisation dynamic in a changing and market economy and in a situation of uncertainty.

Primacy of Planning

Planning is the foundation of the entire management activity/process. Infact, planning provides the basis from which all functions of management arise[8]. Planning precedes other functions like organising, directing, staffing and controlling. There would be nothing to organise, recruit and select, motivate and control without planning. The idea of primacy of planning emphasises the fact that planning takes precedence over all other functions of management.

Individuals and organisations may muddle along reacting to environmental changes without a clear idea of what they have to attain without a plan. Organisations and people associated with them enhance their motivation and get inspiration that helps to encounter the obstacles with proper planning.

Further, it is said that managers cannot know how they should organise various resources – human, physical and financial – and purposes of such organisations[9]. Managers cannot recruit, select, train people and lead them without a plan. Without a plan, controlling will be an exercise in futility. Thus, planning precedes all other management functions and activities.

Many times, we come across with several concepts of planning. In fact, we are confused due to the narrow difference among them. It would be appropriate, at this juncture to understand them clearly. They are nothing but types of plans. Now we shall study and understand them.

(D) TYPES/HIERARCHY OF PLANS

Some authors treat the philosophy, purpose, objective, strategies, policies, procedures, rules, programmes and budgets as levels/hierarchy of plans while other authors including Harold Koontz *et.al.*,[10] deal as types of plans.

Types/Hierarchy of plans includes philosophy, purpose, objectives, strategies, policies, procedures and rules, programmes and budgets (See Fig.4.1). Now we shall discuss each of these types of plans.

(i) **Philosophy:** Organisations are part of society. They exist because they perform an important function in the society. Many organisations define the role that they wish to play in society in terms of philosophy. The concern for an interest in philosophy of the top management of an organisation has been steadily increasing since World War II. A philosophy is a system of thought.

A managerial philosophy that is commonly accepted is a requisite for a common scale of values in the country. Hence the philosophy of the company should have unity of thought and action in the accomplishment of economic objectives of a country. Philosophy is based on the needs and problems of society and economy of the country. Thus, philosophy bridges the gap between society and the company.

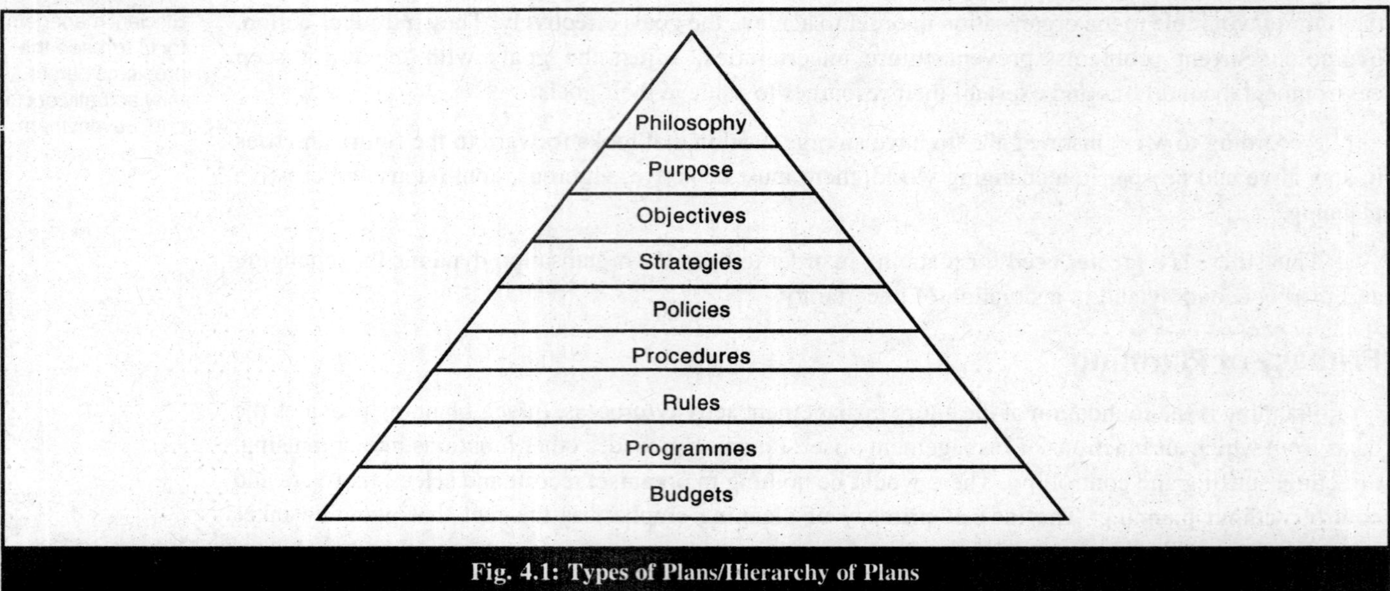

Fig. 4.1: Types of Plans/Hierarchy of Plans

The philosophy of Bank of Madhura Ltd. is: 'A vibrant bank committed to for example excellence in performance through customer satisfaction.'

Oil and Natural Gas Commission (ONGC) states its philosophy as: "To stimulate, continue and accelerate efforts to develop and maximise the contribution of the energy sector to the economy of the country."

(ii) **Purpose:** Every kind of organised group activities or operations has a purpose. For example, the purpose of a bank is to accept deposits and grant loans and advances.

(iii) **Objectives:** Objectives are the ends towards which organisational activity is aimed. Organisational objectives represent not only the end point of planning but also the end towards organising, staffing, directing and controlling point. For example, the objective of the bank may be to contribute to the socio-economic objectives of the country. Every department may have its own objectives which may not be completely the same as of the bank. For example, the objectives of the Advance Department may be to grant loans to socially and economically weaker sections of the community. This objective certainly contributes to the attainment of overall objectives of the bank.

(iv) **Strategies:** Strategy is determination of the basic long-term objectives of an enterprise and the adoption of courses of action and allocation of resources necessary to achieve these goals. Thus, a bank has to state its long-term goal, say, maximisation of customer satisfaction, profit maximisation or contribution to the maximum extent for the socio-economic uplift of the country. Thus, the management has to finalise the course of action like deposit mobilisation, granting of loans etc. and allocate resources of all types like men, material, machine and money to attain the goal.

(v) **Policies:** Policies are general statements or understandings which guide or direct thinking and action in decision-making.[11] However, all policies are not statements.

(vi) **Procedures and Rules:** Procedures are plans that establish a desired method of handling future activities. They are guides to action rather than thinking. They detail the exact manner in which a certain activity must be accomplished. For example, the procedures of granting loans which include inviting application, scrutinising application, verifying facts, appraising projects,

sanctioning loans, disbursing the loan amounts, supervising, following up end-use, recovering etc. Rules spell out specific required action or non-action allowing no discretion. For example, charging of 10 per cent rate of interest on housing loans.

(vii) **Programmes:** These are complexes of goals, policies, procedures, rules task assignment, steps to be taken, resources to be employed and other elements necessary to carry out a given course of action. They are ordinarily supported by necessary budgets[12] of the organisation.

(viii) **Budget:** A budget is a statement of expected results in terms of members. It may be referred to as a numerical programme. Cash budget, sales budget, capital expenditure budget are some of the examples of budget.

Other Classification of Types of Plans

Different authors deal types of plan differently. However, the following are dealt as types of plans in this edition of the book. They are:

Types of plans include: Strategic plans, tactics plans, operational plans and time horizons plans.

- Strategic plans
- Tactical plans
- Operational plans
- Time Horizons of plans: These include:
  - Long-range plans
  - Intermediate-range plans
  - Short-range plans.

Strategic Plans

Strategic plan is a comprehensive, unified and integrated plan of the total organisation. Strategic plans are formulated and implemented to achieve strategies. Normally strategic plans are formulated/crafted by top level management of an organisation. Normally strategic plans cover long-range of the time horizons.

1. *Introduction*

As we have discussed earlier, strategic management is a process or series of steps. The basic steps of the strategic management process are (presented in figure 4.2): *(a)* identifying or defining business mission, purpose and objectives, *(b)* environmental (including global) analysis to identity present and future opportunities and threats, *(c)* organisational analysis to assess the strengths and weaknesses of the firm, *(d)* developing alternative strategies and choosing the best strategy, *(e)* strategy implementation, and *(f)* strategic evaluation and control.

2. *Steps of Strategic Management Process*

Now we, look at each of these steps and their places in strategic management system.

Step 1: **Identifying/Defining Business Mission, Purpose and Objectives:** Identifying or defining an organisation's existing mission, purpose and objectives is the logical starting point as they lay foundation for strategic management. Every organisation has a mission, purpose and objectives, even if these elements are not consciously designed, written and communicated. These elements relate the organisation with the society and states that it has to achieve for itself and to the society.

Exhibit 4.1 Differences Between Operational Planning and Strategic Planning

Operational Planning	Strategic Planning
1. Concerned with goals derived from established objectives.	1. Concerned with the identification and evaluation of new objectives and strategies.
2. Goals usually have been validated through extensive past experience.	2. New objectives and strategies can be highly debatable; experience within the organisation or in other companies may be minimal.
3. Goals are reduced to specific such-goals for functional units.	3. Objectives usually are evaluated primarily for corporate significance.
4. Managers tend to identify with functions or professions and to be preoccupied with means.	4. Management needs a corporate point of view oriented to the environment.
5. Managers obtain evidence of their performance against goals relatively promptly.	5. Evidence of the merit of new objectives or strategies is often available only after several years.
6. Incentives, formal and social are tied to operating goals.	6. Incentives are at best only loosely associated with planning.
7. The "rules of the game" become well understood. Experienced individuals feel competent and secure.	7. New fields of endeavour may be considered. Past experience may not provide competence in a "new game".
8. The issues are immediate, concrete and familiar.	8. Issues are abstract and deferrable (to some extent) and may be unfamiliar.

(**Source:** Robert Mainer, "The Impact of Strategic Planning on Executive Behaviour," a special commentary, Boston Consulting Group, Boston, 1968, pp. 4-5.)

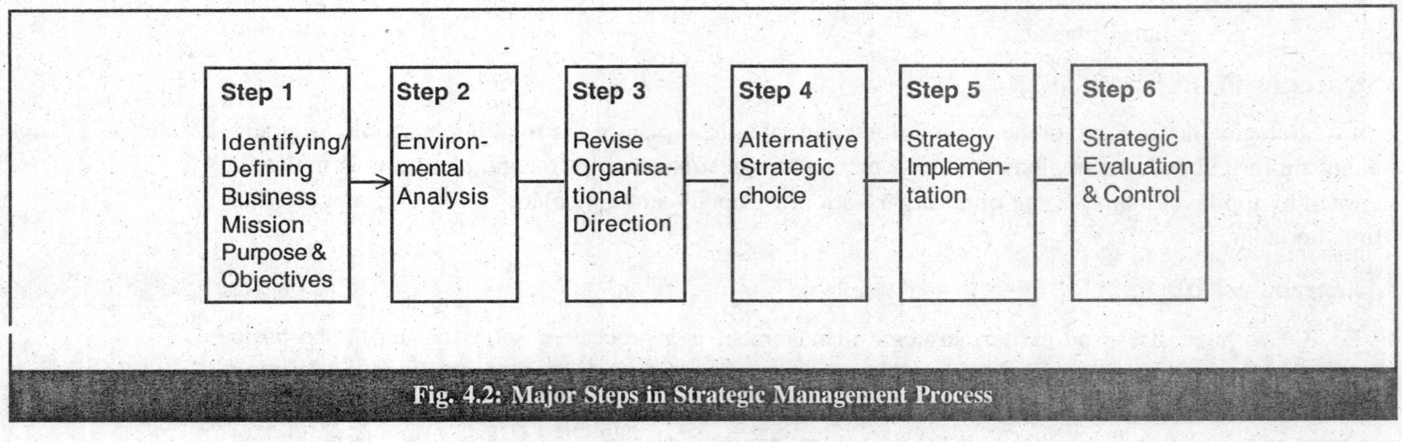

Fig. 4.2: Major Steps in Strategic Management Process

Step 2: **Environmental Analysis:** Environmental factors — both internal environment and external environment — are analysed to: *(i)* identify changes in the environment, *(ii)* identify present and future threats and opportunities, and *(iii)* assess critically its own strengths and weaknesses. Organisational environment encompasses all factors both inside and outside the organisation that can influence the organisation positively and negatively. Environmental factors may help in building a sustainable competitive advantage. Exhibit 4.2 depicts some environmental factors to monitor for strategic management.

Managers must understand the purpose of environmental analysis and recognise the multiple organisational environments in which they operate.

Step 3: **Revise Organisational Direction:** A thorough analysis of organisation's environment pinpoints its strengths, weaknesses, opportunities and threats (SWOT). This can often help management to reaffirm or revise its organisational direction.

Exhibit 4.2 Some Environmental Factors to Monitor for Strategic Management

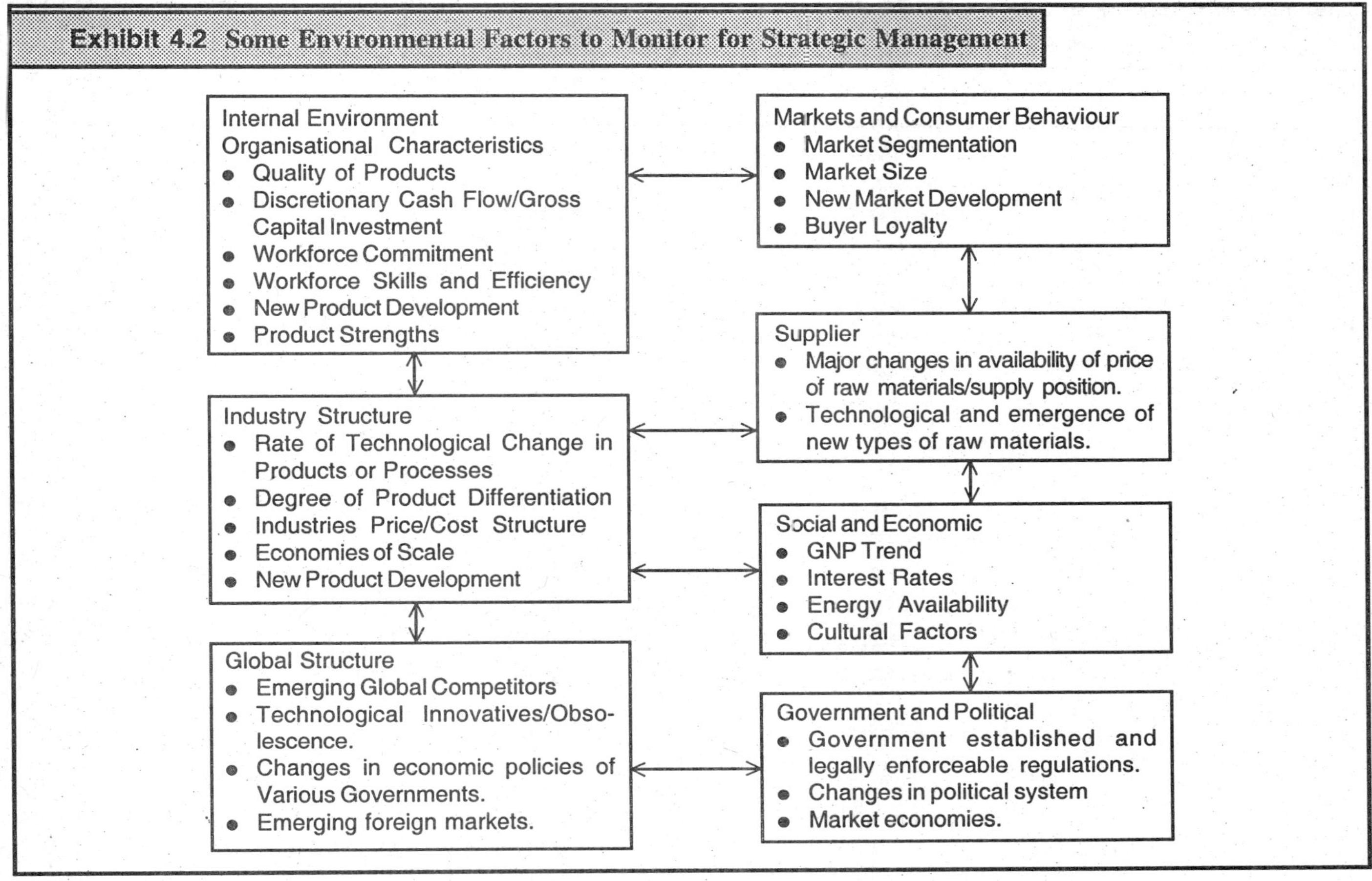

(**Source**: Modified version from Samuel C. Certo and J. Paul Peter, op.cit., p. 16.)

***Step 4:* Strategic Alternatives and Choice:** Many alternative strategies are formulated based on possible options and in the light of organisational analysis and environmental appraisal. Alternative strategies will be ranked based on the SWOT analysis. The best strategy out of the alternatives will be chosen.

The steps from identification of business mission, purpose and objectives of alternative strategies and choice can be grouped into the broad step of strategy formulation.

***Step 5:* Strategy Implementation:** The fifth step of strategic management process is the implementation of strategy. The logically developed strategy is to be put into action. The organisation can not reap the benefits of strategic management, unless the strategy is effectively implemented.

The managers should have clear vision and idea about the competitor's strategy, organisation's culture, handling change, skills of the managers-in-charge of implementation and the like. The progress from the stage of identification of business mission, purpose and objectives to the stage of achieving desired performance must overcome many obstacles. Eight sources of frequent breakdowns that can hinder a manager's navigation are presented in Exhibit 4.3.

***Step 6:* Strategic Evaluation and Control:** The final step of strategic management process is strategic evaluation and control. It focuses on monitoring and evaluating the strategic management process in order to improve it and ensure that it functions properly. The managers must understand the process of strategic control and the role of strategic audit to perform the task of control successfully.

Exhibit 4.3 Potential Breakdown between Planning and Implementation

1. A customer focus does not drive the planning process.
2. Planners do not organise their information to support action by those who implement the plans.
3. The strategic planning process fails to invite input from those who will implement the plan.
4. Plans are fragmented, piecemeal or insufficient.
5. The organisation does not encourage risk-takers or champions.
6. Those responsible for implementation lack the skills they need to carry out their roles.
7. The organisation lacks an adequate system for measuring the results of implementation efforts.
8. The organisation does not adequately recognise or reinforce the accomplishments and victories of its implementation "heroes".

(**Source:** William Sandy, "Avoid the Breakdowns between Planning and Implementation." Journal of Business Strategy, September-October 1991, p. 30.)

Tactical Plans

Tactical plans are a set of procedures for translating broad strategic goals and plans into specific plans and goals that are relevant to distinct portion of the organisation like market share, retention of human resources and cost of procuring finance. Thus, tactical plans aim at achieving tactical goals and implement a particular segment of the company's plan. Tactical plans provide detailed actions based on the strategy for a particular department or unit. These plans cover shorter time horizons compared to strategic and long-range plans. Middle level managers mostly deal with the tactical plans.

Operational Plans

Operational plans are normally designed by the lower level managers based on the tactical plans. Operational plans are courses of action that are to be carried out in day to day activities. Tactical plans indicate day to day and detailed actions to be carried out at departmental or unit level. Operational plans are normally based on strategic plans, intermediate plans, internal environment of the organisation, and ground realities.

Time-Horizons of Plans

Organisational plans are formulated based on time frame viz., long-range plans, intermediate plans and short-range plans.

Long-range Plan: Long range plans normally deal with strategic plans covering 2 years to 10 years and above. Multinational companies (MNCs) and large domestic companies formulate long range plans over 20 years. In fact, software companies formulate long range plans just for one year, whereas steel and machinery industries view 20 years and above as long range. Thus, the time horizon of the long range plan varies from one company to the other based on the size of the company and the nature of the industry to which it belongs.

The basic question in considering any sort of long-range planning is: Why should a firm attempt to look into the future? These are three basic reasons: *(i)* The first reason for looking into the future in a systematic way to understand the future implications of present decisions, *(ii)* The second reason for looking into the future in a systematic way is in a sense the observe of the first. As well as considering the future implications of present decisions, it is necessary to examine the present implication of future events, *(iii)* The third reason for looking into the future in a systematic way is to provide such motivation and such a mechanism.

Intermediate Term Plans

Intermediate term plans mostly deal with tactical plans normally covering one to two years. Intermediate plans deal with specific aspects of long-term plans. Intermediate plans assure significance when the long term environment is unclear and is critical to scan and assess. Thus, managers, particularly at middle level follow the intermediate plans during the periods of uncertainty. However, intermediate plans focus on a particular aspect of long-term plan.

Short-term Plans

Short-term plans normally cover the time horizon upto one year. In fact, it would be upto one month of time horizon for software industry. Thus, the time horizon may vary from industry to industry. Short-term plans normally deals with operational plans and act as guidelines for lower level managers in their day to day activities.

Normally short-term plans are based on intermediate plans and flexible in order to react to the environmental changes and ground realities. Thus, short-term plans are both action plans and reaction plans. They are action plans because, they are based on long and intermediate/medium term plans and are basically action-oriented. They are also reaction plans because they are modified based on environmental shifts, changes in management shifts and other ground realities. Thus, they react to the changes.

Fig. 4.3 presents types of plans, time horizon and management levels.

Time Horizon	Top-Level Management	Medium-Level Management	Lower-Level Management
Time	Long Range Plans	Intermediate Range Plans	Short Range Plans
Types	Strategic Plans	Tactical Plans	Operational Plans

Types of Plans

Fig. 4.3: Matrix of Types of Plans, Time Horizon an d Management Levels

Now we shall discuss the advantages and limitations of planning.

Purpose of Planning

The purpose of planning is to offset uncertainty and changes to focus attention on objectives, to make operations as economical as possible, to facilitate control, to help in coordination and to increase organisational effectiveness.

Having studied various aspects of planning, now we study the process of planning.

(E) STEPS IN THE PROCESS OF PLANNING

Planning is a continuous process. Planning is an organisations plan for the total business or any part of the business including the departments or any part of it. For example, organisations plan for diversification or introduction of a new product, entry into a foreign market, introduction of new technology etc.

The steps in planning include:

***(i)* Being Aware of Opportunities and Strengths:** Business firms analyse both internal environment and external environment. Analysis of the internal environment reveals organisation's strengths and weaknesses. Analysis of an external environment includes the factors which are characterised as technological, economic, political, international and natural. Analysis of these factors reveal the opportunities offered by the external environment and threats posed by the external environment. Thus the business firms should be aware of the opportunities and strengths. For example, increase in middle income group is an opportunity for consumer goods industry. Business firms can plan to match the organisation's strengths with the environmental opportunities, thus knowing the opportunities and strengths is the first step of planning.

***(ii)* Establishing Objectives and Goals:** Business firms have to formulate objectives. Objectives are the ends towards which activity is aimed. They also represent ends towards which organising, staffing, directing and controlling are aimed at. The organisations formulate objectives not only for the entire enterprise but also for each department, unit and sub-unit. The departmental objectives are related to the enterprise objectives and strategically contribute to achieve them.

Objectives provide direction to the organisational plans. Organisational objectives control the departmental objectives and the sub units' objectives. Managers and subordinates formulate the objectives in collaboration by exchanging their ideas and views.

***(iii)* Developing Premises:** The next step is getting acceptance from the employees regarding the planning premises like forecast, policies etc. Managers also get the acceptance of others regarding the assumption of the environment. All the managers involved in planning should have a common understanding about the planning premises. Forecast is an important planning premise. Forecasting premises include:

- What will be the population?
- What new markets will emerge?
- What will be the new products?
- What will be the supply of the competitors?
- What will be the new technologies?
- What will be the future prices?
- What will be the salary levels of employees?
- What will be the new trends in financial markets? and
- What political factors will affect the business?

These premises are more important, critical and strategic for formulating and finalising plans.

***(iv)* Determining Alternative Courses:** The managers have to develop alternative courses. There would be several ways to achieve the predetermined objectives. The objective of profit maximisation can be achieved through the following alternative courses.

- through forward linkage of the business
- through backward linkage of the business
- through expansion of the capacity
- through diversification

- through joint ventures and
- through mergers and acquisitions.

Thus, managers have to develop alternative courses.

***(v)* Evaluating Alternative Courses:** Managers have to evaluate the alternative course. Each alternative course has to be analysed in terms of its strengths and weaknesses. In addition, each alternative should also be analysed in terms of the opportunities for implementation of the course of action and the threats or challenges posed by the environment in implementing the course of action. Thus, each alternative course of action has to be evaluated in terms of strength, weakness, opportunity and threat (SWOT) analysis.

***(vi)* Selecting a Course:** After evaluating the alternative courses based on the SWOT analysis, a manager has to rank them based on relative strengths and opportunities of each alternative. The alternative with highest strengths and opportunities and with the lowest threats and weaknesses would be ranked as number one while the last rank would be assigned to the alternative course with relatively lowest strengths and opportunities and highest threats and weaknesses. Then the manager selects the alternative for which rank number one is assigned.

***(vii)* Formulating Derivative Plans:** Managers have to prepare derivative plans after finalising the main and the basic plan. These plans are essential to support and achieve the basic plan.

***(viii)* Budgeting:** The final step is converting the plans and derivative plans into budgets. The budgets provide clear direction in numerical terms. They also provide clear programmes to be achieved. These budgets include capital budgets, financial budgets, material budgets, production budgets, sales budgets, human resource budgets etc.

(F) ADVANTAGES AND LIMITATIONS OF PLANNING

Advantages of Planning

All organisational activities have to be undertaken as per planning. In addition, all organisations formulate objectives and planning helps in the achievement of these objectives and goals. Further, planning helps for the entire business process from the stage of procuring machinery and material to the stage of selling the products. The advantages of planning include:

(i) **Optimum Utilisation of Resources**: As indicated earlier, planning enhances efficiency. Efficiency requires optimum utilisation of all inputs. Further, it also requires optimum utilisation of machinery, men and other resources.

(ii) **Economy in Operations**: Planning eliminates the unnecessary operations in production, marketing and other functions. In addition, it reduces the purchase price of material and other inputs. These result in economy in operations.

(iii) **Reduces Uncertainties**: Planning process estimates the future trends of the external environments, initiates the steps to prepare for meeting the future challenges and converting some of the future threats into opportunities. Thus, planning reduces uncertainties.

(iv) **Strengthens Competitive Ability**: An organisation's competitive ability depends upon its strengths and matching these strengths with the environmental opportunities. Planning helps the organisation to build the strengths, reduce the weaknesses, foresee the environmental opportunities and match the strengths with the opportunities. Thus, planning helps for improving the organisation's competitive abilities.

(v) **Effective Coordination**: Coordination is linking various sections and departments through network. Planning incorporates coordination in its process. In fact, the planning process provides the detailed process of programming of activities which would result in effective coordination.

(vi) **Acts as Change Agent**: Planning helps to predict the future trends and also manipulate the environmental factors. Planning decides what should be done in terms of innovative product design, technology, marketing alliances etc. and bring the change before it is implemented by other companies. Thus, planning process acts as change agent.

(vii) **Motivation**: Planning encourages subordinates to participate in formulating and finalising the plans. Employee participation in planning satisfies their need for involvement and belongingness. This in turn will meet the employees' social and esteem needs. Thus, planning process motivates the employees.

(viii) **Effective Control**: Planning provides the detailed programming for implementation of various activities. Control function is based on the plans. The detailed plans provide guidelines for effective control. Though planning has many advantages, it has certain limitations. Now, we shall discuss the limitations of planning.

Limitations of Planning

Planning is highly essential for carrying out various types of business activities. However, the planning function suffers from certain limitations/obstacles. They are:

(i) **Unreliability of Forecasts**: Planners forecast future trends based on the past trends by the help of statistical techniques. But a number of environmental factors change between the planning and execution periods. Consequently, the forecasts become unreliable and redundant. (See Box 4.1).

Box 4.1: Unreliability Planning and Wal-Mart Stumbles while going Global in Chile

Having grown in fits and starts, Wal-Mart's international unit has a new game plan. Can it master world markets?

Chile

Chilean shoppers strolling through the aisles of their local D&S supermarket recently came across something not usually offered by the discounter: Apple (AAPL) iPods. That's not the only change coming for the 224-store chain, which sold a majority stake to Walmart earlier this year for $1.6 billion. (It now owns about 75% of D&S.)

In acquiring D&S (short for Distribución y Servicio), the nation's leading grocer and third-largest retailer, Walmart hopes to cement its dominance in Latin America, where it is by far the biggest retailer with $38 billion in sales, estimates research firm Planet Retail, double that of its closest rival, Carrefour. In Chile, Walmart enters a market that has long been inhospitable to foreign retailers. Home Depot (HD), Carrefour, and J.C. Penney are among the companies that have tried, and failed, to make it in Chile, a nation of 17 million with the sixth-largest retail market in Latin America.

Rather than go it alone, as others have attempted, Walmart cultivated close ties with D&S for more than a decade: Bob L. Martin, who ran the international division in the 1990s, says he first visited Chile in 1997. D&S, in turn, modeled much of its business practices on Walmart, looking to Bentonville "as an icon," says Claudio Pizarro, a professor at the University of Chile. (Walmart also imports products like salmon from Chile.)

Financial Services a Draw

Walmart has increased D&S's expansion budget from $150 million to $250 million, which will go toward opening nearly 70 stores this year, many of them small stores that cater to lower-income shoppers, according to Vicente Trius, Walmart

Latin America's president and CEO.The appeal of D&S goes well beyond its stores. About 1.7 million Chileans carry a Presto card issued by its financial services unit, up from 1.2 million in 2004. "There is a saying here that large retailers generate sales with [stores] and earnings with their credit cards," says Rodrigo Rivera, a partner with the Boston Consulting Group in Santiago.

Indeed, some South American retail chains generate upwards of 70% of their profits from financial services, analysts estimate. (At D&S that figure is just 17%.) Walmart already offers financial services in Mexico and Brazil, though its attempts to launch a bank in the U.S. have failed. The retailer is keen to grow the Presto business by adding more low-risk services such as selling life insurance for outside vendors. Achieving the right balance between local knowledge and global scale is not easy. "We're in the early stages," says McMillon. "But we know you can't run the world from one place."

(**Source**: http://finance.yahoo.com/career-work/article/107960/wal-marts-painful-lessons)

(ii) **Time Consuming**: Planning process involves a number of steps, as discussed earlier. In addition, forecast of future events is based on a number of statistical tools. Planning process requires a lot of time to perform all these activities and to make planning effective and systematic.

(iii) **High Cost**: The planning process is not only time consuming but also expensive. The planning process requires vast data and information to be collected and processed. In addition, it requires use of statistical techniques and services of a number of personnel. As such, planning is an expensive activity.

(iv) **Organisational Politics**: Though the planning process is based on a systematic and sequential process, sometimes the influential leaders dominate the planning process. Consequently, planning takes the approach or trend determined by the influential managers. Thus, organisational politics also takes place in the planning process.

(v) **Inflexibility**: Liberalisation and globalisation made the change and adaptability as the order of the day in the business world. Modern business firms have realised that they should change before change changes them. But planning makes most of the organisational activities inflexible and static, which are unsuitable to the present day business environment.

Conclusion

Though certain limitations of planning tend to make the planning activity less effective, planning is highly essential, even during the highly volatile business environmental situations. In fact, planning is a fundamental and basic management function.

(G) PLANNING PRACTICES IN JAPAN, USA AND CHINA

Different countries follow different management practices influenced by several factors including the culture of the country. Productivity levels in Japan are higher than that of USA which is primarily due to the Japanese culture of collectivism. Most of the USA companies started adapting Japanese management practices.

Planning in Japan

Government and business though their joint efforts undertake planning for economic growth and international competitiveness. These plans enabled for harmonising monetary, fiscal and human resource policies and for developing industrial sector. Thus the economic environment has become predictable to the businesses for planning. Consequently decision making, selecting objectives, formulating goals and strategies have become less risky. Japanese emphasise on long-term goals rather than short-term.

Planning in USA

In contrast to the Japanese managers, American managers plan for short-term result as they are under pressure from the stakeholders to report for profits every year. Added to this, American managers frequently change their jobs. The plans of government and business are not in collaborative effort as in Japan. Therefore, complete certainty in predicting the future is not possible.

Planning in China

Most of the Chinese businesses are under state ownership. Only some private companies entered the market recently. Chinese businesses plan for both long-term as well as short-term. Top level at the Government, State Planning Commission prepares 5-year plans and businesses prepare their plans accordingly. Lower level managers prepare short run plans based on the long-term plans. Chinese think strategically, even though they may not prepare strategies formally. Chinese use alliances in their planning process. Organisational goals and individual goals are not aligned completely as the achievement of organisational goals may not contribute to the achievement of individual goals/plans.

Table 4.1 presents comparison of planning in Japan, USA and China.

Table 4.1: Comparison of Planning in Japan, USA and China

Factor	*Japan*	*USA*	*China*
Plan Period	Long-term	Short-term	Long and Short-terms
Individual/Group	Group	Individual	Top-down, participation at lower levels

KEY TERMS

- Management
- Planning
- Goal
- Purpose
- Budget
- Operation Plan
- Unit Level Objectives
- Performance Appraisal
- Mission
- Strategy
- Philosophy
- Rule
- Change Agent
- Tactical Plan
- Targets
- Strategy
- Decisional Roles
- Forecasting
- Procedure
- Programmes
- Strategic Plan
- Goals
- Vision

QUESTIONS

1. Define the term planning. Differentiate planning from forecasting.
2. Why and how planning is primary function of management?
3. Discuss different types of plans with examples.
4. Comment on the planning process and explain various steps in the planning process.
5. "Planning is not an exact science." Critically comment.
6. Discuss various levels of planning. Explain the process of strategic planning.

REFERENCES

1. Harld Koontz and Cyril O' Donnel, "*Essentials of Management*" TMH, 2001, p. 62.
2. Alford and Beatly, *op.cit.*
3. James A.F. Stoner and Edward Freeman, "*Management* ", Prentice-Hall of India (P) Ltd., 1992, p. 186.
4. George R. Terry and Stephen G. Franklin "*Principles of Management*" All India Traveller book Seller, New Delhi, 1998, p. 198.
5. Hurley M.E., "*Business Administration*", Prentice Hall of India'(P) Ltd, New Delhi, 1997, p. 198.
6. George R. Terry and Stephen G. Franklin.
7. Leon C.Megginson *et.al*, "*Management-Concepts and Applications*", Harper & Row, New York, 1983, p. 113.
8. Davis R.C. "*Research in Management During 1950s in Arthur*", E. Warner (ed) "*Research Needs in Business during 1950s*", School of Business, Indiana University, Bloomington, 1950, p. 2.
9. *Ibid.*
10. Harold Koontz, Heinz Weihrich and A.Ramachandra Aryasri, "*Principles of Management*", Tata McGraw-Hill Company Limited, New Delhi, 2008, p. 3.3.
11. Harold Koontz and Cyril O'Donnel, *op.cit.*, p. 66-67.

CHAPTER **5**

OBJECTIVES OF BUSINESS

Chapter Outline

(A) Introduction
(B) Formulating Objectives
(C) Characteristics of Effective Objectives
(D) Importance of Objectives
(E) Nature of Objectives
(F) Formulation of Objectives
(G) Reasons for Change of Objectives
(H) Management by Objectives
- Key Terms
- Questions
- References

Learning Objectives

After studying this Chapter, you should be able to:

✓ Understand the hierarchy of objectives viz., organisational objectives, departmental objectives and unit level objectives.

✓ Explain different areas of objectives.

✓ Discuss the characteristics, importance and nature of objectives.

✓ Know the methods and process of formulation of objectives.

✓ Appraise the guidelines for formulating objectives.

✓ Evaluate the reasons for change of objectives.

✓ Understand the meaning and process of Management by Objectives.

✓ Know the prerequisites for installing and essentials of MBO programme.

(A) INTRODUCTION

The accomplishment of purpose or mission of an organisation requires the formulation of a number of objectives. Achievement of the organisational objectives, in turn, requires the formulation and fulfilment of departmental and unit goals. As presented in Fig. 5.1, objectives can be structured as a hierarchy.

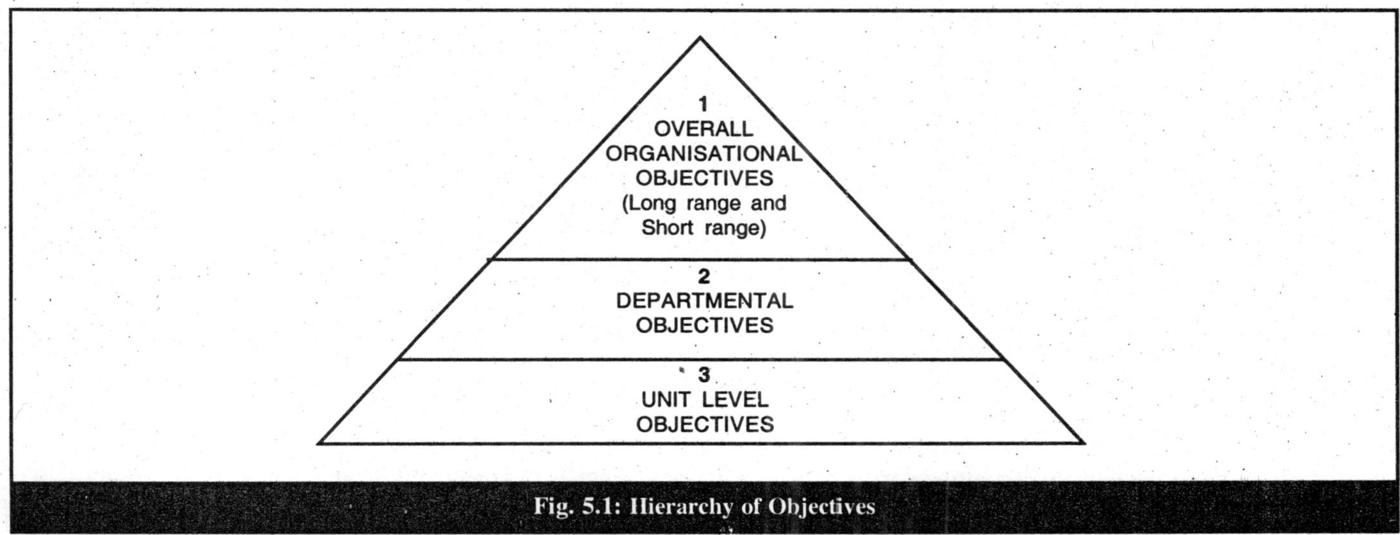

Fig. 5.1: Hierarchy of Objectives

Long-range objectives specify the results that are desired in pursuing the organisation's mission and normally extend beyond the current financial year of the organisation. These objectives are notably speculative for distant years. Short-range objectives are performance targets, normally of less than one year's duration, that are used by the management to achieve the organisation's long-range objectives. The selection of short-range objectives is from an evaluation of priorities relating to long-range objectives. Departmental objectives, both long-range and short-range, are formulated based on both objectives of the organisation. Unit objectives are generally specific and are drawn from the departmental objectives.

Objectives Vs Goals

The terms, objectives and goals are differentiated by some managers based on generality and specificity of what an organisation seeks to achieve. For example, the objective of an organisation is to improve its profitability whereas one of the goals of the organisation is to increase earning per share by 20% during the current financial year compared to the last financial year. (See Box 5.1). Thus, objectives are open-ended attributes and goals are close-ended attributes which are precise and expressed in specific terms. However, some managers use these two terms synonymously. We shall also use these two terms synonymously in this text for convenience purpose.

Objectives are open-ended whereas goals are closed-ended.

Box 5.1: SMART Goals

All businesses need to set goals for themselves or for the products or services they are launching. What does your company, product or service hope to achieve?

Setting goals are important. They focus the company on specific aims over a period of time and can motivate staff to meet the objectives set.

*A simple acronym used to set goals is called **SMART objectives.** SMART stands for:*

1. Specific – Goals should specify what they want to achieve.

2. Measurable – You should be able to measure whether you are meeting the goals or not.

3. Achievable - Are the goals you set, achievable and attainable?

4. Realistic – Can you realistically achieve the goals with the resources you have?

5. Time – When do you want to achieve the set goals?

Examples of SMART Goals:

There are a number of business goals, which an organisation can set:

- ***Market share objectives:** Goals can be set to achieve a certain level of market share within a specified time. E.g. obtain 3% market share of the mobile phone industry by 2004.*
- ***To increase profit:** A goal maybe to increase sales 10% from 2003 – 2004.*
- ***To survive:** The hard times the business is currently in.*
- ***To grow:** The business may set an objective to grow by 15% year on year for the next five years.*
- ***To** increase **brand awareness** over a specified period of time.*

(**Source:** Adapted from http://learnmarketing.net/smart.htm.)

(B) FORMULATING OBJECTIVES

The mission and directional course are converted into designated performance outcomes in the process of formulating objectives. Objectives represent a managerial commitment to achieve specified results in a specified period of time. This clearly spells out the quantity and quality of performance to be achieved, the time period, the process and the person who is responsible for the achievement of the objective.

An organisation's mission statement will just be a window-dressing, unless it is translated into measurable and specific performance targets and managers are pressurised to achieve these targets. Thus, objective formulation is a critical step in the strategic management process. It is viewed that companies whose managers formulate objectives for each key result area and then actively pursue actions to achieve their performance targets will out-perform the companies whose managers operate with hopes and mere good intentions.[1]

Performance objectives must be stated in quantifiable or measurable terms. They must also contain a deadline for achievement.

Objectives are set for all areas and departments of an organisation. Though the objectives can vary widely from one organisation to another organisation, they can be broadly divided into:

***(i)* Profitability:** Profitability objectives are expressed in terms of profits, return on investment, earnings per share, profits to sales etc. For example, to increase return on investment. (See Box 5.2).

Box 5.2: Objectives of Coca Cola Company Ltd.

Mainly all companies' objectives are to survive, maximize their profits and to expand their business, however, from when Coca Cola had started, over the years they had achieved these objectives. So the company have come up with six strategic objectives to provide the company with a framework for the company's success. In 2003, every function of The Coca-Cola Company integrated these priorities into their business plans. And this year, they will continue to establish these priorities, and their benefits into every aspect of the business.

Coca Cola's Six Priorities

1. Accelerate carbonated soft-drinks growth led by coca cola

Coca Cola leads with their strengths. Carbonated soft drinks remain their most profitable business and Coca Cola is the most popular brand in the world. This strategy paves the way for growth.

> 2. Selectively broaden our family of beverage brands to drive profitable growth
>
> Enormous opportunity exists in categories such as juice and juice drinks, bottled water, teas, energy drinks, coffee and more.
>
> 3. Grow system profitability and capability together with our bottling partners
>
> Coca Cola is a company of relationships, and one of our most important relationships is the one we share with our bottling partners. In 2003, those relationships became more profitable and productive.
>
> 4. Serve customers with creativity and consistency to generate growth across all channels
>
> We will continually strive to increase growth for the customers' businesses, helping create a context for the company's growth.
>
> 5. Direct investments to highest-potential areas across markets
>
> Coca Cola tailor their business approach to the individual marketplace based on its stage of development. In this way, we direct our investments in a way that makes the most business sense.
>
> 6. Drive efficiency and cost-effectiveness everywhere
>
> By leveraging technology, creating alignment across business units and achieving economies of scale, we are able to operate with more efficiency.

(**Source:** Adapted from:http://www.123helpme.com/view.asp?id=148943)

(ii) **Markets:** Objectives are expressed in terms of the share of the market, total rupee sales or total quantity of sales.

(iii) **Productivity:** This pertains to the level of goods and/or services produced by an organisation relative to the resources used in the production process. Organisations which use fewer resources to produce specified levels of products are said to be more productive than organisations requiring more resources to produce at the same level.

(iv) **Innovation:** This refers to change made to improve methods of conducting organisational business. Organisational objectives should indicate innovations which the organisation desires to implement.

(v) **Product:** These objectives are expressed in terms of sales and profitability by product line or product, target dates for development of new products and others.

(vi) **Financial Resources:** These objectives are expressed in terms of the capital structure, new issues of common stock, cash-flow, working capital, dividend payments and collection periods.

(vii) **Physical Facilities:** These objectives are expressed in terms of machinery and equipment, square feet, fixed costs, units of production and other measures.

(viii) **Organisation Structure and Activities:** They are stated in terms of changes to be made in the policies of organisational structure or projects to be undertaken.

(ix) **Manager's Performance and Development:** These objectives are related to the quality and rate of development of managerial skills, knowledge and performance. Development of managerial performance is very important from the viewpoint of the long-run success of the company and achievement of other objectives of the company.

(x) **Employee Performance and Attitude:** It related to the development of skills, knowledge and performance of non-managerial employees of the company. This area is also related to the development of the favourable attitude of the employees towards the organisation. The significance of these considerations should be stressed through the formulation of organisational objectives.

(xi) **Customer Service:** This is related to the quality of the product, pre-sales and post-sales service, delivery times, promptly attending to customer complaints, price, package and the like.

(xii) **Social Responsibility:** They are related to the obligation of business towards the society with a view to contribute to its welfare. Today, these objectives have become common to all the companies. For example, to contribute to the medical facilities of the community where the company is located.[2]

Key performance areas and core problems that affect objectives are presented in Exhibit 5.1.

Exhibit 5.1 Key Performance Areas and Core Problems Affecting Objectives

Drucker's Key Performance Areas: *Peter Drucker has argued that well-managed businesses focus organisational efforts on eight key performance areas:*

(i) Market standing — *the specification of market segments and the share of each segment sought.*

(ii) Innovation — *the extent of business involvement in developing new products and services.*

(iii) Productivity — *the way the firm is going to measure its efficiency. (Options include processing and outputs discussed earlier).*

(iv) Physical and financial resources — *the acquisition and efficient use of resources (inputs).*

(v) Profitability — *identification of desired levels of profitability to be used (10 percent RoI, 7 percent profit margin).*

(vi) Manager's performance and development — *criteria for evaluating the performance of managers and the design of training and development programs to assist managers in reaching their potential.*

(vii) Worker's performance and attitude — *criteria for evaluating the performance of operative employees and organisational efforts to maintain positive employee attitudes towards their jobs and the firm.*

(viii) Public responsibility — *the role of the firm in meeting the needs of the society and actions to be taken to enhance the firm's public image.*

Drucker's list of key performance areas was developed for business organisations. Other organisations, non-profit organisations and government agencies find some of Drucker's areas (such as profitability) inappropriate.

Bennis's Core Problems: *Warren Bennis identified core problems facing all organisations. They often select one or more of these problem areas as an area of primary importance to the organisation and incorporate it into mission statements and strategic plans. Core problem areas include the following:*

(i) Integration — *combining individual needs and organisational goals into a mutually rewarding work environment, perhaps 'buying' more humanistic values at the expense of 'efficiency.'*

(ii) Social influence — *distributing power and authority among top managers and subordinates. Organisational growth, separation of management and ownership, technology, broader product mixes, international operations and unions have made sharing power and authority necessary in most organisations.*

(iii) Collaboration — *managing and resolving conflicts. Specialisation, professionalism and interdependence increase the opportunity for conflict and necessitate collaboration to manage or resolve it.*

(iv) Adaptation — *responding to environment-induced changes. Technology, research and development and deepening organisational interdependence with other facets of the environment require careful monitoring.*

(v) Identity — *achieving clarity in, consensus on and commitment to the organisation's mission statement. Organisational complexity and diversity can lead to different orientations within sub-systems unless primary tasks of the organisation are regularly reinforced.*

(**Source:** Adapted from P. Drucker, *Management Tasks, Responsibilities, Practices*, Harper & Row, New York, 1974, p. 100 and W.G. Bennis, *Organisational Development*, Addison Wesley, Reading, Mass, 1969, pp. 26-32.)

(C) CHARACTERISTICS OF EFFECTIVE OBJECTIVES

Characteristics: Specific, measurable, changing, consistent of long-run and shot run.

All organisations formulate objectives in one form or the other. The utility of objectives is determined by their level of effectiveness. The important guidelines for the formulation of effective objectives include:

(i) **Specific Objectives:** It is clear to know exactly what is to be achieved, when, how and by whom, when the objectives are formulated specifically. All organisational members know and understand

what is expected of them, if the objectives are specific. Further, they eliminate confusion. More specific objectives make it easier for the management to develop realistic strategies. Thus, effective and specific objectives provide a foundation on which managers can construct appropriate organisational strategies.

***(ii)* Level of Effort:** Objectives should be realistic and ground realities should be taken into consideration while putting in effort. Objectives should be set to that level, at which employers can extend themselves somewhat to achieve them. They should not be set at very high level at which employees become frustrated and stop trying to achieve them. Objectives that challenge employees' abilities are generally more interesting and more motivating than easily attained objectives.[3] Therefore, managers should establish challengeable but reachable organisational objectives, and all employees should share this view.

***(iii)* Changing Objectives:** Both internal environment and relevant external environments change continuously. These changes sometimes make the established objectives irrelevant. Therefore, the management should continuously assess and monitor the environmental changes and reformulate the objectives accordingly. In fact, managers must encourage all employees to identify changes and suggest required changes in the objectives.

***(iv)* Measurable Objectives:** The objectives should be measurable in quantitative terms like 12% increase in profit per share over last year's profit. A measurable objective is an objective stated in such a way that an attempt to attain it can be compared to the objective itself to determine whether it actually has been attained.

***(v)* Consistent Long-run and Short-run Objectives:** Organisational objectives that reflect a desirable mix of timeframes and that support one another should be established. Long-term objectives must be consistent with the organisational vision and mission, while short-term objectives must be consistent with long-run objectives. In short, short-run objectives should be derived from and lead to the attainment of long-run objectives.[4]

(D) IMPORTANCE OF OBJECTIVES

Why do organisations formulate objectives? And what is their importance? The following factors explain the need for and importance of objectives.[5]

Objectives are important as they link mission and goals.

***(i)* Objectives help to define the organisation in its environment:** The organisations justify their existence to their stakeholders in the environment like customers, government, creditors and society at large.

***(ii)* Objectives help in coordinating decisions and decision-makers:** Stated objectives impose some constraints on the behaviour of employees and modify it towards the desirable direction. It coordinates the decision-making process by different employees.

***(iii)* Objectives help in formulating strategies:** Mission statements are translated into objectives which are the basis for formulating strategies.

***(iv)* Objectives provide standards for assessing organisational performance:** They provide not only the direction to move to the organisation but also provide ultimate goals and targets that the organisation is expected to achieve. These targets and goals become standards to judge organisational performance. Organisations, without clear objectives, will not have clear basis for evaluating their performance or success. (See Box 5.3).

Box 5.3: Objectives of Aultech Group

- *maintain and strengthen market position in Eastern European markets;*
- *develop export operations for increasing competitiveness and extending experience;*
- *develop and reinforce the Company's production facilities using advanced manufacturing processes and modern equipment;*
- *create and market new products with the highest price to quality ratio;*
- *encourage the entire personnel to deliver uncompromisingly high level of product quality and customer service;*
- *maintain the reputation of a technological leader, a stable and reliable business partner.*

(**Source**: Adapted from: http://www.alutech-company.com/about/mission.htm)

***(v)* Objectives are more tangible targets than mission statements:** Mission statements are general as they are expected to be fulfilled in the long run. As such, mission statements are not more tangible, whereas the objectives are the translated versions of the mission statement and as such they are more tangible. For example, the mission of Rayalaseema Passenger and Goods Transport is, '*providing transportation to the common man*' and one of the objectives is fixing the lowest passenger tariff compared to rail transport and any other road transport.

***(vi)* Objectives help to reflect changes in the environment:** Objectives are revised to reflect the changes in the internal and external environment from time to time. Fig. 5.2 presents the changes in objectives.

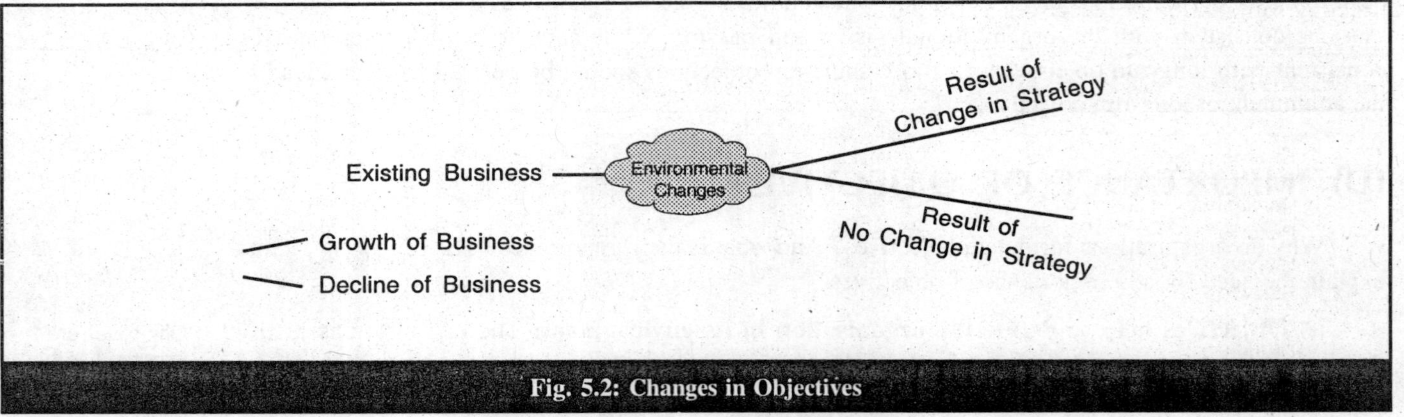

Fig. 5.2: Changes in Objectives

(E) NATURE OF OBJECTIVES

Different organisations pursue different objectives from time to time. These objectives include: profit making, efficiency, employee satisfaction, employee development, quality of products or services for customers, good corporate citizenship and the like:

- All but the simplest organisations pursue multiple objectives.
- The objectives pursued are given a time weighing by strategists.
- Since there are multiple objectives in the short-run at any one time, normally some of the objectives are weighed more heavily than others.
- Strategists should establish priorities for each objective among all the objectives at corporate and strategic business unit levels.

- There are many ways to measure and define the achievement of each objective.
- The implementation phase of strategic management involves clarifying the measurement of achievement of objectives.
- There is a difference between official objectives and operative objectives. Operative objectives are ends actually sought by the organisation. Official objectives are ends which firms seek on official occasions such as public statements to general audiences.
- There may be limits to the attainment of some goals
- Objectives are not strategies.

(F) FORMULATION OF OBJECTIVES

Top management finalises and selects the objectives developed by the managers. The choices are affected by several factors like the realities of external environment and external power relationships, realities of the enterprise's resources and internal power relationships, the value system and goals of the top executives and past strategy and development of the enterprise.

Mintzberg has advanced a theory about formulation of objectives that combines the stakeholder forces with the internal power relationships. He believes that power results from interactions of internal and external coalitions. The external coalition includes: *owners, suppliers, unions and the public*. These groups influence the firm through social norms, specific constraints, pressure campaigns, direct controls and membership on the board of directors. He specifies six pure power configurations affecting formulation of objectives as presented in Exhibit 5.2.

Exhibit 5.2 Six Pure Power Configurations Affecting Objectives Formulation

External Coalition	*Internal Coalition*	*Power Configuration*
Dominated	Bureaucratic	The Instrument
Passive	Bureaucratic	The Closed System
Passive	Personalised	The Autocracy
Passive	Ideologic	The Missionary
Passive	Professional	The Meritocracy
Divided	Politicised	The Political Arena

(**Source**: Henry Mintzberg, *Power In and Around Organisations*, Prentice-Hall, Englewood Cliffs, N.J., 1983, p. 307.)

The internal coalition includes top management, middle level managers, operators, analysts and support staff. These groups influence the firm through the personnel control system, the bureaucratic control system, the political system and the system of ideology.

Thus, the top manager sets the objectives subject to the environment. They are set by a complex interplay of past and present, internal and external role players.

The third factor affecting the formulation of objectives is the value system of the top executives. These values will influence the perception of the advantages and disadvantages of strategic action and the choice of objectives. Exhibit 5.3 presents the extremes of six selected values.

Exhibit 5.3 Values Towards Various Groups in the Strategic Situation

Value(Lowest Degree)	Value(Highest Degree)
1. Very Combative	Very passive
2. Very Innovative	Non-innovative
3. Risk-Oriented	Risk aversive
4. Quality	Quantity
5. Autocratic	Participative
6. Personal Goals	Shareholder's goals.

The fourth factor affecting the formulation of mission and objectives is the awareness by management of the past development of the firm. Factors influencing the formulation of objectives are shown in Fig. 5.3.

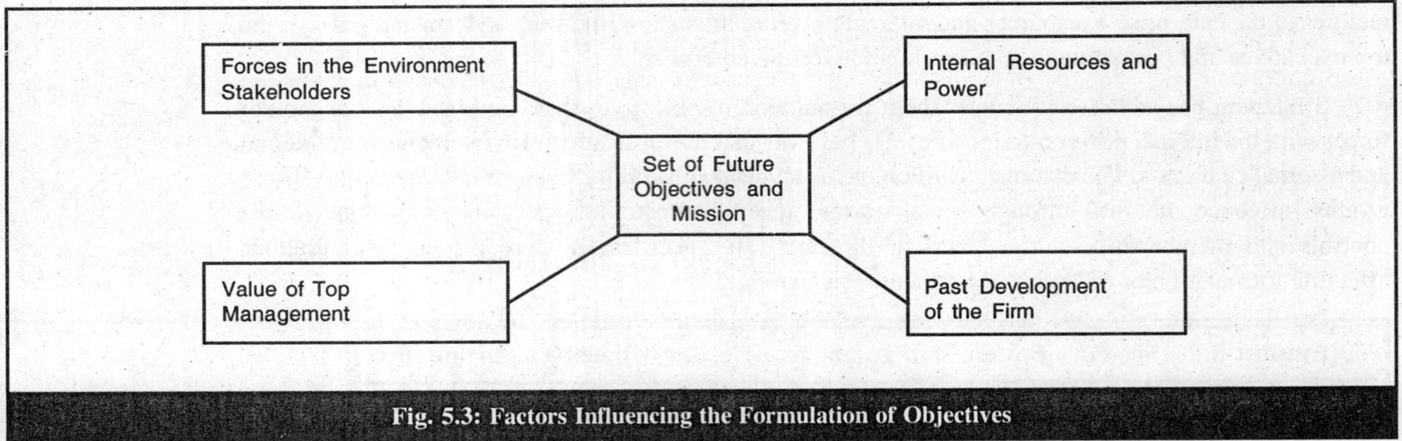

Fig. 5.3: Factors Influencing the Formulation of Objectives

Guidelines for Formulating Objectives

Managers should formulate objectives with great care as they serve as basis for organisational activities. The following guidelines are taken into account while formulating the objectives:

***(i)* Involve all those employees responsible for carrying out the objectives:** The management should identify and involve all those employees responsible for implementing the objectives. The people at the helm of affairs have better knowledge of the activities. They know best what can be achieved. These people should be encouraged to participate in the process of objective formulation. Persons involved in the process of establishment of objectives have a strong commitment to achieve them. They gain a feeling of belongingness and importance. The top management should allow their subordinates to participate in the process, encourage them to express their views and ideas. These ideas should be discussed jointly and modified, if necessary before finalising the objectives. However, during the period of crisis, the top management can formulate the objectives on its own and impose them on their subordinates, by explaining the reasons for such imposition. This practice makes the employees to commit themselves to achieve the objectives.

***(ii)* All objectives within an organisation should support the overall objectives:** The overall organisational objectives should be the basis for the objectives of different departments like finance, human resources, marketing, production and research and development. In turn, the unit level objectives should be formulated based on the departmental objectives. In other words, objectives should be mutually consistent throughout the organisation.

***(iii)* Objectives should have some 'reach':** Normally, most people put their effort to achieve the objectives when there is a reasonable challenge. People are motivated when a feeling of accomplishment can be given. Therefore, objectives formulated should provide some amount of challenge for accomplishing them.

***(iv)* Objectives should be realistic:** They should not only provide challenging jobs but also be realistic from the viewpoint of both internal and external environmental opportunities and threats or hindrances. It is also better to guard against trying to attain too much in a short period. In other words, objectives should not be set with a great ambition. A simply stated objective can be remembered.

***(v)* They should be contemporary as well as innovative:** The manager should keep the objectives up-to-date. In other words, the manager should review the objectives periodically based on the changes in the organisational priorities and changes in the external environment and make revisions, if necessary. In addition, the objectives should not be routine. The manager should invite creative ideas from the employees and incorporate the same in formulating the objectives. In fact, innovative objectives are highly essential for organisations in the market economies.

***(vi)* The number of objectives for each manager should not be too many:** Too many factors cause confusion and neglect while too few factors permit waste and inefficiency. A long list of objectives diminishes the efficiency of major objectives with undue emphasis in minor objectives. Three or four objectives can be maximum to a manager at one point of time. If there are more objectives, they can be assigned to managers in a phased way.

***(vii)* Objectives should be inconsistent with the mission:** The managers should formulate the objectives in consistent with the company's mission (see Fig. 6.4).

***(viii)* Objectives should be ranked according to their relative priority:** If the number of objectives are is more than two, they should be ranked according to their relative priority. This practice gives clear guidelines to the manager and avoids confusion. A manager can attend to the first rank objective initially and after accomplishing it, he can attend to the second rank and so on so forth. This practice helps the manager to allocate his resources and efforts accordingly and improves managerial efficiency. The normal human tendency of working on easily achievable objectives and delaying working on more difficult objectives can be minimised by this ranking method.

***(ix)* They should be in balance within a given enterprise:** The various objectives should not collectively point to an excess of any one condition. For example, the objective of customer service may be overstressed to the detriment of the objective of profit improvement. Similarly the objective of management development should be in balance with the growth and profit objective of the overall organisation.

Process of Formulating Objectives

Having discussed various aspects of organisational direction in terms of mission and objectives, we shall now discuss the process of formulating organisational objectives.

Process includes: environmental analysis, vision, mission, organisational objectives and specific activities.

Step 1: Environmental Analysis: The first step should reflect on the results of environmental analysis. Environmental analysis should provide managers with adequate information and data for reflection. The data and information from all the levels of environment — general, specific, operating and internal — should be collected. A cross-functional analysis of data and information and its results provide a basis for the establishment of organisational direction, in terms of both mission and objectives.

Step 2: Vision and Mission: Environmental analysis serves as a foundation for the development and formulation of vision and mission. Managers should understand the information and data derived from the environment, its analysis and better equip themselves to have a visionary reflection. This reflection helps them to formulate and write organisational vision. Organisational vision, in turn, becomes a solid foundation for establishing organisational mission. Managers should view the organisational mission by relating it to the societal needs. This stage helps the managers to write their mission statement.

Vision and mission statements reflect the organisation's relationship to its environment. This helps the organisation to increase its long-run profitability besides identifying its core values and direction to fulfil the vision.

Step 3: Organisational Objectives: Organisational vision and the mission serve as the basis for development of appropriate organisational objectives. Managers view that objectives should be in consistent with the organisational vision and mission.

Organisations tend to evolve through stages in formulating the objectives more precisely.

(i) Formulation of general objectives, usually not in written form,

(ii) Formulation of general objectives, in written form,

(iii) Formulation of specific objectives and;

(iv) Ranking of specific objectives.

Step 4: Specific Targets: After the objectives are formulated by the top management of the organisation, they should be translated into specific targets (See Exhibit 5.4) by the middle and lower level management. These specific targets help for the effective achievement of objectives at different levels.

Exhibit 5.4 Translation of Objectives into Specific Targets

Corporate Level Objectives	*Corporate and/or Unit Levels Specific Targets*
(1) Improve Return on Capital	(1) Increase return on equity capital employed (after interest and taxes) from 15% to 18% in the next three years.
(2) Improve Overall Profit	(2) Increase overall profit margin from 5% to 8% in the next three years.
(3) Increase Shareholders' Return	(3) Increase earning per equity share from 10% to 15% in the next three years.
(4) Increase Sales	(4) *(a)* Increase sales in Andhra Pradesh in the next 3 years three times of the sales in 1997. *(b)* Penetrate into the market of Karnataka in 1998 and sell up to 5% of sales in Andhra Pradesh. *(c)* Start export to Eritrea in 1998 at least 10% of the company sales.
(5) Increase Manufacturing	(5) *(a)* Increase capital productivity by 10% in 1998. *(b)* Install new technology.
(6) Improve Industrial Relations	(6) *(a)* Settle 70% of the employee grievances in 1998 *(b)* Make the company strike-free by 1999.

(G) REASONS FOR CHANGE OF OBJECTIVES

Objectives may change due to gap between de-sized and expected states.

Generally organisations tend towards stability. Even then, their objectives change over time. Objectives may change on the basis of gap between expected and desired states. These expected and desired states are influenced by some factors. These factors would lead to different perceptions regarding the gaps between goals and how the future goal states might be arrived at. The following are the reasons for change in mission and objectives.

(i) **Change in Goal Orientation:** The goal orientations are altered by the aspiration levels of managers. The managers' aspiration levels change from time to time based on the past achievements of the organisation.

(ii) **Crisis Situations:** The crisis situations like economic liberalisation or any other change due to shift in government policy force the organisations to change their mission. Therefore, the organisations adapt their mission and objectives to the conditions of crisis situations.

(iii) **Changes in the Demands from Coalition Group:** With changes in the strengths and weaknesses of the members of the coalition group and changes in the opportunities and threats of the external environment, the members change their interest. In addition, change in the government policies and international environment change the power configuration of the group. These changes make the enterprise shift from its state to the new state of business. This brings change in the mission and objectives of the enterprise.

(iv) **Changes in the Normal life cycle of the Enterprise:** As the life cycle of the human beings have different stages, the life cycle of the enterprise also has different stages. As the goals of human beings undergo changes from one stage to another, the mission and objectives of an enterprise also undergo changes from one stage to another of its life cycle due to changes in aspiration, needs etc. Exhibit 5.5 presents the change in organisational objectives and strategic focus at different stages.

Exhibit 5.5 Organisational Objectives and Strategic Focus at Different Stages of Organisational Life Cycle

Stage of Organisational Life Cycle	*Organisational Objectives*	*Strategic Focus for an Organisation*
1. Incorporation	Survival-create new entity	Identify an entrepreneurial idea and find resources
2. Establishment	Define Mission and Search environment	Define products, markets and functions to offer
3. Growth	Quantitative Growth	Increase market share; claim more territory
4. Uniqueness	Achieve uniqueness and establish niche	Redefine products, markets and functions.
5. Consolidation	Qualitative growth — gain reputation	Reap rewards, mine markets for benefits
6. Stability	Stabilise and contribute to society	Maintain position with stability
7. Reposition	Survival	Procreate and retrench parts that are no longer healthy.

(**Source**: Modified version from Lawrence R. Jauch and William F. Glueck, *Business Policy* and *Strategic Management*, McGraw-Hill Book Company, New York, 1988, p. 72.)

(H) MANAGEMENT BY OBJECTIVES

Management by Objectives (MBO) is a successful philosophy of management. It replaces the traditional philosophy of 'management by domination.' It was popularised as an approach to planning by Peter F.Drucker in 1954 in his famous book *The Practice of Management*. Since that time, it has acquired momentum and of late it has become a movement.

There are many MBO type programmes like 'management by results', 'goal management', 'work planning and review', 'goals and control'. These programmes are similar in nature inspite of the difference in names.

According to Howell, the concept of MBO has passed through different stages of management development, *viz.*

MBO's result-oriented and non-specialist operational management process.

(i) MBO for performance appraisal,

(ii) for integrating the individuals with the organisation and

(iii) for long-range planning.

Management by objectives has been defined as *a result-oriented, non-specialist, operational managerial process for the effective utilisation of material, physical and human resources of the organisation, by integrating the individual with the organisation and organisation with the environment.*

In other words, MBO is a process by which managers at different levels and their subordinates work together in identifying goals and establishing objectives, consistent with these goals and attaining them.[6] Thus, MBO is not only an aid to planning but also a motivating factor.

The Process of MBO

***(i)* Preliminary Setting of Objectives at the Top Level:** The managers at the top level set the overall objectives by taking planning premises into account. These objectives set by the superiors are preliminary as they must be regarded as tentative and subject to modification as the entire chain on verifiable objectives is worked out by subordinates.[7] Verifiable objectives are developed in terms of profits, market share, growth, expansion etc.

***(ii)* Clarification of Goals:** The relationship between the results expected and the responsibility for attaining them should be established as every goal and sub-goal should be someone's clear responsibility and accountability.

***(iii)* Setting of Subordinates' Objectives:** The organisation's objectives should be accomplished by a number of individuals, if all the individuals are to be jointly made responsible for attaining its overall objectives. Therefore, each individual should be assigned a specific task and he must know in advance what he is expected to achieve. In view of this, the subordinates' objectives should also be set in conformity with the preliminary objectives of the company. In some cases, the preliminary objectives of the organisation may be modified or changed in view of abilities, strengths and weaknesses of the subordinates and their objectives.[8]

***(iv)* Recycling of Objectives:** In fact, the final objectives are neither set at the top nor at the bottom. As discussed earlier, they are set after thorough consultations and discussions between the superiors and subordinates. Thus, it is a joint process requiring interaction and recycling among staff. This process creates a feeling of commitment and involvement of all staff at various levels.[9]

***(v)* Performance Appraisal:** Each employee should evaluate his accomplishment with the objectives set with the help of his superior. This appraisal provides him scope for correction and further improvement.

Pre-requisites for Installing MBO Programme

MBO is a philosophy rather than a technique. Hence its installation requires a basic change in the organizational culture and environment. To be effective, an MBO Programme requires the following:[10]

(i) The purpose and the area of MBO should be defined clearly as MBO is a means but not an end in itself.

(ii) Since the top management plays a crucial role, its favourable attitude and support is a must.

(iii) Employees who will be involved in the programme should be prepared mentally and psychologically for it. This requires a systematic training and management development programme.

(iv) Participation of superiors and subordinates in setting organisational objectives, superiors' objectives, subordinates' objectives, and their ongoing performance, periodical review of progress and final review and appraisal of the performance is highly essential.

(v) Each employee should be provided with feed-back information for self-direction and self-control.

(vi) MBO programmes should be implemented at all levels, including the strategic business unit level and the department level. Formally, there should be direct linkage between MBO and the reward system.

Essentials of MBO Programme

Management by Objectives seeks to integrate the firm's objectives with individual goals and satisfaction of its managers. The essentials of the MBO programme are:[11]

(i) Regular critical review and restatement of an organisation's overall tactical and strategic plans.

(ii) Clarification with each manager of his key results and performance standards.

(iii) Acceptance by each manager of his contribution and commitment to these results and standards.

(iv) Establishment of strict procedures for control and self-control of progress, performance and potential review.

(v) Provision of imaginative MBO development programmes.

(vi) Provision of conditions in which these results can be achieved:

(a) an effective organisation and

(b) sound managerial control information.

KEY TERMS

- Objectives
- Recycling Objectives
- Departmental Objectives
- Management by Objectives
- Short Run Objectives
- Measurable Objectives
- Unit Level Objectives
- Organisational Objectives
- Long Run Objectives
- Performance Appraisal
- Goals
- Mission
- Targets
- Vision
- Strategy

QUESTIONS

1. Differentiate the organisational objectives from those of departmental and unit level objectives.
2. Discuss various areas of objectives.
3. Write short notes on:
   - Nature of objectives
   - Characteristics of objectives
   - Importance of objectives
   - Guidelines for formulating objectives
4. Explain the methods and process of formulation of objectives.
5. Why should management change the objectives?
6. What is MBO? Explain the process of MBO. How do you install an MBO programme?

REFERENCES

1. Arthur A. Thompson and Jr. A.J. Strickland III, *op. cit.*, pp. 23-24.
2. Samuel C. Certo and J. Paul Peter, *op. cit.*, pp. 64-65.
3. Frederick Herzberg, "*One More Time: How Do You Motivate Employees*," *Harvard Business Review*, January-February 1968, pp. 53-62.
4. Samuel C. Certo and J. Paul Peter, *op. cit.*, pp. 65-67.
5. Lawrence R. Jauch and William F. Glueck, *op. cit.*, p. 65.
6. George R. Terry and Stephen G. Franklin, *op. cit.*, pp. 141-142.
7. *Ibid.*, pp. 62-64.
8. Samuel C. Certo and J. Paul Peter, *op. cit.*, p. 67.
9. Lawrence R. Jauch and William F. Glueck, *op. cit.*, p. 75.
10. *Ibid.*
11. *Ibid.*, pp. 71-72.

DECISION MAKING

"It is not that they can't see the solution. It is that they can't see the problem."

— Charles F. Kettering

Chapter Outline

(A) Introduction
(B) Problem and Opportunity Finding
(C) Nature of Managerial Decision Making
(D) Approaches to Decision Making
(E) Types of Decisions
(F) Process of Decision Making
(G) Boards and Committees in Decision Making: Group Decision Making
(H) Tools and Techniques of Decision Making
(I) Decision Making under Abnormal Conditions
(J) Decision Making Practices Abroad
- Key Terms
- Questions
- References

Learning Objectives

After studying this Chapter, you should be able to:

✓ Define decision making and understand the importance of decision making.
✓ Analyse the problems and identify the opportunities in the process of decision making.
✓ Understand the nature of managerial decision making.
✓ Discuss the Rational Model to decision making.
✓ Analyse various types of decisions
✓ Discuss the process of and various steps involved in the decision making.
✓ Have a bird's eye view of tools and techniques of decision making.
✓ Understand the decision making practices abroad.

(A) INTRODUCTION

All managers continuously make decisions regarding all kinds of problems, issues, opportunities, threats etc. In fact, management is decision making. In other words, the most important part of management is making decisions. All functions of management *viz.*, planning, organising, directing, staffing and controlling involves decision making. Similarly, all business activities from the beginning to the end, like type of business to start, type of product, sourcing of raw materials, finance, human resources, where to locate the factory, the production process, type of technology, how much to produce, whether to buy or make some of the components, where to market? to whom to sell? at what price? how to maintain the relations with the customer? expansion or diversification of the business in case of getting profits and how to retrench the loss making business operations etc., are important issues for decision making.

There are a number of alternatives for each of these issues, problems etc. Therefore, managers have to select the best alternative at the right time. This involves decision making. Decision making depends upon the type of organisation structure *i.e.*, tall structure and flat structure. In case of tall structure, authority to make the decisions is centralized at various levels. In case of flat structure, the authority to make the decisions is decentralised or spread at many points.

Meaning and Definition

Decision making is the process of choosing the best from among the alternative solutions under a given set of circumstances.

Now we shall discuss the meaning of decision making based on this analysis.

Decision making is the process of choosing the best among the available alternatives with a purpose under a given set of circumstances.

Harold Koontz and Heinz Weihrich define decision making as "selection of a course of action from among alternatives, it is the core of planning".

Decision making: Selection of course of action from among alternatives.

John A Pearce and Richard B. Robinson define decision making as, "the process of choosing a course of action from two or more alternatives."

The analysis of these definitions present the following facts:

- Identify the purpose or goal, based on which decision has to be made.
- Analyse the set of circumstances, conditions or ground realities which set the norms for decision making.
- Decision making is a process of identifying the issues, collecting information and data, analyse them, and generate or develop necessary inputs for developing alternative solutions.
- Develop alternative solutions to solve the problem or ways to deal with the situation.
- Evaluate the alternative solutions and choose the best solution.
- Implement the selected solution.

Importance of Decision Making

Managers perform all their functions and activities through decision making. In addition, making the decision in right time values much to the organisation rather than making a right decision in the wrong time. Managers in the business world, often fail to make a decision in the right time and allow the competitors to grab the opportunities. As such, managers have to make not only the right decisions but make them in the right time. Otherwise, the problems remain or magnify and culminate into a crisis.

Decision making process helps the management to procure necessary data and information. Thus, it helps in information management. In addition, decision making helps to initiate and complete the action of all the activities of the management in the right time. Decision making further helps in the formulation of strategies and implement them. Thus, decision making plays an important role in the management of a company. Now we shall discuss the Approaches to decision making.

(B) PROBLEM AND OPPORTUNITY FINDING

The strategic manager before planning and making strategic decision, must foresee the probable problems that the company will face in the future. A problem well stated is half solved. Hence, strategic managers must know the difference between problem analysis and decision making. A problem is a deviation from standard or a desired level of performance, to which a person is committed to find a solution.

Approaches to Problem Solving

The major approaches to solve management problems are: *(i)* Routine, *(ii)* Scientific, *(iii)* Decisional *(iv)* Creative and Quantitative. (Fig. 6.1)

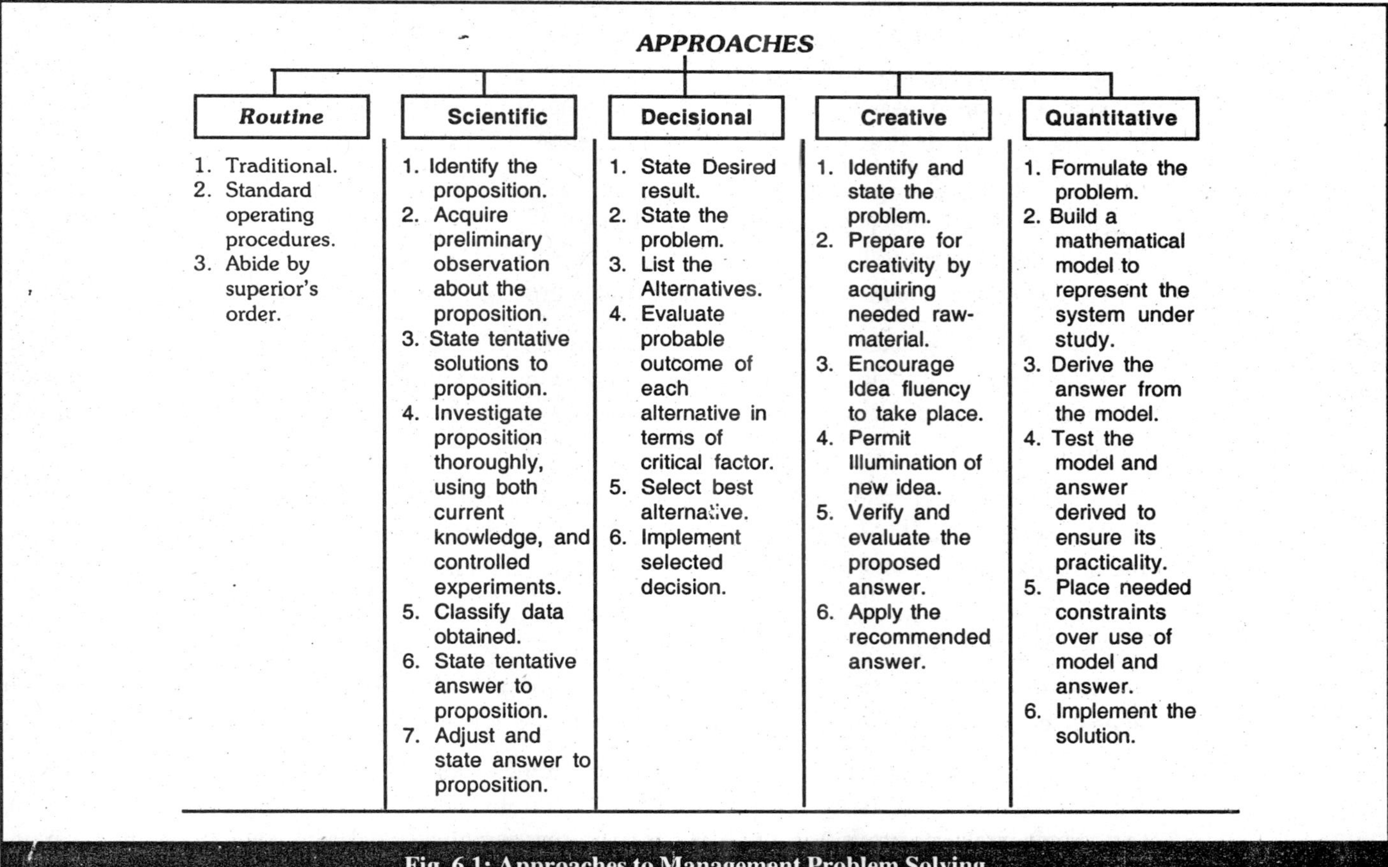

Fig. 6.1: Approaches to Management Problem Solving

(i) **Routine Approach:**This approach involves solving the problem through traditional or routine means. It does mean that applying the solution for the similar problem. Standard operating procedures are used for solving the problem. The standard operating procedure specifies the actions to be taken under specified conditions.

(ii) **Scientific Approach:** Kepner and Tregoe model of scientific approach states that, "What a manager needs for effective problem analysis is an orderly system for processing information, a system in which certain steps follow others in a fixed order."[1] Exhibit 6.1 presents the seven basic concepts of problem analysis outlined by Kepner and Tregoe.

Exhibit 6.1 Kepner-Tregoe Concepts of Problem Analysis

1. A problem analyser has an expected standard of performance against which to compare actual performance.
2. A problem is a deviation from a standard of performance (good or bad).
3. A deviation from standard must be precisely identified, located and diversified.
4. There is always something distinguishing that which has been affected from that which has not.
5. The cause of a problem is always a change that has taken place through some distinctive feature, mechanism or condition to produce a new, unwanted effect.
6. The possible causes of a deviation are deduced from the relevant changes found in analysing the problem.
7. The most likely cause of deviation is one that exactly explains all the facts in the specification of the problem.

(iii) **Decisional Approach:** Decisional approach is one of the most common and popular of all approaches. A decision may solve the management problem, which is the barrier to obtaining the desired result. In this approach, alternative solutions to solve the problem identified are developed and evaluated. Usually the evaluation is on the basis of least cost, conforms with legal requirements, the quickest, the best quality or the best quantity. This basis is called as critical factor.

(iv) **Creative Approach:** Some managers feel that decision making should not be viewed as mechanical steps following one another in a sequential and logical order. The decision-maker should be given freedom to study the information, human resources, facilities involved and concentrate on the possible outcome. Creativity should be used in this process.

The decision-maker should be given freedom to utilise his ideas, views etc., in the process of decision making. A positive attitude, imagination, ability to establish new relationships along modern lines are basic requirements for applyinig creative approach. The steps to follow creative method include:

(i) identify and state the problem, *(ii)* prepare for creativity by acquiring needed raw materials, *(iii)* encourage idea fluency to take place, *(iv)* permit illumination of new idea, *(v)* verify and evaluate the proposed answer and *(vi)* apply the recommended answer.

As the right hemisphere of human brain is responsible for our creativity, subjective, spontaneous and holistic thought processes, whilst, left hemisphere is responsible for the logical, analytical and systematic thought processes, managers (decision makers) should be given exercises to use right hemisphere and bring about a synergistic result with the left side of the brain.[2]

Often, we get a doubt that, when does the idea or the creative material begin to flow? One may get a creative idea while walking, relaxing, watching out through a window, listening to slow music, sitting in a temple or church, travelling alone by bus or train or aeroplane etc. Usually with little or no warning the creative person "starts clicking" and the creative ideas and innovative suggestions begin to flow.[3]

(v) **Quantitative Approach:** The emphasis in quantitative approach to problem analysis is on mathematical modeling of systems. Different results are obtained by substituting different mathematical

values for the variables of the equations. The results so obtained, are evaluated in keeping with the requirements of the stated problem. The computer is of great assistance in this method.

Potential Problem Analysis

Prevention is better than cure even for management problems. Therefore, the managers should foresee the probable occurrence of problems and prevent them before they occur. The steps to prevent potential problems include:

(i) Think all major potential problems that might arise from the proposed action.

(ii) Describe each potential problem. Identify accurately each problem, revealing precisely the what, where and when of it.

(iii) Classify the potential problems by their degree of risk.

(iv) Identify the possible causes for each high risk problem. Determine priority and concentrate on those problems most threatening to the management plan.

(v) Assess the probability of occurrence for the causes of each major potential problem.

(vi) Decide how to handle the most serious potential problems.

Managers often fail to follow a systematic procedure described above in problem solving due to the following reasons:

(i) Managers are preoccupied with the day to day routine problems and consequently prevent the future problems.

(ii) Managers fail to foresee the potential problems.

(iii) Failure to analyse the critical consequences of a managerial action.

(iv) Managers feel that plan suggestions are nearly infallible.

Guides to Improve Managerial Problem Solving

The problem solving to be effective by managers must be free from bias and subjective feelings as much as possible. Constructive team/group working together will result in making effective decisions. Exhibit 6.2. provides guidelines for effective problem solving in organisations.

Exhibit 6.2 Guides to Improve Your Problem Solving

1. *Review quickly all the elements of the problem so that a composite entity of the entire problem is obtained.* This focuses attention upon the "big picture" and avoids seeing the problem is a mosaic of numerous individual considerations. Also, pertinent relationships are more easily disclosed, the memory is relieved, and the mental capacity is enlarged.
2. *Try a change in the manner in which the problem is expressed.* Switching from verbal terms to a mathematical model, graph, or numbers to represent the problem may shed new and wanted light on the task. If dealing with non-verbal terms, try stating the problem in simple action terms.
3. *Consider the work environment and try rear-ranging the space and time characteristics of the problem.* This can help in revealing known and common patterns that originally are hidden by an unfamiliar arrangement. Stating the identifical relationships in a different and perhaps more normal manner can contribute to the solution.
4. *Evaluate your own ideas and those of others constructively.* Guard against complacency in accepting your own ideas. They may be brilliant, but also consider the insights of others wrestling with the same or similar problems.
5. *Discuss problem with others.* This practice forces you to restate all the aspects of the problem and in so doing brings out considerations requiring further attention not considered in the tentative solution. It also requires a relating of the fundamentals so that the listener knows what is being considered. By such communication, obscure and inconsistent points are uncovered; and furthermore, the listener, by asking questions, reveals gaps which appear inconsistent and inadequate, thus pointing out areas for bettering the problem solution.

(**Source:** George R. Terry, Op. cit., p. 84.)

(C) NATURE OF MANAGERIAL DECISION MAKING

1. Introduction

Managers in the business world, often fail to make a decision in right time and allow the opportunities be grabbed by the competitors and the problems remain or magnify and culminate into a crisis. Decisions should be taken in right time and implemented after problems have been thoroughly analysed. Decision making means to come to a conclusion and implement it. Decision making is defined as "the selection based on some criteria of one behaviour alternative from two or more possible alternatives." The need for decision making arises only when there are two or more alternative solutions for a problem.

Values and Alternatives: To select one solution from the available alternatives, each alternative should be evaluated in terms of probable outcome in comparison with other alternative solutions. The comparison should be based on values in terms of financial, social, psychological, technological and political. These values are conflicting with each other and make the decision making process a critical one. Concentrating on the important facets of the problem will help in reducing the conflict. However, taking strategic decisions is much more complicated task.

2. Types of Decisions

Decisions are classified into routine and strategic or programmed and non-programmed decisions. Routine or programmed decisions are taken by an established or systematic procedure. The decision-maker, in general, knows the situation in routine or programmable decisions. Managerial decisions covered by policies, procedures, and rules are taken by following established guidelines.

Strategic or nonprogrammed decisions have little or no precedent. They are relatively unstructured and generally require a more creative approach. The decision maker must develop a procedure to be followed. Generally, it is difficult to make non-programmed decisions compared to programmed decisions.[4]

3. Traditional Process of Decision Making

Decision making process involves identification of the problems, searching the environment for conditions requiring a decision, developing and analysing possible alternatives selecting the best alternative solution and execute the solution to achieve the objectives/goals or solve the problem.

The steps involved in the process of decision making are:

(i) Identification of problem(s) to be solved or determination of objectives to be achieved.

(ii) Searching the environment for conditions requiring a decision.

(iii) Developing the possible alternative solutions.

(iv) Analysing each alternative solution in terms of its ability to solve the problem or to achieve the determined objectives.

(v) Selecting the best alternative solution.

(vi) Executing the solution to solve the problem or to achieve the objectives.

Earnest B. Archer, proposed a nine-phase decision process. The phases are:

Phase 1: Monitor the decision environment.

Phase 2: Define the decision problem or situation.

Phase 3: Specify decision objectives.

Phase 4: Diagnose the decision problem or situation.

Phase 5: Develop alternative solutions or courses of action.

Phase 6: Establishing the methodology or criteria for appraising alternatives

Phase 7: Appraise alternative solutions or courses of action.

Phase 8: Choose the best alternative solution or course of action.

Phase 9: Implement the best alternative solution or course of action.[5]

4. Strategic Decision

Most part of the strategic management is done through strategic decision making. Strategic decision making is not only crucial but also critical and complex. Strategic decisions are made by the top level management and by the strategists whereas the operational decisions are made by the managers at lower levels. Strategic decisions are related to the contribution to the organisational objectives and goals significantly. They determine the direction and destination of the organisation.

5. Characteristics of Strategic Decisions

The characteristics of strategic decisions are:

(i) The strategic decision is a major one which affects either the total organisation or the major part of the organisation.

(ii) Even though, operational decisions also contribute towards the achievement of organisational objectives, contribution of strategic decision towards the achievement of organisational objectives is phenomenal and direct. In fact, strategic decisions determine the destiny of the organisation.

(iii) Strategic decisions may introduce change in the organisational policies, practices, businesses, customers, product mix, human resource policies, financing sources etc.

(iv) Strategic decision requires interweaving a number of factors, requires development of alternatives in view of increasing environmental demands.

(v) Strategic decision making requires trade-offs between conflicting factors. (See Exhibit 6.3).

Exhibit 6.3 The Characteristics of Strategic Decision

Strategic decisions are concerned with:

- The scope of an organisation's activities.
- The matching of an organisation's activities to its environment.
- The matching of the activities of an organisation to its resource capability.
- The allocation and reallocation of major resources in an organisation.
- The values, expectations and goals of those influencing strategy.
- The direction an organisation will move in the long-run.
- Implications for change throughout the organisation — they are therefore likely to be complex in nature.

(**Source:** Gerry Johnson and Kevan Scholes, "Exploring Corporate Strategy," Prentice-Hall, New York, 1988, p. 8.)

6. Elements of Strategic Decisions

The basic elements of strategic decisions are: *(i)* achievement of objective or desired result through the implementation of the decision, result element, *(ii)* a course of action or plan indicating the work to be done in order to achieve the objective — the action element, and *(iii)* inculcating the character of commitment among the employees responsible for implementation of strategic decision — the commitment element.

(i) *Result Element:* Strategies are formulated with a specific objective of either grabbing the market leadership or technology leadership or profit leadership. Completeness of a strategy should clearly specify the pertinent result element to be achieved. It requires the clear specification of a matching action element so as to achieve objectives.

(ii) *Action Element:* Strategic decision is action oriented. A decision may be interpreted as the intervening variable which may ultimately lead to the end-result variables. The action element of strategic decision clearly states what work must be done, how, by whom and when in order to achieve the results.

(iii) *Commitment Element:* Commitment element is most important to put the strategy into action and achieve the results. Commitment element includes commitment of financial resources, top management commitment, commitment of executives and employees. Further, specific time period for commitment of resources should also be indicated.[6]

(D) APPROACHES TO DECISION MAKING

Different theories have suggested different approaches of decision making. These approaches are discussed hereunder:

(a) The Intuitive-Emotional Approach

This approach is based on 'gut-feelings' of the decision makers

Decision-maker takes decisions based on intuition which is characterised by the use of hunches, inner feelings or the 'gut-feeling' of the decision maker. Decision maker who makes decisions based on intuition, practices management exclusively as an art. This decision maker prefers habit or experience, relative thinking, and instinct using the unconscious cognitive process. The decision maker takes into account a number of alternatives into consideration, but simultaneously jumps one step in analysis and search to another and back again.[7]

Most of the managers suddenly become emotional and nothing can change their minds. George Odiorne has stated the following emotional factors which can adversely affect decision makers:

1. They fasten on the big lie stick with it.
2. They are attracted to scandalous issues and heighten their significance.
3. They press every fact into a normal pattern.
4. They overlook everything except the immediately useful.
5. They have an affinity for romantic stories and find such information more significant than any other kind including hard evidence.[8]

This type of emotional attachments are possible and can lead to poor decisions.

The intuitive decision maker is normally an activist, fast mover, incisely questions situations and finds unique solutions to difficult problems. Some theorists prescribe intuitive approach of decision making. (See Box 6.1).

Box 6.1: Decision making in Japanese Trading Companies

The research task on strategic decisions making in Japanese trading companies was conducted over a twelve-month period between 2000-2001, at five well-known Japanese kaisha headquartered in Tokyo. Results from the study indicate that the prominence of distinctive Japanese managerial practices such as nemawashi and settai in developing information sources. As well it was it was found that these practices strongly influence how information sources are accessed. Executive decision-makers from the Presidential level to Divisional Manager level who participated in this study where emphatic in the belief that strategic decision making in most situations is reliant upon the network of information sources cultivated by discoing-makers as well as their skill in accessing the various sources and experiences.

(**Source**: http://jmo.e-contentmanagement.com/archives/vol/9/issue/1/article/403/strategic-decisionmaking-in-japanese-trading)

The supporters of intuition or judgement point out that in many cases, judgement may lead to better decisions than optimising techniques. They also argue that analytical models are only tools to help the decision maker to refine judgement.

The opponents of this approach argue that:

(i) It does not effectively use all the tools available to modern decision-makers and

(ii) The rational approach ensures that adequate attention is given to consequences of decisions before big mistakes are committed.[9]

Considering the views of both supporters and opponents of this approach, it is suggested that the managers who wish to improve their intuition might try to:

(i) Becoming more involved by filling their minds with facts and experiences in the areas where their future decisions will be made;

(ii) Practicing intuitive decision making and keeping a score on how well such decisions turned out;

(iii) Developing an awareness that hunches can help in decision making;[10]

(iv) Becoming aware of biases and allow for them. Undiscovered biases do the most damage, and

(v) Seek out independent opinions. It is always good to seek the opinion of some person who has no vested interest in the decision.[11]

(b) The Rational Model Approach

In this approach, the decision maker is intelligent and rational

In the rational-analytical approach, the decision maker, is intelligent and rational. The decision maker makes the choice, in full awareness of all available feasible alternatives, to maximise advantages. The decision maker considers all alternatives as well as consequences of all possible choices, orders these consequences in the light of a fixed scale of preferences, and chooses the alternative that procures the maximum gain.[12]

The rational approval to decision making includes the following steps:

(i) Recognise the need for a decision;

(ii) Establish, rank and weigh criteria;

(iii) Gather available information and data;

(iv) Identify possible alternatives;

(v) Evaluate each alternative with respect to all criteria; and

(vi) Select the best alternative.

Assumption of Rational Approach

The rational approach is based on the concept of 'economic man'. This concept views that people behave rationally and that their behaviour is based on the following assumptions:

(i) People have clearly defined criteria, and the relative weights which they assign to these criteria are stable;

(ii) People have knowledge of all relevant alternatives;

(iii) People have the ability to evaluate each alternative with respect to all the criteria and arrive at an overall rating for each alternative;

(iv) People have the self-discipline to choose the alternative which rates the highest (they will not manipulate the system).[13]

Challenges of the Rational Model

Rational-analytical approach is the oldest decision theory. It prescribes a rational, conscious, systematic and analytical approach. This has been challenged because:

(i) The decision-maker is often not a unique actor but part of a multiparty decision situation;

(ii) Decision-makers are not rational enough or informed enough to consider all alternatives or know all the consequences. And information is costly;

(iii) Decision-makers take decisions with more than a maximisation of objectives in mind. They tend to, "satisfice" *i.e.,* make a decision expected to yield a satisfactory, as opposed to an "optimal" outcome. Besides, the objective may change;[14]

(iv) Decision-maker makes decisions based on limited knowledge or less perfect information;

(v) The most difficult stage in the decision process may be the evaluation or the prediction of outcomes for the various alternatives;

(vi) The problem is the temptation to manipulate the information and choose a favoured; but not necessarily the best; alternative. This temptation may come from within the decision-maker or it may be created by external forces.[15]

(c) Satisficing Approach

As discussed earlier, "economic man" assumptions are generally unrealistic. Herbert Simon developed the principle of bounded rationality. This principle states that: "the capacity of the human mind for formulating and solving complex problems is very small compared with the size of the problems whose solution is required for objectively rational behaviour — or even for a reasonable approximation to such objective rationality."[16]

The principle of bounded rationality states that there are definite limits to human rationality. Based on the principle of bounded rationality, Herbert Simon proposed a decision theory of the "administrative man." The assumptions of the theory are:

1. A person's knowledge of alternatives and criteria is limited.
2. People act on the basis of a simplified, ill-structured, mental abstraction of the real world; this abstraction is influenced by personal perceptions, biases, and so on and so forth.
3. People do not attempt to optimise but will take the first alternative which satisfies their current level of aspiration. This is called satisficing.
4. An individual's level of aspiration concerning a decision fluctuates upward and downward depending on the values of most recently found alternatives.

These assumptions explain that limits exist to human rationality. Therefore, an individual must take decisions based on limited and incomplete knowledge. In view of this, the individual decision maker cannot optimise but only satisfice.

Optimising means choosing the best possible alternative. Satisficing means choosing the first alternative that meets the decision maker's minimum standard of satisfaction. Minimum standard of satisfaction *i.e.,* criteria for aspiration depends on the current level of aspiration. Level of aspiration refers to the level of performance that a person expects to attain and it is determined by the person's prior success and failures.[17]

Satisfying approach to decision making is presented in Figure 6.2. If the decision maker is satisfied that an acceptable alternative has been found, it is selected otherwise, the decision maker searches for an additional alternative.

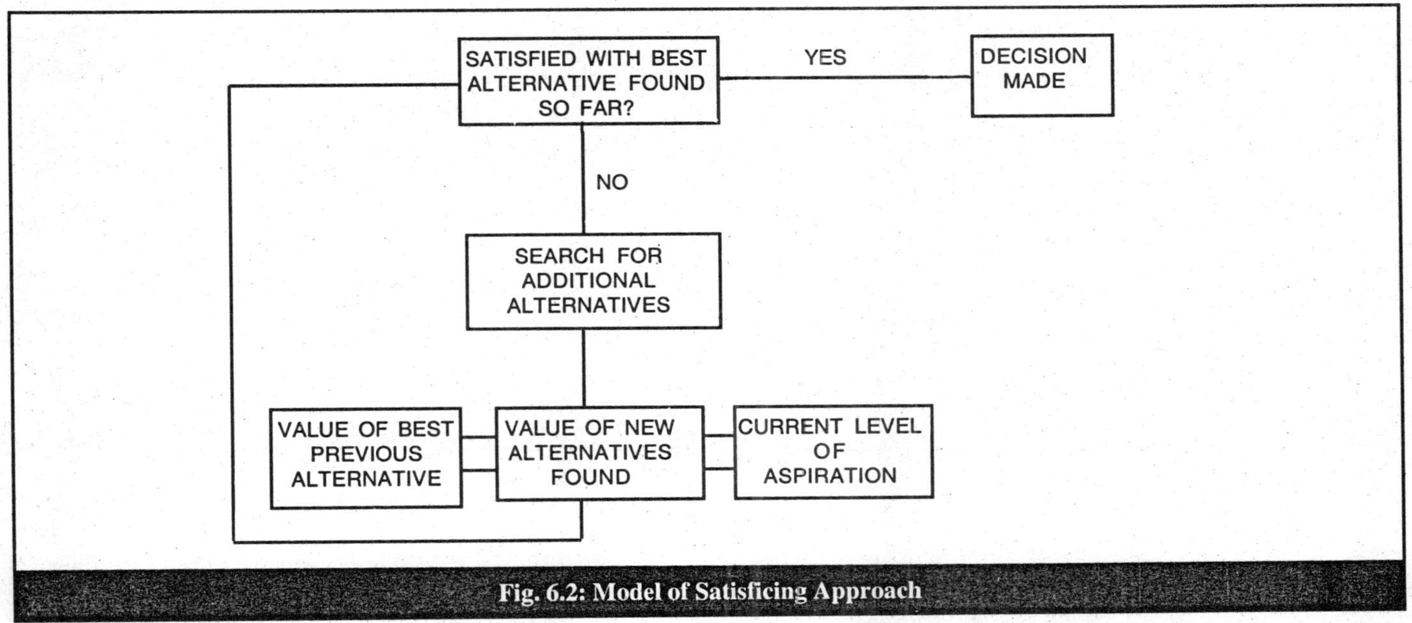

Fig. 6.2: Model of Satisficing Approach

(**Source:** Adapted from James G. March and Herbert A. Simon, "Organisations," John Wiley & Sons, New York, 1958, p. 49.)

The value of best previous alternative and current level of aspiration influence the value of alternative found. This, in turn, indicates whether or not the decision maker is satisfied with best alternative found so far? If the decision maker is satisfied with the best alternative found, he selects that alternative as decision. Otherwise, he searches for additional alternatives and continues the process. The value of best previous alternative and current level of aspiration are influenced by the value of new alternative found. In fact, it is mutual impact.

(d) Political-Behavioural Approach

Normally decisions made by organisations affect a variety of people and organisations. Hence, another view suggests that the corporations must consider all the people and organisations in making decisions. Corporations interact with a variety of stakeholders as the corporation and its stakeholders are mutually dependent on each other.

The employees exchange their human resources for fair salaries, benefits and harmonious industrial and human relations. Customers exchange their money for qualitative products and courteous services. Shareholders exchange their money for high rate of dividend and safety of their capital.

Government provides security and protection and in turn expects payment of taxes regularly. Financial institutions exchange their finance for high rate of interest, security of principal amount and regular payment of interest. Suppliers of inputs expects fair terms of trade and continuous business. Competitors exchange information through chamber of commerce, trade and industry for mutual existence and development. The dealers expects continuous business. Thus, a stakeholder is an individual or organisation who can affect or is affected by the decision making and achievement of organisational purpose and objective.

As stated, every stakeholder gives something to the corporation and expects something in return. Similarly, the corporation also gives something to its stakeholders and expects in return. The corporation can have more power, if it maintains favourable relations with the stakeholders compared to other corporations. More powerful stakeholders have better terms of exchange and, therefore, have more influence on decisions. In fact, the corporations depend on such powerful stakeholders. (See Box 6.2).

Box 6.2: Strategic Decision making Traps

"There are a series of traps that people fall into [in making decisions], that lead to incorrect judgements being reached, whatever the quality of the preceding analysis. The incidence of this is high. The cost, given that these are strategic decisions, is commensurately large..."Pragmatism leads to at least two biases that impact strategic decision making.

1. *Fact-based bias... we like to make decisions based on facts,[but]... To make strategic decisions, we need to be guided by a 'theory' that allows us to act before all the facts are in... a causal theory about the future - 'if we do this, then the following will happen' - lies at the heart of strategic decision making. We cannot wait for all the facts.*
2. *'Cut-through' bias... The second consequence of a pragmatic mindset is that it drives people to 'cut-through' and jump to a decision, by making a call. It is the other side of the fact-based bias. We wait for the facts, get impatient and cut-through...Unless it is done with great skill, it can lead to wrong decisions.*

"Following are the traps that people fall into. Trap one - over-simplification.Trap two - embedded assumptions...Many decisions are based on embedded assumptions that are not discussed, assumptions that often turn out to be wrong.

Trap three - incomplete criteria... Many important decisions are made without an explicit, agreed set of criteria... Strategic decisions will have multiple options, to be tested against multiple criteria... multiple weightings and multiple time periods. The human brain cannot reliably cope with such levels of complexity.In these circumstances, a formal, explicit process will yield a surer judgement...

To avoid these traps, make the decision process visible. Work hard to consider the whole problem at the same time. This provides a great incentive to expedite the process. Identify important embedded assumptions. And spend real time talking through the decision criteria, weightings and scoring. This way, the decision process will do justice to the hard work done in fact gathering and analysis. Better decisions are the expected result."

(**Source**: http://bizzbangbuzz.blogspot.com/2008/02/strategic-decision making-traps.html [Accessed on 09/09/09])

The stakeholders, influence the decisions of the corporation depending upon their strength. If the labour unions are strong and have strong political affiliation, they can influence the managerial decisions. In fact such union get even their unreasonable demands met by the management. Similarly, if the number of shareholders is relatively less, they can influence the decision regarding payment of high rate of dividend versus high reserves. Powerful dealers influence the corporation regarding the terms and conditions of trade.

In view of these factors, corporations do a juggling act to meet the demands of various stakeholders. The corporation should balance through political compromise the competiting demands of different stakeholders in making decisions. This process helps for a coalition of interests that will support the decision.

This is a descriptive theory suggesting a decision making within the alternatives available. Decisions are made through a mutual negotiations and consultation among all the stakeholders who affect and/or are affected by the decision. The negotiations/consultations are based on the rule of the power sharing game between the organisation and the stakeholders.

A Synthesis: The decision-maker being a human being is a mix of the rational and the emotional. Environment is a mixture of analysable and chaotic change and pressures. Therefore, decisions are made in a typically human way, using the rational, conscious analysis and intuitive, unconscious 'gut feeling' in light of political realities. Blending of these prescriptive and descriptive approaches helps to understand how decision-makers operate.[18]

(E) TYPES OF DECISIONS

Decisions are of different types *viz.*, operational and strategic, major and minor decisions, programmed and non-programmed decisions, simple and complex decisions, long-run and short-run decisions, and individual and group decisions.

Strategic vs Operational Decisions

Strategic decisions are related to unified, integrated and comprehensive issues of the organisation. These decisions are related to contribution to the organisational objectives significantly. These decisions affect the total organisation or the major part of it. They require trade-offs between conflicting factors. For example, diversification, introducing a new product and vertical integration are strategic decisions.

Strategic decisions are concerned with:

- the total or major part of the organisation,
- the matching of organisational factors to the external environmental factors,
- allocation and reallocation of organisation's resources,
- the values, expectations and goals of the organisation,
- the organisational direction and
- the change throughout the organisation.

Operational decisions are selected to the operational activities of the company which are routine in nature. These are supportive areas of the organisation. These decisions require less analysis and concentration. They do not change the organisational direction. For example, sanctioning of increments to employees, paying the bill of suppliers of raw materials, extending the due date for delivery etc. are operational decisions.

Operational decision are based on operational activities

Major and Minor Decisions

Major decisions are also called important decisions which affect the policies of the company, the total company or major portion of the company. These decisions influence almost all the functional areas of the company. These decisions do not repeat frequently.

Minor decisions are also called *unimportant* decisions. These decisions affect only one functional area to which it belongs. Most of these decisions are made at the lower level.

Programmed and Non-programmed Decisions

Programmed decisions are those which are made based on the company's policy, budget procedures etc. These decisions are made in response to routine and repetitive situations or problems. Managers develop programmes for the repetitive issues. For example, (i) increase of dearness allowance for employees at 2% of basic pay when the cost of living index increases by 10% and (ii) pay the money back to the customer, if the product is not in accordance with the customer's specifications.

Non-repetitive, peculiar, complex and most important, novel and unstructured problem are non-programmed decisions. Downsizing of employees, removal of regional office and demarketing are some of the examples for non-programmed decisions. Management cannot formulate a programme for these decisions as they are novel. Exhibit 6.4 presents the differences between programmed and non-programmed decisions.

Exhibit 6.4 Differences between Programmed and Non-programmed Decisions

	Programmed	*Non-programmed*
Type	Repetitive and Routine	Novel, complex, non-routine
Examples	Payment of DA Product delivery Attending to customer grievances Borrowing for working capital	New Product Introduction Downsizing Merger and expansion Public issue of equity shares
Procedures	Policies, procedures, budgets Rules and Regulations	Creative problem solving

Simple and Complex Decisions

As indicated earlier, a number of variables affect the decision making process. These variables include growth in population, cost of living, industrial growth, marketing growth etc.

If the number of variables affecting a decision are more, such decisions are called complex decisions. For example, wage increase is affected by a number of variables like employee productivity, trade union influence, government policies, profitability of the company etc. As such, this decision is called *complex decision*.

On the other hand, if the number of variables affecting the decision are less, such decisions are called *simple decisions*. For example, decisions regarding sanctioning of educational loan to an employee is influenced by a few factors like employee's children's educational level. As such, these decisions are called simple decisions.

Long-run Decisions and Short-run Decisions

Decisions affecting the long run plans, activities and business are called *long run decisions*. These decisions include: plant location, entering new markets and joint venture programmes.

Decisions affecting short run plans, activities and business are called *short run decisions*. These decisions include: sources of finances for working capital, over time payment for employees, offering special discounts for clearance sale etc.

Individual Vs. Group Decisions

Decision taken by an individual employee or manager are called *individual decisions*. These decisions are mostly routine, simple, repetitive and programmed decisions.

Decisions made by a group of people are called *group decisions*. Group decisions include: strategic decisions, non-programmed, complex and strategic decisions. Team decisions and committee decisions are also group decisions.

We will discuss group decisions in detail at a later stage. Now we shall discuss the process of decision making.

(F) PROCESS OF DECISION MAKING

Though we have studied different approaches to decision making, the research suggests us to understand the process of decision making, which actually takes place in organisations and give rise to decisions. There are five steps in the process of decision making (Fig. 6.3). They are:

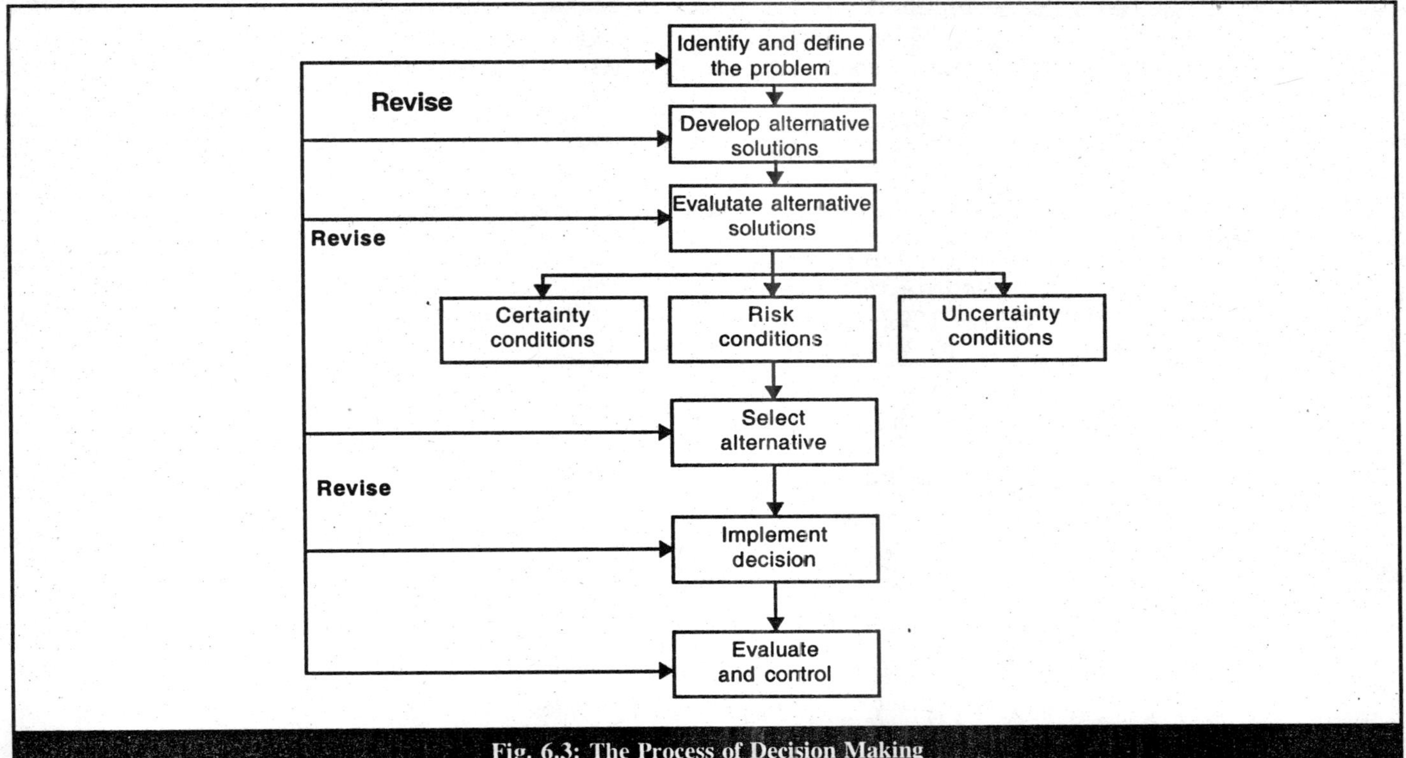

Fig. 6.3: The Process of Decision Making

Step 1: Problem Awareness

Indentifying the problem is the major task

Mostly individual employees identify the problems in various areas. Individuals, when they get a 'gut feeling' that something is wrong, they identify the problem. The awareness of a problem mostly occurs to employees at the grass-root level like sales people, machine operators, finance assistants, human resource assistants etc. This awareness is likely to develop through a period of 'incubations' in which managers sense various stimuli that confirm and define a developing picture of a problem. Norburn and Grinyer call this stimuli as 'signals' or 'ear twitchers' and are of three types:

- Internal performance measurements like level of turnover or profit performance.
- Customer reaction particularly to the quality and price of the products and/or services and
- Changes in the environment, particularly in terms of competitive action, technological change and economic conditions.

These three factors together provide a picture of the deviation of an organisation's circumstances from the planned or expected one. This can be the deviation from a normal traαing pattern.

The accumulation of stimuli will clearly indicate the existence of the problem in the organisation. This 'triggering point,' will soon be highlighted by the formal information system in the form of decline in sales, profit and increase in the rejection level in the production department.

Successful business performance depends upon the ability of the management in sensing its environment. Therefore, managers should respond when the problem is identified by the individual employees at the bottom level. (See Box 6.3).

Box 6.3: How Companies Make Good Decisions: McKinsey Global Survey Results

Do strong decision making processes lead to good decisions? This McKinsey survey highlights several process steps that are strongly associated with good financial and operational outcomes. In the survey, we asked executives from around the world about a specific capital or human-resources decision their companies made in the course of normal business. We learned who was involved, what drove the decisions, how deep the analysis was, how unfettered the discussions, and how and where politics were involved. Respondents also described the financial and operational outcomes of the decisions.[1]

The results highlight the hard business benefits—such as increased profits and rapid implementation—of several decision making disciplines. These disciplines include ensuring that people with the right skills and experience are included in decision making, making decisions based on transparent criteria and a robust fact base, and ensuring that the person who will be responsible for implementing a decision is involved in making that decision. Finally, although corporate politics sometimes seems to undermine strong decision making, some types of consensus-building and alliances apparently can help create good outcomes.

(**Source:** http://www.mckinseyquarterly.com/Strategy/Strategic_Thinking How_companies_make_good_decisions_McKinsey_Global_Survey_Results_2282)

Step 2: Problem Diagnosis

Information should be the basis for diagnosis

After the individual employees are aware of the problem and it is informed to the managers, managers will gather the information and define the problem.

Information, may be gathered in the following ways:

(i) Information may be explored to determine the facts of the problem in detail. Such information may be gathered on a verbal and informal basis.

(ii) Rationalise the information and stimuli relevant to the problem so as to clarify the situation.

(iii) Act diplomatically to establish peer groups or those of political support for individual views of the problem.

Try to define the problem through debates and discussions and also get an organisational view or consensus on the problem to be solved. The problem, then may take a clear shape by interweaving managerial experience of the executives and political process in the organisations. Some executives, may not accept to proceed or define the problem and ask for additional information or the triggering of a different problem owing to different managerial experience and different views in view of social and political process. In such a situation, the process reverts back to the stage of triggering.

Step 3: Development of Alternative Solutions

After the problem is diagnosed clearly, the tendency of managers is that of searching for ready made solutions. They do this process: *(i)* through memory search in which the managers seek for known, existing or attempted solutions, or *(ii)* passive search which entails waiting for possible solutions to be offered. If the managers fail in these two searches, they search for the past experiences of themselves and other managers. If they fail to find a solution even through this method, they attempt to designing solutions.

They start designing or developing solutions through a vague idea, gradually improve it, refine it by recycling it through selection routes back into problem identification or through further searches. This process of developing solutions takes place through discussions, debates, consultations and brainstorming sessions and by sharing management wisdom and experience. This can take place both in the form of structured and unstructured team works. The solutions once developed are to be refined until they are developed to the stage of perfection within the available human and other resources of the organisation.

Step 4: Evaluation of Alternative Solutions

After the alternative solutions are developed, the solutions have to be formally evaluated based on their inherent strengths and weaknesses and also based on the environmental threats and opportunities for implementation. The solutions are to be ranked on the basis of their weights in terms of strengths and opportunities after eliminating the non-viable solutions in view of their weaknesses and environmental threats for implementation.

Evaluation is for ranking the solutions

Step 5: Selection of the Best Solution

After the formal evaluation and ranking is completed, the managers tend to re-evaluate the solutions based on the managerial judgement followed by political bargaining as the formal evaluation is not the predominant criterion for assessing the feasibility in practice. Therefore, the techniques for evaluation of solutions also include social and political process. Quinn suggests that successful managers actively adopt consultation bargaining process in order to challenge prevailing strategic inclinations and generate information from other parts of the organisation. The solutions may also be referred to the senior level to seek authorisation.

David Hickson and his colleagues in their study identified three broad types of decision making processes. They are:

- **Sporadic processes** characterised by many delays and impediments, many sources of influence and information on decision, and therefore, protracted personal interactions and informal negotiation. This type of process exists mostly in public sector organisations
- **Fluid processes** in which there are fewer delays and sources of influence, and more formal channels of communication which takes rather less time and
- **Constricted processes** in which information sources are more readily available and decisions can be taken within groups or by individuals without extensive reference to others in the organisation. This might be the case in a business with a dominant chief executive or where there is an issue which relates primarily to one part of an organisation.

The managers should keep in mind the various processes discussed above while selecting the solution for implementation. If the managers fail to arrive at a consensus, the process may be recycled to search for new designs.

Step 6: Implementation of the Decision

Implementation of the selected solution is a part of the decision making process as the process may be required to be recycled due to impediments in the process of implementation. The managers should secure the support of the top management for allocation of resources, time etc. regarding the implementation of the decision.

A detailed programme of action should be formulated, specifying the minute details of action, people who will execute it, when it will be implemented, who will provide all necessary resources, how it will be implemented and who will coordinate the work. Employees concerned will be entrusted with the work and relevant information should be fed to them before hand. The managers should also ensure for getting the information back about the progress of implementation. If the decision cannot be implemented due to major hurdles in the implementation process, the process may be recycled for possible modification.

Steps to be a good decision-maker are presented in Exhibit 6.5. It will help in taking qualitative decisions.

Exhibit 6.5 Steps to be an Effective Decision Maker

1. Be alert to signals indicating the need for a decision.
2. Make quite uninterrupted time for thinking and reflecting about things to be decided.
3. Set priorities for different decisions.
4. Separate yourself from the problem and solution. How would another person decide the issue?
5. Ask whether the contemplated decision seems honourable and right.
6. Ask whether you will think well of yourself when you review what has resulted from your decision.
7. Have a backing decision, just in case.
8. Take adequate time to reach a decision over the subject. In contrast, don't dig into so many aspects that confusion prevails and no defensive action is taken.

(**Source**: George R.Terry and Stephen G.Franklin, "*Principles of Management*," All India Traveller Bookseller, Delhi, 1987, p. 116.)

(G) BOARDS AND COMMITTEES IN DECISION MAKING: GROUP DECISION MAKING

Board of directors, other boards and various committees are groups. They make decisions in groups and through group decision making process.

A group of people make the decisions jointly by sharing their views, ideas, expertise, experience etc. They participate and involve in all the steps of the process of decision making discussed earlier. Managers who adopt to the group decision making have the advantage of using the expertise of their subordinates. Managers use participative decision making techniques in this regard.

Participation involves the individuals in the decision making process. Some managers make the decision on their own and do not seek any opinion from members of the group. On the other hand, group members themselves do not offer any opinion, even though it is sought by the manager and tell the manager to take the decision on his own. Thus, this is one extreme of no participation at all. The other extreme of participation is that all the members of the group who are affected by the decision are fully involved in the decision making.

The degree of participation is determined by factors like:

- Experience and the expertise of the group leader
- Expertise of the group members
- Nature of the task: Strategic, important, critical, routine
- Dynamism on the part of group members
- Openness of the group leader
- Difference of opinion, attitude etc.
- Employee empowerment and freedom
- Degree of upward communication and
- Organisational culture.

Methods of Group Decision Making

The different methods of group decision making are:

- **The Majority Wins Scheme:** The group chooses the alternative solution which is initially supported by the majority of the members.
- **The Truth Wins Scheme:** Group member gather complete information, discuss the problem in detail and recognise that approach which is objectively correct.
- **The Two-thirds Majority Scheme:** In this method, the decision which is supported by two-thirds of the group members is made.
- **The First-Shift Rule:** In this method, the opinion first expressed by any member of the group is taken as the decision.
- **Status-quo Rule:** In this method, the group members tend to maintain the existing decisions.

Techniques of Group Decision Making

Group decision making techniques include:

(i) The Delphi Technique

Members with expertise and relevant information concerning an issue are selected to make the decision regarding that issue. Questionnaires are sent to the group members who record their answers in writing. The group members do not meet face-to-face. Replies of all the members to the questionnaires are summarised and feedback to them are sent for review. They are asked to make the decisions again in view of the additional information. This process is repeated until a satisfactory decision is made.

This technique is mostly used for the decisions relating to demand forecast, project market trends, identify future problems, predict the future state of finance, production etc.

Success of this technique depends on:

- Seriousness of the group members
- Expertise of the group members
- Availability of adequate time
- Written communication skills of the members
- Level of involvement and motivation of the members
- Level of effectiveness of summarisation of responses
- Use of information technology like e-mail, voice-mail and chatting.

Advantages: The advantages of Delphi technique include:

- Ego problems and related issues of face-to-face interaction can be avoided
- Efficient use of expert time
- Avoidance of interpersonal problems
- Enough time is given for reflection and analysis by respondents. and
- Utmost care can be taken.

(ii) Nominal Group Technique

Group members have minimal interaction prior to making a decision. The steps involved in nominal group decision making are:

(i) Group members are brought together and presented with a problem.

(ii) Members develop the solutions independently and write them on cards.

(iii) They share their ideas with each other in a structured format (all members get an opportunity in a round table format).

(iv) Members ask questions just to get clarifications during a brief session.

(v) Group members individually select the best alternative and inform through a secret ballot.

(vi) The group decision is announced.

Advantages: Advantages of this technique are:

- All members get equal opportunity for participation.
- No member can dominate the discussion.
- Decision can be taken in the right time due to control of time.
- Expertise of each member is used independently.
- Ego problems and interpersonal problems are solved.

Disadvantages: Disadvantages of this technique include:

- The procedure is too rigid.
- Members may be frustrated.
- Members cannot have interpersonal relations.
- Group cohesiveness cannot be ensured and
- Ideas can not be cross-fertilised.

(iii) Brainstorming Technique

This technique is used to encourage creative thinking in groups of around eight members. Brainstorming is built on the following lines:

- Generate as many ideas as possible.
- Be creative, free-wheeling and imaginative.
- Build upon (piggy back), extend or combine earlier ideas and
- Withhold criticism of others' ideas.

The success of this technique depends upon the members' ability to listen to others, use this interaction as a stimulus to spark new ideas and feel free to express them. Further, even the idiotic and impracticable ideas should also be encouraged. More number of ideas should be encouraged so that eventually higher quality ideas would be generated.

Advantages: Advantages of this technique include:

- Group members would be enthusiastic, involved immensely and emotional.
- Broader participation of the members.
- High task orientation and also high relation orientation will be maintained.
- Members have a sense of belongingness and the final product is the team effort.

Disadvantages: Disadvantages of this technique are:

- Some members may fear that their ideas may be looked down by others.
- Criticism of ideas kills creativity.
- Some people may dominate the process of decision making.

(iv) Dialectic Decision Methods

This method ensures generation of alternatives seriously, detailed discussion on each of the alternatives and selecting the alternative or developing a new alternative. The incomplete discussions, analysis and making the decisions quickly, discourage some group members from participating in the group decision making. This technique solves this problem.

(v) Decision-Tree

As we have discussed earlier, alternative solutions are generated in the decision making process. Each of these alternative decisions are evaluated before ranking the solutions. The decision tree is a model in the form of a graphic tool that charts the steps to consider in evaluating each alternative solution in the decision making. The main points of the decision tree are:

- Using the information acquired in preparing to make the decision.
- Recognising the sequential nature of the decision making process.
- Decision tree is a graphic outline of the future choices that the decisions made in the present will lead to.
- Decision tree helps managers to evaluate and arrange the information in order and
- Decision tree enables managers to introduce a degree of quantifiability.

Figure 6.4 shows the decision tree of a car manufacturing company. The company has to make a decision whether to make or buy the wipers.

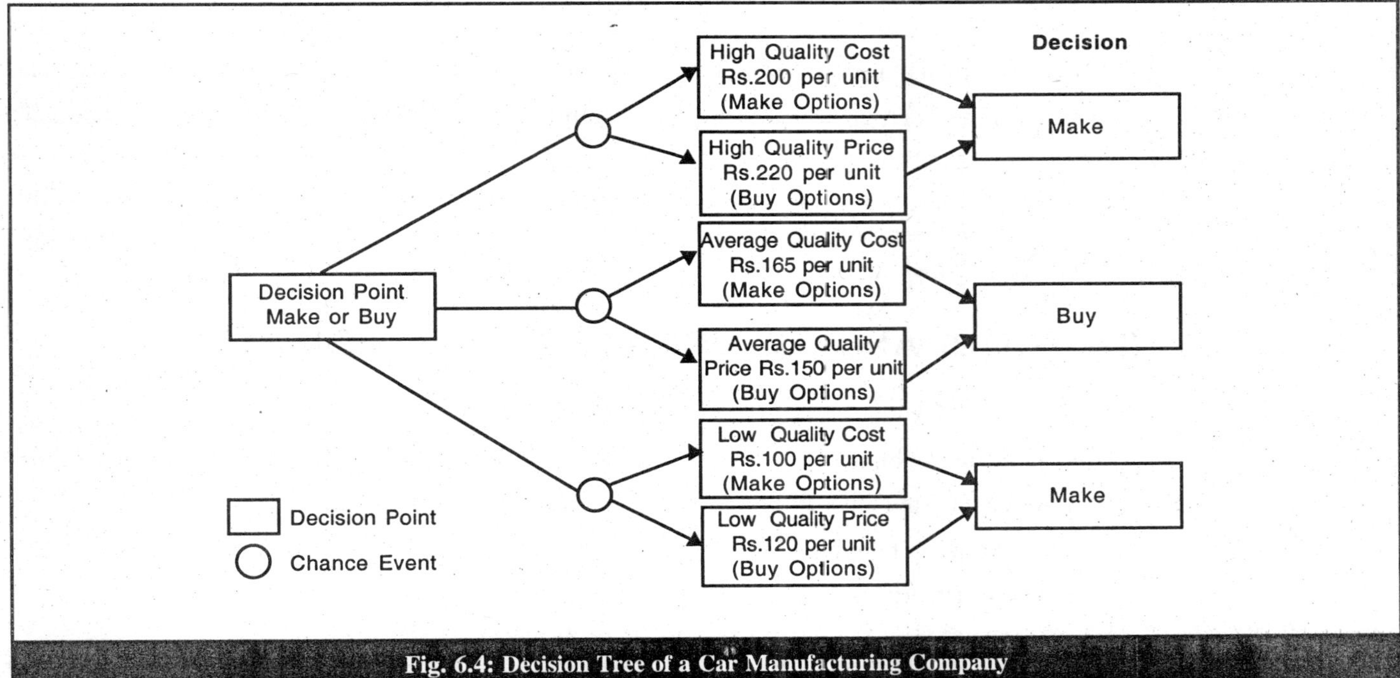

Fig. 6.4: Decision Tree of a Car Manufacturing Company

It is observed from the figure that the car manufacturing company has to take a decision whether to make the wipers or to buy them from other companies. The company has three chance events for each of these two alternatives. Managers make the decision based on the information and quantified data provided in the decision tree.

Potential Benefits of Group Decision Making

Group decision is superior to individual decision

Group Decision Making Leads to Creativity: The counter and encounter process of the group activity over the ideas and issues lead to creativity and innovation. Creativity provides competitive edge to the companies over the competitors. Creativity is the process of combining responses or ideas of individuals or groups in novel ways. The group activity through brain storming, active involvement and interaction may result in creativity and innovation. Divergent thinking is a person's ability to generate novel but appropriate responses to questions and problems. It may lead to creativity.

Group decision making is normally superior to individual decision making as:

- The sum total of the group's knowledge and skill are greater,
- The group has a much wider range of alternatives in the decision process,
- The impact of synergy and
- It facilitates and enhances acceptance of the decision by group members-particularly in strategic issues.

Limitations of Group Decision Making

However, there are certain limitations of group decision making. They are:

- One person may dominate or control the entire process of group decision making,
- The social pressure of conformity,
- Winning an issue becomes more important than the issue itself due to competition within the group,
- Groups tend to accept the first potentially positive solution and give little attention to others,
- Unanimous group decisions are consistently most risky than the average of individual decisions and
- Indifference of the members in the decision making process as "everybody's responsibility is nobody's responsibility." Exhibit 6.6 presents the potential benefits and limitations of group decision making.

(H) TOOLS AND TECHNIQUES OF DECISION MAKING

Tools and techniques of decision making include:

- Operations Research
- Decision Tree
- Linear programming
- Game Theory

Exhibit 6.6 Potential Benefits and Limitations of Group Decision Making

Potential Benefits

- The sum total of the Group's knowledge is greater than that of the total of all individual members of the group due to the impact of synergy.
- Group process develops a much wider range of alternatives in the decision process.
- Participation in the decision making process increases the acceptance of the decision by group members.
- Group members better understand the decision and the alternatives considered.
- Members feel more job satisfaction.
- Extensive information sharing.

Limitations

- One individual may dominate and/or control the group.
- Social pressures to confirm can inhibit group members.
- Competition can develop to such an extent that winning becomes more important than the issue itself.
- Groups have a tendency to accept the first potentially positive solution, while giving little attention to other solutions.
- Group decision is time consuming.
- Group decision is costly.
- Group decision sometimes results in indecision.
- Argumentation stifles creativity and
- Game playing among members.

(**Source**: Modified Version: Leslie W. Rue and Lloyd L. Byars, "Management," Richard D.Irwin Inc., Homewood, 1986, p. 106.)

- Queuing Theory
- Brain Storming
- Delphi Technique
- Nominal Group Techniques
- Dialetic Decision Methods.

Operations Research: Operations research is the application of specific methods, tools and techniques to operations of systems with optimum solution to the problems.[19] Operations research presents in the logical approach to a real problem, by quantifying the variables to the problem. It concentrates on goals in a problem area, hurdles to the solution, overcoming the hurdles in reaching the goal. It quantifies all these variables in the process. (See Box 6.4).

Box 6.4: Data Warehouses: Improve Decision Making with Coherent Views of Data

The ability to make quick, well-informed decisions is critical to competitiveness and growth for most companies. Read the white paper to see how data warehouse solutions can deliver business insight across virtually any business process or function. You will also learn how they're particularly valuable for understanding sales, profiling customers, and analyzing business costs.

The ability to make quick, well-informed decisions is critical to competitiveness and growth for small and large companies alike. In recent years, most companies have seen the amount of customer and company data in legacy systems, desktops, servers and intranets increase dramatically. Yet a lack of integration between systems makes it nearly impossible for companies to use the valuable data within disparate systems to their advantage. In many cases, instead of relying on hard data based on historical trends to drive strategic direction, decision makers rely heavily on experience, limited—sometimes outdated— information and intuition. Siloed data also makes it more challenging to comply with changing regulations.

Data warehouses—which can provide a manageable, cost-effective central repository of company-wide data—can help you take control of growing data volumes. And with the help of online analytical processing (OLAP) and data mining tools, data warehouses can help you drive a business strategy based on documented trends rather than best guesses.

(**Source**: http://www.webbuyersguide.com/resource/white-paper/14702/Data-Warehouses-Improve-Strategic-Decision Making-with-Coherent-Views-of-Data [Accessed on 09.09.09])

Decision Tree: This technique is already explained in group decision making in this chapter.

Linear Programming: Linear programming helps in making decisions with regard to optimum allocation of resources viz., financial, human, material, machines, space, time etc., among various purposes. It is a mathematical technique with objective function establishing proportional relationships between/among variables. It establishes the linear relationship that additional input produces the output in the same proportion.

Game Theory: Game theory is the logic of rational decisions. It provides solutions for competitive problems taking into considerations the situations, the probable actions by the competitors, expected outcome and choosing a right action.

Queuing Theory: Queuing theory deals with ques or waiting lines of a group of items ready to receive the service or operation in the process. Queuing theory presents a mathematical solution to the problem of long queue versus a short/nil queue. This theory considers cost associated, outcome expected, time and alternate use of resources. The characters involved in the decision making are: (i) number of servers waiting at the service stations, (ii) capacity and efficiency of the servers, (iii) number of service facilities, (iv) average arrival rate, (v) average service rate, (vi) average length of queue, (vii) average waiting time and (viii) average time spent in the system.[20]

Brain Storming, Delphi, Nominal and Dialetic Techniques: These techniques are discussed in 'Group Decision Making' section in this chapter.

(I) DECISION MAKING UNDER ABNORMAL CONDITIONS

Conditions under which decisions are made vary widely. Some conditions are normal while other conditions involve uncertainties and risk. In fact, different managers behave differently. The same conditions are perceived as simple by some managers while they are perceived s uncertainties by others.

Managers sometimes fail to see the problems and also avoid or tend to postpone decision making as decision making is challenging. The characteristics of decision making that make it challenging are:

- Uncertainty and Risks
- Conflict
- Absence of Structure

Uncertainty and Risks

The conditions of certainty include: availability of all data and information necessary to make a decision, certainty of implementation of decision completely and certainty of expected outcome of the decision. In fact, conditions of certainty for complicated and strategic issues take place rarely.

Uncertainty: Uncertainty is opposite to the conditions of certainty. Conditions of uncertainty include: absence or non-availability of required data and information, less probability for implementation of the decision as planned and for the occurrence of expected outcome. Decision makers under the conditions of uncertainty mostly depend on their experiences, intuitions and imagination of the process of future conditions, implementation and outcome of the decision. Decision makers, under the conditions of uncertainty follow intuitive approach discussed under approaches to decision making.

Risk: The conditions of risk include the probability of perfect implementation of the decision and probability of expected outcome are less than 100 per cent. The risk involves loss of money, time, other resources invested, reputation and negative consequences on other aspects of the business.

Conditions of risk and risk taking are different. Conditions of risk taking include: available information and data indicate the problems in implementation of decision and the output of the decision would be different from the desired or expected. Entrepreneurs and leaders prefer to take risk in order to add more value or create something beyond the normal outcome. (See Box 6.5).

Box 6.5: Flaws in Strategic Decision Making: McKinsey Global Survey Results

Irrational thinking doesn't just affect individual economic decisions; it affects corporate strategic planning as well. These results highlight the practices of companies that have made successful strategic decisions—and also reveal what the same companies have gotten wrong. Since its inception nearly three decades ago, behavioral economics has upset the pristine premise of classical economic theory—the view that individuals will always behave rationally to achieve the best possible outcome. Today it's clear that the vagaries of individual and group psychology can cause irrational decision making by both individuals and organizations, resulting in less than ideal outcomes. Even the best-designed strategic-planning processes don't always lead to optimal decisions. A recent survey by McKinsey attempts to assess the frequency and intensity of the most common managerial biases in companies. Specifically, we asked executives about a single recent strategic decision at their companies that had a clearly satisfactory or unsatisfactory outcome, focusing on the role that various biases may have played.

It's evident from the results that satisfactory outcomes are associated with less bias, thanks to robust debate, an objective assessment of facts, and a realistic assessment of corporate capabilities. A few clear paths to making successful decisions also are apparent. But even when a decision had a satisfactory outcome, executives note several areas where their companies aren't all that effective, such as aligning incentives with strategic objectives and forecasting competitors' reactions. Also notable is that companies that typically...

Since its inception nearly three decades ago, behavioral economics has upset the pristine premise of classical economic theory—the view that individuals will always behave rationally to achieve the best possible outcome. Today it's clear that the vagaries of individual and group psychology can cause irrational decision making by both individuals and organizations, resulting in less than ideal outcomes. Even the best-designed strategic-planning processes don't always lead to optimal decisions. A recent survey by McKinsey attempts to assess the frequency and intensity of the most common managerial biases in companies. Specifically, we asked executives about a single recent strategic decision at their companies that had a clearly satisfactory or unsatisfactory outcome, focusing on the role that various biases may have played. It's evident from the results that satisfactory outcomes are associated with less bias, thanks to robust debate, an objective assessment of facts, and a realistic assessment of corporate capabilities. A few clear paths to making successful decisions also are apparent. But even when a decision had a satisfactory outcome, executives note several areas where their companies aren't all that effective, such as aligning incentives with strategic objectives and forecasting competitors' reactions.[2] Also notable is that companies that typically...

(**Source**: http://www.mckinseyquarterly.com/Strategy/Strategic_Thinking/Flaws_in_strategic_decision_making_McKinsey_Global_Survey_Results_2284?gp=1 (09/09/09))

Managers prefer to manager or avoid risk as the cost of risk, sometimes is more than the investment in the entire project.

Conflict

Conditions of conflict include the existence of opposing pressures from different sources. The pressures are due to psychological, sociological and political factors.

Psychological conflicts are due to perceptual differences of different managers based on their backgrounds, difference in understanding and interpreting data and information and differences in evaluating alternatives.

Conflicts also arise between two managers based on their professional background and the department to which they belong. For example, marketing manager prefer more investment in materials whereas finance and production managers prefer less investment in materials.

Lack of Structure

There is no mathematical formula and clearcut procedure or structure for decision making. However, there may be structures for routine decisions. Decisions based on structures are of two types viz., programmed decisions and nonprogrammed decisions.

Programmed decisions are those decisions which were encountered and made before with more or less established procedures, rules, programme consequences and outcome. Non-programmed decisions are novel, complex and critical and which were not encountered and made earlier. So the procedure, rules, structure and answers are not established ones. Table 6.1 presents the destinations between programmed and nonprogrammed decisions.

Table 6.1: Distinctions between Programmed Decisions and Nonprogrammed Decisions

Types	Programmed Decisions	Nonprogrammed Decisions
Type of Problem	Frequent, Routine	Novel, Strategic
Certainty	Certain of cause and effect relationship	Uncertain of cause and effect relationship
Procedure	Based on policies, rules and clear procedure	Ambiguity, intuition creative based
Outcome	Clear and certain	Unclear and Risky

(J) DECISION MAKING PRACTICES ABROAD

Decision making practices vary from country to country based on country's culture and other factors.

Decision Making in Japan

Decision making in Japan is mostly group décision making

Japanese emphasise on understanding and analysing a problem and the development of alternative solutions. Managers at the top concentrate on critical decisions. In fact, employees at the lower level also participate in the decision making process. Employees at the lower level make non-critical decisions and submit them to the top for approval. Employees at various levels discuss the problems and decisions, before a final decision is made by the top. Though the top can reject a decision made at the lower level, it asks the subordinates for further study.

Decisions are made through the '*ringi*' process under which a proposal document is prepared by the persons who will be affected by the decision and is circulated among various managers for additions, deletions, modifications etc. Thus the problem is analysed and discussed from different perspectives at different levels before it reaches top management.

Thus, almost all the people who are affected by the problem, who will implement the solution directly or indirectly are involved in the decision making.

Decision Making in the USA: Decisions in the USA are basically made by individuals. Therefore, the individuals who make the decision sell it to others who implement it or affected by it. In fact, these individuals are with varied values, ideas, perceptions. Thus the decision making is easy, but implementing it is difficult.

Decision Making in China: Strategic decisions are made by top level managers, while operational decisions are made by the lower level managers. Central Planning Bureau of the Government makes all strategic decisions affecting the economy. This does not allow flexibility or adaptability in doing business in China. In fact, managers also do not prefer change as it affects their privileges and operations.

Table 6.2 presents comparison of decision making practices in Japan, USA and China.

Table 6.2: Comparison of Decision Making Practices in Japan, USA and China

Factor	Japan	USA	China
Individual Vs.Collective	Collective	Individual	Committees at the top, individuals at lower level
Involvement	Involvement of many people	A few people	Top down. Participation at lower level
Critical Decisions	Top down	Initiation at the top	Top down
Speed of Making	Slow	Fast	Slow
Implementation	Fast	Slow	Slow

(**Source:** Adapted from Heinz Weihrich and Harold Koontz, "Management", Tata McGraw Hill, New Delhi, 2002, p.227.)

KEY TERMS

- Decision Making
- Intutive-Emotional approach
- Boards and Committees
- Political Behavioural Approach
- Rational Model
- Group Decision Making
- Decision Tree
- Strategic Decisions
- Rational Model
- Operations Research

QUESTIONS

1. What is decision making? Explain the importance of decision making in an organisation.
2. What are different types of decisions? Explain with examples their utility in different business activities.
3. Explain different approaches to decision making. Discuss supporting and opposing views of each approach.
4. Discuss in detail the process of decision making.
5. Discuss the superiority of group decision making over individual decision making.
6. What are the techniques of group decision making? Explain its potential benefits.
7. What are the tools and techniques of decision making?
8. What is the rational model of decision making? Discuss its assumptions and criticisms levelled against it.
9. How do boards and committees make decisions?
10. Discuss decision making practices abroad.

REFERENCES

1. Charles H. Kepner and Benjamin B. Tregoe, "The Rational Manager," McGraw-Hill, New York, 1965, p. 40.
2. George Prince, "Putting the other Half of the Brain to work," Training, November 1978, pp. 58-59.
3. George R. Terry and Stephen G. Franklin, "Principles of Management," All India Traveller Book Seller, Delhi, 1987, pp. 76-80.
4. George R. Terry and Stephen G. Franklin, op.cit., pp. 79-85.
5. L.M. Prasad, "Business Policy and Strategy," Paramount Publishers, Surat, 1985, pp. 33-34.
6. Lawrence R. Jauch and William F. Glueck, op.cit., p. 21.
7. George S. Odiorne, "Management and the Activity Trap," Harper & Row, New York, 1974, pp.128-129 and George S. Odiorne, "The Change Resisters," Prentice Hall, Englewood Cliffs, 1981, pp. 15-25.

8. Lawrence R. Jauch and William F. Glueck, op.cit., p. 21.
9. George R. Terry and Stephen G. Franklin, op.cit., p. 94.
10. George S. Odiorne, "Management and the Activity Trap," op.cit., pp. 142-144.
11. Lawrence R. Jauch and William F. Glueck, op.cit., p. 20.
12. Leslie W. Rue and Lloyd L. Byars, op.cit., p. 97.
13. Lawrence R. Jauch and William F. Glueck, op.cit., p. 21.
14. Leslie W. Rue and Lloyd L. Byar, op.cit., p. 98.
15. Herbert A. Simon, "Model of Man," John Wiley & Sons, New York, 1957, p.198.
16. Leslie W. Rue and Lloyd L. Byars, op.cit., p. 99.
17. Lawrence R. Jauch and William F. Glueck, op.cit., pp. 22-23.
18. Gerry Johnson, "Strategic Change and the Management Process," Basil Blackwell, 1987.
19. C.W.Churchman, R.L.Ackoff and E.L.Arnoff, "Introduction to Operations Research". John Wiley, New York, 1977, p.3.
20. L.M.Prasad, "Principles and Practice of Management". Sultan Chand & Sons, New Delhi, 2001, pp.273-74.

CHAPTER 7

DELEGATION, DECENTRALISATION AND SPAN OF MANAGEMENT

Chapter Outline

(A) Introduction
(B) Delegation of Authority
(C) Centralisation and Decentralisation
(D) Span of Management
- Key Terms
- Questions
- References

Learning Objectives

After studying this Chapter, you should be able to:

- ✓ Know the meanings of and differences among authority, responsibility and accountability.
- ✓ Understand the concept of span of management, factors affecting spans and relevance of span of management to delegation.
- ✓ Explain the meaning, principles, benefits and barriers of delegation.
- ✓ Analyse how to make delegation effective?
- ✓ Understand the concepts of centralisation and decentralisation and their effects on organisation structure and management.

(A) INTRODUCTION

L.A.Allen defines an organisation as "the process of identifying and grouping the work to be performed, defining and delegating responsibility and authority and establishing relationships for the purpose of enabling the people to work most effectively together in accomplishing objectives."[1] The relationships that exist in an organisation may be formal and/or informal.

The manager describes organisational relationships in a written and graphic manner. He/she tells the participants to do certain things in a specified manner, to obey orders from designated individuals, and to work co-operatively with others. Formal organisation is built on the relationships of authority responsibility, accountability span of management, delegation, centralisation and decentralisation. Now, we discuss these concepts.

Authority

Authority is the right to give orders

Authority is the right to give orders and the power to extract obedience. It is the right to decide what should be done or the right to do it oneself or to require someone else to do it. An authority is the power to command or to extract action from others in the process of discharging the delegated responsibility. Thus, authority is derived from responsibility just as responsibility is derived from functions. The important principle of authority is:

Authority and responsibility should be equal. In other words, the required amount of authority should be delegated to discharge responsibility. This principle avoids misuse of authority and at the same time helps in the proper discharge of responsibility.

Responsibility

Responsibility is one's obligation

Edwin B. Flippo defined responsibility as "one's obligation to perform the functions assigned to the best of one's ability in accordance with directions received."[2] Responsibility is derived from function which is the origin for relationship. Hence, it is called *functional derivative*. The important principles which could be observed in delegating responsibility are:

- Absence of overlapping responsibilities *i.e.*, one function should not be assigned to more than one individual employee.
- Functional similarity which facilitates specialisation should be taken into consideration while delegating responsibility.
- Clear identification of responsibility limits.
- Avoidance of gaps in delegation of responsibility.
- Unnecessary function or responsibility which does not contribute to organisational goals should not be entrusted.

Though, a certain part of the responsibility is delegated to the subordinate, the original and entire amount of the responsibility still rests with the superior.

Accountability

Accountability is the requirement of answerability

Accountability is the requirement of answerability for one's performance. It is the opposite phase of responsibility in the sense that responsibility flows downward while accountability flows from bottom to top for proper performance. If one has been delegated with co-equal authority and responsibility, he can logically be held accountable for results. While authority is delegated from a superior to a subordinate, where as accountability is created. In other words, accountability is derived from authority. Thus, responsibility is a functional derivative, authority is derived from responsibility and accountability is derived from authority. The important principle of accountability is single accountability. That is each person is accountable to only one superior. Divided accountability is undesirable as it confuses the subordinate.

(B) DELEGATION OF AUTHORITY

Every manager in the organisation has to perform certain activities/tasks which are assigned to him. Managers require authority in order to perform the activities assigned to him by his superiors. Hence, superiors delegate the necessary authority to their subordinates.

Meaning

Most of the managers fail to delegate because they fail to understand the meaning of delegation. The process of giving authority to a subordinate in order to perform the assigned activities by a superior is called *delegation of authority*.

Delegation is the process of giving authority

"Delegation is the process a manager follows in dividing the work assigned to him so that he performs only that part which he can perform effectively and so get others help him with the remaining work."[3]

Delegation is the instrument of responsibility and authority of another and the creation of accountability for performance. It is to be noted that the person who delegates authority and responsibility will not be relieved of the final responsibility and accountability.

Nature of Delegation

Nature of delegation includes:

- It gives direction to a manager in performing his duties
- It has dual characteristics in the sense that though the authority is delegated, it is still retained with the superior
- It can be modified even after the action is over
- Manager cannot delegate authority which he does not possess
- It may be specific or general and
- It is an art rather than a science.

Informal Delegation

Formal delegation is effective to the extent of formal authority and responsibility. Informal delegation occurs because people want to do something and not because they are not instructed to do it. It often takes place as people want to cut delays and get things done quickly and effectively. In informal delegation, the delegation could be bottom-up and lateral, in addition to top-down. As in the case of informal organisation, informal delegation also has plus and minus points. In view of this, the management should wisely use the informal delegation as the delegation is mostly an art rather than a science.

Informal delegation also takes place as people want to do something

Principles of Delegation

Managers have to follow the following principles in order to make the delegation effective.

(i) **Delegation of Results Expected:** Managers have to clearly know the activities to be performed by the subordinates and the results to be achieved by the subordinates. Managers have to delegate the necessary authority and responsibility to produce the results.

(ii) **Co-equal Authority and Responsibility:** Managers should delegate equal authority and responsibility. It means that the amount of authority that is to be delegated should be enough to discharge the responsibility. The authority may be misused, if it is more than the responsibility. In contrast, if the authority is less than the responsibility, the subordinate cannot discharge the authority.

(iii) **Absoluteness of Responsibility:** The superior holds responsibility though he delegates it to his subordinates. Therefore, the responsibility of subordinates to their superiors is absolute.

(iv) **Creation of Accountability:** The subordinates who receive both authority and responsibility should be accountable for their responsibility of completing the activities as specified and for their authority of using various resources. Thus, the delegation of authority and responsibility should create accountability on the part of the subordinates.

(v) **Unity of Command:** We have studied the principle of unity of command while studying Henry Fayol's 14 principles. Unity of command indicates that the subordinate should receive orders, instructions and commands from one superior only. Therefore, the authority and responsibility should be delegated to a subordinate by only one superior.

(vi) **Limits of Authority:** Superiors cannot delegate all the authority they have to their subordinates as they are finally responsible for the success or failure of their departmental functioning. Therefore, they delegate part of the authority to their subordinates. Subordinates should know the limits of the authority delegated to them while exercising the authority and also discharging their responsibilities. Now, we shall discuss the benefits advantages of delegation.

Benefits of Delegation

Delegation of authority and responsibility provides the basic energy to the organisational activities. The benefits of delegation include (see Table 7.1):

Table 7.1: Benefits and Barriers of Delegation

Benefits	Barriers
• Relieves the Managers from routine work	• Fear of loss of power
• Helps the Managers to concentrate on policy issues	• Avoidance of risk
• Basis for effective functions	• Lack of confidence in subordinates
• Effective and timely decisions	• Autocratic style
• Empowers and develops subordinates	• Fear of misuse of authority
• Satisfaction to subordinates	• Overconfidence of subordinates

(i) **Relief to the Manager from routine work and concentration on policy issues:** Managers are burdened with the heavy work relating to policy matters, strategic issues and routine activities. Managers normally delegate the responsibility of carrying out routine

activities to their subordinates. This process of delegation relieves them from the heavy workload and concentrate on important areas like policy and strategic issues.

(ii) **Basis for Effective Functioning:** Delegation of authority creates relationships and links among various jobs in the organisation. This relationship enables the smooth flow of organisational activities.

(iii) **Effective and Timely Decisions:** Delegation of authority and responsibility to the subordinates to the lowest level of the organisation enhances the number of decision points. Each decision point has less number of decisions to be made. Hence, it enables the managers at each decision point to make decisions effectively and timely.

(iv) **Empower and Develop Subordinates:** Delegation process encourages the subordinates to make decisions relating to their areas. Therefore, subordinates are trained to equip with all the necessary skills, knowledge etc. to make the decisions and implement them. Thus, they are empowered to decide their activities and develop strategies to implement or execute them.

(v) **Satisfaction to Subordinates:** Subordinates derive the satisfaction for doing a meaningful and challenging task. In addition, they have the opportunity to utilise their skills and knowledge.

(vi) **Effective utilisation of organisational human resources:** Responsibilities are delegated to all the subordinates depending upon their skills, knowledge, abilities, attitudes and emotions. Therefore, these organisational human resources can be effectively utilised.

However, there are certain barriers to delegation. Now, we shall discuss these barriers.

Barriers to Delegation

Delegation is limited due to the barriers

Delegation provides various benefits to the superior, subordinates and the organisation in general. But certain factors do hinder the process of delegation. These include:

(i) **Fear of Loss of Power:** Superiors feel that they lose power by delegating their authority. They also feel that their subordinates become powerful. This fear hinders some of the managers from delegating their authority and responsibility.

(ii) **Avoidance of Risk:** Some subordinates are not ready to accept responsibility as they do not want to take risk. So they try to encourage the superior to exercise the authority and act as the leader.

(iii) **Lack of Confidence in Subordinates:** Some superiors always view their subordinates as children, who cannot think and act independently. They also view that subordinates have to learn a lot and get experience to accept responsibility. Consequently such superiors show lack of confidence in subordinates and as such they hesitate to delegate authority.

(iv) **Autocratic Style:** Some managers are autocrats. They never consult others and do not allow others to make decisions. They never part with their authority.

(v) **Fear of Misuse of Authority:** Some managers feel that the subordinates misuse the authority or use the authority excessively and as such they fail to delegate.

(vi) **Overconfidence of the superiors:** Some superiors have overconfidence in themselves and feel that they do things better than their subordinates. As such they do not want to delegate their authority.

Art of Delegation

Delegation is mostly an art rather than science. As such managers should have necessary skills of delegation.

Most managers fail to delegate not because they are unaware of the principles[4] but because they take least interest in applying the principles to practice owing to their personal attitudes like receptiveness, willingness to let go, willingness to let others make mistakes, willingness to trust subordinates, willingness to establish and view broad controls.

In view of these limitations in delegation, the manager has to-

- Define assignments in the light of results expected and then delegate the necessary authority;
- Select the right man based on the job analysis;
- Establish and maintain open lines of communication;
- Use appropriate control techniques and
- Reward the superiors who delegate authority appropriately and assume the authority properly.

Most of the managers fail to delegate adequate authority owing to their love for authority and their personality factors. Fear of being exposed, control of the managers over the position they have succeeded, underestimation of subordinates' ability and improper estimation of required authority are other reasons for inadequate delegation.

How to Make Delegation Effective?

The problem of delegation is essentially one of human leadership. Hence, the management has to create appropriate climate, allow the others to develop, should have faith in the subordinates' ability and educate them to overcome fear:

- Management should establish clear-cut goals and define authority and responsibility clearly, motivate the subordinates through stimulation, group cohesiveness, organisational influences, appropriate leadership, counselling and communication.
- Delegation should be complete when arrangements are made for guidance, coaching, supervision, direction, communication and control.
- Managers who delegate authority should make a clear-cut assignment, delegate the details of coordination, specify progress information needed, provide counselling, guidance and adequate training which should be followed up by appraisal of current performance, counselling for improvement and coaching on the job.

Another concept that influences the organisation design is centralisation and decentralisation, which is close to delegation.

(C) CENTRALISATION AND DECENTRALISATION

The concept of organisational centralisation and decentralisation is closely related to the concept of span of control. The degree of centralisation or decentralisation affects the span of management and therefore, influences management.

Decentralisation may be viewed as an extension of delegation. It is the situation which exists as a result of systematic delegation of authority throughout the organisation. Thus, centralisation and decentralisation are two opposite situations. There are some misunderstandings about decentralisation, such as decentralisation is a type of organisation and it is equal to physical dispersion. But, to state clearly, decentralisation is not a type of organisation and is distinct from physical dispersion. Further, decentralisation to the complete extent, *i.e.*, delegation of entire authority to the lowest possible extent, is not practicable and viable.

Centralisation

Centralisation is reservation of authority at the central point.

Centralisation is the systematic and consistent reservation of authority at the central point within the organisation. If a manager reserves work, he has to reserve the authority also. In some cases, managers delegate work without delegating authority necessary to carry out the work. In such cases, the decisions are taken by those people who do not actually perform the work.

Every manager should reserve certain amount of authority for those decisions which are of strategic nature and which cannot be taken by the managers at the lowest level objectively and perspective.

Advantages of Centralisation

- **Facilitates Personal Supervision:** Centralisation helps for personal supervison. In some organisations particularly in the production activities the supervisor or manager has to closely supervise the activities in order to prevent the possible poor quality or deviations from the plans. In such case centralisation of authority and responsibility help the organisation better.
- **Provides Personal Leadership:** Some people need inspiration, influence and direction directly from the leader. Similarly, certain activities need information directly from the leader. In such cases centralisation provides for direct and personal leadership.
- **Promotes Integration and Co-ordination:** Organisational activities and business process is divided into parts for the purpose of convenience. They need to be integrated and coordinated for getting final and unified product or activity. As such the divided processes need to be co-ordinated and integrated. Centralisation provide for the integration and co-ordination.
- **Promotes Uniform Action:** Organisations ultimately provide unified product to the customer which needs uniform action to be performed at each level. Centralisation promotes uniform action.
- **To Handle Emergent Situation:** Emergency situations need flow of authority, resources, information etc. From one point or place only. Centralisation provides for it. Emergency situations can be efficiently managed through centralisation of authority.

Disadvantages of Centralisation

- **Delay in Communication:** Top management commounicates the information to all levels in the organisation as the authority is centralised. As such management may fail to communicate the information within the right line.
- **Delay in Decision-Making:** Top level management has to process all necessary data and information, identify the organisation problems, develop the alternative solutions and make the final decision. Top management takes relatively more time to perform all the sub functions of decision making. As such decision making is delayed in centralisation. (See Box 7.1).

- **Fail to Pay Proper Alternative on Policy Issues:** Centralisation process requires the top management to concentrate both on routine issues and policy issues. Routine issues normally draw most part of the time pay due attention on strategic and policy issues.
- **Under Utilisation of Organisational Human Resources:** People in the organisation are not delegated with authority and responsibilitions under centralisation. Hence, they do not perform most of the important functions in the company and do not use their potentialities fully.
- **Employee Dissatisfaction:** Most of the people under centralisation system perform routine activities. They cannot perform meaningful and challenging work. Hence, majority of the employees are dissatisfied with their job irrespective of salary levels.

Box 7.1: Consequence of Centralisation: Wal-Mart Stumbles while going Global

Having grown in fits and starts; Wal-Mart's international unit has a new game plan. Can it master world markets?

It's rare that a $100 billion business can be marginalized, but such is the case with the international arm of Wal-Mart Stores (WMT). As a stand-alone company, it would rank among the top five global retailers. Inside the $401 billion retail giant, though, the business has traditionally received short shrift. Its Bentonville (Ark.) headquarters is underwhelming—a drab, largely windowless, one-story structure named after Bill Mitchell, a former Walmart executive whom nobody seems to remember.

Since venturing into Mexico in 1991, Walmart International has grown haphazardly. During the 1990s the retailer exported its big-box, low-price model. While that strategy worked in North America, the results were so bad in Germany and Korea that Walmart withdrew from those countries in 2006. In response, Michael T. Duke, the former international chief and current CEO, gave local managers more autonomy while instituting more stringent financial goals for each region.

The results are mixed: International sales rose 11.5% in the second quarter (before the impact of exchange rate fluctuations), while U.S. sales barely budged. But over the past few years, operating profit margins have declined on the international side, which now has 3,805 stores operating under 53 distinct banners in 15 markets. As international chief C. Douglas McMillon says, Walmart is "progressing from being a domestic company with an international division to being a global company."

A Tale of Four Countries

The trick is how to get there. Four countries illustrate the challenges the world's largest retailer will face in the coming years as it seeks new sources of global growth. In Japan, managers are trying to revitalize a business that has hemorrhaged money for years—weighed down by a ho-hum brand, the country's byzantine distribution system, and cultural resistance to the discount model. In India, restrictions on foreign ownership have forced the company to team up with conglomerate Bharti, an odd coupling that has so far resulted in one store. Walmart has spent more than five years in Russia, maintaining a team of 30 executives who are still trying to plot an entry strategy at a time when other foreign retailers, like Carrefour, are bulking up their presence. And in Chile, a decade-long courtship finally led to the acquisition of the country's leading supermarket chain earlier this year, bringing with it a different business model, based in part on financial services.

All four demonstrate the perilous but potentially lucrative terrain that lies outside the saturated retail markets of Europe and North America. And Walmart's success will ultimately hinge on its ability to learn from past mistakes and adapt quickly to the shifting realities of these markets. Ahead, a look at the company's strategies.

(**Source**: http://finance.yahoo.com/career-work/article/107960/wal-marts-painful-lessons)

Decentralisation

It refers to the systematic effort to delegate to the lowest levels all authority except that which can only be exercised at central points. It proceeds at different rates to different levels and for different functions within the same company. It generally spreads level by level from the top to the bottom. Decentralisation can be accomplished to a certain extent in a functional type of organisation structure.

Effort to delegate to the lowest levels.

The decision to decentralise is complex as it involves a major change in the company's philosophy of management. The factors which dictate divisionalisation also dictate decentralisation. These factors include easing the burden of top executives from routine matters, to facilitate diversification, to provide product market and customers' emphasis, to encourage the development of the managers and to motivate people.[5] Factors determining the degree of decentralisation are:

- Cost pertaining to the decision;
- Desire for uniformity of policy;
- Size of the organisation;
- Number of levels in the organisation structure;
- History of the enterprise;
- Philosophy of the management;
- Decision for independence;
- Availability of managers with skill, knowledge and ability;
- Availability and use of control techniques;
- Need for decentralised performance in different geographical areas;
- Business dynamics and the need for adaptability to the situation and
- Influence of internal and external environmental factors.[6]

How to make Decentralisation Effective?

The management has to take the following steps while decentralising authority:

- Establishment of appropriate centralisation of authority to the required level;
- Development of managers in the areas of decision-making skill, interpersonal skills, job knowledge, organisation knowledge, technical knowledge, general knowledge, etc;
- Providing for communication and coordination and
- Establishment of adequate control techniques and providing for appropriate follow-up.

Benefits of Decentralisation

Decentralisation benefits the superiors, subordinates and the organisation in general. These benefits include:

- ***Effective Communication***: Decentralisation provides for a number of communication points and thereby reduces the number of persons or stages between the sender and the receiver of the communication. This process enhances the effectiveness of communication.
- ***Reduces Red-tapism***: Decentralisation reduces the supervisory levels in the organisations and thereby reduces the degree of red-tapism.
- ***Fast Decision-Making***: Decentralisation enhances the decision points. Each decision point is very close to the helm of affairs. Each decision point gets the necessary and accurate information quickly. Thus, it provides an environment for fast decision-making.
- ***Enhances Employee Job Satisfaction***: Decentralisation increases authority and decision making points. Most of the employees get the opportunity of managerial positions. They

get the freedom and autonomy to make the decisions, use their authority and make use of their talents. This process in turn leads to job satisfaction.

- ***Executive Development***: Decentralisation enhances the managerial positions. Existing employees acquire skills of decision making, handling various situations, directing skills etc., leading to development of a number of executives in the organisation.
- ***Competitive Advantage***: Decentralisation enables the managers and employees to be innovative and creative due to the autonomy and freedom it provides. In addition, the other benefits of decentralisation enable the organisation to produce the products at low cost of high quality and have other competitive advantages.

Decentralisation, further enables the managers to specialse in those activities in which they have expertise. Managers may specialise in line activities or in staff activities. Now, we shall discuss the line and staff relationships, which are critical for organisation design, authority, responsibility etc.

(D) SPAN OF MANAGEMENT

Span of management number of subordinates who report directly to the superior.

The span of management refers to the number of subordinates who report directly to the superior. It is also known as the number of subordinates who are efficiently managed by a single superior manager. If the subordinates who report to a superior are more in number, it is called the 'wide span' and the vice versa is called the 'narrow span.' The wide span results in a less number of levels in the organisation hierarchy (flat organisation) and thereby expedites the communication process. But this span is challenging to a manager as the manager has to supervise, direct, control a number of subordinates performing different types of activities. On the other hand, narrow span results in close and personalized relationships between the manager and his subordinates and it leads to tall organisations.

Factors Affecting Span of Management

The problem of any manager is to decide the proper number of subordinates to be managed or controlled. It is basically a behavioural question and varies with such factors like:

- Ability, leadership skills and styles of the manager;
- Position of manager in the organisation structure;
- Possible conflicts between superior and subordinates;
- Faith in subordinate's performance;
- Degree of team work;
- Nature of the work to be performed by the subordinates;
- Training received by the subordinates;
- Clarity of delegation of authority and responsibility;
- Clarity of plans, policies and programmes;
- Use of objective standards;
- Rates of change of policies, objectives, organization structure etc.;
- Use of communication techniques and
- Amount of personal contact needed.

V.A. Graicunas analysed the problem of subordinate-superior relationships in his paper on "*Relationship in Organisation.*"[7] He developed a mathematical formula which illustrates the number of relationships between the superior and the subordinates. He feels that the number of relationships increases geometrically based on the increase in the number of subordinates. He points out that the superior has to take into consideration not only the direct relationships between himself and the subordinates but also the relationships with different groups of subordinates and the gross relationships among all the subordinates. The number of these relationships naturally varies with the number of subordinates to be managed. While the superior's direct relationship increases with the proportionate increase in the number of subordinates, the group and cross relationship increases much more than proportionately. Total number of all possible relationships can be calculated on the basis of the following formula:

$$n\frac{2^n}{2}+n-1$$ where n = number of subordinates managed by a superior.

For example, the number of all possible relationships is 95 where the number of subordinates is 5.

Though there are certain criticisms against this formula, as it does not deal with the actual performance, this formula gives some picture about the possible relations. This certainly helps the manager in building up of optimal span depending upon the factors discussed above.

Lyndall F. Urwick concluded that the executives cannot supervise more than five or at the most six subordinates directly.[8] This number seems to be ideal as managers cannot supervise more number of subordinates effectively and too narrow spans would result in under-utilisation of the management's capabilities. However, the determination of size of the span is also influenced by the nature, amount, mode and extent of delegation of authority and responsibility.

Creation and maintenance of relationships in formal organisations depend upon delegation of authority and responsibility to the lower level employees or subordinates. Now, we shall discuss the delegation of authority and responsibility.

KEY TERMS

- Authority
- Responsibility
- Accountability
- Delegation
- Informal Delegation
- Centralisation
- Decentralisation
- Span of Management
- Formal Delegation

QUESTIONS

1. What is authority? Differentiate authority from responsibility and accountability.
2. What is span of management? Explain the factors those affect the span of management.
3. What is delegation of authority? Explain the principles of delegation.
4. What are the benefits and barriers of delegation?
5. How do you make delegation effective?
6. What is centralisation? How does it differ from decentralisation?
7. What are the benefits of decentralisation?

REFERENCES

1. Louis A. Allen, "*Management and Organisation*," McGraw-Hill, Auckland, 1958.
2. Edwin B. Flippo, *op.cit*., p.99.

3. Louis A. Allen, *op.cit.*, pp. 156-171.
4. Louis A. Allen, *op.cit.*, pp. 156-171.
5. Harold Kountz, Cyril O'Donnel and Weihrich, *op.cit.*, pp. 262-269.
6. *Ibid.*
7. Lathur, G. and Lyndall, F. W. (Eds.), *op.cit.*, pp. 183-187.
8. Urwick Lyndall, F., *"Scientific Principles and Organisation,"* American Management Association, New York, 1938, p. 8.

CHAPTER **8**

DIRECTING (MORALE, COMMITTEES AND COORDINATING

Chapter Outline

Learning Objectives

After studying this Chapter, you should be able to:

- ✓ Know the meaning and features of Direction
- ✓ Understand the importance of Direction
- ✓ Analyse the Principles of Direction
- ✓ Explain the meaning and importance of Morale
- ✓ Identify the factors affecting Morale
- ✓ Understand the measurement of Morale
- ✓ Evaluate the influence of Morale on productivity
- ✓ Understand the warnings of low Morale and how to improve Morale
- ✓ Know the meaning and types of Committees
- ✓ Analyse the merits and demerits of Committees
- ✓ Know the meaning of Co-ordination and analyse the pre-requisites of Co-ordination
- ✓ State the techniques and types of Co-ordination

(A) DIRECTING

Mr. N. R. Narayanamurthy, mentor of Infosys, makes his employees believe in themselves, the organisation, its value system and the philosophy including its targets. He tells the employees how to achieve the targets. He shares his ideas, opinions, attitudes etc. with all his subordinates. Sometimes he orders them, sometimes he counsels them and sometimes he consults them. Thus, he informs and instructs the employees how to do their job and achieve the targets. All these efforts of Mr.Narayanamurthy are called direction.

As we have discussed in chapter 1, management is getting things done by people. This process requires directing the people, motivating them and leading them towards doing the work. The managers have to direct the people, tell them how to do the work and order them to achieve the targets after they plan and organise various activities. All these activities constitute direction. Now we shall discuss the definition of direction.

Definitions

- **Haimann** defines the term direction as "the process and techniques utilised in issuing instructions and making certain that operations are carried on as originally planned."[1]

Leading the subordinates to contribute to the objectives

- According to **Harold Koontz and Cyril O'Donnel**, direction is "the interpersonal aspect of managing by which subordinates are led to understand and contribute effectively to the attainment of enterprise objectives."[2]
- **Earnest Dale** defines direction as "telling the people what to do and seeing that they do it to the best of their ability. It includes making assignments, corresponding procedures, seeing that mistakes are corrected, provided on-the-job instructions and of course, issuing orders."[3]
- **Urwick and Breach** define the direction as "the guidance, the inspiration, the leadership of those men and women that constitute the real core of the responsibilities of management."[4]

Analysis of these definitions reveals the following features of direction:

Features of Direction

Features: Contribution to objectives issuing orders, leading and motivating

- The end of direction is achievement of enterprise plans and objectives.
- Direction techniques are: issuing orders, instruments and commands and inspiration of people.
- Leading the subordinates and
- Motivating, guiding and inspiring the employees to utilise their human resources to the maximum extent.

Importance of Direction

Planning and organising do not ensure getting the things done. Things are done by the people only, even in high technology industries. This is because people have to handle certain tasks even in high technology-based industries. People do the work and carry out the activities effectively only when they are inspired and motivated. Thus, people need to be directed to carry out the organisational activities and contribute to the organisational goals.

Organisational goals are achieved through direction. In other words, the efficient direction makes the people to handle machines, materials and money properly and contribute to the organisational goals. In addition, direction plays an important role in:

- Leading the people towards the organisational goals.
- Motivating and inspiring the people towards the predetermined tasks.
- Communicating the data, information, attitudes, behaviours, morale and satisfaction levels etc.
- Influencing group behaviours, interpersonal behaviour and
- Determining and improving morale and employee job satisfaction.

In fact, direction makes the difference between two organisations. Organisations with the same kind of resources including human resources perform differently. This is mostly due to the level of efficiency of direction. The organisation with right direction perform better than the other organisation with the same kind of resources.

Thus, direction plays a significant role in achieving organisational goals. Now, we shall discuss what kind of principles make direction an important and crucial function of management.

Principles of Direction

Managers have to direct the subordinates towards organisational objectives and goals. Therefore, first managers have to understand the goals properly. In fact, the wise managers direct the subordinates even in formulating organisational objectives and goals. The principles of direction are:

Coordinate the individual objectives with organisational objectives

***(i)* Balance between individual objectives and organizational objectives:** Organisational objectives, goals and strategies are prime for the survival and development of not only the company but the individual employees of the company. But the objectives of individual employees, sometimes may not contribute to the achievement of organisational goals. In fact, some of the individual goals contradict organisational objectives. For example, some employees dealing with the suppliers of materials, market intermediaries and finance intermediaries maximize their personal income even though it costs the organisation through unethical practices, contradict the achievement of organisational objectives. In such cases, the managers have to mould the employee needs through counselling and change the individual objectives towards the organisational objectives.

It does not mean that always the individuals have to modify their goals to suit them to organisational goals. The organisations do also modify their objectives/goals to suit with the employees' skills, knowledge attitude. For example, Bharat Petroleum Corporation Limited postponed its computerisation programme due to non-availability of suitable personnel from 1997 to 1999. Thus, both the individual and organisational objectives are to be balanced with each other for their effective achievement.

***(ii)* Unity of Command:** The principle of unity of command implies that the subordinates should receive the orders and instructions from only one superior in order to avoid the confusion and uniformity of the orders and instructions. But this principle is regarded as a traditional principle during these days of competition and team work. Members in the team receive orders from more than one member, balance the conflicting orders and prioritise them before implementation. This leads to selection of the best ideas and implement them.

***(iii)* Effective Communication:** Direction is ordering and instructing subordinates. Ordering and instructing the subordinates is possible through efficient communication. In addition, counselling the subordinates, telling them how to do job etc. can be done through effective communication.

(iv) **Leading the People:** Leading is influencing the people. Leadership is the process whereby one individual influences other members of the group towards the attainment of defined group or organisational goals. Thus most part of direction involves leading the people.

(v) **Maximising the Employee Productivity:** Human resources of the employees can be effectively used only through direction. Otherwise, the skills and knowledge of the employees may not be used for the right purpose. The efficient use of human resources would in turn result in efficient use of all other resources like material, machines and money. This in turn results in maximisation of employee productivity.

(vi) **Direct Supervision:** Every manager should supervise their subordinates face-to-face and through direct contact. This in turn avoids misunderstanding and enhances proper understanding between the superior and subordinates. Further, this enhances employee loyalty, commitment and a sense of belongingness.

(vii) **Feed-forward and Feedback:** Managers while directing with their subordinates provide the information necessary to prevent the possible deviations in the process of achievement of organisational objectives. Thus, most part of the direction is to feed the information forward to the subordinates through counselling and instructions.

Some deviations take place even though management takes all possible care. Then managers find the reasons for failure from the subordinates and suggest the means for correcting events and ensure that such deviations will not take place in the future.

(viii) **Integrated and Comprehensive Approach:** Strategy is an integrated and comprehensive plan that relates to the strategic advantages of the firm to the challenges of the environment. It is designed to ensure that the basic objectives of the enterprise are achieved though proper execution by the organisation. Direction integrates money, material, machines and human resources. This integrated approach enables the managers to implement the strategies and in turn achieve the organisational goals.

(ix) **Controllability:** Managers plan the activities, organise various resources and facilities and induce the employees to achieve the organisational goals. Sometimes, the employees may fail to achieve the goals. In such cases, the managers find the reasons for variation between plan and actual and order the employees to correct the deviations and exert their resources for achievement of these objectives.

Managers direct their employees through: *(i)* Motivation *(ii)* Leading *(iii)* Communicating. Effective direction leads to high employee morale and job satisfaction. Now we shall study the dimensions of morale in detail.

(B) MORALE

Morale is purely emotional

Mr. Chitanya of Infosys tells, "I tell you whatever I have in my mind i.e. Inf[illegible]s really an exceptional company to work. I really contribute the best to my customer and the community. My boss need not tell me that I should produce the best quality, at lowest cost with superior speed. I am highly satisfied with my job and the company. Therefore, I should make my customer and then my boss happy." This is what we call 'Morale'.

Morale is purely emotional. It is an attitude of an employee towards his job, his superior and his organisation. This may range from very high to very low. It is not a static thing but it changes depending on working conditions, superiors, fellow-workers, pay and so on. When a particular employee has a favourable attitude towards his work, he is said to have high morale. In the organisational context, we usually talk of group morale as each person has an influence over the other's morale.

Definition

Edwin B. Flippo defines morale as "a mental condition or attitude of individuals and groups, which determines their willingness to cooperate. Good morale is evidenced by employee enthusiasm, voluntary conformance with regulations and orders and willingness to cooperate with others in the accomplishment of an organisation's objectives. Poor morale is evidenced by surliness, insubordination, a feeling of discouragement and dislike of the job, company and associates."[5]

Michael J. Jucius defines "Morale as a state of mind or of a willingness to work which in turn affects individuals and organisational objectives. "He explains it in detail by answering the following questions:

(1) "What is it?" — It is an attitude of mind, and 'esprit de corps,' a state of well being and an emotional force.

(2) "Where does it reside?" — It resides in the minds, attitudes and emotions of individuals as members of a group.

(3) "Whom does it affect?" — It affects employees and executives in their interactions immediately and ultimately, the customer and the community.

(4) "What does it affect?" — It affects willingness to work and cooperate in the best interest of the enterprise and ultimately output, quality of output and costs of operations."[6]

Importance of Morale

Morale plays a vital role in the organisation's success. High morale keeps the employees loyal to the job, profession and organisation. This leads to employee commitment and sincerity. The committed and sincere employees plan not only their individual work but also the work of the group and the entire department. Further, the committed employees contribute their human resources to the maximum extent to the job. It leads to improved performance and productivity. Further,

High morale keeps the employees loyal to jobs

- High level morale contributes to sound superior-subordinate relations.
- High morale leads to employee satisfaction. The satisfied employee stays with the organisation continuously. It reduces employee turnover and absenteeism.
- High level morale and employee satisfaction reduce employee grievances. Further, satisfied employees follow the company rules and regulations. It reduces employee indiscipline.
- High morale leads to employee commitment to industrial peace by avoiding the occurrence of industrial disputes.
- Morale helps the employees to build teams easily to maximise their contribution. Further, the modern techniques of human resources management like empowerment can be easily practiced. (See Box 8.1).

Box 8.1: Measures to Boost Morale

- *Make the new employees feel part of the organisation*
- *Let the employees interact with superiors, customers etc.*
- *Use tea and lunch breaks for informal conversation*
- *Understand the company culture*
- *Explain job responsibilities and rewards clearly*
- *Make sure that orientation reflects the reality of the company's internal world and*
- *Gain full participation from new employees*

(**Source:** Human Capital, Febrary 2000, p. 46)

- Further, implementation of enterprise resource planning and business process re-engineering can be possible with the employees of high morale.

In essence, morale results in:

- High level commitment, sincerity and employee loyalty
- Reduction in absenteeism and labour turnover
- Reduction in grievances and increase in discipline
- Reduction in industrial conflicts
- Sound superior-subordinate relations
- Reduction in accidents
- Increase in employee pride
- Team building
- Employee empowerment and
- Easy implementation of Enterprise Resource Planning and Business Process Re-engineering.

Individual and Group Morale

Group morale reflects the esprit de corps.

Morale may be concerned with an individual. An *individual's morale* is related to knowing one's own expectations and living up to them. If one is clear of his own needs and how to satisfy them most of the time, his morale is high. An individual's morale is a single person's attitude towards life, *whereas group morale* reflects the general *esprit de corps* of a collective group of personalities. Group morale is everyone's concern and it must be practiced continually, for it is never ultimately achieved and is constantly changing.

Group morale and the morale of the individual are interrelated but not necessarily identical. They have an effect on each other. It is conceivable that an individual's own personal perception of existing conditions as they relate to himself may be high, and the group's perception of conditions may be low or vice versa, but more usually the two share common feelings.

Factors Affecting Morale

Roach determined that there are twelve factors that influence morale:

- General workers' attitude towards the company.
- Employees' attitude towards the supervisor.
- The level of satisfaction with job standards.
- The level of consideration the supervisor shows to his subordinates.
- The work load and the work pressure level.
- The treatment of individuals by the management.
- The level of workers' pride in the company and its activities.
- The level of workers' satisfaction with salaries.
- Worker's reactions to the formal communication network in an organisation.
- Intrinsic job satisfaction level of the workers.
- Worker satisfaction with progress and opportunities for further progression and
- The worker's attitude towards fellow workers.

Measurement of Morale

Since morale is a subjective concept, there are some difficulties associated with its measurement. Employees are naturally reluctant to express their true attitude towards work and the management. For this reason, the questionnaire method has the least significance as a technique of measurement. The following are the popular methods of morale measurement:

Morale can be measured though: observations, attitude surveys and company records.

- Observations
- Attitude surveys and
- Company records.

Observation

A keen observation of employees' behaviour, talk and gestures should help the manager to identify any change in the level of morale. On identifying this, the manager should immediately think of a remedial action in order to restore the morale at its previous level.

Attitude Surveys

Attitude surveys are conducted mainly in two ways: (a) Interview method and (b) Questionnaire method.

(a) ***Interview Method:*** Under this method, a face-to-face talk is carried out with the employee. The interviewer asks several persons about their feelings and opinions on various aspects of their jobs and the organisation. One of the disadvantages of this method is that it is uneconomical, if the work group is large.

(b) ***Questionnaire Method:*** In this method of morale-measurement, a questionnaire is served to the employees asking them about their opinions on all factors that affect morale.

Company Records and Reports

Certain reports from the personnel department provide the information as to labour turnover, rate of absenteeism, number of workers' grievances, the number of goods rejected, strikes and such other things, which are indicators of the level of morale.

Morale and Productivity*

Since morale manifests itself in the attitudes of workers, it is important to know about the results of high morale and low morale. One of the most unpredictable effects of the level of morale is its impact upon worker productivity. The review of the research studies does not show a direct relationship between morale and productivity. For example, the studies performed by **Katz and Vroom** showed no consistent relationship between a specific level morale and the productivity of the workers. Productivity sometimes is high with high morale, but at other times may be low even when morale is high and vice versa.

Herzberg found that in 54 per cent of the studies, high morale was related to high productivity while in 35 per cent of the studies, morale and productivity did not reveal relationship. In 11 per cent of the studies, high morale was associated with low productivity. Evidences support the view that the level of satisfaction was directly related to performance on the job. **Gellermen** points out that "poor morale can cause strike, feathers-bedding, malingering and allied reactions which can lower the productivity of any kind of job. Moreover, lower morale may lead to odd higher rates of turnover, absenteeism and accidents."

* Treatment from C.B.Mamoria, *op.cit.*

On the contrary, **Davis** finds some positive relationship between morale and productivity. But it is not absolute relationship. An increase in morale may either cause increase or decrease in productivity. A high morale reflects a predisposition to be more productive if attempts are made to provide effective leadership and coordinate various technical production factors.

On the basis of several research studies, **Miller and Form** have given four combinations of productivity and morale, viz.: *(i)* high productivity-high morale; (ii) low productivity-high morale; (iii) high productivity-low morale and (iv) low productivity-low morale. For this type of combination, social dynamics in the work group have been responsible.

High Productivity-High Morale: This *situation* is likely to occur when group goals (such as pride in work groups, group recognition etc.) are satisfied, where individual goals including freedom on work, good wage rates, intrinsic job interest etc. are satisfied, leading to motivation of the employees to accomplish high standards of performance and where high productivity leads to high morale which in turn, reinforces high productivity.

Low Productivity-High Morale: This *situation* may occur when individual goals, rather than those causing high productivity (such as desires for good working conditions, pleasant fellow workers, etc.) are satisfied, where the individual behaviour is determined by informal groups causing restriction of output, where supervisors lack technical and administrative skills thus lowering productivity of high morale group and where workers lack adequate skills or training leading to low-productivity by high morale.

High Productivity-Low Morale: In this *situation,* the supervisor is only able to increase productivity through his skills or planning ability rather than through motivation, where supervisory practices give rise to high productivity by use of penalty (such as loss of pay or loss of job).

Low Productivity-Low Morale: This *situation* occurs where factors obtained in combination of high-productivity-high morale are lacking.

It will thus be observed that there is a complexity of relationship between morale and productivity.

If a worker's attitudes/perceptions lead to a state of high morale, other positive effects may result with high morale and workers tend to exhibit a willingness to co-operate; employees tend to be more satisfied with existing conditions; they tend to be more willing to observe company rules; labourers are careful in handling company property and equipment; workers show a loyalty and respect towards their company; people work together harmoniously and individuals do their job without grumbling. High morale also tends to reduce absenteeism, tardiness and employee turnover.

If morale is low, many of the effects will be just the opposite of the effects stated above.

Morale and Performance

Relationship between morale and performance is unclear

It has been pointed that "there is a little evidence in the available literature that employee attitudes bear any relationship to performance on the job." The evidence available is rather confusing. There are three schools of thought and probably all are correct to some extent.

- *First,* there are some who assert that high satisfaction leads to high performance. The Hawthorne studies of 1930s seem to support this view, as do findings of other studies.
- *Second,* others take an opposite view. For example, Lyman Porter and Lawler say that satisfaction results from high performance; because most people experience satisfaction by accomplishing more tasks, like manufacturing a radio or clinching a sale.

- *Third,* still others claim that there is no consistent relationship between morale and performance. Vroom found significant relationship between morale and performance in only 5 out of 22 studies undertaken by him.

Warning Signs of Low Morale

Signs of low morale are generally not noticed till it is obviously low or when something has gone amiss. By the time the management recognises the fact that morale has deteriorated, it is faced with one crisis or another. Perceptive managers are, therefore, constantly on the look-out for clues to any deterioration in the morale of the employees.

High rate of observation, labour turnover, strikes etc. are warning signs of low morale.

Among the more significant of the warning signals of low morale are:

- High rate of absenteeism
- Tardiness
- High labour turnover
- Strikes and sabotage
- Lack of pride in work and
- Wastage and spoilage.

Maintenance of Morale

Having assessed the level of prevailing employee morale, the management can determine the need for maintenance and improvement of morale. If the management feels that there is such a need, there are two ways by which it can maintain and improve the morale, viz. preventive measures and remedial measures.

Preventive Measures

Preventive measures prevent regression in the level of morale. These measures include:

- **Creation of the whole job:** Creating and assigning the whole job to a single worker with a view to satisfy his need for achievement.
- **Job enrichment:** Designing the vertical slice of the tasks into a job and assigning it to an employee satisfies his needs for recognition, responsibility, growth etc.
- **Modifying the work environment:** Creating and providing a conducive and challenging work environment.
- **Flexible working hours:** 'Development of Human Resources' and flexible working hours provide freedom to the worker in doing the job and in attending to his personal affairs.
- **Job rotation:** Job rotation reduces monotony of work and boredom and thus increases morale.
- **Point individual prosperity in company prosperity:** If the management can show to the worker that there is scope for his prosperity in the company, there can be better motivation for the worker to strive towards the company goals.
- **Adaptation of "how-shall-we-do it" attitude:** By adapting this kind of attitude, the management can give the worker a feeling that he has made the decision himself which makes any job easier for the management to make workers accept its decisions. This is nothing but what participative management preaches.

Improvement of Morale

Organisations formulate strategies to improve morale

Whenever something is found to be wrong with the workers, it is obvious that there must be some cause of this situation. It may be that the policies or practices of the company are defective, or that if executives are at fault, or that the views of those whose morale is low do not agree with those of the company or of its executives.

In such cases, a three-fold action may be initiated:

- In the *first place*, it is essential to change *the policy or to correct it immediately.* Employees do not lose their respect for the boss who admits his mistakes; but they cannot respect one who makes too many; and they may have contempt for one who refuses to admit his mistakes.
- *Second, misconceptions should be removed, and the correct positions should be explained to the employees.*
- *Third, a reasonable attempt should be made to educate and convince the employees.*

In this respect, the following three-point plan may be adopted even when the morale of the employees is good:

- In the first place, it must be decided that a particular person will be responsible for the execution of the plan. Each executive should be told, preferably in writing, what he should do to improve the general morale of the employees; he should know the extent of his authority and what his relations with other departments should be.
- A morale-building programme should be based on a clear conception of the theory that underlines it. A written statement should be prepared, clearly outlining the relationship between the company's objectives and personal objectives and the process of integrating the interests of the two, and mentioning the results of good morale.
- Specific morale duties should be outlined for every executive.

Besides these, since morale is determined largely by worker's perception's and attitudes, the management should work upon the conditions that define these perceptions. For example: Managers can concentrate on supervisory styles, company policies, working conditions and other factors external to and out of the control of the worker to see that such factors are employee-oriented. Leadership styles that support the worker and encourage him may be applied.

(C) COMMITTEES

Committees are formed whenever group decision-making is necessary on strategic issues after thorough investigation. A committee is a formal group of individuals who meet regularly to solve strategic problems. Executive Committees are entrusted with decision-making powers. However, some committees are constituted to offer advices for decision-making by the chief executive.

Nature of Committees

Committees are formed whenever group activity is necessary

Some committees are horizontal and formed with the representatives from all functional departments like production, marketing, finance and human resources. Committees' management is a form of group management. It provides well balanced and competent advice for the executives. It integrates the concepts and knowledge of cross functional areas. It provides the integration of ideas of various executives. It provides voluntary acceptance and interested execution of plans, polices though participation. Also, it provides new ideas though group discussion and deliberations.

Group Decision-Making

Committee members meet regularly, exchange their ideas and interact with each other. they counter the ideas generated and encounter the ideas and ultimately make efficient decisions through information generation, sharing and development.

Types of Committees

Committees are of four types. They are Strategic committees, Executive committees, Advisory committees and Joint action committees.

Types of committees include: Strategic, executive, advisory, joint action etc.

- **Strategic Committees:** These committees are formed to formulate strategies and make strategic decisions.
- **Executive Committees:** These committees are empowered with the decision-making of operational issues and executing or implementing strategic issues.
- **Advisory Committees:** These committees are constituted with the Senior and experienced executives in order to offer advices to the chief executive and in crisis situations. These committees have authority to offer advises but not to take decision or implementing decisions.
- **Joint Action Committees:** These committees are constituted when decisions are to be implemented by a group of employees drawn from various departments.

Reasons for Using Committees

Committees are constituted and used for the following reasons:

- **Multi-management Issues:** Certain issues need multi-management approach in solving them. Committees are used to deal with such issues.
- **Expertise:** Committees are used to have the expertise of various managers in making decisions.
- **Team Approach:** Committees are used when the execution is to be done through/by teams.
- **Innovativeness/Creativity:** Committees are used when the business or managerial activity needs innovation in problem solving.
- **Nobody to bell the cat:** Committees are used when no one in the company wants to take the risk or responsibility of dealing with a particular issue or person.
- **Delay the Decisions:** Management entrust the decisions to the committee when it would like to delay the decision-making.
- **Strategic/Critical Issues:** Management constitute committees to deal with the strategic and critical issues.

Merits of Committees

The following are the merits of committees:

Committees produce sound decisions, coordination, empowerment and participation.

- **Sound Decisions:** Committees are known for sound and efficient decisions as they make decisions after thorough discussions and investigations.
- **Rational Decisions:** Committees reduce emotions and irrational behaviour of the individuals. Hence, the decisions committees make would be rational.

- **Availability of Expertise:** Experts are drawn as member of committees. Therefore, they provide rich knowledge and expertise for managerial activities.
- **Coordination:** Coordination among departments of the organisation becomes easy and automatic as committee members are drawn from various departments.
- **A Holistic Approach:** Committees present a holistic approach for decisions and managerial activities as they present an integrated and total picture from all dimensions of the issues.
- **Participative Management:** Committees automatically provide for the practice of employee.
- **Employee Empowerment:** Committee members are empowered to take decisions and implement them within their area. Therefore, employee empowerment can be practiced.
- **Management Training:** Committees are used to train the managers of one department in the knowledge of other departments.

Demerits of Committees

Though the committees are useful, they are not used widely after globalisation due to demerits associated with them. They are:

- **Time consumption:** Committees consume a lot of time in making the decisions due to diversified views and inability of the members to accept others' views.
- **Cost of decisions:** Decisions made by committees are costly due to involvement of time and experts. The cost of decisions, sometimes, may be more than the outcome of the decisions.
- **Impracticability of Decisions:** Committee members offer impractical advice as their role is limited to advisory and staff, in some issues.
- **Indecisions:** Committee members, sometimes, fail to make decisions due to their ego clashes.
- **Absence of Seriousness:** Committee members may not have seriousness to their duty as everybody's responsibility is nobody's responsibility. It is viewed in the lighter vein that committee means 'join for tea.'
- **Domination:** One or two members may dominate the proceedings of the committee. As such the committee decisions may not represent holistic view.
- **Fail to see the total:** Some members may be indifferent or submissive. As such the committee cannot see the issue from all angles or the total picture.

(D) CO-ORDINATION

Business operations are performed by a number of departments and individual employees based on plans, objectives and goals. The total business operations include procuring of raw material, producing the products, mobilizing and managing financial resources, acquiring the required human resources, providing them to various departments, marketing the product etc. Each department performs only one kind of operation based on its specialization. Similarly, each employee also performs one kind of operations based on his/her specialization. These activities need to be coordinated as each individual employee and department perform the business activities from their perspective rather than from the perspective of organizational objectives.

Definitions

According to Alan C.Reiley and James D.Mooney, coordination is the, "orderly arrangement of group effort, to provide unity of action in the pursuit of common purpose." George R.Terry defines coordination as the task of "blending efforts in order to ensure the successful attainment of an objective. It is accomplished by means of planning, organizing, actuating and controlling."

Coordination: Orderly arrangement of group effort to provide unity of action.

It is observed from these definitions that coordination is part of all managerial functions of planning, organizing, staffing, directing and controlling. Managers coordinate various activities while performing managerial functions. For example, marketing manager coordinates the activities of all regional marketing executives in estimating demand for products, in assessing the customers' preferences regarding product design, quality, price etc. Similarly, the marketing manager coordinates the activities of his department relating to product design and development with those of production department. Similarly, all functional managers also coordinate the activities of not only their departments but with those of other departments of the organisation. Further, managers coordinate the planning function with organizing and controlling functions.

Need for Coordination

Coordination is essential for the effective performance of organizational activities due to the following reasons.

Coordination is necessary due to: team-work functional differentiation, unity in diversity etc.

Team Work: Most of the modern organisations designed the organisations based on the team structure. Teams consist of employees from various functional areas, with various skills and background. This nature of teams makes the coordination essential for integration of skills, knowledge etc.

Functional Differentiation: Business activities are divided into jobs, units, sections and departments. Each employee performs his/her job and group of employees perform the functions of a department. Departments cannot achieve organizational objectives unless they are interlinked and coordinated. Therefore, coordination is needed to ensure the achievement of organizational goals and objectives.

Unity in Diversity: There would be a number of employees with different backgrounds, culture, capabilities, skills, values etc. These diversities inhibit the organisation in achieving its objectives, unless these diversities are coordinated, unified and directed towards organizational goals.

Division of work and specialization: Most of the organisations are structured based on the principles of division of work and specialization. These aspects develop the islands of activities and hinder the companies from achieving their goals. Therefore, coordination is needed to interlink these islands and allow the managers to think comprehensively.

Prerequisites for Effective Coordination

Coordination programme to be effective should have the following requisites.

Start Before the Plan: Coordination should start even before the plans are formulated and finalized. The plans should be coordinated with the environmental factors.

End After Control: Coordination ends only after the control function. Control function has to be coordinated with the planning function in order to ensure that the plans are achieved.

Continuous Process: Coordination is a continuous process. The organizational activities are to be networked and the network should continue uninterrupredly so as to ensure continuous workflow.

Dynamism: Coordination should be dynamic in order to foresee the environmental changes and infuse their consequences into the network of oganisational activities before the competitors adopt it. Therefore coordination should be dynamic.

Direct Personal Contact: Coordination can be effective, if the superior establishes and maintains direct personal contact and direction with his subordinates.

Effective Communication: Communication without distortions, gaps etc. make the coordination perfect.

Flat Organisation Structure: Flat organisation structure allows the employees to interact and communicate freely and frequently with their superiors. Further the superiors also interact with his/her subordinates with an open mind, which in turn make the coordination effective.

Leadership: Democratic and participative leadership allow the employees and leader to communicate with each other frequently. Further, they encourage the subordinates to express their ideas, view points etc. regarding their activities. Thus, they enable the coordination effective.

Now, we shall discuss the techniques of coordination.

Techniques of Coordination

Techniques of coordination include: Chain of command, team work, clear objectives etc.

(i) **Chain of Command:** The organizational hierarchy specifies the line of command. The line of command indicates the authority and responsibility relationships between superior and subordinate. Superior co-ordinates the activities of his/her subordinates through the line of command.

(ii) **Team Work:** Organisations through the team structures coordinate the activities. People interact closely, share their ideas, share the work etc., through which they coordinate their activities effectively.

(iii) **Clear Objectives:** Clear objectives specify the areas of activities of each department and each employee. They also specify the process of achievement of objectives. This process indicates the networking and co-ordinating process.

(iv) **Procedures and Programmes:** Procedures and programmes clearly specify the way the activities to be performed, the order and the sequence the issues are linked to each other. Thus the detailed procedures and programmes make the co-ordination effective.

(v) **Liaison Departments:** Business firms establish liaison departments or offices or managers to co-ordinate the activities of the departments, branches and offices. Regional offices co-ordinate the activities of the branch offices, zonal offices, regional offices and the central office coordinates the operations of zonal offices.

(vi) **Intranet:** The revolution in the information technology brought significant strides in coordination. Coordination based on predetermined plans, programmes, budgets would be fast and easy when the activities of the company are placed in the intranet of the company.

Now, we shall discuss the different types of co-ordination.

Types of Coordination

Coordination is basically of two types viz.

(i) Internal Coordination

Internal coordination refers to the coordination of activities within the organisation. These activities include production, marketing, human resources and finance operations. Internal coordination is of three types viz., vertical coordination, horizontal coordination and circle coordination.

Vertical Coordination: Coordination of activities/operations of different levels in the organizational hierarchy is referred to as vertical coordination. Production manager coordinates the activities of Assistant Production Managers in-charge of purchase of raw materials, stores, product design, quality control etc. Thus, under vertical coordination, the superior coordinates the activities of his/her subordinates.

Horizontal Coordination: Coordination of activities of the same level of an organizational hierarchy is called horizontal coordination. Production Manager coordinates the activities relating to the designing of new product with marketing manager, human resource manager and finance manager under horizontal coordination.

Circle Coordination: Circle coordination refers to multi-dimensional or all round coordination. It includes vertical, horizontal and cross-wise coordination. Coordination of activities relating to procuring of raw material, product design, producing the product, acquiring the people, finance, delivering the product to the customer and rendering the customer service etc., are examples of circle coordination.

(ii) External Coordination

External coordination refers to linking the organisation with various external agencies. In fact, the business firms have to operate in accordance with the requirements and abilities of the external agencies. These external agencies include:

- Suppliers of raw material and various inputs
- Market intermediaries like wholesalers, retailers etc.
- Competitors
- Customers
- Suppliers of technology, equipment etc.
- Banks and Financial Institutions
- Consultancy Firms
- Government
- Chamber of Commerce and Industry
- Employees Unions and Federations
- Society at large

Problems of Coordination

Though coordination is essential, it would be difficult to establish effective coordination due to the following problems.

Interpersonal Relations: Unsound interpersonal relations and ego-clashes result in poor coordination.

Approaches towards the achievement of Goals: Different employees and departments adopt different approaches to achieve the same objectives and goals. This would result the coordination difficult.

Adjustment to organizational structure: Sometimes managers' styles do not match with the requirements of the organisation structure. These situations would result in poor coordination.

Organisational policies: Organisational political activities do not allow the coordination to be effective.

KEY TERMS

- Direction
- Productivity
- Feedback
- Measurement of Morale
- Control
- Morale
- Motivating
- Group Morale
- Communication
- Low Morale
- Leading
- Individual Morale
- Feedforward
- Performance
- Objectives

QUESTIONS

1. What is direction? Explain the features of direction.
2. Define the term 'direction.' Explain in detail the principles of direction.
3. What is morale? Explain the importance of morale.
4. What is individual and group morale? Analyse the factors that affect morale.
5. How do you measure morale?
6. Explain the relationship among morale, productivity and performance.
7. What are the warnings of low morale?
8. How do you maintain and improve morale?

REFERENCES

1. Haimann, *op.cit.*, p. 341.
2. Harold Koontz and Cyril O'Donnel, *op.cit.*, p. 234.
3. Earnest Dale, *op.cit.*, p. 211.
4. Urwick and Breach, *op.cit.*, p. 131.
5. Edwin B. Flippo, *op.cit.*, pp. 416-417.
6. Michael J. Jucius, *op.cit.*, p. 422.

CHAPTER 9

CONTROLLING

Chapter Outline

(A) Introduction
(B) Feedback and Feed-forward Control
(C) Basic Process of Control
(D) Control Techniques
(E) Problems of Control Process
(F) Requirements for Effective Control
(G) Overall Control Techniques
(H) Global Control
- Key Terms
- Questions
- References

Learning Objectives

After studying this Chapter, you should be able to:

✓ Understand the meaning of and need for managerial control
✓ Discuss various steps in the managerial control process
✓ Appraise different types of control
✓ Know the essential conditions for effective control
✓ Identify the problems of control
✓ Evaluate different types of control techniques with an emphasis on budgets.
✓ Know the meaning, objectives, importance and activities of managment audit.
✓ Discuss the concept of self audit.

(A) INTRODUCTION

Managers formulate mission, objectives, strategies and plans, organise the people and resources and direct the people to implement the plans to achieve the objectives. To what extent do the people achieve the objectives? To what extent the facilities and people contributed for the implementation of plans? Did the environmental factors affect the implementation of plans? We have to review the total process to answer these questions. In addition, we have to study control to answer these questions.

Once the strategy is formulated and implemented, there is no guarantee that the strategy could be implemented as it is designed and also that the strategy generates the results aimed at. Therefore, the strategist has to evaluate the strategy and its programme to assess whether the implementation of the strategy is as per the strategic plan or not. Further, a number of deviations either in the external environment or in the organisational environment may take place. These deviations may necessitate a change in the strategy. These changes also require evaluation and control. Initially we shall study the meaning of control and differences between strategic control and operational control.

Definition of Control

Control consists in verifying whether everything occurs in conformity with the plan adopted, the instructions issued and principles established.

Control consists of making something happen the way it was planned to happen.[1] According to Henri Fayol, *control consists in verifying whether everything occurs in conformity with the plan adopted, the instructions issued and principles established.* It's objective is to point out weaknesses and errors in order to rectify them and prevent recurrence. It operates on everything, things, people and actions.[2] The control function includes three procedures *viz. (i)* measuring actual performance, *(ii)* comparing actual performance to standards and *(iii)* taking corrective action to ensure that planned events actually occur. Fig.9.1 shows the model of control process.

Strategic Control

Strategic control focuses on monitoring and evaluating the strategic management process to ensure that it functions in the right direction. Strategic control aims at achieving the results planned at the time of strategy formulation. Strategic control is a special type of organisational control.

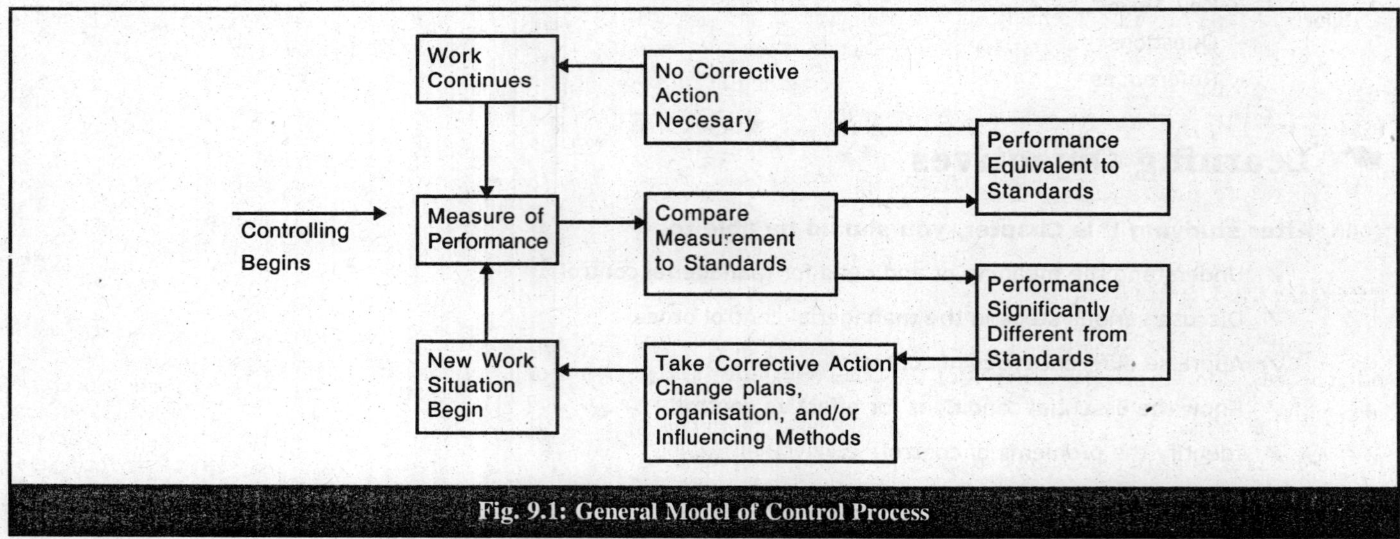

Fig. 9.1: General Model of Control Process

(**Source:** Samuel C. Certo, *Modern Management*, 1994, p. 436).

Thus, strategic control provides feedback about various steps of strategic management to know whether the strategic management processes are appropriate, compatible and functioning in the desirable direction.[3]

Operational Control

Operational control deals with monitoring and evaluating the operations to ensure that organisational issues and operations function in the right direction. Operational control aims at achieving the results as planned. Operational control focuses on various routine aspects of the production, marketing, human resources and financial issues in the company.

Operational control mostly deals with performance of the company in the direction decided in advance. Similarly, it deals with the allocation and utilisation of various organisational resources like materials, spare parts, human resources, machinery, financial resources, etc. Managers at the middle level and lower level control the operations at the direction of the top level management.

Exhibit 9.1 depicts the differences between strategic control and operational control.

Exhibit 9.1 Differences Between Strategic Control and Operational Control

Attribute	*Strategic Control*	*Operational Control*
1. Basic question	"Are we moving in the right direction?"	"How are we performing?"
2. Aim	Proactive, continuous questioning of the basic direction of strategy	Allocation and use of organisational resources
3. Main concern	'Steering' the organisation's future direction	Action control
4. Focus	External environment	Internal organisation
5. Time horizon	Long-term	Short-term
6. Exercise of control	Exclusively by top management, may be through lower-level support	Mainly by executive or middle-level management on the direction of the top management
7. Main techniques	Environmental scanning, information gathering, questioning and review	Budgets, schedules and MBO

(**Source**: Adapted from J.A. Pearce III and R.B. Robinson, Jr. Strategic Management: Strategy Formulation and Implementation (3rd edn.), (Homewood, III. Richard D. Irwin, 1988), pp. 404-419. Quoted in Azhar Kazmi, op. cit., p. 319).

(B) FEEDBACK AND FEED-WARD CONTROL

There are three types of control viz. feedback control, concurrent control and feed-forward control.

Feedback Control

Feedback control focuses on organisational activities and operations after they are completed. In other words, control process starts after the completion of the operations or activities. This control is also called *postmortem control*.

Feedback control focuses on organisational activities and operations after they are completed.

Feedback control plays three roles at the operating level:

- It provides the necessary information to the operating manager to evaluate overall organisational effectiveness.
- It is useful as a basis for evaluating and rewarding employees and
- It alerts the operating managers who need to adjust or modify their activities.

Feedback control also plays a vital role at the strategic level. It provides necessary information to managers in formulating and modifying their strategies. Further, it provides information for strategic evaluation and control.

Concurrent Control

Concurrent control seeks to affect control while the work is in progress.

Concurrent control seeks to affect control while the work is in progress. In other words, control is applied while the operations are in progress. For example, Compaq computers has set thirty four check points in its assembly line for successful production of Laptop computers. Checks at all these thirty four points ensure that the laptop computer is produced perfectly. Concurrent control at the operating level ensures that the operations are being performed successfully in accordance with the plans. Concurrent control at the strategic level focuses on quarterly results regarding the implementation process of the strategies.

Feed-forward Control

Managers or Supervisors in feed-forward control identify the critical issues for the successful performance of organisational activities.

Managers or Supervisors in feed-forward control identify the critical issues for the successful performance of organisational activities. They foresee the possible deviations in these critical issues and suggest to the employees regarding the preventive steps to be taken before implementation of the plan. They feed such information to the employees before the implementation of organisational activities or plans.

Thus, managers in feed-forward control foresee the possible deviations, choose the best inputs, prevent the deviations before they take place and implement the plans.

Feed-forward at the operating level emphasises on careful selection of inputs and formulation of policies and procedures to head off anticipated deviations.[6] Feed-forward control, at the strategic level, alerts the strategists to key and unanticipated environmental changes that may affect the strategies and objectives and to take preventive steps in order to control the possible deviations or to modify the strategies.

Essentials of Feed-forward Control: Essentials of feed-forward control include:

- Analyse the planning and controlling systems thoroughly
- Identify critical input variables
- Observe the environmental changes very closely and identify the factors that would affect the plan implementation process.
- Develop a model and Review the model regularly regarding the continuation of interrelationship among the input variables
- Collect the data on input variables and enter them into the system
- Identify the variations in input variables before the implementation process starts and
- Correct the variations in input variables. If it is not possible, then modify the plan or strategy before the implementation process starts.

Though managerial control is the last function, it should be performed successfully in order to get desirable results. As such, now, we shall discuss the essential conditions for effective control.

With this basic understanding, now, we shall discuss the process of control.

(C) BASIC PROCESS OF CONTROL

The managerial control process consists of six steps (Fig. 9.2) The top management initially must decide what elements of the environment and the organisation need to be monitored, evaluated and controlled. The four key areas to be monitored and controlled are: the macro environment, mission and objectives, the industry environment and internal operations.

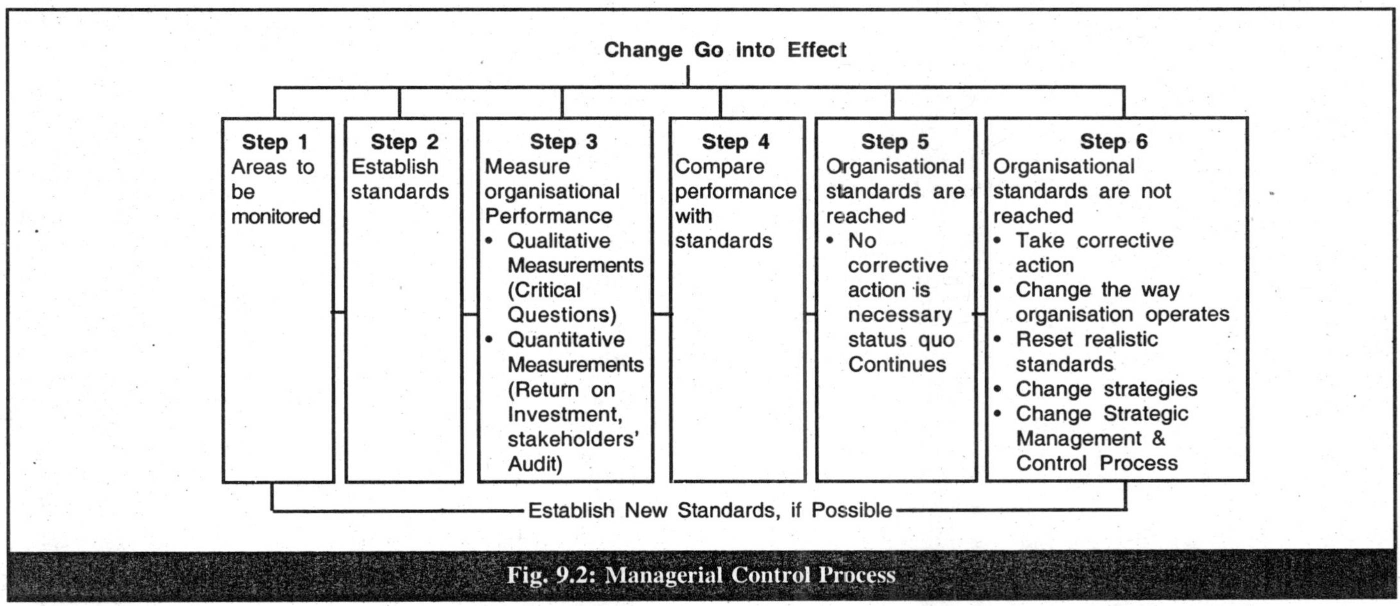

Fig. 9.2: Managerial Control Process

(**Source:** Modified Version From: Wright, Pringle and Kroll, op. cit., p. 202 and Samuel C. Certo and J. Paul Peter, op. cit., p. 150).

Step 1: Key Areas to be Monitored

Macro-environment: As stated earlier, one of the key areas to be monitored is the macro-environment of the company. This area should be focused first. Normally individual companies cannot influence the environment significantly. But the external environmental forces must be continuously monitored as the changes in the environment influence the implementation of the plans of the company.

Mission and Objectives: This includes modifying any one or more of the areas like company's mission, objectives, plans, goals, strategy formulation and implementation. The modification depends upon the nature and degree of changes and shifts in the environment.

Industry Environment: The manager also monitors and controls the industry related environment. The environmental forces may not be as they were planned. The changes in the environment may provide new opportunities or pose new threats. The plan, therefore, should be modified accordingly.

The industry environment of the future should be considered by the top management for the purpose of evaluation and control.

Internal Operations: The manager has to evaluate the internal operations continuously in view of the changes in the macro-environment and industry environment. The manager has to introduce changes in internal operations when changes in the environment affect the plans.

Step 2: Establishing Standards

Evaluating an organisational performance is normally based on certain standards. These standards may be the previous year's achievements or the competitor's records or the fresh standards established by the management. Qualitative judgements like the qualitative features of the product or service in the last year may be used. Quantitative measures like Return on Investment (ROI), Return on sales may also be used for judging the performance. Companies should establish the standards for evaluating the performance of the strategies taking several factors into consideration.

The standards may include:

- Quality of Products/Services.
- Quantity of Products to be Produced.
- Quality of Management.
- Innovativeness/Creativity.
- Long-term investment value.
- Volume of sales and/or market share.
- Financial soundness in terms of return on investment, return on equity capital, market price of the share, earning per share etc.
- Community and environmental responsibility in terms of amount spent on community development, variety of facilities provided to the community, programmes undertaken for environmental protection and ecological balance etc.
- Soundness of human resources management in terms of percentage of employee grievances redressed, employee satisfaction rate, employee turnover rate, industrial relations situation etc.
- Ability to attract, develop and retain competent and skilled people.
- Use of company's assets.
- Production targets, rate of capacity utilisation, design of new products, new uses of existing products, rate of customer complaints about the product quality, suitability of ingredients etc.
- Corporate image among the customers and general public.
- Market place performance.
- Standards relating to the organisational variables include freedom and autonomy, level of control, responsibility, formal organisation and degree of formality and informal organisation scope for innovation and creativity.

Step 3: Measuring Performance

The manager has to measure the performance of various areas of the organisation before taking an action. Performance may be measured through quantitative terms or qualitative terms. Reports and statements help to measure the actual performance through quantitative terms and managerial observations help to measure performance through qualitative terms. Production, sales, profitability, staff cost etc. can be measured through quantitative terms and quality of the product, employee's performance, attitude etc. can be measured through qualitative terms.

Step 4: Compare Performance with Standards

Once the performance of different aspects of the organisation is measured, it should be compared with the predetermined standards. Standards are set to achieve the already formulated organisational goals and plans. Organisational standards are yardsticks and benchmarks that place organisational performance in perspective.[4] The manager should set standards for all performance areas of the organisation based on organisational goals and strategies. Normally, the standards vary from one company to the other company. Further, they also vary from time to time in the same company. The standards developed by General Electric Company can be used as model standards. These standards include.

- **Profitability Standards:** They include how much gross profit, net profit, return on investment, earning per share, percentage of profit to sales, the company should earn in a given time period.
- **Market Position Standards:** These standards include total sales, sales region-wise and product-wise, market share, marketing costs, customer service, customer satisfaction, price, customer loyalty shifts from or to other organisation's products etc.
- **Productivity Standards:** These standards indicate the performance of the organisation in terms of conversion of inputs into output. These standards include capital productivity, labour productivity, material productivity etc.
- **Product Leadership Standards:** They include the innovations and modifications in products to increase the new uses of the existing product, developing new products with new uses etc.
- **Human Resources Standards:** These standards include providing competitive salaries, benefits and different aspects of quality of work life. They also include human resources performance, productivity, turnover rates, absenteeism rates providing challenging and creative jobs etc.
- **Employee Attitude Standards:** They include employees' favourable attitude towards the nature of work, organisation, salaries, benefits, working environment, quality of work life, treatment by superiors etc.
- **Social Responsibility Standards:** All organisations discharge their responsibilities towards different sections of the society. These standards are related to the services of organisations towards community, government, employees, suppliers, creditors etc.
- **Standards Reflecting Balance between Short-range and Long-range Goals:** Short-range and long-range strategies should be balanced successfully. Standards in these areas should bring balance between these two goals.

Step 5: Take No Action, if Performance is in Harmony with Standards

If the performances of various organisational areas match with the standards, the manager need not take any action. He should just allow the process to continue. However, he can try to improve the performance above the standards, if it would be possible, without having any negative impact on the existing process.

Step 6: Take Corrective Action, if necessary

Managers should take necessary corrective action, if performance is not in harmony with standards. If the deviation is positive *i.e.* performance is above the standards continuously, revises the standards. On the contrary, if performance is below standard, take steps to improve the performance. (See Fig 9.3).

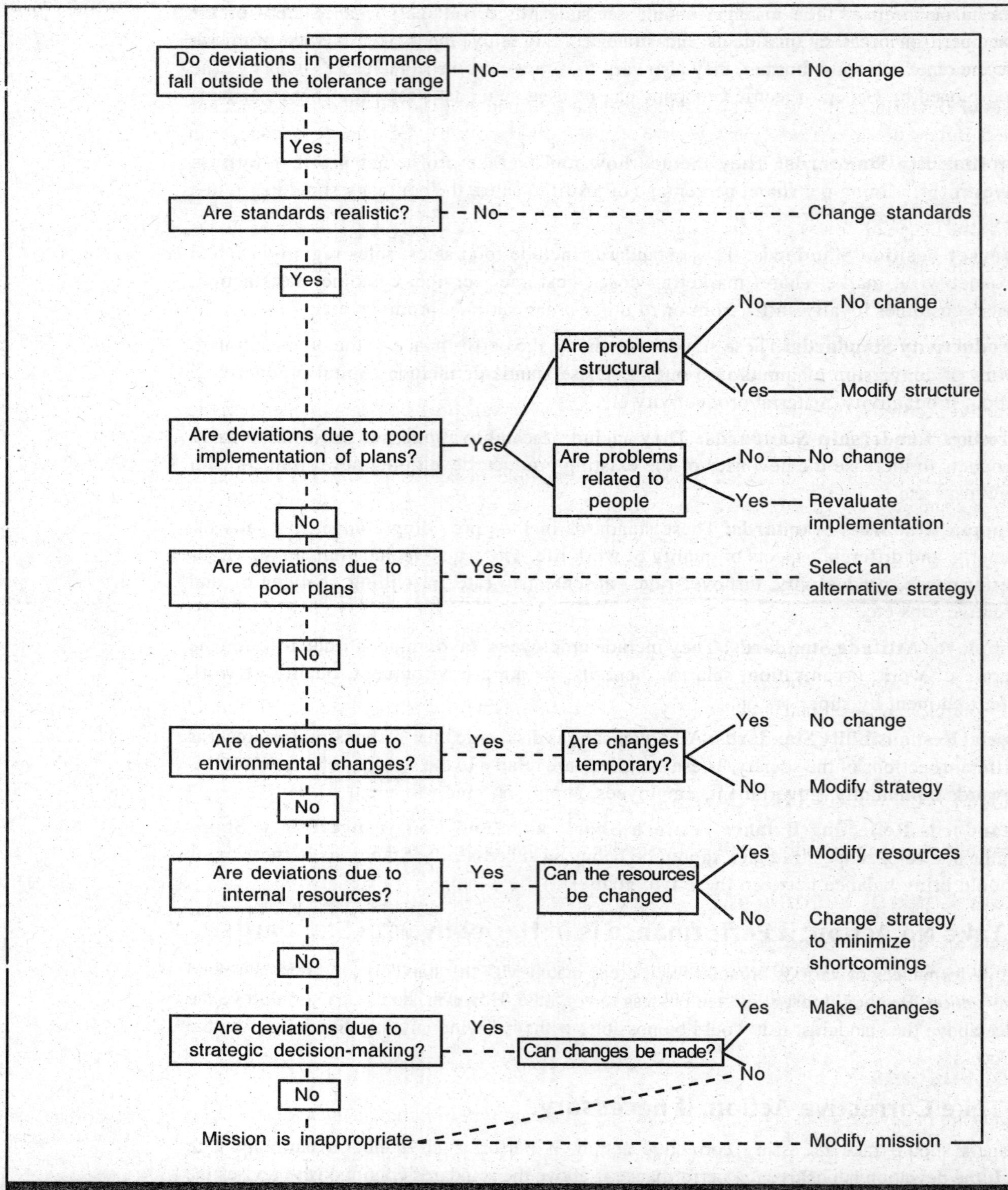

Fig. 9.3: Determining Reasons for Deviations

(**Source:** Joe G. Thomas, op. cit., p. 340).

Now, we shall discuss the non-budgetary control techniques.

The managers compare the performance with standards. If they find any deviation between the standards and performance, they should take corrective action to bridge the gap between the standards and performance.

Causes of Deviations: It is very easy to conclude that someone made a mistake, when deviations are identified. But the deviations maybe the result of an unexpected move by a competitor, or changes in external environment. Therefore, the manager should consider the following before making a decision, in this regard:

- Was the cause of deviation internal or external?
- Was the cause random, or should it have been anticipated?
- Is the change temporary or permanent?
- Are the present plans still appropriate?
- Does the organisation have the capacity to respond to the change needed?[5]

Corrective Action: Corrective action may be defined as change in a company's operations to ensure that it can more effectively and efficiently reach its goals and perform its established standards.

Plans that do not achieve standards produce three possible responses *viz.(i)* to revise plans, *(ii)* to change standards and *(iii)* to take corrective action in the existing process without changing standards and plans. Change in plans may require a 'fine tuning' of the existing strategy or complete changes in plans. If it is realised that the existing standards are unrealistic under the present conditions, the manager should reset the standards taking the existing conditions into consideration.

Corrective action may be as simple as to increase the price or may be as complex as change the chief executive officer. Deviations require re-examination of the company's mission, objectives, relationship to its environment, internal strengths, weaknesses and plans. After having an idea of the process of control, now we shall study the types of control. Now, we shall discuss the control techniques.

(D) CONTROL TECHNIQUES

Control techniques are broadly classified into budgetary techniques and non-budgetary techniques.

Budgetary Control Techniques

Budgets are plans for a specific period in numerical terms. They are statements of expected outcome in financial terms, physical terms, human resources terms etc. Budgets would be the basis for delegation of authority and responsibility without loss of control. The budgets would provide orderliness in controlling.

Types of Budgets

Types of budgetary control techniques include capital expenditure budgets, cash budgets, space and materials budget etc.

Budgets are of several types. Now, we discuss the important types of budgets mentioned below:

(i) **Capital Expenditure Budgets:** Companies basically require capital for establishing manufacturing facilities, marketing network, marketing the product/service, employing and developing the people etc. They formulate budgets before acquiring and incurring capital expenditure. Capital expenditure budgets specify the estimates of the amount of capital required for land, buildings, plant, equipment, machinery, technology, minimum level of materials etc. The actual expenditure is compared with the budgeted capital

expenditure and steps are taken to control the deviations regarding the future capital expenditure.

(ii) **Cash Budgets:** Cash budgets provide the estimates of cash receipts and disbursements. The actual cash receipts and disbursements are compared with the estimates, if the deviations are negative. Deviations and causes are identified and steps are taken to control the deviations, Cash budgets are highly essential in order to ensure required amount of cash to meet the obligations.

(iii) **Time, Space and Materials Budget:** Budgets need not be specified in financial and physical terms. They can be specified in other quantifiable terms like time and space. Time is more important in the business organisations. Time-based budgets are direct labour hours and machine-hours rate. Space budgets include square-feet required and actually allocated for each machine or office. Materials budgets include estimation of materials of various kinds needed and actually allocated. All these budgets help to control the allocations.

(iv) **Production Budgets:** They specify the amount of the estimated output, estimated materials, human resources etc. These budgets help to control the production hindering factors and ensure the production as ensured.

(v) **Sales Budgets:** Sales budgets specify the amount of estimated sales. They help to estimate the sales, identify the factors hindering sales and control these factors. These budgets help to ensure the estimated sales and are more advantageous to the management as a controlling technique for ensuring the achievement of plans and strategies.

(vi) **Zero-Based Budgeting:** The recent budgeting technique is the zero-based budgeting. Organisational programmes for all the departments are divided into packages. Each package focuses on its own goals, activities and resources. Though the different departments are in various levels of development, the starting of the budgets of all packages would start at a base of zero. All costs or expenditures are calculated afresh for each budget period avoiding the past changes. Zero-based budget is useful for starting the programmes or activities afresh, ignoring the different stages of the packages.

Advantages of Budgetary Control Techniques

The advantages of budgets as control techniques include:

(i) **Clear Guidelines for Action and Control:** Budgets are for a specific time framework. Therefore, it is clear to the managers regarding the time framework for the achievement of results. Similarly, budgets indicate the numerical values regarding the estimations in financial and physical values. Thus, they provide clear guidelines for managerial action and control.

(ii) **Coordination:** Budgets are prepared for various departments and functional areas. Further, a master budget is also prepared by coordinating all the departmental budgets. Thus, budgets help in the coordination of entire organisational activities.

(iii) **Encourage Team Effort:** Employees at different levels in the departments are involved in preparing budgets. All the employees work like a team in budget preparation. Therefore, budgets encourage team work.

(iv) **Creative Ideas:** The combined and comprehensive efforts of all the employees in budget preparation storm their brains, bring creative ideas and enable the organisation to meet the future challenges.

Despite these advantages, there are certain dangers in budgets. Now, we shall discuss these dangers in budgeting.

Dangers in Budgeting

(i) **Overbudgeting:** The departments compete among themselves for the limited resources. As such, the departments over-budget their requirements. Ultimately, the budget estimates become unrealistic.

(ii) **Overriding Enterprise Goals:** Normally budgets are based on organisational goals. But various departments formulate their budgets by over estimating the budget figures of their respective departments without considering the total organisational resources. In this process, each department concentrates on formulating their own budgets leaving the goals. Consequently, the budget estimates override the enterprise goals.

(iii) **Hiding Inefficiencies:** Managers present reports that they achieved the budget estimates by preparing low budget estimates. Thus, managers hide their inefficiencies by making low budget estimates.

(iv) **Causing Inflexibility:** Budgets are prepared for a specific period and are presented in detailed values. As such, budgets are rigid and do not provide any adaptability to the changing environmental conditions.

Non-Budgetary Control Techniques

These include statistical data, special reports and analysis, operational audit and personal observations.

(i) **Statistical Data:** Statistical data provide the basis for performing a number of activities for the present and the future. Future, data act as a control technique for the present operations.

(ii) **Special Reports and Analyses:** Accounting reports, financial reports, personnel reports, sales reports etc. provide information for reporting and control.

(iii) **Operational Audit:** Operational audit is also known as *internal audit*. Internal audit specifies the results of financial operations of the company including the company sales, profits, cost of salary etc. Operational audit compares the results of one year with those of another year and helps as a control technique.

(iv) **Personal Observations:** Personal observations are more powerful control devices. Managers observe the various activities and operations including production, sales, human resources and finance. They check them against the standards and take the controlling steps.

Operations Research Techniques of Controlling

Operations research is the application of scientific/mathematical methods or techniques and tools to the solution of operating business problems or business system. Operations research techniques of control include:

Operations research techniques of controlling are linear programming, queuing theory, simulation, game theory etc.

(i) **Linear Programming:** It is a mathematical technique for directing the most efficient use of raw materials, manpower, tools of production, or capital toward a goal. It solves the product mix and distribution problems.

(ii) **Inventory Theory:** Inventory theory emphasises on minimising costs of holding inventories, procurement of inventories, shortage of inventories etc.This theory suggests

how much to buy, when to buy etc., in order to minimise the cost of inventory without affecting production schedules.

(iii) **Queuing Theory:** It attempts to minimise the costs of providing service and reduces customers waiting-time. For example, introduction of 'Sudarshana Chakra' at Tirumala.

(iv) **Simulation:** It sets a model which is similar to a real life situation. Simulation means the duplication of the essence of the system or activity without actually attaining reality itself.

(v) **Decision Theory:** It is used in risky and uncertain situations in order to take the decision which results in minimum loss and maximum benefit.

(vi) **Game Theory:** It is used to determine the optimum strategy in a competitive situation.

(vii) **Network Analysis:** The important operations research techniques are network models which are mostly used in many scheduling situations as sequencing models *viz.*, Critical Path Method (CPM) and Programme Evaluation and Review Technique (PERT). Both are planning techniques and tools of controlling.

PERT is employed to calculate the total time required to complete a project and also identify the possible problems that may arise towards delay of the project completion. CPM is identifying the critical areas in project implementation which deserve the attention in the control process. PERT enables the management to observe the project implementation, the actual, compare them with the planned standards, identify deviations, if any and take corrective measures. However, PERT/CPM is a technique for focusing our attention on the danger signals or potential bottlenecks shown by the critical path. Management can take remedial action in right time for completing the project in an optimum time. PERT/CPM is a forward as well as backward technique.

PERT/CPM also help management in:

(i) finding out total events/activities and their interrelationship with each other.

(ii) finding out optimum time for each event with a view to calculate total time required to complete a project.

(iii) planning a project, implementing the project, in meeting the desired goals of timely completion of the project with optimum use of available human, material and financial resources.

Advantages of PERT/CPM Techniques

(i) They cover all the phases of project management: (a) project planning, (b) time and resource estimation, (c) basic scheduling, (d) time-cost-tradeoffs, (e) resource allocation, (f) project control.

(ii) They enable the managers to plan as accurately as possible

(iii) They help management in identifying the favourable factors in project implementation and maximise them.

(iv) They help in taking preventive measures as they identify the possible bottlenecks in the project implementation.

(v) PERT is an effective means of communication. Network methods (CPM/PERT) provide a clear, unambiguous way of documenting the plans, schedules and communicating the time and cost performance of the projects to the project team and upper management.

(vi) PERT/CPM methods, if properly developed by the project team, can encourage team feeling and build project confidence in completing projects in the required time span. The

clear delineation of activities can aid in allocating responsibilities to achieve the project objectives. Lower management is motivated as the people are involved in the project execution.

Limitations of CPM/PERT

(i) CPM assumes that there is a certain time for the activity performance. In real life, the assumed time interval may not be realised.

(ii) CPM does not offer statistical analysis in determination of estimates of time.

(iii) CPM is a static planning model and not a dynamic controlling device. Any change in the network leads to repetition of the entire evaluation.

(iv) PERT is not suitable for routine planning of recurrent events.

(v) PERT gives emphasis only to time and not to costs.

(E) PROBLEMS OF CONTROL PROCESS

Problems in the control process arise due to dynamism of the environment, information overload, defective standards, employee resistance etc.

(i) **Dynamism of the Environment:** The external environment consists of STEPIN factors viz., Social, Technical, Economic, Political, International and Natural. These factors are dynamic in nature, changing both in kind and magnitude. The environmental conditions which would be in existence at the time of making plans may not be in existence when they are in the implementation stage. Though the measures are taken to feed the information of changes to the implementation mechanism, sometimes it would be highly difficult to the planners to foresee the environmental changes. These changes would subsequently affect the effectiveness of control system. (See Box 9.1).

Box 9.1: Failure to Control: Krispy Kreme Lost its way

The once-hugely popular doughnut chain lost money selling something cheap and delicious. What happened

There's a truism among investors that you should invest in what you know, understand, and like. It's a common sense strategy: You spot something new. It's special. It's useful or innovative. It's cool and affordable. Let me buy some of that!

Related Quotes

Krispy Kreme had been a popular doughnut chain in the South since 1937, but remained unknown to the rest of us until about 1996. That's when the first Krispy Kreme popped up in New York City, on West 23rd Street. Believe it or not, the town went nuts.

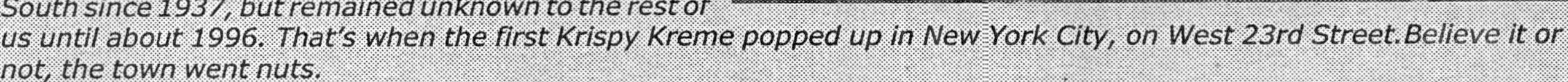

Doughnuts are a major food group in New York, where people eat many of their meals while walking. These fabulous new doughnuts were favorably reviewed by local newspapers. Lines formed when the "Hot Doughnuts" sign was lit. The two young men who owned the franchise were extolled as modern entrepreneurs.

I lived one block away from the store, and thought Krispy Kremes were a much better thing than sliced bread. I was soon as knowledgeable about the product as any potential investor could be. Krispy Kreme went public in 2000. Luckily, by then I was living out of the country and didn't hear about it. After all, what could go wrong? Just about everything. Krispy Kreme stock hit a high of about $49 in 2003. Then it started on a long downward spiral, losing about 90% of its value. This company had problems that had nothing to do with its doughnut recipe.

It over-expanded and took on crushing debt. There were allegations of management misconduct. Some franchises went bankrupt. Competition was fierce in the cheap eats category. More people started consuming healthy foods. In short, Krispy Kreme managed to lose money selling something that is both cheap and delicious.

Now the company is under new management and seems to be on a bit of a roll. Since February, when its share price hovered around $1, it has climbed steadily, topping $4 a share before settling at $3.49 as of October 8, 2009. It has fewer and smaller stores, but is parking them in strategic locations around the world. Is there hope for Krispy Kreme? Apparently, the answer is "maybe."

At the end of September, Standard & Poor's raised its outlook on the company's junk credit ratings to Stable from Negative (still just above "highly speculative") and indicated that its sales declines had slowed and cost pressures would ease. In its latest quarterly report, the company announced it was close to breaking even, and reported a 5.9% increase in year-over-year, same-store sales for company-owned locations.

The company even got some good press recently, if you want to call it that. A new junk-food craze involves a bacon cheeseburger sandwiched between two Krispy Kremes (Original Glazed). It weighs in at 1,500 calories, give or take a few. (With this company's luck, everyone who eats one will have a coronary within the hour.)

*So, taking the common sense investing strategy to its illogical conclusion, what about **McDonald's** (MCD)?*

*You hate it, right? Everybody says they do. Nutritionists condemn it as a major cause of the American obesity crisis. Fat teens have tried to sue it for damages. French farmers demonstrated when it started expanding its presence there. In India, people rioted — all because of a little fib about what those French fries were fried in. For more, see **Bad Boys of Business: McDonald's.***

McDonald's will announce its latest quarterly earnings on October 22, when it's expected to report earnings of $1.10 per share on revenues of $6.09 billion. The company's sales grew 4.5% last year. So much for tough competition in the fast-food industry. Meanwhile, the company's share price over the past five years has climbed steadily from the mid-20s to mid-50s. They also pay a dividend, currently 3.87%.

So, if there's a shred of truth in the common sense investing strategy, maybe it's this: Forget about everything you understand, think is new or wonderful, or ought to take the world by storm. Instead, watch what everybody else is doing. Pretty soon, what they'll be doing at The Louvre in Paris is eating at the city's newest McDonald's restaurant. They probably needed one because those on the nearby Rue de Rivoli and Champs Elysee are always overcrowded.Nothing contained in this article is intended as a solicitation for business of any kind or for investment in the firm.

(**Source**: http://finance.yahoo.com/news/The-Tragedy-of-Krispy-minyanville-220090191.html?x=0)

(ii) **Information Overload:** The emergence of information technology including internet enabled the controlling system to procure too much information. Generation of too much of information makes the control system difficult and sometimes unmanageable.

(iii) **Defective Standards:** As discussed earlier, standards are the basis for control. Sometimes the planners fail to design the realistic standards. If the standards are too high, it would be impossible for the subordinates to achieve them. If the standards are too low, then the subordinates' capacity and time are underutilized. In both these cases, the standards are defective and it would be difficult to implement the controls.

(iv) **Employees' Resistance:** It is the general human tendency that people do not like someone to control their operations. They prefer to do the work but not to be controlled by someone else. As such, employees also resist the control of their activities by somebody else including their superiors.

The problems of control process can be minimised by adapting the following essential conditions for effective control.

(F) REQUIREMENTS FOR EFFECTIVE CONTROL

Requirements for effective control include design control to plans and strategies, individual managers etc.

Essential conditions for effective control include:

(i) **Design Controls to Plans and Strategies:** Plans and strategies are the basis for control. In fact, the purpose of control is to ensure the effective implementation of plans and strategies. Therefore, the control techniques should reflect the plans and strategies that they are designed to follow.

(ii) **Design Controls to Individual Managers:** Individual managers have to implement the plans and strategies. Thus, they are the monitoring points for the execution. As such, control techniques and systems should be designed to individual managers.

(iii) **Controls Pointing up Exceptions at Critical Points:** There would be critical points in the implementation process of plans. For example, rating of the company is a critical point in the plan of raising the equity capital. The control techniques should concentrate on such critical areas.

(iv) **Objectivity of Controls:** There should be objectivity in measuring the performance of the employers in terms of implementation of plans and strategies. Therefore, management should objectively determine the standards of performance. Subsequently, the operations can be controlled based on these objective standards.

(v) **Flexibility of Controls:** Environment under which the plans are implemented is dynamic and ever-changing. The unforeseen circumstances make the plans and strategies vulnerable to the environmental changes. Therefore, the control standards should be flexible and adaptable to these changes.

(vi) **Compatibility of the Control System and Organisational Culture:** Organisational culture is developed over the period and relatively stable in the short run. It gets modified mostly in the long run and slowly. As such the control system should be designed based on the organisational culture.

(vii) **Economy of Controls:** As discussed earlier, controls are necessary to ensure the proper implementation of the plans. But the cost of the control system and techniques should not be more than the savings derived from them. Thus controls should result in economies to the organisation.

Though these factors are taken into consideration while designing the control system, yet various problems crop up in the control process.

Like other functions, it is also difficult to perform controlling functions due to the problems associated with it.

(G) OVERALL CONTROL TECHNIQUES

Management Audit

Management audit is relatively of recent origin. It is concerned with the evaluation of company's mission, objectives, strategies, organisational structure, policies, programmes and the utilisation of various resources including the human resources against bench marks in order to find deviations and make recommendations for improvement.

Definition

William F.Kelly defines the term management audit as, "a critical review of an organisational structure and administration. Its purpose is making recommendations for adjustment and improvement. An audit may involve a whole company structure or be restricted to one of its parts such as a division or department."

Objectives of Management Audit

Objectives of management audit include:

- To find the level of achievement of strategies, goals and objectives
- To find the suitability of the organisation structure to the organisational strategies
- To observe the degree and direction of utilisation of various resources in tune with the organisational strategies
- To identify the deviations against the set standards or the benchmarks of the industry
- To suggest the measures to correct the deviations, if any and to improve the management system
- To help the management in improving the execution aspect of policies, objectives etc.

Importance of Management Audit

Management audit play pivotal role in making the company efficient due to the following reasons:

- Management Audit sets the policies and objectives right in view of changing environment, competitors' strategies, changes in technology, consumers' preferences etc.
- It helps the management in improving its systems in view of developments or creations in management principles, techniques and approaches
- It helps the management in improving its performance in execution of policies and in utilising resources
- It sets the direction of objectives policies and business definition
- It provides scope to the business to interact openly with the environment and maxmises the benefit of the environmental opportunities and controlling the effects of environmental threats

Activities of Management Auditor

Management auditor performs the following activities:

- Scanning external environment
- Scanning the company's vision, mission, objectives, philosophy, policies, goals and strategies
- Evaluating the industry benchmarks in terms of objectives, strategies, organisational structure, profitability, productivity etc.
- Evaluating the internal environment of the company in terms of benchmarks
- Evaluate the key managers, their capabilities, styles and performance
- Evaluate the current management styles and approaches in another companies also
- Evaluate the potentialities of managers and their creative skills
- Evaluate freedom and autonomy provided to employees in order to make use of their talents
- Evaluate the degree of involvement of managers in policy making as well as execution.

Self Audit

Audit can be undertaken by the outsiders or by the manager himself/herself. Individual manager can be provided with the details of benchmarks or standards and organisational expectations in order to audit his own performance, potentialities and the direction. He/she can evaluate himself in terms of his/her styles, involvement, commitment and direction against the company objectives, external environment, competition strategies etc.

Audit can be undertaken by the outsiders or by the manager himself/ herself.

Manager knows about his job, relevant internal environment and the management styles. As such he can audit his activities more efficiently than the outsiders. This system enhances his self satisfaction as his/her ego will not be at stake.

However, if he fails to see himself completely and objectively, self audit cannot produce results. Further, his/her inefficiencies may not produce accurate results. Therefore, self audit and evaluation by the external auditor may reduce the limitations of self audit.

Human Resource Accounting: Human resource accounting deals with cost of and contribution of human resources to the organisation. Cost of employee includes cost of manpower planning, recruitment, selection, induction, placement, training, development, wages and benefits etc. Employee contribution is the money value of employee service which can be measured by labour productivity or value added by human resources.

Cost of human resources may be taken as standard. Employee performance can be measured in terms of employee contribution to the organisation. Employee performance can be taken as positive when contribution is more than the cost and performance can be viewed as negative, it cost is more than the contribution.

Positive performance can be measured in terms of percentage and excess of employee contribution over the cost of employee. Similarly, negative performance can be calculated in terms of percentage of deficit in employee contribution compared to the cost of employee.

Strategic Audit

A strategic audit is an execution and evaluation of organisation's operations affected by the strategy implementation. Strategic audit may be very comprehensive, emphasising all facets of a strategic management process. It may also be narrowly focused, emphasising only on a single part of the process such as environmental process. Strategic audit may be quite formal adhering to organisational rules and procedures. It may be quite informal providing freedom and autonomy to the managers to take decisions. The strategic audit must work to integrate related functions. Hence, the strategic audits are carried out by cross-functional teams of managers.[6]

A strategic audit is an execution and evaluation of organi-sation's operations affected by the strategy implementation.

There is no universally accepted single method of strategic audit. Each organisation can formulate its own method depending upon its need. Exhibit 9.2 presents a worthwhile set of general guidelines on how to conduct a strategic audit.

Exhibit 9.2 How to Conduct a Strategic Audit

A strategic audit is conducted in three phases: diagnosis to identify how, where, and in what priority in-depth analyses need to be made; focused analysis; and generation and testing of recommendations. Objectivity and the ability to ask critical, probing questions are key requirements for conducting a strategic audit.

Phase One: Diagnosis

1. Review key documents such as:
   (a) Strategic plan
   (b) Business or operational plans

(*c*) Organizational arrangements

(*d*) Major policies governing matters such as resource allocation and performance measurement

2. Review financial, market, and operational performance against benchmarks and industry norms to identify key variances and emerging trends.
3. Gain an understanding of:

(*a*) Principal roles, responsibilities, and reporting relationships

(*b*) Decision-making process and major decisions made

(*c*) Resources, including physical facilities, capital, management, and technology

(*d*) Interrelationships between functional staff member and businesses or operating units

4. Identify strategic implications of strategy for organization structure, behaviour patterns, systems, and processes — define interrelationships and linkage to strategy.
5. Determine internal and external perspectives.

(*a*) Survey the attitudes and perceptions of senior and middle managers and other key employees to assess the extent to which they are consistent with the strategic direction of the firm. One way to accomplish this task is through carefully focused interviews and/or questionnaires to ask employees to identify and make trade-offs among the objectives and variables they consider most important.

(*b*) Interview a carefully selected sample of customers and prospective customers and other key external sources to understand their view of the company.

6. Identify aspects of the strategy that are working well. Formulate hypotheses regarding problems and opportunities for improvement based on the findings above. Define how and in what order to pursue each.

Phase Two: Focused Analysis

1. Test the hypotheses concerning problems and opportunitists for improvement through analysis of specific issues. Identify interrelationships and dependencies among components of the strategic system.
2. Formulate conclusions as to weaknesses in strategy formulation, implementation deficiencies, or interactions between the two.

Phase Three: Recommendations

1. Develop alternative solutions to problems and ways of capitalizing on opportunities. Test these alternatives in light of their resource requirements, risks, rewards, priorities, and other applicable measures.
2. Develop specific recommendations to produce an integrated, measurable, and time-phased action plan to improve strategic results.

(**Source:** Adapted from A.J. Prager and M.B. Shea, "The Strategic Audit," in The Strategic Management Handbook, ed. K.J. Albert (New York: McGraw-Hill, 1983), pp. 8-14.

Strategic Audit Measurement Methods

Generally accepted methods may be used to measure organisational performance. These methods can be broadly divided into two categories *viz., (i)* Qualitative Methods and *(ii)* Quantitative Methods. Exhibit 9.3 presents Key Strategy Evaluation Questions.

Exhibit 9.3 Key Strategy-Evaluation Questions

1. Do you feel that the strategic-management system exists to provide service to you in your day-to-day work? How has it helped you in this respect?
2. Has the strategic-management system provided the service that you feel was promised at the start of its design and implementation? In which areas has it failed and excelled, in your opinion?
3. Do you consider that the strategic-management system has been implemented with due regard to costs and benefits? Are there any areas in which you consider the costs to be excessive?
4. Do you feel comfortable using the system? Could more attention have been paid to matching the output of the system to your needs and if so, of, in what areas?
5. Is the system flexible enough in your opinion? If not, where should changes be made?
6. Do you still keep a personal store of information in a notebook or elsewhere? If so, will you share that information with the system? Do you see any benefits in so doing?
7. Do you think that the strategic-management system is still evolving? Can you influence this evolution and, if not, why not?
8. Does the system provide you with timely, relevant, and accurate information? Are there any areas of deficiency in this respect?
9. Do you think that the strategic-management system makes too much use of complex procedures and models? Can you suggest areas in which less complicated techniques might be used to advantage?

10. Do you consider that there has been sufficient attention paid to the confidentiality and security of the information in the system? Can you suggest areas for improvement of these aspects of its operation?

(**Source:** K.J. Radford, Information Systems for Strategic Decisions, 1978, pp. 220-21.)

Qualitative Organisational Measurements

Qualitative measurements are in the form of non-numerical data that are subjectively summarised. These measurements are organised and provided to the strategists for decision making and strategy control action. Critical questions are designed to reflect important facets of organisational operations. Answers to these questions form as the basis for measurements. There is no universally acceptable list of questions by all companies. However, Exhibit 9.4 presents a list of useful questions of quantitative organisational measurements.

Exhibit 9.4 Sample Questions for Qualitative Organisational Measurement

- Are financial policies with respect to investment, dividends, and financing consistent with the opportunities likely to be available?
- Has the company defined the market segments in which it intends to operate specifically with respect to both product lines and market segments? Has it clearly defined the key capabilities it needs to succeed?
- Does the company have a viable plan for developing a significant and defensible superiority over competitors based on these capabilities?
- Will the business segments in which the company operates provide adequate opportunities for achieving corporate objectives? Do they appear attractive enough to draw an excessive amount of investment to the market from potential competitors? Is the company providing adequately for developing attractive new investment opportunities?
- Are the management, financial, technical, and other resources of the company really adequate to justify an expectation of maintaining superiority over competitors in key capabilities?
- Does the company have operations in which it cannot reasonably expect to outperform competitors? If so, can managers expect these operations to generate adequate returns on invested capital? Is there any justification for investing further in such operations, even just to maintain them?
- Has the company selected business segments that can reinforce each other by contributing jointly to the development of key capabilities? Do competitors combine operations in ways that give them superiority in the key resource areas? Can the company's scope of operations be revised to improve its chances against competitors?
- To the extent that operations are diversified, has the company recognized and provided for the special management and control system this requires?

(**Source:** Milton Lauenstein, "Keeping Your Corporate Strategy on Track," *Journal of Business Strategy 2*, No. 1 (Summer 1981), p. 64.)

Seymour Tilles in his paper on, "How to Evaluate Corporate Strategy," mentioned several important questions to measure organisational performance qualitatively. These questions include:

1. Is organisational strategy internally consistent? Internal consistency is concerned to the cumulative impact of various strategies on organisation. Are strategies conflicting with each other. Strategies should also be judged by their relationship with other organisational initiatives.

2. Is the organisation's strategy consistent with its environment? Normally organisational strategies are formulated based on the industry's environment and general environment.

Similarly, the strategies are modified based on the environmental changes. The strategist should see, whether the strategies are consistent with the present and future environmental factors or not? These environmental factors include: Present and future regulations of the Government, Customers taste and preferences, trends of labour supply, technology changes, competitors' products and demand. Many organisational problems can be solved easily, if the management brings the balance between the strategy and the environment.

3. Is organisational strategy appropriate, given organisational resources? Strategy implementation invariably requires the allocation of sufficient resources. Therefore, the strategist should enquire, whether the existing organisational resources are sufficient to carry out a proposed strategy. The strategist should not implement the strategy, without the allocation of sufficient money, material, machines/technology and human resources.

4. Is the Time Horizon of the strategy appropriate? Organisational strategies are formulated to achieve specific goals within a time framework. The strategist should require whether the time framework, under the existing circumstances is realistic and acceptable? Organisational goals cannot be achieved satisfactorily, if there is inconsistency between these two variables:

Qualitative measurement methods are efficient and are useful. But applying them relies mostly on human judgement. Conclusion based on such methods should be drawn carefully due to the subjectivity of the judgement.

Quantitative Organisational Measurements: Under quantitative organisational measurements of the performance of strategy implementation is taken place in the form of numerical data. The numerical data can be summarised and organised to draw conclusions and to recommend strategic action. Quantitative measurements can be used to evaluate: *(i)* number of units produced per time period, *(ii)* cost of production, cost of marketing, *(iii)* productivity and production efficiency levels, *(iv)* Employee turnover, absenteeism levels, *(v)* sales and sales growth market shares, *(vi)* Profit-gross, net, earning per share, dividend rate, return on equity, market price of the share, *(vii)* Cost of production, *(viii)* cost of marketing etc.

Organisations design and use their own methods to evaluate the performance quantitatively. The commonly used methods include:

Return on Investment: Return on investment is widely used as a measure of organisational performance

$$\text{Return on Investment (ROI)} = \frac{\text{Amount of Income per year}}{\text{Total investment during that year}}$$

Management calculates the return on investment for consecutive years or consecutive quarters and compares the values over the period to measure the performance. It has its advantages and limitations (Exhibit 9.5). Managers can use the ROI along with other measures of organisational performance in view of its limitations.

Exhibit 9.5 Advantages and Limitations of ROI Performance Measures

Advantages

1. ROI is a single comprehensive figure influenced by everything that happens in a firm.
2. It measures how well the division manager uses the assets of the company to generate profits. It is also a good way to check on the accuracy of capital investment proposals.
3. It is a common denominator that can be compared among many entities.
4. It provides an incentive to use existing assets efficiently.
5. It provides an incentive to acquire new assets only when doing so would increase the firm's return.

Limitations

1. ROI is very sensitive to depreciation policy. Variances in depreciation write-offs between divisions affect their ROI performance. Accelerated depreciation techniques reduce ROI, conflicting with capital budgeting discounted cash flow analysis.
2. ROI is sensitive to book value. Older plants with more fully depreciated assets have relatively lower investment bases than newer plants, increasing ROI. (Note also that inflation can skew asset values and ROI.) Managers might be tempted to hold down asset investment or dispose of assets in order to increase ROI performance.
3. In many firms that use ROI, one division sells to another, so transfer pricing affects the measure. Expenses incurred affect profit. Since, in theory, the transfer price should be based on the total impact on firm profit, some investment center managers are bound to suffer. Equitable transfer prices are difficult to determine.

4. If one division operates in favourable industry conditions and another division operates in an industry with unfavourable conditions, the former division will automatically look better than the other.
5. ROI reflects a short time span. The performance of division managers should be measured in the long run. This is top management's time-span capacity.
6. The business cycle strongly affects ROI performance, often despite managerial performance.

(**Source:** Excerpt from James M. Higgins, Organisational Policy and Strategic Management: Text And Cases.)

2. Stakeholders' Audit: Stakeholders are the people who have a stake in the company. They are interested in the company's activities as they are significantly affected by the company's objectives.[11] The organisational stakeholders include: *(i)* shareholders or owners of the company who are interested in dividend, market price the share, *(ii)* Trade unions and employees interested in favourable wages, benefits, conditions of employment and better quality of work life, *(iii)* creditors interested in company's liquidity position and ability to repay the debts with interest in right time, *(iv)* suppliers interested in retaining the organisation as a good customer, *(v)* government interested in keeping the organisation as a good tax payer, maintaining the congenial industrial relations, maintaining the ecological balance, and contributing to solve the social and economic problems of the country, *(vi)* social interest groups such as consumer protection associations and environmental protection associations *(vii)* customers who expect a qualitative product/service at a reasonable price, prompt service and favourable conditions of sales.

Stakeholders audit is one of the measures of organisational performance. Exhibit 9.6 provides stakeholder groups and measures to assess both the short run and long run impact they may have on organisational performance.

Exhibit 9.6 Stakeholder Groups and their impact on Organisational Performance

Stakeholder Category	*Near-Term Performance Measures*	*Long-Term Performance Measures*
Customers	Sales (value and volume) New customers Number of new customer needs met	Growth in sales Turnover in customer base Ability to control price
Suppliers	Cost of raw material Delivery time Inventory Availability of raw materials	Growth rates of Raw materials costs Delivery time Inventory New ideas from suppliers
Financial Community	EPS[a] Street Stock price Number of "buy" lists[b] ROE[c]	Ability to sell strategy to Wall Growth in ROE
Employees	Number of suggestions Productivity Number of grievances	Number of internal promotions Turnover
Congress	Number of new pieces of legislation that affect the firm Access to key members and staff	Number of new regulations that affect the industry Ratio of cooperative to competitive encounters
Consumer advocates	Number of meetings Number of hostile encounters Number of coalitions formed Number of legal actions advocates[d]	Number of changes in policy due to consumer advocates Number of calls for help initiated by consumer

Environmentalists	Number of meetings Number of hostile encounters Number of coalitions formed Number of Environmental Protection Agency complaints Number of legal actions	Number of changes in policy due to environmentalists Number of calls for help initiated by environmentalists

a Earnings per share.
h Lists from which financial brokers recommend stock purchases for their clients.
c Return on equity.
d Calls in which consumer advocates attempt to enlist others in action against a company.

(**Source:** Adapted from Edward Freeman Strategic Management: A Stakeholder Approach, Boston: Pitman Publishing.)

3. Standards:

Profitability Standards: These standards include how much gross profit, net profit, return on investment, earning per share, percentage of profit to sales the company should earn in a given time period.

Market Position Standards: These standards include total sales, sales-region-wise and product-wise, market share, marketing costs, customer service, customer satisfaction, price, customer loyalty shifts from other organisations' products etc.

Productivity Standards: These standards indicate the performance of the organisation in terms of conversion of inputs into outputs. These standards include capital productivity, labour productivity, material productivity etc.

Product Leadership Standards: These standards include the innovations and modifications in products to increase the new uses of the existing product, developing new products with new uses etc.

Human Resource Standards: Human resource standards include providing competitive salaries, benefits and different aspects of quality of worklife. These standards also include human resource performance, productivity, turnover rates, absenteeism rates etc.

Employee Attitude Standards: Employee attitude standards include employees' favourable attitude towards the nature of work, organisation, salaries, benefits, working environment, quantity of work life, treatment by superiors etc.

Social Responsibility Standards: All organisations discharge their responsibilities towards different sections of the society. These standards are related to the services of the organisations towards community, government, employees, suppliers, creditors etc.

Standards Reflecting Balance between Short-range and Long-range Goals: Short-range and long-range strategies should be balanced successfully. Standards in these areas should bring balance between short-range and long-range goals.

Management Information System (MIS)

A management information system is a formal computer-assisted organisational function designed to provide managers with information to help their decision-making.

A management information system is a formal computer-assisted organisational function designed to provide managers with information to help their decision-making. The important use of such information is to support strategic control. There are six steps in the operation of MIS (Fig. 9.4).

Managers at different levels of the organisation perform different functions and therefore, they need different kinds of information. MIS should be flexible to provide different kinds of information to the managers at various levels. Exhibit 9.7 presents typical activities performed by top management, middle management and junior management.

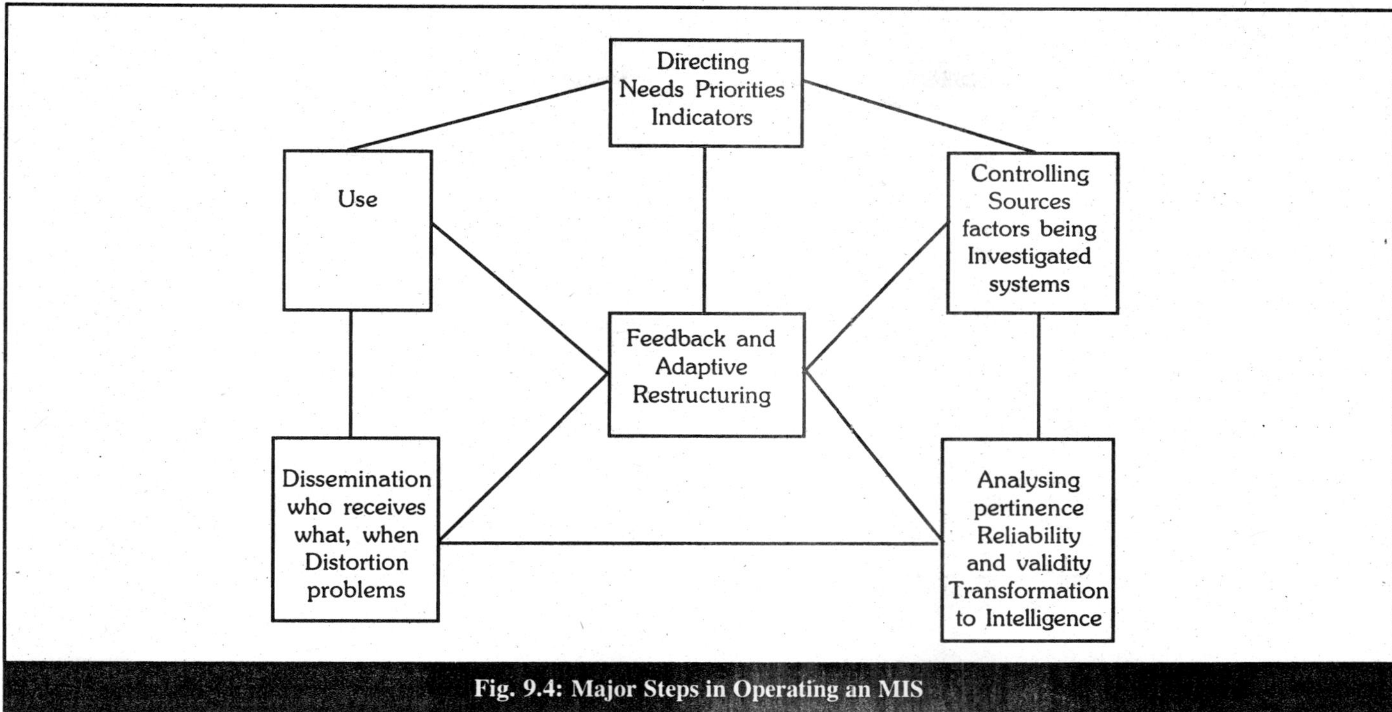

Fig. 9.4: Major Steps in Operating an MIS

(**Source:** Samuel C. Certo and J. Paul Peter, op. cit., p. 152.)

Exhibit 9.7 Typical Activities of Managers at Various Organisational Levels

Organizational Level	*Characteristics of Activities*	*Sample Activities*
Top management	Future oriented Significant uncertainty Significant subjective assessment Strategic management emphasis	Establishing organizational direction Performing environmental analysis Developing organizational strategies
Middle management	Somewhat future oriented (less than top-management activities) Emphasis on implementation of strategies	Marking short-term forecasts Budgeting Human resource planning
Supervisory management	Emphasis on daily production Emphasis on daily performance that reflects organizational strategy and contributes to attaining long-term goals	Assigning jobs to specific workers Managing inventory Supervising workers Handling worker complaints Maintaining organizational procedures and rules

(**Source:** Samuel C. Certo and Paul Peter, op. cit., p. 153.)

Since the success of the strategic control depends on the efficient functioning of MIS, the strategists should monitor the functioning of MIS continuously. The strategists should be aware of the symptoms of a malfunctioning MIS (Exhibit 9.8) and set the MIS in the right direction and in right time.

Exhibit 9.8 Symptoms of a Malfunctioning MIS

Operational Symptoms	*Psychological Symptoms*	*Report Content Symptoms*
Large physical inventory adjustments Capital expenditure overruns Unexplained changes from year to year in operating results Uncertain direction of company growth Unexplained cost variances No order backlog awareness No internal discussion of reported data Insufficient knowledge about competition Purchasing parts from outside vendors that the firm could make itself Failure of investments in facilities, or in programs such as R&D and advertising	Surprise at financial results Poor attitude of executives about usefulness of information Lack of understanding of financial information by nonfinancial executives Lack of concern for environmental changes Excessive homework	Excessive use of large tables of numbers Multiple preparation and distribution of identical data Disagreements among information from different sources Lack of periodic comparative and trend information Late information Too little or excess detail Inaccurate information Lack of standards for comparison Failure to identify variances by cause and responsibility Inadequate externally generated information

(**Source:** Institute for Practitioners in Work-Study, Organization, and Methods, Middlesex, England, Management Sciences 4, No. 5 (September-October 1967), pp. 15-24.)

Management Decision Support System

A management decision support system is an independent set of decision aids that helps managers make relatively unstructured, perhaps nonrecurring decisions. Fig. 9.5 presents information needs of executives responsible for strategic control in their firms and the internal functions responsible for finding, interpreting and passing on critical information to top managers.

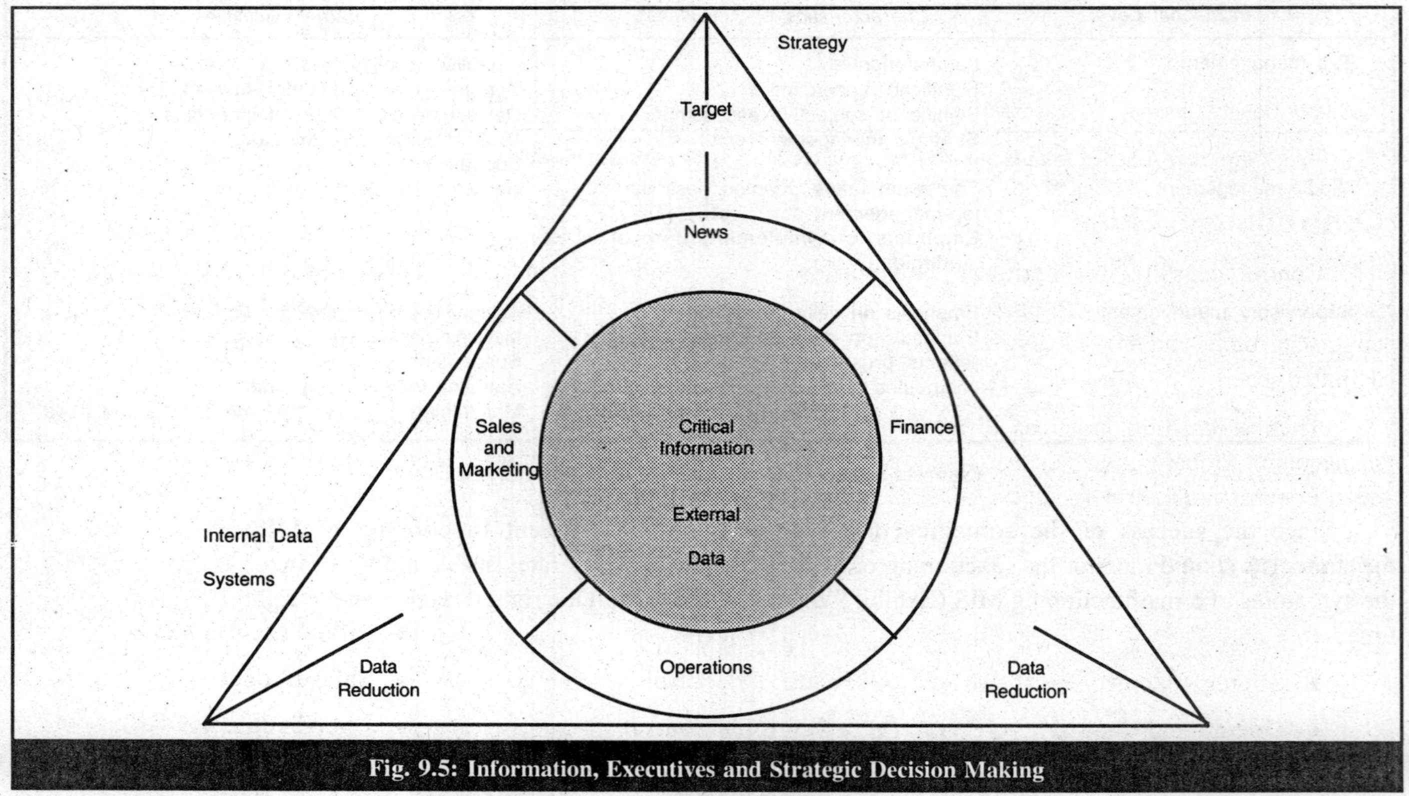

Fig. 9.5: Information, Executives and Strategic Decision Making

(**Source:** Robin Matthews and Anthony Shoebridge, "EIS - A Guide for Executives," Long Range Planning, Vol. 25, No. 6, December 1992, p. 98.)

(H) GLOBAL CONTROLLING

Culture of the country influence the management practices including controlling. Though controlling concept specify a clear-cut procedure, companies in practice many not follow them strictly.

Controlling in Japan

The Japanese culture of collectivism collaboration, and open-door policy influence control practices profoundly, the team work culture in Japan makes managers part of employees rather than separate from them. Therefore, the emphasis is on group performance though individual performance can also be measured against objectives. Control in Japan is more on the process than on the numbers. Employees at the grass route level also involve in quality control through quality circles. Thus control in Japan is more of a group process.

Controlling in USA

Controlling in USA is more of a step by step procedure discussed earlier. In other words, specific targets are established, superior measures the performance of the subordinate, identify the deviations and initiates corrective measures, if necessary. Group performance in USA companies may suffer as the companies concentrate on individual performance.

Table 9.1 presents controlling practices in Japan, USA and China.

Table 9.1: Controlling Practices in Japan, USA and China

Factor	*Japan*	*USA*	*China*
Who controls?	Peers	Superior	Group Leader/Superior
Control Focus	Group Performance	Individual Performance	Primarily on Group Secondary: Individual
Point	Saving Face	Fixing blame	Try to save face
Quality Control Circles	Extensive use	Limited use	Limited use

(**Source:** Adapted from Heinz Weihrich and Harold Koontz, "Management", *op.cit.*, p.697.)

Controlling in China

Control focus in China is primarily on group leader and secondarily on individuals. Chinese control practices are a blend of both Japanese and USA practices. Factory managers are held responsible for targets/standards and individuals are held responsible at the secondary stage. Quality circles are used on a limited scale.

Thus controlling practices differ from country to country based on the culture. However, managers of global companies learn from other countries and introduce practices that are superior in other countries in their companies. Thus, global companies use the best-fit practices.

KEY TERMS

- Control
- Strategic Control
- Operational Control
- Standards
- Deviations
- Feedback Control
- Concurrent Control
- Feed-forward Control
- Production Budget
- Sales Budget
- Over-budgeting
- Special Reports

- Performance
- Corrective Action
- Management Audit
- Capital Expenditure Budget
- Cash Budget
- Self Audit
- Operational Audit
- Personal Observations
- Measurement

QUESTIONS

1. Define the term control. Discuss the need for managerial control.
2. Discuss in detail the process of managerial control.
3. Explain different kinds of control. Which kind of control is most desirable?
4. Outline the essential conditions for control.
5. What are the problems of control? How do you minimise them?
6. What are the different types of budgets? State their advantages as control techniques.
7. What is management audit? Explain the importance and objectives of management audit.
8. Discuss the activities of management audit.
9. Discuss the concept of self audit.

REFERENCES

1. Robert N. Anthony, *The Management Control Function*, Harvard Business School Press, Boston, 1988.
2. Henri Fayol, *General and Industrial Management*, Pitman Publishing, London, 1949, p. 107.
3. Fred R. David, op. cit., p. 325.
4. R. Kaufman, *Preparing Useful Performance Indicators*, Training and Development Journal, September 1989, pp. 80-83.
5. John A. Pearce and Richard B. Robinson, *Management*, McGraw-Hill, New York, 1989, p. 584-586.
6. Harold Kooutz and Heinz Weihrich, *Essentials of Management*, McGraw-Hill, 1990, p. 393.

CHAPTER **10**

RECENT TRENDS AND PARADIGM SHIFTS IN MANAGEMENT PRINCIPLES

Chapter Outline

(A) Introduction
(B) Deregulated Environment
(C) Competition and Customisation
(D) Paradigm Shifts in Management Principles
(E) Conclusion: Situational Approach to management Principles
- Key Terms
- Questions
- References

Learning Objectives

After studying this Chapter, you should be able to:

✓ Understand the impact of globalisation and information technology on competition;

✓ Study the effects of deregulated economic policies on business;

✓ Analyse the cause and effect relationship between competition and customisation; and

✓ Study the paradigm shifts in management principles due to deregulation of economies, competition and customisation in the areas of division of labour, specialisation, unity of command, individual accountability, team work, standardisation, systems approach, leadership styles, motivational patterns, organisation structure patterns and the like.

(A) INTRODUCTION

The business across the border of the countries had been carried out since times immemorial. The post World War II period witnessed an unexpected expansion of national companies of mostly capitalistic countries into international or multinational companies. The post 1990s period has given greater fillip to international business due to globalisation of world economies along with the strides in information technology. Thus the phenomenal change in economic and technological environments brought significant changes in the business. Though the business environment comprises of social, technical, economic, political, international and natural environments, the type of economic system that a country adapts decides the major part of the environment. Most of the countries initially adapted capitalistic economic systems and later shifted to communistic/socialistic or mixed economic system/ socialistic pattern of societies as a result of revolutions or demands of the masses. These types of economic systems necessitated the Governments to play the role of businessmen also as a part of discharging their responsibilities of being the custodian of the nation. This role made the Governments to use the public sector mainly as a means to achieve their objectives and control the private sector toward its ends. As such the economic environment in such countries did not allow either the domestic or foreign businesses to formulate and implement competitive strategies and to give the best to the customer. In deed businesses formulated non-competitive strategies centred on the Governments' protective policies Management strategies in various companies in these countries-derivates of corporate strategies.[1]

(B) DEREGULATED ENVIRONMENT

Governments in capitalistic economic systems, in contrast, provide free and deregulated environment to the business to operate and formulate competitive corporate as well as management strategies. Further, globalisation provides free and deregulated environment for the business in all those countries whose economies are opened for the rest of the globe. As such businesses in such economies centre their strategies on customer, and treat all resources equally for the purpose of winning the customer deliciousness. The deregulated environment created by the Governments and /or globalisation discourages most of the business regulative institutions or measures which hampers the freedom of the business to operate competitively. As such the terms and conditions of management are mostly determined by the market forces. Therefore, management principles, structure and pattern are based on the theme of the corporate strategies that, in turn, are shaped mostly by the country's economic system and/or globalisation. Thus, globalisation along with capitalistic economic system results in insignificant role for business regulating devices including institutions.[2]

(C) COMPETITION AND CUSTOMISATION

Globalisation tends to result in exchange of the cultures across the globe, location of manufacturing centres and/or various business processes in and spread of markets to various countries. Thus globalisation led to internationalisation of capital, human resources, markets, material, management and manufacturing posing sever competition to the companies of developing countries from multinational and translational companies not only in their home counties but also in various foreign countries wherever they operate. This multidimensional competition made the companies to align and realign all of their strategies, operations and resources including human resources around the customer and adapted customisation approach. Customisation approach to business was in fact, the earliest approach and it is coming back in a different degree. This process has its impact on management of various resources.[3]

(D) PARADIGM SHIFTS IN MANAGEMENT PRINCIPLES

At this point of time, most of the economies in the world including the erstwhile communistic counties have chosen capitalistic pattern of society/ market economies in view of the limitations of communism and /or due to the conditions laid by International Monetary Fund and World Bank. This global trend along with the huge fiscal deficit and crisis in balance of payments forced the Governments of various countries including that of India to create a favourable climate for restoration of capitalistic tendencies or markets economic situations. Capitalistic trends along with innovations of information technology brought paradigm shifts in the principles and practices of management. Now, we shall discuss the paradigm shifts in the principles and practice of management (See Table 10.1).

Table 10.1: Traditional and Modern Management Principles

S.No.	Traditional Principles	Modern Principles
1	Division of Labour and Specialisation	Multi-skills and Generalisation
2	Unity of Command, Unity of direction and scalar chain	Multiple superiors, Diverse direction, vector chain(point-to-point)
3	Standardisation, separation of planning and doing	Customisation, Combine planning and doing
4	Fixed System Approach	Goal-oriented flexi-system
5	Individual-based management-authority, responsibility and accountability	Team-based management-authority, responsibility and accountability
6	Individual Authenticity- Boss	Shared Authenticity
7	Manager as a Boss	Manager as a Leader
8	Tall Organisation structure	Flat/ virtual organization structure
9	Money as a significant motivator	Significant motivators: Achievement, involvement, freedom and empowerment
10	Autocratic, participative and democratic styles of leadership	Transformational, transactional and developmental leadership
11	Middle management- must for coordination	Middle management-Redundant
12	Junior Management- Strategy implementers	Junior management: Innovators and strategists
13	Change: resist	Change-order of the day. So invite and initiate
14	Craft strategy based on Strategic Fit principle	Craft strategy based on Strategic Intent principle
15	Production: Market whatever you can produce	Produce whatever you can Market
16	Exhibitive Objective: Maximisation of shareholders' wealth	Maximisation of Employee satisfaction. Satisfied employees serve the customers efficiently and satisfied customers enhance business and profits. Increased profits maximize shareholders' wealth.

(**Source**: P.Subba Rao, *Management at Cross-Roads*, Unpublished Teaching Notes, University of Papua New Guinea, 2007.)

Specialisation vs. Generalisation

Adam Smith during 1700s advocated division of labour and specialization. It is found that the specialization has become a hindrance in the process of customer service and convenience. As such businesses have shifted to multi-skills and generalistion in order to meet the global benchmarks and customer conveniences.

Unity of Command vs. Multiple Directions

Henry Fayol's principles like unity of command, unity of direction and scalar chain were prominent before globalization. Later, it was found that these principles resulted in killing the initiatives and innovations of team work as well as other knowledgeable employees in the organization. Consequently, businesses started adapting multiple leaders/ supervisors, diverse directions and point-to-point in place of scalar chain.[4]

Diversions in Principles of Scientific Management

F.W.Taylor suggested standardization and separation of planning and doing. Various businesses discovered that competitive environment favours customization over standardization as customization leads to customer satisfaction and thus enhances business volume. In addition, businesses found that every human being has innovative and creative ideas. Making use of such ideas is paramount for business growth. This concept led to employee involvement, employee participation and employee empowerment program that contradict the principle of separation of planning and doing. Hence, the principle of separation of planning and doing is relegated by the principle of combining these tow functions.

System Approach vs. Goal-Oriented Flexi-system

Systems approach suggests thinking and doing as per the pre-fixed approach. But the changing environmental factors and competitive situations can be addressed efficiently with the flexible and goal-oriented approach. Hence, businesses started adopting flexible and goal-oriented systems approach.

Individual vs. Team-Based Management

Traditionally businesses used to prefer individual responsibility, authority and accountability. But the societies built around team/ joint effort achieved higher level productivity than the individualistic societies. Further, research found that team work results in synergy, innovations and higher productivity in addition to resulting in stress-free work environment. Consequently, businesses have shifted to team-based management from individual-based management.

Individualistic Authenticity vs. Shared Authenticity

Traditionally, it was believed that the boss/leader/superior is always right as they normally expected to possess higher order skills, knowledge and expertise. But the ever-growing knowledge and changing environment eroded this assumption. Consequently, it is learnt that everyone has his/her own strengths and weaknesses. The shared knowledge can wipe-out the weaknesses and enhance the strengths. Therefore, businesses have started in relying on shared authenticity over individualistic authenticity.

Manager: Boss vs. Leader

Managers used to feel that they know everything and as such used to assume the role of a boss undermining the capacities and expertise of subordinates. But, of late managers realized that subordinates also have skills, knowledge and expertise and they only need direction and motivation. As such the managers started assuming the role of a leader to provide direction to the competent people, involving and empowering them, transforming them, inspiring them and developing them.

Organisation Structure: Flat vs. Virtual

Businesses traditionally used to structure vertical organizations based on classical principles. Later they shifted to virtual structure in order to serve the customer wherever, whenever and however he/she needs either products or services or both. Thus, business to-day tends to structure organizations based on virtual structures.

Shifts in Motivating Factors

Traditionally managers feel that money is the major motivating factor. Of late, businesses found that other factors like a sense of achievement, involvement and freedom/ empowerment motivate employees significantly. As such, businesses started designing various employee involvement and empowerment programs to motivate employees.

Paradigm Shifts in Leadership Styles

Popularly known leadership styles are autocratic, participative and democratic. The recent developments in leadership styles are charismatic, developmental, transactional and transformational. Business leaders of late practicing developmental and transformational styles to explore the untapped potentialities of employees in order to develop distinctive human competencies.

Middle Management: Coordinative Level or a Redundant Hierarchy?

Middle level management was initially created to coordinate the activities between the operational and strategic level. The recent strides in information technology and on-line activities enabled the business to coordinate the activities automatically. Consequently, middle level management in some organizations has become redundant.

Junior Management: Innovators and Strategists

Initially junior management was responsible for carrying-out the commands of the top level management and implementing the strategies. But the junior managers of late are highly educated and possess innovative and strategic skills. Businesses after realizing these shifts started using the junior level managers for crafting strategies. Thus the junior mangers are also involved in strategy crafting.

Change Management

Businesses used to plan the change and push the change plans down for implementation. Employees used to resist change. But, the businesses as well as employees after the recent globalization an economic recession and their aftermath realized that the change is the order of the day. Consequently, they realized that 'Change before change changes you'. As such employees started inviting the change rather than resisting the change.

Strategic Fit vs Strategic Intent

Initially businesses used to craft strategies using strategic fit concept by aligning organizational strengths and weaknesses with the external opportunities and threats. But businesses learned that most efficient companies craft strategies by manipulating strengths and opportunities of the environment based on the intention (intent) of the management.

Market Whatever You Can Produce vs. Produce Whatever You Can Market

Initially businesses' strategy used to be 'market whatever they can produce' without enhancing organizational efficiency. This was due to low level competition. But the competition consequent upon globalization made the businesses to understand the customer needs, design the products and services accordingly and produce. Thus, the businesses started to shift towards producing whatever they can market.

(E) CONCLUSION: SITUATIONAL APPROACH TO MANAGEMENT PRINCIPLES

Businesses tend to adopt flexible principles of management depending upon situation and strategy. For example some businesses structure organizations based on tall structure while more advanced businesses adapt virtual structure. Same business firm during the growth stage go for flat structure and adopt tall structure during economic recession. Some organizations adapt division of labour and specialization while other organizations adapt multi skills and generalizations. Unity of command principle during recession and multi-directional command principle during economic boom are appropriate. Thus, businesses should follow flexible and adaptable management principles depending upon situations as no management principle is right for all situations and no management principle is wrong for all situations.

KEY TERMS

- Management
- Competition
- Standardisation
- Market Production
- Strategic Intent
- Globalisation
- Customisation
- Unity of Command
- Accountability
- Team Work Individual Responsibility
- Information Technology
- Division of Labour
- Unity of Direction
- Strategic Fit

QUESTIONS

1. What is the impact of globalization on competition?
2. What is the impact of competition on customization?
3. Explain the impact of customization on standardization?
4. Discuss the impact of globalistion on various principles of management.
5. Discuss the flexible nature of management principles.

REFERENCES

1. P.Subba Rao, "Globalization: Is It Driving Industrial Relations in A Reverse Gear?" Journal of Social and Economic Policy, Vol.2, No.1, June 2005, pp. 53-54.
2. P.Subba Rao, "Impact of Globalization on Human Resource Management", GITAM Journal of Management, Vol.3, No.1, January-June, 2005, pp. 71-72.
3. Ibid.,p.73.
4. P.Subba Rao," Management at Cross-Roads", Unpublished Teaching Notes, University of Papua New Guinea, 2007.

PART - B

ORGANISATIONAL BEHAVIOUR

CHAPTER 11

INTRODUCTION TO ORGANISATIONAL BEHAVIOUR

Chapter Outline

Learning Objectives

After studying this Chapter, you should be able to:

- ✓ Analyse the causes for similarities and dissimilarities among individuals;
- ✓ Discuss various models of man like economic man, social man organisational man, self-actualisation man and complex man;
- ✓ Understand the need for study of organisational behaviour;
- ✓ Know the meaning and features of organisational behaviour;
- ✓ Know the factors responsible for increase in diversity of human resources;
- ✓ Analyse the contributions of various disciplines to organisational behaviour; and
- ✓ Understand the model of organisational behaviour.

(A) NATURE OF MAN

Humans may be physically alike but not behaviourally. In fact, the same person behaves differently in different situations. This is due to the influence of various factors. The important among them include: various models of man, *i.e.,* Economic Man, Social Man, Organisational Man, Self-actualising Man, Complex Man, Impulsive Man and Compulsive Man. As such, human behaviour is complex and dynamic. The study of human behaviour is presented in Fig. 11.1.

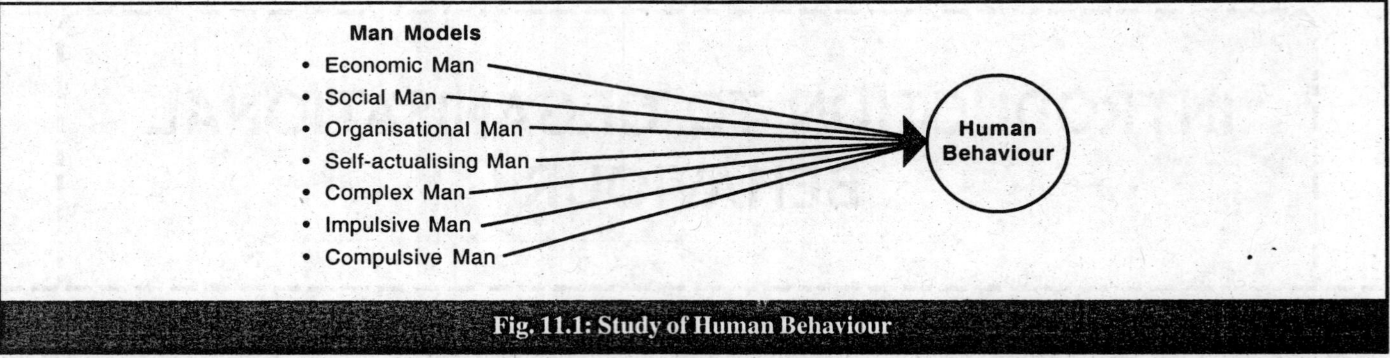

Fig. 11.1: Study of Human Behaviour

We often come across with a number and variety of people in different situations, organisations and societal set-ups. These people may be similar or dissimilar with each other in *(i)* physical features like height, weight, body structure, facial dimensions, etc., *(ii)* psychological factors like attitudes, values, opinions, perception, leadership, etc., *(iii)* social factors like activeness, shyness, interactive, etc. and *(iv)* in human resources like skills, knowledge, abilities, commitment, values, beliefs, etc.

People are also similar as well as dissimilar in professions or occupations, interests, likes, dislikes, etc.

People are also similar as well as dissimilar in professions or occupations, interests, likes, dislikes, etc. There are scientists, technical experts, management experts, engineers, politicians, business people, etc. We come across with great personalities in different fields and also mentally instable personalities. Some people like musicians, painters and dancers have in-born talents whereas other people like scientists and engineers have the acquired skills. We come across with people like Mahatma Gandhi, Nelson Mandela, Abraham Lincon, Mother Theresa on one side and like Bin Laden and Veerappan on the other.

It is clear that the cognitive abilities of the people *viz.,* aptitudes, attitudes, intellectual abilities, interests, etc., physical traits, social interactive skills, religious beliefs do not exist in the same extent in all the people. As such, it can be said that no two individuals are alike and each individual is unique in himself or herself. However, we find some similarities too in different individuals.

Similarities in Individuals

We find some people with similar physical features; psychological, social attributes and abilities and religious beliefs within the broader limits. In other words, individuals may not be identically equal to one another but differ from one another within certain limits.

Sir Francis Galton conducted studies in 1896, on the extent of genetic inheritance in human beings by devising sensory motor tests to examine similarities or differences among individuals. According to these studies, individuals are similar with each other within certain limits. We find people with similar physical characteristics like height, weight, body structure, facial design, etc. The psychological attributes of the people in general are distributed in a particular manner. The psychological attributes and physical characteristics of the majority of the people are normal in an average. The psychological attributes and physical characters of a few people are above or below average. A normal distribution curve is obtained when the scores of the physical and psychological attributes are plotted (See Fig. 11.2).

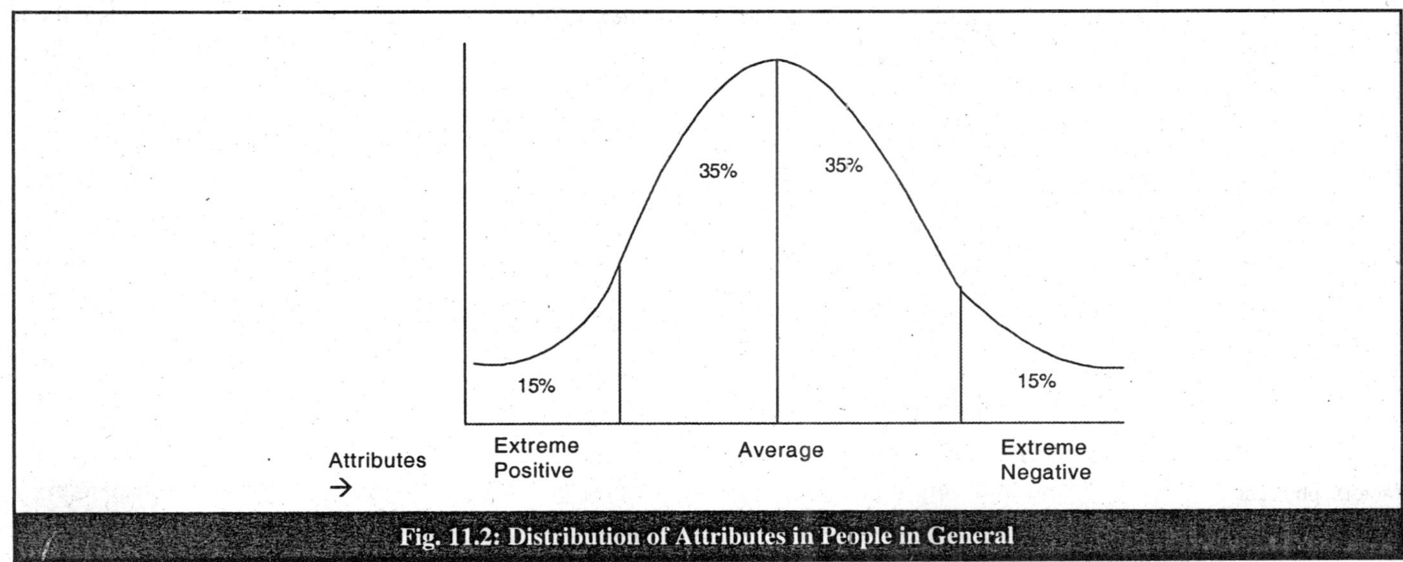

Fig. 11.2: Distribution of Attributes in People in General

It is clear that majority of the people have average attributes (35% plus 35% = 70%). Thus, majority of the people are with similar attributes and characteristics. There would be similar attributes even among the people with above average scores. For example, Mahatma Gandhi and Nelson Mandela. The common attributes would be average risk taking, moderate dynamism, rational thinking, positive attitudes, democratic leadership style, passing the buck and the like.

However, it is viewed that the physical characteristics, psychological attributes, social values and religious beliefs vary among individuals within each broad category. Now, we shall discuss individual differences.

Individual Differences

Individuals differ from one another within the broad spectrum. What are the factors that produce these differences? Are these differences significant in real life situations? Do these differences affect behaviour? The factors that influence individual differences are classified into three categories. Individual behaviour is a complex phenomenon. We should understand the total human being by studying the total man concept. Some individuals attach importance to extrinsic rewards while some other individuals attach credence to intrinsic rewards. Some individuals prefer challenging and risky jobs while others prefer routine and secure jobs. Some people prefer salaries linked to performance, while others prefer uniform salaries for all irrespective of individual performance. Similarly, people do also differ in tolerance for tension, stress and ambiguity. Thus, individuals differ from each other within a broad spectrum. Now, we shall discuss the factors of individual differences. (See the Exhibit 11.1).

Exhibit 11.1 Factors Affecting Individual Differences

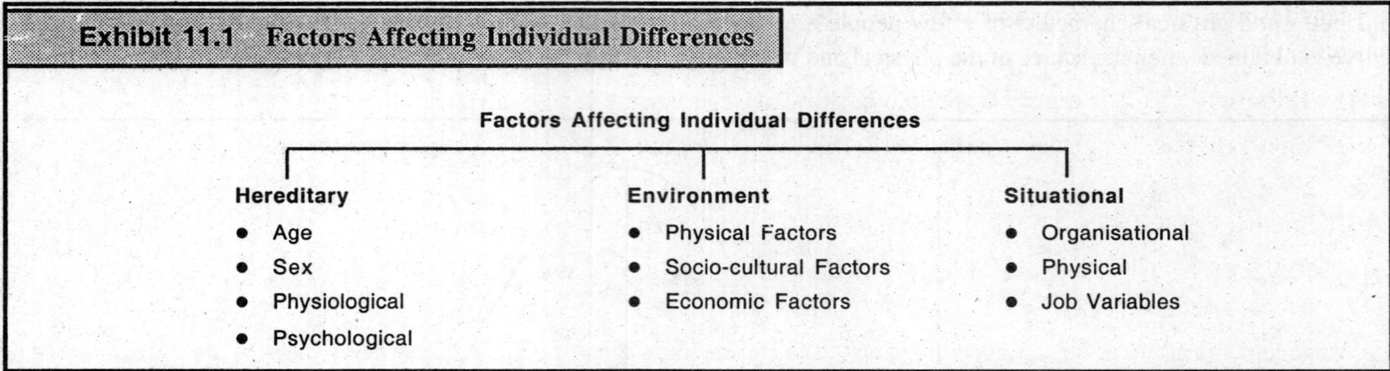

The factors that contribute for individual differences include: hereditary factors, environmental factors, physical factors, socio-cultural factors, economic factors and situational factors.

The factors that contribute for individual differences include: hereditary factors, environmental factors, physical factors, socio-cultural factors, economic factors and situational factors.

Now, we shall look into these factors.

(i) **Hereditary Factors:** Even two people do not have identical heredity. Hereditary factors include height, weight, skin colour and other physiological and psychological factors. Psychological variables include perception, learning, leadership, motivation, attitudes, values, emotions, and the like.

(ii) **Environmental Factors:** Environmental factors include physical, socio-cultural and economic factors.

- *Physical Factors:* Physical factors include climate, demographical factors, etc. People live under diverse physical conditions. The body structure and facial, skin colour, hair, etc., vary from one geographical area to the other. Structures of the people vary based on the physical factors. Eating habits, dressing habits and other cultural factors depend upon the physical factors.
- *Socio-cultural Factors:* The socio-cultural factors include the family, neighbourhood, school, college, university, working place and other social groups and institutions transmitting socio-cultural values, attitudes, likes and dislikes, aspirations, moral standards, living habits, eating habits, dressing habits, behaving towards others, etc.
- *Economic Factors:* Economic position of a person influences different aspects of his development, *viz.*, Physical, motivational, emotional, social, education, living, career, interacting with others, etc.

(iii) **Situational Factors:** Situational variables affecting individual differences include type of organisation or institution, type of supervision, training received, type of incentives, social and cultural environment at workplace, methods of work, work design, conditions of equipment and machinery and physical work environment.

The individual differences result in variations in individual behaviour and performance in terms of perception, personality, motivation and other behavioural issues.

Individual differences are the result of the interactive product of hereditary, environmental and situational factors.

Implications of Individual Differences

The individual differences result in variations in individual behaviour and performance in terms of perception, personality, motivation and other behavioural issues.

Further, different jobs need different job behaviours. Individuals with different behavioural patterns are essential to perform the jobs which need varied behaviours. A research study conducted at the Texas Instruments establishes that different types of individuals prefer different behavioural and managerial patterns. They are:

(i) **Tribalistic:** This category of people prefer directive, strong leadership from their boss.

(ii) **Ego-Centric:** This category of people desire to work alone in their own entrepreneurial style.

(iii) **Socio-Centric:** This category of people seek social relationship from their job.

(iv) **Existential:** This category of people strives for satisfying the growth and self-fulfilment needs from their jobs.

Management should understand the individual differences in order to understand their behaviours and assign the appropriate jobs to the individuals based on their behaviour.

Now, we study the different models of man to understand the individual differences further.

Managers try to understand individual differences in order to understand human behaviour and accordingly assign different jobs to different people. In other words, managers understand individual differences in order to make a balance between the individual behaviour and job demands. Managers make assumptions about man while understanding their differences. These assumptions resulted in developing various models of man. Schein and William H.Whyte Jr. have developed five models of man viz.,

(i) Economic Man, *(ii)* Social Man, *(iii)* Organisational Man, *(iv)* Self-Actualising Man, *(v)* Complex Man, *(iv)* Impulsive Man, and *(v)* Compulsive Man.

Now, we shall study these models.

Economic Man

This model is built around the assumptions that man's behaviour is based on his income levels or salary levels — works more and better when his/her wage/salary is more and works less when the wage/salary is low. He or she starts making contributions to the job only when salary/incentive is assured.

This model is built around the assumptions that man's behaviour is based on his income levels or salary levels.

In addition, man evaluates the cost of his efforts, to the value of the salary. He compares the cost and returns and prefers to contribute to the job when the returns are more than the cost of his contributions. Further, he also evaluates the available alternative income sources for his/her efforts and selects those alternative sources which yield highest income. Thus, the man prefers to maximise his satisfaction level through monetary emoluments. He/she also prefers to equalise marginal efforts and marginal inducement of the work.

Assumptions: This model is built on the following assumptions:

- Man is basically motivated by economic incentives like salary and fringe benefits and he/she prefers to maximise them for his efforts.
- The feelings of the man need to be controlled and moulded towards rationality from their irrational state.
- Organisations manipulate the economic incentives in order to get more work as man is passive.
- Organisation can predict human behaviour through controlloing economic incentives.

Social Man

Man is a social animal. Man lives within the society. He can't live in isolation.

Man is a social animal. Man lives within the society. He cannot live in isolation. He prefers to create and develop social relations with other members of the society like affiliation, belongingness, acceptance by the others, association with others, etc. Individuals would like to satisfy their social needs. As such, individuals can be motivated by satisfying their social needs.

Assumptions: This model is developed based on the following assumptions:

- Individuals can be contended by satisfying their social needs. Individuals are satisfied by creating and maintaining social relationship with others.
- Man values the social relationship more than the appeasement by the management through economic incentives. As such, man is more responsive to social relations and group pressures rather than management's efforts to bring them within their fold through economic incentives.
- Management can motivate the individuals by satisfying their social needs only.
- Managements should design the jobs in such a way that they provide the opportunity to the employees to satisfy their social needs.

Elton Mayo's experiments and human relations approach to management and organisational behaviour were designed on the basis of this model.

Organisational Man

An organisational man is committed and loyal to the organisation, works and lives along with others by involving, interacting and associating with others.

People live in the society by co-operating, associating and interacting with other members of the society. Similarly, employees in an organisation work and live along with others by co-operating, interacting and associating with others. Thus, an organisational man is committed and loyal to the organisation, works and lives along with others by involving, interacting and associating with others. Thus, organisational man model is an extension to social man model. William Whyte developed this model. According to this model, individuals sacrifice their needs for the sake of the satisfaction and requirement of a group or an organisation. Henry Fayol's principle of subordination of individual interest to the general interest supports this model. Social ethics and social responsibilities guide the individuals in sacrificing their needs for the achievement of organisational needs.

Assumptions: According to Whyte, social ethics guide organisational man based on the following assumptions:

- Group and collaborative activities contribute for creativity. Individual by himself cannot be creative. In other words, the interactive and collaborative work is more meaningful as it has synergitical impact, *i.e.,* the whole is greater than the sum of the individual contributions.
- Man prefers to live and work along with others as his belonging and affiliation needs are ultimate.
- Individual and social needs are balanced by eliminating the conflicts between them by creating an organisation and also by applying scientific methods.

Self-actualising Man

Individual employees are satisfied when they achieve something

Individual employees are satisfied when they achieve something different and create certain special things by using their capabilities, potentialities and distinctive abilities. This model criticises that organisations assign the work to individuals which may not be challenging and creative, and as such an organisational man cannot be satisfied. Similarly, this model also criticises the social man on the ground that employees are not satisfied with the group and social relations. Thus, this model specifies that employee behaviour depends upon the challenging and creative work which exploits employee potentialities. Employees are satisfied most when they achieve and create something special. Self-actualising man behaves constructively and efficiently.

different and create certain special things by using their capabilities.

Assumptions: The assumptions of self-actualisation model include:

- The human needs are hierarchical in the order of physiological needs, safety needs, social needs, esteem needs and self-actualisation needs. People satisfy their needs one after the other. They get ultimate satisfaction when they satisfy their self-actualisation needs. Satisfied needs are no more motivators. Therefore, self-actualisation needs provide greatest satisfaction to the employees.
- Employee behaviour is changed from one level of needs to another level.
- External incentives and controls do not affect the employees as human beings are self-motivated and self-controlled.
- There would be conflict between organisational man and self-actualisation man.

Complex Man

Various models of man discussed earlier analyse the man from only one aspect or the other. All these models could not specify the human behaviour independently. Predicting and managing human behaviour is a complex task as human behaviour can be determined by as set of complex variables. Further, the actual human behaviour may not be in accordance with the established cause-effect relationship. Thus, human behaviour is quite complex and hence more unpredictable.

Predicting and managing human behaviour is a complex task as complex variables determine human behaviour.

Assumptions: This model is built based on the following assumptions:

- Man is motivated by a set of complex variables and factors. These complex variables include physiological, psychological, social, political, religious, climatic and geographical factors.
- Interaction of the employees with the organisation enables them to learn motives.
- Variations in terms of need pattern, behaviour, direction and control do exist among people.
- Human behaviour cannot be understood, even though the needs are understood due to the absence of cause-effect relationship.
- Man can behave differently in similar situations due to the absence of cause-effect relationship.

This model establishes that complex man presents a particular pattern of human behaviour.

Impulsive Man

According to this concept, man acts and reacts spontaneously. The impelling forces result in sudden inclination to act. The impulsive forces make the man to act all on a sudden without any rational reasoning. It would be highly difficult to predict the behaviour of impulsive man.

Compulsive Man

A number of factors, *viz.*, social, cultural, political, economic, natural factors affect human behaviour. In addition, the personality factors of other influential persons particularly superiors, subordinates and colleagues, company policies, rules and regulations, customers and other stockholders' behaviour affect the behaviour of an employee. Compulsive man does not act or react quickly. He takes

Compulsive man does not act or react quickly. He/she takes into consideration the influence of various factors, situations and personalities.

into consideration the influence of various factors, situations and personalities, collect the necessary data and information and analyses the interactive output of these factors. He then evaluates the consequences of this output and behaves in a more desirable way. Thus, the behaviour of individuals turns compulsive.

Subordinates are delegated with the responsibility and authority. They are naturally accountable for their activities. Globalisation, liberalisation and privatisation resulted in severe competition. The competition led the subordinates to achieve the targets and benchmarks in the limited span of time. Some subordinates are unable to achieve their targets due to high competition and prefer to withdraw from the job. In addition, subordinates fail to act and behave as per the expectations of the superiors. Subordinates prefer to withdraw from the situation when they fail to meet the expectations of the superiors, job and the company.

Thus, globalisation along with information technology make the jobs competitive and challenging. This results in increase in withdrawal behaviours of some employees and enhance the job satisfaction of others.

As discussed earlier, the different models of man indicate various diversified characteristics. These varied characteristics result in diversified human behaviour.

This in turn, influences the behaviour of the people at work in an organisation. In addition, the process of globalisation results in conglomeration of people with diversified culture in one organisation, which in turn, complicates understanding of human behaviour. Added to this, the strides in information technology led to the complexity of understanding human behaviour.

Having studied the human behaviour in general, we shall now look into the human behaviour related to organisations.

(B) WHAT IS ORGANISATIONAL BEHAVIOUR?

Today's organisations face the challenges of understanding, predicting and managing the employee behaviour due to the consequences of diversity. In fact, human behaviour is complex and dynamic. The study of human behaviour helps to understand varied behaviour of diversified groups and take steps to unify the diversified behaviour and channelise these unified behavioural aspects towards the organisational strategies and goals (see Fig. 11.3).

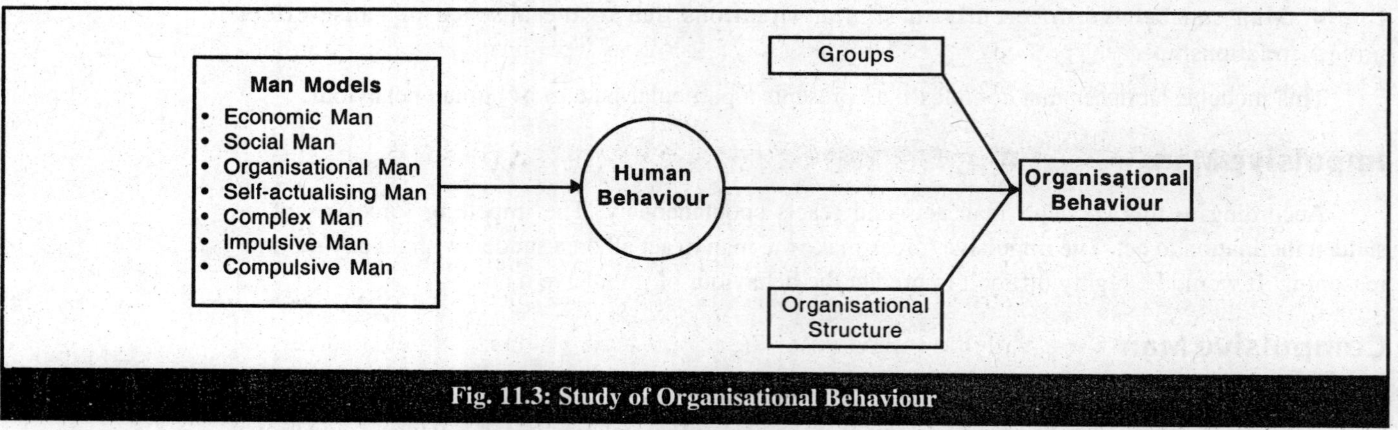

Fig. 11.3: Study of Organisational Behaviour

It is clear from the above figure that the human behaviour in organisations when it is interacted with the groups, results in group behaviour and when it interacts with the structures it takes the shape of organisational behaviour.

Why should we understand the diversified human behaviour and unify it? The answer to this question is:

People are the competitive advantage for today's organisations. (See Exhibit 11.2).

Exhibit 11.2 People as a Competitive Advantage

"The fact of the matter is that human resources do make a difference. As successful real world organisations ranging from Chrysler to General Electricals to Microsoft and Wipro, Hindustan Levers, Infosys Technologies, Reliance, etc., to a posh departmental store and a newly established company have discovered, people may be the substantial competitive advantage that an organisation has in our globalised and informationalised world. The importance of various functions, technology and information systems is given. But these simply level the playing field in the competitive battles ahead. The people, their ideas, their productivity, their adaptability to change and their capacity to learn—at all levels of organisation—are the competitive advantage, now and especially in the 'four anys' (anybody, any place, any time, anyway) environment of the future.

(**Source:** Don L.Bohl, Fred Luthans, John W.Slocum Jr., and Richard M.Hodgetts, "*Ideas that Will Shape in Future of Management Practices*," Organisational Dynamics, Summer, 1996, p. 8).

Most of the organisations have realised that people with diversified skills, behaviour, etc., are the major strength and strategies can be formulated from these assets. Further, these diversified people with their innovative skills, smart working and commitment to the business are useful as a major competitive advantage to those firms which possess them. Though the modern organisations had downsized their operations, delayered their structures, implemented TQM programmes, installed information technology and gone international, still the lasting competitive advantage comes through human resources and the way they are managed.[3]

Further, it is found by the research studies that the efficient human resource management has positive impact on productivity and financial performance of the companies.[4]

Thus, understanding diversified human behaviour, unify it in accordance with organisational requirements and direct it towards organisational strategies are necessary not only for efficient human resources management but also for the success of organisations.

The next logical question is what is human behaviour? How can it be unified and directed towards organisational strategies?

Mr. Ramana, an employee in the production department of Ballarpur Industries, behaves politely with his supervisor but rudely with other managers of the company when he meets them in a group consisting of trade union leaders. Human beings behave differently as individuals, as members of groups and organisations. The study of behaviour of human beings as individuals, members of groups and organisation is referred to as organisational behaviour.

(C) DEFINITIONS OF ORGANISATIONAL BEHAVIOUR

- John W. Newstrom and Keith Davis define the term organisational behaviour as, "the study and application of knowledge about how people as individuals and as groups – act within organisations. It strives to identify ways in which people can act more effectively."[5]

  This definition deals with the behaviour of the people as individuals and as members of groups within the organisations. It also deals with diverting the human behaviour towards organisational requirements.

- Stephen P. Robbins defines organisational behaviour as "a field of study that investigates the impact that individuals, groups and structures have on behaviour within organisations for the purpose of applying such knowledge toward improving an organisation's effectiveness."[6]

This definition deals with the development of knowledge regarding the behaviour induced by individuals, groups and structures in an organisation. It also deals with utilization of such knowledge for enhancing organisational effectiveness.

- Steven L. McShane and Mary Ann Von Glinow define organisational behaviour as "the study of what people think, feel and do in and around organisations."[7] The authors view that organisational behaviour includes the study of the impact of individual, team and structural characteristics on behaviour in organisations and understanding and predicting the impact of these behaviours on organisational success.

Organisational behaviour can be defined as studying, predicting and managing human behaviour caused by individuals, groups and structures towards the requirements of organisational strategies.

- Fred Luthans defines organisational behaviour as "the understanding, prediction and management of human behaviour in organisations."[8]

  This definition seems to be simple and comprehensive. But further analysis is necessary to understand it thoroughly.

- Organisational behaviour can be defined as studying, predicting and managing human behaviour caused by individuals, groups and structures towards the requirements of organisational strategies.

Analysis of these definitions indicates the following features of organisational behaviour.

(D) FEATURES OF ORGANISATIONAL BEHAVIOUR

Interactive Process of Three Levels: Behaviour of people in organiations can't be judged exclusively based on individual behaviour of employees. Human behaviour is caused by individuals, groups and structures of the organisations. For example, the tall structures make the individuals to be rule minded and behave mechanically. The flat structures modify the individual to be innovative, creative, challenging and committed and ultimately persuade them to be result – oriented.

- Human behaviour can be predicted, studied, transformed and managed. This can be done to some extent but not completely as required or anticipated.
- Understand the organizational strategies, type of human behaviour necessary for their implementation and manage the people to exert the behaviour necessary for effecting strategy implementation to the maximum extent possible.
- The purpose of organisational behaviour is to enhance organisational efficiency and effectiveness.
- Organisational behaviour is a multidisciplinary subject, that involves various disciplines.

Psychology

Psychologists study and attempt to understand human behaviour.

Psychology is the science that studies the human behaviour which has its origin to philosophy and physiology. Psychology contributes maximum inputs to organisational behaviour. Psychology studies, predict and manage the behaviour of human beings and animals. Psychologists study and attempt to understand human behaviour. Psychologists who contributed to the discipline of organizational behaviour include learning theorists, personality theorists, counselling psychologists, and industrial and organizational psychologists. Industrial and organizational psychologists contributed to the areas of fatigue, boredom and other working conditions pertaining to the job. In addition, they also contributed to learning, perception, personality, leadership, qualities, emotions, training, job satisfaction, motivation, communication, performance management, employee selection, job and team design and stress management. Psychology developed into a number of fields like clinical, experimental, military, organizational, industrial, and social psychology. Organisational psychology deals with various areas like perception and work motivation that are the integral parts of organizational behaviour. Psychology developed various tests for selection of employees. The psychological concepts relevant to organisational behaviour include:

- Perception
- Personality
- Motivation
- Learning
- Job Satisfaction
- Training
- Communication
- Emotions
- Leadership
- Values
- Attitudes
- Selection
- Risk-taking

Psychology helps to understand and ameliorate individual behaviour and interpersonal behaviour.

Sociology

Sociology — the science of society — deals with the society as a whole rather than individuals. Sociology also made significant contributions to organisational behaviour. Sociology studies the human beings in groups, formal and informal organizations. In addition, Sociology contributes to the social and cultural environment. Sociologists contributed to organizational culture, formal organizations, informal organizations, communication, leadership and power and politics. The contributions of sociology to organisational behaviour include:

- Group Dynamics
- Teamwork
- Communication
- Power and Politics
- Organisation Theory
- Organisation Design
- Organisation Change
- Intergroup Conflict and Behaviour

Social Psychology

Social psychology is the blend of psychology and certain sociology concepts. Social-psychology deals with the influence of one individual on others and vice versa. The major contribution of social psychology is understanding the need for change, designing change process, predicting the possible resistance and developing strategies to avoid such resistances. Further it contributes to shifts in attitudes, communication patterns, group patterns, group conflicts and power politics. Contributions of social psychology to organisational behaviour include:

Social-psychology deals with the influence of one individual on others and vice versa.

- Attitude Change
- Group Process
- Group Interaction
- Communication
- Change Management
- Group Decision-making

Anthropology

Anthropology is the science of human behaviour. Anthropology studies the societies in order to understand the human beings and their activities. Anthropologists contributed to the work culture, human environment, values, attitudes and beliefs of different organizations in different countries. Anthropologists' contributions to organizational behaviour includes organizational culture, organizational environment, cultural differences among various countries. Cultural anthropology deals with the origin of culture and pattern of human behaviour particularly organisational behaviour. The contributions of Anthropology to organisational behaviour include:

- Cross Culture
- Comparative Values
- Comparative Attitudes
- Organisational Culture
- Organisational Environment

Political Science

Political Science predicts studies and manages the behaviour of individuals and groups in the political environment. The contributions of political scientists to organizational behaviour include organizational power and politics, conflicts due to organizational structures and group conflicts. The contributions of political science to organisational behaviour include:

- Structuring Conflict
- Allocation of Power
- Political Behaviour
- Decision-making

Engineering and Technology

Engineering — the applied science of energy and matter — has contributed significantly to the organizational behaviour. Engineering contributes to the work design and thereby job design. In fact F.W. Taylor, the Father of Scientific Management, has designed time study and motion study that has significant contributions to organizational behaviour. Taylor has developed performance appraisal, piece-rate system and human productivity. Technology is application of knowledge. Technology influences the human behaviour directly and significantly by influencing job designs, relationship between employees, machinery, organisational structure, working styles of employees, etc. The contributions of technology to organisational behaviour include:

- Perception
- Work Environment
- Communication
- Teamwork

Information technology still makes phenomenal contributions to organisational behaviour. They include:

- Team Dynamics
- Decision-making
- Communication
- Knowledge Management

Management

Management is getting things done by the people. Management deals with supervising people in their activities to contribute to organizational goals. In other words, people are directed and motivated to get the things done. Thus, management contributes to organisational behaviour in building decision-making models, communication patterns, leadership styles, etc. Management after psychology makes significant contributions to organizational behaviour. Its contributions include people management, decision-making, communication, leadership, motivation, job design, organisational structure, job satisfaction, group management and change management. Management contributions to organisational behaviour include:

- Decision-making
- Communication
- Leadership
- Organisational Structure
- Motivation
- Predict the Behavioural Requirements of Organisational Strategies and
- Manage the Behaviour towards the Strategic Requirements.

Economics

Economics is the science which studies human behaviour as a relationship between ends and scarce means which have alternative uses. The major contribution of Economics to organsiational behaviour is treating human being as an economic man. Therefore, Economics contributes to motivational theories and practices. The contributions of Economics to organisational behaviour include:

- Motivation
- Decision-making
- Learning

Medicine

Medicine is the applied science of healing or treatment of diseases to enhance an individual's health and lifespan[9]. Thus, medicine has concerns for physical as well as psychological health of a human being.[10] Medicine of late deals with psycho-physical diseases like hypertension, occupational health hazards as well as health problems related to industrial nature, environments, etc.[11]

The significant contributions of medicine to organizational behaviour include:

- Organizational Stressors
- Hypertension
- Frustration

Thus, various disciplines contribute to the development of organisational behaviour as a multi-discipline ary characteristic.

Human behaviour in organisations is caused by individuals as individuals, as member of groups and structures of the organisations. Figure 11.4 presents the model of organisational behaviour.

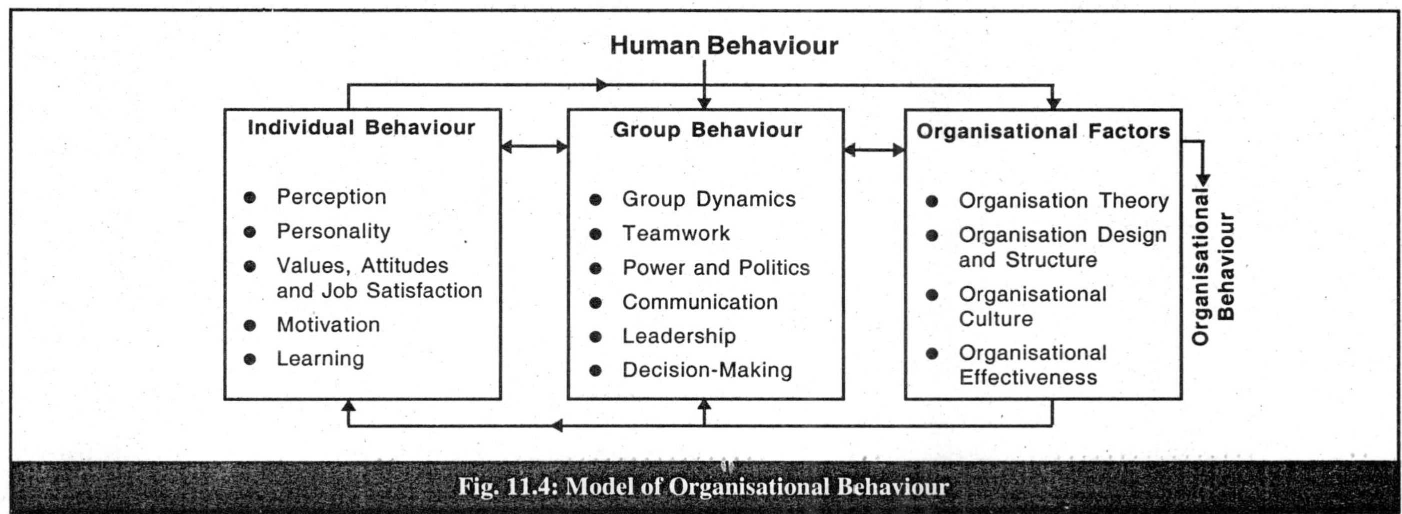

Fig. 11.4: Model of Organisational Behaviour

(E) NATURE OF ORGANISATIONAL BEHAVIOUR

We in our daily activities come across with various types of organizations like public sector, private sector, manufacturing, service, economic, social, and religious organizations. Organisations are economic and social entities in which a number of individuals and groups perform multifarious tasks in order to attain common goals. Thus, organizations are structured social systems consisting of groups and individuals working together to achieve common goals. People work as individuals as well as members of groups based on the pre-determined goals. Organisational behaviour is concerned with the behavioural aspects of individuals, groups and total organization. In fact organization mainly consists of people whether it is a manufacturing or service, profit-oriented or non-profit oriented, organization.

Now we study the different aspects of nature of organizational behaviour.

Multidisciplinary Course

As discussed earlier, organizational behaviour draws knowledge and concepts from various disciplines like psychology, sociology, social-psychology, economics, commerce, management, medicine and anthropology. Thus, organizational behaviour systematically crafts various behavioural concepts by integrating the knowledge drawn from various disciplines.

Organizational behaviour draws knowledge and concepts from various disciplines like psychology, sociology, social-psychology, economics, commerce, management, medicine, anthropology.

Application of Scientific Methods to Practical Managerial Problems

Organisationl behaviour draws knowledge from various disciplines using various scientific methods. The scientific methods used by organizational behaviour may not be as scientific, sophisticated and mature as the pure science disciplines like Mathematics, Physics and Chemistry. However, Organisational Behaviour's approach is scientific in nature as it seeks to develop knowledge by using empirical and research approach. Thus organizational behaviour observes the behaviour systematically and measures the behaviour using scientific instruments. Managers measure the behaviour of employees by using instruments and by using 5-degree scale as depicted in the Exhibit 11.3:

Exhibit 11.3 Transactional Analysis: Know Your Ego States—Model Instrument to Measure Behaviour

For each statement, allocate a score (as given below), to show how much your behaivour is like the way, as reflected by the statement. As all statements are true for all of us sometime or other, please go by what is true for you, often. Please BASE your Score, in general, on Work Situations and place it in the box:

Not true for	(1)	☐	Generally true of me	(3)	☐ Sometimes true of me
	(2)	☐	Nearly always true for me	(4)	☐
Always completely true	(5)	☐			

1	☐	I tell others firmly, how they should behave.
2	☐	I think deliberately, before carrying out a job.
3	☐	I carry out jobs as per instructions of my superiors.
4	☐	I show sympathy towards people having problems.
5.	☐	I enjoy the company of other people.
6.	☐	I take care of others' needs.
7.	☐	I am systematic/logical, in doing things.
8.	☐	I give instructions to others, on how to do their job properly.
9.	☐	I express my feelings to others, without feeling embarrassed about it.
10.	☐	I am comfortable only when I practise usual etiquette, towards people.

The results of these instruments are used for managing employee behaviour and in general human resources. Thus, organizational behaviour concepts are used in human resource management as in case of using the properties of Physics by engineers and use of engineering data for testing the theories of Physics.

Interactive Analysis of Three Levels

Organisational behaviour deals with the human behaviour at three levels viz., individual level, group level and organisational level.

Organisational behaviour deals with the human behaviour at three levels, viz., individual level, group level and organizational level. In addition, it also deals with the influence of each level of behaviour on other levels. In other words it deals with the influence of individual behaviour on group behaviour and *vice-versa*. If also deals with individual behaviour on organizational behaviour and *vice-versa* in addition to influencing group behaviour on organizational behaviour and *vice-versa*. Individuals can't act on their own as human beings are social animals and interact with others in the society. In addition, they behave according to the social norms, values and ethics. For example, if the norm of a society is to follow the elders, though they are incompetent or wrong, employees of such societies prefer to follow the instructions of the superior even though superior is incompetent or wrong. Similarly, groups take care of individual values and norms of their members into consideration, before shaping the group values and norms as well as group behaviour.

Groups' and individuals' behaviour influences the behaviour of the individuals in the organization. In other words, organisation's values and norms are determined by the norms of various groups and individuals operating in it. In addition, organizations also influence the groups' and individuals' norms and values. For example, the same individual behaves differently in a public sector orgnization and in a private sector organization. Employees in public sector organization do not exert all their resources for the contribution of organizational goals where-as the same employees, if join a private sector organization, exert their resources for the organisation's performance.

Thus, organizational behaviour analyses human behaviour in an integrated, unified and comprehensive manner of the three levels as presented in Fig. 11.5.

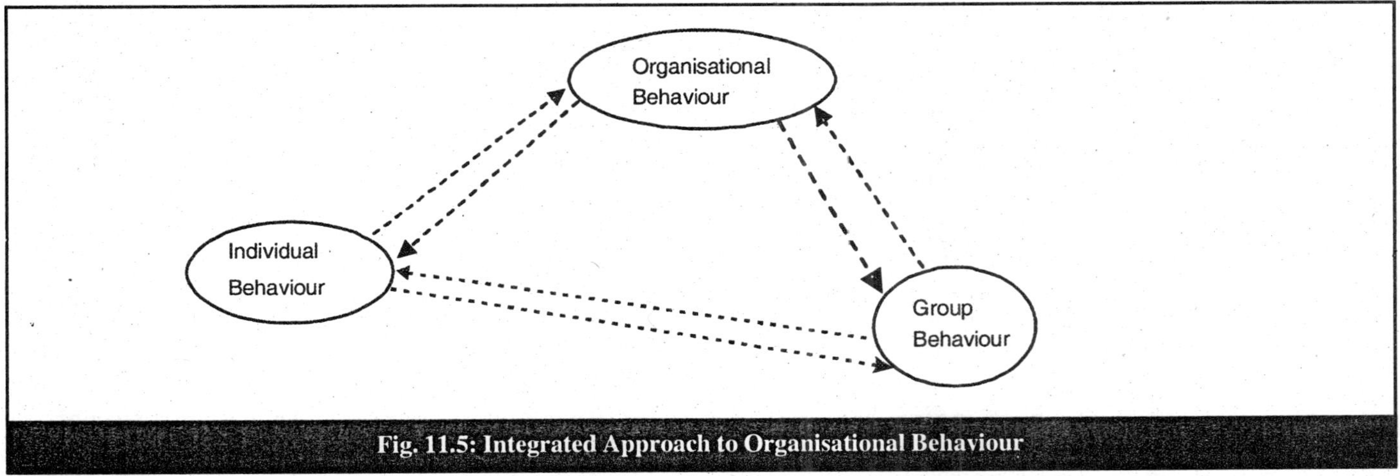

Fig. 11.5: Integrated Approach to Organisational Behaviour

Quality of Work Life and Organizational Behaviour

Employees at the grass roots level experience a sense of frustration because of low level of wages, poor working conditions, unfavourable terms of employment, inhuman treatment by their superiors and the like whereas managerial personnel feel frustrated because of alienation over their conditions of employment, interpersonal conflicts, role conflicts, job pressures, lack of freedom in work, absence of challenging work, etc.

Certain values were attributed to work in the past. Work was worship and people had sincerity and commitment to work. But today's employee would not believe in such values of work. He works for his salary, he works hard if the conditions of work are conducive and congenial and terms of employment are favourable to him. As such, the work norms have been changing from time-to-time.

Work norms in modern industrial society indicate that *(i)* employee's role in industry is different from his role in the family, *(ii)* superior knows the best and he has the right to impose on the subordinates, *(iii)* rules are for employees and they have to follow them, and *(iv)* employer has the right to layoff the workers due to marketing and technological factors.

Employees also experience alienation which may result from poor design of socio-technical systems. Alienation is a feeling of powerlessness, lack of meaning, loneliness, boredom, lack of ego, involvement and lack of attachment to job.[1] The workers at the lower level are not happy with their work due to tight schedule, speed of machine, close watch and supervision and less social interaction. Even the ministerial staff complain that they are unhappy with the job due to routine nature of work and fixation of schedules, standards and targets. Thus, job discontent is due to the limited scope of the job, short cycle of operations, lack of opportunity to exercise discretion, initiative, existence of bureaucratic controls, oppressive supervision, low wages, poor working conditions, etc.

Job discontent and job pressures have their substantial effect on employees' health in the form of reduction in general happiness, increase in smoking, drinking, putting on excess body weight, etc. Frustration would further cause heart disease, joint pain, etc. Frustration might also be due to absence of recognition, tedious work, unsound relations with co-workers, poor working conditions, low self-esteem, occupational stress, work overload, monotony, fatigue, time pressures, lack of stability, security, etc. In view of the contemporary managerial problems, the present day employees are much concerned about high wages, better benefits, challenging job, etc.

Quality of work life improvements are defined as any activity which takes place at every level of an organisation, which seeks greater organisational effectiveness through the enhancement of human dignity and growth ... a process through which the stockholders in the organisation — management, unions and employees — learn how to work together better to determine for themselves what actions, changes and improvements are desirable and workable in order to achieve the twin and simultaneous goals of an improved quality of life at work for all members of the organisation and greater effectiveness for both the company and the unions.

Organisational behaviour deals with various aspects of quality of work life like frustration, alienation, employee relations, self-esteem and the like.

Organisational Behaviour and Organisational Effectiveness

Though we use the term 'organisational effectiveness' more often, it is rather difficult to define the term precisely. This is because; the finance manager equates effectiveness with return on investment or market capitalization while the marketing manager equates effectiveness with increase in sales. The human resources managers prefer to mean effectiveness with employee satisfaction while Research and Development Managers mean effectiveness to innovations. However, there are certain comprehensive definitions on effectiveness.

According to Amitai Etizioni, effectiveness is "the degree to which an organisation realizes its goals." Paul E. Mott defines effectiveness as, "the ability of an organisation to mobilize its centres of power for action — production and adaptation." Thus, organisational effectiveness is more concerned with the achievement of organisational objectives. The term efficiency is used quite closely to project effectiveness.

Organisational behaviour helps to understanding, predicting and managing human behaviour, in such a way that such managed behaviour contributes to the achievement of organizational goals. Thus, organisational behaviour contributes to the organizational effectiveness.

Individual Behaviour

Behaviour of an individual employee is influenced by several factors like the individual's mental make-up, family background, educational background, social and cultural background, geographical region, personality traits, values, attitudes, opinions, etc. Individual behaviour is studied through perception, personality, values, attitudes, job satisfaction and motivation.

Behaviour of an individual employee is influenced by several factors.

- **Perception** refers to a complex cognitive process that yields a unique picture of the world that may be quite different from reality. Individuals behave in accordance with their perceptual world or impressions.
- **Personality** is the sum total of ways in which an individual reacts and interacts with others. Hereditary factors, environmental factors and situational factors determine personality.
- **Values** are the basic convictions that a "specific mode of conduct or end-state of existence is personally or socially preferable to an opposite or converse mode of conduct or end-state of existence."[9]
- **Attitudes** are evaluative statements – either favourable or unfavourable — concerning objects, people or events.
- **Job satisfaction** refers to a person's feeling of satisfaction on the job, which acts as a motivation to work.
- **Motivation** is the process that account for an individual's intensity, direction and "persistence of effort toward attaining a goal".
- **Learning** is relatively a process of effecting permanent change in behaviour that occurs as a result of experience.

Group Behaviour

An integrated and comprehensive behaviour of people in a group is referred to as *group behaviour*. Group behaviour is studied through group dynamics, teams, communication, power and politics, leadership and decision-making.

An integrated and comprehensive behaviour of people in a group is referred to as *group behaviour*.

- **Group Dynamics:** Groups are formed with a specific purpose. They exist for some time until the purpose is achieved and then disband or adjourn. Groups are both formal and informal. Other types of groups include: command groups, task groups, interest groups and friendship groups. Groups behave and function based on its norms.
- **Teamwork:** Teamwork is a group whose individual efforts result in a performance that is greater than the sum of the individual inputs. Different types of teams include: problem solving teams, self-managed work teams, cross-functional teams and virtual teams.
- **Power and Politics:** Power refers to the ability of the people to acquire resources and award them to various people in organisations.
- **Communication:** Communication is transferring of information and understanding the meaning of it. Communication may be formal or informal, downward, upward, horizontal and cross-wise.

- **Leadership:** Leadership is the ability to influence and guide a group towards achieving the preset goals. Leadership styles include autocratic, benevolent autocratic, participative and democratic style.
- **Decision-making:** Decision-making is developing alternative solutions to a problem and selecting the best solution from among the alternatives available.

Organisational Factors

Organisational structure is dividing, grouping and coordinating the job tasks. Job tasks may be structured with respect to departments, functions, geographical areas, products or services.

- **Organisational Theory:** Organisational theory refers to various models of structuring various activities in relation to work and jobs in order to build relationships among people, goals, etc.
- **Organisational Design:** Organisational design is formulating the philosophy for coordinating the job tasks. One philosophy is narrow bandwidth which results in narrow and specialised jobs. Narrow bandwidth is a common characteristic of tall organisations. Another philosophy is wider bandwidth which leads to flat structures.
- **Organisational Culture:** Organisational culture is a "pattern of basic assumption — invented, discovered or deployed by a given group as it learns to cope with its problems of external adaptation and internal integration — that has worked well enough to be considered valuable and, therefore, to be taught to new members as the correct way to perceive, think and feel in relation to those problems."[12]
- **Organisational Effectiveness:** Organisational effectiveness refers to selecting the right objectives and goals depending upon the environment and social goals of the country in which the company is operating.

Organisational Behaviour

Organisational behaviour is studying the behaviour of individuals and groups. Organisational behaviour studies the behaviour systematically, how people behave under a variety of situations and conditions. It also studies why people behave as they do. Thus, it identifies the reasons for the behaviour.

Organisational behaviour predicts the future behaviour of employees. Managers predict the future behaviour of employees as per the past behaviour of the employees, employee traits, values and future situations.

If the predicted behaviour is not in accordance with the requirements of organisational strategies, managers mould the employee behaviour towards organisational requirements by changing the reward system, organizational structure, leadership pattern and styles, group norms, etc. Thus, managers manage the overall behaviour of the employees in an organisation.

(F) SIGNIFICANCE OF ORGANISATIONAL BEHAVIOUR

The difference between two organizations is attributed to the commitment, attitude, aptitude, values, norms and performance of employees.

The difference between two organizations is attributed to the commitment, attitude, aptitude, values, norms and performance of employees. These factors along with other factors determine the human behaviour. The other factors include social, cultural, political, economic and structural. All these factors influence the behaviour of human resources.

Human Behaviour and Human Resources

Human resources play a crucial role in the development process of modern economics. Arthur Lewis observed "there are great differences in development between countries which seem to have roughly equal resources, so it is necessary to enquire into the difference in human behaviour." It is often felt that, though the exploitation of natural resources, availability of physical and financial resources and international aid play prominent roles in the growth of modern economies, none of these factors is more significant than efficient and committed human resource. It is in fact, said that all development comes from the human behaviour.

Human Behaviour in the Nation's Well-being

A nation with abundance of physical resources will not benefit itself unless human resources make use of them. In fact human resources are solely responsible for making use of national resources and for the transformation of traditional economies into the modern and industrial economies. Lack of organisation of human resources is largely responsible for the backwardness of the nation.[14] Countries are underdeveloped because their people's behaviours are inappropriate for economic development. In essence, "the difference in the level of economic development of the countries is largely a reflection of the differences in the types of their behaviour...."[15] The key element in this proposition is that the values, attitudes, commitment, aptitude, general orientation and quality of the people of a country determine its economic development. The shift from manufacturing to service and from service to knowledge and the increasing pace of technological upgradation are making human behaviour the ingredient of the nation's well-being and growth.[16]

Human Behaviour and Organisational Performance

Organisational performance can be measured against organizational objectives like market share, rate of profit, product innovation, customer satisfaction and employee satisfaction. Appropriate human behaviour contributes to the employees' commitment towards organizational goals. In effect, employee values, attitude and other behavioural issues shape the employee behaviour that would be appropriate for achieving organizational performance. Thus, appropriate human behaviour contributes for the organizational performance.

Strategy is a unified, comprehensive and integrated course of plan/action. Crafting and implementing strategy depend on employee commitment to organizational strategies. Employee commitment in its turn depends on appropriate leadership style, human values, self-motivation, appropriate perception and learning. Thus, behavioural issues of employees determine the level of success in crafting and achieving organizational strategies.

Appropriate and adaptable human behaviour enables the organization to develop employee commitment to the orgnisational strategies. In addition, appropriate behaviour encourages the employees to acquire and develop required hard skills like technical skills, knowledge and competency. Organisations do also invest in the development of technical skills and knowledge of those employees whose behaviour is quite appropriate for the achievement of organizational strategies. Thus, appropriate behaviour provides an opportunity for the development of distinctive competence of employees that enable them to craft and achieve distinctive strategies.

Human Behaviour and Strategic Advantages

Strategic advantages include achieving low cost advantage, high quality, superior customer service, innovations and superior speed in producing and delivering a product/ service. Committed employees with appropriate technical skills contribute to achieve highest human efficiency, which in turn makes the operations at the lowest cost. In addition, the committed minds contribute to innovation and other strategic advantages like superior customer service and superior speed. Thus, appropriate human behaviour contributes for building up of strategic advantages of the firms.

Human Behaviour and Efficient Human Resource Management

Appropriate human behaviour helps for positive and efficient human resource management in terms employee satisfaction, fair treatment of employees, training and continuous learning, performance management, employee counselling, mentoring, building teams, congenial superior-subordinate relations as well as human relations, sound salary and benefits. Thus, appropriate behaviour brings about efficient management of human resources.

Thus, appropriate human behaviour helps not only efficient human resource management but also envisages strategic management which ultimately leads to achieving high level of organizational performance.

KEY TERMS

- Globalisation
- Information Technology
- Structures
- Diversity in Human Resources
- Organisational Behaviour
- Economic Man
- Individual Behaviour
- Group Behaviour
- Benchmarking
- Manage Behaviour
- Psychology
- Management
- Economics
- Predict Behaviour
- Nature of Man
- Human Behaviour
- Anthropology
- TQM
- Political Science
- Models of Man
- Sociology

QUESTIONS

1. What are the similarities and dissimilarities among individuals?
2. Why do people behave and act differently in various situations?
3. Discuss various models of man with their implication on organisational behaviour.
4. Explain the factors that magnified the significance of organisational behaviour.
5. What is diversity in human resource? How does it affect human behaviour?
6. Define the term organisational behaviour. Explain the features of organisational behaviour.
7. Explain the relationship between strategic management and organisational behaviour.
8. Analyse the contributions of various disciplines to organisational behaviour.
9. Discuss the nature of man. Explain various models of man in detail.

REFERENCES

1. Michael Hammer and James Champy, "*Reengineering the Corporation:A Manifesto for Business Revolution*," Harper Collins, New York, 1993, p. 32.
2. Fred Luthans, "*Organisational Behaviour*," McGraw Hill, Boston, 1998, p. 36.
3. Jeffery Pfeffer, "*Competitive Advantage Through People*," Harvard Business School, Boston, 1994.
4. Mark A.Huselid, "*The Impact of Human Resource Management Practices on Turnover, Productivity and Corporate Financial Performance*," Academy of Management Journal, 1995, pp. 635-672.
5. John W.Newstorm and Keith Davis, "*Organisational Behaviour*," Tata McGraw Hill Publishing Company Ltd., New Delhi, 1998, p. 5.

6. Stephen P.Robbins, "*Organisational Behaviour*," Prentice Hall of India (P) Ltd., New Delhi, 2000, p. 6.
7. Steven L.McShane and Mary Ann Von Glinow, "*Organisational Behaviour*," Tata McGraw Hill Publishing Co.Ltd., New Delhi, 2001, p. 4.
8. Fred Luthans, *op.cit.*, p. 16.
9. Debra L. Nelson and James C. Quick, "*Organizational Behaviour*", Thomson, New Delhi, 2008, p.6.
10. H.B. Elikind, "Preventive Management: Mental Hygiene in Industry", B.C. Forbes, New York, 1931.
11. J.C. Quick, "Occupational Health Psychology: Historical Roots and Future Directions, Health Psychology,18, 1999.
12. M.Roxeach, "*The Nature of Human Values*," Free Press, New York, 1973, p. 5.
13. Edgar H.Schein, "*Organisational Culture and Leadership*," Jossey-Bass, San Francisco, 1985, p. 9.
14. Lewis Arthur, *The History of Economic Growth*, George Allen & Urwin Ltd., London, 1965, p. (ii).
15. Leon C. Megginson, *Personnel,* Richard D. Irwin Inc., Home-wood, Illinois, 1972, p. 14.
16. Myrdal Gunnar, *Asian Drama*, Penguin Books Ltd., Middlesex, 1968.

CHAPTER 12

VALUES, ATTITUDES, EMOTIONS, MOODS AND JOB SATISFACTION

Chapter Outline

(A) Values
(B) Attitudes
(C) Emotions and Moods
(D) Job Satisfaction
— Key Terms
— Questions
— References

Learning Objectives

After studying this Chapter, you should be able to:

✓ Understand the meaning, significance and values;
✓ Analyse the values in different cultures;
✓ Explain the meaning of attitudes and functions of attitudes;
✓ Comment on the changes in attitudes and enabling factors;
✓ Explain the theory and meaning of job satisfaction; and
✓ Analyse the factors affecting job satisfaction.

(A) VALUES

Most of the Westerners consume beef which is personally and socially preferable by them. Indians, particularly Hindus, do not normally consume beef as the basic conviction is that cows are God and they give milk. This basic conviction is personally and socially preferable to Hindus because it is the value of Hindus treating the cow as a sacred animal that dissuades them from consuming beef.

One of the food processing companies defends its action of using apple essence rather than actual apple in its products as the action results in less cost and competitive advantage. This company says: "earning profit by any means is our value." This company believes that the end state of earning profit for existence is its value. These two examples give you a general idea of what value is? Now, we shall discuss the formal definition of value.

Meaning of Values

Rokeach defines values as "basic convictions that a specific mode of conduct or end-state of existence is personally or socially preferable to an opposite or converse mode of conduct or end state of existence."[1]

We can draw the characteristics of values based on this definition. They are:

- Values contain a judgmental element.
- It carries individual or group ideas regarding which is good, is bad and which is preferable.
- Conduct or end-state of existence is important as it has content attributes.
- It also has an intensity attribute which specifies how important the conduct or end-state of existence is.
- Individual's value in terms of intensity can be ranked, which is called *value system*.

Value System

Value system is a hierarchy based on the ranking of an individual's value in terms of their intensity. This system is identified by the relative importance assigned to such values as freedom, pleasure, self-respect, honesty, obedience and equality.[2] Values tend to be relatively stable and enduring.[3]

Value system is a hierarchy based on the ranking of an individual's value in terms of their intensity.

Significance of Values

Values play a significant role in organisational behaviour. Values are the basis for the study of:

- Attitudes,
- Perception,
- Motivation,
- Morale,
- Formation of preconceived notions, and
- Satisfaction and frustration

Values indicate the preferred behaviour of the employee in the organisation over others. (See Box 12.1) For example, organisations prefer the employees to be innovative and creative on the job rather than doing the routine work. Similarly, organisations prefer the employees at work during the working hours and not in the canteen. This value system indicates how the employees should behave.

Box 12.1: Traditional Values Keep TATAs' Going....

The redoubtable Ratan Tata was awarded the Outstanding Businessman of the Year award by the Mumbai-based Indian Merchant Chamber.

Ratan Tata not just runs one of the biggest and most professional groups in the country, but he also has managed (God knows how) to keep the legendary Tata values alive. Indeed, over the past three years, Tata has been constantly raising the bat across group companies, disbanding cliques, pushing senior executives to do better, and focusing on shareholder value. Tata has been continuing the same old values set from the very inception. The maximum concern of values include maximistation of shareholders' wealth, giving maximum value to the customers for their money, giving the society back its due share and acting as a good corporate citizen.

One of the most spectacular effects of that is the turnaround at Tata Steel, which made Ratan proud by recently bagging the National Award for Excellence in Corporate Governance. Tata's maxim: Compete on a global basis.

(**Source:** Ratan Tata, Chairman, Tata Group, *Business Today*, April 21, 2001.)

Values influence attitudes and behaviour.[4] Normally employees view that promotions are based on either merit or seniority or merit-cum-seniority. But the employees tend to be frustrated when they know that the promotions in an organisation are based on reservations.

Thus, the values help to form attitudes, perceptions, morale and determine employee behaviour in an organisation.

Types of Values

Values which influence different areas of behaviour are classified into terminal values and instrumental values by Milton Rokeach in his *Rokeach Value Survey.*

- Terminal values refer to desirable end-states of existence. Individuals would like to achieve these values during his/her lifetime.
- Instrumental values refer to preferable modes of behaviour or means of achieving the terminal values.[5]

Exhibit 12.1 presents the terminal and instrumental values in this survey.

Exhibit 12.1 Terminal and Instrumental Values in Rokeach Value Survey

Terminal Values	Instrumental Values
A comfortable life (a prosperous life)	Ambitious (hardworking, aspiring)
An exciting life (a stimulating, active life)	
A sense of accomplishment (lasting contribution)	
A world at peace (free of war and conflict)	
A world of beauty (beauty of nature and the arts)	
Equality (brotherhood, equal opportunity for all)	
Family security (taking care of loved ones)	
Freedom (independence, free choice)	
Happiness (contentedness)	
Inner harmony (freedom from inner conflict)	
Mature love (sexual and spiritual intimacy)	
National love (protection from attack)	
Pleasure (an enjoyable, leisurely life)	
Salvation (saved, eternal life)	
Self-respect (self-esteem)	
Social recognition (respect, admiration)	
True friendship (close compnionship)	
Wisdom (a mature understanding of life)	

(**Source:** M. Rokeach, *The Nature of Human Values* (New York: The Free Press, 1973).

It is confirmed by different studies that *Rokeach Value Survey's* values vary among groups. People in the same occupations or categories tend to hold similar values.[6] Exhibit 12.2 presents mean value ranking of executives, union members and activists.

Shalom Schwartz's Value Classification

Shalom Schwartz classified values under four major categories viz., openness to change, conservation, self-transcendence and self-enhancement. Openness to change implies that a person thinks differently, innovatively and creatively. The person is self-motivated, self-stimulated, excited and self-directed. Conservation is opposite to openness to change. Conservation indicates that a person prefers status quo and he/she maintains conformity to social values, norms and expectations, security (safety and stability) and tradition (preservation of status quo). Self-transcendence refers to promotion of welfare of others and nature. It indicates the benevolence (concern for others) and universalism (concern for all people and nature). Self-enhancement is opposite to self-transcendence and it indicates that a person is motivated by self-interest (achievement of personal goals) and acquiring power to dominate others. These values are applicable to individuals as well as for organizations.[7]

Shalom Schwartz classified values under four major categories viz., openness to change, conservation, self-transcendence and self-enhancement.

Value Congruence

Value congruence is the situation where the values of two units are similar. Normally, personal values of individual employees and organizational values vary. Employees under such situations have various options like tendering job resignation, modifying personal values to suit organizational values and influencing the top management/strategic managers of the organization to change the organizational values to individual personal values of majority of the employees. The last two options result in value congruence.

Value congruence is the situation where the values of two units are similar.

Mr. Pratap has joined as the procurement officer of South-Pacific International Hospital in June 2009. He is from a traditional Hindu family from Bangalore and has grown in a traditional society and developed a value of honesty and non-corruptive. In other words, he never offered bribing to others as well as he never accepted any kind of bribe, whatsoever. He faced a conflicting value situation when he imported medical equipment for his hospital from India. The operations manager, his superior, informed him the value of custom officials is that they release the medical equipment in one month, if no bribe is offered and alternatively, they release the medical equipment in 24 hours if appropriate bribe is offered. Therefore, the South-Pacific Hospital offers bribe to custom officials in the airport in order to get the medical equipment released in 24 hours in order to save the lives of patients who are in critical condition. Mr. Pratap after evaluating the nature of the company where he is currently working and knowing a few situations where the patients died in the past when the South-Pacific International Hospital followed the value of non-corruption changed his value. This shift to suit the individual values with organizational value is called value congruence. Individual values and organizational values mostly differ. As many as 76% of executives in a study expressed that conflicts between their values and organizational values exist. The prospective managers in a study indicated that they will have to take business decisions that conflict with their individual values so as to safeeguard organisational interests.[8]

Values in Different Cultures

Cultures vary from country to country due to variations in climatic conditions, economic conditions, physical security issues and the like. Culture, in turn, influences the formation, development and maintenance of values. Since the cultures vary across the globe, values also vary accordingly.

Cultures vary from country to country due to variations in climatic conditions, economic conditions, physical security issues and the like.

Exhibit 12.2 Mean Value Ranking of Executives, Union Members, and Activists (Top Five Only)

Executives		Union Members		Activists	
Terminal	**Instrumental**	**Terminal**	**Instrumental**	**Terminal**	**Instrumental**
1. Self-respect	1. Honest	1. Family security	1. Responsible	1. Equality	1. Honest
2. Family	2. Responsible	2. Freedom	2. Honest	2. A world of peace	2. Helpful
3. Freedom	3. Capable	3. Happiness	3. Courageous	3. Family security	3. Courageous
4. A sense of accomplishment	4. Ambitious	4. Self-respect	4. Independent	4. Self-respect	4. Responsible
5. Happiness	5. Independent	5. Mature love	5. Capable	5. Freedom	5. Capable

(**Source:** M. Rokeach, *The Nature of Human Values* (New York: The Free Press, 1973).

Geert Hofstede surveyed more than 116,000 IBM employees in 40 countries about their work-related cultures. He classified the values into five categories based on his survey. They are: power distance, individualism vs. collectivism, quantity of life vs. quality of life, uncertainty avoidance and long-term vs. short-term orientation.[7]

- ***Power Distance:*** It is a national culture attribute describing the extent to which a society accepts that power is distributed unequally in institutions and organisations. Equal power distribution is called low power distance and extremely unequal power distribution is called high power distance.
- ***Individualism vs. Collectivism:*** Individualism is the degree to which people in a country prefer to act as individuals rather than a member of a group. Low individualism is collectivism.[8]
- ***Quantity of Life vs. Quality of Life:*** Quantity of life is the degree to which values like assertiveness, the acquisition of money and material goods and competition. Quality of life is the degree to which people value relationships and show sensitivity and concern for the welfare of others.[9]
- ***Uncertainty Avoidance:*** It is the degree to which people in a country prefer structured over unstructured situations. People with high score on uncertainty avoidance have increased level of anxiety resulting in greater nervousness, stress and aggressiveness.
- ***Long-Term vs. Short-Term Orientation:*** Long-term orientation is a national culture attribute that emphasises the future, thrift and persistence. Short-term orientation is a national culture attribute that emphasises the past and present, respect for tradition and fulfilling social obligation. People with short-term orientation emphasises on tradition and fulfilling social obligations.[10] Exhibit 12.3 presents rating of these five dimensions in different countries.

Exhibit 12.3 indicates the cultural dimensions in different countries. Power distance is high in China, France, Russia, West Africa, etc. This indicates that power is distributed unequally in these countries whereas it is distributed equally in USA, Netherlands and Germany as the power distance is low.

People work as individuals in France, Germany and USA, as individualism is high in these countries. People work in groups in China, Indonesia, West Africa and Japan.

Exhibit 12.3 Examples of Cultural Dimensions

Power Country	Distance	Quantity Individualism	Uncertainty of Life	Long-Term Avoidance	Orientation
China	High	Low	Moderate	Moderate	High
France	High	Low	Moderate	High	Low
Germany	Low	High	High	Moderate	Moderate
Hong Kong	High	Low	High	Low	High
Indonesia	High	Low	Moderate	Low	Low
Japan	Moderate	Moderate	High	Moderate	Moderate
Netherlands	Low	High	Low	Moderate	Moderate
Russia	High	Moderate	Low	High	Low
United States	Low	High	High	Low	Low
West Africa	High	Low	Moderate	Moderate	Low

(**Source:** M. Rokeach, *The Nature of Human Values* (New York: The Free Press, 1973).

People prefer quantity of life in Germany and USA to quality life and the vice versa is true in case of Netherlands, Russia and China. People of France and Russia have increased level of anxiety, stress and aggressiveness and the opposite is true in case of USA, Hong Kong and Indonesia.

People in China and Hong Kong have future value thrift and persistence while people of West Africa, USA, Russia and Japan emphasise on fulfilling social obligations.

Having analysed the values in various countries, now we shall discuss the next concept, i.e. attitudes.

(B) ATTITUDES

"*Attitudes are evaluative statements – either favourable or unfavourable – concerning objects, people or events. They reflect how one feels about something.*"[11] Attitudes and values are interrelated.

Attitudes are evaluative statements – either favourable or unfavourable – concerning objects, people or events. They reflect how one feels about something.

We often listen to a number of statements like:

Our boss is highly humanistic.... Management of Southern Automobiles Limited shows unconcern towards its employees.... Treatment in Usha Hospitals is excellent.... Operations of Rediffmail.com are extremely fast.

The analysis of above statements indicates that they are evaluative of either favourable or unfavourable or good or bad of people, objects or events. This is the meaning of attitude. Now, we shall understand the formal definition of attitude.

Mr. Bhat works in the Finance Department of Ruchi Foods. He always suggests for low quality raw material in order to reduce the cost of production. This practice of the company is labelled as an unethical practice by the customers, which in turn affected the quality of products of the company, performance of production and marketing departments, sales and profitability. Then the Production Manager and Marketing Manager of the company avoided Mr. Bhat in the process of decision-making.

Here, the belief that "being unethical is wrong," is the cognitive component of an attitude. Production and Marketing Managers of Ruchi Foods did not like Mr. Bhat as the latter suggests unethical practices. This stage is the effective component of an attitude. Affect is the emotional or feeling segment of an attitude. Finally, the avoidance of Mr. Bhat in the decision-making process is the outcome which is called behavioural component of an attitude.

Thus, the components of the attitude are:

- **Cognitive**: Cognitive component of an attitude is the opinion or belief segment.
- **Affective**: Affective component of an attitude is the emotional or feeling segment.
- **Behavioural**: Behavioural component of an attitude is an intention to behave in a certain way towards someone or something.

Attitudes and Behaviour

The above example clearly indicates that attitudes determine the behaviour. So we can predict and understand that the behaviour of people is based on attitudes. They are comparatively less stable than values. Producing low cost product is viewed as ethical as the low income customers get the opportunity to consume it. For example, Akai and Aiwa produced colour TVs at ₹.10,000 when other companies produced at around ₹20,000. This provided an opportunity to low income group people to buy colour TVs.

Employees follow the orders of their boss, if they have positive attitude towards their boss. Attitudes are more important as they affect and determine job behaviour. Positive attitudes result in positive behaviour and vice versa. Management should develop positive attitudes among employees in view of positive relationship between attitudes and behaviour.

Attitudes of creative people include: curiosity, seeing problems as interesting and acceptable, confronting challenge, constructive discontent, optimism, suspending judgment, etc. (See Box 12.2).

Box 12.2: Nine Attitudes of Highly Creative People

1. Curiosity

I've written previously on the topic of curiosity because I'm convinced that it is an essential skill to build as a blogger. Learning to ask 'why', 'what if' and 'I wonder...' are great questions to build into your life if you want to be a more creative person.

2. Seeing Problems as Interesting and Acceptable

One of the problems of the Western mindset is that we often see problems or obstacles in life as unacceptable parts of life. We avoid pain or suppress it when it comes and in doing so don't often see and feel symptoms that are there to tell us something important. Creative people see problems as a natural and normal part of life - in fact they often have a fascination with problems and are drawn to them.

3. Confronting Challenge

Many of the most creative ideas throughout history have come from people facing a challenge or crisis and rather than running from it asking 'how can I overcome this'?

4. Constructive Discontent

Creative people often have an acute awareness of what's wrong with the world around them - however they are constructive about this awareness and won't allow themselves to get bogged down in grumbling about it - they take their discontent and let it be a motivation to doing something constructive.

5. Optimism

Creative people generally have a deeply held belief that most (if not all) problems can be solved. No challenge is too big to be overcome and no problem cannot be solved (this doesn't mean they're always happy or never depressed - but they don't generally get stumped by a challenge).

6. Suspending Judgment

The ability to hold off on judging or critiquing an idea is important in the process of creativity. Often great ideas start as crazy ones - if critique is applied too early the idea will be killed and never developed into something useful and useable. (note - this doesn't mean there is never a time for critique or judgement in the creative process - it's actually key - but there is a time and place for it).

7. Seeing Hurdles as leading to improvements and solutions

This relates to some of the above - but by 'hurdles' I mean problems and mistakes in the creative process itself. Sometimes it's on the journey of developing an idea that the real magic happens and it's often out of the little problems or mistakes that the idea is actually improved.

8. Perseverance

Creative people who actually see their ideas come to fruition have the ability to stick with their ideas and see them through - even when the going gets tough. This is what sets apart the great from the good in this whole sphere. Stickability is key.

9. Flexible Imagination

I love watching a truly creative person at work when they're 'on fire'. They have this amazing ability to see a problem or challenge and it's many potential solutions simultaneously and they have an intuitive knack at being able to bring previously disconnected ideas together in flashes of brilliance that seem so simple - yet which are so impossible to dream up for the average person.

Is Creativity tied to Personality Type or Can it be Learned?

As I read through this list of traits of creative people - the question that I find myself asking is whether creativity is tied to personality type or whether it can be learned.

My own uneducated answer to this question is - 'yes'.

Some people are just creative - they don't train themselves to think like they do and they often don't even know that they are any different from the rest of us - it's just who they are.

However I believe that we can all enhance our ability to be creative over time.

Tomorrow I'm going to round off this mini-series of posts on creativity by suggesting a few practical things that those of us wanting to enhance our creativity might build into our lives.

http://www.problogger.net/archives/2007/05/09/9-attitudes-of-highly-creative-people/(Accessed on 13/08/09)

Attitudes influence behaviour by performing several functions. Now, we shall discuss these functions.

Functions of Attitudes

A study of the functions of attitudes is necessary as attitudes influence behaviour of employees at work.

- The study of attitudes help in predicting employee behaviour at work. For example, retrenchment of one employee led to resignations of many employees in Prudential Capital and Investments Limited due to negative attitude towards retrenchment.
- The study of attitudes is significant as it helps the people adapt to their work environment.

According to Katz, attitudes perform four important functions in this process.[12]

(i) **The Adjustment Function:** Employees form positive attitudes towards their superiors when their expressed and unexpressed problems are solved by the superiors. For example, increase in salary, help in promotions, training, coaching, providing transport facilities, health facilities, counselling facilities, maintaining social and human relations. Positive attitudes help the employees to adjust to the organisation and to the jobs and *vice versa.*

(ii) **The Ego-Defensive Function:** Attitudes help the people in defending their self-images and serve in justifying the action and defending the ego.

Mr. Iyyer, Manager of Hewlett-Packard (HP) India, always argues with Mr. Badal, his subordinate. Sometimes he picks up a quarrel with him, whenever the latter proposes innovative ideas. He tells him that his ideas are trash and irrelevant. Mr.Badal on the other hand challenges the arguments of Mr. Iyyer saying that he has outdated and traditional views when he proposes innovative ideas. These challenges and counter challenges are quite possible in HP as it provides transparency and empowerment in its administration.

Mr. Iyyer defends himself by believing and repeating his attitude that "boss is always right." Mr. Badal, on the other hand, defends himself by repeating his attitude that, "youth is more innovative as far as information technology is concerned."

(iii) **The Value-Expressive Function:** Attitudes provide the employees with a basis for expressing their values.

Mr. Pratap's (of Reebok) value is that the product should be designed around the desirability of the customer rather than exciting to the customer. He tells his subordinates, "the company lives for long-time and grows steadily by serving more desirable needs of the customer not not by creating excitement."

(iv) **The Knowledge Function:** Trade Union Leaders in A.P. Lighting Limited used to have a negative attitude towards management and therefore, they used to impress the workers that all management communications were false. Workers easily believed the trade union leaders, but not the management. Thus, the standard attitude of the trade union towards management frames of reference and allow the people to organise and explain the world around them.[13]

Attitudes which perform various functions are not static, they go on changing based on the changes in culture and values. Now, we shall discuss changing attitudes.

Changing Attitudes

We observe a few changes in the attitudes. Exhibit 4.4 presents the past and present attitudes.

The analysis of the past and present attitudes presented in the exhibit indicate that attitudes change faster than the culture.The old values protecting each economy through self-dependence is changed to self-reliance due to opening of the economy to the globe.

Management, of late have realised that people use their full potentiality only when they are provided with freedom.

Managements used to believe that bureaucratic organisations only enhance organisational effectiveness and profitabilty of the companies. But management, of late have realised that people use their full potentiality only when they are provided with freedom. This made managements to believe in the new attitude that organic and humanistic structures only make the companies more productive and profitable than bureaucratic organisations. (see Box 12.3).

Box 12.3: Shifts in Attitudes: Air India chargesheets airhostess in molestation case

Delhi, Oct. 29 — Air India's inquiry committee has charge sheeted airhostess Komal Singh, who had levelled molestation charges against two pilots, for violating the national carrier's conduct rule. "Singh has been issued a charge sheet for violation of conduct rule and for not complying with the company policy," an Air India spokesperson said on Thursday.

Air India had constituted the panel to investigate a scuffle between co-pilot Aditya Chopra and flight purser Amit Khanna onboard a Sharjah-Lucknow-Delhi flight on October 3. Singh, who alleged that the two pilots molested her in the cockpit, had lodged a police complaint against them. "She has also been accused of insubordination and disobeying seniors," said an airline official.

The committee was formed on October 6 to investigate the mid-air scuffle between co-pilot Aditya Chopra and flight purser Amit Khanna onboard a Sharjah-Lucknow-Delhi flight IC 884.

The five-member panel is headed by a senior woman and included the member of an NGO.

The National Commission for Women (NCW) which is also investigating the allegations of the airhostess, meanwhile, is apparently drawing a different conclusion. While its report is yet to be compiled, officials indicated that Singh was not on the "wrong side".

Source: http://in.news.yahoo.com/32/20091030/1053/tnl-ai-chargesheets-airhostess-in-molest_1.html (Accessed on 30/10/2009).

Thus, attitudes go on changing with the new knowledge developed based on research. (See Exhibit 12.4).

However, the process of attitudinal change is prevented by certain barriers.

Exhibit 12.4 Past and Present Attitudes

Sl. No.	*Past Attitudes*	*Present Attitudes*
1.	Economies need to be protected from the rest of the globe. As such tariffs and duties were imposed.	Economies need to be opened for enhancing the efficiency of the domestic economy. As such tariffs, quotes, etc. are removed and the concept of Globalisation is emerged.
2.	Bureaucratic organisational structures were best suitable.	Organic and humanistic structures are best suitable.
3.	Authority was centralized.	Authority is decentralized.
4	Management by control.	Management by autonomy and empowerment.
5	Workers work better as individuals.	Employees perform better as members of Teams.
6	Workers try to avoid the work.	Employees create the work and take it

Barriers to Attitudinal Change

There are two barriers which prevent the change process of attitudes. They are:

- **Prior Commitments:** Prior commitment occurs when people feel a commitment to a particular course of action and are unwilling to change.[14] For example, Mr. Kulkarni, President of Railway Trade Union who committed to the workers that he would get 100% salary hike in 1974 was reluctant to change his attitude even after learning that the company is financially weak.
- **Result of Inadequate Information:** Inadequate information does not allow the people to change their attitudes. Managers of Raymond used to say that they have changed to democratic style of working. But workers said, let the management prove it, as we do not have evidences to that effect.

However, the process of attitudinal change should be allowed to continue as world economy is rapidly changing. In fact, change is the order of the day in the 21st Century. There are certain measures which enable the change process.

Now, we shall discuss the measures those enabling measures of changing attitudes.

- **Providing Additional Information:** We recall the example of A.P. Lightings Limited. Trade Union leaders created a gap between the workers and Management. Management provided additional information to the workers through a third party, i.e., Consultant and changed the workers' attitude in its favour. Thus, the attitudes can be changed by providing additional information.
- **Use of Fear:** The staff of a private hospital were irregular to their duties as their attitude was: "Health facility is Seller's market." The Managing Director wanted to change the attitude of the doctors by creating terror, i.e., fear of retrenchment. Then the human resource manager suggested that staff may reject the message of retrenchment because it is too threatening. Hence, he advised the Managing Director to introduce a scheme of salary cut proportionate to the degree of irregularity. This scheme changed the attitudes of the staff. Thus, a proportionate degree of fear changes the attitudes.
- **Resolving discrepancies:** Canteen employees of IPCL resisted the automation and mechanization process in their canteen as they viewed that management would retrench the excessive staff. The human resource manager resolved the discrepancies through consultation and finally transferring the excessive staff to other departments. This made the workers change their attitude and welcomed the automation and mechanization process.

The theory of cognitive dissonance says that people try to actively reduce the dissonance by attitude and behaviour change.[15] Thus, resolving discrepancies enable the change process.

Influence of Friends and Peers: Mr. Satyanarayana of Hindustan Cables Limited had the attitude that "employees should exert all their energies for the company and behave ethically." He had a confrontation with many employees in the company as the behaviour of the latter were against to his attitude. His friends and peers in the company influenced him directly and indirectly and made him to change his attitude that "employees in public sector organisations do not exert all their energies for the company." Thus, friends and peers though persuation can change attitudes.

The Co-opting Approach: Ms. Mayawathi was always criticizing her boss — the Purchasing Manager in IPCL – for his delay in decision-making. Then the boss co-opted her in a committee for purchasing inputs. She experienced the procedural formalities and the controlling points in the bureaucracy. Since then she stopped criticizing her boss and changed her attitude towards the boss. Thus, co-opting means involving the people who are dissatisfied with a situation to understand the things and change their attitudes.

Human Resource is considered to be the most valuable asset in any organisation. It is the sum-total of inherent abilities, acquired knowledge and skills represented by the talents and aptitudes of the employed persons who comprise executives, supervisors and the rank and file employees. It may be noted here that human resources should be utilised to the maximum possible extent, in order to achieve individual and organisational goals. It is thus the employee's performance which ultimately decides and attainment of goals. However, the employee performance is to a large extent, influenced by motivation and job satisfaction.

(C) EMOTIONS AND MOODS

Emotions are reactions to a person's acts and the consequences of an event. Emotions include a feel of happiness, being glad, a feel of angry, a feel of surprise and a feel of suspicion.

Emotions are intense feelings that are directed at someone or something.[16] Moods are feelings that tend to be less intense than emotions and that often, though not always, lack a contextual stimulus.[17] Emotions are reactions to a person's acts and the consequences of an event. Emotions include a feel of happiness, being glad, a feel of angry, a feel of surprise and a feel of suspicion. A feel of surprise when you see your childhood friend, a feel of irritation when your wife becomes crazy over purchase of a gold belt for her whose cost is beyond your current ability to buy, angry over your subordinate who is hopelessly inefficient in grasping a new technique are some examples of emotions. Moods are not the consequences of persons' actions and events. (See Box 12.4).

Box 12.4: Emotions and Acts: Chicago Blackhawks F Kane arrested in Buffalo

Chicago Blackhawks star Patrick Kane(notes) was charged with attacking a cab driver in his hometown Sunday, a beating that police said was triggered when the driver did not have 20 cents in change to give the player and his cousin.

Buffalo police said the 20-year-old Kane and his 21-year-old cousin, James Kane, had apparently caught a cab from the city's downtown nightclub district at about 4 a.m. The cab driver suffered cuts to his face and his glasses were damaged, police spokesman Michael DeGeorge said.

Both men were charged with felony robbery and misdemeanor counts of theft of services and criminal mischief. Patrick Kane pleaded not guilty in City Court on Sunday, WIVB-TV reported. It was not immediately clear when James Kane will appear in court.

The driver said he was punched and hit by both men because he did not have 20 cents in change to give them, according to the police report. A message left at the home of Patrick Kane's parents was not immediately returned Sunday afternoon. Relatives who answered his grandfather's phone and his mother's cell phone declined to comment and could not say whether either Kane had an attorney. A Blackhawks' spokesman said the team is aware of the allegations against Kane.

> *"He is a big part of our organization and a team leader and we stand behind him," spokesman Brandon Faber said. "As we are still collecting all the facts, it would be premature to comment further at this time." On Thursday, Patrick Kane was at a Buffalo ice drink where he played hockey as a child to help Mayor Byron Brown announce funding for improvements. He said at the time he was happy to have time "to hang out back home in Buffalo."*
>
> *"The best thing about it is my friends treat me like I'm a regular kid," said Kane, the first overall pick in the 2007 NHL draft. "They don't treat me like a celebrity or whatever they might treat me like in Chicago."*

Source: http://www.google.com/hostednews/ap/article/ALeqM5jz7wxsbGjui3s-j8txZOhokXO1lwD99VIQC00 (Accessed on 12/08/09)

Thus, emotions are caused by specific events. They are very brief in duration, and normally lasts for a few seconds. Emotions are specific and numerous in nature like anger, fear, sadness, happiness, disgust, surprise, etc. Emotions are normally accompanied by distinct facial expressions and are action-oriented in nature. Moods are often caused by general and unclear factors or actions. Moods last longer than emotions, normally hours or days. Moods are more general and are normally not indicated by distinct expressions. Emotions are cognitive in nature.[16]

Affection, emotions and moods are interdependent on each other and inseparable in practice and/or experience. Affection is the broad range of feelings that people experience. Strong and deep emotions result in moods. For example, an emotion of happiness of salary hike would result in positive mood towards the job. Happiness of the salary hike may stay for some time, but the positive mood of the job would stay for longer until the change in other factors like increase in price, design of new jobs and development of new careers.

Types of Emotions: The result and experience of emotions can be of the following types:

- Anger
- Embarrassment
- Hate
- Jealousy
- Frustration
- Pride
- Wonder
- Sadness
- Disgust
- Surprise
- Joy
- Disappointment
- Love
- Hatred
- Contentment
- Happiness
- Hope
- Fear
- Enthusiasm
- Affection
- Desire

Aspects of Emotions

The aspects of emotions include: Biology of emotions, intensity, frequency and duration, and rationality of emotions.

The Biology of Emotions

Limbic system of brain is the source for all kinds of emotions.

Limbic system of brain is the source for all kinds of emotions.[18] Generally, inactive state of the limbic system produces happy state of emotions like joy, happy, contentment and satisfaction. Normally, active or "heats up" state of limbic system produces the emotions like anger, jealous, and guilt. Limbic system of all people may not work in the same phase. Limbic systems of moderately depressed people and women work actively or heats up when it encounters with negative information. As such women and relatively depressed people are more susceptible to depression than undepressed men. Hence, women and depressed men are more likely to be emotionally bonded.[19] Similarly, women are normally more depressed than men as limbic system of women works actively. It does not mean that all women are depressed and all men are free from depression.

Biological emotions, some time result some deals impulsive rather than compulsive. Consequently, some deals that are based on emotions may face the problems of sustainability and/or continuity.

Intensity

Different jobs require different kinds of emotions. For example, judges, pilots, traffic controllers, police officers and human resource managers are expected to control emotions and be calm. In contrast, lecturers, receptionists, public speakers, chief executive officers, political personalities and sales people are expected to express emotions relevant to the situation. Business executives exhibit their emotions towards politicians to control and manage the impact of political decisions/environmental factors on business. Box 12.5 presents the emotions of Chief Executives of certain companies with regard to the impact of Mr. Obama's policy decisions on their businesses. Thus, people express different emotions based on the job factors. Different people express different emotions for the same stimuli as their personality factors influence the process of generation of emotions. The outcome of emotions is the interaction between the personality factors of an individual and the job/situational factors.

Box 12.5: CEOs Emotions and Moods about Obama's Performance

To some top executives, President Barack Obama is "rapidly socializing the United States." Others see his initiatives on everything from healthcare reform to the saving of GM as crucial for sparing the U.S. from even deeper economic trouble. We quizzed numerous leaders of small, medium, and large companies on how they think the President has fared in his first six months in office. Some give him a failing grade; others, top marks. Read on to see what these business leaders think of the CEO-in-chief.

***Angela F. Braly:** CEO, WellPoint, the nation's biggest health insurer.*

Employers are struggling to provide health benefits while remaining competitive in the global economy and many Americans worry an illness will devastate their financial security. Both are already bearing the brunt of an existing cost shift to private insurers from Medicare and Medicaid. Unfortunately, many in Congress are proposing to shift the burden even further by expanding government-run health care. As Medicare shows us, a government-run health plan would not address the underlying issues of cost and quality. Case in point: Medicare is predicted to be bankrupt by 2017.

The President is doing the right thing by bringing in leaders from hospitals, physicians, nurses, employers, advocacy groups, and private insurers, among others. Only by working together will we be able to develop a sustainable solution for America's health care system.

***Michael S. Dell:** Founder and CEO, Dell*

There are some aspects of what is in the economic recovery act around broadband, healthcare, and IT spending that we think are good things. We're concerned, like many, that one word that seems to be missing from a lot of discussions is "competitiveness." How do all of these things make America more competitive? It's a word that should be used more in Washington.

***Mohamed El-Erian:** CEO and co-chief investment officer of Pimco*

The most interesting thing is the mess he inherited and the extent he has to pursue two different agendas Â—there's the agenda he came in with and the agenda to stabilize a rapidly imploding US economy. The big gamble is that he has tried to pursue both simultaneously. That's going to define his first term. So far the evidence is mixed. On one side he has been able to stabilize the financial centre and institute major structural reforms. And he still maintains enormous popularity with the American people.

On the negative side, the jobs picture is worse than anticipated, and unemployment itself is becoming a big policy challenge. It's going from being a lagging indicator to being a leading indicator. The major issue people are going to second guess in the next six months is his decision to pursue both agendas. Was that the right one or should have he done it sequentially?

He inherited a real mess, not just a mess, but one that requires him to make difficult decisions. I voted for Obama, and I'm a supporter. I've been impressed by how bold he has been on the political front, and how quickly he came up the learning curve in terms of the trade-offs involved. You see it very explicitly: Three weeks ago, for example, he talked about yes, fiscal stimulus was important and it avoided bigger problems Â—yet there are also longer-term fiscal sustainability challenges. The notion that we get is that he understands what the issues are and he's making active choices as opposed to reactive choices.

***Robert Greifeld:** CEO, Nasdaq OMX*

What I like is the fact that the President recognizes that we have a number of pressing issues and is endeavouring to attack or approach these issues with hopefully innovative solutions. The counterpoint to that is that you do grow concerned that they might try to do too much too soon or to overreach in a particular area and run the risk of rendering all efforts either neutered or ineffectual.

He's exceeded my expectations with respect to the managerial ability to craft and attempt to execute a wide-ranging agenda. I would have assumed that the natural realities of the office and what's required to move legislation would have narrowed the agenda.

Within the leadership of the business community, there is concern and I would say that the attitude is not so much wait-and-see, but wary. They're wary with respect to trade policy. They're wary with respect to tax policy and obviously are also concerned with the burden of health-care costs. There's a fair amount of trepidation in the business community and what the Administration policies might mean to their success in the future. In terms of the concern in the business community, I think, it is greater today than it was back in November.

On the stimulus package: I don't believe the stimulus has had a noticeable impact on the economy as of yet. I think it is somewhat misguided to be calling for additional stimulus. We need to get the stimulus that was approved into the economy, flowing through our different activities.

***Jeffrey Katzenberg:** CEO, Dreamworks Animation SKG*

(Katzenberg was an early Obama supporter and is still very much in the President's corner.)

I don't think that any President in modern history has had to face a deeper or more difficult or more complicated set of issues from the first moment he set foot in the White House, and I think he has done an exceptional job of methodically working his way through that horrendous set of problems. He had to make a lot of decisions, and some of them will be wrong, but many, many of them will turn out right.

On tax hikes: Unfortunately, that's not been a level playing field and there has been an unhealthy concentration of wealth in this country. Those days are over.

***Jeffrey B. Kindler:** CEO, Pfizer*

Obama's health-care reform is making more progress than a lot of people would have predicted. We're on the verge of a bill coming out of the House that's clearly going to happen. Right now there's some challenges in the Senate because of the potentially significant differences between the two committees there. The biggest challenge is this issue around the public plan. The other is how do we pay for it? Those are big issues. How they're going to get resolved within the time frame people have in mind, I'm not an expert on that. On any given day you'll hear harmony or disharmony. But yeah, I do sense a considerable amount of progress.

I do think that we have to accept the reality that the vast majority of the people in this country get their insurance from employers and if we create a system that provides an incentive for employers to not provide their employees with insurance, then under certain scenarios huge numbers of people under public option would move out of the employer system into the public system. That would not be a good outcome because it would impose a tremendous financial burden on the taxpayers.

***W. James McNerney Jr. :** CEO, Boeing*

A level playing field for American companies and workers in international markets is more important than ever. I see clear evidence that the Administration understands the issue and its importance to U.S. economic health.

***Duncan L. Niederauer:** CEO of NYSE Euronext, operator of the New York Stock Exchange*

The sense of optimism that is continuously communicated by the Administration is not only important, but necessary. The expectations for him generally speaking were so incredibly high when he took office. He's done a reasonably good job of living up to those. I have seen a number of instances where President Obama really is doing what we all hoped he would by reaching out to the stakeholders, decision-makers, potential influencers, and people who have expertise in various arenas. I know a number of people, including myself, who have been invited to the White House for various discussions. A lot of leaders wouldn't do that. The President's communication skills are very strong, as you would have expected. But he and the Administration have taken on so much, they're multitasking beyond expectations. I do like the reaching-out approach. It will serve him very well as we tackle all these rather meaty issues.

On tax policy: A place where I do not think they struck the right chord was on the tax proposal involving overseas earnings of multinational corporations headquartered in the U.S. The overwhelming view from that constituent group is that if that proposal were to go through, it would at best require a lot of U.S.-headquartered companies to eliminate jobs to reduce costs to make up for the increased tax burden. More challengingly for the United States, it would encourage a lot of these companies to contemplate being incorporated elsewhere and potentially moving jobs out of this country and moving headquarters and operations abroad. I hope the Administration listens to the feedback and reconsiders their position.

On regulation: We all know we need some regulatory reform here and to bring the opaque markets out of the shadows and into the light. But there's a real danger, in our view, that there ends up being excessive regulation that stifles creation of new business and new jobs.

***Charles R. Schwab:** Founder and Chairman, Charles Schwab, the San Francisco-based discount brokerage*

We've got to restore business confidence. We've restored the individual's confidence. The banking system seems to be doing okay. What we haven't done is restore the confidence of the people who create the jobs. There are six million businesses with more than one employee. What would it take to get each one to hire one more? If I had a magic wand,

I'd create some kind of incentive. The biggest uncertainty is: Where are taxes going to go? The quicker you bring certainty, the quicker you restore confidence.

Donald J. Trump: *CEO, the Trump Organization*

I would hire him. He's handled the tremendous mess he walked into very well. He still has a daunting task ahead of him but he appears to be equal to the challenge. He has kept his eye on both national and international issues and his visits to foreign countries have shown him to be warmly received, which is certainly a change from the last Administration. I believe he should pay more attention to OPEC and what's going on there, but overall I believe he's done a very good job.

Source: http://finance.yahoo.com/career-work/article/107453/ceos-rate-obamas-performance.html?mod=career-leadership (Accessed on 15/08/09)

Frequency and Duration

As indicated earlier the expressed emotion is the outcome of personality factors and job/ situational demands for a particular type of emotions. People take-up the jobs or involve themselves in such situations as and when their personality factors and situational demands for a particular type of emotion match with each other. In addition, people take-up the jobs even their personality factors don't match with the job/situational demands for a particular type of emotion if, the frequency of mismatch is relatively less and the duration of maintaining such an emotion is relatively for a shorter period. Otherwise, they can't cope-up with such a job/ situation.

Rationality of Emotions

Free expression of emotions sometime undermines the credibility or professionalism of the person, while it is essential for performance of certain jobs. Expression of sadness and job dissatisfaction at every situation would result in loss of job or assigning a low performance rate by the superior. Expression of extreme emotions like crying when the employee is sad and fighting when the employee is angry would harm the career goals. Non-expression of emotions would result in misunderstanding the employee's reactions to the management policies and practices. Therefore, employees should rationalize their emotions to avoid the negative consequences of expression of emotions to the extreme levels.

Sources of Emotions and Moods

Sources of emotions and moods include: personality, work overload vs relaxation times, weather, stress, social activities, sleep, exercise, age and gender. Now, we shall study how these factors act as sources of emotions and moods.

Personality

Different people experience and express different emotions at the same time and from the same input. Personality of the individuals is one of the important factors that influence them to experience varied emotions. Individuals with personality traits like reserved experience balanced emotion while people with outgoing/highly social personality trait may experience happy emotion from a situation of a social gathering involving liquor party. Similarly, people with submissive personality trait feel harassed while the people with dominant personality trait feel routine office procedure when superior communicates the low performance scores to the subordinates. Thus, personality traits act as sources of emotions.

Gender

As indicated earlier women express and experience emotions in a greater degree than men. In fact, women are more sensitive than men. Women experience emotions more intensively and express emotions both positive and negative more frequently than men. In addition women are more comfort in expressing emotions and in reading nonverbal and paralinguistic cues than men.[19]

Age

Some of us may feel that young people may experience happy and other positive emotions and older people may experience sad and negative emotions. But, one research study found that people between the age of 18 and 94 tend to experience less negative emotions and have positive moods for longer periods.[20] Thus, the study concludes that emotional experience tends to be positive with the progressive of age.

Stress

We come across the word 'stress' everyday. Managers, financiers, government officials, administrators, politicians, students and also housewives experience stress. Stress has its effects on all walks of life. To manage stress effectively, it is important to understand nature and effects of stress. Stress can be explained *basically as pressure upon a person's psychological system which arises out of complexity or intensity of one's work life*. Though stress is basically upon a person's psychological set-up, it also in turn affects his/her physical and behavioural systems. The sources of stress can be individual, organisational and social. More than often stress is viewed in negative terms. In fact the negative aspect, *i.e.*, **distress** is only one form of stress. But there is also positive aspect of stress which is called as **Eustress.**

People experience different emotions when they are under stressful situations compared to that under normal situations. People experience negative emotions like anger, jealousy and hatred during distress situations and positive emotions like happiness and joy. Similarly, people experience positive emotions under eustress situations. Thus, the employees under stressful circumstances experience negative emotions. Overwork and the work that causes strain also causes stress and result in experiencing negative emotions and moods. People become irresistible when they are under stress. Box 12.6 presents the emotions of irresistible men.

Box 12.6: SEVEN Emotions of Irresistible Men

We're not going to lie. A man boasting abs chiseled to perfection and biceps that pop just enough when flexed (without shredding shirts He-Man style) will no doubt turn our heads. And even if caught mid check-him-out glance, we're not about to look away. Fit, toned bodies are the result of hard work and dedication to a healthy lifestyle. We certainly pay homage to that. But for a man to achieve a skyrocketing score on the sexiness scale there's got to be more to him than physical assets. Throw in these seven traits and he's guaranteed irresistible.

1. He Has Mastered The Wink. *We don't know how they learn the technique but some guys really have the Richard-Gere wink down pat. There's an art to this wink and getting it right can be tricky. It's more suave and smoky than cheeky and laughable. He's comfortable giving this signal and has the timing to the tee. Done right, this move is pure sexy. Caveat: The wink can be tricky to pull off. Practice first.*

2. He Radiates Calm. *It's sending shivers up our spine just thinking about how powerful a man's calm presence can be. Neurotic or hyper or frenzied is stressful, no matter how busy the man or what his excuse. But if he's got cool written all over his face and his gaze is pure steady and peaceful his sex appeal will shoot through the roof (think old-school James Dean). We women can unwillingly fall into the trap of over-worrying about things we can't control. A man who sets us at ease by reminding us how things always manage to work out in the end is absolutely hot. Read: 3 Secrets To Exuding Sexy.*

3. He Takes Care of Himself. *Look, we're not saying it's a certain height or build that matters. If he keeps his body in relatively good shape this shows us he knows how to take care of himself. It also clues us in that he sets health as a priority. What's more, if he's active, working out even a few times a week, the endorphins his body is producing during gym sessions are sure to keep him in good spirits and energized. The bottom line: If he takes good care of himself he's likely to take good care of his partner (or at least help keep her motivated to do so). That's a turn-on. Read: Play Together: Top Sports For Couples.*

4. He's Got Style. *We don't want to give the wrong idea here. This is not to say he has to be one certain type of style, and that mimicking a prescribed "it" style is a surefire path to sexy (whether that's clean-cut, tattooed-up or punked-out). Not at all. Rather, what's attractive in a guy is that he has a style at all, a way of dressing that reflects in some way who he is and what he's into. A guy who wakes up hum-drum and throws the same dingy shirt and pair of jeans on everyday? Not sexy. At all.*

*5. **He Has A Manly Scent.** Sounds so animalistic, we know. No man can control his natural scent, and it turns out our DNA compatibility dictates who smells good to us, anyway. But, every guy can augment his essence with a spritz (one will do just fine) of cologne. As long as it's not overdone, a man with a strong scent has the potential to drive women wild.*

*6. **He Is Affectionate.** Though we women try not to let on, affection (be it an arm around the shoulder or hand on the leg) lights us up like fireflies. Consider it your secret weapon. By affection, we do mean to include expressing your feelings through words, such as "I love you." It's amazing how many hot men fall short of sexy just for lack of articulating and showing their love. Let's put it this way: There are guys who reach out to their partner while driving, and there are guys who keep both hands on the wheel and eyes straight ahead. The lads of the former group qualify for sexy.*

*7. **He Laughs Loud, Hard, Often.** No news flash here. Comedy is highly enticing. It's worth noting though that there are different types of humor. The insecure comedy that's based on putting others down or calling them names doesn't gibe with us. But give us fun-loving, belly-jiggling jokes and laughter and you'll head straight to the top of the sexiness charts.*

(**Source:** http://shine.yahoo.com/channel/sex/7-traits-of-irresistible-men-491994/ (Accessed on 02/08/20009.)

Social Activities

Social activities have their bearing on experiencing emotions. People experience positive emotions when they are in social activities like birthday parties, marriages, success celebrative parties. Similarly, people celebrate social functions when they are in good moods. For example, when an employee is in good mood due to his/her promotion tends to organize a social get together and a party to share his joy. Thus, people experience positive emotions when they are in social gatherings experiencing good moods would like to organize social gatherings to share their good moods with others.

Weather

Whether is conducive when the temperature is around 25^0 C. The temperature during summer in most of the South Indian cities would be around 45^0 C. People during summer in these cities and towns are irritated even for small deviations from their comfort and think negatively and pickup quarrels with others. Thus, they experience negative moods. In fact even the University and College Lecturers and Professors who normally are in good moods get irritated during summer classes when the students pose questions. In contrast, people with temperamental and tense personality traits feel relaxed and positive moods and emotions during comfortable climate of around 25^0 C. Thus, the weather influences the types of emotions.

Sleep

People with less than the normal sleep of eight hours would experience negative emotions like sad and unhappiness. For example, employees with less than normal sleep fail to perform the job properly the next day and they experience negative emotions.

Physical Exercise, Yoga and Meditation

Physical exercises can relax the body and yoga and meditation help both body and mind relaxation. Both are used traditionally to keep body and mind fit. Some organisations have successfully introduced yoga and meditations as a technique of mind relaxation and management. Physical exercises, yoga and meditation would result in mind as well as body relaxation that would enable the people to experience positive emotions and moods so that they become more creative.

Overload vs. Relaxation Times

People, particularly employees, work seriously during week-days and they get tired during such periods. They experience negative moods and emotions during the times of overload situations of week days. In contrast, people during the week-end relax to recoup and recover from the stress and overstrain. People during such period of relaxation experience positive moods and emotions.

Emotional Intelligence

Knowing how to identify and manage emotions can help in building and sustaining an 'emotionally intelligent' workplace. As the rules of work are changing, people are not only being judged on their IQ and educational qualification. A new concept of 'Emotional Intelligence' (EI) is gaining popularity among companies. EI means the ability to manage both personal and professional emotions and apply them for career progression. The best part about EI is that it can be learnt and HR managers are working towards developing it in their organisations, Aditi Joshi tells more..

What Is Emotional Intelligence?

Emotional intelligence, EI, can be defined differently by different people. For some, it is about being a "nice guy", while others find it too hard to believe that even emotions can be intelligent. While different theories and researches have been undertaken to define EI, in layman's terms emotional intelligence is the ability to perceive emotions, to access and generate emotions so as to assist thought. In simple terms emotional intelligence is the ability to reason with, and about emotions; it combines feelings with thinking and vice versa. And at workplace, emotional intelligence defines a set of skills, or competencies, which provides HR professionals, managers, and any one in the world of work, with a comprehensive tool to define, measure and develop emotional skills. Thus, emotional intelligence can be defined as the capacity to recognise our own feelings and those of others, for motivating ourselves and managing emotions well in our social interactions. Thus, emotional intelligence is capacity to balance the mind and brain with the situational requirements.

In simple terms emotional intelligence is the ability to reason with, and about emotions; it combines feelings with thinking and vice versa.

Source: http://sports.yahoo.com/nfl/blog/shutdown_corner/post/Fail-Redskins-Ladell-Betts-has-name-misspelled?urn=nfl,183018 (Accessed on 15/08/09)

Why is Emotional Intelligence Critical to Workplace Performance?

It takes more than technical skills to be successful. Emotional intelligence or the ability to restrain negative feelings such as anger and self-doubt and to focus on positive ones such as confidence and congeniality are the key determinants of an individual's career growth. Not only do superiors and corporate leaders need high doses of emotional intelligence, but every job demands it too. People skills run parallel to the concept of emotional intelligence and its application at workplace. HR experts point that emotional intelligence matters twice as much as technical and analytic skill combined for star performances, and the higher people move up in the company, the more crucial emotional intelligence becomes.

A display of emotions like anxiety on new project, happiness over the promotion, fear of losing job, tension of the board meeting and alike, can take place in the workplace. The way an individual manages his/her emotions can convey critical information about his/her performance at work: for example, happiness indicates satisfaction levels while tension depicts nervousness, etc.

Steps in Emotional Intelligence

Here are a few steps that can help an individual identify his emotional intelligence and use it effectively at his workplace:

1. Identifying Emotions

This is very important. One needs to be aware of his/her own feelings and emotions so that one is not blinded by emotions. Similarly, being aware of other's emotions is a key to developing strong relationships with colleagues.

2. Understanding Emotions

Knowing what motivates people, understanding their point of view and handling team interactions help in building the framework of emotional intelligence.

3. Managing Emotions

Like the way one manages a scheduler, one can learn to manage one's emotions as well. It means being aware of those individual emotions that have valuable information and their application to solve problems. For example: If one is feeling sad, one needs to find out the reason for this and solve the problem. If one is angry there ought to be a reason for the frustration. Find out the reason and solve the problem. If one is anxious, one needs to find out the reason for the worry, and solve the problem. Likewise, if one is joyous, one needs to find out the reason for the happiness and make use of it beneficially in the future.

4. Using Emotional Intelligence on the Job

Management experts opine that almost seventy per cent of management problem-solving happens in the mind, and only thirty per cent through analytical techniques. The business community has embraced the concept of emotional intelligence and its importance, but the challenge that lies ahead is to demonstrate that such competencies can be acquired and when they are, they significantly impact employee performance.

Now the Question: How Can EI, be Used for Career Development?

Judicious application of emotional intelligence can lead to management development, team effectiveness, and right selection of employees.

Management Development: Managers who focus on their technical skills do not manage, they're just in charge. Understanding and enhancing emotional intelligence enhances management skills.

Team Effectiveness: Teams are more than the sum of the individual parts. The glue, which holds teams together, can be supplied by emotional intelligence.

Selection: Hiring decisions can be better informed through the use of a thorough job analysis and an ability-based measure of emotional intelligence.

Emotional Intelligence and Management Development

Emotional intelligence, defined as a set of abilities, may assist managers in several, critical ways:

- Making planning more flexible.
- Motivating themselves and others.
- Making more informed decisions.

Flexible Planning

Managers who are emotionally intelligent use their emotions to adapt their plans. They do not ignore uncomfortable facts. Emotionally intelligent behaviour helps managers plan better in many ways:

- Change plans to meet the need of the moment.
- Adapt to the situation.
- Consider a variety of possible actions.
- Come up with alternate plans.
- Avoid doing consistently the same thing.
- Avoid sticking to a plan which is not working.

Motivation

Emotionally intelligent managers are able to understand their emotions, and those of others, which helps them to motivate their staff, and themselves. Emotionally intelligent managers are capable to:

- Get people to keep going, even when they want to give up.
- Get people to try again after failing at something.
- Motivate others.
- Motivate self.
- Get things done.

Decision-Making

Managers are called upon to make decisions everyday. Decisions based upon strong emotions, when the emotions are not dealt within a constructive way, can be bad decisions. Emotionally intelligent managers make better decisions in the following ways:

- Use emotions to improve their thinking.
- See things clearly even when feelings are strong.
- Make good, solid decisions although they may be angry at the time.
- Don't react out of anger.
- Balance their thoughts and their feelings.
- Make decisions based on their head and their heart.
- Don't let strong emotions blind them.

Emotional Intelligence and Team Effectiveness

When one works in a team environment, the skills of emotional intelligence become even more important to the job. One of the keys is to work effectively and efficiently with others. Another way in which emotional intelligence can help an individual in the teamwork is by helping to generate new and creative ideas and solutions to problems.

Creative Thinking

All teams require its members to come up with solutions to problems. Sometimes the problems are very complex, at other times they are quite simple. Yet, all problems require creative thought to generate ideal solutions. Emotional intelligence helps an individual to think creatively in many ways:

- View problems from multiple perspectives
- Have many new and creative ideas
- Be inventive
- Generate original ideas and solutions
- See new solutions

Social Effectiveness

When one works in a team, or even with just one person, social effectiveness allows the person to accomplish goals working with other people. Emotional intelligence can help an individual to work with others in these ways:

- Enjoyable to be with
- Good at influencing people
- Build consensus
- Believable and trusting
- Empathetic

Where Does Emotional Intelligence Fit in Terms of Workplace Success?

Emotional intelligence is not the sole predictor of workplace success, career satisfaction, or leadership effectiveness. It is one of many important components. Part of being an educated user of emotional intelligence means understanding that it is not and should not be thought of as a replacement or substitute for ability, knowledge or job skills. Emotional intelligence — people skills — enhances one's success, but it does not guarantee it in the absence of suitable skills.

Emotional intelligence always helps the individual. It is a good thing to have. But other skills and competencies are also important. Emotional intelligence is applying intuition and emotion to problem-solving. Emotional intelligence strengthens one's self-leadership and interpersonal relationships, and fortunately, it is a skill that can be learnt. The key role and importance of applying emotional intelligence, at workplace is that it lets the individual explore how emotional forces are managed in the workplace and how the consequences of managed work performance lead to business success. It adds new layers of meaning to one's daily work experience, lending insight to personal feelings and to dealings with others in the workplace.[21]

(D) JOB SATISFACTION

Job satisfaction refers to a person's feeling of satisfaction on the job, which acts as a motivation to work.

Job satisfaction refers to a person's feeling of satisfaction on the job, which acts as a motivation to work. It is not the self-satisfaction, happiness or self-contentment but the satisfaction on the job.

Job satisfaction relates to the total relationship between an individual and the employer for which he is paid. Satisfaction means the simple feeling of attainment of any goal or objective. Job dissatisfaction brings an absence of of motivation at work. Research workers differently describe the factors contributing to job satisfaction and job dissatisfaction. Hoppock describes job satisfaction as, "any combination of psychological, physiological and environmental circumstances that cause and person truthfully to say I am satisfied with my job."[22]

Job satisfaction is defined as the, "pleasurable emotional state resulting from the appraisal of one's job as achieving or facilitating the achievement of one's job values."[23] In contrast job dissatisfaction is defined as "the unpleasurable emotional state resulting from the appraisal of one's job as frustrating or blocking the attainment of one's job values or as entailing disvalues."[24] However, both satisfaction and dissatisfaction were seen as, "a function of the perceived relationship between what one perceives it as offering or entailing."[25]

Theories of Job Satisfaction

There are vital differences among experts about the concept of job satisfaction. Basically, there are four approaches/theories of job satisfaction.

They are: *(i)* Fulfilment theory, *(ii)* Discrepancy theory, *(iii)* Equity theory, and *(iv)* Two-factor theory.

(i) **Fulfilment Theory:** The proponents of this theory measure satisfaction in terms of rewards a person receives or the extent to which his needs are satisfied. Further, they thought that there is a direct/positive relationship between job satisfaction and the actual satisfaction of the expected needs. The main difficulty in this approach is that job satisfaction as observed by willing, is not only a function of what a person receives but also what he feels he should receive as there would be considerable difference in the actuals and expectations of persons. Thus, job satisfaction cannot be regarded as merely a function of how much a person receives from his job. Another important factor/variable that should be included to predict job satisfaction accurately is the strength of the individuals' desire of his level of aspiration in a particular area. This led to the development of the discrepancy theory of job satisfaction.

(ii) **Discrepancy Theory:** The proponents of this theory argue that satisfaction is the function of what a person actually receives from his job situation and what he thinks he should receive or what he expects to receive. When the actual satisfaction derived is less than expected satisfaction, it results in dissatisfaction. As discussed earlier, "Job satisfaction and dissatisfaction are functions of the perceived relationship between what one wants from one's job and what one perceives it is offering."[26] This approach does not make it clear whether or not over-satisfaction is a part of dissatisfaction and if so, how does it differ from dissatisfaction. This led to the development of equity theory of job satisfaction.

(iii) **Equity Theory:** The proponents of this theory are of the view that a person's satisfaction is determined by his perceived equity, which in turn is determined by his input-output balance compared to his comparison of others' input-output balance. Input-output balance is the perceived ratio of what a person receives from his job relative to what he contributes to the job. This theory is of the view that both rewards — over rewards as well as under rewards lead to dissatisfaction. An under-reward causes feelings of unfair treatment while over-reward leads to feelings of guilt and discomfort among employees.

(iv) **Two-factor Theory:** As discussed earlier, this theory was developed by Herzberg, Manusner, Peterson and Capwell who identified certain factors as satisfiers and dissatisfiers.[27] Factors such as achievement, recognition, responsibility, etc., are satisfiers, the presence of which causes satisfaction but their absence does not result in dissatisfaction. On the other hand, factors such as supervision, salary, working conditions, etc., are dissatisfiers, the absence of which causes dissatisfaction. Their presence, however, does not result in job satisfaction. The studies designed to test their theory failed to give any support to this theory, as it seems that a person can get both satisfaction and dissatisfaction at the same time, which is not a valid proposition.

Factors of Job Satisfaction

Job satisfaction refers to a general attitude which an employee retains on account of many specific attitudes in the following areas: *(i)* Job satisfaction, *(ii)* Individual characteristics, and *(iii)* Relationships outside the job. There are different factors on which job satisfaction depends. Important among them are discussed hereunder.

(i) **Personal Factors:** They include workers' sex, education, age, marital status and their personal characteristics, family background, socio-economic background and the like.

(ii) **Factors Inherent in the Job:** These factors have recently been studied and found to be important in the selection of employees. Instead of being guided by their co-workers and supervisors, the skilled workers would rather like to be guided by their own inclination to choose jobs in consideration of 'what they have to do'. These factors include: the work

itself, conditions, influence of internal and external environment on the job which are uncontrolled by the management, etc.

(iii) **Factors Controlled by the Management:** The nature of supervision, job security, kind of work group, wage rate, promotional opportunities, transfer policy, duration of work and sense of responsibilities are factors controlled by management. All these factors greatly influence the workers. These factors motivate the workers and provide a sense of job satisfaction.

Though performance and job satisfaction are influenced by different set of factors, these two can be related if management links rewards to performance. It is viewed that job satisfaction is a consequence of performance rather than a cause of it. Satisfaction strongly influences the productive efficiency of an organisation whereas absenteeism, employee turnover, alcholism, irresponsibility, non-commitment are the result of job dissatisfaction. However, job satisfaction or dissatisfaction forms opinions about the job and the organisation which result in boosting up employee morale.

KEY TERMS

- Values
- Collectivism
- Attitudes
- Emotions
- Job Satisfaction
- Discrepancies
- Co-opting
- Moods
- Power Distance
- Value System
- Cognitive
- Emotional Intelligence
- Personal Factors
- Peers
- Attitude Changes

QUESTIONS

1. Define the term 'Values.' Explain the significance of values and values in different cultures.
2. What are attitudes? Explain the functions of attitudes.
3. What are the changes in attitudes? Explain the enabling measures of changing attitudes.
4. What is job satisfaction? Discuss various theories of job satisfaction.
5. Explain various factors those affect job satisfaction in an organisation.

REFERENCES

1. M.Rokeach, "*The Nature of Human Values*," Free Press, New York, 1973, p. 5.
2. Stephen P.Robbins, "*Organisational Behaviour*," Prentice Hall, New Delhi, 2000, p. 62.
3. M.Rokeah and S.J.Ball-Rokeah, "*Stability and Change in American Value Priorities 1968-1981*," American Psychologist, May 1989, pp. 775-784.
4. B.M.Meglino and E.C.Ravlin, "*Individual Values in Organisation:Concepts, Controversies and Research*," Journal of Management, Vol.24, No.3, 1998, pp. 351-389.
5. Stephen P.Robbins, *op.cit.*, p. 63.
6. J.M.Munson and B.Z.Posner, "*The Factorial Validity of a Modified Rokeah Value Survey for Four Diverse Samples*," Educational and Psychological Measurement, Winter, 1980, pp. 1073-1079.
7. G.Hofstede, "*Culture's Consequences:International Differences in work Related Values*," Sage, Beverly Hills, 1980.
8. Stephen P.Robbins, *op.cit.*, p. 66.
9. Hofstede called this dimension masculinity vs. femininity, while Robbins called this Quantity of life vs. Quality of life.
10. Stephen P.Robbins, *op.cit.*, p. 66.
11. *Ibid.*, p. 68.

12. D.Katz, "*The Functional Approach to the Study of Attitudes*," The Journal of Opinion Quarterly, Summer, 1960, pp. 163-204.
13. Fred Luthans, *op.cit.*, p. 123.
14. *Ibid.*, p. 124.
15. Leon Festinger, "*A Theory of Cognitive Dissonance*," Stanford University, 1957.
16. Stephen P. Robbins et.al., "Organisational Behaviour", Person, 2007, p. 293.
17. J. Nolte, "The Human Brain", Mosby, St. Louis, 2002.
18. R.C. Gur et.al., "Sex Differences in Tempro-Limbicc and Frontol Brain Volumes of Healthy Adults", Cerebral Cortex, 12:9, Semptember 2009, pp. 998-1003.
19. J.A.Hall, "Non-verbal Sex Differences", Johns Hopkins Press, Baltimore, 1984.
20. L.L.Carstensen et.al., Journal of Personality and Social Psychology, 79:4, 200, p. 644.
21. N.H. Frijda, "Moods, Emotion Episodes and Emotions", Guilford Press New York, 1993, p. 381.
22. H.M. Weiss and R. Cropanzano, "Affective Events Theory", Research in Organisational Behaviour, Vol. 18, pp. 17-19.
23. Hoppock, R., *Job Satisfaction,* Harper, New York, 1935.
24. E.A.Locke, "What is Job Satisfaction", Organisational Behaviour and Human Performance, Vol.4, No.4, 1969, p.316, cited in G.James Francis and Gene Milbourn Jr. *Human Behaviour in the Work Environment,* Goodyear Publishing Co., Inc., California, 1980, p.70.
25. *Ibid.*
26. *Ibid.*
27. Nerzberg *et al., The Motivation to Work*, New York, 1959.

CHAPTER 13

PERSONALITY

☛ Chapter Outline

(A) Introduction
(B) What is Personality
(C) Personality Traits
(D) Determinants of Personality
(E) Personality Development
(F) Personality Theories
(G) Personality and Organisational Behaviour
(H) Type 'A' and Type 'B' Personalities
— Key Terms
— Questions
— References

☛ Learning Objectives

After studying this Chapter, you should be able to:

✓ Know the meaning of Personality and Personality Traits;
✓ Analyse the Significant Personality Traits viz., the Big Five;
✓ Understand the Self-concept;
✓ Explain Personality Development Theories; and
✓ Interrelate the Personality Development and Employee Behaviour and Job Performance.

(A) INTRODUCTION : CHANGING TIMES : NEED FOR CHANGED PERSONALITY

Until the liberalization of economies in various countries, environment was relatively static. Consequently, the jobs were secured. In other words, it was almost impossible for the companies to fire the employees.

But, privatisation, liberalization and globalisation changed this scenario. Competition caused by the economic liberalizations, led to the downsizing, de-layering, job sharing, talent management, retention, retrenchment and other massive layoffs. With this change losing a job has become a common feature in India as has been in the western world. Some public sector and private sector companies adapted the retrenchment strategies either voluntarily or compulsorily. However, the economic boom and particularly the boom in software industry, pharmaceutical and other sun-rising industries created a number of jobs. Added to this the man-made economic boom resulted in creation of a number of jobs. Thus, the economic boom opened up a number of jobs in various industries particularly in software industry during 1991 and 2007. Slowly, employees shifted to software industry by learning new skills.

The recent economic recession in various industries after 2007 resulted in loss of jobs and issue of pink slips to the employees in significant number of companies particularly in software and retail industries. The young male and female employees were shocked of this new culture of hiring and firing.

Thus, hiring, firing and rehiring culture entered in their minds. Similarly, learning continuously in order to acquire the status of employability from time to time has also entered the young minds. Indians today learnt that the days of 'lifetime employment' have gone. They also learnt that they will get jobs only, if they learn and acquire new and employable skills continuously.

Today, we need the people with versatile personality traits. The individuals should have and develop multiple traits and need to change them depending upon circumstances.

Mahatma Gandhi designed the non-violence strategy whereas Subash Chandra Bose designed the aggressive strategy for the attainment of Independence to India. Bin Laden diverted innocent Muslim youth towards violence and terrorism in the name of God whereas Nelson Mandela directed the South Africans towards a peaceful transformation based on Gandhian principles of non-violence *(Ahimsa)*. Dhirubhai Ambani (See Box 13.1) adopted aggressive expansion policy for Reliance whereas Ratan Tata followed the strategy of slow and steady growth for Tata. Narayana Murthy of Infosys followed a middle path silently. Even in the normal business activities, we come across several types of people. Some of them are competitive while others are contented. Some people are aggressive whereas others are quiet. Why do people vary so widely? To answer this question, we should know the concept of personality.

Box 13.1: Dhirubhai Ambani Built India's Largest Private Sector Company

Achievements: *Dhirubhai Ambani built India's largest private sector company. Created an equity cult in the Indian capital market. Reliance is the first Indian company to feature in Forbes 500 list.*

Dhirubhai Ambani was the most enterprising Indian entrepreneur. His life journey is reminiscent of the rags to riches story. He is remembered as the one who rewrote Indian corporate history and built a truly global corporate group.

Dhirubhai Ambani alias Dhirajlal Hirachand Ambani was born on December 28, 1932, at Chorwad, Gujarat, into a Modh family. His father was a school teacher. Dhirubhai Ambani started his entrepreneurial career by selling "bhajias" to pilgrims in Mount Girnar over the weekends.

After doing his matriculation at the age of 16, Dhirubhai moved to Aden, Yemen. He worked there as a gas station attendant, and as a clerk in an oil company. He returned to India in 1958 with Rs 50,000 and set up a textile trading company.

Assisted by his two sons, Mukesh and Anil, Dhirubhai Ambani built India's largest private sector company, Reliance India Limited, from a scratch. Over time his business has diversified into a core specialisation in petrochemicals with additional interests in telecommunications, information technology, energy, power, retail, textiles, infrastructure services, capital markets, and logistics.

Dhirubhai Ambani is credited with shaping India's equity culture, attracting millions of retail investors in a market till then dominated by financial institutions. Dhirubhai revolutionised capital markets. From nothing, he generated billions of rupees in wealth for those who put their trust in his companies. His efforts helped create an 'equity cult' in the Indian capital market. With innovative instruments like the convertible debenture, Reliance quickly became a favourite of the stock market in the 1980s.

In 1992, Reliance became the first Indian company to raise money in global markets, its high credit-taking in international markets limited only by India's sovereign rating. Reliance also became the first Indian company to feature in Forbes 500 list.

Dhirubhai Ambani was named the Indian Entrepreneur of the 20th Century by the Federation of Indian Chambers of Commerce and Industry (FICCI). A poll conducted by The Times of India in 2000 voted him "greatest creator of wealth in the century".

Dhirubhai Ambani died on July 6, 2002, at Mumbai.

(**Source:** http://www.iloveindia.com/indian-heroes/dhirubhai-ambani.html)

(B) WHAT IS PERSONALITY?

What does personality mean? People use different terms like good, popular, strong, honest, weak, polite, etc., to denote personality. Behavioural scientists and common people define personality from different perspectives.

The word personality can be traced to the Latin words 'per sona' which are translated as "to speak through." According to Gordon Allport, personality is "the dynamic organization within the individual of those psychological systems that determine his unique adjustments to his environment."[1]

Fred Luthans defines the term personality as, "how people affect others and how they understand and view themselves, as well as their pattern of inner and outer measurable traits and the person-situation intervention."[2]

Personality devotes for the methods of affecting others, reacting to others' actions and interacting with others.

Robbins defines personality as, "the sum total of ways in which an individual reacts to and interacts with others."[3]

Thus, personality devotes for the methods of affecting others, reacting to others' actions and interacting with others. These methods are chosen by individuals based on several factors. Important one among these are their traits. Now, we shall study personality traits.

(C) PERSONALITY TRAITS

According to Luthans, the way people affect others as per their personality traits. Personality traits include: height, weight, facial features, colour, dimension, etc. Personality traits are enduring characteristics like shyness, submissiveness, laziness, timidity, loyalty, dynamism, aggressiveness, creativity, etc., exhibited in a large number of situations.

Allport and Odbert identified 17,953 personality traits. It is highly difficult to predict the individual behaviour based on such a large number of traits. R.B. Cattell reduced this number to 171. He further reduced them to 16 personality factors, or primary traits (See Table 13.1). The 16-factors are found to be generally steady and constant sources of behaviour. They help in predicting individual behaviour in specific situations. Box 13.2 presents personality traits of effective leaders.

Table 13.1: Sixteen Primary Traits

1.	Reserved	Vs.	Outgoing
2.	Less intelligent	Vs.	More intelligent
3.	Affected by feelings	Vs.	Emotionally stable
4.	Submissive	Vs.	Dominant
5.	Serious	Vs.	Happy-go-lucky
6.	Expedient	Vs.	Conscientious
7.	Timid	Vs.	Venturesome
8.	Tough-minded	Vs.	Sensitive
9.	Trusting	Vs.	Suspicious
10.	Practical	Vs.	Imaginative
11.	Forthright	Vs.	Shrewd
12.	Self-assured	Vs.	Apprehensive
13.	Conservative	Vs.	Experimenting
14.	Group dependent	Vs.	Self-sufficient
15.	Uncontrolled	Vs.	Controlled
16.	Relaxed	Vs.	Tense

(**Source:** Stephen P. Robbins, "Organisational Behaviour," *op.cit.*, p. 94.)

Box 13.2: Personality Traits of Effective Leaders

What makes an effective leader? Why are people naturally attracted to some individuals and follow their lead while others have to work hard at coalescing others behind them and in the end are not particularly effective?And are there secret ingredients that go into making effective leaders? If so, what are they and why are they so important? In this article, which is one of a two-part series, we'll cover the first five of ten traits that most all effective leaders exhibit. Assertiveness – Absolutely essential to being a leader, the ability to be forthright in expressing demands, opinions, feelings, and attitudes is a key component of success.Assertiveness actually helps leaders in their performance of many tasks and especially in identifying and achieving goals. To lead, you must be prepared to confront your followers about their mistakes, make legitimate demands, demand higher performance, and always set high expectations of yourself and others. Enthusiasm – Leaders know enthusiasm is contagious. Others react positively to it almost instantly. They also know without it, it's virtually impossible to expect others to follow. Yet enthusiasm is one of the easiest traits to develop in yourself. People don't follow leaders who are boring and dull. Moreover, the leader knows he or she must frame his or her vision and mission in an enthusiastic way for others to want to make it their own. Enthusiasm fully developed is charisma. While genuinely rare, leaders who have transformed themselves into charismatic are able to easily enroll others to "buy in" and follow. Warmth – Warmth is actually the glue that holds it all together. In fact, without warmth, a leader cannot build the rapport between himself and others that's critical to leading. Frankly, warmth is not only wanted and needed by everyone, but it's one of the key ingredients for emotional support of others that holds the group together. It's also another important component of charisma. People expect their leaders to have warmth – don't disappoint them. Self-Awareness & Objectivity – Effective leaders have developed the ability to quickly assess the strengths and limitations of and others. This allows them to capitalise upon strengths, and build-up weaknesses to convert them into strengths. A good leader also recognizes that attempting to change others is not nearly as effective as simply noticing the way others are "wired" and using those already present patterns to achieve success. High Tolerance For Frustration – Simply stated, the ability to cope with and quickly overcome the inevitable roadblocks that will come. Others will watch closely how you respond when frustrated. How you act when things are going well is easy. How you respond when the going gets tough is far more difficult. Many leaders have lost their followers having failed in this trait. Other leaders have actually cemented and grown their following by rising to the occasion and showing that in good situations or bad, their ability to stay focused while not become upset and frustrated is strong.

http://www.google.co.in/search?q=personality&hl=en&sa=2 (Accessed on 12/08/09)

The Myers-Briggs Type Indicator

This is a 100-question personality test asking the respondents how they usually feel or act in particular situations. This is one of the most widely used personality tests.

According to the answers given by individuals they are classified as:

- **E**xtroverts or **I**ntroverts (E or I)
- **S**ensitive or I**n**tuitive (S or N)
- **T**hinking or **F**eeling (T or F)
- **P**erceiving or **J**udging (P or J)

These arrangements are classified into 16 personality traits (as shown in Table 13.1).

People with **INTJ** viz., introverted, intuitive, thinking and judging have original minds, and great drive for their own ideas and purposes. Their characters are sceptical, critical, independent, determined and often stubborn.

ESTJs are: organizers, realistic, logical, analytical, decisive and have a natural inclination towards business/mechanics.

ENTPs are conceptualisers, innovative, individualistic and versatile entrepreneurs, resourceful in solving challenging problems.

A recent book reported that the persons who created successful companies (Apple Computer, Honda Motors, Microsoft, Sony, Federal Express, etc.) are intuitive thinkers (**NTs**).[4]

Big Five Model

Personality traits of an executive/ supervisor influences the behaviour of the employees in an organisation.

Personality traits of an executive/spervisor influences the behaviour of the employees in an organisation. Personality traits like talkative, smiling, exhibitive in facial expressions and assertiveness are highly appropriate for executives to inspire, motivate and lead the subordinates. Similarly, traits like openness and frankness of the managers reduce dysfunctional activities and conflicts and enable the subordinates to concentrate on work related activities and increase productivity. *Mr. Jayasankaran of Delta Airlines attracts and impresses his subordinates due to his impressive height. Mr. Vasanta Rao of L&T is highly sociable. His subordinates are impressed with the way he conducts the meetings and directs his juniors.*

The major personality traits which influence the job behaviour and job performance are labelled as the 'Big-Five Personality Traits.' These traits have emerged from the Research Studies.[5] They are:

1. **Extroversion:** Sociable, talkative and assertive.
2. **Agreeableness:** Good natured, cooperative and trusting.
3. **Conscientiousness:** Responsible, dependable, persistent and achievement-oriented.
4. **Emotional Stability:** Calm, self-confident, secure, tense, insecure and nervous.
5. **Openness to Experience:** Imaginative and artistically sensitive.

Extreme traits of the 'Big Five' intellectual[6] are presented in Exhibit 13.1.

Now, we discuss these big-five personality traits in detail.

1. Extroversion

People get the energy from their preference of extroversion or introversion.

People get the energy from their preference of extroversion or introversion. The people who prefer extroversion get the energy from their interactions with other people. The people who prefer introversion get energy by spending time or doing the activities by themselves. Extroversion type people develop and maintain wide-range of social network while the introversion type people narrow down their relationships to a few people.

According to Jung, even the introverts possess social skills, but prefer internal world of ideas, thoughts and concepts.[7] In fact certain societies encourage and reward extroverts. Extroverts at workplace, prefer variety and they don't mind the interruptions at workplace by people/ coworkers. They prefer relationships over quality and quantity of output. In contrast, the introverts prefer complete concentration and least disturbances at workplace by people/coworkers and telephone calls. They prefer quality and quantity of output over relationships.[8] Introverts prefer to work in isolation and concentrate on performance.

Extroversion represents a person's interest in the external world. Person's interest in the external world can be exhibited through sociability, talkativeness/gregariousness and assertiveness. Thus, this dimension deals with relationships with others. Extroverts are assertive, sociable, talkative, gregarious people and introverts are reserved, timid and quiet.

Exhibit 13.1 Extreme Traits of the BIG FIVE

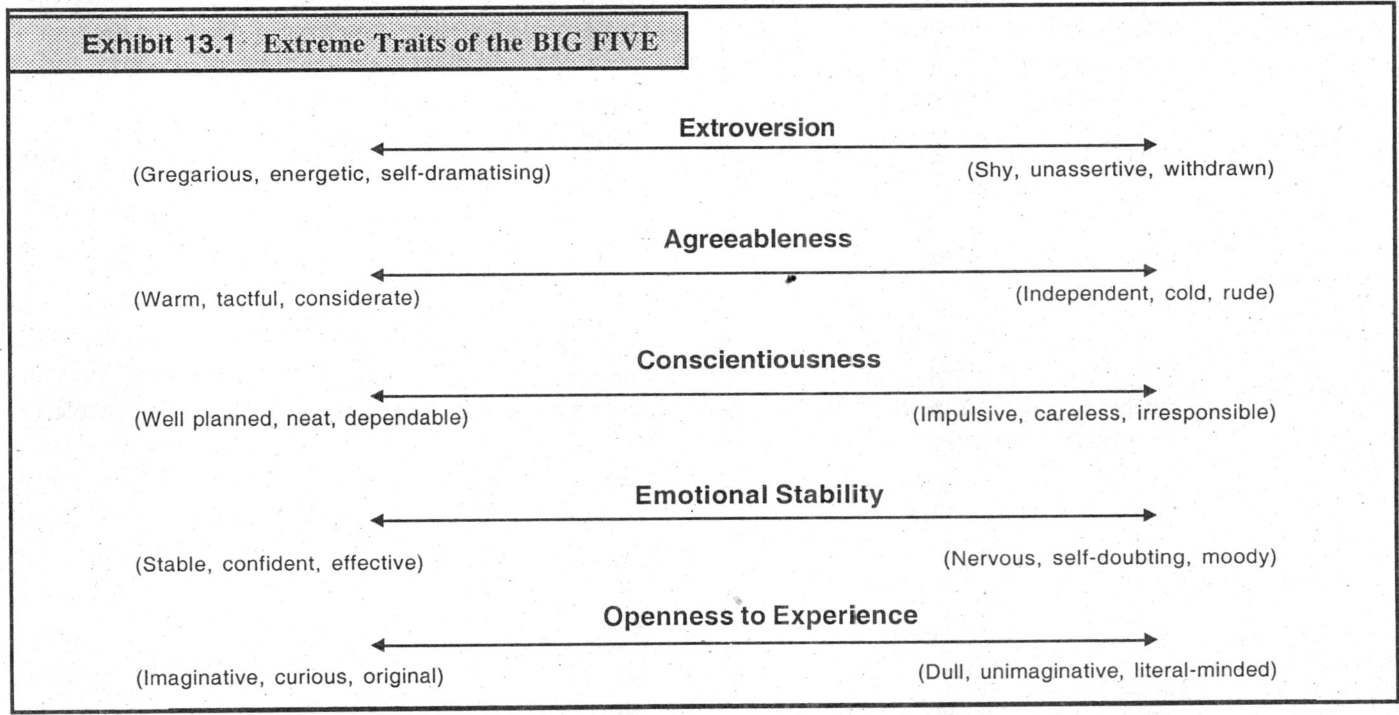

(**Source:** Modified version from Don Hellriegel, John W.Slocum Jr. and Richard W.Woodman, "*Organisational Behaviour*", Southwestern, Singapore, 2001, p. 41).

(a) **Sociability:** Sociability is the ability of a person in maintaining interrelationship within a social group. Some executives possess the trait of maintaining social relations with their subordinates. They visit the subordinate's houses, enquire about the subordinates' health, financial, family, children's educational and marriage issues. They participate in various social functions organized by the subordinates.

The employees with high social skills create, nurture and develop social networks. Such employees never feel the social relations as disturbance even at the workplace. Sociability of executives and superiors tend to result in positive job behaviour and improved job performance of subordinates.

Mr. Ravi, Human Resources Manager of Nutrine Confectionary Ltd., has been highly sociable, visits the employees' families and monitors their welfare. During one summer when there was heavy demand for chocolates, employees refused to work beyond the scheduled hours despite his repeated requests. Then Mr. Ravi arranged for a social get-together of the employees' family members and explained to them the demands of the company regarding overtime work. The convinced family members influenced the employees to concede to the demand of the HR Manager. Thus, the sociability trait of Mr. Ravi resulted in positive job behaviour and enhanced the production of the company.

***(b)* Talkative:** People with talkative skills are with open-mind and speak their mind to others. They disseminate and share information with others without any hesitation. They also voice various issues, ventilate employee grievances and proact on various organizational and employee issues. Many executives, with their speaking skills attract and influence the subordinates regarding their job behaviour and performance. Mr. Mahajan of Grindwell Norton is a skilled speaker. He is good at making presentations. He talks on various issues and attracts the employees and major customers. He makes enquiries with the employees regarding their family issues, welfare, etc. His subordinates are influenced by his abilities of voicing on various issues of the company, jobs, their personal issues, etc.

***(c)* Assertive:** Assertiveness is confirming one's own ideas or actions confidently or defending oneself and/or others through positive arguments, declaring strongly or laying claims. Subordinates like the assertive character of their boss and mould their job behaviour and performance to his expectations. Mr. Rajiv of Mukand Industries never counts down on his employees though they commit mistakes. In fact, he appreciates and defends them publicly. He calls them for discussions privately and makes them realize their mistakes. Similarly, he also defends himself through arguments, systematic analysis backed up with reasoning and cause-effect presentations. He attracts and influences his subordinates through his assertiveness.

2. Agreeableness

Highly agreeable people are cooperative, warm and trusting, whereas less agreeable people are cold, disagreeable and antagonistic. Individuals with agreeable traits think from the view- point of their employees or clients, accept the proposals, needs or requests of the employees. Employees' job behaviour and job performance is influenced with such a trait. Individuals with such a trait are good natured, cooperative and trusting.

Mr. Uday of Kotak Mahindra enters into the shoes of his employees and customers and analyses the issues and problems from their point of view. Added to this, his positive attitude towards others makes him to exhibit his trait of accepting the proposals or requests or needs of his subordinates. His subordinates are influenced positively by his trait of agreeableness.

Good nature includes respecting the employees' ideas, views, opinions, values and considering them in decision-making.

***(a)* Good Natured:** Good nature includes respecting the employees' ideas, views, opinions, values and considering them in decision-making. Further, it includes involving the employees in decision-making, helping and guiding them in their work. Good nature of the superiors influence the job behaviour and performance of the subordinates positively.

Mr. Chowdary of Voltas respects the ideas, values and opinion of each of his subordinates. He encourages their participation in various activities and involvement in decision-making. They visit the workplace of his subordinates, offers suggestions, guide them and help them in their work. Employees in Voltas are influenced by the good nature and treatment given by Mr. Chowdary.

***(b)* Cooperative:** Cooperative traits regarding attitude and practice of superiors of an organization help the company in moulding the job behaviour and increasing the job performance.

Mr. Singh of Max India works jointly with his colleagues and subordinates, though, he has an independent work and independent office. Further, he shares his resources, time and expertise for the efficient performance of his subordinates and colleagues. Singh's cooperation in attitude and practice influenced the job behaviour and performance of Max India to a greater extent through positive reciprocation of employees.

***(c)* Trusting:** Trust is worthiness of being relied upon or confidence in the truth of anything. It is resting on the integrity. Executives with the trait of trusting provide autonomy to the people, enable them to realize their potentialities and rise to the expectations of their boss. Executives can concentrate on strategic and policy issues.

Mr. Premji of WIPRO entrusts the work, broadly fixes the targets and gives freedom to the employees to achieve the targets. He proudly says that his employees achieve targets beyond his expectations. His employees happily reciprocate that their boss trusts them, which changed their behaviour and enhanced their performance. (See Box 13.3).

Box 13.3: Mukesh Ambani: Trusting Personality

Trusting Personality

It was not easy task for Mukesh Ambani to prove his efficiency and business acumen in a nation where parallel economy prevails. His dream of becoming famous and successful kept himself bang on to his goals. After bagging a chemical engineering degree, and an MBA degree from Stanford University, Mukesh started to work hard for business enhancements. With his unique business ideas he founded the Reliance Communications that roars in the telecom sector of India. Beside telecommunication, he eyed at the market and perceived the growing trend on the retail sector. He endeavoured to invest in retail and again established the Reliance Fresh brand.

The innovative approach

Time and again with the thrust of tasting more and more success, Mukesh came up with unique business brands. He initiated in starting up a diamond jewellery business. Mukesh Ambani is icon for the guys who want to be famous and are ready to put up efforts. In the year 2006, as per the data provided by Forbes Magazine, Mukesh Ambani is considered to be the second richest person of India. In different seminars, he repeatedly pronounced the mantra of his success, and it can be a nice experience for the guys to listen to his valuable suggestions.

http://mukeshambani.crazybillionaire.org/mukeshambani.php (Accessed on 28/11/2009).

3. Conscientiousness

Conscientiousness refers to governing or regulating the work activity by conscience. Conscientiousness is a measure of reliability. Persons with a high level of conscientiousness are reliable, organized, dependable and persistent; while persons with a low level are easily distracted, disorganised and unreliable. The conscientiousness trait of the executive changes the job behaviour and enhances the job performance of the subordinates. The conscientiousness trait includes responsibility, dependability, persistency and achievement-oriented.

Mr. Rajesh Chowdary, an executive of Bharat Heavy Plates and Vessels Limited (BHPVL) had no real pressure of work and responsibility to spend longer hours in the company, take risks, exert his energies, etc. But he worked sincerely beyond the expectations of the organisational culture and his colleagues. The responsive trait of Mr. Chowdary changed the work culture of his department to a considerable extent.

(a) Responsible: Responsible trait is responding readily to discharge one's own obligations towards others and the organisation. The responsible trait of the individuals enables them to take up the work activities with or without delegation, and makes the superiors to concentrate on policy issues. This process improves the job performance of the employees and moulds the employee behaviour towards organisational requirements.

(b) Dependable: Subordinates commit themselves to organizational goals, take up the responsibility and carryout the organizational activities that contribute to the strategy even they are not assigned to them. Such subordinates are dependable. Employees with dependable traits maximize organizational performance. Thus, the dependable trait of the employees improves their job performance.

Mr. Prakash Singhal of Escorts frequently takes up the work activities of the company depending upon the situation, without being assigned to him by his boss. His boss feels that Mr. Prakash is dependable and the work he takes up or which is assigned to him need not be followed up.

(c) Persistent: Persistent trait refers to the behaviour of rendering the services or doing the work continuously at a steady pace without any opposition. The persistent trait influences job behaviour and performance.

Mr.John of Dr. Reddy's Lab reacts to the needs of his subordinates and organisational requirements continuously, steadily at a fast rate without any opposition. This persistent trait of Mr. John influenced the behaviour of his subordinates significantly.

(d) Achievement-oriented: Employees translate the objectives into achievable goals based on ground realities and conditions and achieve the goals to a large extent. The achievement oriented trait of employees improves their job performance and mould the job behaviour of others and shapes work culture. (See Box 13.4).

Box 13.4: Achievement and Risk-oriented Traits of Ratan Tata

Risk-taker's dream: Ratan Tata

"We need to be bolder and willing to take bigger risks abroad," Ratan Tata had said THE WEEK *in an interview in May 2005. That was at a time when the Tata group had taken a big leap abroad with acquisitions by Tata Motors and Tata Steel. It had also become the third largest player in the world in the branded tea business. Tata Motors' acquisitions in Korea and Spain in 2005 made it the world's fifth largest truck maker and the third largest bus chassis maker. Tata Steel's buy of Singapore's NatSteel did not add much to capacity, but made it a strong regional player.*

Perhaps, Corus was on the Tata radar even then. Perhaps Ratan Tata had an inkling that Tata Steel would grow from being a regional player to a global one, practically overnight, when he said, "I am sure at some point we will go beyond the Tetley scale." For the Tata group, the objective of this aggressive expansion abroad is not just acquisition for the sake of acquisition. "Going into select geographies is not just to exploit commercial opportunities but where the group will have a development role in that country," Tata had said.

In all its acquisitions, local managers have remained, with Tata Sons people on hand to provide guidance and to ensure corporate governance. "We are far more tolerant of differences than many American and eastern companies," Alan Rosling, executive director, told The Week *then. As the group's footprints in foreign markets have grown, Tata Sons, which owns a controlling interest in the bigger group companies, has been building a philosophy to institutionalise the process. Templates and models for institutionalising the group support for such acquisitions are now in place.*

"We have created a very small group to look at our growth internationally," Tata said. An important criterion for the top team is how well the acquired company will fit into the Tata value system. "Chemistry is an extremely important issue," Tata said. "We do a lot of homework to make sure the acquired company fits into our culture and value system. If we find that a company follows practices that we are not in agreement with, we would not go into it."

As the group grows across geographies, it is getting noticed for its quality, pricing and services. Emphasis rests as much on gaining mind-share for the group as on gaining market share. "We have created a common brand and built brand discipline," said Tata, when asked about making brand Tata an international one. "Now we are spending money to promote the brand in the countries we are in.... The group now has more visibility, we are less shy of the media and we have more media coverage." That is certainly true of the Corus acquisition.

Ratan Tata, the soft-spoken man of steel

Ratan Tata showed that grace, composure and nerves of steel can sit easy on the same personality, as he marked an audacious milestone in his career as Tata group chairman by winning over Anglo-Dutch steel maker Corus Group with a bid worth $12.1 billion. In venturing into new areas, fighting corruption in his own industrial empire and in going ahead with his car plant in West Bengal despite protests over land acquisition, the 69-year-old has shown that he does not budge an inch once he has made up his mind.

After he took over the mantle of Tata Sons, the group's holding company, from legendary patriarch JRD Tata, everyone - from close lieutenants to outsiders and experts - was sceptical of his ability to manage such a large and diversified empire with around 85 companies in a salt-to-software range. His grit and determination are best epitomised in what he said in an interview. "I am unfortunately a person, who has often said: You put a gun to my head and pull the trigger or take the gun away, I won't move my head." That is a rare insight into a man who protects his privacy, integrity and patriotism in equal measures. The acquisition of Corus comes in the 100th year of Tata Steel. That should make the centenary celebrations more sweet. The Corus deal is a "defining moment for Tata Steel," Tata had said after launching a recommended bid for Corus.

Much before corporate governance became a buzzword in India Inc, Ratan Tata did not hesitate to file a criminal case against one of his perceived lieutenants and other top executives of the group for allegedly defrauding one of his companies. Throughout his career, which began as a management trainee in Tata Steel, he has displayed enormous courage in taking assignments that critics had written off even before they had taken off. The Indica Car project is a case in point.

When Indica was unveiled in 1998 in Delhi, the then Industry Minister Murasoli Maran termed it the "modern Kohinoor of India". From there, after a series of build-outs and acquisitions, Corus could well be a logical jewel in Tata's crown. Several observers had nearly written off the Indica project, some had even said the project could mark the beginning of the end of Tata Motors. It did not. Nobody now is questioning whether Tata Motors can live up to the promise of producing a "people's car" in the price bracket of Rs 1 lakh. Tata is fiercely patriotic. In 1998, he stepped in immediately to douse a nationwide rumour that there was a salt shortage. Tata issued full-page advertisements, in national interest, stating that there was no supply crisis of salt and citizens need not hoard kilos of salt in their homes.

The man called Ratan

Ratan Tata's 'Corus Conquest' is just the beginning of the Indian industrial saga of 'How the West was won'. There are instances in history which reveal that often the time makes the man; World War II made the man Churchill, British Raj and Indian Independence struggle made the man Gandhi. Contrary to such instances, Ratan from the days of his youth was making the man in himself and was already 'made' when the time came.

Ratan's is a story of struggle, perseverance, survival and success covering a long period of more than four decades. When he was very young, a shattered Nelco was thrown in his lap. From the shambles it was, how it has survived as a company is a wonder. It was not in the best period of automobile industry that Ratan was made vice-chairman and then chairman of Telco (now known as Tata Motors). Facing him immediately thereafter in Telco was the worst of the industrial labour unrest led by Rajan Nair.

The tough, cool and calculated handling of Telco by Ratan during those turbulent times almost gave an answer to the oft-repeated question, after JRD who? Tisco and Indian Hotels, before his becoming the Chairman, were not free from controversies and once again it was after a stiff resistance and struggle that he preserved and protected the shareholders' interest in these companies.

The Tata Group, which during those days was under a serious threat of disintegration with strong satraps like Russi Mody, Darbari Seth, Ajit Kelkar and other contenders at play, was held together singly by Ratan under his strong and visionary leadership. With Ratan's taking over as the undisputed leader of the Tata Group, he embarked upon consolidation and expansion in key strategic arrears. The opening up of the national and global economy provided the time and opportunity for which the man had already made himself.

'Corus Conquest' is the culmination of this process of making the man and certainly not the end. What will hold Ratan in one good solid piece and take him further and higher are his extremely high ethical standards, a wide international vision and perseverance. All these attributes have been tested often in most disturbing times. Ratan's contribution to the Tata Group in particular and to the Indian industry in general is not less significant than that of its founder, Jamsetji Tata.

Ratan's achievements in strengthening the group in critical times and providing leadership to the Indian industry in the national and international economy are equally praiseworthy. The licence and permit raj which followed the Indian independence had harshly restricted the growth of the Tata Group and therefore, in fairness to JRD, it may be stated that his hands were tied.

But it was good fortune for the Tata Group that, when the time came, Ratan had already made himself; and he seized the challenges and opportunities, steering the group way ahead of others with enviable grace and dignity. Ratan will go down in the Indian history as one of the greatest industrialists of all times. His contribution to the Indian industry through the Tata Group is extremely valuable and everlasting. He will be long remembered for his rare and unique adherence to noble principles, astute business acumen, inner steel-like strength, inherent fairness to the shareholders and business associates and dignified demeanour all the time.

The Bombay House biz wiz

The late patriarch JRD Tata, ambitious as he was, could not have foreseen that the industrial group he had built so painstakingly would be taken to such heights by his chosen successor. The conquest of Anglo-Dutch steel maker Corus Group plc by Tata Steel under Ratan Tata's leadership is a giant achievement, even by the Tata group's standards.

About 15 years ago, when JRD decided to pass the baton on to the then 53-year-old Ratan Tata, his close lieutenants had opposed the move: Ratan Tata was too young and inexperienced, they said. The old guard at Bombay House — Rusi Mody, Darbari Seth and Ajit Kerkar, in charge of steel, chemicals and hospitality respectively — had their own vision for the company. But the suave and soft-spoken Ratan Tata was determined to take the group to new heights.

In one of the biggest gambles of his life, Ratan Tata put everything at stake at Tata Motors to give the country its first indigenously manufactured 'people's car'. At a time when foreign carmakers were confidently tightening their grip on *the Indian market, Ratan went ahead with his grandiose vision and the result, the ubiquitous Indica, is on Indian roads and in select export markets. It was, for Ratan, the first indication that he could take on foreign competitors.*

Ratan Tata articulated his vision for the salt-to-software group with 86 companies in 3 phases over 15 years. In the first phase, he was primarily engaged in cleaning the empire's Augean stables that comprised slothful chieftains who drained resources and ran personal fiefdoms. Next, he started scouting around for management professionals. In the second phase, Tata put together a management team that combined Indian traits with a global vision.

The Tatas had a strong management cadre and were known to groom management graduates from the Tata Administrative Services. But there was need for fresh blood and thinking, which came from the likes of R Gopalakrishnan, Kishore Chaukar and Alan Rosling along with inhouse bosses: J J Irani, Ishaat Hussain, N A Soonawala and R K Krishna Kumar. "The biggest change that is happening on a continuous basis is that of distribution of leadership. "It's like someone creating a 100-piece orchestra," says Gopalakrishnan, executive director at Tata Sons, the group's holding company into which he moved from Hindustan Lever. "Ratan Tata has the unique ability to smell the winds of globalisation much before many of us," says Krishna Kumar, vice-chairman, India Hotels. "The changes that the Tata Group has undergone is entirely in sync with globalisation.

The Chairman's initiatives are in response to the winds of change that have been blowing ever since the Berlin Wall fell," he adds. With designs on the world following the management shakeup, Ratan Tata unleashed the tiger. This was the beginning of the third phase. After 2000, the Tata empire has gone on a shopping spree across the world. The mandate was clear. Each business segment should be strong enough to survive and thrive in the global market.

Gopalakrishnan says, "Ratan Tata gives his team the licence to be bold. But no major decisions will happen without consultation." Nobody, for instance, now raises eyebrows about the feasibility of the 'people's car' in the price bracket of Rs 1lakh. Ratan Tata is a man of determination, says investment banker Uday Kotak. "Nothing he says is casual or off-hand. When he speaks, he means business." The Corus deal, adds Kotak, is the biggest example of Tata's "courage and vision, which made India proud and a force to reckon within the global canvas".

So, what makes Ratan Tata so confident? Industry observers say Tata not only preaches ethics and corporate governance, but implements them in letter and spirit. He has the ability to call a spade a spade. Much before 'corporate governance' became a catch phrase with India Inc, Tata did not hesitate to file a criminal case against one of his perceived close lieutenants and a top executive of the group for allegedly defrauding one of his companies.

New frontiers have also been nurtured. F C Kohli and JRD Tata created a hen that laid the golden eggs — Tata Consultancy Services (TCS), the country's biggest software company, which was listed on Indian bourses in 2004. Before its listing, it was a cash cow for Tata Sons. Now, Tata Sons' holding of 80 per cent in TCS, which has a market capitalisation of Rs 1,26,500 crore, is worth over Rs 100,000 crore. A marginal dilution can generate enough cash for Tata Sons to gobble up many companies through a leveraged buyout route using the acquired company's assets to pay for the acquisition.

Source: http://www.thevaryouth.com/tata.htm (Accessed on 12/08/09)

4. Emotional Stability

Some executives absorb the actions, reactions, views, feelings, attitudes, outcome of activities, etc., and maintain stability of their emotions. Consequently, they tend to be calm, self-confident and secure. People with negative scores tend to be nervous, anxious, depressed and insecure.

5. Openness to Experience

Executives are expected to be open to new job experiences, learn, absorb and integrate them with their previous experiences and knowledge. This trait includes imaginative, artistically sensitive, intellectual, creative and curious people. Those with low level of openness are conventional and go along with the familiar.

(a) **Imaginative:** All the business ventures come into existence only after they cross the stage of imaginative or projective. In fact all the business activities also cross this stage and as such, all the employees are expected to possess the imaginative trait. In fact, those who imagine much, achieve much.

(b) **Artistically Sensitive:** Employees should be sensitive to all types of changes in the environment and imagination. Employees with this trait learn much from the environment and use such knowledge for the improvement of the job performance.

(*c*) **Intellectual:** The intellectual trait enables the individuals to think and analyse rationally and understand systematically. This trait helps the employee to make efficient decisions and enhance the job behaviour.

Big Five Traits and Job Performance

The research studies conclude that:

- Individuals who are dependable, reliable, careful, thorough, able to plan, organised, hardworking, persistent and achievement-oriented tend to have high job performance in most occupations.[7]
- Individuals with high conscientiousness develop higher levels of job knowledge as they exert great levels of effort on their job. This, in turn results in higher levels of job performance.
- There is a positive relationship between Personality Traits and Job Satisfaction. (See Box 13.5).

Box 13.5: Relationship between Personality Traits and Job Satisfaction — Research Results

To understand the relationship between job involvement, job satisfaction, and personality traits among health volunteers in one Taiwan community. It is not easy to retain voluntary workers as part of health programmes even though they have been trained. Previous research has shown that in order to increase job involvement, volunteers must effectively fulfil their needs to achieve and obtain job satisfaction. Design and sample: Cross-sectional design. Surveys were mailed to 317 health volunteers at community health centres in I-lan County, northern Taiwan; 213 complete responses (67%) were received. Methods: The survey instrument included sociodemographic items and scales measuring locus of control, achievement orientation, job involvement, and job satisfaction. Results: Most respondents (94.8%) were female and their average age was 49.6 years. In terms of personality traits, most volunteers showed internal control orientation. Explainable variance for the prediction of job involvement from a combination of participation frequency, on-job training, achievement orientation, and job satisfaction was 33.6%. Conclusions: The results suggest that there is a need to strengthen cooperative relationships among volunteers by initiating well-planned volunteer training programmes and growth groups. These should involve the empowerment concept with the aim of enhancing the volunteers' interpersonal relationships and job satisfaction.

http://www3.interscience.wiley.com/journal/118533689/abstract?CRETRY=1&SRETRY=0 (Accessed on 15/08/09)

The Self-concept

Almost all the people try to understand themselves by virtue of their qualities, characters, actions, reactions, responses, etc. This process in personality theory is called the self-concept. This process involves the interaction of the background, one's own psychology, values, social, economic, religious and other internal factors of oneself. The concepts of self-esteem and self-efficacy are concerned with self-concept.

Mr. Michael of Human Resources Department of Lipton perceived in 1992 that he has the skills and competence of solving issues of the proposed corporate merger with Brooke Bond. This perception is referred to as self-esteem.

People's self-esteem is concerned with their self-perceived competence and self-image.[8] When Lipton merged with Brooke-Bond, Mr. Michael perceived that he could counsel and train the employees regarding the cultural diversity issues of the former Brooke Bond employees. This is called *self-efficacy*. Self-efficacy has to do with self-perceptions of how well a person can cope with situations as they arise.[9]

Thus, self-esteem is concerned with the perceived competence while self-efficacy deals with the perceived performance based on the situation.

(D) DETERMINANTS OF PERSONALITY

It has been viewed after a long debate that leaders are both born and made, *i.e.*, heredity.

There has been a debate whether the leaders are born or made? It has been viewed after a long debate that leaders are both born and made, *i.e.*, heredity. Similarly, there has been an argument as to whether personality is determined at birth or is the result of individual's interaction with the environment. Added to this, it is also argued that situation is another factor that determines personality. Now, we shall discuss these three broad determinants of personality.

According to the heredity approach, the individual's personality is influenced by the molecular structure of the genes located in the chromosomes.

Heredity

Certain physical and psychological characteristics like facial attractiveness, temperament, gender, muscle composition, energy level, biological rhythms, etc., either substantially or partly are inherited from one's parents. They are inherited by the parents' biological, physiological and psychological make-up.

Research studies show that traits like shyness, fear, height distress are mostly caused by inherited genetic characteristics.[10] They also show that genetics accounts for around 50 per cent of personality differences and more than 30 per cent of the variation in occupational and leisure interests. However, it is strongly argued that personality factors are not completely dictated by heredity, but they are also determined by the environment.

Now, we shall study another determinant factor of personality, i.e., Environment.

Environment

Environmental factors are those factors which encircle us and which influence our behaviour.

Environmental factors are those factors which encircle us and which influence our behaviour. Culture is the most important factor among the environmental factors that influence personality. Most of the Indians are humble, obedient, tolerant, non-violent, non-materialistic, non-competitive and tend to sacrifice. Hindu religious texts, saints, parents and elders teach these cultural values.

Japanese are industrious, obedient, dependent and non-violent. Buddhist religious texts and monks and elders taught these values. While the westerners are independent, competitive, industrious, ambitious and aggressive as the independent western society/culture, parents and teachers in the schools infused these cultural values in them.

Culture is the complex of beliefs, values, norms, opinions and attitudes which are shared by individuals of contemporary period and transmitted from generation to generation. Culture is learnt from the family members, friends, peers, social groups, teachers, etc.

Thus, culture is considered as the major determinant of the personality as it determines what and how an individual learns. For example, a young boy of a family with docile nature was adopted by another family with aggressive nature. The boy turned into an aggressive guy when he grew up.

Many Indians who normally avoid the work, come late to the workplaces and are less quality conscious in Indian organisations behave quiet differently in western organisations. They respond and adjust to the demands of the work environment of the companies in the west.

Thus, culture shapes the personality of an individual, in addition to heredity. Stephen P. Robbins views that heredity sets the parameters or outer limits while culture makes the individual to adjust himself/herself to the demands and requirements of the environment.

Now, we shall discuss the third factor, i.e., situation.

Situation

Situations change based on the shifts in environmental factors. The stable economic environment before 1990s has turned into a more dynamic and volatile environment due to globalization of world economies and information technology innovations. These shifts led to more competitive and challenging situations during 1991 and 2007. These situations changed into recessionary and shirking situations consequent upon economic meltdown throughout the globe after 2007. Managers changed their managing styles in crafting and implementing strategies based on these shifts in situations. Job demands vary depending upon situations and employees change their traits depending up on situational demands. Women managers have started to grow to the levels of chief executive officers of the companies and accept challenges along with men. (See Box 13.6). Managers adapt creative and growth strategies during economic boom periods and adapt retrenchment and conservative strategies during economic recession. Thus, exhibitive personality traits change based on situational demands.

Box 13.6: Kiran Mazumdar Shaw- CEO of India's Biggest Biotechnology Company

Born: *March 23, 1953*

Achievement: *Chairman & Managing Director of Biocon Ltd; Felicitated with Padmashri (1989) and Padma Bhushan (2005).*

Kiran Mazumdar Shaw is the Chairman & Managing Director of Biocon Ltd, India's biggest biotechnology company. In 2004, she became India's richest woman.

Kiran Mazumdar Shaw was born on March 23, 1953 in Bangalore. She had her schooling at Bishop Cotton Girls School and Mount Carmel College at Bangalore. After completing her B.Sc. in Zoology from Bangalore University in 1973, she went to Ballarat University in Melbourne, Australia and qualified as a master brewer.

Kiran Mazumdar Shaw started her professional career as trainee brewer in Carlton & United Beverages in 1974. In 1978, she joined as Trainee Manager with Biocon Biochemicals Limited in Ireland. In the same year, Kiran Mazumdar Shaw founded Biocon India in collaboration with Biocon Biochemicals Limited, with a capital of Rs.10,000. She initially faced many problems regarding funds for her business. Banks were hesitant to give loan to her as biotechnology was a totally new field at that point of time and she was a woman entrepreneur, which was a rare phenomenon.

Biocon's initial operation was to extract an enzyme from papaya. Under Kiran Mazumdar Shaw's stewardship Biocon transformed from an industrial enzymes company to an integrated biopharmaceutical company with strategic research initiatives. Today, Biocon is recognised as India's pioneering biotech enterprise. In 2004, Biocon came up with an IPO and the issue was over-subscribed by over 30 times. Post-IPO, Kiran Mazumdar Shaw held close to 40% of the stock of the company and was regarded as India's richest woman with an estimated worth of Rs. 2,100 crore.

Kiran Mazumdar Shaw is the recipient of several prestigious awards. These include ET Businesswoman of the Year, Best Woman Entrepreneur, Model Employer, Ernst & Young's Entrepreneur of the Year Award for Life Sciences & Healthcare, Leading Exporter, Outstanding Citizen, Technology Pioneer, etc. Government of India also felicitated her with Padmashri (1989) and Padma Bhushan (2005).

Source: http://www.iloveindia.com/indian-heroes/kiran-mazumdar-shaw.html# (Accessed on 12/11/2009).

Mr. Agarwal of IFCI normally works coolly by designing routine strategies. But, he suddenly changed his work style and started working seriously and designing innovative strategies when the market value of the equity share fell down from Rs. 45 to Rs. 11. Thus, the stable personality of Mr. Agarwal changed, consequent upon the situational demands.

Japanese started working hard, innovatively and competitively consequent upon the effect of World War II. Similarly, many business executives also started working competitively consequent upon globalisation. Thus, situational factors also influence the personality.

Different situations demand different aspects of one's personality. Therefore, individual's personality changes in order to meet the situational demands. Individual's personality changes in different situations though it is normally stable and constant. Thus, the situational requirements influence the effects of heredity and environment on personality.[11]

Situations like temple, classroom, working place, employment interview, boss's chamber, saint's sanctuary and the like regulate the behaviour of the individuals to a greater extent based upon the situational requirements.

We may conclude that heredity, environment and situation influence personality. Heredity states the outer limits of the personality, while environment develops the personality relevant to the normal circumstances and the situation influences the individual to realise and exhibit his potential personality in tune with its requirements. Thus, the interactive conglomeration of heredity, environment and situation makes the individual personality.

(E) PERSONALITY DEVELOPMENT

Various physiological and psychological stages occur in the development of the human personality. There are a number of well known stage theories of personality development. Theories provided by Sigmund Freud, Erikson, Levinson, Hall and Argyris are relevant to understand organisational behaviour.

Freudian Stages

Sigmund Freud first formulated a systematic stage theory. According to Freud, childhood events have a bearing on adult behaviour and consciousness. He believes that there are five stages of psychological development which influence the personality development, *viz.*, oral, anal, phallic, latency and genital.

Stage 1: The Oral Stage

This stage is from the birth up to the age of one year. Infants during this stage depend on others for survival. The biological drives are reduced through the mouth. Mouth remains an important erogenous zone throughout life. Excessive or insufficient amounts of stimulation during this stage may lead to the development of an oral-passive personality in adulthood, with the characteristics of exploitation and domination of others.[12]

Stage 2: The Anal Stage

This stage is from the age of one year to age of three years. The liberal energy is focused on the anal region during this stage. The harsh and repressive toilet training given during this stage may result in anal-retentive personality with the characteristics of punctuality, orderliness, obstinacy, stinginess and cleanliness. The other side of the toilet training will develop an anal-aggressive personality with traits like disorderliness, hostility, destructiveness and cruelty.[13]

Stage 3: The Phallic Stage

This stage starts at the age of three years and ends at the age of four. This stage focusses on psychosexual development. Freud believes that children during this stage identify themselves with the parents of the same sex. Children at this stage are generally interested in the genitals. The Oedipus complex or conflict occurs during this stage, which results in both loving and hating parents. If this conflict is unresolved, it would lead to severe anxiety and guilt feelings affecting normal personality development.

Stage 4: The Latency Period

This stage occurs between the 4 and 6 years of age. The children during this stage shift their interest from sexual issues and seeking gratification of the libido to the social knowledge and skills needed for work. Children develop the interest in developing social relations with classmates and friends. Similarly, they develop the basic skills necessary for their work by understanding the basics of environments with the entry in schools.

Stage 5: The Genital Stage

This stage occurs during adolescence to adulthood and sexual interest is re-emerged during this stage. Interest in and awareness towards the opposite sex increase during this stage.

Freud mostly relied on sex to explain stages in personality development. As such, this theory was criticised and paved the way for the development of other theories based on stages of personality development. Erikson's stages of personality development are important among them.

Erikson's Stages of Personality Development

Erikson believed in paying more attention on the social aspects of personality development rather than sexual aspects. He felt that social issues are more important in the process of personality development and development of human relationships. According to Erikson, individuals face psycho-social crisis in each stage of personality development. Each crisis should be aptly resolved in order to have a normal and fulfilling personality. Crisis is a turning point in an individual's development. Erikson proposed eight stages of personality development.

Erikson believed in paying more attention on the social aspects of personality development rather than sexual aspects.

Stage 1: Infancy Stage

This stage runs up to the age of one year. Success in this stage brings pursuit of affection, gratification of needs, recognition, etc. Failure in this stage results in consistent abuse, deprivation of love, too early or hard weaning and artistic isolation.

Stage 2: Early Childhood

This stage runs from the age of one year to three years. The success in this stage makes the child to view self as a person in his/her own right apart from parents. The failure in this stage results in feeling of inadequacy, doubting the self, etc.

Stage 3: Play Age

This stage runs from four years to five years of age. The success in this stage makes the individual to be initiative, imitative, anticipates the future and imaginative. Vice-versa is true in case of failure in this stage.

Stage 4: School Age

This stage is from the age of six to eleven years. The successful individual during this stage is industrious, develops scholastic and social competencies, undertakes real tasks, etc. Failure in this stage develops inferiority complex, poor work culture, avoids competition, etc.

Stage 5: Puberty and Adolescence

This stage occurs during the age of 12 to 20 years. The successful individual during this stage identifies himself with egos and with failure the individual experiences role confusion.

Stage 6: Young Adulthood

This stage is from 20 to 24 years of age. The successful individual develops the capacity to commit himself to others. Failure to meet requirements of this stage keeps the individual in isolation. The individual avoids intimacy and seeks interpersonal encounters.

Stage 7: Middle Adulthood

This stage runs between the age of 25 years to 65 years. The successful individual in this stage is productive and creative for self and others and the failing individual tends to self love, personal impoverishment and has a feeling of hopelessness and meaninglessness.

Stage 8: Late Adulthood

This is the stage of old age. The successful individual during this stage develop integrity. He appreciates continuity of past, present and future. The failing candidate finds no meaning in life and no faith in self and others.

Adult Life Stages

Daniel Levinson believed that, "the life structure evolves through a relatively orderly sequence throughout the adult years."[14] He believed that there was little variability in the following four identifiable but stable periods.

Stable Periods

1. Entering the adult world (22 years to 28 years of age)
2. Settling down (33 years to 40 years of age)
3. Entering middle adulthood (45 years to 50 years of age) and
4. Culmination of middle adulthood (55 years to 60 years of age)

Transitional Periods

He identified four transitional periods:

1. **Age-thirty transition (Age 28 to 33):** During this period, individuals think of promotions, shift in lifestyles, developing new relationships, building networks, etc.

2. **Mid-life transition (Age 40 to 45):** During this period, individuals prefer to change jobs, broader relationships, wider the networks, and set new goals in the career as well as in life etc due to increasing responsibilities.

3. **Age-fifty transition (Age 50 to 55):** During this stage, individuals are content with their achievement. They prefer stability in career and life. However, they try to make a change before the end of career, if the environment favours them.

4. **Late adult transition (Age 60 to 65):** During this stage, individuals try to have a second career by switching over to a convenient and tension free job with an average income. This stage is the post retirement stage.

Hall's Career Stage Model

Hall has developed an overall model for career stages. There are four major career stages. These four career stages are:

Career Stage 1: Exploration

This stage includes searching for an identity, undergoing self-examination, role try outs, taking up of different jobs; unstable and less productive. This stage runs from 15 years to 25 years of age.

Career Stage 2: Establishment

This stage includes settling down, need for intimacy, growing and productive period. This stage runs from 25 years to 45 years of age.

Career Stage 3: Maintenance

Person levels off into a highly productive plateau, need for generativist, assumes paternalistic role/ mentor. This stage runs from 45 years to 65 years of age.

Career Stage 4: Decline

This stage indicates the need for integrity (need to feel satisfied with his/her life choices and overall career). This stage normally takes place after the age of 65 years.

Immaturity to Maturity Approach

Chris Argyris, a well known organisational behaviour theorist, has identified specific dimensions of human personality in a departure from the strict stage approach, i.e., immaturity to maturity approach.

Chris Argyris proposes that human personality progresses along a continuum from immaturity as an infant to maturity as an adult (See Table 13.2).

Argyrs clarifies that all persons may not reach for all dimensions on the mature end of the continuum. He further clarifies that:

- Personality depends upon individual's perception, self-concept, adaptation and adjustment in addition to the dimensions shown in the table.
- The dimensions continually change in degree from infant to adult stages.
- This model does not predict specific behaviour, but provides a method of describing and measuring the growth of any individual in the culture.
- These dimensions are based upon latent characteristics of the personality.[15]

Table 13.2: The Argyris Immaturity-Maturity Continuum

Immaturity (as an Infant) Characteristics	Maturity (as an Adult) Characteristics
Passivity	Activity
Dependence	Independence
Few ways of behaving	Diverse behaviour
Shallow interests	Deep interests
Short-term perspective	Long time perspective
Subordinate position	Superordinate position
Lack of self-awareness	Self-awareness and control

(**Source:** Fred Luthans, Organisational Behaviour, p. 188.)

(F) PERSONALITY THEORIES

Psychologists and other human behaviour theorists developed personality theories based on research studies. These personality theories are grouped into psychoanalytic theories, socio-psychological theories, trait theories and holistic theories. Now, we shall discuss the psychoanalytic theories.

Psychoanalytical Theory

Various psychologists contributed to the development of psychoanalytic theory. These psychologists include: Sigmund Freud, Carl Jung, Alfred Adler, Karen Horney and Eric Fromm. Sigmund Freud made significant contributions to the theory compared to other psychologists. On the basis of his research, freud concluded that unconscious framework motivates the man mostly. There are three aspects in the unconscious framework, *viz*., The Id, the Ego and the Super ego. These three aspects are interrelated with each other.

The Id

The Id is the primary principle of all human life. It is the mental agency containing everything inherited. It seeks gratification for biological needs. It is the unconscious part of human personality. The biological needs include: hunger, thirst and sexual needs. These needs would be the driving force for thinking and behaving throughout the life. According to the Id, the man removes the tension of unsatisfied biological needs by forming a mental image of the object which would satisfy the needs. Thus, the Id concept is related to the imaginary and illusionary world.

The Ego

The ego is related to the reality principle. It is the conscious and logical part of human personality. Ego is based on the realities of the external environment through intellect and reason. The Id wants immediate pleasure through imagination while the ego wants a real pleasure. For example, a fresh management graduate develops a mental image of a General Manager's position in a multinational company. This is the essence of the Id concept. The job market, competition from other candidates like CAs, ICWAs, MHRM, CFAs, etc., and recession in the industry make him to realize the reality and aspire for a junior management position. This is the essence of the ego concept. The interactive functioning between the Id and the Ego results in many conflicting situations like the fresh management graduate aspiring for a General Manager's position and forced to accept a junior management's position by the environment. Super ego provides necessary support to the ego in resolving the conflict.

Super Ego

Super ego represents a system of personal and societal values, norms, ethics and attitudes. It acts as an ethical constraint on behaviour. This can be treated as conscience. Super ego acts as a norm to the ego in order to determine which behaviour is right and which behaviour is wrong. For example, expressing the individual employee's opinions and ideas is wrong in the public sector while the same behaviour is right in the private sector based on their respective norms and culture.

Thus, the super ego judges whether the behaviour/action is correct or incorrect based on the culture, norms and values of the society concerned.

Though this theory makes significant contributions, it is criticised as:

- It suffers from scientific verification;
- It does not give total picture of the behaviour emerging from personality; and
- It does not take the social factors into consideration.

The personality theory which is developed by taking the social factors into consideration is the socio-psychological theory of personality.

Socio-Psychological Theory

The personality of Late Dhirubhai Ambani of Reliance Industries had been shaped by the society's needs for petroleum products at competitive prices, telecommunications needs for fast communications at the lowest prices and his psychological needs like achievement, involvement etc. Similarly, the personality of Dr. Anji Reddy of Dr. Reddy's Laboratories is shaped by the society's need for qualitative medicines at the affordable price by the people of third world countries and his psychological need for achieving something different from others. Thus, the society's needs and psychological factors of the individual shape the personality. The individual and the society cannot live in isolation. These two interact with and are interdependent on each other. The individual contributes to the achievement of society's needs. Similarly, society assists the individual in fulfilling his needs.

The psychological factors of the individual and the sociological factors of the society interact with each other. Thus, this theory is inclusive of social factors and psychological factors. Contributors to this theory include: Adler, Fromm, Horney and Sullivan. Social variables are significant factors in this theory while biological factors are significant in psychoanalytical theory. Behavioural motivation is conscious according to socio-psychological theory.

The psychological factors of the individual and the sociological factors of the society interact with each other.

The contributions of the socio-psychologists are as follows:

Fromm stressed on the importance of social context. These contributions include: building social relations, making the work more social relevance, making the employee to have the feel of social sets in his work and output.

Sullivan and Horney stressed on interpersonal behaviour. These contributions include: developing transactional abilities, viewing the people positively, developing positive attitude, etc.

Adler emphasised on different variables. These contributions include: career, networking, religious beliefs, balancing family and work requirements, etc.

Horney stressed on predominant interpersonal behaviours like being compliant, aggressive and detached. Compliant people are dependent on others, aggressive people are motivated by the need for power and detached people are self-sufficient.[16]

Managers have to shape the personality of their employees through the interaction and interrelation of social and psychological needs. Now, we shall study the trait factor theory.

Trait Factor Theory

Allport and Cattell contributed to the development of trait factor theory. Allport differentiated common traits from personal dispositions. Common traits are used to compare people. He identified six types of values, *viz*., religious, social, economic, political, aesthetic and theoretical. Personal dispositions are completely unique from individual to individual. This uniqueness emphasises the psychology of the individual.[17] Cattell developed similar set of traits, *viz*., surface traits and source traits.

Surface and Source Traits

Surface traits include wise-foolish, affectionate-cold, sociable-seclusive, honest-dishonest, etc. Individuals keep their actual feelings inside and exhibit the traits desirable by the situation. Individuals would like to be good to others at their own cost. Similarly, individuals maintain social relations, develop friendship and networks.

Source traits include Maturity-realism, good nature and trustworthiness, critical-suspicious, etc. Individuals with source traits possess characteristics like maturity of mind, judgmental, analysing and understanding people and situations more accurately.

Trait theory helps to find out relationship between traits and behaviour. This theory recognises continuity of behaviour.

Now, we shall study the holistic or self-theory of personality.

Holistic/Self-Theory of Personality

The personality theories discussed earlier, deal with the personality from one or the other aspect only. Self-theory deals with the personality from all aspects and as such it provides the holistic approach. It emphasises on the totality of the human behaviour. This theory is also known as *organismic theory*. This theory treats the organism as a whole. The contributors to this theory include Alfred Maslow, Herzberg and Lewin. Carl Rogers is the major contributor to this theory. According to him, there are four factors in self-concept, *viz*., self-image, ideal self, looking glass-self and real self.

Self-Image

Self-image is the way one sees himself/herself. Self-image is the set of beliefs of oneself who or what he is. Mr. Vijay K. Rekhi, CEO of Spirits Division of UB Group sees himself as a leader who brings the skills of each individual member of his team to the forefront.

Ideal Self

Ideal self denotes the way one would like to be. The self-image is the reality of a person while the ideal self is the ideal position as expected/perceived by him. The ideal self motivates the person. Mr. Vijay of UB Group would like to be the leader who manages the overall environment of his company. This view of Mr. Vijay is called the ideal self.

Looking Glass-self

Looking glass-self is the perception of an individual about how others perceive his/her characteristics and qualities. Looking glass-self is perception of others' perception and is the outcome of face-to-face interaction with others from the very beginning of life. Ms. Kalpana, Executive Director of ICICI, perceives that her followers perceive her as intellectual and has the ability to satisfy the customers. This act is called 'looking glass-self.'

Real Life

The real life is what one actually is. In other words, real life is the real characteristics, values and attitudes of one self. The person adjusts and readjusts himself based on the responses of others and the environmental influences.

Self-concept helps the person in perceiving others, other things and himself. The person cautiously behaves as the average person is not particularly well acquainted with himself. Self-concept helps in perception and overall behaviour.

Thus, personality influences behaviour of the people in organisations. Now, we shall study the influence of personality on organisational behaviour.

(G) PERSONALITY AND ORGANISATIONAL BEHAVIOUR

The CEO of Gillette India says, he retains the employees with originality, confidence, dependency and self-dramatizing traits even during recessionary periods as they perform better even in adverse situations. He also says, he fires the employees with irresponsibility, self-doubting, uncommunicative, rude and unassertive traits even in boom conditions as their behaviour does not match the organisational expectations. His views indicate that personality has direct influence on behaviour and performance of the people. Even the research findings indicate the same. Hence, we should study the influence of personality on organisational behaviour. Specific personality traits, among others, influence the behaviour significantly. They are: locus of control, self-monitoring, and type A and type B personality.

Locus of Control

Locus of control refers to the degree to which people believe that they plan, direct and control their life and career. People generally believe that they have control over their own lives. Locus of control is the extent to which people believe that they can control the events affecting them. Locus of control may be internal or external.

Locus of control refers to the degree to which people believe that they plan, direct and control their life and career.

Internal locus of control refers that the people believe that they plan, direct and control their lives and career to the complete extent. External locus of control refers that the people believe that their lives and career is planned, directed and controlled to the complete extent by external factors and forces. The newly appointed CEO of Visakhapatnam Steel Plant of Steel Authority of India Limited (SAIL) believed that his traits could basically turn around the sick plant while the CEO of Hindustan Cables Limited (HCL) believed that the financial assistance from the Government of India could turn around the sick company in 2001. The former one is the internal locus of control whereas the latter refers to the external locus of control.

Internal locus of control

Internal locus of control is the belief of an individual that his/her behaviour determines many of the events in his/her life. People with moderately strong internal locus of control are successful in their jobs, career and lives. They also perform their job better, cope better in stressful situations and are satisfied with the challenging jobs and performance-based rewards.[18]

External locus of control

External locus of control is the belief of an individual that chance, luck, fate or other people determine what happens to him/her. People who believe in the external locus of control view that external environment or god or fate determines what should happen to them and it will happen. People with moderately strong external locus of control may not be successful in their jobs, career and lives.

Research studies reported that the executives with the internal locus of control formulated innovative strategies compared to those with external locus of control. They invested more in R&D, introduced new products ahead of the competitors and changed product lines drastically. They formulated aggressive strategies for the future.[19]

Self-Efficacy and Self-Monitoring

Self-Efficacy

Confidence in one's own abilities and capacities in carryingout a task to the levels of specific performance successfully is referred to as self-efficacy.[20] People with high self-efficacy take-up the activity with confidence, plan appropriately, and implement the activities with full confidence and normally complete the activity to the specific level of performance successfully. Judgments of self-efficacy consists of three aspects, viz.,

People acquire general beliefs/ expectations about their abilities and capacities, cognitive resources and strengths needed to achieve their goals as well as events and situations.

- Magnitude – the level of confidence of the individual in his/her own confidence.
- Strength – the degree of confidence that the individual can do the activity to the level of desired performance level.
- Generality – the extent to which the magnitude and strength of one situation or task is extended to other situations and tasks.[21]

General Self-Efficacy: People acquire general beliefs/ expectations about their abilities and capacities, cognitive resources and strengths needed to achieve their goals as well as events and situations.[22] Such beliefs /expectations are known as general self-efficacy. These beliefs are stable over period.

Self-monitoring is the sensitivity and ability of an individual to adapt to the situational demands or cues. High self-monitors change their behaviour easily based on the situational requirements while the low self-monitors reveal their moods and personal traits which may contradict situational requirements.

Employees with high self-monitoring tend to be better conversationalists, better leaders, work efficiently with people of different departments (boundary-spanning positions), are more likely to be promoted/selected for better jobs.

The CEO of LG realised that the sales of the company were declining due to the cultural change. He immediately changed his leadership style and created empowered teams. This change in behaviour enabled the employees to develop a new refrigerator which could store the traditional Korean food. This product turned the company into a profit-making company. Adjustment of the behaviour of the CEO of LG is called *self-monitoring*.

(H) TYPE 'A' AND TYPE 'B' PERSONALITIES

Mr. Ramana Rao of Hindustan Beverages Limited is excessively competitive towards his rival company, takes his office work home, never enjoys leisure time, and experiences a chronic sense of time urgency. His personality is termed as Type 'A' personality. The personality with opposite traits is called Type 'B' personality.

Type A Personality

Type A personality is aggressively involved in a chronic, incessant struggle to achieve more and more in lesser and lesser time, and, if required to do so, against the opposing efforts of other things or other persons.

Type A personality is "aggressively involved in a chronic, incessant struggle to achieve more and more in lesser and lesser time, and, if required to do so, against the opposing efforts of other things or other persons."[20] This type of personality is treated as positive personality in North American culture and an undesirable personality in the Indian culture.

Profile of Type A Personality is:

- Always moving, walking rapidly, talking and eating rapidly
- Impatient
- Does two things at the same time
- Not coping up with leisure time
- Is obsessed with numbers
- Measuring success with quantity
- Aggressive and competitive and
- Always under time pressure.

Type B Personality

Type B personalities are exactly opposite to Type A. These personalities are "rarely harried by the desire to obtain a widely increasing number of things or participate in an endless growing series of events in ever-decreasing amount of time."[21]

Profile of Type B personality:

- Is not concerned about time, patient, mild mannered and never in a hurry
- Does not brag
- Plays for fun and not to win
- Relaxes without guilt
- Has no pressing deadlines.

Types A and B and Job Performance

Type B personalities are exactly opposite to Type A.

Normally, it is viewed that Type-A persons are superior to Type-B people. Type-A people produce more even under distractions and disturbing situations than Type-B people. In addition Type A perform more difficult and challenging jobs. Type A employees are highly competitive and poorly creative. They suit to the routine activities. Their behaviour can be easily predictable. These people concentrate on quantity and results rather than quality. Type A people fail to perform the jobs those require patience and judgment. Type-As are too hurry to complete the work ahead of time. Thus, Type-As are suitable for time bound jobs, rather than creative, administrative and managerial jobs.

Type B personalities can reach higher positions as promotions, "usually go to those who are wise rather than to those who are merely hasty, to those who are tactful rather than to those who are hostile and to those who are creative rather than to those who are merely agile in competitive strife."[22] Surveys reveal that most of top executives are Type-B category rather than Type-A category.[23]

We can't conclude that Type-Bs are superior to type-As as both these two categories have their own strengths. Type-As are suitable for jobs involving time pressure and solitary work, whereas Type-Bs are suitable for jobs involving complex judgment and creativity. Therefore, organizations have to select either Type-A or Type-B depending upon job-candidate fit.

Type-'A's Burn themselves, but Provide Light to the Company

Type-A burns themselves, but provides light to the company.

Type-A employees are aggressive and competitive, overwork for the company and work even under critical and crisis situations. There are certain situations when the employees forget their conveniences and trouble themselves to meet the deadlines and conveniences of customers and other company's stakeholders. Type-A employees in the process of meeting the challenges of the company on time and sometimes even before the deadlines burn themselves in the sense that their health as well as causing inconveniences to their family members. (See Box 13.7).

Box 13.7: Life is to Live, but not Burn for Others!

Six software professionals under the age of 33 have died and 2 top executives from renowned software companies have become paralyzed because of stress-related heart ailments in the last six months in Chennai, says a study by Mitran Foundation, a Bangalore-based voluntary association of practising doctors. "All the six who died, and the two who became invalid, had no family history of heart attacks or any pre-history of heart ailments or paralysis. They were all in their prime, between 27 and 33 years, and handled challenging projects at work in their respective companies. They worked long and continuous hours. The end struck them very suddenly, and it looked as if their hearts refused to take any more stress," said Dr Dwarakanath, director of Mitran Foundation, who has studied stress components in 40 software companies in Chennai during the last six months.

The study, conducted at a cost of Rs 45 lakh, covered more than 4,000 software professionals from 80 companies who were in service for a minimum of three years. The e-mail responses were scientifically tabulated and the findings were ready in 2002. Dr Dwarakanath, who was the late Dhirubhai Ambani's personal stress management consultant, said questionnaires extracting every minute detail were sent to the respondents. The personal background, family history and personal characteristics of these individuals were assessed and it was found that the stress in these professionals was only due to work pressure. All other factors were eliminated. "Our study confirmed that the number of suicides, divorces, heart ailments, BP and diabetes patients and mental depression are the highest in the software industry. The fancy salaries of software professionals are no longer something to rejoice about," Dr. Dwarakanath said.

We found that the software industry has simply no routine. Deadlines hang before them and everyday they chase new problems. During weekends more than 60 per cent of the vehicles are found parked in the office complexes. There is no physical exercise and new food habits favoured by pizza culture fuel the problem. Cervical spondilitis and wrist problems due to uncomfortable handling of the computer mouse, eye problems and discomfort in bowel movements are common. The stress for couples where both are employed in the IT industry is the worst. The simple step of taking time off from work for three months allowed an IT couple wanting a child for years to conceive one," Dr Dwarakanath said.

M.T.R. Venukopalan, senior training coordinator, Covansys India, acknowledged that "IT professionals were the most stressed individuals. Even if the company sponsors a movie or self-care lecture, not many attend them," he said. Jyothsana, a travel coordinator for Temenos India Pvt Ltd, expressed concern for the young employees who complain of back and knee pains. She acknowledged that IT professionals require a specific eating and physical exercise routine to ease their stress. "Our lives are becoming mechanical, guided only by deadlines," she said.

So think again if you are staying late in the office regularly. Think again about your family. Think again about your social life and health. Work is essential. Your contribution to the goal should be great. But, please don't make it a habit to stay late.

Don't skip your breakfast/lunch/dinner. None of these are equated by Pizza, breads / Biscuits / Wafers / Chat items. This will save your life, as life is not worth living without the eyes. During a recent visit to an optician, one of my friends was told of an exercise for the eyes by a specialist doctor in the US that he termed as 20-20-20. It is apt for all of us and also for people who spend long hours in front of the computer for various activities.

Source: http://akssara.blogspot.com/2006/10/about-professionals-health.html (Accessed on 15/08/09)

Type-Bs Relax Themselves, but Cost to the Company

Type-Bs relax themselves, but cost to the company.

Type-B employees relax without guilt, enjoy life and don't meet the deadlines. Therefore, such employees meet their goals rather than contributing to the company's goals and meeting the needs of the customers. Type-B employees spend more than enough time with their family members and friends. They also relax and enjoy music and never in hurry in meeting deadlines. In fact, they feel that situations and events wait for them rather than otherwise. Thus, they enjoy themselves even at the cost of the company and its stakeholders and particularly the customers. (See Box 13.8).

Box 13.8: Type-Bs: Care Themselves, Not the Customers/ Company!

Ms. Jennett has been working as an airhostess of XYZ Airlines. She attended a party and spent time leisurely and reported for duty 30 minutes late, but fifteen minutes before the departure the flight. Later she found that she forgot to bring her passport and coolly informed the pilot about the same. Then the pilot asked her to go home and get her passport as it is most essential for her to complete her duty. She came with her passport after an hour and the flight took off after 1 hour fifteen minutes of the scheduled time. The flight landed at the destination one hour fifteen minutes late. Consequently, some travellers missed their connecting flights. She never felt that she committed a mistake or caused inconvenience to the customers. But of course, the airlines incurred heavy expenditure for providing hotel accommodation to the travellers, who missed the connecting flights.

Types A and B and Interpersonal Relations

The tasks of managers involve getting things done by others and as such they have to maintain sound interpersonal relations. Type-B employees are relaxed and therefore maintain sound relations with subordinates. Type-A employees are impatient, irritable and always in hurry and as such they also push their subordinates towards completions of jobs based on time. In addition Type-As lose temper and lash out at subordinates. As such Type-As may more involve in inter-personal conflict. Research studies also suggest that Type-As are more aggressive, and involve in dysfunctional conflicts and counterproductive behaviour.

Therefore though the Type-A would turnout more volume of work than Type-Bs; they disturb the interpersonal relations. So Type-As are best fit for the jobs that can be performed in isolation. Type-Bs are suitable for supervisory and executive positions.

Globalisation, Competition and Personalities A and B

The economic liberalizations along with the strides in information technology led to competition. Competition in its turn placed the customer at the significant place and the companies compete among themselves to win over the customer by providing the high qualitative product at the place and time of the convenience of the customer. Consequently, the companies started pressuring the employees to perform their jobs based on the time and convenience of the customers. Employees of Type-A personality category meet the deadlines of the companies and as well as customers. Thus, the companies prefer Type-A employees to meet the targets. (See Box 13.9)

Box 13.9: Personalities A and B and Competitive Situations: Research Results

Friedman & Rosenman identified a pattern of behaviour that they believed contributed to heart disease; they called it Type A behaviour. Type A behavior is characterized as the behaviour pattern of individuals who are competitive, impatient, hostile and always striving to do more in less time. Type B behaviour is the pattern exhibited by people who are calmer, more patient, and less hurried less competitive. Three of the most common characteristics of an individual who exhibits Type A personality are time urgency, competitiveness, and achievement striving. An individual with Type A behaviour tends to be impatient, hurries under pressure and is prompt and often early for appointments. Though past literature inferred that in a competitive situation, Type A individuals would perform a task with greater speed than Type B individuals, the results were inconsistent with the hypothesis because they did indeed correspond with previous research as was expected. It was hypothesized that Type A personalities will have faster recall speeds in competitive situations whereas the recall speed of Type B personalities should be the same as Type A personalities in non-competitive circumstances. The results are in agreement with my hypothesis such that personality type does affect recall speed and that depends on whether the task is competitive or non-competitive. The results also showed a main effect for competition between Type A and Type B individuals with an interaction. The interaction exhibits that recall scores depend on the personality level and competition. *Though past literature inferred that in a competitive situation, Type A individuals would perform a task with greater speed than Type B individuals, the results were inconsistent with the hypothesis because they did indeed correspond with previous research as was expected. It was hypothesized that Type A personalities will have faster recall speeds in competitive situations whereas the recall speed of Type B personalities should be the same as Type A personalities in non-competitive circumstances. The results are in agreement with my hypothesis such that personality type does affect recall speed and that depends on whether the task is competitive or non-competitive. The results also showed a main effect for competition between Type A and Type B individuals with an interaction. The interaction exhibits that recall scores depend on the personality level and competition.*

Source: http://web.sbu.edu/psychology/lavin/carolyn.htm (Accessed on 12/08/09)

Most of the executives during economic boom used to be aggressive, fast in decision- making, formulating and implementing strategies. In fact, such executives could exploit the opportunities provided by the environment and win over their competitors like Richard Branson (see Box 13.10). Most of the CEOs of sun rising industries like software companies, pharmaceutical companies and biotechnology companies used to be dynamic, fast and hurry in making and implementing decisions as well as acting. Even the executives of other companies also acquired the traits of personality-A in order to be competitive and exploit the opportunities of the growing markets. In other words, they used to be situational in adapting to personality-A characteristics. Thus, Personality- A is more apt for economic boom situations. Box 13.10 provides the suitability of personality of Mr. Richard Brason, CEO of Virgin Group of companies, to the economic boom situations. He has been dynamic, hurry and fast in carrying out the activities and to exploit the opportunities by breaking the traditional management practices followed by business giants like British Airways and Qantas Airways.

Thus, Personality-A type of the people are more appropriate during the economic boom periods even for executive positions as they proact and react faster than Personality-B type of the people.

However, economic recessionary situations would be different that of economic boom situations. There would be competition among companies to reduce the cost of operations in order to save the cost and to achieve the survival and sustainability strategies of the companies during economic recessionary periods. Executives of various companies have started making-decision fast and act dynamically even during recessionary periods. Thus, executives of Personality-A traits perform fast to meet the competition under varying conditions. Thus, personality-A is appropriate when the economic situations are volatile.

Box 13.10: Richard Branson's Personality and Competition

Richard Branson

Richard Branson at Virgin Atlantic Global Flyer planned

Born: *18 July 1950*

Birthplace: *Surrey, England*

Best known as: *Founder of the Virgin business empire.*

A billionaire businessman with a taste for derring-do, Richard Branson is the founder and CEO of the mega-corporation known as the Virgin Group. Branson's first business was music: he began selling records by mail order in 1970, opened a shop in London in 1971, and in 1972 added a music studio. Virgin Records was launched a year later and soon became force in the music business, signing hot 1970s and '80s acts like the Sex Pistols, Phil Collins and Boy George. Rather than rest on his laurels, Branson branched out into a dizzying array of businesses bearing the Virgin name: Virgin Atlantic Airways, Virgin Megastores (sellers of music and books), Virgin Mobile (phone service), along with cosmetics, car sales, health clubs, and many other concerns. Jovial, aggressive, and never shy about self-promotion, Branson put himself at the forefront of the Virgin publicity machine and made himself one of the best-known businessmen in Britain and the world. Branson also has made a hobby of record-breaking travel adventures: in 1986 he made the fastest-ever crossing of the Atlantic Ocean on his boat Virgin Atlantic Challenger II *and a year later became the first to cross the Atlantic in a hot air balloon in his* Virgin Atlantic Flyer. *In the 1990s he also joined fellow-businessman Steve Fossett in several failed attempts to circle the globe non-stop in a hot air balloon. In 2006 he made headlines by pledging to devote all personal profits from his transporation companies for 10 years to developing renewable energy technologies. Branson's autobiography,* Losing My Virginity, *was published in 1998. He was knighted by Queen Elizabeth II in 1999.*

Extra credit: *The first artist to sign with Virgin Records was Michael Oldfield, whose album* Tubular Bells *was featured on the soundtrack of the movie* The Exorcist *and subsequently sold over 15 million copies... According to his autobiography, Branson is dyslexic... Virgin Music was sold to Thorn EMI in 1992; Branson started a fresh label, V2, in 1996.*

Branson formed Virgin Atlantic Airways in 1984, launched Virgin Mobile in 1999, Virgin Blue in Australia in 2000. He was 9th in the Sunday Times Rich List 2006, worth just over £3 billion. Branson wrote in his autobiography of the decision to start an airline:

"My interest in life comes from setting myself huge, apparently unachievable challenges and trying to rise above them...from the perspective of wanting to live life to the full, I felt that I had to attempt it".

In 1992, Branson took what many saw as being one of his riskier business exploits by entering into the railway business. Virgin Trains won the franchises for the former Intercity West Coast and Cross-Country sectors of British Rail. Launched with the usual Branson fanfare with promises of new high-tech tilting trains and enhanced levels of service, Virgin Trains soon ran into problems with the rolling stock and infrastructure it had inherited from British Rail. The company's reputation was almost irreversibly damaged in the late 1990s as it struggled to make trains reliably run on time while it awaited the modernisation of the West Coast Main Line, and the arrival of new rolling stock.

Virgin acquired European short-haul airline Euro Belgian Airlines in 1996 and renamed it Virgin Express. In 2006 the airline was merged with SN Brussels Airlines forming Brussels Airlines. It also started a national airline based in Nigeria, called Virgin Nigeria. Another airline, Virgin America, began flying out of the San Francisco International Airport in August 2007. Branson has also developed a Virgin Cola brand and even a Virgin Vodka brand, which has not been a very successful enterprise. As a consequence of these lacklustre performers, the satirical British fortnightly magazine Private Eye *has been critical of Branson and his companies (see* Private Eye *image caption).*[9]

After the so-called campaign of "dirty tricks" (see expanded reference in Virgin Atlantic Airways), Branson sued rival airline British Airways for libel in 1992. John King, then chairman of British Airways, counter-sued, and the case went to trial in 1993. British Airways, faced with likely defeat, settled the case, giving £500,000 to Branson and a further £110,000 to his airline and had to pay legal fees of up to £3 million. Branson divided his compensation (the so-called "BA bonus") among his staff.

On 25 September 2004, Branson announced the signing of a deal under which a new space tourism company, Virgin Galactic, will license the technology behind Spaceship One—funded by Microsoft co-Founder Paul Allen and designed by legendary American aeronautical engineer and visionary Burt Rutan—to take paying passengers into suborbital space. Virgin Galactic (wholly owned by Virgin Group) plans to make flights available to the public by late 2009 with tickets priced at US$200,000 using Scaled Composites White Knight Two.

Branson's next venture with the Virgin group is Virgin Fuels, which is set to respond to global warming and exploit the recent spike in fuel costs by offering a revolutionary, cheaper fuel for automobiles and, in the near future, aircraft. Branson has stated that he was formerly a global warming sceptic and was influenced in his decision by a breakfast meeting with Al Gore.

Branson has been tagged as a "transformational leader" in the management lexicon, with his maverick strategies and his stress on the Virgin Group as an organization driven on informality and information, one that is bottom-heavy rather than strangled by top-level management.

Source: http://www.infoplease.com/biography/var/richardbranson.html and http://en.wikipedia.org/wiki/Richard_Branson (Accessed on 08/08/2009)

Fundamental Interpersonal Relations Orientation- Behaviour (FIRO-B)

Fundamental Interpersonal Relations Orientations-Behaviour(FIRO-B) assesses the impact of individual's social traits on others. It also examines individual's adjustment and compatibility with others. FIRO-B measures the degree to which a person associates with others in terms of inclusion viz., moving towards and moving away from people. It also measures the extent to which a person controls himself as well as others. Its measurement regarding affection reflects the degree to which a person emotionally involved with others.

Thus, this instrument measures a person's characteristics with regard to:

(1) Inclusion in social settings for satisfying the needs like belongingness and recognition; (I- Score)

(2) Control others in a social setting by influencing, assuming responsibility, making decisions affecting others, leading others and dominating people; (C-Score)

(3) Affection in terms of emotional bondage, closeness, warmth and sensitivity. (A-Score)

This instrument also measures:

(1) A person's expressed and manifested behaviour that can be observed by others in the areas on inclusion, control and affection; (E-Scores)

(2) A person's wanted behaviour that refers what a person wants from other people in terms of inclusion, affection and control, which is less directly observable by others.(W-Scores)

This instrument's scores present the results as follows:

(1) Low E(I) score indicates that a person is uncomfortable around people and tends to move away from them. Such people are termed as 'under social'.

(2) High E(I) score indicates that a person is comfortable in social settings and tends to move towards others. Such people are termed as 'over social'.

(3) Low W(I) score indicates that a person is selective about with whom he/she associates.

(4) High W(I) score indicates that a person has a strong need to belong and be accepted.

(5) Low E(C) score indicates that a person avoids of making decisions and assuming responsibility.

(6) High E (C) score indicates that a person can and does take on responsibilities involved in leadership roles. Such persons are termed as 'autocrats'.

(7) Low W(C) score indicates that a person does not want others to control him/her and does not want others to make decisions for them.

(8) High W(C) score for women indicates that women are learned to tolerate the men's dominance.

(9) High W(C) score for men indicates that men have dependency needs and expect others to make decisions for them.

(10) Low E(A) score indicates that person is cautious about initiating the development of close and deep relationships. These persons are called 'under social'.

(11) High E(A) scores indicate that persons can readily become emotionally involved in relationships and they develop deep relationships with others. These persons are termed as 'over personal'.

(12) Low W(A) scores indicate that a person is very selective about with whom he/she forms deep relationships.

(13) High W(A) scores indicate that persons want others to initiate close and deep relationships with them.

Machiavellianism

Profile of a Machiavellian is someone who views and manipulates others purely for personal gain

Machiavellianism has its origin to Niccolo Michiavelli, who wrote in 16th century on how to gain and use power.[23] Profile of a Machiavellian is someone who views and manipulates others purely for personal gain. Some people manipulate others in the social settings, while some others view manipulation as sinful and deceitful. Some other people view manipulation as an essential strategy to succeed in career. Psychologists have developed instruments to measure a person's Machiavellian orientation. A personality high in Mach:

- Tends to behave in consistent with the basic principles of Machiavellianism;
- Tends to approach situations logically and thoughtfully and possess the ability to lie to achieve personal goals;
- Tends to be reluctant to be swayed by loyalty, friendship, past promises, and opinions of others; and
- Tends to influence others.[24]

Thus, personalities high in Mach manipulate more, win more are persuaded less and persuade others more. The performance/outcome of high Machs is superior when situation is based on (1) face-to-face interactions rather than indirect interaction, (2) autonomy rather than based on bureaucratic rules and regulations, and (3) emotional involvement with less details.[25]

High Machs would be suitable for jobs that require negotiation skills like marketing, project managers and labour contract negotiators subject to the presence of the situations mentioned above. However, the success of high Machs poses ethical challenges of means adapted to achieve the goals.

KEY TERMS

- Personality
- Maturity
- Agreeableness
- Emotional Stability
- Learning
- External Locus of Control
- Self-Concept
- External Locus of Control
- Ego
- Personality 'A'
- Locus of Control
- Internal Locus of Control
- Extroversion
- Conscientiousness
- Openness to Experience
- FIRO-B
- Machiavellianism
- Traits
- The Id
- Super Ego
- Personality 'B'
- Self-Efficacy

QUESTIONS

1. What is Personality?
2. Explain the personality traits. State in detail the big five personality traits.
3. What is self-concept? Explain with examples.
4. Analyse various personality development theories
5. Who do you interrelate the personality development and employee behaviour and job performance?
6. What is locus of control? Discuss the characters of persons having internal and external locus of control.
7. What is FIRO-B? Analyse the personality characters of people with varied scores of expressed and wanted behaviours.
8. What are the different characters of people of personality A and personality B types?

REFERENCES

1. G. W. Allport, *"Personality:A Psychological Interpretation,"* Rinehart & Winston, New York, 1937, p. 48.
2. Fred Luthans, "*Organisational Behaviour*," McGraw Hill, New York, 1995, p. 114.
3. Stephen P. Robbins, "*Organisational Behaviour*," Prentice Hall of India (P) Ltd., New Delhi, 2000, p. 92.
4. G.N.Landrum, "*Profiles of Genius*," Prometheus, 1993.
5. Murray R. Barrick and Michael K. Mount, "*Autonomy as a Moderator of the Relationship Between the Big Five Personality Dimensions and Job Performance*," Journal of Applied Psychology, February 1993, p. 111.
6. M. K. Mount, M. R. Barrick and J. P. Strauss, "*Validity of Observes Ratings of the Big Five Personality Factors*," Journal of Applied Psychology, April 1994, p. 272.
7. O. Kroeger and J. M. Thusen, "Type Talk", Delacorret Press, New York, 1988.
8. Debra l. Nelson and James Campbell Quick, "Organisational Behaviour", Thomson, New Delhi,2008, pp. 91-92.
9. R. L. Hotz, "*Genetics Not Parenting, Key to Temperament, Studies Say*," Los Angeles Times, February 20, 1994, p. 41.
10. Daniel Levinson, "*The Seasons of a Man's Life*," Knopf, New York, 1978, p. 49.
11. Chris Agyris, "*Personality and Organisation*," Harper, New York, 1957, pp. 51-53.
12. R. C. Carson, "*Personality*," in M. R. Rosenzweig and L.W.Porter (eds.), Annual Review of Psychology, Vol.27, 1976, p. 10.
13. Abraham K.Korman, "*The Psychology of Motivation*," Prentice Hall, N.J., 1974, p. 227.
14. Larry A. Hjelle and Danniel J. Ziegler, "*Personality Theories, Basic Assumptions, Research and Applications*," McGraw Hill, New York, 1976, p. 32.
15. *Ibid.*
16. Karen Horney, "*Neurotic Personality of Our Times*," New York, Norton, 1937.
17. Gordon W. Allport, "*Personality*," Henry Holt, New York, 1937, pp. 43-47.
18. J. M. Howell and B. J. Avolio, "*Transactional Leadership, Locus of Control and Support for Innovation*," Journal of Applied Psychology, 78(1993), pp. 891-902.
19. D.Miller and J. M. Toulouse, "*Chief Executive Personality and Corporate Strategy and Structure*," Management Science, 32(1986), pp. 1389-1409.
20. M.Synder, "*Public Appearences/Private Realities*," The Psychology of Self-Monitoring, W.H.Freeman, New York, 1987.
21. M.Kilduff and D. V. Day, "*Do Chameleous Get Ahead? The Effects of Self-monitoring on Managerial Careers*," Academy of Management Journal, 37(1994), pp. 1047-60.
22. M.Friedman and R. H. Rossman, "*Type A Behaviour and Your Heart*," Alfred A.Knof, New York, 1984, p. 84.
23. *Ibid.*, pp. 84-85.
24. *Ibid.*, p. 86.
25. Niccolo Michiavelli, "The Prince, Trans, George Bull", Middlesex, Penguin, 1961.
26. Wood et.al, "Organisational Behaviour", John Wiley & Sons Australia Ltd., 2001, p. 108.
27. Quoted in Robbins et.al., "Organisational Behaviour", Pearson, New Delhi, 2007, p. 129.

CHAPTER **14**

PERCEPTION AND LEARNING

☛ Chapter Outline

☛ Learning Objectives

After studying this Chapter, you should be able to:

✓ Know the meaning of perception and differentiate perception from sensation;
✓ Analyse the perceptual process, viz., perceptual inputs, perceptual throughputs and perceptual output;
✓ Understand the perceptual throughputs like external and internal environmental factors;
✓ Understand the relationship between personality and perception;
✓ Know how the perceptual output leads to behaviour;
✓ Identify various factors those hinder the perception accurately;
✓ Discuss how to perceive accurately;
✓ Analyse why and how people impress others; and
✓ Explain the meaning of learning and various learning theories.

(A) WHAT IS PERCEPTION?

Cognition and cognitive process precede perception. The study of these two terms make the understanding of perception ease and systematic. Therefore, we discuss the two terms viz., cognition and cognitive process before we study the meaning of perception.

Cognition is the act of knowing an item of information. Cognition precedes behaviour. It provides input into a person's thinking and perception. Information can be known from the stimulus like overt and covert physical factors, social and cultural factors, technological and mechanical factors, environmental factors and the international factors. Information can be known through the sensory organs like eyes, ears, nose, mouth and skin.

Cognitive process is a complex one as it involves the collection of information from many sources and through different sensory organs, supply this information to the cognitive mediators, arranging the information in a sequential order. (See Fig. 14.1).

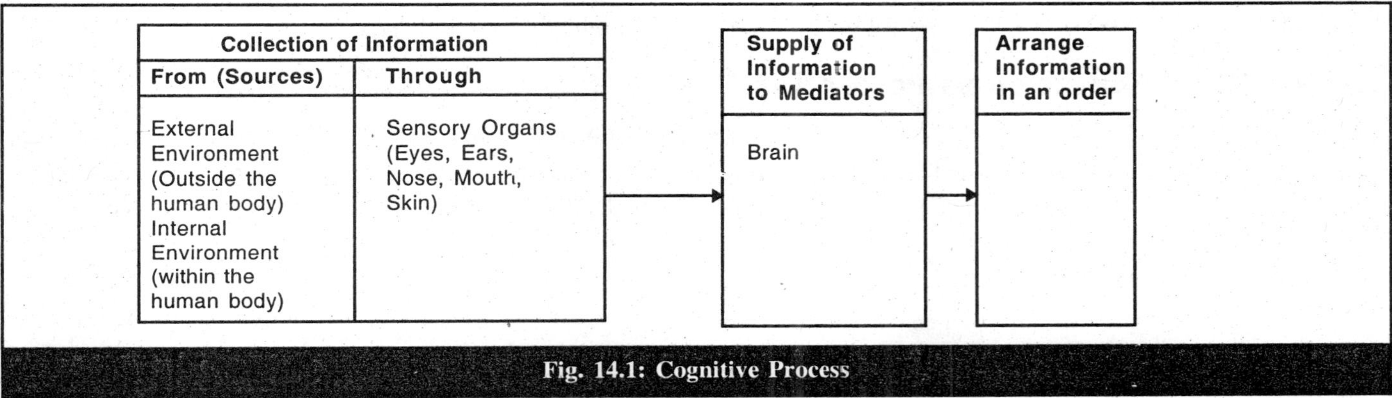

Fig. 14.1: Cognitive Process

Perception is not necessarily just what one sees with his own eyes or what one listens with his own ears. Perception is a unique interpretation of the situation, not an exact recording of it. Fred Luthans defines the term perception as a very complex cognitive process that yields a unique picture of the world, a picture that may be quite different from reality.[1]

Perception is the process of receiving, selecting, organising, interpreting, checking and reacting to sensory stimuli or data.

Having discussed the definition on perception provided by Fred Luthans, we shall now discuss other definitions for further clarity.

Uma Sekharan defines perception as, "the process through which people select, organise and interpret or attach meaning to events happening in the environment."[2]

Stephen P. Robbins defines perception as "a process by which individuals organise and interpret their sensory impressions in order to give meaning to their environments."[3]

Udai Pareek *et al* define perception as, "the process of receiving, selecting, organising, interpreting, checking and reacting to sensory stimuli or data."[4]

We will further discuss the meaning of perception with the help of a case example for further clarity. Mr. Prakash is Personal Assistant of the General Manager of Federal Express. It was 4th August 2009 and Mr. Prakash attended the office at 9.45 a.m. and he went directly to the production department to get the production records to place it before the meeting scheduled to be held at 10.30 a.m. on the same day at the General Manager's Chamber. He completed his business in the production department by 10.20 a.m. and returned to the General Manager's chambers.

The General Manager came to his office at 10 a.m. He wanted to have a discussion with Mr. Prakash regarding the arrangements for the day's meeting. He was thinking that Mr. Prakash has not yet (i.e., 10.25 a.m. of 4th August, 2009) come to the office.

The General Manager was very much angry with Mr. Prakash and scolded him for being late to office and he immediately went to the meeting without giving any scope to Mr.Prakash to answer. What is your view in this case? Your view is your perception. The General Manager did not see Mr. Prakash in his office or he did not hear from anybody that Mr. Prakash has come to the office before 10.25 a.m. Therefore, his cognitive process provided him the picture that Mr. Prakash was not available in the office on time. Thus, it yielded this unique picture to the General Manager. In fact, the reality was that Mr. Prakash had come to the office even before 10.00 a.m. and he had been on duty up to 10.20 a.m. in the production department. Therefore, the unique picture that the General Manager's cognitive process yielded is quite different from the reality. Thus, perception is the picture, yielded by the cognitive process which need not be the reality or the correct one.

Some people may be confused with the meaning of perception with that of sensation. Therefore, now we discuss the differences between sensation and perception.

Sensory organs like eyes and ears collect the data from the environment. The physical senses are vision, touch, smell, taste and hearing.

Sensation vs Perception

Sensory organs like eyes and ears collect the data from the environment. The physical senses are vision, touch, smell, taste and hearing. These are the five senses. Some of us believe in the sixth sense — "intuition." The physical senses are bombarded by numerous external and internal stimuli.

Stimuli

Stimuli is an enabling or disabling factor to act or not to act within an individual. Stimuli is of two types *viz.*, external stimuli and internal stimuli.

External stimuli include heat waves in the summer, cold waves in the winter, light waves in the day time, sound waves of a factory, smell from the kitchen/garden.

Internal stimuli include food passing through the digestive system, internal comfort or discomfort and actions and reactions caused by the physiological functioning.

Sensation is the experience we get by touching a baby, seeing a picture or an incident, listening to a conversation, smelling a flower or tasting food.

For example, yesterday you saw your subordinate sharing information with your boss in the latter's chamber and overheard the former referring your name in their conversation. In this example, sensation is observing your boss and the subordinate and listening to their conversation. Perception is more than seeing and listening, it is broader than sensation.

Perception is a complicated interaction of selection, organisation and interpretation. Now, we extend the same example. The addition to this example is that, yesterday you have warned your subordinate regarding his inefficiency in achieving the targets. Therefore, you perceived that your subordinate is lodging a complaint against you with your boss.

Thus, the perceptual process is broader and complex. It organises and interprets the raw data collected by the senses both from internal and external sources. Further, perceptual process adds to and subtracts from the data collected by the senses as per your imagination. Thus, sensation is part of the perceptual process. And perceptual process is broader and complex than sensation.

With this background of the meaning of perception and the difference between sensation and perception, we shall now discuss the perceptual process.

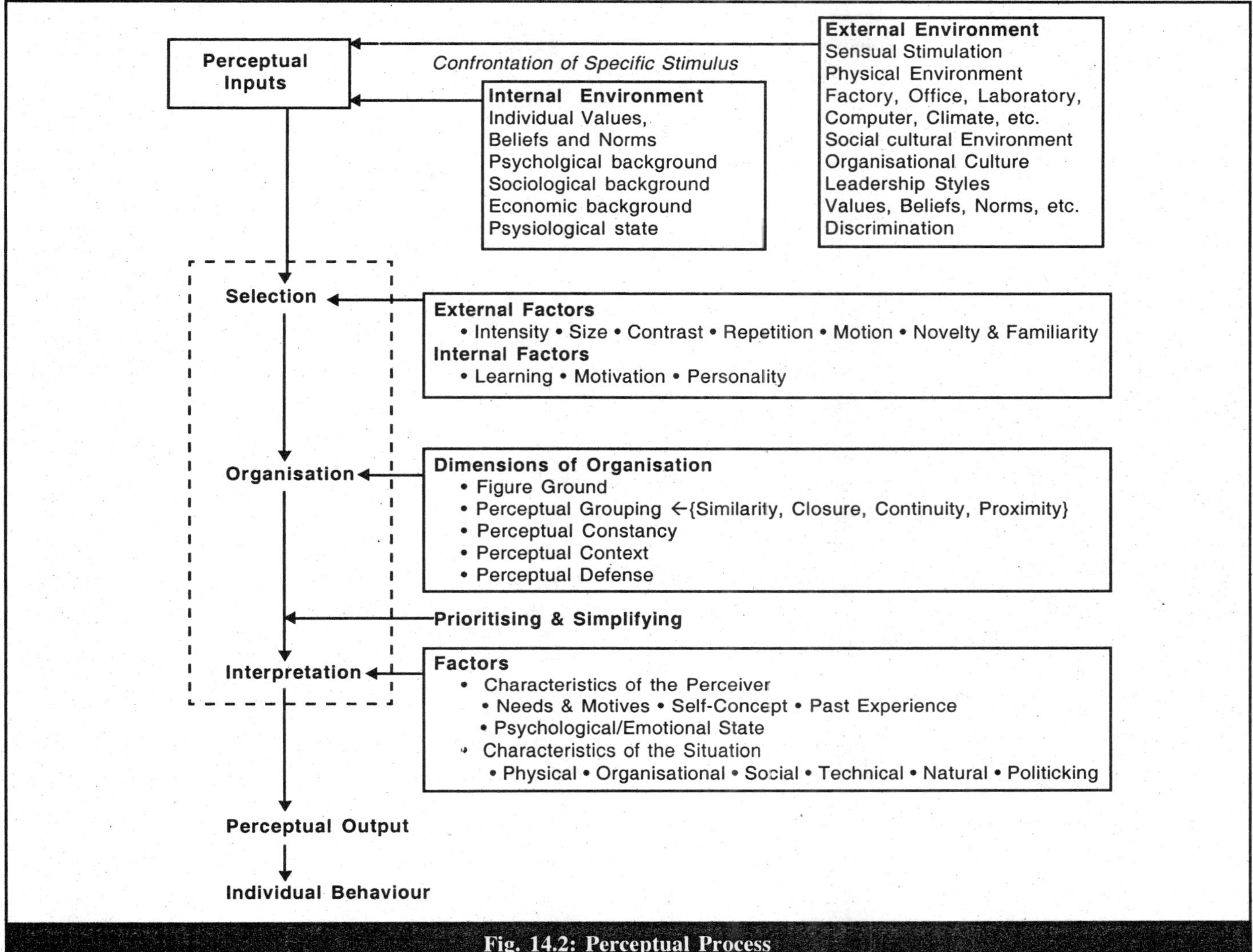

Fig. 14.2: Perceptual Process

Elements in Perception

Elements involved in perception are:

- Involvement of an individual;
- Process;
- Receiving, selecting and organising sensory stimuli and data;
- Yield a picture of the environment;
- That picture varies between the reality and just opposite to the environment.

The information we receive from the environment like objects, events and people are the perceptual inputs. These inputs are transformed through the perceptual mechanism like selection, organisation and interpretation as the output. The transformation mechanism is called *throughput*. The output is the perception. The perception may be the opinions, feelings, values, attitudes, conclusions, etc. These influence the decisions and behaviours. Fig. 14.2 presents the perceptual process model.

(C) PERCEPTUAL INPUTS

Perceptual inputs include all stimuli that exist in the external environment like classroom, laboratory, Socio-cultural environment, Technological Environment, etc.

Perceptual inputs include all stimuli that exist in the external environment like classroom, laboratory, Socio-cultural environment, Technological environment, Economic environment, Political/physical environment, International environment and Natural environment (STEPIN). We might have learned (or will learn) these environmental factors in the course on "Business Environment." Business environment provides inputs for the perceptions regarding business/organisational decisions and behaviours. And the general environment provides the inputs for the perceptions regarding general decisions and behaviours. (See Box 14.1).

Box 14.1: What Americans are Perceiving?

Nearly a year after the presidential election, the national mood takes a turn, a poll shows. Jobs, health care, war

- *Gas prices, supply up*
- *New home*

The Wall Street Journal

Americans are growing increasingly pessimistic about the economy after a mild upswing of attitudes in September. But Republicans haven't been able to profit politically from the economic gloom, according to a new Wall Street Journal/NBC News poll.

The survey found a country in a decidedly negative mood, nearly a year after the election of President Barack Obama. For the first time during the Obama presidency, a majority of Americans sees the country as being on the wrong track.

Fifty-eight per cent of those polled say the economic slide still has ways to go, up from 52% in September and back to the level of pessimism expressed in July. Only 29% said the economy had "pretty much hit bottom," down from 35% last month.

But a dark national view of how everybody in Washington is conducting the public's business appears to be preventing Republicans from benefiting from concerns about the direction of the country or the Democrat-led government's handling of the economy, as the minority party often does.

In fact, disapproval of the Republican Party actually has ticked upward, along with the public's general pessimism. Asked which political party should control Congress after next year's midterm elections, Democrats now hold a clear edge over the GOP, 46% to 38%, a month after the Republicans were nearly as popular. In September, the Democratic edge was 43% to 40%.

"There was a bounce-back surge for Republicans, and that's stalled," said Bill McInturff, a Republican pollster who conducted the Wall Street Journal/NBC News poll with Democratic pollster Peter Hart.

Source: http://finance.yahoo.com/banking-budgeting/article/108035/gloom-spreads-on-economy-but-gop-doesnt-gain (Accessed on 20/12/2009).

As stated earlier, perceptual throughputs comprise selection, organisation and interpretation. These throughputs transform the inputs into output.

(D) PERCEPTUAL SELECTION

The perceptual selectivity is based on the external and internal environment factors.

Mr. Prakash — the dynamic executive under the competitive environment is always bombarded by numerous stimuli like factory noise, conversations of his subordinates, movement of a number of people, outside noises from cars, trains, planes and his internal initiative to outperform his competitors, etc. Yet, he selects his computer to know the strategies of his competitors through the internet.

Similarly, we are also confronted by numerous stimuli every time. The stimuli below our conscious threshold is called 'subliminal perception.' Though numerous stimuli affect us, some of us select the food based on the smell, some select summer due to heat, and so on. Why do people select different stimuli. The answer for this is found in perceptual selectivity.

The perceptual selectivity is based on the external and internal environment factors. Now, we shall study the influence of external environmental factors on selectivity.

External Environmental Factors

The external environmental factors influencing selectivity are discussed below:

***(i)* Intensity:** We select the stimuli from the numerous environmental stimuli based on the intensity. The intensities include loud noise, bright light, strong odour over the soft noise, dim light and weak odour.

The audio advertisers use intensity to gain the attention of the prospective customers. The superiors use loud voice to caution/warn the subordinates. Sometimes the teachers raise the pitch of their voice to make the students attentive during the post-lunch sessions. The principle of intensity, though a small one, plays significant role in perceptual selectivity. Mr. Kiran – a supervisor was walking around the factory. He was bombarded by the machine's sound, the discussions of the workers in the factory, etc. But he was attracted by the huge cry made by the workers who were demanding six hours of work rather than the present eight hours of work a day. This was due to intensity of the sound.

***(ii)* Size:** The perceptual selectivity principle here is that, "the larger the object, the more likely it will be perceived." We normally see and get attracted by the large size objects rather than smaller objects. Normally, the human resource manager perceives a 6 foot and 90 kgs trade union leader over the 5 foot and 50 kgs trade union leader. A large size bus rather than a bicycle is perceived by a traffic policeman or a striker. Larger companies prefer to issue full-page advertisement rather than a few lines in the classified category as the large sized advertisements are more perceived by the customers than those in the classified category.

***(iii)* Contrast:** Recently we watch the advertisements like the following on TV:

"Are you tired due to heavy mental work?" Yes!

"Do not use the foods like these as they are not enough for your child. Our food is complete and planned. Therefore, use our food for your child."

"You are not expected to see, taste and use this product...."

Companies present this type of advertisement as the people perceive external stimuli which they do not expect.

Companies present this type of advertisement because customers select the stimuli of the product against the background of other products.

Thus, the contrast principle states that, "external stimuli which stand out against the background or which are not what people are expecting will receive their attention."[6]

Fig. 14.3 presents the perceptual principle.

The black circle in Fig. 14.3 (a) seems to be larger than that of Fig. 14.3 (b) from a naked eye. But, in reality on measurement, both the black circles in Fig. 14.3 (a) and 14.3 (b) are of the same size.

This is due to the varying size of the background white circles in both the figures. White background circles of Fig. 14.3 (b) are smaller than those of Fig. 14.3 (a) and this makes us feel that the black circle of Fig. 14.3 (a) is bigger than that in Fig. 14.3 (b). But the black circles in both the figures are of the same size. This is due to the difference in the contrast.

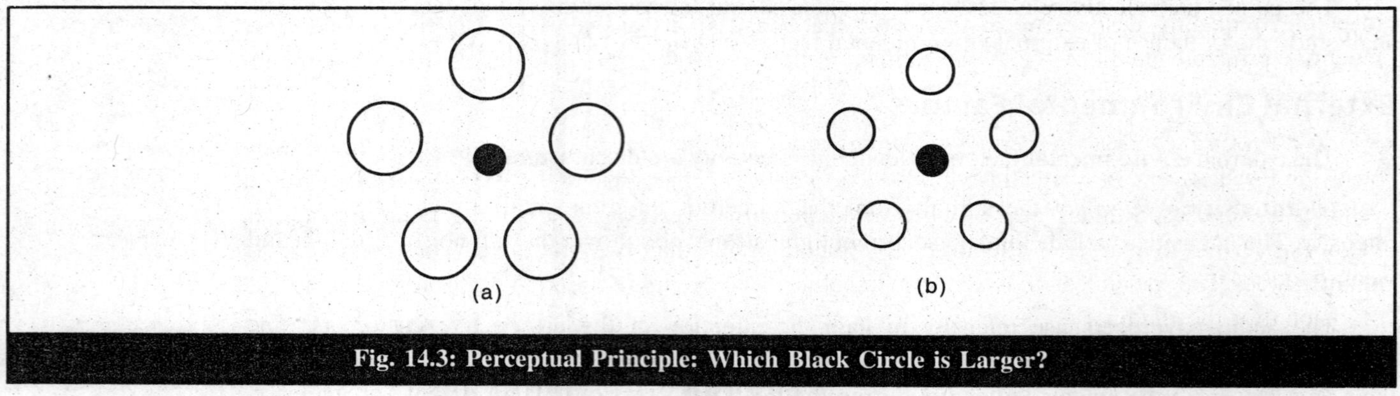

Fig. 14.3: Perceptual Principle: Which Black Circle is Larger?

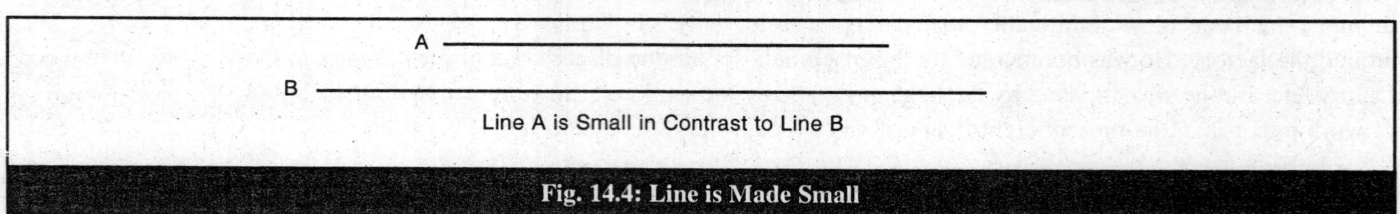

Fig. 14.4: Line is Made Small

Fig. 14.4 above shows two lines A and B. Line A is smaller in contrast to line B.

These lines can be perceived in two different ways

(i) Line B is viewed as long because of the presence of line A

(ii) If you see the above figure without line B, Line A cannot be viewed as short.

Bank of Baroda employed 1,000 clerks in 1971 to meet its manpower requirements due to the massive expansion. The IQ level of these 1,000 clerks varied widely. The Bank of Baroda Training College planned to train these clerks in a batch of 50 each. It divided the batches based on the regions ignoring the IQ level. In each batch, 8 to 10 clerks used to learn at a fast rate and 10-15 clerks used to learn at very slow rate and felt that they were insulted. Faculty of the training college had the feedback from the trainees regarding this issue.

The Principal and faculty of the training college divided the batches based on the selection score (written test score + interview score) of the trainees in the second phase of the training. The second phase of the training programme proved to be successful as the high IQ trainees used to learn at a fast rate. The low IQ trainees also had a homogeneous group and therefore, the feeling of being insulted was avoided. Thus, avoidance of contrast helped the trainees and the training colleges. Similar principle is also followed in dividing the sections for 'Intermediate Course' students in residential junior colleges in Andhra Pradesh.

***(iv)* Repetition:** The repetition principle is that a repeated external stimulus is more attention-getting than a single one. Trade unions include the significant demands in the agendas of the collective bargaining meetings frequently to draw the attention of the top management and the human resources manager. Similar examples include frequent instructions by the superiors to the poor performers and frequent advertisements by the fast moving consumer goods manufacturing/marketing companies.

Mr. Michael Benson, an MBA student at the School of Business Administration, University of Papua New Guinea was not initially selected for internship by any company in Port Moresby. The convener of MBA Programme informed Mr. Benson that the internship would be arranged for him in a premier company in a couple of weeks. But Mr. Benson used to meet the MBA Convener at least twice a day to remind him of the internship placement. When the convener asked Mr. Benson, "Why do you meet me frequently despite my assurance of placement?", his answer was that he was using the repetitive principle taught by the Organisational Behaviour professor to get the convener's attention to get placement as soon as possible.

(v) **Motion:** During the periods of strikes and agitations, agitators mostly destroy the moving buses and vehicles as moving objects draw the attention rather than stationery objects like parked vehicles and houses. Similarly, the moving production processes, conveyer belts, moving trucks in the factory receive the workers' attention very much rather than the stationary equipment and its maintenance.[7] The principle here is that, moving objects receive more attention of the people in the field of vision than the stationary objects do.

The companies follow this principle in their advertisements and incorporate mostly moving parts and objects in the advertisements. (See Box 14.2).

Box 14.2: Fail: Redskins' Ladell Betts has Name Misspelled on Back of Jersey

By Chris Chase

Four months after the Washington Nationals sent two players onto the field with "NATINLS" written across their jerseys, the NFL team in the nation's capital is following suit. Washington Redskins running back Ladell Betts played last night's preseason game in Baltimore with his last name misspelled on the back of his jersey:

Hmm ... Maybe it wasn't as much of a mistake as it was a Freudian slip by the Redskins equipment staff. As evidenced by the 2008 stats that were displayed on screen, Betts could certainly stand to be more like Jerome Bettis.

After the game, Betts was informed of the error and told Dan Steinberg of the DC Sports Bog:

"Actually, I do like Jerome Bettis, but I don't prefer to have his name on my back," he said. "I wasn't upset or anything. I think the equipment people felt bad, but I wasn't mad at them."

With his "I ain't mad at cha" attitude, Betts is like a modern day 2pac. Perhaps his understanding will result in a nice thankk ewe noat frum tha ekwipment staf.

Source: http://sports.yahoo.com/nfl/blog/shutdown_corner/post/Fail-Redskins-Ladell-Betts-has-name-misspelled?urn=nfl,183018 (Accessed on 15/08/09).

(vi) **Novelty and Familiarity:** Novelty and familiarity principle is that either a novel or a familiar external situation can serve as an attention drawer. Both novelty and unfamiliarity would fail to draw the attention as nothing can be drawn out of it. It is said that the efficient managers do the same thing differently. Example for novelty and familiarity is the job rotation. Here, employee is familiar one whereas the new job is the novel one. Computerisation of many jobs in commercial banks resulted in novelty in doing the familiar job. Talapatra Paper Mills Employees' Union had been demanding the management for the payment of dearness allowance due to increase in cost of living since 2007. Management did not concede to this demand of workers despite the frequent demands until 2009. The Union resorted to a novel technique of representing the problem by the employees' wives in September 2009. Then this issue had drawn the attention of the top management when their wives explained their problems in managing the family budgets. The management immediately accepted the demand and paid

the dearness allowance. In this example, the demand of dearness allowance was familiar but representation of the demand by the employees' wives was novel which had drawn the attention of the management.

Computer aided teaching also brings the novelty in teaching and learning the familiar courses and topics/subjects.

Environmental Factors

So far we have discussed various external factors which influence perceptual selectivity. Now shall we discuss the internal factors influencing the perceptual selectivity. Individual's physiological and psychological makeup influence their learning, motivation and personality. Learning, personality and motivation of an individual, in turn, influence the perceptual selectivity. Internal factors include:

Learning and Perception

Learning, personality and motivation of an individual, influence the perceptual selectivity.

Dr. P. S. Rao had been teaching the course on 'Organisational Behaviour.'

He used to write the following on the board:

"which bind them to get her as a social entity."

Nearly 80 per cent of the students used to read the sentence as

"which bind them **to get her** as a social entity."

While remaining 20 per cent of the students used to read the sentence correctly as

"which bind them **together** as a social entity."

It took a few seconds for the 80 per cent of the students to realize that there are two unnecessary gaps (in fact, it is something wrong).

The 20 per cent of the students who got it right used to read it correctly as 'together' due to their familiarity with the sentence from prior learning. Thus, these students are perceptually set to read the three independent words as a single word as: 'Together.'

Read the matter in the triangle given below.

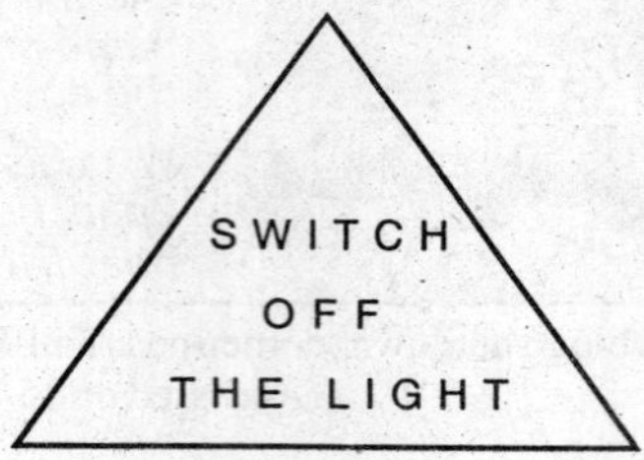

So, What did you read?

SWITCH OFF THE LIGHT

If yes, read the matter given in the triangle again.

Did you notice any difference?

The matter given in the triangle is:

SWITCH OFF ***THE THE*** *LIGHT*

There are two "THE" in the sentence.

Most of us read this spontaneously as 'switch off the light,' without realising that there is something wrong. The mistake is the word 'The' which is printed twice. This is due to our familiarity from prior learning, that we are perceptually set to read as 'switch off the light.'

These two examples show that learning affects set by creating an expectancy to perceive in a certain manner. Expectancies play a vital role in the cognitive explanations of behaviour. In essence, we see and listen what we expect to see and listen.[8] This can be further understood by pronouncing the following word very slowly.

M-A-T-H-E-M-A-T-I-C-S

If we pronounce this word as '**Mat-He-Mat-Ics**' we are caught in a verbal response set. A number of similar examples are as follows:

O-F-F-I-C-E

If we pronounce the word as '**Off-Ice**' we are caught in a verbal response set.

M-A-N-A-G-E-M-E-N-T

Similarly, if we pronounce the word as '**Man-Age-Ment**' we are caught in a verbal response set.

The most classical example for explaining the impact of learning on development of perceptual set is 'young lady-old lady experiment' as presented in Fig. 14.5.

Fig. 14.5(a): Ambiguous Picture of an Young Woman

Observations from figure 14.5(a), (b), (c).

1. If we see only figure 14.5(a), we perceive that it is a figure of a young lady.
2. If we compare figure (a) with (b), we perceive that lady in figure (a) is young and the lady in figure (b) is old.
3. If we compare figure (a) with figure (c), we perceive that lady in figure (a) is old and the lady in figure (c) is young.

4. If we compare figure (c) with (b), we perceive that lady in figure (c) is young and the lady in figure (b) is old.
5. If we compare all the three, then we perceive that lady in figure (a) is a mix figure of young and old ladies; lady in figure (b) is old lady and lady in figure (c) is young lady.

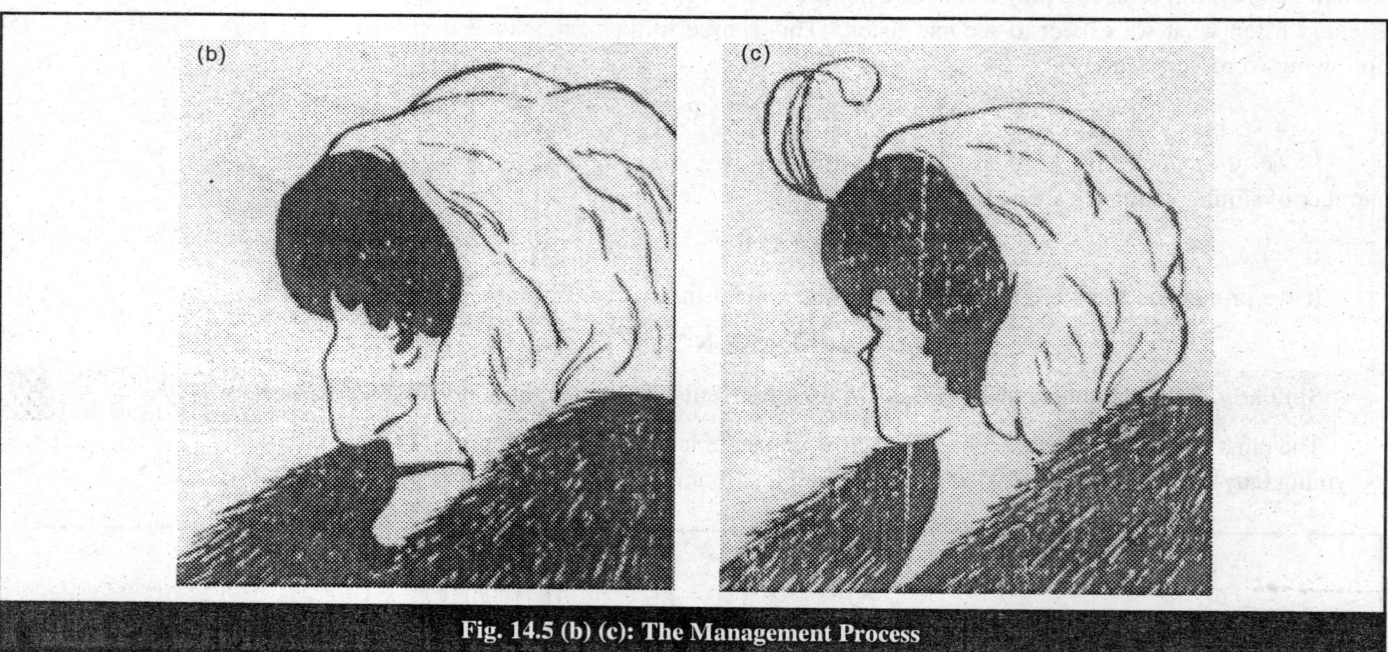

Fig. 14.5 (b) (c): The Management Process

If we see the figures independently, we cannot make the distinction as stated earlier. Therefore, it is clear that perceptual set, *i.e.,* comparing one against another gives us a picture close to reality. Thus, learning plays a significant role in developing perceptual set.

Now, we present other varieties of commonly used illusions to present the impact of the learned set on perception. Fig. 14.6 presents the two-three-pronged objects.

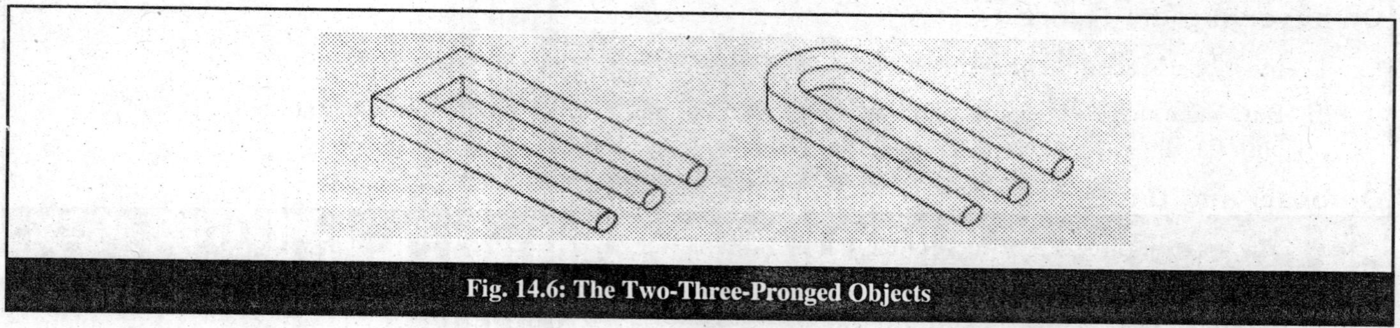

Fig. 14.6: The Two-Three-Pronged Objects

Our perception:

1. If we see the above figures spontaneously, we perceive that there are three pronged objects.
2. If we see the above figures closely and calmly, we observe that there are only two pronged circles, which is correct.

These objects are drawn in contrary to common perceptions of such objects.

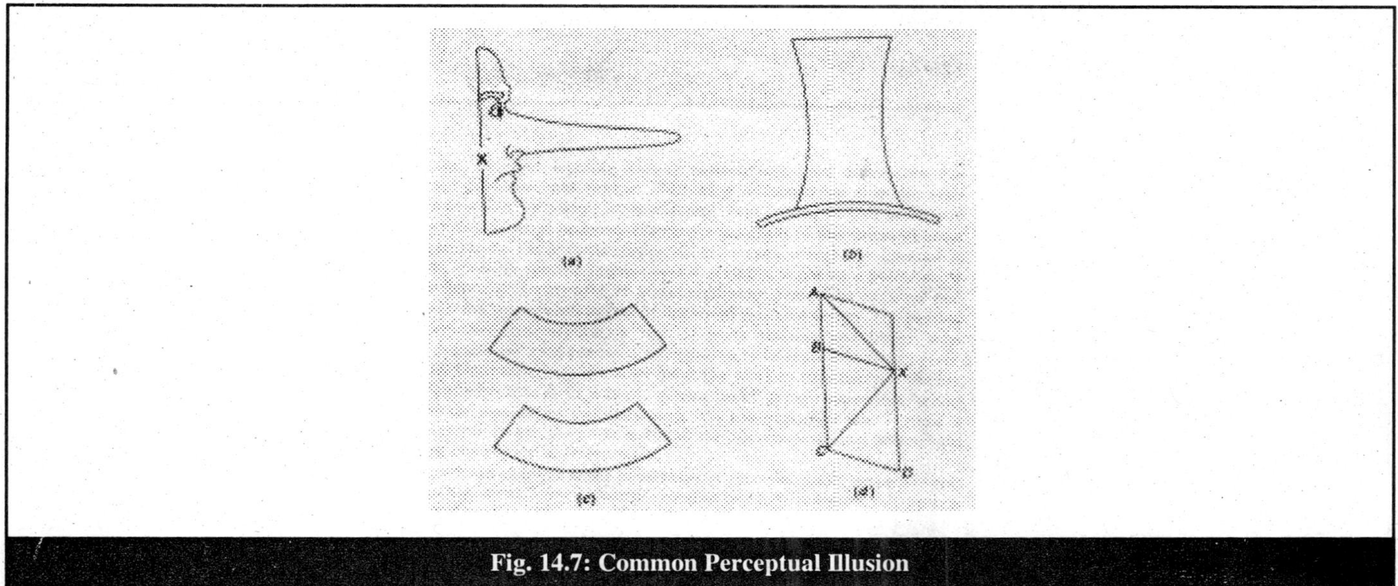

Fig. 14.7: Common Perceptual Illusion

Fig. 14.7 also presents common perceptual illusions. Illusion may be a form of perception that badly distorts reality.

On observing the Figure 14.7(a)

1. We perceive from the figure(a) that the length of nose is larger than the height of the face.
2. But, when these dimensions are measured with the scale, you will find that length of nose is equal to the height of the face.

On observing the Figure 14.7(b)

1. Most of us feel that the height of the hat is more than the width of the brim.
2. But, when these dimensions are measured you will find that both the dimensions are the same.

On observing the Figure 14.7(c)

1. Most of us feel that the dimensions of the upper figure are larger than the lower figure.
2. But, when these dimensions are measured with the measures of scale, you will find that both the dimensions are the same.

On observing the Figure 14.7(d), we feel the following:

1. The length of line CX is more than that the line XD
2. The length of line XD is more than that the line AD
3. When these dimensions are measured, you will find that the dimensions of the lines CX, XD and AD are identically equal.

On Observing the Figure 14.8, We Perceive the Following:

1. Person (c) in the figure is the tallest
2. Person (b) in the figure is tall
3. Person (a) in the figure is short

4. When you measure the height of these three figures, you will find that the heights of all the three are same.

Fig. 14.8: Role of Learning in Perception

We perceived differently from the actual in the above figures due to the strong role played by the learned set in perception process. This figure presents the role that the learned set plays a more stronger role in perception compared to the previous figures.

Perceptual set in the workplace

Normally, different employees perceive either differently or on the same line from the same set of real things at the workplace. The chief executive officer of the newly established company told the leaders of the three unions, "The Company cannot pay the bonus to you."

The leaders of the three unions were cross-checked to know their perception.[9] Though the statement is unclear, ambiguous and indicating negative view, all the three leaders expressed positively that the company now pays good salaries though it cannot pay bonus as it is in the initial stage of establishment. Thus, perception may be favourable and positive but the statement seems to be negative. Further, all the people may perceive in the same way.

Strong Brief Cases Ltd. observed the decline in sales. The General Manager organized the meeting of all the functional managers to find out the reason for the decline in the sales of their products and to develop the alternative strategies to improve the sales. The production manager identified the problem of poor maintenance of machines, the finance manager identified the problem of heavy working capital, marketing manager identified the problem of less promotional efforts and the human resources manager identified the problem of obsolete skills of the employees. Thus, the different managers perceive the same situation/problem in completely different ways at the workplace.

Motivation and Perception

Similarly, workers and management perceive the company's financial position quite differently in collective bargaining meetings while meeting the workers' demands.

The concept of motivation is explained in the chapter on 'Motivation.' Maslow's hierarchy of needs include: physiological needs, security needs, social needs, esteem needs and self-actualisation needs. The motives play a significant role in perception.

The physiological needs like sex, food and shelter play a dominant role in perception. The Indian culture suppresses sex and hence, sex is the unfulfilled need for many teenagers in this society. As such, visual/audio deal with sex acts as an attention-drawer. This is more so in eastern countries compared to the western countries. Food and consumer goods were a major attention drawer in India before the 1970s. But, food and consumer goods lost appeal as an attention getter after 1990s in our country due to increase in incomes and living standard.

The Indian culture of living together in a social set-up satisfies the social needs of the people even in business and industrial organisations. Therefore, this is a fulfilled need for many people at the workplace in India unlike in the western countries. As such, this need does not have any appeal as an attention-getter.

The preachers of Hindu religion reduce the desires/needs of esteem like high need for power, achievement and recognition. But, modern Indian culture is slowly tending towards the departure from the Hindu religion dominated Indian culture. Therefore, the mention about esteem needs started acting as an attention-getter.

Personality and Perception

Information technology, computerization, officeless offices, home-cum-offices, paperless offices and business process reengineering and enterprise resource planning brought radical changes in the line of thinking and personalities between the young managers and the senior managers.

The senior managers view that the young managers change at a fast rate unnecessarily resulting in wastage in resources and methods. Whilst the young managers perceive that the old managers resist change, if not, move very slowly resulting in becoming the back number in these days of severe competition.

Similar personality differences can also be perceived between male executives and female executives and between the old generation and the younger generation people. Thus, the people of different age groups, sex, backgrounds and values perceive the world around them quite differently.

Professional Experience and Knowledge: Professional/occupational experience and knowledge also play a vital role in developing perceptual set. Further, they also help in attracting the attention of the perceiver. For example, the chief medical officer of a chemical company went to the production department to see the production manager who is a friend of the former. The personal assistant of the production manager informed him that his boss is in the factory. He went into the factory and met the production manager. Later, the production manager was explaining the new technology that the company adopted recently to the Chief medical officer. He identified the areas in the new technology that would cause lung disease to the operators out of his professional knowledge. All the other employees could not identify this.

Paranoid Perception: The person who is the victim of a situation or an event cannot perceive the events like most others who are not the parties to it. For example, the one who is denied promotion can perceive that injustice was done to him and his cognition won't select any other factor which would give him the indication that he is less qualified or less experienced or less efficient than the one who was promoted. Thus, the perceptual field of the emotionally disturbed person differs from that of the others. The disturbed person suffers from excessive repression, projection, distortion of reality and highly individual based interpretation such persons behave in an inflexible manner due to the feeling of insecurity.

(E) PERCEPTUAL ORGANISATION

After selecting the inputs from the external environment, based on the influences of the internal environmental factors, we have to organize the inputs in a logical and sequential manner. Therefore, perceptual organisation is the next logical step in the perception process.

The data and information have to be organised in a logical and sequential way in order to get a meaningful whole. For example, Mr. Chandra, a superior, receives the following information and data from internal and external stimuli regarding his subordinate Mr. Surya.

- Mr. Surya reported late to office today by an hour and half. This is the third time he has reported the office late.
- He started from home much earlier than he normally does and went to the other office to hand over an envelope in person.
- Mr. Prakash, Mr. Chandra's boss, gave an envelope to Mr. Surya yesterday and asked him to handover the envelope before coming to this office was not known to Mr. Chandra.

Mr. Chandra cannot draw any conclusion unless he organizes these data and information. After organising these data and information, Mr. Chandra concludes that Mr. Surya was on official duty today, and therefore, he was not late to the office.

The dimensions of the perceptual organization include:

Figure-Ground

Perceived object or person or event stands out distinct from its background and occupies the cognitive space of the individual.

We organise information and data based on the figure-ground principle. This principle states that the perceived object or person or event stands out distinct from its background and occupies the cognitive space of the individual.[10] The perceived objects stand out as separable from their general background.

For example, the employees during their probation give top priority for their performance rating given by their superiors rather than on the other activities including their relations with their colleagues.

Fig. 14.9 presents another figure-ground example.

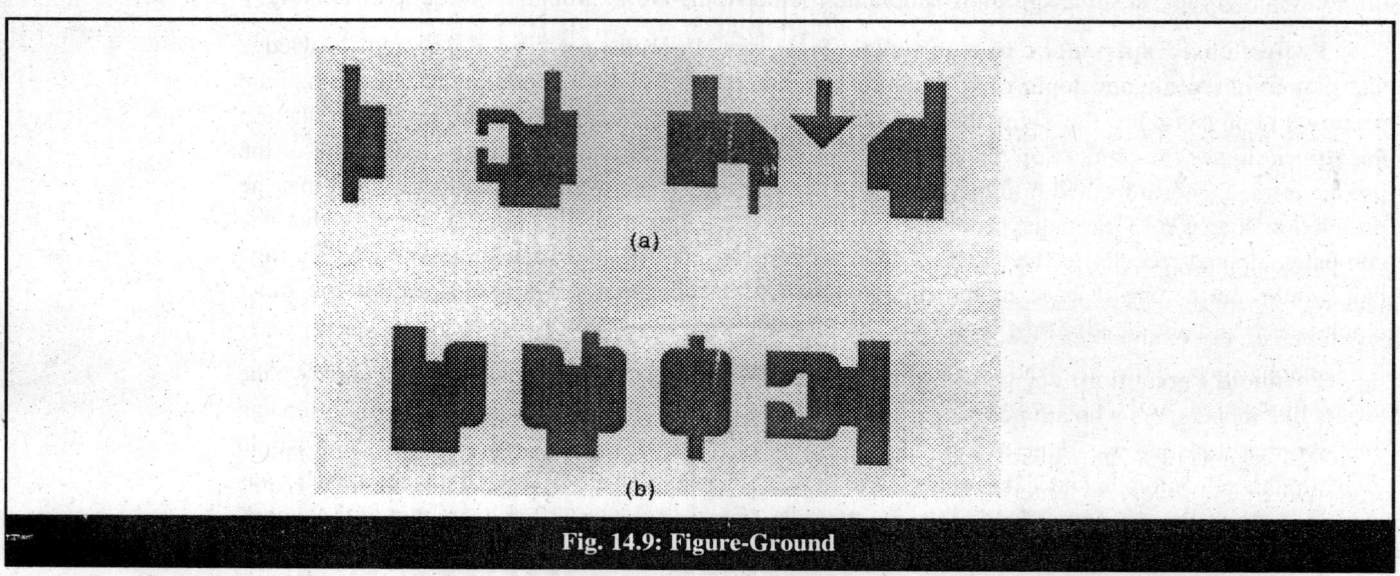

Fig. 14.9: Figure-Ground

(**Source:** Jerome Kagen and Ernest Haveman, Psychology:An Introduction, Harcourt Brace and World, 1968, p. 166)

Observations from the Figure 14.9 include:

1. We perceive an irregular shape of black portion against the white portion.
2. If we close the white portion around (not within) each of the upper figures and read the white portion within each figure, we can get the word **FLY**
3. Similarly, if we close the white portion around (not within) each of the lower figures and read the white portion within each figure, we can get the word **TIE.**

We perceive an irregular shape against a white background at the first glance. If we closely observe the black background and the white portion within the black background, we can observe the words 'FLY' and 'TIE.' This example presents that perceptual selectivity will influence perceptual organization. Normally, we find the black letters against the white background in the books. But it is opposite in Fig. 14.9 because the letters are in white and black is the background.

Fig. 14.10 presents reversible figure ground.

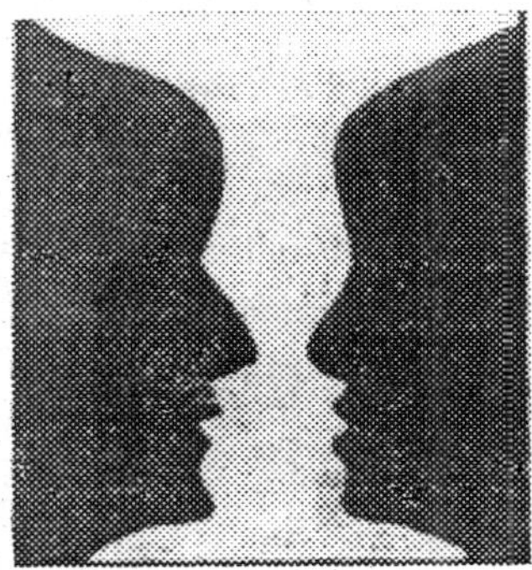

Fig. 14.10: Reversible Figure-Ground

Observations from the figure 14.10 include:

1. We observe a rough picture of black and white portions
2. If we observe the black portion by closing the white portion, we see two rough profiles: one of a male and other of a female.
3. If we take the white portion by closing the black portion, we see the shape like a white vase.

Perceptual Grouping

Perceptual grouping is the tendency to join/club individual stimuli together into recognisable and meaningful patterns. If we perceive objects of people with similar characteristics, we tend to group them together. For example, if we see the students at the University Canteen, discussing the concepts of organisational behaviour, we tend to group them as 'Management Students.' We tend to group the constellations of stimuli together by the following factors:

***(i)* Similarity:** Principle of similarity states that we perceive the objects of stimuli as one group or a common group, if there is greater similarity of stimuli among them. When we see the children with the same uniform, we group them as the students of a single school. Similarly, we can also group the employees of B.H.E.L. based on their uniform. We can group those who wear the turban on their head as 'Sikhs.' Fig. 14.11 presents the similarity principle.

A	B	C	D	E	F
X	X	X	X	X	X
÷	÷	÷	÷	÷	÷
?	?	?	?	?	?
$	$	$	$	$	$

Fig. 14.11: Similarity Principle

Observations from the figure 14.11 include:

1. On the first impression, we immediately see the horizontal arrangement (columns) of the letters or symbols due to their similarity like ABC... or XXX.. but we do not observe the vertical arrangement (rows) as they are dissimilar to each other and also difficult to comprehend them
2. Thus, similarity of objects plays vital role in grouping the objects.

***(ii)* Closure:** The principle of closure states that we sometimes perceive a whole when one does not actually exist. People connect and link the information, data and knowledge that are close to each other to make a meaning for the whole of the linked data, information and knowledge. People bridge the gaps by using the background, previous experiences, established norms, traditions, principles and theory. Our perceptual process will close the gaps which are unfilled from sensory inputs. For example, 3 3 = 6. We easily perceive that it is 3+3=6, even when the symbol '+' is missing here. It is quite common that members of an informal organisation see a whole that does not exist.

Highly specialist managers or technical experts often fail to integrate their activities with other employees/experts in the same department or line. Hence, shift towards generalisation took place in the recent times and under business process reengineering.

Most of the modern art, movie making and cartoons need us to close the gaps and make the whole unlike traditional art. Observe Fig. 14.12, which clearly shows that the perceiver perceives the whole circle, triangle and rectangle.

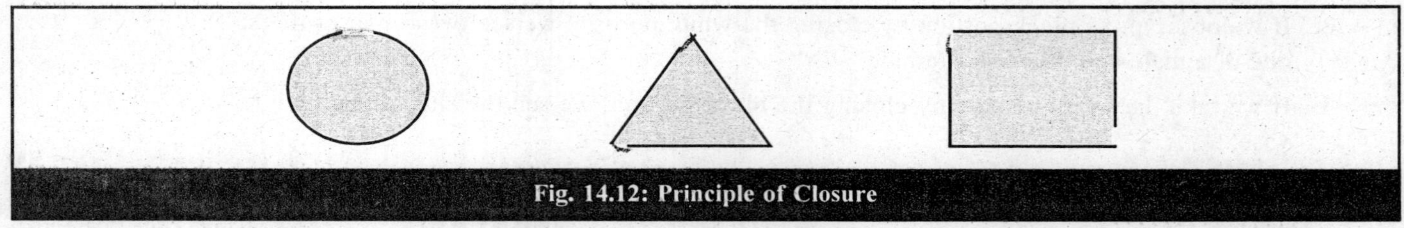

Fig. 14.12: Principle of Closure

Observations from the Figure 14.12 include:

1. We observe gaps in the circle, triangle and rectangle;
2. With our previous experience, we perceive that the first figure is a circle, second a triangle and third figure as a rectangle on closure of gaps; and
3. The closing-up of the gaps is due to our past experience.

Mr. Chaitanya had been working as an Assistant in the Marketing Department of Southern Footwear Ltd. The Marketing Manager asked Mr. Chaitanya on 10th December 1999 at 4.00 p.m. to go to the Production Manager of Quality Leathers Ltd. and handover an envelope before 5 p.m. on the same day before going home. The firm Quality Leathers Ltd. is situated in one of the suburban areas of the city. Mr. Chaitanya went to the firm, handed over the letter and went into a liquor shop around 5.30 p.m. due to heavy rain on his way back to home. The liquor shop was housed in a hut. The hut collapsed due to heavy rain and wind. He along with 8 others died.

The management of Southern Footwear Ltd. consulted the lawyer to know whether the company should pay compensation? The lawyer advised the company that it need not pay any compensation as Mr. Chaitanya died in the liquor shop most probably after consuming liquor. But the marketing manager recommended for the payment of compensation as Mr. Chaitanya never drinks, and therefore, he went into the hut seeking shelter only.

Here, the marketing manager perceives the whole incident, even when the information regarding the alcohol consumption by Mr. Chaitanya is not available.

Thus, we say that the perceiver perceives the whole.

(iii) **Continuity:** Some of us may confuse continuity with closure. There is a little but clear difference between continuity and closure. Closure provides missing stimuli while the continuity principle says that we will tend to perceive continuous lines or patterns. We observe the following numbers:

2,4,6,8,10,12,....

The continuity principle says that the number after 12 is 14. This type of continuity is normal in mathematics. But it leads to inflexible or non-creative thinking on the part of the members of the organisation. Therefore, we can view that continuity can greatly influence the system design of organisational structure. However, continuity limits the innovative ideas or designs or creative flow of information.

(iv) **Proximity:** The principle of proximity indicates that a group of stimuli which are close together will be perceived as a whole pattern of parts belonging together. Thus, all the managers' performance is perceived as a single whole and similar to each other.

The Chief Marketing Manager of Software Exports (India) Ltd., organised a meeting of the marketing managers. Twenty marketing managers attended the meeting. Out of the 20, two managers did extremely well and achieved 120% of the targets and the performance of the remaining 18 regional marketing managers was quite discouraging. The Chief Marketing Manager while addressing the members expressed his dissatisfaction saying that: "I am very much unhappy with the performance of the regional marketing managers...." The chief marketing manager grouped all the regional marketing managers into one due to proximity of nature of jobs, though the performance of a few regional mangers was really good.

Social Identity

Social identity is determined by complex combination of various factors like gender, demographic, income level, social status based on community, ethnicity, race, organization and the like. It is distinguished by the uncommon factor in the group. For example, teacher is distinguished himself/herself when he/she is among the students in a classroom setting. Similarly, a medical doctor is distinguished himself/herself in a hospital setting.

Social identity is determined by complex combination of various factors like gender, demographic, income level, social status based on community, ethnicity, race, organization and the like.

Social identity theory explains how we perceive ourselves as well as others in a social setting. This theory explains how and why people homogenise others and categorize them based on certain traits. For example, we categorize the youth as dynamic, students as aggressive and old as emotionally stable and judgmental. People view more favourable features of their group rather than other group. People perceive themselves as favourable and based on certain traits.

Perceptual Constancy

So far, we have discussed various factors that influence the perceptual organisation. Further, we discussed earlier that various factors influence the perceptual process. These factors complicate the task of perceptual organisation and perceptual process. But, Mr. Bharat Joshi, Production Supervisor of Parle Biscuits Limited expresses that every day he perceives the same raw material like wheat powder, sugar, salt, etc., same machines, same tools and almost same employees. We can state here that the size, design, shape, colour and location of the objects are almost constant. This feature is referred to as the principle of perceptual constancy. It indicates a sense of stability in the dynamic world. Perceptual constancy principle permits us to have some constancy in a tremendously variable and highly complex world. Perceptual constancy makes the perceptual organisation simple.

Perceptual Context

Organisational culture, structure, mission, objectives and strategies are the context in which employees and customers perceive the company activities, policies and objectives. In addition, company products, services, activities, social responsibilities and business ethics also form a basis for forming perception of employees, customers as well as general public. Our perceptions regarding quality of the services of Air India — a public sector transport corporation — in contrast to the private sector transport organisations and other public sector organisations are perceptually set accordingly.

Mr. Kishore Bajaj was leaving for Paris from New York by Air India flight. He came to J.F.K. Airport just 30 minutes before the check-in time. He verified his bag and other attaches for his ticket and passport. He could get the passport, but failed to locate his ticket. He recollected at the moment that he placed his ticket in the cupboard in the hotel.

He spontaneously took a decision to go back to the hotel and go to Paris the next day, rather than requesting the officer concerned to permit him to travel by the scheduled flight simply due to the assumption that officers of Air India work by rules like bureaucrats.[11]

The context of the public sector organisational culture and organisational structure of Air India influenced the perception process of Mr. Kishore Bajaj. This is what is called perceptual context.

Perceptual Defence

We may build a defence (i.e. a block/a refusal to recognise) against stimuli or situational events in the context that are personally or culturally unacceptable or threatening. Perceptual defence is closely related to perceptual context.[12]

Mr. Joshi has been working as a subordinate of Mr. Pandey in Pure Chemicals Ltd. Mr. Joshi had a problem regarding his working hours. He approached the trade union leaders for solving the problem rather than his superior. Trade Union leaders referred the issue to Mr. Pandey for settlement. Mr. Pandey was surprised at the act of Mr. Joshi for not informing him of the problem first.

Mr. Pandey called Mr. Joshi and asked him the reason for not expressing the problem to him first. Mr. Joshi replied, "I had enough experience with you regarding the grievance redressal, when I informed you first." The block developed by Mr. Joshi against stimuli/situational events can be referred to as 'Perceptual Defence.'

Prioritising and Simplifying

Managers every day receive lot of queries, demands, clarifications and information from superiors, colleagues, employees, customers, public, government departments and the like. They will not attend to all these queries and demands with equal attention due to limited time, resources, talents and abilities. Therefore, they prioritise the queries, demands, clarifications and rank them in the order of importance and urgency and select an issue to act upon it. This process simplifies the activities to be performed. Then they attend to and perform them with ease. Dr. Ramana Murthy, Human Resources Manager, Pinakini Soft Drinks Ltd. receives a number of representations from employees, problems from the trade union leaders, memos from production manager, requests from marketing manager and orders from the general manager. He arranges all these as per the importance and urgency of each item and makes a priority list. Thus, he simplifies the complex data and information and perceives the important and urgent issues by keeping the other issues as pending. This is prioritising and simplifying.

Managers prioritise the queries, demands, clarifications and rank them in the order of importance and urgency and select an issue to act upon it.

(F) INTERPRETATION

The perceiver after selecting and organizing the stimuli/information has to interpret them in order to make a sensible meaning. The sensible meaning, thus arrived will help the perceiver to make decisions or to act in the situation. The perceiver cannot draw any meaning without the interpretation. The perceiver uses his/her assumptions of people, things, objects and situations. He/she makes attributions, uses his/her judgmental skills, distorts information, adds/deletes information, brings his/her own subjective feelings, opinions and emotions in interpreting and drawing the meaning. Sometimes, the perceiver tries to fabricate the meaning based on his/her biases. The perceiver should be emotionally free to interpret and to draw bias-free meanings. Bias and absence of seriousness on the part of the perceiver tend to distort/ignore some stimuli/information which is unpleasant to him/her. Therefore, our perceptions based on cognitive preferences could not reflect the reality.

The perceiver should be emotionally free to interpret and to draw bias-free meanings.

Dr. Ramesh has been working as a scientist in Sital Refrigerators Ltd., Mumbai. His wife forgets many things. She dumps many vegetables and other things in the refrigerator and forgets to utilise them later. Consequently, they get spoiled. He warned his wife many times but in vain. He organised this information, used his judgmental skills and abilities and interpreted the information in such a way that this is not only the problem (forgetfulness) of his wife or other housewives, but the problem with the limited functions of refrigerators available in the market. Then he started researching on how to develop new functions to the existing refrigerators, which would indicate the housewives regarding the expiry time of the articles stored in it. Ultimately he succeeded in his research and his company released the new product. Dr. Ramesh interpreted the information through his judgmental skills before actually perceiving the problem.

Thus, a number of factors affect the interpretation process. These factors also influence the perceptual thought process. Having discussed the core system of perceptual process (or perceptual throughput process), now we shall discuss various subsystems (or factors affecting perceptual throughput process) of perceptual process.

Factors Affecting Interpretation Process

Various factors that affect perceptual thought process are:

- Characteristics of the perceiver, and
- Characteristics of the situation.

Characteristics of the Perceiver

Perceiver's characteristics significantly influence his thought process. The perceiver's thought process, in turn, help the perceptual throught process. The characteristics of the perceiver which influence this process include:

(a) Needs and Motives: Needs and motives of the perceiver play a significant role in perceptual process or in perceiving things. In other words the perceiver is influenced by his/her needs and motives in perceiving the objects. The employees who have the strong power prefer to see the promotional opportunity from the power perspective whereas the employee with the need for money perceive the promotion from salary perspective.

S. K. Institute of Management (SKIM) offers dual specialisation in its MBA programme. Mr. Chaitanya and Mr. Prasanth did their MBA with specialisations in Marketing Management and Human Resources Management in 2006 from SKIM. Mr. Chaitanya was interested in taking up marketing job while Mr. Prasanth was interested in taking up human resource job.

Both of them got the jobs in July 2006 as Marketing Executives in Natco Pharma Ltd. The Chief Marketing Manager in the Marketing Executives' Meeting told Mr. Chaitanya that the target for him was increased from 1,00,000 units in 2006 to 1,50,000 units in 2008. He accepted the new target. In fact, he was confident of achieving the new target as his needs and motives were to be recognised by the boss as the high achiever.

The Chief Marketing Manager told the same thing to Mr. Prasanth also, who immediately reacted negatively and informed his boss that it would be impossible to achieve the new target. This reaction was mostly due to his needs and motives of leading a peaceful and comfortable life without any challenges and risks.

Mr. Chaitanya could perceive the new target as a possible and achievable one and Mr. Prasanth perceived the same thing quite differently and negatively. This difference was due to the variation in needs and motives of these two executives.

(b) Self-Concept: Self concept explains how we perceive ourselves. Some of us, perceive ourselves as high achievers and we can perform and attain anything. Others view themselves as low achievers. Our self concept determines how we perceive others. Those who feel themselves to be high achievers, perceive the others, as encouraging and opportunistic. The vice versa, i.e., perceiving the outside world as discouraging and threatening is true in case of those who perceive themselves as low achievers. Those who perceive themselves in a realistic manner can also perceive others, situations and the outside world close to reality.

(c) Past Experience: Past experience provides knowledge and sets the mind to do things in a certain way. In addition, it builds relationships with several people and institutions. These derivatives of past experience influence the perceiver to perceive the things as they happened in the past.

Mr. Madhu Joshi has been working in a public sector commercial bank. He offered suggestions frequently to the general manager (advances) regarding following the guidelines in sanctioning loans to the industries in which politicians are the directors of the company. The general manager did not care for them. Then he decided that bosses do not listen to their subordinates and therefore, better not to offer any suggestions in future. Later, the general manager sought the advice of Mr. Madhu. But Mr. Madhu refused to offer suggestions.

Thus, our past experiences mould the way we perceive the present situations, persons and the world.

(d) Current Psychological/Emotional State: The current psychological/emotional situation of a person influences his perception process very much. For example, if a person is not given promotion, but in turn his junior is given promotion, he feels distressed accompanied with insecurity. Then he perceives even opportunities as threats. Similarly, employees facing the problems at home perceive negativity at the work place and vice versa.

Characteristics of the Situation

Managers behave differently in different situation based on situational characteristics. Leaders assume autocratic style when the situation is urgent as well as routine. In other words leaders perceive the routine situations as those that do not require additional inputs and thus assume autocratic style. The strategic situations need additional and talented inputs from managers as well as their subordinates in the process of decision-making. Therefore, leaders assume democratic style during the strategic situations. Thus, the characteristics of the situations influence the leaders to perceive the styles.

The strategic situations need additional and talented inputs from managers as well as their subordinates in the process of decision-making.

Mr. Pillai is the Human Resources Manager of Pragati Chemicals Ltd., Chennai. He receives the workers' grievances like a bureaucrat at office and just like a friend at home. Therefore, trade union leaders meet him at his home, and present their problems. He promises them to redress the issues. In fact, he solves them and fulfills his promises.

The home environment brings the congenial social, psychological and physical situation to Mr. Pillai, whereas the organisational physical setting makes him to assume organisational formal roles. Thus, the characteristics of the situation like physical, social, organisational etc. influence the perceptual thought process.

(G) PERCEPTUAL OUTPUT

The information selected from the external environment through the stimuli is organised and interpreted by one cognitive process. This interpretation turns into the perceptual output. In other words, it is the perception. Perception is in various forms like attitude, opinion, view, feeling and the like. For example, a superior expresses his opinion regarding his subordinate. Employees express their view about their working conditions. Customers express their attitude towards the quality and utility of the products/services.

(H) INDIVIDUAL BEHAVIOUR

Perception in the form of attitude, opinion, feeling, etc., influence the behaviour. Employees who feel satisfied regarding their job contribute maximum to their job. Job satisfaction results in the maximum contribution to the job. In other words, maximum contribution to the job is the behaviour.

(I) BARRIERS TO PERCEPTUAL ACCURACY

The analysis of perceptual process indicates that perception is a complex process and it is influenced by a number of factors. Added to this, cognitive process plays a vital role in interpreting the information. Since, human nature is complex they cannot be objective regarding their judgments where environment is involved. A number of factors, objects and situations hinder our judgment about other people. We can perceive accurately, if these hindering factors are either eliminated or controlled. These hindering factors are also known as *barriers* to perceptual accuracy. They are:

A number of factors hinder our judgment about other people, objects and situations.

(i) Stereotyping

We normally tend to classify/categorise people and events into already known or perceived categories. Such tendency is termed as 'Stereotyping.'

We have certain pre-established categories with certain characteristics and attributes based on the occupational/professional characteristics. We approach doctors, judges and teachers with most positive and obedience attributes, whereas policemen with fear and submissive attributes. When a drug addict or an alcoholic approaches us, we perceive them most negatively.

Mr. Srinivas, a newly appointed Accountant in the Department of Finance of Bharat Cables Limited entered the Department of Finance of the company. He saw a gentleman dressed in a full-suit and tie, carrying a brief case entering the room of the Chief Finance Manager. Mr. Srinivas perceived that the gentleman is the Chief Finance Manager as we normally perceive that the managers are in full-suit and necktie. But that gentleman was a cashier and carrying cash in the brief case and he was on his way to the bank.

The perception of Mr. Srinivas was based on stereotype impressions.

The other stereotypes are:

- Age stereotype, and
- Sex role stereotype.

Age Stereotype: Age is one of the stereotypes which influences the organisational environment. We presume physical qualities, psychological qualities and intellectual qualities based on the age. The stereotypes of the young people include:

- Dynamic and dashing
- Quick decision-making
- More creative and innovative ideas
- More physical capacities
- Highly interested in new techniques and new methods
- Highly active.

The stereotypes of the older employees, as found by Rosen and Jerdee,[13] are as follows:

- More resistant to organisational change
- Less creative and innovative
- Less likely to take calculated risks
- More conservative in nature
- Lower in physical capacity
- Less interested in learning new techniques
- Less capable of learning new techniques
- Gray hair.

Sex-Role Stereotypes: We normally stereotype men and women into separate and distinct categories. The stereotypes of men include:

- Tough leadership
- Task centred leader rather than human relationist
- High self-confidence
- High competitiveness
- Highly ambitiousness
- Detailed analytical ability.

Stereotypes of the women employees include:

- Highly emotional
- Highly impulsive and submissive

- Highly human-relationists and inter-personal relationists
- Low self-confidence
- Less ambitious
- More commitment and loyalty
- Highly tolerant.

These steoreotypes dominate/influence us to perceive the objects/people/incidents in a pre-categorised or predetermined structure. Hence, stereotyping hinders us from perceiving the objects as objectively as possible.

(ii) Halo Effect

Halo effect is the tendency of perceiving a person/object or situation on the basis of a single trait/characteristic.

Halo effect is the tendency of perceiving a person/object or situation on the basis of a single trait/characteristic. For example, Mr. Raman of Industrial Finance Corporation attends the office on time every day while all other colleagues attend the office at least 15 minutes late. But Mr. Raman is not efficient in job performance. But the manager of the branch ranked his performance as the best simply based on his punctuality in coming to the office.

The halo effect is likely to be related to our own self-image. The managers who are also technically competent, would view his/her subordinates more favourably who are technically competent than those who are not. The one trait of the subordinate influences us in perceiving. Halo effects may be positive or negative. They act as a screen blocking the perceiver from perceiving or judging the objects/people/situations as objectively as possible.

(iii) Selective Perceptions

Selective perception is to single out certain aspects of the environment due to defence mechanisms and other human limitations. Selective perception is also due to the reinforcement of values and beliefs.

Normally, we observe that the production manager perceives the organisational problem from the point of view of the production activities while the marketing manager perceives the same problem from the point of view of the marketing activities. The selection perception hinders us to analyse the problem from the multi-dimensional and comprehensive view. Hence, we fail to perceive the total environment from the multidimensional point of view.

Mr. Chakravarti, Chief Marketing Manager of Global Exports Limited had been very much concerned with the Exports to the Middle East. He organised a meeting of all General Managers (Marketing). Mr. Chakravarti discussed all the issues with the General Manager, who was in-charge of Middle East ignoring other general managers. This situation is due to selective perception.

(iv) Attribution

Attribution is the way/method of explaining the causes for another's behaviour or their own behaviour. We explain the causes for our success like intelligence, presence of mind, competence etc., and causes for others' failure as unfavourable environmental factors. Thus, attribution is the process by which people draw conclusions about the factors that influence our own or another's behaviour.[14]

We tend to attribute certain factors as responsible for occurrence of an event or outcome. These factors can be internal or external. Internal factors include intelligence, dynamism, skill, practical, efficiency, trusting, etc., of an individual. Customer satisfaction may be attributed to the dynamism and practical of the sales person. This attribution is called internal attribution. In contrast customer satisfaction may be attributed to the external factors like deployment of more resources by the company or the customer does not have need for additional service. Thus, we tend to attribute the success of the sales person in satisfying the customer to the external factors. Such attribution is called external attribution. So, people tend to attribute internal factors perceive the success due to the intelligence of one's own and those tend to attribute external factors perceive the success due to luck or availability of resources.

Attribution is of two types *viz.,* (a) dispositional attributions and (b) situational attributions. Dispositional attributions refer to internal factors for one's own or others' behaviour. These internal factors include personality traits, motivation, intelligence, ability, etc. Situational attributions refer to external factors for one's own or other's behaviour.

Attributions play an important role in perception at the workplace and organisational situations. People behave as they do. Why determine several reasons for the behaviours of the people. Harold Kelley proposed a model, which tends to explain how people determine about the other's behaviour.[15] This model suggests three major factors on which people focus while making casual attributions. These factors are:

***(a)* Consistency Cues:** If a person behaves in the same way in different situations that behaviour is viewed as consistently similar. The reasons for such behaviour can be considered as internally generated. Otherwise, the varying behaviour from poor to excellent may be viewed as the outcome of the external factors.

Mr. Mohan has been working as a recovery manager in Central Bank since 1974 and his recovery performance has been consistently below average. Mr. Naveen of Research and Development department of Natco Pharma Limited has been consistently developing innovative products. Thus, the performances of Mr. Mohan and Mr. Naveen have been consistent though, it is positive in case of the latter and negative in case of the former.

***(b)* Consensus Cues:** Consensus is behaving in the same fashion as others behave in the same situation under the same circumstances. Private sector employees normally work seriously and with commitment and as such behaving in a private sector company is viewed as consensus behaviour. In contrast employees in public sector with relatively less commitment and employees working in public sector with relatively less commitment are viewed as consensus. Thus, consensus is behaving like most of the others in the same or similar organizations behave including carrying out activities, following organizational work culture, values and ethics.

Mr. Phani Kumar, Senior Production Manager of TELCO took his subordinate and immediately admitted him in emergency ward of the company hospital when the latter met with an accident in the factory. Thus, Mr. Phani Kumar behaved as others behave in such situations. This is called *consensus*.

Mr. Sharma committed himself to his job and the organisation when almost all of his colleagues resorted to moonlighting. Thus, he behaved differently from other people. This might be due to his self motivation generated by his internal factors. Thus, an employee behaves differently from other employees of the same organisation or behaves differently than expected, when the expectations are based upon the expected behaviour of other employees. Then this behaviour is viewed as revealing the employee's true motives and these motives are considered to be internally generated.[16]

***(c)* Distinctiveness Cues:** Distinctiveness refers to the extent to which the same person behaves in the same way in different circumstances. Different circumstances may be highly positive, negative, challenging, crisis, critical, growing business, decline business, boom and recessionary. To behave in the same way in different circumstances, the person should have full commitment, intelligence, adaptability, presence of mind and vigour.

Mr. Chaitanya of Wadia Industries Limited performed his job as Marketing Manager extremely well. When the employees' morale came down, he was transferred to Human Resources Management Department. His performance was extremely well in this department also. Thus, he did his job with the same level of performance as the Head of R&D Department of the same company. Thus, he behaved in the same level in different situations.

Fundamental Attribution Error: We tend to measure the behaviour of other people through their internal characteristics rather than the external environmental factors. This is called *fundamental attribution error*. The attribution error is defined as "the tendency to underestimate the impact of external causes of behaviour and to overestimate the impact of internal causes when trying to understand why people behave the way they do."[17]

(v) Distortions

As explained earlier, we use perceptual defence mechanism. Sometimes we distort what we see. Sometimes we totally avoid viewing or seeing what actually exists. We avoid viewing the reality when we don't like the situation or the situation is quite contrary to our expectations or the situation is against our values/accepted social and ethical values or when we don't dare to involve ourselves in such a situation.

Mr. Prakash expected 'excellent' rating (self concept) while his boss rated him as 'poor.' Mr. Prakash viewed that his boss is partial (possible distortion of facts). There is direct relation between the perceived threat to a person's self-concept and the likelihood of a defensive response to perceived data.

(vi) Projection

The superior who is a hard worker assigns the same character of hard working to his subordinates in appraising them. The American superiors assign punctuality to their subordinates while the Japanese bosses assign the character of working together to their subordinates in appraising their performance.

Projection takes place when one's own personal attributes are assigned to others.

(vii) Similar-to-me Effect

People tend to perceive others similar to them when others have one or a few characteristics similar to them. These characteristics include work habits, values, beliefs, intelligence, skills, demographic factors and the like.

(viii) First Impression Error

We form an opinion about others, when we meet and interact with them for the first time. This is called first impression. First impression influences some people very much and they perceive other areas also based on first impression, may be positive or negative. First impression, mostly may not pose the correct and total picture of others due to various factors — both internal and external — that influence momentarily.

(ix) Self-Fulfilling Prophecies: The Pygmalion Effect and the Golem Effect

Perceptions influence behaviour in the real world. Self fulfilling prophecy is behaving towards others in consistent with expectations about them. For example Mr. Michael — a superior forms a positive view of the potentialities of a particular subordinate Mr. Johnson and thereby forms high job expectations. Mr. Michael starts motivating and supporting Mr. Johnson in his job performance including providing training and empowering. This practice, in turn enables Mr. Johnson to achieve highest performance. The opposite is also true in the sense that if Mr. Michael forms a negative view about the potentialities of Mr. Thomas, and thereby forms low job expectations, the former starts discouraging and disabling the latter at the job that would result in poor job performance of Mr. Thomas.

Thus, self-fulfilling prophecies can mostly be two forms, i.e., positive and negative. Sometimes it can also be neutral. Positive and high expectations would result in high job performance of the subordinate. This is known as Pygmalion effect. This effect was demonstrated in a study of Israeli soldiers who were taking a combat command course in a training programme.[18] All the four instructors were told that certain trainees, who were selected at random, have high potentialities whereas all other trainees have normal or low potentialities. This resulted in taking special attention, providing encouragement and support of the selected trainees by the instructors. At the end of the programme, the selected trainees achieved highest performance/test scores.

As explained earlier, the negative view of potentialities and low expectation of performance would result in poor job performance. This is referred to as Golem effect. Researchers found that the instructors were informed that certain paratrooper has poor potentialities compared to others and the ultimate end performance of these paratroopers in the training programme was poor.[19]

Fig 14.13 depicts the summary of Golem effect, Pygmalion effect and general case of self-fulfilling prophecy.

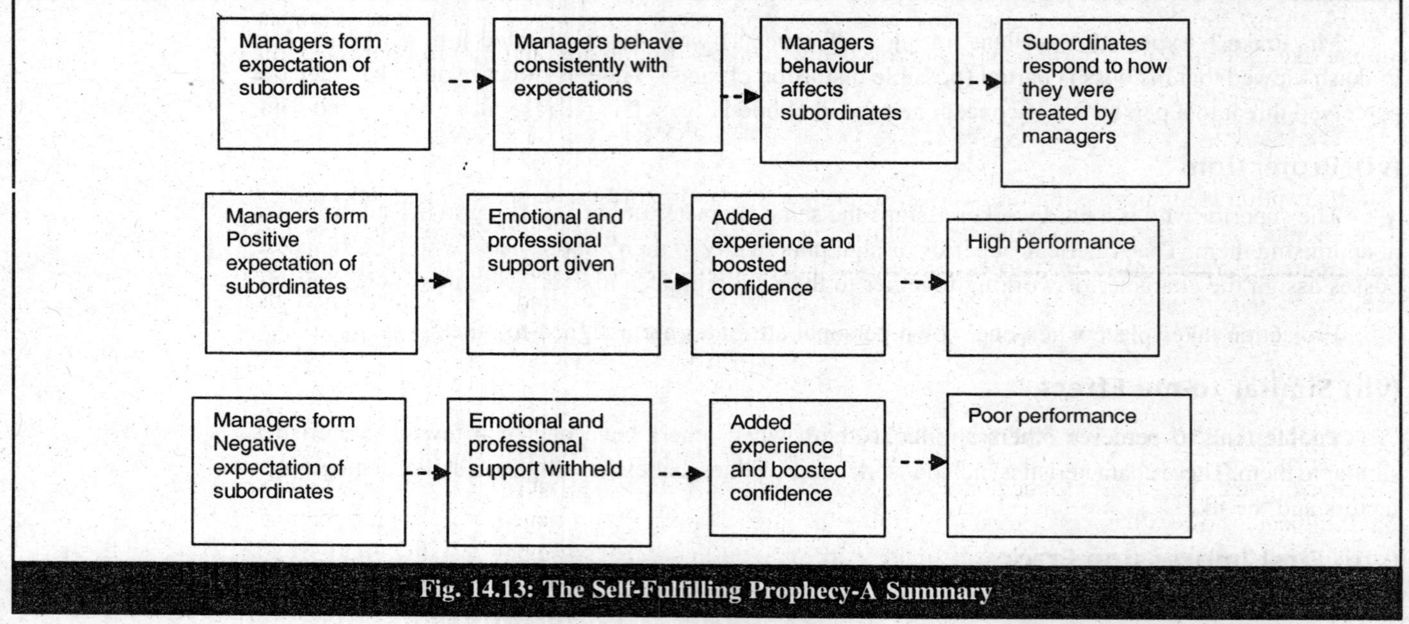

Fig. 14.13: The Self-Fulfilling Prophecy-A Summary

(**Source:** Modified version from Eden, D., "Leadership and Expectations" in R. Vecchio (ED.), "Leadership: Understanding the Dynamics of Power and Influence in Organisations, University of Nortedame Press,1997, pp.177.)

These barriers reduce the accuracy of perception. This in turn deviates the behaviour from the expected behaviour. Hence, we should perceive the objects/people/situations as accurately as possible.

How to Perceive Accurately?

Perceptual barriers can be minimized and the accuracy of the perception can be enhanced by enhancing perceptual skills.

Perceptual barriers can be minimized and the accuracy of the perception can be enhanced by enhancing perceptual skills. Perceptual skills can be enhanced by adopting the following measures:

- Knowing oneself more accurately
- Assessing and knowing the others more exactly
- Being empathic
- Having positive attitudes
- Enhancing one's self-concept
- Taking a conscious effort to reduce the perceptual barriers

- Open and two-way communication with the employees
- Develop the habit of analysing the incidents/people/objects from the multi-dimensional point of view
- Avoid attributions
- Get complete information from multi-sources regarding an object/incident/a person and organize, interpret and perceive from the data.
- Be in the adult ego state, so that you would be a rational decision-maker. It does mean that your internal factors would be in control.
- Avoid other perceptual distortions that bias our perception
- Avoid inappropriate attributions.

These measures help us to perceive other people, objects and situations as accurately as possible. But most of the subordinates working in various companies are concerned about how their superiors perceive them? In fact most of us also think, how our friends perceive us, how our colleagues view us and the like. In turn, we prefer to behave appropriately to others' preferences in order to impress them.

(J) PERCEPTION: ORGANISATIONAL APPLICATIONS

Perception is applicable not only in social settings, but at organizational settings and workplaces also. In fact, it produces or damages employee performance, customer service, product design, product quality, financial performance, building corporate image and the like. It affects various human resource management functions and customer service functions directly and some other functions indirectly. To be specific, perception affects performance appraisal, impression management and corporate image.

Perception and Performance Appraisal

Performance here refers to the degree of accomplishment of the tasks that make up an individual's job. It indicates how well an individual is fulfilling the job demands. Performance appraisal is a method of evaluating the behaviour of employees in the work spot, normally including both the quantitative and qualitative aspects of job performance. Often the term is confused with effort, but performance is always measured in terms of results and not efforts. Some of the important features of performance appraisal may be captured thus:

- Performance appraisal is the systematic description of an employee's job-relevant accomplishments and failures.
- The basic purpose is to find out how well the employee is performing the job and to establish a plan of improvement.
- Appraisals are arranged periodically according to a definite plan.

Perception affects the measurement and comparison of it with the standards. Expectations of superiors in terms of performance standards rather than actually set standards influence the performance appraisal. Research studies found that superiors' expectations rather than actual performance standards were considered in appraising the performance of bank tellers. In addition performance is measured depending on the characteristics of the perceived.

The perceiver's characteristics affect performance appraisal in the form of rating biases. The problem with subjective measure (is that rating which is not verifiable by others) has the opportunity for bias. The perceiver's biases include: *(a)* halo effect, *(b)* the error of central tendency, *(c)* the leniency and strictness biases, *(d)* personal prejudice and *(e)* the recency effect.

(a) ***Halo Effect:*** It is the tendency of the perceiver to depend excessively on the rating of one trait or behavioural consideration in rating all other traits or behavioural considerations. One way of minimising the halo effect is appraising all the employees by one trait before going to rate them on the basis of another trait.

(b) ***The Error of Central Tendency:*** Some perceiver follow play safe policy in rating by rating all the employees around the middle point of the rating scale and they avoid rating the people at both the extremes of the scale. They follow play safe policy because of answerability to the management or lack of knowledge about the job and the person he is rating or has least interest in his job.

(c) ***The Leniency and Strictness:*** The leniency bias crops when some perceivers have a tendency liberalise their rating by assigning higher rates consistently. Such ratings do not serve any purpose. It should be noticed that is assigning consistently low rates also is equally demaging.

(d) ***Personal Prejudice:*** If the perceiver dislikes any employee or any group, he may rate them at the lower end, which may distort the rating purpose and affect the career of the employees concerned.

(e) ***The Recency Effect:*** The perceivers generally remember the recent actions of the employee at the time of rating and rate them on the basis of these recent actions — favourable or unfavourable — rather than on the whole activities.

The other areas of perception those affect performance appraisal include various problems of perception like: attribution, similar-to-me effect and first impression effect.

Impression Management

The purpose of impression management or self-presentation is to regulate or monitor what others perceive of us. We mostly tend to try to present ourselves in a socially desirable or acceptable way in order to impress others. The employees tend to present themselves in an acceptable way to their superiors in order to be rated high in the performance appraisal or to be considered for continuation of employment or promotion or salary increase and the like.

The impression management strategies include enhancing the positive behavioural outcomes and reducing the negative behavioural outcomes.

The impression management strategies (See Table 14.1) include enhancing the positive behavioural outcomes and reducing the negative behavioural outcomes. In addition, the employees would like to give the impression that they are capable of more than what they really are. In addition, they use other strategies like hiding the weaknesses, dissociation with the trouble-makers, apologising for their mistakes, associating with the positive impression-makers and the like.

Impression Management and Employment Interviews

Normally, most of the candidates try to impress the interview panel and market themselves in one way or the other. The impression techniques that the candidates use include dressing, speaking and elaborating acts. A study summarized the impression techniques by interviewees in a campus recruitment interviews (See Table 14.1). In fact the interviewers also responded favourably to these techniques. Thus, the candidates became successful in interviews by following these techniques.

Table 14.1: Impression Management Techniques Used by Job Interviewees

Impression Management Technique	Description	Frequency of using Technique
Self-promotion	Directly describing oneself in a positive manner of the situation at hand (for example: I am a sincere employee).	100%
Personal Stories	Describing past events that make oneself look good (for example: I used to work until 8 p.m. in my previous job).	96%
Opinion Conformity	Expressing beliefs that are assumed to be held by the target (for example: I agreeing with you-interview panel member).	54%
Entitlements	Claiming responsibility for successful past events (for example: I was responsible for profits of my company in 2010).	50%
Other Enhancement	Making statements that flatter, praise or compliment the interviewers (for example: Your company earned profits only because of your efforts)	46%

(**Source:** Adapted from Jerald Greenberg and Robert A. Baron, "Behaviour in Organisations", Prentice Hall of India (P) Ltd., New Delhi, 2007, p. 54.)

Impression Management by Organisations: Corporate Image

Like individuals, corporations also impress their stakeholders with respect to different aspects. For example, companies use recruitment advertisements to impress prospective employees, use issue of share advertisement to impress upon the prospective shareholders and use marketing advertisements to impress current and future customers.

Companies also use their annual reports to impress all kinds of stakeholders. Companies publish annual reports projecting their image with highly attractive material, good photographs, success stories, significant achievements and data.

Another impresive management technique used by companies is creating employer brand. Employer brand carries various human resource management aspects in particular and business — both internal and external — aspects in general in order to attract, utilise and retain talent. Thus, employer brand creates employee friendly image of the employer, builds healthy working relationships between employer and employees, enhances self-esteem and organisational loyalty of the employees and there by creating a perception of stabiling in production and growth.

The Best Employer Brands

Business Today Mercer-TNS Survey: The Business Today Mercer-TNS Survey identified the top 10 best employers in India for the year 2006. They are:

Rank	*Name of the Company*
1	Infosys
2	MindTree Consulting
3	Satyam Computer Services
4	Dr. Reddy's Labs
5	Sapient
6	Agilent Technologies
7	Johnson and Johnson
8	Covansys
9	HCL Comnet
10	HSBC

The fast growing information and knowledge make learning as the order of the day not only for individual but also for the organisations. People learn not only information but the behaviour. Therefore, we should understand the concept of learning in order to understand the behaviour of the individuals, groups and the organisation.

(K) LEARNING

Need for Learning in Organisations

Human resources play a critical role in implementing organizational strategies and achieving goals. Different strategies need different kinds of employee behaviour. For example, the growth strategies need transformational leadership styles, employee empowerment and adult-adult ego states. Retrenchment strategies need parent-child ego states and autocratic leadership style. Thus, efficient achievement of different strategies desire different behaviours. Employees are expected to acquire the desirable work behaviour based on strategies to achieve organisational goals. In other words, employees change their behaviours depending up on shifts in strategies. Employees change their behaviours by learning new competencies, knowledge, beliefs, values and the like.

Meaning

Learning is a relatively permanent change in knowledge or observable behaviour that results from practice or experience.

Learning is a relatively permanent change in knowledge or observable behaviour that results from practice or experience.[20] People acquire new competencies, skills, knowledge, values, beliefs, norms, cause and effect relationships, and the like based on either one's own experience or others' experience or research output.

This learning influences the individuals to change their knowledge or wisdom and/or observable behaviour. All learning may not result in observable behaviour as all learning may not result in performance. Performance need motivation and commitment to use the learned knowledge and acquired competency on to the job for the benefit of the organization.

Ms. Hima Bindu joined a private biscuit manufacturing company as Marketing Executive after working for 10 years in a public sector company. Most of the decisions were made by the Chief Marketing Manager and they were pushed down for implementation in the public sector company. As such Ms. Hima Bindu never offered any suggestion in her previous company.

Mr. Ramesh, the Chief Marketing Manager of the private biscuit company organised the Marketing Executives meet in Chennai and sought the suggestions for the product modification and development. Many marketing executives offered suggestions. But Ms. Hima Bindu could not offer any suggestion, though she had the idea of a new product (*i.e.*, cashew mixed biscuits) in her mind due to the culture of her previous company. The meeting was concluded.

The rival company after six months could increase their market share by three per cent by introducing cashew mixed biscuits. Ms. Hima Bindu felt very bad for her failure in transmitting the idea she had in her mind.

Ms. Hima Bindu offered a suggestion to the Chief Marketing Manager even before it is sought in the next Marketing Executives' Meet. This suggestion was relating to introduction of new variety of biscuits mixed with very small pieces of curry leaves and spices. The Chief Marketing Manager appreciated Ms. Hima Bindu and implemented the idea. This enabled the company to improve its marketing share by five per cent within one year. Since then, Ms. Hima Bindu changed her behaviour in offering suggestions. This relatively permanent change in Ms. Hima Bindu's behaviour occurred as a result of her experience is called Learning. According to Stephen P. Robbins learning is, "any relatively permanent change in behaviour that occurs as a result of experience."[21]

Ms. Hima Bindu has learnt that follower should respond as and when there is a request from the leader. Otherwise, the organisation would not be benefited by the valuable ideas of its employees. Further she felt that, leaders in the public sector mostly follow autocratic style and as such they do not seek the ideas or suggestions from the subordinates. Hima Bindu learnt from her experience that the leaders in private sector mostly follow participative style and they welcome the ideas and suggestions from the followers for the organisational effectiveness and improvisation. This experience resulted in a permanent change in Hima Bindu's behaviour in offering suggestions to her superior.

Forms of Learning

There are many forms of learning.[22] Learning takes place through education, training, management development programmes, self-observation of various activities. Individuals primarily learn through various formal and informal education programmes. Formal education programmes are offered by schools, colleges, universities, technical, vocational training institutions as well as open and distance educational institutions. Informal education is provided by the parents and other family members, peers and various social and religious organizations.

Various organizations provide job training to prepare the candidates for jobs. In addition, organizations provide training and management development programmes to their employees to provide job skills. Individuals learn through these educational, training and management development programmes.

In addition, individuals learn by observing others while performing various activities. Similarly, individuals learn through converting the ideas, imaginations and assumptions into practise as well as through various research activities.

Learning Principles

Models of human learning are studied in order to find out the reasons for fast and accurate learning. The principles of learning developed by Sikula[23] are as follows:

(a) All human beings can learn.

(b) An individual must be motivated to learn.

(c) Learning is active and not passive.

(d) Learners may acquire knowledge more rapidly with guidance. Feedback ensures improvement in speed and accuracy of learning.

(e) Appropriate material (like case studies, tools, problems, reading, etc.) should be provided.

(f) Time must be provided to practise learning.

(g) Learning methods should be varied. Variety of methods should be introduced to off-set fatigue and boredom.

(h) The learner must secure satisfaction from learning. Education must fulfill human needs, desires and expectations.

(i) Learners need reinforcement of correct behaviour.

(j) Standards of performance should be set for the learner.

(k) Different levels of learning exist.

(l) Learning is an adjustment on the part of an individual.

(m) Individual differences play a large part in effectiveness of the learning process.

(n) Learning is a cumulative process.

(o) Ego involvement is widely regarded as a major factor in learning.

(p) The rate of learning decreases when complex skills are involved.

(q) Learning is closely related to attention and concentration.

(r) Learning involves long-run retention and immediate acquisition of knowledge.

(s) Accuracy deserves generally more emphasis than speed.

(t) Learning should be relatively based.

(u) Learning should be goal-oriented.

Exhibit 14.1 depicts leaning principles.

Exhibit 14.1 Learning Principles

1. Learning requires purposeful activity.
2. Learning is a process of the whole individual.
3. Learning is problem solving. Challenging problems stimulate learning.
4. Learning is based on past experiences.
5. Learning results from stimulation through the senses.
6. The more vivid and intense the impressions, the greater the chance of remembering.
7. Interest is essential to effective learning. Learning requires motivation.
8. Friendly competition stimulates learning.
9. e gnition and credit provide strong incentives for learning.
10. eople learn more when they are held to account and made to feel responsible for learning.
11. owing 'why' makes learning more effective.
12. Knowledge of the standards required makes learning more effective.
13. Things should be taught the way they are to be used.
14. Teaching should be logical or orderly.
15. The most effective learning results when initial learning is followed immediately by application.
16. Early successes increase chances for effective learning.
17. Repetition, accompanied by constant effort toward improvement, makes for effective development of skill.
18. Feelings of both teacher and student affect learning.
19. Students learn many things in addition to skills and information (attitudes, interests, appreciations, etc.)
20. Continuous evaluation is essential to effective learning.

Source: William J. Micheels, p. 6, quoted in M.N. Rudrabasavaraj, *op. cit.*, pp. 150-151.

Learning Patterns

Trainers need some understanding of the patterns in which new skills are learned. The employee is likely to find him/her unusually clumsy during the early stages of learning. This can be called discouraging stage. After the employees adjust him/her to the environment, he learns at a fast rate. A 'plateau' develops after the lapse of more training time due to a loss of motivation and lack of break in training schedule and time. The trainee reaches the next stage when he is motivated by the trainer and/ or some break or pause in time and training process is given. The trainee at this stage learns at a fast rate.[24] Special repetition of the course leads the trainee to reach the stage of over-learning.

Thus, it is clear that, learning rarely takes place at a constant rate. It varies according to the difficulty of the task, ability of the individual and physical factors. However, the rate of learning varies from one individual to another.

Characteristics of Learning Process

(1) Learning is a continuous process.

(2) People learn through their actual personal experience, simulated experience and from other's experience (by using the knowledge which represents experience of others).

(3) People learn step by step, from known to unknown and simple to complex.

(4) There is a need for repetition in teaching to improve skill and to learn perfectly.

(5) Practice makes a man perfect. Hence, opportunity should be created to use, transfer the skills, knowledge and abilities acquired through learning. It gives satisfaction to the learner.

(6) Conflicts in learning: Conflict in learning arises when the trainer knows or has developed some habits which are incorrect in terms of the method being learned.

The Climate for Learning

Conducive climate is highly essential for serious participation, attentiveness, creation of interest, and sincerity of learner. Climate for learning consists of working conditions, relationship with other trainees, and trainers/instructors, conditions for relaxation, freedom, scope for social interaction, and formation of social groups.

Conducive climate for learning should be provided in view of its significance in training. It consists of ideal physical and psychological environment. Ideal physical environment, consisting of suitable location with space, adequate accommodation, audio-visual aids, air conditioning, ventilation, lighting and other facilities like canteen, facilities for relaxation, should be provided. Ideal psychological environment, consisting business atmosphere, friendly environment, frequent communication, follow-up regarding performance and progress, enthusiastic, helpful and broad minded trainer, etc., should be created and provided. Provision for measuring learner's progress through tests should also be made in order to regulate, correct and follow-up the training programmes.

Learning Problems

The instructor should have the knowledge of the possible learning problems. He should identify the problems of trainees and take steps to solve them. The possible learning problems are:

(a) Lack of knowledge, skill, aptitude and favourable attitude.

(b) Knowledge and skill not being applied.

(c) Existence of anti-learning factors: Most operational situations contain a number of elements which will restrict the development of learning regardless the methods employed.

(d) Psychological problems like fear and shy.

(e) Inability to transfer of learning to operational situation.

(f) Heavy dependence on repetition, demonstration and practice.

(g) Unwilling to change.

(h) Lack of interest about the knowledge of results.

(i) Absence of self-motivation.

(j) Negative attitude about involvement and participation.[25]

Learning efficiency depends up on the effectiveness of teaching and training. Now, we shall study teaching principles.

Teaching Principles

In addition to learning principles, teaching principles should also be taken care of to make training effective some of the teaching principles are given below:

(a) The employee must be taught to practise the correct method of work.

(b) Job analysis and motion study techniques should be used.

(c) Job training under actual working conditions should be preferred to class room training.

(*d*) Emphasis should be given more on accuracy than speed.

(*e*) Teaching should be at different time intervals.

(*f*) It should be recognised that it is easier to train young workers than old workers due to their decreasing adaptability with the increase in age. Exhibit 14.2 shows principles of teaching basic skills and Exhibit 14.3 shows principles of teaching basic Physical Movements.

Exhibit 14.2 Principles of Teaching Basic Skills

1. The worker must be taught and must practise only correct methods of work. This is the basic principle.
2. First establish the best way of doing a job — use job analysis and/or time and motion study techniques.
3. Follow the principles of best movements in work.
4. Job training under actual working conditions is superior to classroom and formal training.
5. *Emphasise accuracy* first - speed second.
6. Training is more efficient when distributed over short periods of time.
7. Remember the practice aims — efficiency increases with repetition of the task. However, you should expect learning plateaus when no apparent progress is made, followed by additional spurts of improvement. Therefore, you should carry out distributed practice over longer period than is commonly believed (otherwise workers settle down at production speeds lower than their real abilities).
8. *When* a plateau is reached, use incentives and other devices to get *more* improvement.
9. Age and learning: You can train older workers as well as younger ones. Learning ability does not deteriorate rapidly with age - instead, older workers have learned more bad habits and therefore need retaining.

(**Source:** Morris Viteles, Quoted in *Ibid.*, pp. 151-152.)

Exhibit 14.3 Principles of Teaching Basic Physical Movements

1. Successive movements should be so related that one movement passes easily into that which follows, each ending in a position favourable for the beginning of the next movement.
2. The order of movements should be so arranged that little direct attention is needed for passage from one to another. In other words, they should be so arranged that the mind can attend to the final aim or end of the operation instead of being distracted by the work of initiating successively the several movements which are involved in a task.
3. The sequence of movements is to be so framed that an easy rhythm can be established in the automatic performance of the various elements of operation.
4. From the principles stated above follows the corollary that continuous movement is preferable to angular movements involving sudden changes in the direction of movement.
5. The number of movements should be reduced as far as possible within the scope of limitations suggested above. In general, reducing the number of movements will facilitate a rhythmic method of working and automation as a means of reducing the volitional direction of work.
6. Simultaneous use of both hands should be encouraged.
7. When a forcible stroke is required, the direction of movement and placement of material should be so arranged that, as far as practicable, the stroke is delivered when it has reached its greatest momentum.

(**Source:** *Ibid.*)

Learning efficiency depends on training effectiveness in addition to teaching. Now, we shall study the principles of training.

Principles of Training

Providing training in the knowledge of different skills is a complex process. A number of principles have been evolved which can be followed as guidelines by the trainees. Some of them are as follows:

(*1*) ***Motivation:*** As the effectiveness of an employee depends on how well he is motivated by management, the effectiveness of learning also depends on motivation. In other words, the trainee will acquire a new skill or knowledge thoroughly and quickly if he or she is highly motivated. Thus, the training must be related to the desires of the trainee such as more wages or better job, recognition, status, promotion, etc. The trainer should find out the proper ways to motivate experienced employees who are already enjoying better facilities in case of retraining.

(2) ***Progress Information:*** It has been found by various research studies that there is a relation between learning rapidly and effectively and providing right information specifically, and as such the trainer should not give excessive information or information that can be misinterpreted. The trainee also wants to learn a new skill without much difficulty and without handing too much or receiving excessive information or wrong type of progressive information. So, the trainer has to provide only the required amount of progressive information specifically to the trainee.

(3) ***Reinforcement:*** The effectiveness of the trainee in learning new skills or acquiring new knowledge should be reinforced by means of rewards and punishments. Examples of positive reinforcement are promotions, rise in pay, getting accolades, etc. Punishments are considered as negative reinforcements. Management should take care to award the successful trainees quite positively to retain their spirit and mental aspirations intact.

The management can punish the trainees whose behaviour is undesirable. But the consequences of such punishments have their long-run ill effect on the trainer as well as on the management. Hence, the management should take much care while instituting negative reinforcements.

(4) ***Practice:*** A trainee should actively participate in the training programmes in order to make the the process an effective one. Continuous and long prastice is highly essential for effective learning. Jobs are broken down into elements from which the fundamental, physical, sensory and mental skills are extracted. Training exercises should be provided for each skill.

(5) ***Full vs. Part:*** It is not clear whether it is best to teach the complete job at a stretch or dividing the job into parts and teaching each part at a time. If the job is complex and requires a little too long to learn, it is better to teach part of the job separately and then put the parts together into an effective complete job. Generally, the training process should start from the known and proceed to the unknown and from the easy to the difficult when parts are taught. However, the trainer has to teach the trainees based on his judgment on their motivation and convenience.

(6) ***Individual Differences:*** Individual training is costly, and group training is economically viable and advantageous to the organisation. But individuals vary in intelligence and aptitude from person to person. So the trainer has to adjust the training programme to the individual abilities and aptitude. In addition, individual teaching machines and adjustments of differences should be provided. (See Box 14.3).

Box 14.3: How an Android Phone Can Change Your Life?

In the past few months several mobile devices have enmass taken to Google's mobile operating system and launched Android-enabled handsets. In this season of heavy activity around Android phones, comes the big announcement of the launch of version 2.0 of the operating system, also code-named Eclair.

A number of enhancements have been added to the previous version including the much talked-about multi-touch feature and sync. Here's how the Android can up your tech quotient with these new capabilities:

* *Communicate instantly by tapping on the contact, and choosing from all available communication options (Facebook, Twitter, Yahoo! Mail, Gmail, etc)*

* *Availability of an accounts management API to store centrally account-credential information on the device*
* *Supports devices with various screen sizes and resolutions, with three different screens of each of the applications*
* *Multiple email account synchronization, that combines all account into a single email inbox with option of exchange support*
* *New virtual keyboard layout for faster and more accurate typing. The multi-touch ensures that all keys pressed during typing are not skipped.*
* *Bluetooth API allows the device to connect to other nearby devices. This capabilities includes the integration of features of social-interaction and P2P communication*
* *Improved camera controls with digital zoom, a scene mode, white balance controls, macro focus and colour effects*

In the past few months several mobile devices have en mass taken to Google's mobile operating system and launched Android-enabled handsets. In this season of heavy activity around Android phones, comes the big announcement of the launch of version 2.0 of the operating system, also code-named Eclair.

A number of enhancements have been added to the previous version including the much talked-about multi-touch feature and sync. Here's how the Android can up your tech quotient with these new capabilities:

* *Communicate instantly by tapping on the contact, and choosing from all available communication options (Facebook, Twitter, Yahoo! Mail, Gmail, etc)*
* *Availability of an accounts management API to store centrally account-credential information on the device*
* *Supports devices with various screen sizes and resolutions, with three different screens of each of the applications*
* *Multiple email account synchronization, that combines all account into a single email inbox with option of exchange support*
* *New virtual keyboard layout for faster and more accurate typing. The multi-touch ensures that all keys pressed during typing are not skipped.*
* *Bluetooth API allows the device to connect to other nearby devices. This capabilities includes the integration of features of social-interaction and P2P communication*
* *Improved camera controls with digital zoom, a scene mode, white balance controls, macro focus and colour effects.*

Source: http://in.news.yahoo.com/242/20091028/1359/ttc-how-an-android-phone-can-change-your.html

Characteristics of Learning

Learning has the following characteristics:

- **Learning involves change**: As indicated earlier, people acquire new information which is processed in their cognition. This process produces new knowledge. This new knowledge brings changes in their existing pattern of behaviour.
- **Change must be Relatively Permanent**: When the information acquired is converted into knowledge and wisdom, people change their behaviour more or less permanently.
- **Behavioural Issues**: The change in the knowledge and wisdom should produce different attitudes and values. These new attitudes and values should change the behaviour. Then only it is called learning. In other words, the new attitudes and values not accompanied by change in behaviour is not called learning.
- **Experience-based**: Learning is based on experience. Experience may be direct or indirect, personal, through observation or through reading.

Now, we shall discuss the theories of learning.

There are three theories of learning, viz.,

- Behaviouralistic Theories
- Cognitive Theories
- Social Learning Theory

Behaviouralistic Theories

Behaviouralistic theories of learning are developed by the traditional behaviourists like Ivan Pavlov, and John B. Watson. These classical behaviourists attributed learning to the connection between Stimulus and Response (S → R). Whereas, the operant behaviourists particularly B.F. Skinner attributed learning to the consequence, i.e., Response-Stimulus (R → S) connection. The Stimulus → Response connection deals with classical or respondent connection while the Response → Stimulus connection deals with the instrumental or operant conditioning.

Classical Conditioning

The Russian Pioneering behaviourist Ivan Pavlov conducted classical conditioning experiment using dogs as subjects. Classical conditioning came out of experiments to teach dogs to salivate in response to the ringing of a bell. Pavlov measured the amount of Saliva secreted by a dog. Pavlov presented meat powder to the dog (unconditioned stimulus), then he noticed a great deal of salivation (unconditioned response). When he merely rang a bell (neutral stimulus) the dog had no salivation. Next Pavlov presented the meat powder along with ringing the bell. After doing this several times, he rang the bell without presenting the meat. This time the dog salivated to the bell alone. The dog had become classically conditioned to salivate (conditioned response) to the sound of the bell (conditioned stimulus).[26]

The classical conditioning reveals that the stimulus elicits response, i.e., S → R.

Examples of classical conditioning

	Stimulus (S)		Response (R)
	Sees a snake	→	Runs away
The Individual	is ordered by an autocratic manner	→	Says 'Yes' boss
	sees a good book	→	reads it

Skinner felt that classical conditioning cannot explain the more complex human behaviours. He felt that human behaviour affects or is affected by the environment. This behaviour is explained by operant conditioning.

Operant Conditioning

Operant conditioning emphasises that learning occurs as a consequence of behaviour, i.e., R → S. Employees work for more hours to get more salary or not to be fired. If the management pays more salary to those employees who work for more hours, then the employees repeat their behaviour of working for more hours. Paying more salary is called reinforcement. Reinforcement strengthens a behaviour and increases the likelihood of repeating that behaviour. Example of operant conditioning:

	Response (R)	→ Stimulus (S)
The student	studies hard	gets first class
The employee	Commits to the company	is promoted
The businessman	is ethical	maximises wealth
The student	enters the classroom	listens to the lecture

Operant conditioning is more relevant to human learning than classical conditioning. It also explains most of the organisational behaviour aspects. Operant conditioning is used by organisational behaviour researchers to explain the effectiveness of managers.[27]

Cognitive Theories

Cognitive theories emphasise on the cognitive process. Cognitive learning theories establish the relationship between cognitive environmental cues and expectations.

Edward Tolman is a widely recognised cognitive theorist. He conducted an experiment using white rats as subjects. He found that a rat could learn to run through an intricate maze with purpose and direction toward a goal (food). The rat learned to expect that certain cognitive cues associated with the choice point might eventually led to food. Tolman's approach is depicted as S-S (Stimulus-Stimulus). In other words learning is the association between the cue and expectancy.[28]

Employees expect higher salaries, promotions, and high quality of work life. Employees learn that they can achieve their expectations by working productively. The realisation of working productively is the result of cognitive environmental cues. Organisational behaviour researchers are currently concerned about the relationship between cognitions and organisational behaviour.[29]

Now, we shall discuss the social learning theory.

Social learning takes place through reciprocal interactions among people, behaviour and environment. Reciprocal interactions take place by integrating operant and cognitive learning approaches.

Social Learning Theory

People learn through different means like observation of others, direct experiences and indirect experiences. Learning though these various means is called social learning. Social learning theory integrates behavioural concepts, cognitive concepts and environmental determinants. (See Fig 14.14). Social learning takes place through reciprocal interactions among people, behaviour and environment. Reciprocal interactions take place by integrating operant and cognitive learning approaches.[30] This theory draws the inputs from the principles of classical and operant conditioning. It also recognises that learning takes place through various means like vicarious, modelling and self controlling processes.

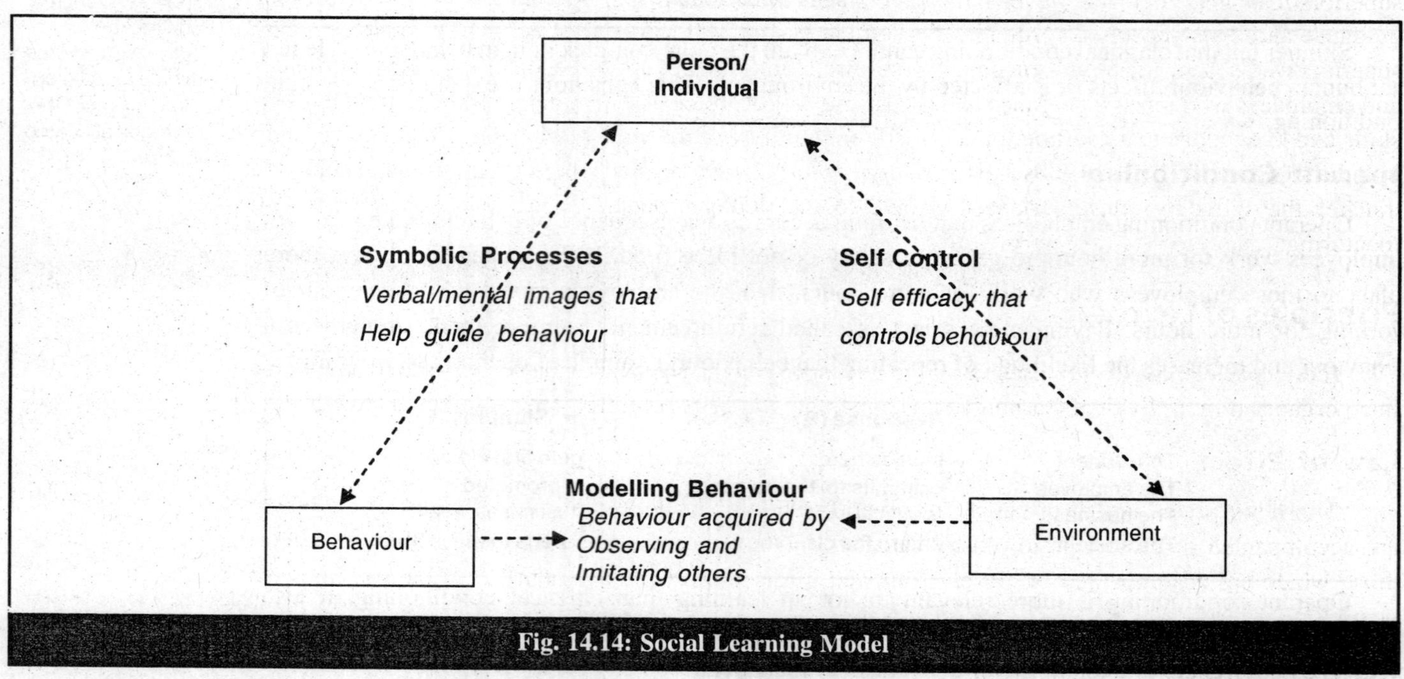

Fig. 14.14: Social Learning Model

(**Source:** Adapted from R. Kreitner and Fred Luthans, "A Social Learning Approach to Behavioural Management", Organisational Dynamics, Autumn, 1984, p. 55.)

It is observed from the figure that individuals learn by observing others, imitate them and modelling them through practice. Employees model their superiors or other managers. Tutors in the university model their lecturers/mentors. Kids model and imitate their big brothers/sisters/parents/ other family members. However, the entire behaviour of individuals is not acquired through imitations. However, the individuals learn through their own verbal and mental images as well as their own self efficacy that controls behaviour. These approaches shape the leaning through imitating the models.

People learn from various role models like parents, teachers, peers, leaders, etc. The influence of models is significant in social learning theory. There are four processes through which the model influences the individuals. These four processes include:

- **Attention Processes:** People learn from the critical features of the models like leadership skills, attractiveness, timely decision-making, etc.
- **Retention Process:** The level of influence of the model depends on the level to what extent the individual remembers the model.
- **Motor Reproduction Processes:** People may at times imitate the models. Children imitate their parents and teachers. This is because, observation is converted into action.
- **Reinforcement Processes:** Individuals prefer to exhibit the behaviour of the model, if such behaviour results in rewards. People pay more attention to and learn the positively reinforced behaviours from the models.

Mentoring

Mentoring is the process of providing guidance and advice by specially selected and trained individuals, in order to help to develop the careers of the proteges allocated to them.

Mentoring is the process of providing guidance and advice by specially selected and trained individuals, in order to help to develop the careers of the proteges allocated to them. Normally, superiors/managers at higher level have special technical and managerial competence and provide guidance and assistance to subordinates in their careers as well as personal issues. The managers and superiors who coach, advice and encourage employees/subordinates are called mentors. The subordinates and employees who receive guidance and advice are called proteges. The older employees transfer their skills and knowledge that can't be found in written literature to the young employees. The caste system in India significantly before 1960s and the *sempai-kohai (Japanese mentoring system) in* Japan helped to transfer the skills by the experienced people to the younger people. Thus, people learn through mentoring.

Principles of Learning

Individual learning in organisations has to be shaped and managed based on behavioural requirements in an organisation. Individual learning is managed with the help of reinforcement and punishment.

Law of Effect

Thorndike stated law of effect as "of several responses made to the same situation, those which are accompanied or closely followed by satisfaction (reinforcement)...will be more likely to occur; those which are accompanied or closely followed to discomfort (punishment)...will be less likely to occur."[31]

Reinforcement

Reinforcement is any act which is rewarding. Reinforcement is anything that increases the strength of response and tends to induce repetitions of the behaviour that preceded the reinforcement.[32] Reinforcement encourages learning. Reinforcement may be positive or negative.

Rewards are outcomes of a behavioural act or outcomes of environmental consequences. Rewards can be extrinsic and intrinsic. Extrinsic rewards are like increase in pay, promotion, and offering a benefit like offering company car. Extrinsic rewards are important external rein- forcers. Which influence employees' behaviours significantly. Extrinsic rewards are of two types, viz., rewards involving budgetary commitments and rewards with no budgetary commitments. Table 14.2 presents types of external rewards.

Table 14.2: Types of External Rewards

Rewards with Budgetary Implications	Rewards with No Budgetary Implications
Salary	Transfer to a powerful job
Allowances	Greetings
Free car	Feedback
Free lunch and refreshments	Appreciation letters
Spacious and furnished offices	Certificates
Free medical benefits	Challenging job
Paid vacation	Employee of month recognition
Promotions	Counselling
Birthday gifts	Mentoring
Performance rewards	Encouragement
Stock options	Sound relations
Family parties	

Reinforces and Behaviour Modifications

Reinforces modify the employee behaviour and thereby group and organizational behaviour. Thus, these reinforces are the organizational behaviour modification forces. These forces include:

- Positive Reinforcement
- Negative Reinforcement
- Punishment
- Extinction

Positive Reinforces

Positive reinforcement strengthens the behaviour and repeats the same behaviour with desirable consequences. For example, Mr. Chandra of Tata Tea produces high quality tea and Mr. Surya, the superior of Mr. Chnadra, pays more bonus to Mr. Chandra. Thus reward is paid after the positive behaviour is exhibited. These positive reinforces (rewards) strengthens the repetition of behaviour (producing high quality tea).

Positive reinforce = Desirable behaviour → Reward → Desirable behaviour

Extrinsic rewards both involving budgetary commitments and non-budgetary commitments act as positive reinforces. Offering rewards should be repeated only when such reward results in desirable behaviour. In contrast, offering a reward is based on the exhibition of desirable behaviour. This contingent behaviour and reward is known as the *law of contingent reinforcement.* Thus, contingent reinforcement indicates that the reward would be delivered only when the desirable behaviour is exhibited, as per the stimulus that is based on response. Reward should be delivered immediately after the exhibition of desirable behaviour in order to maintain employee's state of morale. Otherwise, the employee would be de-motivated and the chances of repeating the desirable behaviour would be reduced. This is known as the law of immediate reinforcement. This law states that the delivery of reward immediately after the exhibition of desired behaviour result in greater reinforcing effect.[33]

Scheduling of Positive Reinforcement

Rewards can be offered continuously as well as at different schedules like annual awards or festive rewards like *Dessara* rewards, *Christmas* rewards and *Ramzan* rewards. Offering rewards continuously is known as continuous reinforcement. Continuous reinforcement is scheduled to offer the rewards each time as and when the desired behaviour is exhibited.

Offering rewards periodically is known as intermittent reinforcement. Intermittent reinforcement states that rewards are offered periodically after the desired behaviour is exhibited. For example, payment of annual performance pay is paid once in a year based on the quality and/or quantity of output produced by an employee. Table 14.3 presents schedule of positive reinforcements.

Table 14.3: Schedule of Positive Reinforcements

Schedule	Description	Effects on Responding
Continuous	Reinforce follows every response	Payment of rewards every time of desirable performance is exhibited;High frequency of reinforcement may lead to early satisfaction;Behaviour weakens rapidly when the reinforces are withheld;Offering reward continuously may reduce the strength of the reward in sustaining employees' performance to produce desired behaviour.
Intermittent	Reinforcer does not follow every response	Capable of producing desirable performance continuously until the reinforce is executed;Low frequency of reinforcement precludes early satiation;Appropriate for stable and high frequency responses.
Fixed Ratio	A fixed number of responses must be emitted before reinforcement occurs	A fixed ratio of 1:1(reinforcement occurs after every response) is the same as a continuous schedule.Tends to produce a high rate of response that is vigorous and steady.
Variable Ratio	A varying or random number of responses must be emitted before reinforcement occurs	Capable of producing a high rate of response that is vigorous. Steady and resistant to extinction.
Fixed Interval	The first response after a specific period of time has elapsed is reinforced.	Produces an uneven response pattern varying from a very slow, unenergetic response immediately following reinforcement to a very fast, vigorous response immediately preceding reinforcement.
Variable Interval	The first response after varying or random periods of time have elapsed is reinforced	Tends to produce a high rate of response that is vigorous, steady and resistant to extinction.

Source: Fred Luthans and Robert Kreitner, "Organisational Behaviour".

Negative Reinforcement/Avoidance

Negative reinforcement also strengthens the behaviour and repeats the same behaviour but by the termination or withdrawal of an undesirable consequence.[34] Thus, negative reinforcement results from withholding a negative consequence when a desirable behaviour occurs. For example, a manager allots an uninteresting work to an employee who reports for duty late for the last five days. When the employee reports for duty on time on the sixth day, the manager allots an interesting work to the employee. Allotting an uninteresting work is negative consequence, reporting for duty late is undesirable behaviour and reporting for duty on time is desirable behaviour. Negative consequence of allotting uninteresting work is withdrawn, when undesirable behaviour is terminated. Employee can be free from negative consequence, by exhibiting desirable behaviour.

Negative Reinforce = Undesirable behaviour → Negative consequence → Desirable Behaviour

Negative reinforcement6 is also called avoidance as the negative consequence is avoided as and when the undesirable behaviour is withdrawn.

Punishment

Punishment is different reinforcement. Reinforcement strengthens and increases the frequency of desirable behaviour. But punishment is different from reinforcement. Punishment is anything that weakens behaviour and tends to decrease its subsequent frequency. For example, imposing the punishment of two per cent salary cut for failing to meet the targets twice in a month in a software company reduced the cases of not meeting the targets from 12% to 0.06% in 2009. Thus, punishment changed the behaviour of the employees in this company from contributing to targets. Even withholding a positive consequence for an undesirable behaviour also amounts to punishment.

One study found that punishment reduced poor performance and enhanced performance of employees. However, the satisfaction levels of employees did not increase. But, punishment demoralises the employees. Employees view punishment as arbitrary. Punishments in the long run will lead to low satisfaction as well as low performance.

Therefore, the human resource managers should always attempt to reinforce instead of punish to enable the employees to learn and change their behaviour in accordance with the behavioural requirements of the organisation.

Problems of Punishment

Punishment is quite undesirable, though sometimes it is quite inevitable to impose punishment to correct undesirable behaviour.

- **Punishments Produce Unintended Results:** Punishments cause discomfort and damage the psychology of both the parties. They also cause emotional and relationship problems. The employees punished may become angry, hostile, frustrated and depressed. These consequences result in even physical fight.
- **Punishments May Not Change Behaviour Permanently:** Punishment is normally taken by employees as negative and it is viewed as a reprimand technique by managers. So employees would like to take revenge against the managers who imposed punishment and pay back with the same or even more tempo. As such, employees wait for an opportunity to revert their negative behaviour. Thus, punishment may not change the negative behaviour permanently.
- **Administrator of Punishments is Viewed as Villain:** Most of the less performing employees view the managers who impose punishments as negatively and as villains in the organization. Further, punishments imposing managers are viewed as creators of unpleasant situations.
- **Punishments May Offset the Effects of Positive Reinforces:** Punishments imposed by a manager may offset the benefits of positive behaviour of positive reinforces.
- **Behavioural Change due to Punishment is Unpredictable:** It is quite difficult to predict the change in the behaviour due to punishments as punishments may fail to bring permanent change in behaviour.

Extinction

Extinction is an attempt to weaken undesirable behaviour by attaching no consequence to it. In other words, it is ignoring the behaviour. Sometimes, employees may not change their behaviour for any kind of reinforcements as well as for punishment. In such cases, extinction is the best alternative available to managers. Extinction helps the managers as well as employees to ease tensions and slowly shift from parent egos to either adult ego or child egos. (Ego states will be dealt in the chapter 'Group

Behaviour'). For example, powerful and sometimes frustrated subordinates may not respond to positive as well as negative reinforces. They also fail to respond to punishments. In such cases extinction is the only alternative strategy available to managers at least for some time. Managers, later can shift to positive reinforce, depending up on the state of mind of the subordinate.

Extinction and Positive Reinforcement

Sometimes extinction may work better along with using positive reinforces on-and-off. When behviour is desirable, manager can make use of positive reinforces and use extinctions when the behaviour is relatively undesirable.

KEY TERMS

- Perception
- Sensation
- Stimuli
- Intensity
- Contrast
- Novelty
- Perceptual Process
- Motivation
- Perceptual Output
- Perceptual Constancy
- Familiarity
- Impressions Management
- Learning
- Halo Effect
- Perceptual Defence
- Motion
- Self Concept
- Stereotype
- Perceptual Throughput
- Attribution
- Distortion
- Projection

QUESTIONS

1. What is perception? How do you differentiate it from sensation?
2. What is perceptual process? Discuss the perceptual inputs, throughputs and output.
3. What is perceptual selectivity? Explain the influence of external environmental factors on perceptual selectivity.
4. How do the internal environmental factors affect the perceptual selectivity?
5. How do you organise the data and information in the perceptual throughput process?
6. Discuss the factors that influence the interpretation of data and information in perception process.
7. Why do people fail to perceive close to reality?
8. Suggest the measures to perceive close to reality.
9. Why and how people impress others?
10. What is learning? Discuss various learning theories.

REFERENCES

1. Fred Luthans, "*Organisational Behaviour*," McGraw Hill Inc., New York, 1995, p. 86.
2. Uma Sekharan, "*Organisational Behaviour*," Tata McGraw Hill Publishing Company Ltd., New Delhi, 1989, p. 41.
3. Stephen P. Robbins, "*Organisational Behaviour*," Prentice-Hall of India (P) Ltd., New Delhi, 1986, p. 83.
4. Udai Pareek et al, "*Behavioural Process in Organisations*," Oxford & IBH Publishing Co., New Delhi, 1981, p. 27.
5. Joseph H. Reitz, "*Behaviour in Organisations*," Richard D. Irwin Inc., Illinois, 1977, p. 129.
6. Fred Luthans, *op.cit.*, p. 90.
7. *Ibid.*, p. 92.
8. *Ibid.*
9. Uma Sekharan, *op.cit.*, p. 43.

10. Fred Luthans, *op.cit.*, p. 101.

11. Uma Sekharan, *op.cit.*, p. 44.

12. B. Rosen and T. H. Jerdee, "*The Nature of Job Related Stereotypes*," Journal of Applied Psychology, Vol. 61, 1976, pp. 180-83.

13. Donald L.McCabe and Jane E. Dutton, "*Making Sense of the Environment:The Role of Perceived Effectiveness*," Human Relations, May 1993, pp. 623-643.

14. Harold Kelley, "*The Process of Casual Attribution*," American Psychologist, Vol. 28, 1973, pp. 107-125.

15. J. S. Chandan, "*Organisational Behaviour*," Vikas Publishing House (P) Ltd., New Delhi, 1994, p. 135.

16. John H. Harvey and Gifford Weary, "*Current Issues in Attribution Theory and Research*," Annual Review of Psychology, Vol. 35, 1984, pp. 427-459.

17. Stephen P.Robbins, "*Organisational Behaviour*", Prentice Hall of India (P) Ltd., New Delhi, 1999, p. 68.

18. Eden, D. "Self-fulfilling Prophecies in Organisations", in J. Greenberg (ed.), "Organisational behaviour", 2002.

19. Oz,S. and Eden D., "Restraining the Golem: Boosting Performance by Changing the Interpretation of Low Scores",Journal of Applied Psychology, 79, pp. 744-754.

20. I.V.Pavlov, "*The work of the Digestive Glands*", Trans,W.H.Thompson, Charles Griffin, London, 1902.

21. Fred Luthans, "*Organisational Behaviour*", McGraw Hill, New York, 1995, p. 199.

22. Wood et.al. "rganisational Behaviour", John Wiley&Sons Australia Ltd.,Milton, 2004, p. 167

23. Andrew F. Sikula, *Personnel Administration and Human Resource, Management,* John Wiley and Sons, New York, 1977.

24. George Strauss and Leonard R. Sayless, Prentice-Hall, New Delhi, 1977, p. 451.

25. J.R. Talbot and C.D. Ellis, *Analysis and Costing of Company Training,* Grower Press, London, 1970, p. 22.

26. *H.M.Weiss, "Learning Theory and Industrial and organizational Psychology", in M.D> Dunnette and L.M. Hough (eds.)," Handbook of Industrial and Organisational Psychology", Consulting Psychologist Press, 1990, pp. 170-221.*

27. Judith L.Komaki, "*Toward Effective Supervision:An Operant analysis and Comparison of Managers at work*", Journal of Applied Psychology, Vol.71, No.2, 1986, pp. 270-279.

28. Fred Luthans, *op.cit.*, p. 201.

29. Ibid., p. 170

30. Dannis A.Gioia and Henry P.Sims, "*Cognition-Behaviour Connections*", Organisational Behaviour and Human Decision Process, Vol.37, 1986, pp. 197-229.

31. Edward L.Thorndike, "*Animal Intelligence*", MacMillan, New York, 1911, p. 244.

32. "Paying Employees Not to go to the Doctor", Business Week, 21 March 1983, p. 150.

33. Fred Luthans, *op.cit.*, p. 203.

34. *Ibid.*, p. 204.

CHAPTER **15**

MOTIVATION: CONCEPTS AND THEORIES

☛ Chapter Outline

(A) Introduction
(B) Motivating
(C) Types of Motivation
(D) Theories of Motivation
— Key Terms
— Questions for Discussion
— References

☛ Learning Objectives

After studying this Chapter, you should be able to:

- ✓ Understand the meaning and the basic motivation concepts like, motivation, motive and motivating;
- ✓ Know different types of motives like primary motives, secondary motives, general motives, power motives, achievement motives and affiliation motives;
- ✓ Explain the significance and nature of motivation;
- ✓ Analyse content theories, process theories and reinforcement theories;
- ✓ Compare and contrast content theories, process theories and reinforcement theories; and
- ✓ Observe the developments of the motivation concepts from the analysis of various motivation theories.

(A) INTRODUCTION

Every human action is the result of a need or desire. One experiences a sort of mental discomfort as long as that need remains unsatisfied in him/her. The moment the action is initiated he/she makes an attempt to get over the discomfort. What causes an action is the need or desire? What causes a need is called the *stimulus*. Therefore, the manager's duty is to create the stimulus that causes a need which initiates action leading to satisfaction. This should be a repetitive process for the action to continue. All this is called 'motivation' in management.[1] Now we shall discuss motives, motivating and motivation.

Motives

The term motive is derived from the Latin word 'movere.' It means 'to move.' 'Motive' is defined as an inner state that energises, activates (or moves) and directs (or channels) the behaviour of individuals towards certain goals.[2] Motives are certain important needs of human beings. These needs have different degrees of potency or strength.

Strong motive creates tension in a person until the need is fulfilled.

The strong need or motive creates high tension or disequilibrium in a person and makes him restless until the need is fulfilled. For example, the need for professional recognition makes the doctor restless until the co-doctors and patients recognize him as an efficient doctor. In order to reduce the tension, the doctor treats the critical cases. Motives induce the individuals to channel their behaviour towards those actions which would reduce the disequilibrium. Thus, motives are drives which energises individuals to an action with a direction. For example, the strong motive of earning large sums of money directs the students to take up the action of studying course which have fast earnings.

Types of Motives

Motives are classified into three categories, *viz., primary motives, general motives and secondary motives.*

Primary Motives

Primary motives are mostly physiological

Psychologists say some motives are unlearned and they are called physiological, biological, unlearned or primary motives. Like, fasting before prayer and fasting during religiously auspicious days. In these cases, secondary motives are stronger over primary motives. These motives include: hunger, sleep, avoidance of pain, sex and material concern. These motives are both unlearned and physiologically based. These motives always do not take precedence over general or secondary motives. General and secondary motives take precedence over primary motives in some situations.

General Motives

The motives which can't be classified either as primary motives or as secondary motives are categorized into general motives. These motives are unlearned but not physiologically based.

Primary movies tend to reduce the tension or stimulation. In contrast, general motives encourage a person to increase the stimulation. Therefore, these needs are also called, 'stimulus motives.' General motives play a significant role in organisational behaviour than primary motives.

General motives include: curiosity, manipulation, activity motives and affection motive. Human curiosity, manipulation and activity drives are quite intense. *The teacher or examiner tries to confuse the student in order to create curiosity to learn deeper or exhibit the potentialities. Similarly, superiors allocate complex work to the subordinates in order to explore the employees' curiosity, manipulation and activity drives. Similarly, employees should also be allowed to exhibit their curiosity, manipulation and activity motives, in order to motivate them.*

Affection motive is closely associated with the sex motive or primary motive and also affiliation motive or secondary motive. Hence, affection motive sometimes is classified as primary motive and sometimes as secondary motive. Affection motive plays a vital role in the organisations as most of the employees, in these days, are deprived of love and affection at home. Further, it plays a vital role in the general society also, due to the adages of, 'Love makes the world go round' and 'Love conquers all.' .

Secondary Motives

General motives play a significant role in organisational behaviour compared to primary motives. But secondary motives play further pivotal role in organisational behaviour. Primary motives do not play a significant role in the developed countries. However, it is not true in case of developing countries like ours. Secondary motives are closely related to learning concepts. Important secondary motives are power, achievement and affiliation. Examples of key secondary needs are presented in Exhibit 15.1.

Strong motive creates tension in a person until the need is fulfilled.

Exhibit 15.1 Examples of Key Secondary Needs

Need for Achievement

- Doing better than competitors
- Attaining or surpassing a difficult goal
- Solving a complex problem
- Carrying out a challenging assignment successfully
- Developing a better way to do something

Need for Security

- Having a secure job
- Being protected against loss of income or economic disaster
- Having protection against illness and disability
- Being protected against physical harm or hazardous conditions
- Avoiding tasks or decisions with a risk of failure and blame

Need for Power

- Influencing people to change their attitudes or behaviour
- Controlling people and activities
- Being in a position of authority over others
- Gaining control over information and resources
- Defeating an opponent or enemy

Need for Status

- Having the right car and wearing the right clothes
- Working for the right company in the right job
- Having a degree from the right university
- Living in the right neighbourhood and belonging to the country club
- Having executive privileges

Need for Affiliation

- Being liked by many people
- Being accepted as part of a group or team
- Working with people who are friendly and cooperative
- Maintaining harmonious relationships and avoiding conflicts
- Participating in pleasant social activities

(**Source:** Adapted from Gary Yukl, *Skills for Managers and Leaders*, Prentice Hall, Englewood Cliffs, N.J., 1990, p. 41. The examples of need for status are developed by Fred Luthans, op.cit., p. 144.)

Motives are also classified as *(i)* power motive, *(ii)* achievement motive, *(iii)* affiliation motive, *(iv)* security motive, and *(v)* status motive. Now, we discuss these motives in detail.

Power Motive

Alfred Adler – a pioneering psychologist advocated the power motive. He submitted a person's overwhelming drive for superiority or power. He developed the concept of 'inferiority complex' and compensation to explain the power need. The power need implies the need to manipulate others or the drive for superiority over other people. According to him, every child experiences a sense of inferiority. People strive for power or superiority in order to overcome the inferiority complex.

The quest for power is quite prominent in almost all areas. The quest for power is more prominent in political fields. Normally, those who are inferior in their profession or occupation in terms of ability, skill and knowledge have more quests for power in order to compensate their feelings of inferiority. (See Box 15.1).

Box 15.1: Helping People to Motivate Themselves

A major function of leaders is to motivate other individuals and groups. (Note that leaders can also focus on motivating themselves when their focus is on self-leadership.) There are approaches to motivating people that are destructive, eg, fear, intimidation, etc. While these approaches can seem very effective in promptly motivating people, the approaches are hurtful, and in addition, they usually only motivate for the short-term. There are also approaches that are constructive, eg, effective delegation, coaching, etc. These approaches can be very effective in motivating others and for long periods of time.

Note that different people can have quite different motivators. For example, some people are motivated by more money, others by more recognition, time off from work, promotions, opportunities for learning, opportunities for socializing and relationships, etc. Therefore, when attempting to motivate people, it's important to identify what motivates them. Ultimately, though, long-term motivation comes from people motivating themselves.

(**Source:** http://managementhelp.org/guiding/motivate/motivate.htm)

Persons in different administrative positions in business, industry, trade unions, government, public service, education, etc., strive for power.

Achievement Motive

David C. McClelland, a Harvard psychologist has been studying on 'achievement motive.' McClelland has written about all aspects of achievement. Characteristics of a high achiever have emerged out of his research. The achievement motive is expressed as a desire to perform in terms of a standard of excellence or to be successful in competitive situations.[3] The prominent characteristics of a high achiever are discussed hereunder.

- **Moderate risk taking:** Common sense tells that high achievers take the risk of higher order. But the research studies conclude that high achievers take moderate risk. Low achievers take either low risk or high risk.
- **Need for immediate feedback:** High achievers need immediate feedback. These people need immediate and clear-cut information about their activities, level and rate of progress. They also need information regarding the contribution of their efforts in achieving organisational goals. The likes of the high achievers include: woodwork and mechanics which provide immediate feedback. Their dislikes include: coin-collection which takes years to develop. High challenging jobs like sales and managerial jobs which are challenging and are evaluated frequently. They dislike teaching, research and development jobs.
- **Satisfaction with accomplishments:** High achievers do not want materialistic rewards. They want intrinsically satisfying rewards. High achievers prefer a complicated and challenging job though it offers less salary compared to a simple job even if it offers higher salary.

- **Preoccupation with the task/activity:** The high achievers, once they select a task completely concentrate on it until it is accomplished. They cannot do two jobs simultaneously or take up another job leaving one job half done. High achievers are quiet and do not boast about themselves or about their accomplishments. They tend to be realistic. They cannot maintain sound human relations with others as they do not allow others to come in their way in achieving their goals and targets. High achievers are more of individualistic nature and may fail to work in a team environment.

Affiliation Motive

Affiliation is a social need

Affiliation is a social need and members prefer to join groups in order to satisfy their need of belongingness/affiliation. Lower level employees have higher intense need to belong to a group. Affiliation motive plays a significant role in human resources management particularly in the area of commitment. Employees' commitment level is enhanced by satisfying their social needs of belonging.

Security Motive

The post-privatisation and globalisation era brought significant changes in the Indian business. The pre-liberalisation period (i.e., before 1991) provided job security to the employees particularly to those in the public sector. Added to this, the fast technological advancement brought significant changes in the structure of employment.

Now, the Indian industry needs less number of people and as such, many industries started retrenching the employees through voluntary retirement scheme. Therefore, security of employment has become a complicated issue. Further, most of the employees have a fear of losing their jobs. Thus, the employees are deprived of the security need.

Status Motive

The capitalistic economic system along with the advanced technology created dynamic organisations. These dynamic organisations created challenging jobs. The candidates with the skills and knowledge suitable to the dynamic jobs are given quite attractive salary, lucrative perks like free house, free car, telephone, club membership, credit card, computer, internet connection and the like. Thus, the status and prestige motive of these dynamic employees is satisfied even though their need for job security is uncared for.

Thus, the status motive of the dynamic people is fulfilled in the free and high technology economies. Exhibit 15.2 presents need hierarchy in different countries.

Having discussed the motives, now, we shall study motivating.

Exhibit 15.2 Need Hierarchy in Different Countries

Country	*Need Priority*
United States and Japan	Self-actualisation, esteem, safety, physiological and social
France	Self-actualisation, esteem, physiological, safety and social
Germany	Self-actualisation, physiological, esteem, social and safety
India	Physiological, self-actualisation, esteem, social and safety
Malawi	Physiological, self-actualisation, esteem, safety and social
China (Esteem needs are not in evidence)	Self-actualisation, safety, physiological and social

(**Source:** Manab Thakur, et al., *International Management*, TMH, 1997, p. 177)

(B) MOTIVATING

Marketing Manager of ABC Pharma Ltd. tells the sales force as: Those who achieve 200% targets will receive 200% of monthly salary as commission and will be promoted as Area Sales Managers. Thus, the marketing manager induced the sales force to engage in extensive sales through the motives of commission and promotion.

Motivating implies that one person induces another person to engage in action or desired work behaviour by ensuring that a channel to direct the motive of the person becomes available and accessible to the person.

Managers play a significant role in motivating the subordinates. They identify employees' talents, skills, creativity and innovative ideas and energise them to put these into action. Thus, the managers motivate their subordinates. Through this action, the managers help convert the innovative and creative ideas of their subordinates into worthwhile actions. Managers play a significant role in motivating their subordinates by channelling the employee's potentialities and work behaviour towards the organisational goals.

Further, the managers also convert a weak desire into a strong desire and motive. This, in turn helps the employee to make use of his potentialities for his benefit and also for the organisation.

The relationship among motive, motivating and motivation is presented in Fig. 15.1.

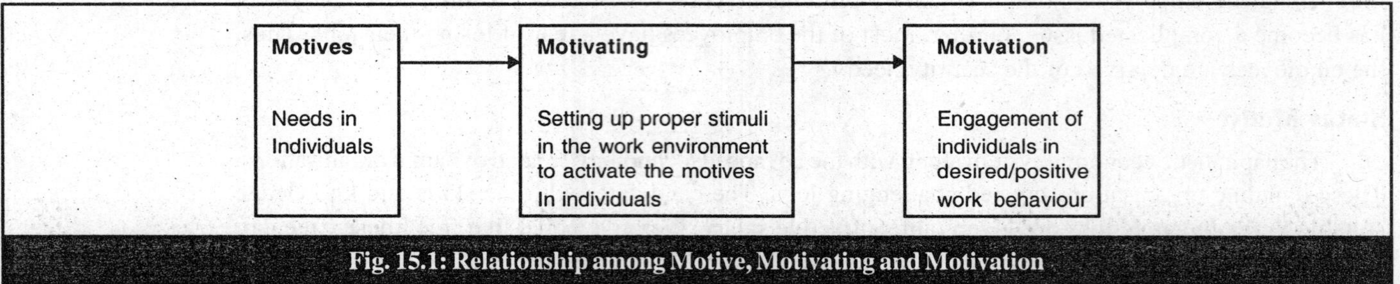

Fig. 15.1: Relationship among Motive, Motivating and Motivation

Motivation

Motivation is derived from the word motive. "A motive is an inner state that energises, activates or moves and directs or channels behaviour towards goals."[4]

"Motivation represents an unsatisfied need which creates a state of tension or disequlibrium, causing the individual to move in a goal directed pattern towards restoring a state of equilibrium by satisfying the need."[5] According to the Encyclopedia of Management, "motivation refers to the degree of readiness of an organization to pursue some designated goal and implies the determination of the nature and locus of the forces, including the degree of readiness."[6]

Motivation is a process that starts with a deficiency

Motivation is a process that starts with a physiological or psychological deficiency or need that activates behaviour or a drive that is aimed at a goal or 'incentive.' Thus, the process of motivation lies in the meaning of and relationship among needs, drives and incentives (Fig. 15.2).

Need	**Drive**	**Goals/Incentives**
(Deficiency)	(Deficiency with Direction)	(Reduction of drives and fulfills deficiencies)

Fig. 15.2: The Basic Motivation Process

Need: Need is deficiency. Needs are created whenever there is a physiological or psychological imbalance.

Drive: Drive is a deficiency with direction. They are action-oriented and provide an emerging thrust towards goal accomplishment.

Incentives: Incentive is anything that will alleviate a need to reduce a drive.

Constant state of tension is the nature of motivated people. The drives towards an activity relieve the tension. The outcome or the result also reduces the tension. Greater activity is needed to reduce the greater tension. The greater activity increases the level of motivation. Thus, greater tension needs greater activity which results in higher motivation. The basic motivation process is presented in Fig. 15.3. This process shows that there are three phases in motivation.

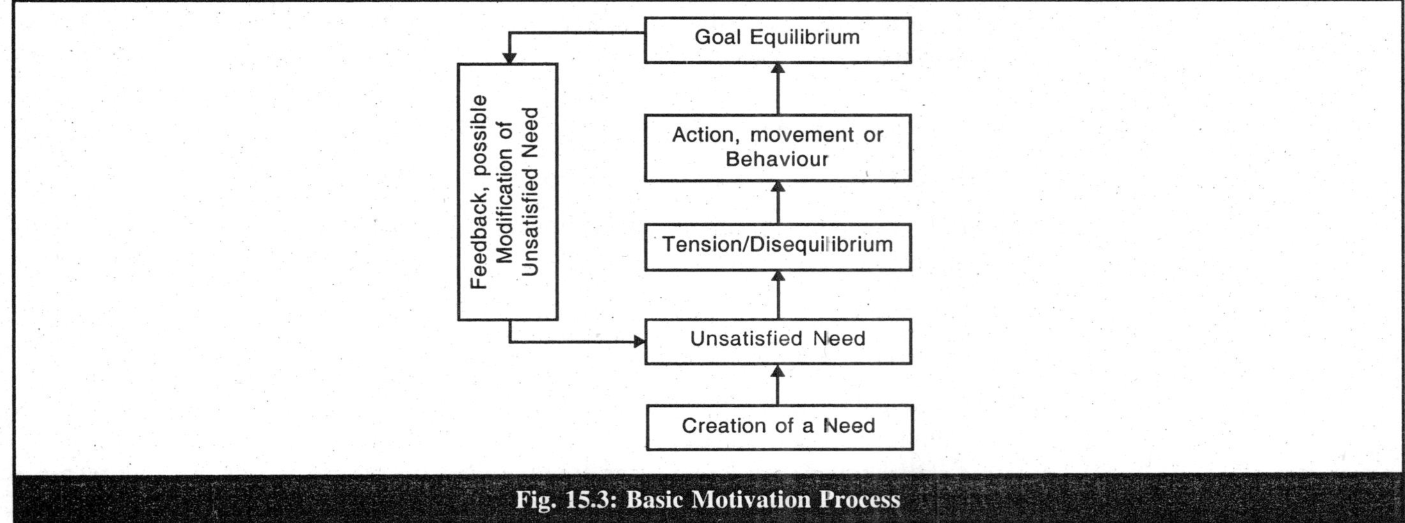

Fig. 15.3: Basic Motivation Process

There are three areas in motivation, *viz.*, motives, motivation and motivating. Let us look at each of them.

The three basic phases of motivation include: Effort, Persistence and Direction.

Effort: The strength of a person's work related behaviour is determined by the amount of effort devoted for the activity. *For example, the salesman of an insurance company can sell more number of insurance policies and of higher value, by devoting a lot of time for and effort in meeting and convincing the prospective customers.*

Persistence: Motivation should be a permanent and an integral part of human beings.[7] Motivation should also be persistence in the efforts. Therefore, individuals put their efforts continuously until the goal is achieved. Once the predetermined goal is achieved, the individual selects or chooses further higher goal. Then the individual puts further additional effort and strives continuously and persistently to achieve the higher goal. *For example, an MBA student has a goal of securing 'A' grade in MBA and puts all the efforts to achieve the goal. Once this goal is achieved, he/she selects another goal of becoming an ERP Consultant and puts an additional effort to achieve this goal.* Thus, high motivation needs higher level of persistent efforts.

Direction: The goal achievement requires a clear direction in addition to persistent hard work. Direction enhances the level and quality of output. The efforts should be directed towards organisational goals. Clear direction ensures that the persistent efforts are put for the right purpose in the right level and in the right time. The candidate who earned MBA degree and would like to become an ERP consultant, directs all his/her time, money, mental and physical inputs to learn necessary skills and become an ERP consultant.

Significance of Motivation

Motivation can be positive or negative

The word 'motivation' is used frequently and prominently by the people of different occupations and professions. *A student says, "Mathematics teacher motivated me a lot positively during my school days and hence, I am very much interested in Mathematics." A salesman says, "the new marketing manager does not motivate the sales force and hence the sales of our company are dwindling these days."*

Further, scientists, researchers, politicians, managers and the like refer to the term 'motivation' quite often. Even, we come across the word, 'motivation' in the Ramayana when Lord Anjaneya was encouraged/motivated by Jambava to fly over the sea by identifying the potentialities of Lord Anjaneya. This is a positive effort of motivation. This simple example tells us what could motivation do. In other words, motivation makes the impossible things possible. Thus, motivation plays an important role in converting the human potentialities into performance that lead to high level achievements.

Further, the importance of motivation can be explained as indicated hereunder:

- Motivation identifies employee potentialities and makes the employee to know his potentialities.
- Motivation converts the potentialities into performance.
- Motivation converts motivated employees into committed and loyal employees.
- Motivated employees explore the alternative methods of performing a task and they select a better method than the existing method. Motivated employees use their *innovative and creative skills, talents,* etc., and offer creative ideas to the management. This factor, in turn results in the upgradation of technology and technical know-how.

Motivated employees contribute to increase in productivity.

- If the employee has a positive attitude towards quality and has also been motivated by the production manager, his concern towards quality increases. The increased concern towards quality results in high quality in production/operations.
- ***Increase in productivity:*** Motivated workers exert all their energies towards the job. This would in turn result in increase in employee efficiency and thereby productivity. Added to this, the committed employees do the work in a better way, and also reduce the wastage, which, in turn, contributes to higher productivity.
- ***Human resources development:*** Motivation results in exploring potentialities, development of skills, knowledge and abilities. This, in turn, leads to the development of human resources.
- Motivated employees behave positively, maintain sound human relations, congenial superior-subordinate relations.
- Motivated employees formulate *efficient strategies* in order to achieve the corporate objectives and compete with the competitors.
- The present day high-technology and software industries depend upon highly self- motivated employees.
- ***Proper utilisation of human resources:*** As indicated earlier, motivation identifies human potentialities and channel them towards organisational objectives. This results in increased efficiency and productivity due to utilisation of human resources where they are appropriately fit.

- ***Optimum utilisation of other resources:*** All other resources without human resources can produce nothing. Human resources make use of all other resources like material and finance and produce products or services. The motivated human resources utilise all other resources to the optimum extent and maximise productivity.
- ***Builds congenial industrial relations:*** Motivation maintains discipline, sound superior-subordinate relations and sound relations among colleagues. This, in turn, leads to congenial industrial relations.
- ***Basis for cooperation:*** Motivation makes the people understand each other completely, leads to group work and team spirit. These, in turn, lead to unreserved cooperation and collaboration among members of a department and organisation.

Nature of Motivation

Motivation is mainly concerned with the directing of employees towards organisational objectives and mission. The nature of motivation is discussed as follows:

All unsatisfied wants are motivators. So motivation is a continuous process

(i) **Motivation is a continuous process:** As we have studied in economics, human wants are unlimited. It is said that, 'Even God cannot satisfy all human wants.' With the satisfaction of one want, another want preferably of the higher order crops up and this process goes on and on. Thus, new wants emerge when the present wants are satisfied. Further, all the wants cannot be satisfied at the same time. Wants are to be satisfied one after another continuously. Hence, motivation is also a continuous and an unending process.

(ii) **Motivation is a psychological concept:** Motivation is concerned with the psychological aspects of the human being. The level of satisfaction, contentment, etc., by using the same reward/incentive varies from person to person. This is due to variations in aspirations, attitudes, feelings and perceptions of the individuals. Thus, motivation is reaction of the organs of the human body to the inducements/incentives offered.

(iii) **The entire individual is motivated:** As stated earlier, motivation is a psychological concept interacting with the total organs of an individual. Further, each individual is an integrated and comprehensive system. The entire system of an individual reacts to the motivation. Thus, the entire individual is motivated.

(iv) **Frustrated individual fails to be motivated:** Some individuals are frustrated despite the rewards due to the wide gap between his/her aspirations and rewards. Some of the frustrated persons become mentally ill and these persons cannot be motivated.

(v) **Goals lead to motivation:** Goals form a part of the motivational process. Goal achievement results in the satisfaction of want. Goal fulfilment leads to reduction of drives and fulfils deficiencies. Thus, goal achievement ends the motivation process.

(vi) **The self-concept as a unifying force:** Self concept is the life position of a person that he formulates about himself during his childhood. He thinks himself in the same way during his life time until and unless a major change takes place in the rest of the life time. Therefore, those who formulated a positive view about themselves during the childhood, will be motivated by themselves in the rest of the life time. And the vice versa is true in case of negative self concept.

Features of Motivation

The analysis of definitions on motivation presents the following features:

1. Motivation is individual's internal feeling: Motivation is a psychological process within individuals. Individual needs/desires are the feelings in the mind of a person regarding the deficiencies. These deficiencies include physical, social and psychological.

2. Motivation is concerned with the total person: Individuals are total persons. They are self-contained. Each individual is an inseparable unit and all his needs are interrelated. The individual feelings in the social area affect his physical and psychological areas also. Individual feelings and motivation is continuous process. They result in continuous and interrelated human behaviour.

3. Motivation = Anticipated values × Perceived probability: Motivation is the product of anticipated values from an action and the perceived probability that these values would be attained by the action. The anticipated value is called 'Valence' and the perceived probability is called 'Expectancy.'[8] Thus, the

Motivation = Valence x Expectancy

Motivation = Valence x Expectancy

4. Motivation is the willingness to exert high levels of effort towards organisational goals, conditioned by the efforts and the ability to satisfy some individual need.

5. Motivation involves the arousal, direction and maintenance of behaviour towards a goal. It is presented in Fig. 15.4.

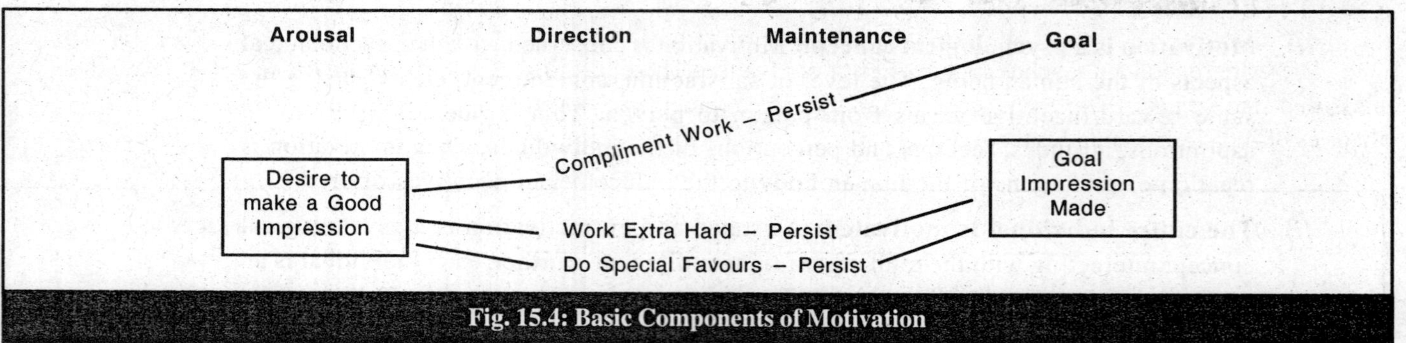

Fig. 15.4: Basic Components of Motivation

(C) TYPES OF MOTIVATION

There are two ways by which people can be motivated. One is a positive approach or pull-mechanism and another is a negative apprcach or push-mechanism.

Positive Motivation or Pull-Mechanism

People are said to be motivated positively when they are shown a reward and the way to achieve it. Such reward may be financial or non-financial. Monetary motivation may include different incentives, wage plans, productive bonus schemes, etc. Non-monetary motivation may include praise for the work, participation in management, social recognition, etc. Monetary incentives provide the worker a better standard of life while non-monetary incentives satisfy the ego of a man. Positive motivation seeks to create an optimistic atmosphere in the enterprise. Positive motivation involves identifying employee potentialities and make him realise the possible result by achieving his potentialities. Positive motivation can be referred as 'Anjaneya type of motivation' in Ramayana.

Negative Motivation or Push-Mechanism

One can get the desired work done by installing a fear complex in the minds of people. In this method of motivation, fear of consequences of doing something or not doing something keeps the worker in the desired direction. This method has got several limitations. Fear creates frustration, a hostile state of mind and an unfavourable attitude towards the job which hinders efficiency and productivity. So the use of it should be kept to its minimum and should be practised discretely.

Steps in Motivation

According to Judicious, the following are the steps that should be adopted in motivation:

(i) **Sizing up:** This step mainly involves understanding of different needs of people. Having assessed the needs, one can determine what motivates them.

(ii) **Preparing a set of motivating tools:** This list of motivators should be prepared based on the revealed needs of the people.

(iii) **Selecting and applying motivators:** Out of the list of motivators, few should be selected and applied wherever and whenever they are needed.

(iv) **Feedback:** Having applied the motivators, it is important to find out how effective had a particular motivator been.

Now, we shall study the important aspect of this Chapter, i.e., Theories of Motivation.

(D) THEORIES OF MOTIVATION

There are several approaches and theories of motivation. These theories of motivation are broadly classified into content theories, process theories and reinforcement theory. The classification of the theories of motivation is presented in Fig. 15.5.

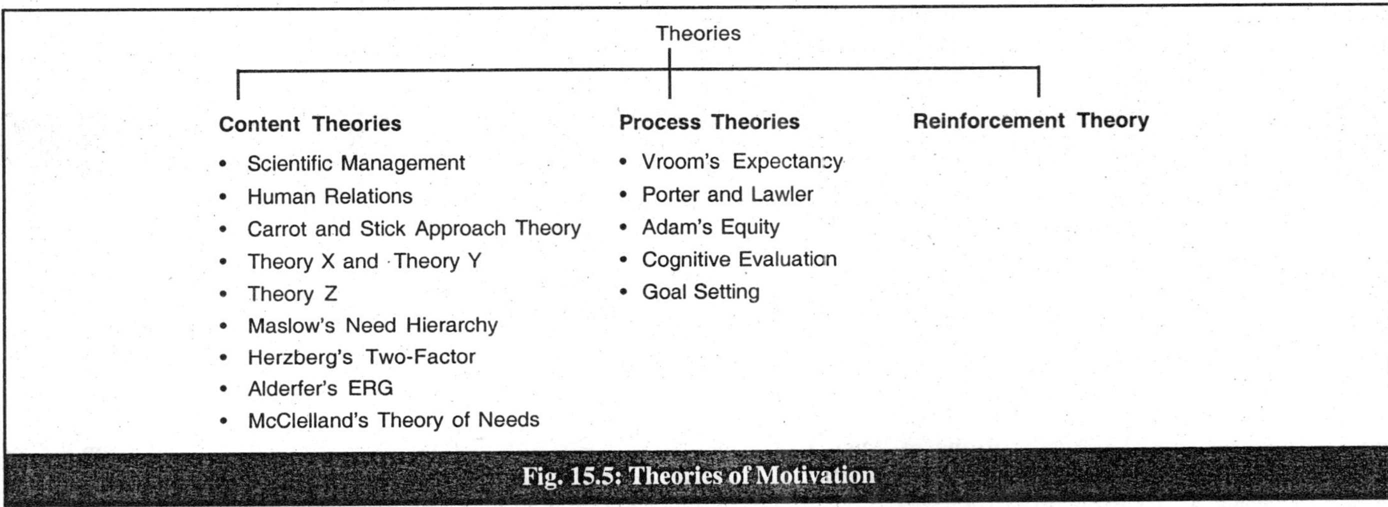

Fig. 15.5: Theories of Motivation

Content Theories of Motivation

Content theories of motivation deal with identifying the needs of the people and how they prioritise them. These needs include wage, salary in order to satisfy physiological drives, incentives, social needs, security needs, recognition, etc.

Content theories are based on the needs of people

Let us now understand in detail the various types of content theories of motivation, viz., Carrot and Stick Approach Theory, Theory X, Theory Y and Theory Z.

Scientific Management and Human Relations

Principles of scientific management emphasise that the employes should be motivated through salary. Principles of human relations emphasise that the employees should be motivated by allowing them to work in groups. These two aspects are discussed in detail in Chapter 2.

Carrot and Stick Approach Theory

This theory advocates that people are motivated to work under two conditions, *viz.*, *(i)* When they are offered rewards and *(ii)* When they are penalised or punished. The rewards are offered for efficient and high performance and punishments or penalties are imposed when the performance is lagging behind of a standard performance.

Vroom and Deci observe: "Organisation - mediated rewards and penalties most clear-cut motivational effects where the outcomes, on the basis of which rewards and penalties are allocated, are under the control of an individual. Where such control is weakened, the motivational advantages tend to break down."

This theory is effective, if the employee's basic needs are not satisfied. If the employee is satisfied with his needs up to a certain extent, he doesn't care of the penalties.

According to Saul W. Gillerman, "The philosophy of management by direction and control is inadequate to motivate because human needs, on which this approach relies, are today unimportant motivators of behaviour. Direction and control are essentially useless in motivating people whose important needs are social and egoistic."

McGregor is of the view that neither the 'hard' nor the soft approach can provide an effective motivation for human effort towards the achievement of orgnisational objectives.

The Carrot approach involves the offer of monetary rewards, non-monetary benefits, providing better working conditions and high quality of work life. The Stick approach supports the theory X assumptions and involves the use of coercion and threat, close supervision and tight control of employee behaviour.

This approach doesn't work in many situations during the third millennium as people do not work for only money and other rewards. The other needs like sense of achievement, interesting work, recognition, involvement in decision-making, etc., play vital role in employee motivation.

Theory X, Theory Y and Theory Z

Douglas McGregor proposed two altogether different views of human beings. One view is basically negative of human beings called Theory X and the other is basically positive of human beings called Theory Y.[9]

Theory X is based on negative aspects of people

Assumptions of Theory X: Theory X is a traditional set of assumptions about people. The assumptions held by managers under Theory X include:

- The typical person dislikes work and will avoid it, if possible;
- The typical person lacks responsibility, has little ambition and seeks security about all; and
- Most people must be coerced, controlled and threatened with punishment to get them to work.

Motivational Aspects of Theory X: Theory X assumes that people are relatively self-centred, indifferent to organisational needs and goals and resistant to change. Managers have to motivate their subordinates through negative motivational techniques like coercion, punishment, threatening and controlling.

Theory X assumptions are mostly applicable in government departmental and public sector organisational situations where people are not basically trusted. And these assumptions are not applicable in private sector organisations where freedom, autonomy and voluntarism are mostly trusted.

Assumptions of Theory Y: Theory Y implies a more positive, human and supportive approach to managing people. The assumptions of Theory Y include:

Theory Y is based on positive aspects of people

- People view work as being as natural as rest or play.
- People will exercise self-direction and self-control, if they are committed to the organisational objectives.
- The average person can learn to accept and/or seek responsibility.
- People are not inherently lazy. They have become that way as a consequence of their experience, and
- People have potential. Under proper conditions, they learn to accept and seek responsibility. They have imagination, ingenuity and creativity that can be applied to work.

Motivational Aspects of Theory Y: These assumptions motivated the managers to develop employee potential and help them release that potential towards the organisational objectives.

Theory Y assumptions are believed mostly by the private sector organisations, where the performance is most essential than the procedure. Private sector organisations motivate the employees by creating proper organisational structures like humanistic and flat structures. The believers of Theory Y design the jobs based on job enrichment techniques. Further the employees are given freedom and autonomy to decide their work, activities, take their own decisions with a view to enhance the organisational performance. Empowerment of employees is a recent technique in this direction.

William Ouchi's Theory Z

Ouchi proposed Theory Z – a hybrid model that blends elements of successful Japanese managerial practice with an assessment of US workers' needs. It focuses heavily on a humanistic philosophy, teamwork and consensus decisions.

Theory Z is based on long-term and total aspects of people

The distinguishing features of Theory Z companies are:

- Long-term employment;
- Non-specialised careers;
- Individual responsibility;
- Concern for the total person;
- Control systems are less formal;
- Consensus decision-making; and
- Slower rates of promotion.

It is believed that Theory Z companies develop close, cooperative, trusting relationships among workers, managers and other groups.

Theory Z emphasizes that industrial teams are created within a stable work environment. This match enables the employee to satisfy his needs for affiliation, independence and control. Further, it contributes for the organisation's needs of high quality and high productivity.

Maruti Udyog Limited in India, Toyota, Honda and Nissan are the best examples for the practices and outcome of Theory Z. These organisations' levels of quality and productivity have been quite higher than those of their competitors in the respective countries. In fact, the rate of absenteeism and number of grievances in these companies are very low compared to those in similar organisations.

Positive Points of Theory Z: The positive points of theory Z are:

- Theory Z companies have made a commendable attempt to adapt Japanese ideas into their organisations.
- This theory is based on shared concern for multiple employee needs.
- Theory Z suggests strong bondage between organisation and its employees.
- Employee involvement is a prominent factor in this theory.
- Theory Z encourages the practice of informal organisation.
- This theory encourages automatic coordination among employees.

Negative Points of Theory Z: Theory Z is not free from criticism due to the following drawbacks.

- It is criticised that this theory is not new. It is an extension of earlier theories which failed to receive popularity;
- It is also criticized that the research supporting this theory is limited;
- The other criticism is that this theory fails to provide useful criteria for helping managers regarding the correct time to use this theory;
- The volatile firms in the software industry, information technology and other high technology industries cannot provide life time employment; and
- Slow rates of promotions frustrate employees.

Despite these limitations or criticisms, Theory Z helps managers in managing human resources efficiently and balancing human behaviour with the organisational environment.

Maslow's Theory of Hierarchy of Needs

Maslow's Theory is based on the hierarchy of five human needs.

The most popular and important content theories of motivation is the Maslow's Theory. According to Maslow, human needs form a hierarchy, starting at the bottom with the physiological needs and ascending to the highest need of self-actualisation as shown in Fig. 15.6. He says when one set of needs are satisfied, they no longer work as motivators as a man seeks to satisfy the next higher level needs.

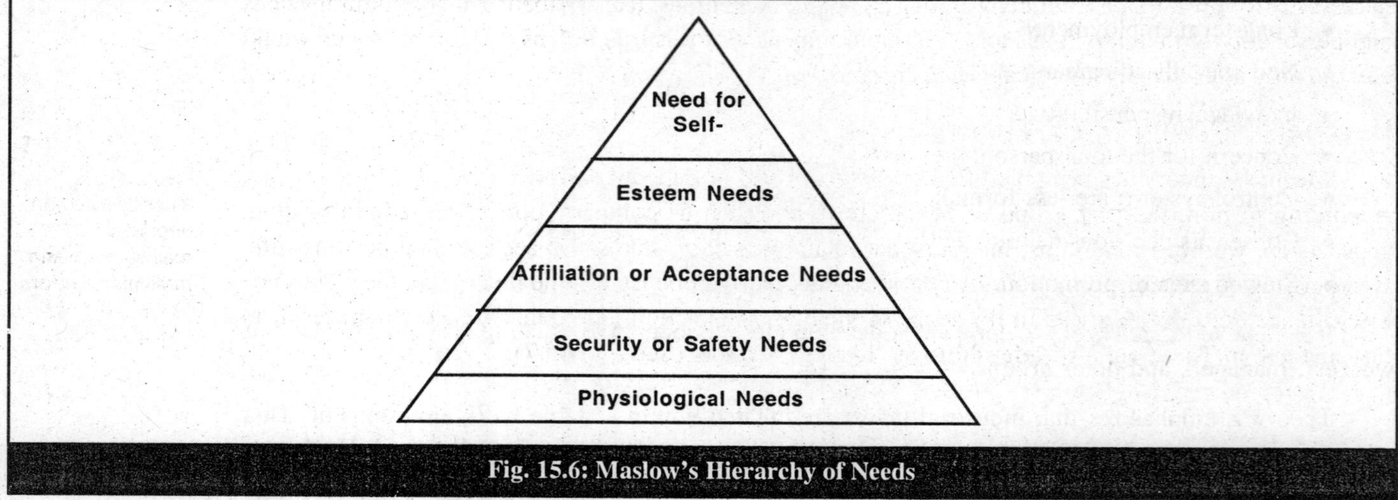

Fig. 15.6: Maslow's Hierarchy of Needs

The Need Hierarchy

(i) **Physiological needs:** These are the basic necessities of human life — food, water, warmth, shelter, sleep and sexual satisfaction. Maslow says that until these needs are satisfied to the required level, man does not aim for the satisfaction of the next higher level needs. As far as work organisation is concerned, these needs include basic needs like *pay, allowance, incentives* and *benefits.*

(ii) **Security/safety needs:** These refer to the need to be free of physical danger or the feeling of loss of food, job or shelter. When the physiological needs are satisfied, man starts thinking of the way by which he can continue to satisfy these physiological needs. Security needs spring up the moment he makes an effort in the direction of providing himself the source of continuity of physiological needs. This is exactly the reason why attitude towards security is an important consideration in choosing the job. These needs as far as work organisation is concerned include: *conformity, security plans, membership in unions, severance pay, etc.*

(iii) **Social needs (affiliation or acceptance needs):** When the physiological and security needs are satisfied, these social needs begin occupying the mind of a man. This is exactly why he looks for the association of other human beings and strives hard to be accepted by its group. Social needs at the workplace include: human relations, formal and informal work groups.

(iv) **Esteem needs:** These needs are power, prestige, status and self-confidence. Every man has a feeling of importance and he wants others to regard him highly. These needs make people aim high and make them achieve something great. These needs for employees include status symbols, awards, promotions, titles, etc.

(v) **Self-actualization needs:** This is the highest need in the hierarchy. This refers to the desire to become what one is capable of becoming. Man tries to maximize his potential and accomplish something, when this need is activated in him.

As indicated earlier, the individuals proceed from physiological needs to safety needs and so on and so forth only when each need is satisfied. If any need is not satisfied, the individual sticks to that need and strives to fulfill that need.

Critical Analysis of Malsow's Theory: The first question that arises is, "Do needs follow hierarchy?" Studies and surveys conducted by experts reveal that needs do follow hierarchy to some extent. But it should be remembered that it cannot be generalised in the sense that needs do not necessarily follow the same hierarchy among all people at all times. It also depends on the cultural values and personality of the individuals and their environment. But it is true that psychological needs would emerge only after the physiological needs are satisfied.

Herzberg's Two-Factor Theory

Herzrberg classified human needs into maintenance and motivating factors

Maslow's theory has been modified by Herzberg and he called it two-factor theory of motivation. According to him, the first group of needs are things such as company policy and administration, supervision, working conditions, interpersonal relations, salary, status, job security and personal life. Herzberg called these factors as '*dissatisfiers*' and not motivators. By this, he means that their presence or existence does not motivate in the sense of yielding satisfaction, but their absence would result in dissatisfaction. These are also referred to as 'hygiene' factors (See Fig. 15.7).

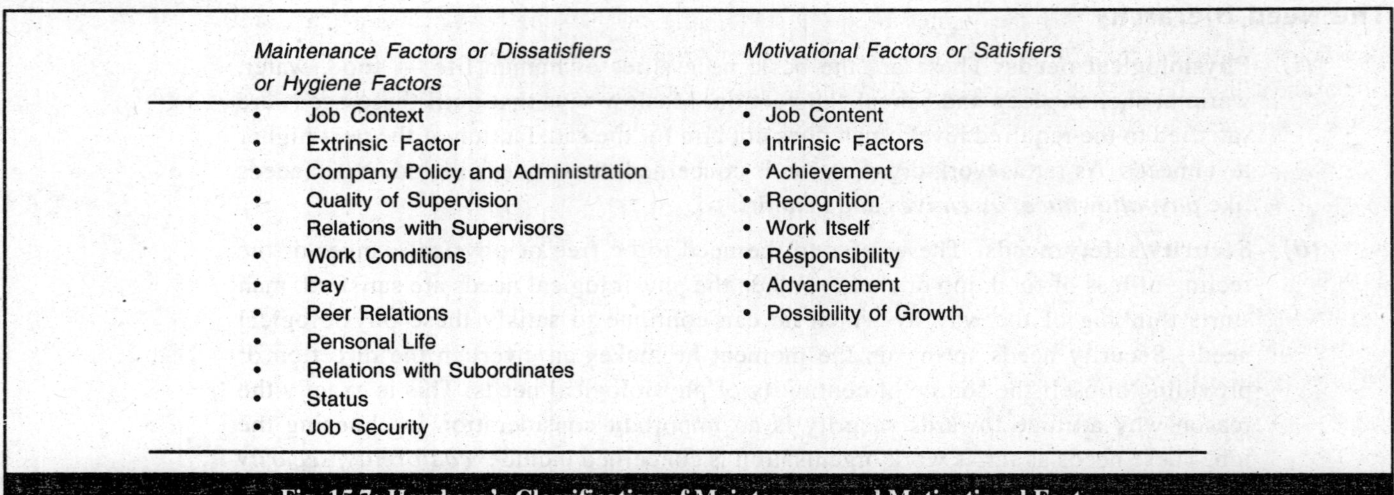

Maintenance Factors or Dissatisfiers or Hygiene Factors	*Motivational Factors or Satisfiers*
• Job Context	• Job Content
• Extrinsic Factor	• Intrinsic Factors
• Company Policy and Administration	• Achievement
• Quality of Supervision	• Recognition
• Relations with Supervisors	• Work Itself
• Work Conditions	• Responsibility
• Pay	• Advancement
• Peer Relations	• Possibility of Growth
• Personal Life	
• Relations with Subordinates	
• Status	
• Job Security	

Fig. 15.7: Herzberg's Classification of Maintenance and Motivational Factors

In the second group are the satisfiers, in the sense that they are motivators. These factors are related to 'job content.' He included the factors like achievement, recognition, challenging work, advancement and growth in this category. Presence of these factors will yield feelings of satisfaction.

Frederick Herzberg's theory is also called *motivation-hygiene theory*. Herzberg believed that individual's relation to work is a basic one. Individual's attitude towards work determines his/her success or failure on the job. Herzberg conducted a study by asking the question: What do people want from their jobs? He asked the respondents to describe situations or events when they felt exceptionally good and bad about their jobs. The responses of the respondents are tabulated as presented in Exhibit 15.3.

Exhibit 15.3 Comparison of Satisfiers and Dissatisfiers

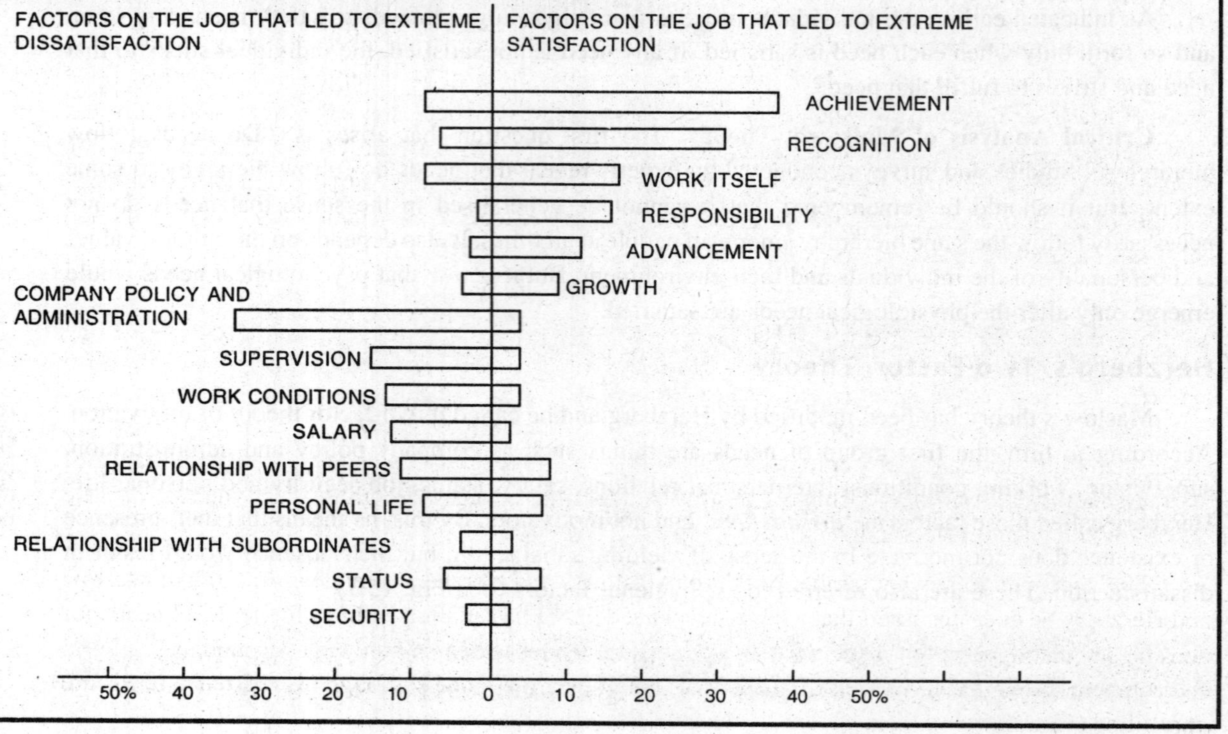

FACTORS ON THE JOB THAT LED TO EXTREME DISSATISFACTION

FACTORS ON THE JOB THAT LED TO EXTREME SATISFACTION

ACHIEVEMENT

RECOGNITION

WORK ITSELF

RESPONSIBILITY

ADVANCEMENT

GROWTH

COMPANY POLICY AND ADMINISTRATION

SUPERVISION

WORK CONDITIONS

SALARY

RELATIONSHIP WITH PEERS

PERSONAL LIFE

RELATIONSHIP WITH SUBORDINATES

STATUS

SECURITY

50% 40 30 20 10 0 10 20 30 40 50%

Herzberg concluded that the replies of the good feeling of the jobs of the respondents are significantly different from those of the bad feelings of the jobs of the respondents. Factors on the right side of the exhibit tend to be related to job satisfaction motivational factor and the factors on the left side of the exhibit tend to be related to job dissatisfaction maintenance factors.

Factors contributed to job satisfaction in the order of their significance include: achievement, recognition, work itself, responsibility, advancement and growth. Those respondents, when they felt good about their job, attributed to these factors. In contrast, when they felt bad about their jobs, they attributed the following factors for being bad on their jobs. These factors in the order of their significance include: company policy and administration, supervision, relationship with supervisor, work conditions, salary, relationship with peers, personal life, relationship with subordinates, status and security (Exhibit 15.3).

Criticisms: This theory suffers from the following criticisms:

- The procedure used by Herzberg is limited by its methodology;
- The reliability of the methodology used by Herzberg is questioned;
- The conclusions of this theory are related to job satisfaction and job dissatisfaction. Therefore, it is not a theory on motivation;
- This theory does not provide measurement to find out the total job satisfaction or job dissatisfaction;
- This theory ignores situational variables; and
- Herzberg did not cover the relationship between job satisfaction and productivity, though he assumed that there is a relationship between these two factors.

However, this theory significantly contributes to the literature on motivation and this theory is known by most of the practising managers. The practising managers practise this theory in motivating their subordinates.

Comparison of Maslow's and Herzberg's Models

If we compare Herzberg and Maslow's models, we can see that Herzberg's theory is not much different from that of Maslow. Most of the maintenance factors of Herzberg come under low level needs of Maslow. Maslow says when the lower level needs are satisfied, they stop being motivators and what Herzberg says is the same in the sense that they are maintenance factors (not motivators). But one particular difference that can be talked off here is that Maslow emphasizes that any unsatisfied need, whether of lower or higher level, will motivate people and Herzberg clearly identifies certain needs and calls them as maintenance factors which can never be motivators.

Alderfer's ERG Theory

Alderfer classified human needs as existence, relatedness and growth needs.

Alderfer also feels that needs should be categorised and that there is basic distinction between lower order and higher order needs. Alderfer identifies three groups of needs, viz., Existence, Relatedness and Growth and that is why his theory is called ERG theory. The existence needs are concerned with survival or physiological well-being. The relatedness needs talk of the importance of interpersonal and social relationships. The growth needs are concerned with the individual's intrinsic desire for personal development.

This theory is somewhat similar to that of Maslow's and Herzberg's models. But unlike Maslow and Herzberg he does not assert that a lower level need has to be satisfied before a higher level need, nor does he say that deprivation is the only way to activate a need. So, a person's background and cultural environment may make him think of relatedness needs or growth needs though his existence needs are unfulfilled (Fig. 15.8).

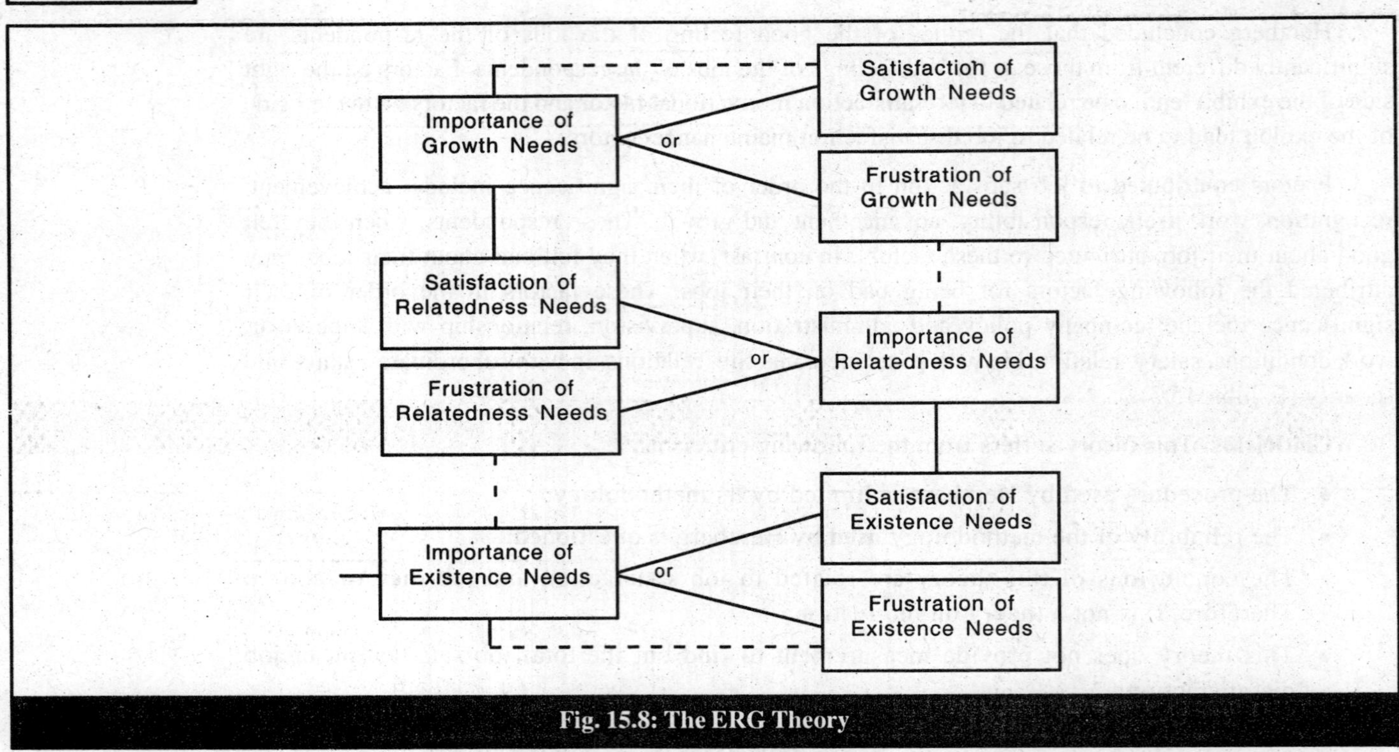

Fig. 15.8: The ERG Theory

McClelland's Theory of Needs

As discussed earlier, McClelland's theory of needs was developed by David McClelland — a Harvard psychologist and his associates.[10] The theory focuses on three needs, viz.

***(i)* Need for achievement:** Need for achievement refers to the drive to excel, to achieve in relation to set standards and to strive to succeed.

McClelland observed from his research that high achievers differentiate themselves from others by doing the same work in different ways. They perform best when they perceive their probability of success as being 0.5. They seek quick feedback on their performance in order to improve or correct the action before it goes wrong. They accept personal responsibility for success or failure.

***(ii)* Need for power:** Need for power refers to the desire to make others behave in a way that they would not otherwise have behaved in. In other words, need for power (nPow) is the desire to have impact, to be influential and control others.

For example, Mr. Chandra Babu Naidu, the then Chief Minister of Andhra Pradesh, has the need for power as he influences the entire government machinery to work like a private organisation towards efficiency, perfectness and service to its customers, *i.e.*, people.

People with high order need for power prefer to be placed in competitive and status oriented situations. They would like to have prestige and gain influence over others.

***(iii)* Need for affiliation**: Need for affiliation refers to the desire for friendly and close interpersonal relationship.

The new employees who come from various places, organisations, educational and social backgrounds normally have the need for affiliation.[11]

Application: The match between the needs and jobs is presented in Fig. 15.9 McClelland's theory has some similarities with the other content theories like Herzberg, Maslow and ERG. These similarities among the content theories are presented in Fig. 15.10.

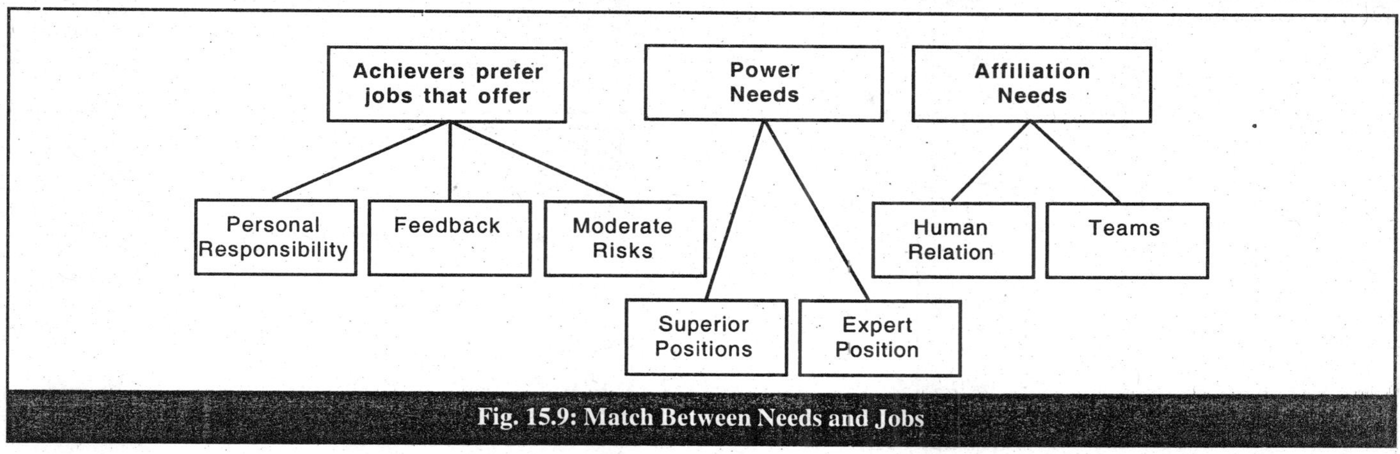

Fig. 15.9: Match Between Needs and Jobs

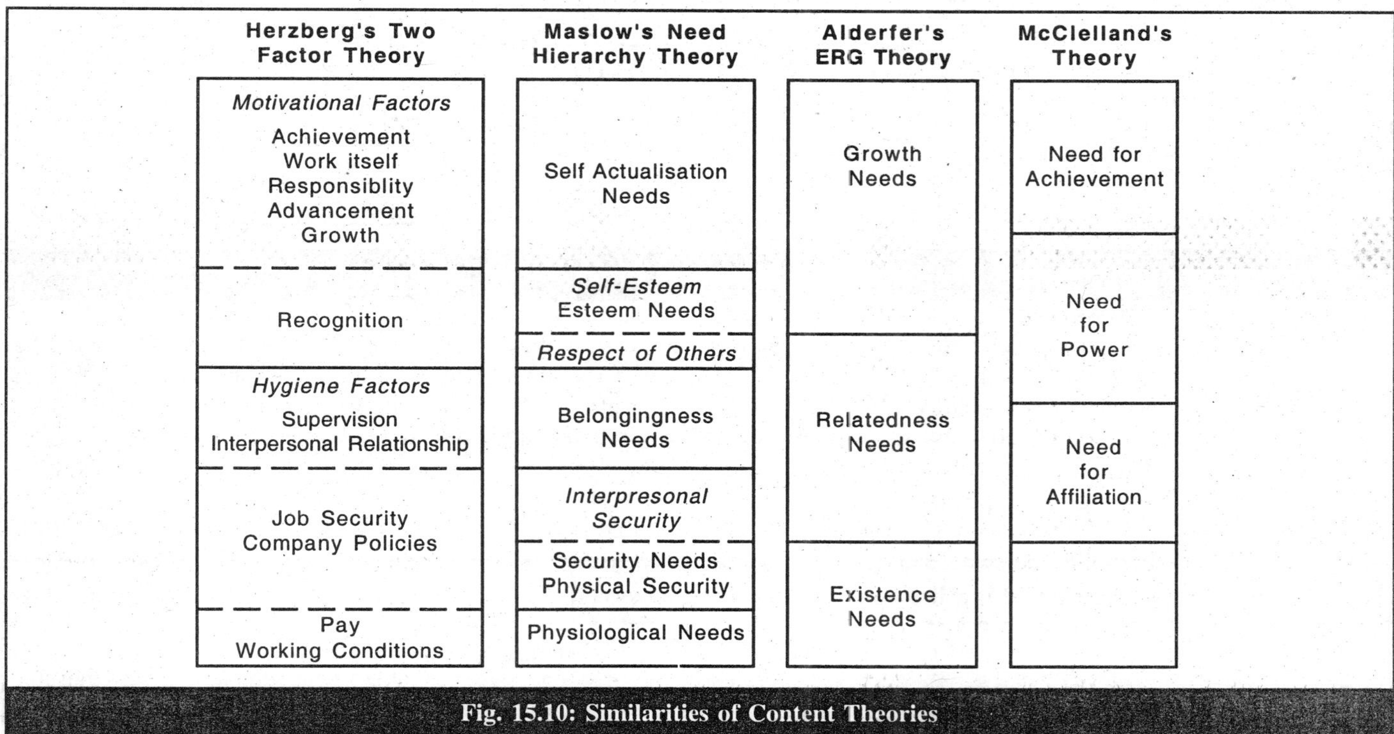

Fig. 15.10: Similarities of Content Theories

(**Source:** Gregary Moorhead and Ricky W. Griffin, *Organisational Behaviour*, p. 146)

The Process Theories of Motivation

The content theories of motivation identify what motivates people, while process theories deal with cognitive antecedents that go into motivation and effort. These theories contribute to the complex processes involved in motivational effort.

Process theories deal with cognitive antecedents

Process theories, include: Vroom's Expectancy Theory, Porter-Lawler Model, Adam's Equity Theory, Cognitive Evaluation Theory and Goal-Setting Theory.

Vroom's Expectancy Theory of Motivation

Victor Vroom felt that content models were inadequate explanations of the complex process of work motivation and he developed a relatively new theory of motivation. According to his theory, motivation of any individual depends on the desired goal and the strength of his expectation of achieving

This theory deals with valence, instrumentality and expectancy

the goal. Vroom's model is built mainly on three concepts — valence, instrumentality and expectancy (See Fig. 15.11).

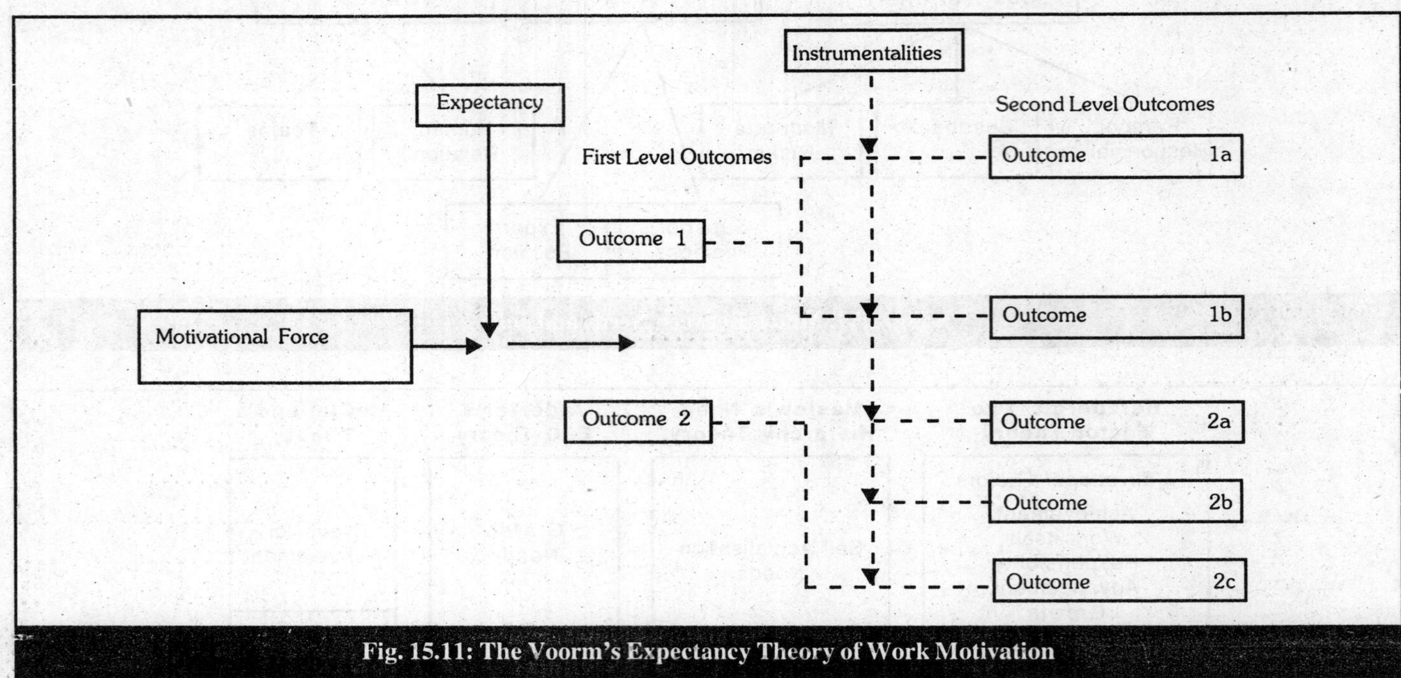

Fig. 15.11: The Voorm's Expectancy Theory of Work Motivation

Valence: Vroom says that valence is the strength of an individual's preference for a particular outcome. It can be taken as an equivalent of value, incentive, attitude and expected utility. For the valence to be positive, the person must prefer attaining the outcome to not attaining the outcome. A valence of zero occurs, when the individual is indifferent towards the outcome. The valence is negative when the individual prefers not attaining outcome to attaining it. This can be observed from the managerial implication of this theory (Exhibit 15.4).

Exhibit 15.4 Managerial implications of Vroom's theory

Key Terms	*The Individual's Question*	*Managerial Implications*
Expectancy	"Can I achieve the desired level of task performance?"	• Select workers with ability • Train workers to use ability • Support ability with organisational resources • Clarify performance goals
Instrumentality	"What work outcomes will be received as a result of the performance?"	• Clarify psychological contracts • Communicate Performance -> reward possibilities • Confirm performance -> reward possibilities by making actual rewards contingent upon performance
Valence	"How highly do I value the work outcomes?"	• Identify individual needs or outcomes • Adjust available rewards to match these

(**Source:** Schermerhorn et al "*Managing Organisational behaviour,*" p. 149)

Instrumentality: Another major input into the valence is the instrumentality of the first level outcome in obtaining desired second level outcome. *For example*, assume that an individual desires promotion and feels that superior performance is a very strong factor in achieving that goal.

His first outcomes are then superior, average or of poor performance. His second level outcome is *promotion*. The first level outcome of high performance thus acquired a positive valence by virtue of its expected relationship to the preferred outcome of second level promotion. In this case, the person is motivated to achieve superior performance because he has desire to be promoted. The superior performance (first level outcome) is seen as being instrumental in obtaining promotion (second level outcome).

Expectancy: The third major variable in Vroom's theory is expectancy. Though expectancy and instrumentality appear to be the same at the first glance, they are quite different. Expectancy is a probability (ranging from 0 to 1) or strength of a belief that a particular action or effort will lead to a particular first level outcome. Instrumentality refers to the degree to which a first level outcome will lead to the second level outcome. Vroom says the sum of these variables is *motivation*.

The Porter and Lawler Model Expectancy Theory

This theory deals with effort, performance, reward and satisfaction

All the content theories assume that satisfaction leads to improved performance. However, it was later found that there is a very low positive relationship between satisfaction and performance. Lyman W. Porter and Edward E. Lawler exploded the complex relationship between motivation, satisfaction and performance (See Fig. 15.12). According to them performance is a function of three important factors, *viz*.,

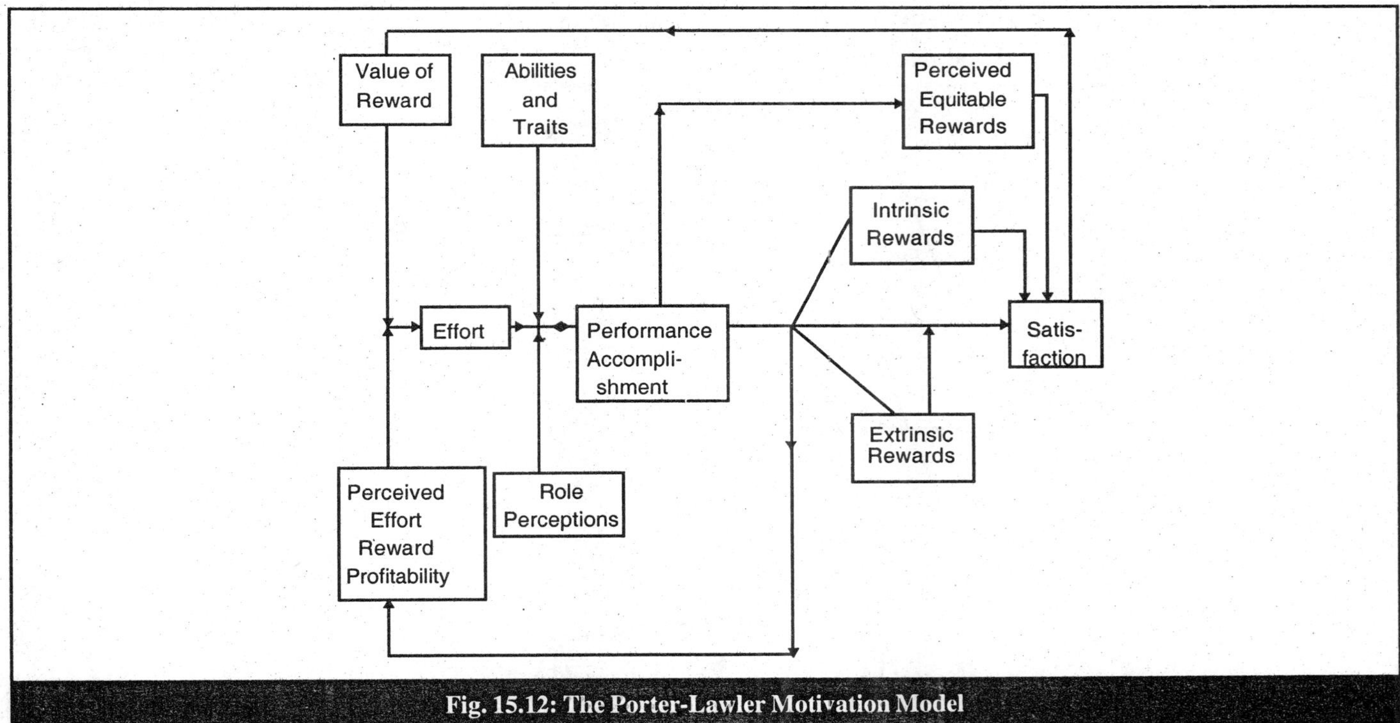

Fig. 15.12: The Porter-Lawler Motivation Model

(i) If an employee wants to perform, he must be motivated;

(ii) Motivation alone does not ensure performance and hence a person must have the necessary abilities and skills as well;

(iii) An employee must have an accurate knowledge of the requirements of the job.

Following are the key-variables in this model:

Effort: Effort does not directly lead to specific levels of performance. Effort is only the amount of energy exerted by an individual to achieve a specific task. It is only the result of the attractiveness of the reward and how he perceives a relation between effort and pay-off. The individual will exert greater effort if he perceives that there is a greater probability that his effort will lead to the reward. So motivation is seen as a force on the employee to expect effort.

Performance: Effort alone is not enough, as performance results only when the effort is continued with the ability. Effort and performance cannot be taken to be the same.

Reward: A person gets intrinsic reward himself by performing a task well. Intrinsic reward will be a feeling of accomplishment. Extrinsic rewards like pay, promotion and status are offered by the organisation.

Satisfaction: The satisfaction depends on the perceived rewards and the actual rewards. If an individual feels that he should have received more for what he had done, it results in dissatisfaction and vice versa.

Thus, motivation and achievement result in satisfaction or dissatisfaction of an employee about the job, organisation, etc.

Equity Theory of Work Motivation

Credit of developing this theory goes to J. Stacy Adams. This theory argues that a major input into job performance and satisfaction is the degree of equity (or inequity) that people perceive in their work situation. Inequality occurs when a person perceives that the ratio of his or her outcomes to inputs and the ratio of other's relevant outcome to inputs are unequal. Fig. 15.13 presents an overview of equity theory of work motivation.

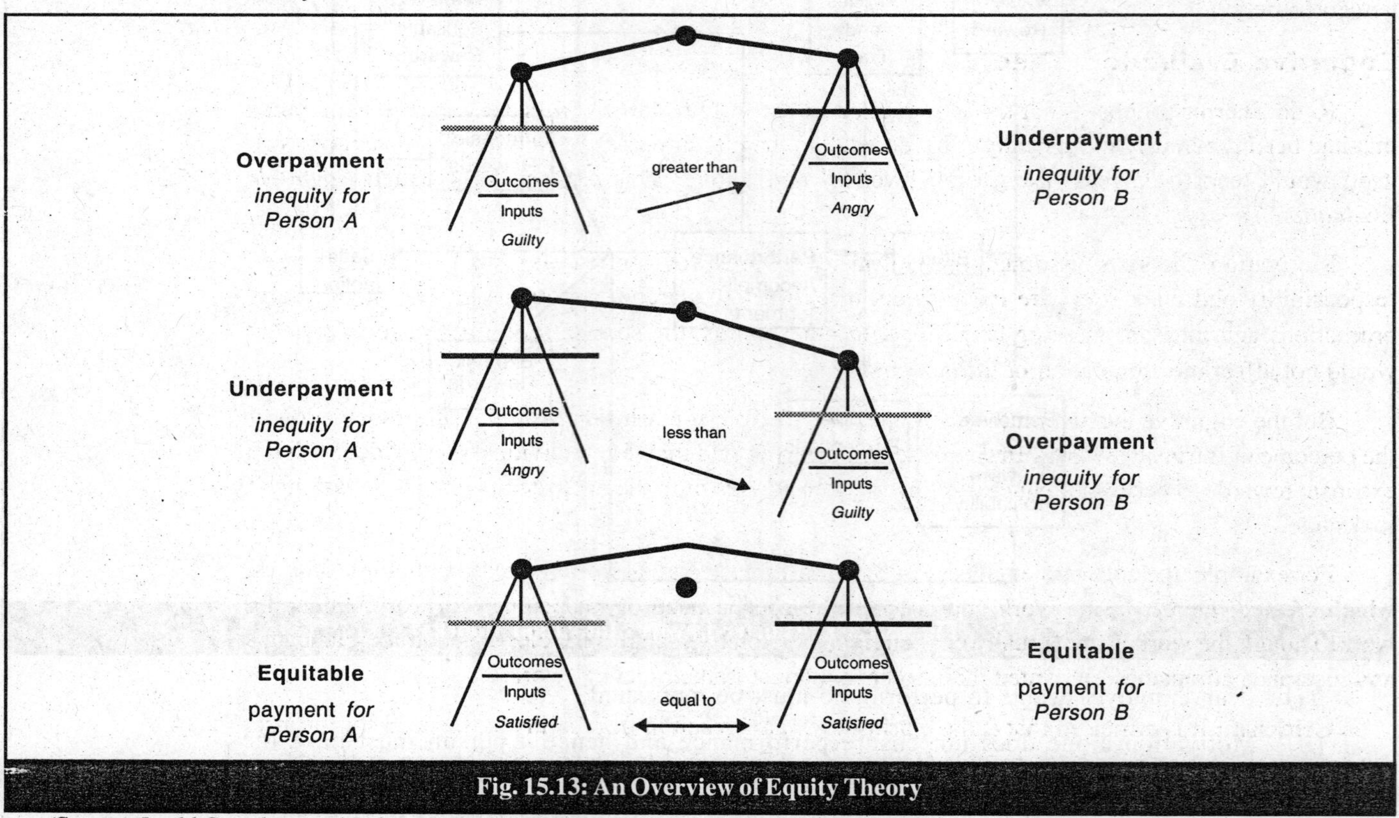

Fig. 15.13: An Overview of Equity Theory

(**Source:** Jerald Greenberg and Robert A. Baron, "*Organisational Behaviour,*" Prentice-Hall of India (P) Ltd., 1999, New Delhi, p. 138.

Schematically this is represented as follows:

Inequity occurs when:

$$\frac{\text{Person's outcomes}}{\text{Person's inputs}} < \frac{\text{Other's outcomes}}{\text{Other's inputs}}$$

$$\frac{\text{Person's outcomes}}{\text{Person's inputs}} > \frac{\text{Other's outcomes}}{\text{Other's inputs}}$$

Equity occurs when:

$$\frac{\text{Person's outcomes}}{\text{Person's inputs}} = \frac{\text{Other's outcomes}}{\text{Other's inputs}}$$

Both the inputs and the outputs of persons and others are based upon the person's perceptions. Age, sex, education, economic and social status, skill, experience, training, effort, education, past performance, present performance, level of difficulty, position in the organisation etc., are examples of perceived input variables. Outcomes consist of rewards like pay, status, promotion and intrinsic interest in the job.

If the person's perceived ratio is not equal to the other's, he or she will strive to restore the ratio to equity. Thus, the work motivation of oneself depends upon other's inputs, output and one's perceived output.[12]

Cognitive Evaluation Theory

R. de Charms proposed that the introduction of extrinsic rewards, *viz.*, salary, benefits and perks that had been previously intrinsically rewarded due to the pleasure associated with the content of work itself would tend to decrease the overall level of motivation.[13] This proposition is called *Cognitive Evaluation Theory*.

Motivation theorists assumed that intrinsic rewards (or motivators) such as achievement, responsibility and work itself are independent of extrinsic rewards (or motivators), *viz.*, high salary, promotions and pleasant working conditions. In other words, the stimulation of extrinsic motivators would not affect the stimulation of intrinsic motivators.

But the cognitive evaluation theory argues that the use of extrinsic rewards result in deviation of the outcome of intrinsic rewards. In simple terms, it can be said that if an individual is provided with the extrinsic rewards to perform an interesting work, it would result in the intrinsic interest in the task itself to decline.

For example, the software engineers in Satyam Infotech Ltd. are offered extremely high salaries, which created interest in the work and reduced the special need of interesting work or challenging work. Though the work is not actually challenging, the lucrative salaries for clerks in commercial banks and insurance companies motivated them to have interest in their clerical work.

Criticism: It is criticised that if the extrinsic rewards result in the decline in the need for intrinsic rewards, organisations need not provide intrinsic rewards, interesting work, challenging work, etc.

Goal-Setting Theory

Edwin Locke in the late 1960s proposed that intentions to work towards a goal are a major source of work motivation.[14] We can determine what should we do? And how much effort we should put in and at what direction? if we know the goals clearly. To be precise, specific goals enhance performance. Difficult goals, when accepted would lead to higher performance than normal goals. Further, feedback contributes to higher performance.[15]

The specificity of the goal itself acts as an internal stimulus. Specific hard goals produce a higher level of performance and output than the generalised goal.

Normally, it is expected that the employee is motivated to achieve higher results if he/she is allowed to participate in goal setting. In fact, the concept of management by objectives (MBO) suggested by Peter F. Drucker, assumes that employee involvement in the setting of objectives contributes to higher output. But research in this respect indicate mixed conclusions.

For example, *BPL executives give clear direction and goal to each employee with minute clarity and specificity. The employees once understand the goals and have clear direction. The executives indicate that this practice resulted in increase in output and also quality and production of zero defect products.*

Self-efficacy refers to an individual's belief of performing a task. The higher the self-efficacy the higher would be the performance. Therefore, the organisation has to create a favourable belief in the individual minds that they are capable of achieving higher performance. This in turn would motivate them towards higher performance.

Reinforcement Theory

Reinforcement theory is also known as *operant conditioning theory*. Principles of learning and conditioning are used in the reinforcement theory to the process of influencing the motivation and job performance of people. B. F. Skinner developed this theory of motivation. According to Skinner, behaviour of people is mostly influenced by its consequences. The actions that result in positive consequence tend to be repeated more often. On the other hand, the actions that result in negative consequence consequence tend to be repeated more often.

Reinforcement

Mr. Bhusan, a salesman in Natco Pharma Ltd., sold 1,500 units in 2009, quite higher than the sales of all other salesmen. Mr. Navneet – Marketing Manager appreciated Mr. Bhusan for his performance. Mr. Bhusan has been motivated by the act of Mr. Navneet. He worked skilfully and enhanced his sales to 1,800 units in 2010. The act of Mr. Navneet is termed as positive reinforcement.

An action is said to be positively reinforcing, if the occurrence of the event following some behaviour makes the behaviour more likely to repeat in the future.

There are four types of reinforcements, *viz.*, positive reinforcement, negative reinforcement, punishment and extinction. The different types of reinforcements are the results of either the application or withdrawal of either pleasant or unpleasant events.

Positive Reinforcement: Following the positive behaviour, the employee is provided with a pleasant or a desirable event like high salary, better benefits, praise, recognition and status. This results in occurrence of the positive behaviour frequently.

Negative Reinforcement: Following the withdrawal of a negative reinforcer (like strict supervision, strict controls, harassment and threatening), the positive behaviour tends to occur more frequently. *For* *example*, the production department of Ruchi Star Hotel is designed on basis of bureaucratic lines. Consequently, there has been strict supervision and controls. It resulted in occurrence of mistakes frequently in the food production. The management realised that humanistic structure is more appropriate to the hotel industry and hence they switched over their activities to humanistic structure. This change resulted in decline in mistakes and improvement in quality and productivity.

Punishment: Some superiors feel that strict control and supervision leads to enhanced performance. Hence, they impose controls. Punishment takes place when an unpleasant or undesirable event occurs following some behaviour and makes the behaviour less likely to occur.[16]

Extinction: Mr. Chandrakant is an able Recovery Officer in State Bank of India, Dharmavaram Branch. He was transferred to Anantapur Branch in 2000. His performance in the Anantapur Branch turned out to be poor while it was excellent in Dharmavaram. The branch manager of Anantapur Branch started giving all his support and encouragement to Mr. Chandrakant in July 2000. Immediately, his performance increased significantly. The branch manager stopped encouraging him in August 2000 due to his busy schedule. Soon, the performance of Mr.Chandrakant has also come down. This situation is called *extinction*. Extinction occurs when the withdrawal of a pleasant or desirable factor results in behaviour becoming less likely to occur in the future.[17]

KEY TERMS

- Motivation
- Motives
- Motivating
- Need
- Drive
- Goal
- Incentives
- Achievement Motives
- Affiliation Motives
- Power Motives
- Reinforcement
- Effort
- Persistance
- Primary Motives
- Secondary Motives
- General Motives
- Positive Motivation
- Negative Motivation
- Physiological Needs
- Security Needs
- Social Needs
- Carrot Motivation
- Esteem Needs
- Self-Actualisation Needs
- Scientific Management
- Human Relations
- Theory X
- Theory Y
- Theory Z
- Expectancy
- Instrumentality
- Valence
- Stick Motivation

QUESTIONS

1. What is motivation? Identify the difference among motive, motivating and motivation.
2. Explain various kinds of motives.
3. Discuss the significance and nature of motivation.
4. Explain the principles of scientific management and human relations approach to motivation.
5. Compare and contrast Maslow's Theory of Motivation, Herzberg Two Factor Theory of Motivation and ERG Theory of Motivation.
7. Examine the carrot - stick approach theory of motivation.
8. Examine the similarities and differences among Theory X, Theory Y and Theory Z.
9. Give a detailed account of Vrooms Expectancy Theory of Motivation.
10. Comment on the Porter and Lawler Expectancy Theory of Motivation.
11. Explain reinforcement theory of motivation.

REFERENCES

1. C. B. Mamoria, op.cit., p. 652.
2. Berelson *et.al., "Human Behaviour,"* Harcourt Brace and World Inc., New York, 1964, p. 240.
3. Marris S. Viteless, *"Motivation and Morale in Industry,"* W. W. Norton & Co., New York, 1953, p. 73.
4. C. B. Mamoria, *op.cit*., p. 652.
5. Berelson and Steiner, "*Human Behaviour*," Harcourt Brace and World Inc., New York, 1964, p. 240.
6. Fred Luthans, *op.cit*., pp. 165-166.
7. L.M.Prasad, *op.cit*., p. 144.
8. F. W. Taylor, "*Shop Management in Scientific Management*," Harper & Row, New York, 1947, pp. 36-37.
9. Douglas McGregor, "*The Human Side of Enterprise*," Cambridge, Mass, 1957.
10. D. C. McClelland, "*The Achieving Society*," Van Nostrand Reinhold, New York, 1961.
11. Stephen P. Robbins, "*Organisational Behaviour*," Prentice Hall of India (P) Ltd., New Delhi, p. 175.

CHAPTER 16

MOTIVATION: APPLICATIONS

☛ Chapter Outline

☛ Learning Objectives

After studying this Chapter, you should be able to:

- ✓ Understand how motivation theories help in designing jobs;
- ✓ Understand how motivation theories and concepts are used in developing the concept of MBO;
- ✓ Know how motivation theories help in designing and developing various Employee Recognition Programmes;
- ✓ Appraise the role of motivation theories in administering salaries and benefits and in designing reward systems and fringe benefits;
- ✓ Interpret the motivation concepts to human psychology and develop employee involvement programmes;
- ✓ Discuss how the quality circles are designed in order to satisfy employee social needs and esteem needs; and
- ✓ Interweave motivation theories to various aspects of human resource management in order to manage the people by enhancing the quality of life at workplace.

(A) INTRODUCTION

We have discussed various motivation concepts and motivation theories in the previous chapter. It has been established that motivation is well applicable to the work environment. Different factors motivate the employees. However, these factors vary from country to country. Exhibit 16.1 presents the factors that motivate the employees across the globe. In this Chapter, focus is on the application of motivation through job design, job enrichment, job enlargement, de-jobbing environment, management by objectives, employee recognition programmes, variable pay, flexible benefits, employee involvement programmes like workers' participation in management and quality circles and quality of work life.

Exhibit 16.1 What Motivates Employees: An International View

USA	*Germany*	*Netherlands*	*Korea*	
• Interesting job • Achievement • Advancement	• Interesting job • Co-workers • Meaningful work	• Interesting Job • Achievement • Co-workers	• Achievement • Security • Interesting job	
Taiwan	***India***	***China***	***Israel***	***Hungry***
• Achievement • Interesting job • Esteem	• Security • Salary & Benefits • Achievement	• Achievement • Use of Ability • Esteem	• Interesting job • Meaningful work • Advancement	• Supervisor • Interesting job • Co-workers

(**Source:** Adapted from Jerald Greenberg and Robert A.Baron, *op.cit.*, p.127)

(B) JOB DESIGN

Job is the process of deciding on the content of a job in terms of its duties and responsibilities.

Job design is defined as the process of deciding on the content of a job in terms of its duties and responsibilities; on the methods to be used in carrying out the job, in terms of techniques, systems and procedures and on the relationships that should exist between the jobholder and his superiors, subordinates and colleagues.[1] Two important goals of job design are: *(i)* to meet the organisational requirements such as higher productivity, operational efficiency, quality of product/service, etc. and *(ii)* to satisfy the needs of the individual employees like interests, challenge, achievement or accomplishment, etc. Finally, the goal of the job design is to integrate the needs of the individual with the organisational requirements.

Job Design Process

Job design process has to start from what activity needs to be done in order to achieve organisational goals. It requires the use of techniques like work study, process planning, organisational methods and organisational analysis. The retaining part of the discussion on the process of job design involves the technical aspects of job design and as such it is outside the scope of this book. The next step of the study is *job design options.*

Job Design Options

Job design options include job rotation, job enlargement and job enrichment.

As discussed earlier, scientifically structured job design motivates the employees for higher efficiency, productivity and generates job satisfaction than the one designed on the basis of the traditional engineering system. Specification should be introduced in job design so that the needs of the employees for accomplishment, recognition, psychological growth, etc., can be satisfied. Personnel departments use a variety of methods to improve jobs such as job rotation, job enlargement and job enrichment. Thus, all this factors include in the job design options.

(C) MANAGEMENT BY OBJECTIVES

Management by Objectives (MBO) is a successful philosophy of management. It replaces the traditional philosophy of 'management by domination.' It was popularised as an approach to planning by Peter F. Drucker in 1954 in his famous book *The Practice of Management.* Since that time, it has acquired momentum and of late it has become a movement.

Employee Recognition Programmes

Rural Development Trust (RDT) is a pioneering voluntary organisation committed to the upliftment of rural poor in Anantapur district of Andhra Pradesh. Mr.Ashok worked in RDT for two years during 1992-94, before doing his MBA programme. He joined Hindustan Machine Tools in September 1996 after completing his MBA. Mr. Ashok says, he was very happy in Rural Development Trust though his monthly salary was Rs.1,500 rather than in Hindustan Machine Tools where it is Rs.10,000. The reasons for this are:

His supervisor in RDT used to praise him for his committed work in the presence of his clients. Consequently, his clients used to treat him as a great person. Further, his supervisor praised him in the annual functions twice in the presence of the top management. His needs for recognition, prestige and achievement were satisfied though his salary was not attractive in RDT.

Organisations started recognizing the employees particularly after liberalization and globalisation in 1991.

Organisations announced a number of employee recognition programmes in order to motivate them:

- Praising the employees in the presence of their colleagues regarding their achievements, excellent performance, etc.
- Providing long-term employment and job security. (See Box 16.1).
- Presenting awards in the annual functions to those employees who are committed, creative and innovative.
- Providing wage/salary increments, benefits, perks and special bonus.
- Inviting the employee and his family members to the company's annual functions and other functions.
- Giving special treatments to the employee and his family members for special events like birthday, marriage day, etc.
- Honouring outstanding employees for their extraordinary accomplishments by giving them prestigious company awards.

Box 16.1: Top 9 Companies With the Best Job Security

With unemployment reaching and expected to surpass 10%, job security is one of the top desires of employees today. Along with good pay and benefits, people want to find a company that's not going to give them a pink slip any time soon.

Here's a group of companies that earn high marks in that regard. Nine companies on Fortune *magazine's* 100 Best Companies to Work For *list for 2009 have never undergone layoffs - ever.*

1. Nugget Market

This company has avoided layoffs because of careful job placement and shrewd labor management. Instead of laying off workers, the 81-year-old grocery store refrains from replacing employees who leave. Its stores are 15 miles from each other, making it easier to fill positions, and employees are trained to fit various roles. The Woodland, Calif.-based supermarket chain filled 173 jobs, for a 22% job growth in the year before the list was released in February.

Sandwiched between Goldman Sachs and Adobe Systems, the store ranked number 10 on the overall list. Store directors make an average of $116,440 in annual salary, and checkers, the most common hourly workers, earn $34,490. The store also offers 100% health care coverage.

2. Devon Energy

An oil and gas producer headquartered in Oklahoma City, this company takes a conservative approach to its finances, yet still treats its employees well. Ranked 13 on the overall list, it started a 401(k) retirement plan featuring company contributions of 11-22%.

Flexible and prudent management helps avoid layoffs. The company, which cut its operating budget before the recession, withholds raises in bad years but gives midyear pay increases in good times.

3. Aflak

Known for its quacking duck ads, this company sells supplement insurance. The company, based in Columbus, keeps its eyes on its budget and ears open to employees. Employee suggestions like telecommuting and flex schedules have saved it millions of dollars. Other company benefits include an onsite fitness center, subsidized gym membership and the largest onsite corporate child care center in Georgia.

4. QuikTrip

Because this 24-hour convenience store is privately held, it can send profits back to its stores and workers instead of shareholders. Smart financial management has helped it thrive in the downturn. It offered over new 1,400 jobs last year. Wages and benefits are so good that over 200 employees have stayed with the company more than 20 years.

5. The Container Store

The storage retailer, based in Coppell, Texas, froze salaries and watched spending to avoid layoffs. Still, it kept expanding last year, opening four stores and adding 70 employees. Extensive employee training makes the company stand out.

6. NuStar Energy

Considering layoffs harmful to company productivity, NuStar management avoids them like the plague. The San Antonio-based pipeline and refinery operator also offers bonuses that can exceed $10,000 and 100% 401(k) matches for up to 6% of pay.

7. Stew Leonard's

Known for flashy store displays, this privately-held grocery chain focuses on customer service and long-term sales rather than short-term earnings. CEO Stew Leonard Jr. says selling groceries is a stable business, which helps avoid layoffs. No matter how the economy is faring, people still have to eat.

8. Scottrade

This privately-held online discount brokerage has cut bonuses instead of cutting employees. A conservative growth strategy has also helped it avoid layoffs.

9. Publix Super Markets

A strong balance sheet with no debt helped this grocery chain acquire 49 stores and hire over 1,250 people last year. In its 79 years, it has never had layoffs. No wonder - it's entirely owned by employees.

Besides never laying off employees, at least as of early this year, companies on the list are also some of the best to work for. Treating employees well means good pay and benefits - two factors that are attracting all the right workers. (Preparation can help you land on your feet after getting the "old heave-ho."

Source: http://finance.yahoo.com/career-work/article/108085/top-9-companies-with-the-best-job-Security.html?mod=career-salary_negotiation (Accessed on 05/02/2010).

Linking Recognition Programmes and Reinforcement Theory

As we have discussed in the earlier chapter, rewarding a behaviour with recognition immediately following that behaviour is likely to encourage its repetition. Therefore, if the management recognises the extraordinary accomplishments of the employees, they are motivated to repeat their extraordinary accomplishments.

Organisations expect efficient performance from their employees in order to contribute to the attainment of the individual goals. Organisations reward their employees who contributed to the achievement of organisational goals. (Fig. 16.1)

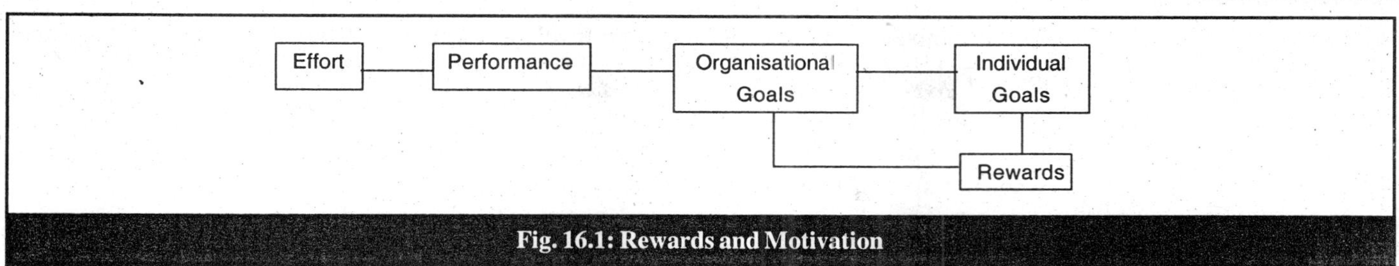

Fig. 16.1: Rewards and Motivation

(D) SOUND SALARY ADMINISTRATION

Management has to formulate and administer the salary policies on sound lines as: *(i)* most of the employees' satisfaction and work performance are based on pay; *(ii)* internal inequalities in pay are more serious to certain employees; *(iii)* employees compare their pay with that of others; *(iv)* employees act only on gross external inequities; *(v)* employee comparisons of pay are uninfluenced by levels of aspirations and pay history; and *(vi)* employees compare the pay of different employees with their skill, knowledge, performance, etc.

Objective of Salary Administration

The objective of wage and salary administration are numerous and sometimes conflict with each other. The important among them are: (See Exhibit 16.2).

Exhibit 16.2 Objectives of Wage and Salary Management

- ***Acquire Qualified Personnel:*** Compensation needs to be high enough to attract applicants. Pay levels must respond to supply and demand of workers in the labour market since employers compete for workers. Premium wages are sometimes needed to attract applicants who are already working for others.
- ***Retain Present Employees:*** Employees may quit when compensation levels are not competitive resulting in higher turnover.
- ***Ensure Equity:*** Compensation management strives for internal and external equity. *Internal equity* requires that pay be related to the relative worth of jobs, so that similar jobs get similar pay. *External equity* means paying workers what comparable workers at other firms in the labour market pay.
- ***Reward Desired Behaviour:*** Pay should reinforce desired behaviours and act as an incentive for those behaviours to occur in the future. Effective compensation plans reward performance, loyalty experience, responsibilities and other behaviours.
- ***Control Costs:*** A rational compensation system helps the organization obtain and retain workers at a reasonable cost. Without effective compensation management, workers could be over or under payed.
- ***Comply with Legal Regulations:*** A sound wage and salary system considers the legal challenges imposed by government and ensures the employer's compliance.
- ***Facilitate Understanding:*** The compensation management system should be easily understood by human resource specialists, operating managers and employees.
- ***Further Administrative Efficiency:*** Wage and salary programs should be designed to be managed efficiently, making optimal use of the human resource information system, although these objectives should be a secondary consideration compared with other objectives.

(**Source:** William B. Werther and Keith Davis, *op. cit.*, p. 414.)

(1) *To acquire qualified competent personnel:* Candidates decide upon their career in a particular organisation mostly on the basis of the amount of remuneration the organisation offers. Qualified and competent people join the best paid organisations. As such, the organisations should aim at payment of salaries at that level, where they can attract competent and qualified people.

(2) *To retain the present employees:* If the salary level does not compare favourably with that of other similar organisations, employees quit the present one and join other organisations.

The organisation must keep the wage levels at the competitive level, in order to prevent such quits.

(3) *To secure internal and external equity:* Internal equity does mean payment of similar wages for similar jobs within the organisation. External equity implies payment of similar wages to similar jobs in comparable organisations.

(4) *To ensure desired behaviour:* Good rewards reinforce desired behaviour like performance, loyalty, accepting new responsibilities and changes, etc.

(5) *To keep labour and administrative costs* in line with the ability of the organisation to pay.

(6) *To protect in public as progressive employers* and to comply with the wage legislations.

(7) *To pay according to the content* and difficulty of the job and in tune with the effort and merit of the employees.

(8) *To facilitate pay roll* administration of budgeting and wage and salary control.

(9) *To simplify collective bargaining* procedures and negotiations.

(10) *To promote organisational* feasibility.

Principles of Salary Administration

Development and administration of sound wages and salary policies are not only important but also complex managerial functions. The complexities stem from the fact that on the one hand, a majority of union management problems and disputes relate to the question of wage payment and on the other, remuneration is often one of the largest components of the cost of production. Thus, it influences the survival and growth of an organisation to the greatest extent.

The influence of remuneration over distribution of income, consumption, savings, employment and prices is significant.

The influence of remuneration over distribution of income, consumption, savings, employment and prices is also significant. This aspect assumes all the greater importance in an undeveloped economy like India where it becomes necessary to take measures for a progressive reduction of the concentration of income and/or to combat inflationary trends. Thus, the wage policy of an organisation should not become an evil to the economy.

There are several principles of wage and salary plans, policies and practices. The important among them are:

(i) Wage and salary plans and policies should be sufficiently flexible;

(ii) Job evaluation must be done scientifically;

(iii) Wage and salary administration plans must always be consistent with overall organisational plans and programmes;

(iv) These plans and programmes should be in conformity with the social and economic objectives of the country like attainment of equality in income distribution and controlling inflationary trends;

(v) Both these plans and programmes should be responsive to the changing local and national conditions; and

(vi) These plans should simplify and expedite other administrative processes.

The Elements of Salary System

Wage and salary system should have relationship with the performance, satisfaction and attainment of goals of an individual. Henderson identified the following elements of wage and salary system:

(i) Identifying the available salary opportunities, their costs, estimating the worth of its members of these salary opportunities and communicating them to employees.

(ii) Relating salary to needs and goals.

(iii) Developing quality, quantity and time standards relating to work and goals.

(iv) Determining the effort necessary to achieve standards.

(v) Measuring the actual performance.

(vi) Comparing the performance with the salary received.

(vii) Measuring the job satisfaction gained by the employees.

(viii) Evaluating the unsatisfied wants and unreached goals of the employees.

(ix) Finding out the dissatisfaction arising from unfulfilled needs and unattained goals.[2]

(x) Adjusting the salary levels accordingly with a view to enabling the employees to reach unreached goals and fulfill the unfulfilled needs.

Wage Differentials

Wage differentials among employees working in the same unit, among different units, occupations, regions and the like are common features of labour markets in various countries. Interpersonal wage differentials are mainly due to variations in personal characteristics like sex, age, skill, knowledge, etc., of employees who work in the same unit and are in the same or similar occupations. Interfirm or interunit wage differentials reflect relative wage levels of workers in different units in the same or similar occupation. These differentials are mostly because of varying abilities of the firms to pay wages. Inter-occupational wage differentials are due to varying requirements of physical skills, endurance, knowledge, etc., varying demand and supply conditions and the like. Inter-area differentials are mainly due to varying demand and supply factors, living costs, abilities of employers to pay and the like.

Wage Differentials and Economy Functions

Wage differentials perform important economic functions like labour productivity, attracting the people to different jobs.

Wage differentials perform important economic functions like labour productivity, attracting the people to different jobs. Since most of the workers are mobile with a view to maximising their earnings, wage differentials reflect in variations in productivity, efficiency of management, maximum utilisation of human forces, etc. Attracting efficient workers, maximisation of employee commitment, development of skills, knowledge, utilisation of human resources, maximisation of productivity can be fulfilled through wage differentials as the latter determines the direct allocation of manpower among different units, occupations and regions so that national production can be maximised. Thus, wage differentials provide an incentive for better allocation of human forces, labour mobility among different regions and the like.

Wage differentials play a pivotal role in a planned economy in the regulation of wages and the development of the national wage policy by allocating the skilled human force on priority basis. Development of new skills, knowledge, etc., is an essential part of human resource development. Shortage of technical and skilled personnel is not only a problem for industries but it creates bottlenecks in the attainment of planned goals. Thus, wage differentials, to a certain extent, are desirable from the viewpoint of national interest. As such, they probably become an essential part of the national wage policy. Complete uniform national wage policy is impracticable and undesirable.

Fringe Benefits

The term *'fringe benefits'* refers to various extra benefits provided to employees in addition to the compensation paid in the form of wage or salary. Balcher defines these benefits as "any wage cost not directly connected with the employees' productive effort, performance, service or sacrifice."[3] Cockmar has defined fringe benefits as "those benefits which are provided by an employer to or for the benefit of an employee and which are not in the form of wages, salaries and time-related payments."

Different terms are used to denote fringe benefits. They are welfare measures, social charges, social security measures, supplements, sub-wages, employee benefits, etc. The ILO described 'fringe benefits' as: "*Wages are often augmented by special cash benefits, by the provision of medical and other services or by payments in kind, that forms part of the wages for expenditure on the goods and services. In addition, workers commonly receive such benefits as holidays with pay, low cost meals, low-rent housing etc. Such additions to the wage proper are sometimes referred to as fringe benefits. Benefits that have no relation to employment or wages should not be regarded as fringe benefits even though they may constitute a significant part of the worker's total income.*"

Fringe benefits are those monetary and non-monetary benefits given to the employees during employment and post-employment period.

Thus, fringe benefits are those monetary and non-monetary benefits given to the employees during employment and post-employment period which are connected with employment but not to the employees' contributions to the organisation.

Coverage of Fringe Benefits

The term 'fringe benefits' covers bonus, social security measures, retirement benefits like provident fund, gratuity, pension, workmen's compensation, housing, medical, canteen, co-operative credit, consumer stores, educational facilities, recreational facilities, financial advice, and so on. Thus, fringe benefits cover a number of employee services and facilities provided by an employer to his employees and in some cases to their family members also. Welfare of the employee and his family members is an effective advertising and also a method of buying the gratitude and loyalty of employees. But while some employers provide these services over and above the legal requirements to make effective use of their workforce,[4] some restrict themselves to those benefits which are legally required.

Need for Extending Fringe Benefits

Most of the organisations have been extending fringe benefits to their employees, year after year, for the following reasons:

(1) *Employee demands:* Employees demand a more and varied types of fringe benefits rather than pay hike because of reduction in tax burden on the part of employees and in view of the galloping price index and cost of living.

(2) *Trade union demands:* Trade unions compete with each other for getting more and a new variety of fringe benefits to their members such as life insurance, beauty clinics. If one union succeeds in getting one benefit, the other union persuades the management to provide a new model fringe. Thus, the competition among trade unions within an organisation results in more and varied benefits.

(3) *Employer's preference:* Employers prefer fringe benefits to pay hike, as fringe benefits motivate the employees for better contribution to the organisation. It improves morale and works as an effective advertisement.

(4) *As a social security:* Social security is a security that society furnishes through an appropriate organisation against certain risks to which its members are exposed. These risks are contingencies of life like accidents and occupational diseases. The employer has to provide various benefits like safety measures, compensation in case of involvement of workers in accidents, medical facilities, etc., with a view to provide security to his employees against various contingencies.

(5) *To improve human relations:* Human relations are maintained when the employees are satisfied economically, socially and psychologically. Fringe benefits satisfy the worker's economic, social and psychological needs. Consumer stores, Credit facilities, canteen, recreational facilities, etc., satisfy the worker's social needs, whereas retirement benefits satisfy some of the psychological problems about the post-retirement life. However, most of the benefits minimise economic problems of the employee. Thus, fringe benefits improve human relations. Exhibit 16.3 presents the need for extending benefits to employees.

Exhibit 16.3 Need for Extending Benefits to Employees

(i) Rising prices and cost of living has brought about incessant demand for provision of extra benefits to the employees.

(ii) Employers too have found that fringe benefits present attractive areas of negotiation when large wage and salary increases are not feasible.

(iii) As organisations have developed more elaborate fringe benefits programmes for their employees, greater pressure has been placed upon competing organisations to match these benefits in order to attract and keep employees within their fold.

(iv) Recognition that fringe benefits are non-taxable rewards has been a major stimulus to their expansion.

(v) Rapid industrialisation, increasingly heavy urbanisation and the growth of a capitalistic economy have made it difficult for most employees to protect themselves against the adverse impact of these developments. Since it was workers who were responsible for production, it was held that employers should accept responsibility for meeting some of the needs of their employees, As a result, some benefits-and-services programmes were adopted by employers.

(vi) The growing volume of labour legislation, particularly social security legislation, made it imperative for employers to share equally with their employees the cost of old age, survivor and disability benefits.

(vii) The growth and strength of trade unions has substantially influenced the growth of company benefits and services.

(viii) Labour scarcity and competition for qualified personnel has led to the initiation, evolution and implementation of a number of compensation plans.

(ix) The management has increasingly realised its responsibility towards its employees and has come to the conclusion that the benefits of increase in productivity resulting from increasing industrialisation should go, at least partly, to the employees who are responsible for it, so that they may be protected against the insecurity arising from unemployment, sickness, injury and old age. Company benefits-and-services programmes are among some of the mechanisms which managers use to supply this security.

(**Source:** Adapted from C.B. Mamoria, *op. cit.*, pp. 552-553.)

Objectives of Fringe Benefits

The important objectives of fringe benefits are:

(1) To create and improve sound industrial relations.

(2) To boost employee morale.

(3) To motivate the employees by identifying and satisfying their unsatisfied needs.

(4) To provide qualitative work environment and an appropriate work life.

(5) To provide security to the employees against social risks like old age benefits and maternity benefits.

(6) To protect the health of the employees and to provide safety to the employees against accidents.

(7) To promote employee's welfare by providing welfare measures like recreation facilities.

(8) To create a sense of belongingness among employees and to retain them. Hence, fringe benefits are called *golden handcuffs*.

(9) To meet requirements of various legislations relating to fringe benefits.

Factors Influencing Fringe Benefits

A number of factors influence the programme of employee benefits. The important among them are:

(i) Absolute and per capita cost of fringe benefits;

(ii) Organisation's financial ability to provide the benefits;

(iii) Employee's deficiencies or needs;

(iv) The bargaining strength of trade unions;

(v) Employees' significance to the organisation;

(vi) Fax benefits to the organisation and individual employees;

(vii) Need for building public image for the organisation;

(viii) Organisation's awareness and policy towards social responsibility; and

(ix) Employee's reactions to the benefits.

Rewards

The employee gets pay satisfaction if the perceived salary is equal to actual salary received.

An organisation has to balance fairly both financial and non-financial rewards and extrinsic and intrinsic rewards. Effective reward system requires not only that the absolute level of compensation paid by an organisation compares favourably but also requires that it satisfies the principle of internal equity and equity with the job content. The employee gets pay satisfaction if the perceived salary is equal to actual salary received as shown in Fig. 16.2. If the actual salary is less than the perceived salary, the employee is dissatisfied with the salary.

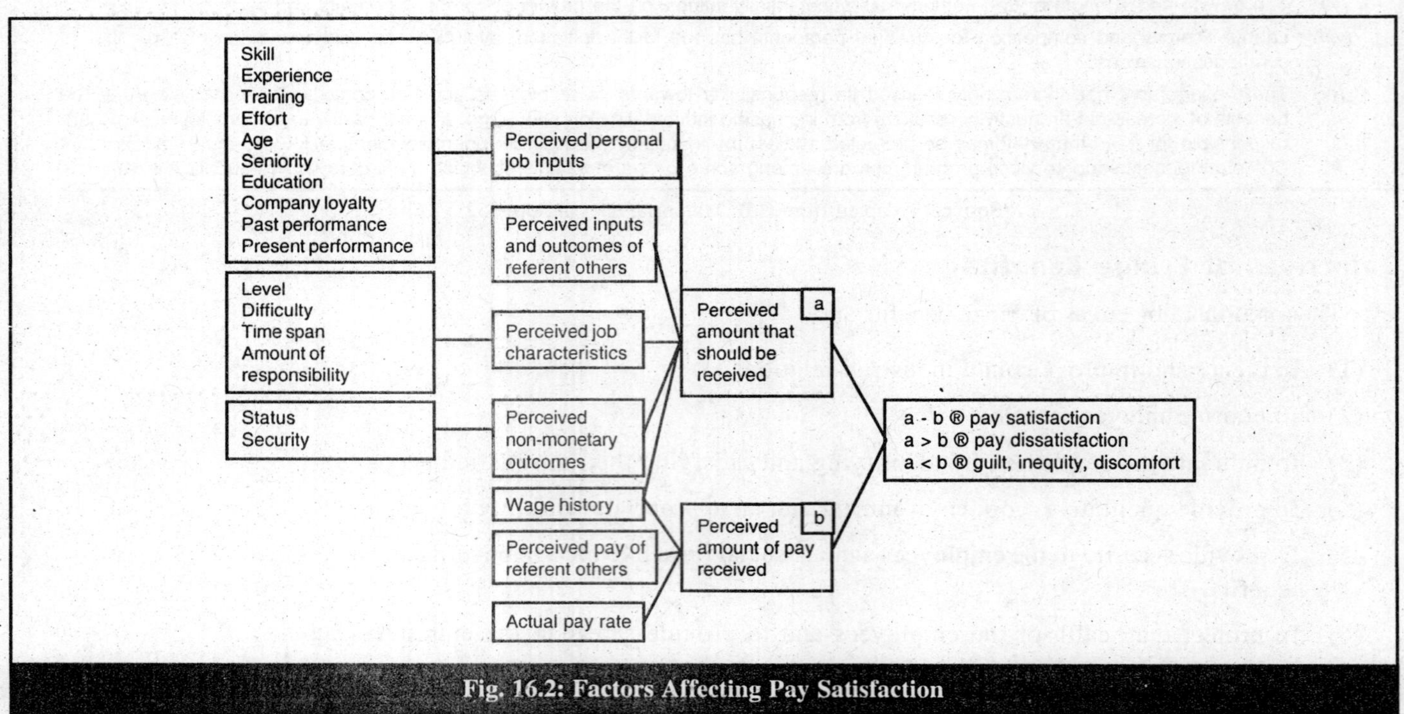

Fig. 16.2: Factors Affecting Pay Satisfaction

(**Source:** John Bernardin and Joyce Russell, *op. cit.*, p. 422).

Types of Rewards: Intrinsic and Extrinsic Rewards

Intrinsic rewards are the satisfiers that the employees get from the job itself. These rewards include pride in one's work, having a feeling of job accomplishment, being member of a team, job enrichment, etc. Extrinsic rewards include wage/salary, fringe benefits, welfare measures, promotions, incentives, etc. These benefits are external to the job and come from the management.

Financial versus Non-Financial Rewards

Rewards are two types viz., financial rewards and non-financial rewards. Financial rewards include wages/salaries, allowances, incentive payments, bonuses, profit sharing and the like. Non-financial rewards include facilities like canteen and conveyance, medical care, paid vacations, paid sick leave, etc. Figure 16.3 presents the structure of rewards.

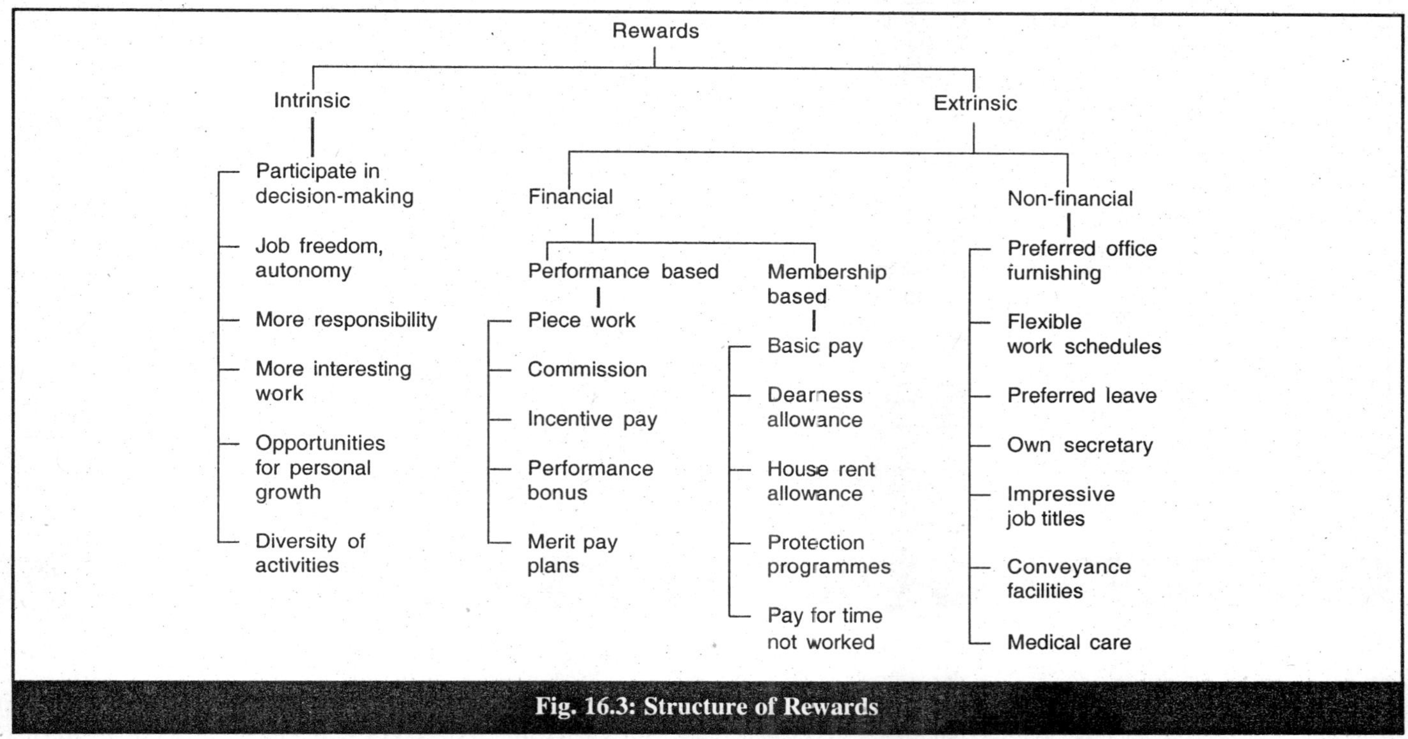

Fig. 16.3: Structure of Rewards

(**Source:** Modified Version of David A. De Cenzo and Stephen P. Robbins, *op. cit.,* p. 414).

Performance-based versus Membership-based Rewards

The rewards that the organisation allocates are based on either performance criteria or membership criteria. Performance-based rewards are exemplified by the use of commissions, incentive pay, piece work, pay plans, group bonuses, etc. Membership rewards are allocated to all employees as they are the employees of the organisation. These include: basic salary/pay, dearness allowance based on the cost of

Non-Monetary Rewards

Management motivates the employees to work efficiently and contribute their potential to a maximum extent. Individuals enhance their contributions in order to achieve organisational goals. Achievement of organisational objectives enables the management to provide more benefits and rewards to the employees. This in turn helps in the achievement of individual objectives (Fig. 16.4).

Achievement of organisational objectives enables the management to provide more benefits and rewards to the employees.

In addition to fringe benefits, the management provides different types of non-monetary rewards. These non-monetary rewards have been mentioned in Fig. 16.5.

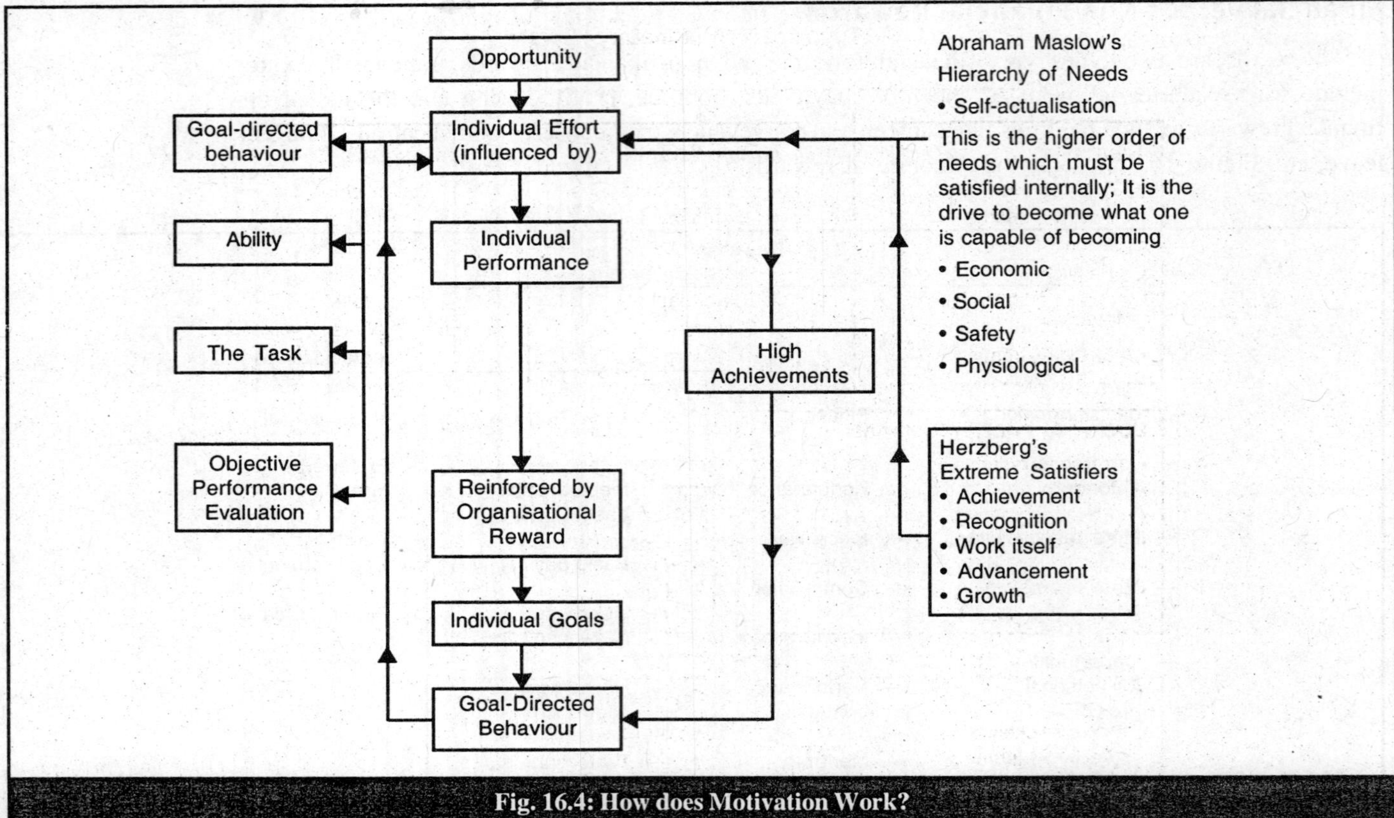

Fig. 16.4: How does Motivation Work?

(i) Treats cover free lunches, festival bashes, coffee breaks, picnics, dinner with the boss, dinner for the family, birthday treats;

(ii) Knick-Knacks cover desk accessories, company watches, tie-pins, brooches, diaries/planners, calendars, wallets and T-shirts;

(iii) Awards include trophies, plaques, citations, certificates, scrolls, letters of appreciation;

(iv) Social Acknowledgment includes informal recognition, recognition at office get-together, socialisation of advice, suggestions, etc.;

(v) Office Environment covers redecoration, flexible hours, etc.

(vi) To kens covers movie tickets, vacation trips, early time-offs, etc.

(vii) On-the-job rewards include increased responsibility, job rotation, training, etc.

Advantages: Advantages of non-monetary rewards include:

(i) Non-monetary rewards motivate employees to perform better;

(ii) They build employee's self-esteem;

(iii) Employees become more loyal to the company;

(iv) These benefits create an atmosphere where change is not resented;

(v) These benefits can be provided without any extra cost; and

(vi) Create a close bond between the company and employee's family.

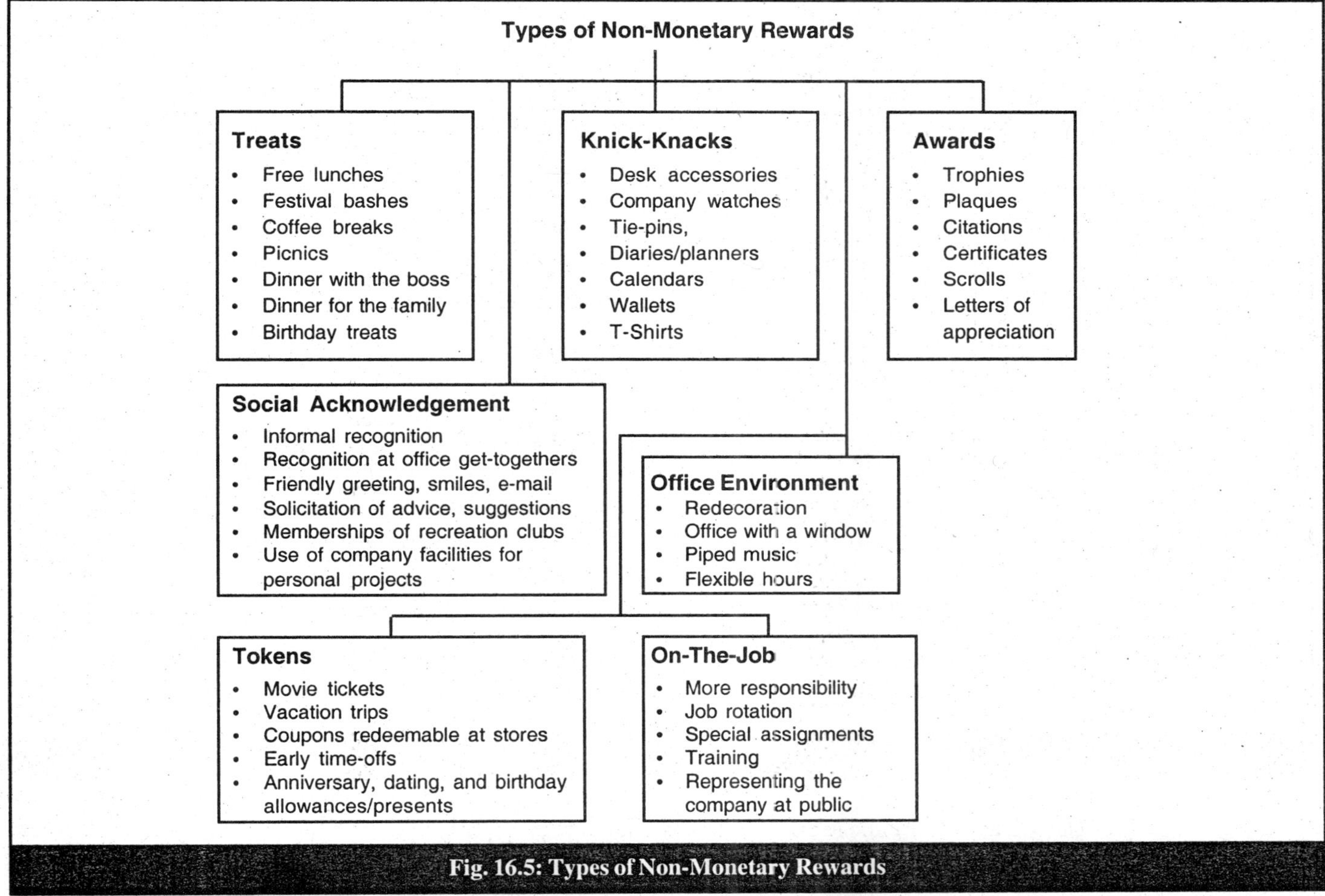

Fig. 16.5: Types of Non-Monetary Rewards

Disadvantages: The non-monetary rewards, despite the advantages discussed above, suffer from the following disadvantages:

(i) They demotivate the employees, if the processes are not transparent;

(ii) These rewards may result in short-sighted and hasty decision-making;

(iii) They may result in unhealthy competition among employees;

(iv) Work intrudes on the home life of employees;

(v) Employees feel that the management concentrates on the non-cost programmes; and

(vi) These rewards will not work, if monetary rewards are not adequate.[5]

Stock-Option Scheme

Stock options are common in many countries. This scheme allows the employees to purchase the shares of the company at a fixed and reduced price. Employees are motivated when the company allows them to buy the shares at a concessional price. The stock options are viewed as performance-based incentives.

Merits: The merits of stock-option scheme are:

(i) This scheme links compensation package closely to performance;

(ii) It enables the companies to retain efficient employees within the company;

(iii) It encourages the employees to work even better;

(iv) It inculcates a sense of ownership and responsibility;

(v) This scheme establishes significance of team effort among employees.

Limitations: The limitations of the scheme are:

(i) This scheme can be used only by the profit-making companies;

(ii) Share prices do not always reflect fundamentals;

(iii) Falling share prices result in loss to employees;

(iv) Unsound stock market conditions cause inconvenience to employees in en-cashing their investment; and

(v) Lack of transparency can earn accusations of favouritism.

(E) EMPLOYEE PARTICIPATION PROGRAMMES

The formal employee involvement programmes include: worker's participation in both management and quality circles.

Organisations today are increasingly involving their employees in various activities. The management realised that employee potentialities can be used to the maximum extent only through involving them in decision-making and the implementation process. The formal employee involvement programmes include: worker's participation in both management and quality circles.

The concept of workers' participation in the management is considered as a mechanism where workers have a say in the decision-making process of an enterprise.

Definition

The concept of workers' participation in management crystallises the concept of Industrial Democracy, and indicates an attempt on the part of an employer to build his employees into a team which works towards the realisation of a common objective.

According to Davis, "It is a mental and emotional involvement of a person in a group situation which encourages him to contribute to goals and share responsibilities in them."

Within the orbit of this definition a continuum, of men management relationship can be conceived:

Workers' Control → Joint Management → Joint Consultation

Workplace Consultation → Management Supremacy

Nature of Participative Management

(a) Participation results from practices which increase the scope for employee's share of influence in decision-making at different tiers of organisational hierarchy with concomitant assumption of responsibility.

(b) The participation has to be at different levels of management: *(i)* at the shop level, *(ii)* at the department level and *(iii)* at the top level. The decision-making at these different levels would assume different patterns in regard to policy formulation and execution.

(c) The participation incorporates the willing acceptance of responsibilities by a body of workers. As they become party to decision-making, the workers have to commit themselves to ensuring their implementation.

(d) The participation is conducted through the mechanism of forums and practices which provide for the association of workers' representatives and

(*e*) The broad goal of participation is to change basically the organisational aspect of production and transfer the management function entirely to the workers so that management becomes 'auto management.'

Formal Vs. Informal

The forms of Workers' Participation in Management depend on the differences in the levels of management, the subject-matter of participation, the strength of the union and the pattern of industrial relations. The important forms in which workers could participate in the management are collective bargaining, joint decision-making, consultation and information sharing. They may take the form of formal organisations like Works Committees, Joint Management Councils or an informal system, for instance, a supervisor consulting a worker before taking any decision in which the latter is interested.

Objectives of Workers' Participation in Management

The main objectives of Workers' Participation in Management include:

(*i*) To promote increased productivity for the advantage of the organisation, workers and society at large;

(*ii*) To provide a better understanding to employees about their role and place in the process of attainment of organisational goals;

(*iii*) To satisfy the workers' social and esteem needs;

(*iv*) To strengthen labour management cooperation and thus maintaining industrial peace and harmony;

(*v*) To develop social education for effective solidarity among the working community and for tapping latent human resources;

(*vi*) An ideological point of view to develop self-management in industry;

(*vii*) An instrument for improving efficiency of the company and establishing harmonious industrial relations;

(*viii*) To build the most dynamic human resources; and

(*ix*) To build the nation through entrepreneurship and economic development.

Participation and Motivation

Participation provides greater autonomy for subordinates and often leads to increasing motivation for:

(*a*) Participation permits a more balanced interaction pattern and therefore, results in less resistance to innovation.

(*b*) It permits members of the group to unfreeze their attitudes and engage in catharsis.

(*c*) It permits leaders to reinforce their position. They enhance their status both by taking a leading part in making the decision and through inducing group members to abide by it.

(*d*) It enables the subordinate to feel that an exchange relationship has been set up since the boss listens to his problems and permits them to be corrected.

(*e*) It may permit the subordinate to feel that doing the job well provides him with an opportunity to demonstrate skills which he values high, *i.e.*, it provides him an opportunity for achievement from work.

(*f*) It subjects the individual to certain group pressures to implement the decision which the group participated in making it.

(F) GROUP INTERACTION

A group is defined as two or more individuals, interacting with and interdependent on each other, who come together to achieve particular objectives: groups may be formal or informal.

A group is defined as two or more individuals, interacting with and interdependent on each other, who come together to achieve particular objectives: groups may be formal or informal. Formal groups are defined and formed by organisational structure with clear-cut assignment, responsibility, accountability rules and norms. Informal groups are the natural formations in the work environment and form in response to the need for social contact. Thus, these groups are not structured and determined by the organisation. These groups satisfy the social needs of their members. The important aspects of group interaction are group goals, participation, leadership norms and cohesiveness.

Group Goals: Groups generally have two types of goals viz., *task goal* and *maintaining the group itself.* Task goal is related to the main function for which the group is formed. The second goal is related to dealing with interpersonal conflict, resolving it and maintaining interpersonal relations. Group members' trusting behaviour will contribute to increased originality, greater emotional stability, less defensive and improved self-control.

Type of Participation in Group: Participation in a group may be voluntary, invited or assigned. If the group activity is effective, members voluntarily join the group in significant numbers.

Some people like experts and specialists are invited to join the groups as members of advisors. Group as a whole and other members of the group are benefited by the interaction of these special members. For example, university professors are invited to be special members on various committees of government, economic bodies, political and social organisations. These institutions are benefited by the rich theoretical base of the professors.

Participation in group is also assigned. The management forms various groups and assigns the membership including talks and responsibilities to various individuals. For example, the personnel manager may form a group with three assistant personnel managers to suggest measures to minimize absenteeism. He assigns three different aspects of the problem like absenteeism among unskilled workers, technical personnel and managerial personnel to the three assistant personnel managers of the group.

Leader: The leader of the group is a must to coordinate and control the members as well as activities - whether it is a formal group or an informal group. Groups may have two types of leaders *viz.,* talks leader and unofficial social leader, as they have two basic objectives *i.e.,* performing the main task and satisfying members' social needs.

Norms: Group norms pertain to the expected behaviour of group members. These norms are normally unwritten in the case of informal groups. The norm of quality circles is openness which helps to solve the problems better.

Cohesiveness: Cohesiveness is the degree of attraction that the group has for its members. This attraction may be in the form of loyalty, sense of belongingness, friendliness and feeling of responsibility for group tasks. Group cohesion can be increased through stability of membership, similar values of members, providing free communication opportunities, physical isolation from the formal control and small size.

With this background about the participative management and group interaction, we now discuss the history of quality circles - the sophisticated technique of participative management.

(G) QUALITY CIRCLE

Definition

A quality circle has been defined as a 'self-governing group of workers with or without their supervisors who voluntarily meet regularly to identify, analyse and solve problems of their work field'. But there is a misconception that quality circle and taskforce are one and the same, quality circle is not a taskforce and the former is broader than the latter.

A quality circle is a 'self-governing group of workers with or without their supervisors who voluntarily meet regularly to identify, analyse and solve problems of their work field'.

A taskforce is a group of most skilled employees selected and appointed by the management, engaged in various functions, with an orientation to problem-solving. The QC is a voluntary association of workers engaged in similar work with an orientation of human relations. QCs are formed to attain specific objectives.

Objectives

The important objectives of quality circles are:

(i) To develop, enhance and utilise human resources effectively;

(ii) To improve quality of products/services, productivity and reduce cost of production per unit of output;

(iii) To satisfy the workers' psychological needs for self-urge, participation, recognition etc., with a view to motivate them. Accomplishment of this objective will ensure enhancement of employee morale and commitment;

(iv) To improve various supervisory skills like leadership, problem solving, inter-personnel and conflict resolution; and

(v) To utilise individual imaginative, creative and innovative skills through participation, creating and developing work interest, inculcating problem solving techniques, etc. Achievement of these objectives effectively requires the use of certain techniques.

Techniques Used for Discussion in Quality Circles

Mainly three techniques are used in discussing various problems at quality circles. They are: (i) Brain storming processes, (ii) Cause and effect or fishbone diagrams and (iii) Sampling and charting methods.

(i) **Brain storming processes:** Under this technique, a complete free environment is created with a view to stimulate creativity. In this free environment, employees' ideas are free from criticism. Hence, employees voice all their worthy as well as less worthy ideas. All these ideas are recorded seriously. This technique is useful to generate as many ideas as possible. Later, the plus and minus points of each idea are discussed before taking a final decision.

(ii) **Cause and effect:** Members are asked to find out the causes for the identified problem. In this process, members identify one important effect of this cause on the problem. Then they identify other causes and their effects. Charting out of those causes and effects resembles the fish bone diagram. Hence, this technique is also called *fishbone diagram.*

(iii) **Sampling and charting methods:** Members of the quality circles observe the events and their consequences in the form of positive or negative results. They chart out all their observations either in sequence or in some other relationship, which gives a clear idea of the problem.

These techniques will work effectively in attaining the objectives only when the organizational structure of QCs is sound and systematic.

Concepts to Make QC Process Effective

The members and leaders of the QC should recognize and practise the following concepts to make the QC process effective:

(a) Persuasion by all the parties concerned that there is more than one way to solve a problem successfully.

(b) Encouragement of all members to clarify and build on each other's ideas.

(c) Periodic summarising of the activities by the leader or a member to ensure common understanding.

(d) Avoidance of heated arguments in favour of one particular position. Vigorous eloquence should not be a substitute for clarity and logic.

(e) Avoidance of such techniques as majority vote and conflicts to obtain group agreement, and

(f) Promotion of constructive disagreements in place of dodging arguments in search of an artificial state of harmony.

(H) QUALITY OF WORKLIFE

Introduction

Employees at the grass roots level experience a sense of frustration because of low level of wages, poor working conditions, unfavourable terms of employment inhuman treatment by their superiors and the like, whereas managerial personnel feel frustrated because of alienation over their conditions of employment, interpersonal conflicts, role conflicts, job pressures, lack of freedom in work, absence of challenging work, etc.

Certain values were attributed to work in the past. Years ago, work was worship and people had sincerity and commitment to work. But today's employee does not believe in such values of work. He works for his salary, he works hard if the conditions of work are conducive and congenial and terms of employment are favourable to him. As such, the work norms have been changing from time to time.

Work norms in modern industrial society indicate that: (i) employee's role in industry is different from his role in the family; (ii) superior knows the best and he has the right to impose on the subordinates; (iii) rules are for employees and they have to follow them and (iv) employer has the right to lay off the worker due to marketing and technological factors.

Meaning

There has been much concern today about the decent wages, convenient working hours, conducive working conditions, etc. The term 'Quality of Worklife' has appeared in Research Journals and the press in the USA only in 1970s. There is no generally acceptable definition about this term. However, some attempts were made to describe the term Quality of Worklife (QWL). It refers to the favourableness or unfavourableness of a job environment for people. QWL means different things to different people. J.Richard and J.Lloy define QWL as *"the degree to which members of a work organisation are able to satisfy important personal needs through their experience in the organisation."*

Improvement in the quality of work life are defined as any activity which takes place at every level of an organisation, which seeks greater organizational effectiveness through the enhancement of human dignity and growth....a process through which the stakeholders in the organisation management, unions and employees learn how to work together better....to determine for themselves what actions, changes and improvements are desirable and workable, in order to achieve the twin and simultaneous goals of an improved quality of life at work for all members of the organisation and greater effectiveness for both the company and the unions.

Improvement in the quality of work life is any activity which takes place at every level of an organisation, which seeks greater organizational effectiveness.

Richard E.Walton explains quality of work life in terms of eight broad conditions of employment that constitute desirable quality of work life (QWL). He proposed the same criteria for measuring QWL. These conditions/criteria include:

1. **Adequate and fair compensation:** There are different opinions about the adequate compensation. The Committee on Fair Wages defined fair wage as "....the wage which is above the minimum wage but below the living age."
2. **Safe and healthy working conditions:** Most of the organisations provide safe and healthy working conditions due to humanitarian requirements and/or legal requirements. In fact, these conditions are a matter of enlightened self-interest.
3. **Opportunity to use and develop human capacities:** Contrary to traditional assumptions, QWL is improved "....to the extent that the worker can exercise more control over his or her work, and the degree to which the job embraces an entire meaningful task...." but not a part of it. Further, QWL provides opportunities like autonomy in work and participation in planning in order to use human capabilities.
4. **Opportunity for career growth:** Opportunities for promotions are limited in case of all categories of employees either due to educational barriers or due to limited openings at the higher level. QWL provides future opportunity for continued growth and security by expanding one's capabilities, knowledge and qualifications.
5. **Social integration in the workforce:** This can be established by creating freedom from prejudice, supporting primary work groups, a sense of community and interpersonnel frankness, egalitarianism and upward mobility.
6. **Constitutionalism in the work organisation:** QWL provides constitutional protection to the employees only to the level of desirability as it hampers workers' satisfaction of doing the job beyond that level. It happens because the management's action is challenged in every action and bureaucratic procedures need to be followed at that level. Constitutional protection is provided to employees on such matters as privacy, free speech, equity and due process. Managements would not interfere with the private life as well as past life of the employee before joining the organization. (See Box 16.2).

Box 16.2: University Backs Scientist Unmasked As Sex Blogger

The university which employs the woman unmasked as the sex blogger and former call girl Belle de Jour has given her its backing, saying her former life has nothing to do with her current job.

Research scientist Dr. Brooke Magnanti works at St Michael's Hospital in Bristol and is employed by the University of Bristol.

She finally revealed that she was the writer behind one of the literary world's biggest secrets in an interview with the Sunday Times.

Her anonymous blogs about life as a high class prostitute earned her a six-figure book deal and inspired an ITV2 series starring Billy Piper entitled Secret Diary of a Call Girl.

A month ago Dr. Magnanti told colleagues at the Bristol Initiative for Research of Child Health about her former job, saying her "massive secret" was making her paranoid.

Barry Taylor, a university spokesman said: "This aspect of her past bears no relevance to her current role at the university."

It is believed she decided to reveal her identity for fear of a tip-off to a national newspaper.

Dr. Magnanti had turned to prostitution in order to make some money while completing her PhD.

She detailed her experiences in an online blog from October 2003.

Writing on her blog yesterday, the 34-year-old said it was a relief to tell all.

"It feels so much better on this side. Not to have to tell lies, hide things from the people I care about."

"To be able to defend what my experience of sex work is like to all the sceptics and doubters."

http://uk.news.yahoo.com/5/20091116/tuk-uni-backs-scientist-unmasked-as-sex-45dbed5.html (Accessed on 12/11/2009).

7. **Work and quality of life:** QWL provides for the balanced relationship among work, non-working factors and family aspects of life. In other words, family life and social life should not be strained by working hours including overtime work, work during inconvenient hours, business travel, transfers, vacations etc.
8. **Social relevance of work:** QWL is concerned about the establishment of social relevance to work in a socially beneficial manner. The workers' self-esteem would be high if his work is useful to the society and vice-versa is also true.

QWL and Productivity

The general perception is that improvement in QWL costs much to the organisation. But it is not so as improvement over the existing salary, working conditions and benefits will not cost much. However, the rate of increase in productivity is higher than the cost of QWL. Thus, increase in QWL results in increase in productivity. But continual increase in QWL eventually leads to reduction in productivity due to increase in cost of output. This is because the worker's output does not increase proportionately after a certain level, even though QWL increases.

Improved QWL leads to improved performance. Performance means not only physical output but also the behaviour of the worker in helping his colleagues in solving job-related problems, accepting orders with enthusiasm, promoting a positive team spirit and accepting temporary unfavourable work conditions without complaint.

KEY TERMS

- Motivation
- Employee Involvement
- Employee Participation
- Job Enlargement
- Job Enrichment
- De-jobbing
- MBO
- Financial Rewards
- Non-financial Rewards
- Job Rotation
- Salary
- Wage Differentials
- Fringe Benefits
- Rewards
- Job Design
- Wage
- Quality Circles
- Leader
- Quality of Worklife

QUESTIONS

1. Discuss in detail the practical implications of different motivation theories.
2. How do you apply various motivation theories in designing jobs.
3. Discuss various job design techniques and explain how do these techniques satisfy various human needs.
4. Why do the employees aspire for recognition? How do you construct employee recognition.
5. How do you use Maslow's Theory of Motivation and Equity Theory of Motivation in fixing and revising wages and salaries.
6. Why do the employees prefer to use their potentialities? Explain to what extent quality circles satisfy this need.
7. How do you design quality of worklife programme to motivate employees in general.
8. Design a programme to satisfy employee self-actualisation needs.
9. Identify employee needs which can be met through the wage differentials and varied benefits programmes.

REFERENCES

1. George Strauss and Leonard R.Sayles, *Personnel*, Prentice Hall, New Delhi, 1977, p. 553.
2. David W.Belcher, *Omnibus Trends in Wage and Salary Administration,* Personnel, Sep-Oct.1964, pp. 45-46.
3. D.W.Balcher, *Fringe Benefits*, South West Publishing Co., Ohio, p. 488.
4. Anshu Tandon, *The Non-Monetary Techniques,* Business Today, January 7-21, 1996, pp. 268-269.
5. Rukmini Parthasarathy, *The Stock Option Technique, Ibid.,* pp. 270-273.

CHAPTER **17**

FOUNDATIONS OF GROUP AND TEAM BEHAVIOUR

☛ Chapter Outline

(A) Group-Introduction
(B) Groups in Organisation
(C) Types of Groups
(D) Stages of Group Formation and Development
(E) Groups at the Workplace
(F) Group Structure
(G) Communication Channel and Network
(H) Teamwork — An Introduction
(I) Types of Teams
(J) Team Building Strategies
(K) Essential Conditions of Team Building
— Key Terms
— Questions
— References

☛ Learning Objectives

After studying this Chapter, you should be able to:

- ✓ Know the meaning of groups, need for formation of groups and types of groups;
- ✓ Analyse the different stages of group formation and development;
- ✓ Differentiate the formal groups from informal groups;
- ✓ Analyse the significance and role of informal groups;
- ✓ Understand the group structure;
- ✓ Know the factors that increase and decrease group cohesiveness;
- ✓ Understand the meaning of teams and the difference between teams and groups;
- ✓ Discuss various types of teams including work teams, project teams and ad hoc teams;
- ✓ Explain various strategies for building teams; and
- ✓ Discuss the conditions for building-up successful teams.

(A) GROUPS-AN INTRODUCTION

Larsen and Toubro (L&T) Limited was hesitant to accept the invitation of the Government of Andhra Pradesh to establish a Cement Factory in Tadipatri, one of the faction areas of Rayalaseema region in the state. However, L&T established its cement plant at Tadipatri after getting assurance from the government for maintaining law and order in view of richness of raw material near Tadipatri.

The management used to experience threats from the local politicians and factionists during the early days of its operation. The company's Human Resources Department (HRD) played a dynamic role in changing the culture of employees drawn from the local areas through whom the factionists mostly operate.

The Human Resources Department consists of around ten human resource managers and is headed by Mr. S.V.Ramana Rao, General Manager (Human Resources). All the human resources managers meet every day at 9 a.m. over a cup of coffee. They exchange the unique problems they have faced on the previous day and the innovative techniques they used to solve them. They also discuss the probability of success of those techniques and offer suggestions for follow up of the issue and for effective implementation of the techniques to the HR Manager who implemented the technique. They also review other activities in the meeting. Thus, the HR managers used to interact with each other in order to provide efficient solutions for current and future HR issues in the company.

This group activity enriched all the HR Managers in dealing with the unique and critical problems faced by the company. This activity resulted in significantly changing the culture of the employees drawn from the local area from the factionalism to corporate professionalism. These employees today think of enhancing their formal educational qualifications through distance learning methods in internet, etc.

The CEO of the company proudly admits that this group activity of the HR department initiated a dynamic and paradigm shift in employee attitude, commitment and culture, which in turn contributed towards higher productivity. Thus, the group activity converted the critical threat into one of the critical opportunities for the company.

Practice of the group process followed at the HR department of L&T, Tadipatri Cement Factory, is not new to the Indian Society. There are mentions of the group practice even in the religious epics like the Mahabharat and the Ramayana. In fact, the Indian joint family system is the resemblance of the group activity. But, Japanese organisations and corporations implemented the group culture in business operations since a long period in the past and thus enhanced its significance. The Indian corporate sector realised the significance, utility and applicability of group process and started implementing in business operations phenomenally after the liberalization and globalisation of business.

Definitions

Now, we shall discuss the formal definition of groups and group process. Stephen P. Robbins defines the term group as 'two or more individuals, interacting and interdependent, who have come together to achieve particular objectives.'[1]

G.C. Homans defines the term group as 'any number of people who share goals, often communicate with each other over a period of time, and are few enough so that each individual may communicate with all the others, person-to-person.'[2]

In the modern days of information technology, people need not physically come together, but they communicate and interact with each other. Thus, there may be virtual coming together. They strive for a common goal. Thus, the bondage of the group is constructed around the common goal or objective.

Group is the combination of two or more people formed with a purpose of achieving their common and shared goals through their interactive effort.

The members of the group share their skills and other resources and achieve their goals through the integrated effort.

With this background, we define the term *group*.

Group is the combination of two or more people formed with a purpose of achieving their common and shared goals through their interactive effort.

Analysis of these definitions would provide us the following features of groups.

Features

The features of group include:

- Combination of two or more individuals;
- Individuals are motivated to come closer physically and/or virtually;
- They come closer to achieve their common and shared goals;
- Group members achieve their common goals through integrated efforts;
- Perceive the group as a unified unit;
- Members contribute different inputs (like skills, knowledge and efforts) in different amounts towards the achievement of group goals; and
- Reach agreements and disagreements through various forms of interaction.[3]

Characteristics of Effective Groups

Groups should function effectively to achieve the goals and purpose. Characteristics of effective groups include:

- Groups should have relaxed, comfortable and informal atmosphere;
- The purpose of the group should be well formulated, understood and accepted by members;
- Members should have good listening skills, patience and participate in task-related discussions;
- Members should express their ideas and feelings without any hesitations and preconceived notions;
- Conflicts and disagreements should take place around the task, but not around the personalities;
- Groups members should aware and mindful of their purpose related functions and activities;
- Group decisions should be based on conscious and agreement but not based on majority voting;
- Group members should have an understanding of each others' strengths and weaknesses, so that each one can try to minimize other's weaknesses through their contribution;
- Group roles should be clearly determined and assigned. However, members should be given freedom to attend to others' work in times of need and emergency.[4]

People come together both physically and or virtually for several purposes or due to various forces. In addition, people join groups to get various kinds of benefits. Now we shall study why people join groups or the need for group formation.

(B) GROUPS IN ORGANISATIONS

Formation of groups is necessary as man is basically a social being. Most of the people prefer to live and work in groups. In addition, the following factors are also responsible for the formation and development of groups:

(i) **Security:** Groups provide security to its members from others in the society, from the threats posed by other groups, insecurity caused by the environmental, climatic, life, economic, social and other factors.

(ii) **Empowerment through sharing of resources:** Groups provide facilities and opportunities to the members to exchange their skills, knowledge, talents, values, etc. Group members exchange their ideas, opinions, skills and talents among themselves. This process enables the individuals to gain more knowledge, strengths, competence and acquire expertise by sharing from each other of the same group. Group members also gain expert power from others. Thus, the group empowers the members.

(iii) **Becoming a leader:** People with leadership skills and with a desire to become a leader enable the formation of the groups. They at least initially lead such groups. For example, outside political leaders used to form groups and convert these groups into trade unions in India during 1940s to 1960s. Some of these important leaders are Mr. Jayaprakash Narayan, Mr.V.V.Giri, Mr. Khandubhai Desai, Mr.George Ferandez and Mr.Shankar Dayal Sharma.

(iv) **Synergy:** Groups provide the benefit of synergy. Synergy takes place when the outcome of the group effort is greater than the sum of the individual contributions of the group members. Group activity results in synergy due to exchange of skills, knowledge, talents and ideas and enhancing them through brain-storming and interactive sessions among the group members.

(v) **Goal attainment:** Organizational goals on most cases can't be achieved by individual efforts. Most of the organisational goals can be achieved by the integration of skills, knowledge and expertise of and coordinated effort of the employees.

(vi) **Status:** People possess enhanced status as a member of a group rather than as individuals. Mr. Ranga Kumar says that he enjoys better status as personnel officer of Human Resources Department of L&T, Tadipatri rather than individually. This is because most of the people in the business and academia didn't recognize him before he joined L&T, Tadipatri.

(vii) **Affiliation needs:** Members can satisfy their social needs by interacting and sharing their social problems with other members of the group. People use on-the-job interactions as a place for satisfying their social needs. Thus, group membership satisfies belonging and affiliation needs of the employees.

(viii) **Self-esteem:** Group membership provides a feeling to the members that they are more worthy as a member of a group than individually.

Now we shall discuss advantages and disadvantages of groups.

Advantages and Disadvantages of Groups

Like any other aspect of an organization, groups also have advantages and disadvantages.

Advantages of groups include:

- People come together to achieve a specific purpose in organizations;
- Groups can enhance organizational productivity through synergy;

- Highly cohesive groups with positive orientation produce results with greater efficiency;
- Groups result in collaborative effort;
- People with complementary skills in a group would produce similar results like those of teams;
- Groups would make highly balanced decisions that involve less risk;
- Groups share information and data openly and efficiently;
- Group work produces best results in collectivism societies like Japan, India and Papua New Guinea;
- Groups formulate more shared and realistic objectives, strategies and goals;
- Group meet individual employee needs and support each other particularly in times of crisis that can't be met otherwise in an organization;
- Groups also meet organizational needs with less cost and other resources requirements due to synergy;

As every coin has two sides, groups have certain disadvantages. We now discuss them.

Disadvantages of Groups Include:

Certain group goals are in conflict with organizational goals.

- Certain group goals are in conflict with organizational goals. For example, achieving highest productivity would be organizational goal while achieving group goal along with protecting members' interest may be the group goal. Under such circumstances, protecting the interest of inefficient employees in a group hinders organizational performance;
- Certain group goals are in conflict with individual goals. For example, efficient employees try to produce more while groups would like to reduce the performance of high performers in order to balance with that of low performers in order to protect the interest of all members;
- Group performance may be affected by dysynergy due to social loafing;
- Highly cohesive groups with negative introduction or improper understanding of group and organizational goal would hamper organizational interest severely;
- Social loafing would hamper group relations due to inequity in contributions;
- Group members with similar opinions and ideas will produce routine decisions while group members with widely varied opinions and ideas will land in indecisions and confrontations;
- As is said that everybody's responsibility is nobody's responsibility, group members may not feel responsibility for results;
- Group members may take less risky decisions as they would like to safeguard group's interest;
- Group members of the same profession and background may not have much to share and fail to get the benefit of sharing and interacting;
- Groups fail to produce results in individualistic societies;
- Members with more of individualism would hamper group interest as well as goals;
- Groups of inappropriate size and structure would produce negative results;
- Mechiavellian and/or political behaviour particularly result in informal groups would result in negative impact of groups in organizations.[5]

Now we shall discuss different types of groups.

(C) TYPES OF GROUPS

Types of groups include: formal, informal, command, task, interest, friendship, primary, coalitions.

As discussed earlier, different people join groups with various purposes or due to the forces of different factors. Consequently, different types of groups are formed. They are:

(i) **Formal Group:** When two or more individuals join together as a group due to the official job structure and job relationship in an organisation, such a group is called *formal group*. Group of production manager, materials manager and quality control manager of a company is an example of formal group.

(ii) **Informal Group:** When two or more individuals join together as a group in order to satisfy their social needs but not due to official job structure and organisational requirements, such a group is called *informal group*. Informal groups are formed out of the common interests, aptitudes, values, opinions, ideas and characteristics of the people. For example, three employees from production department, marketing department and the finance department gather in the company's meeting hall and discuss current economic issues. This is an example of informal group.

(iii) **Command Group:** It is a group of the superior and his/her subordinates. Finance Manager and Assistant Finance Managers of a company form a *command group*. Thus, the command group is a group of individual employees and the manager to whom they report.

(iv) **Task Group:** People working together in order to accomplish a particular task form a *task group*. Task group boundaries are not limited to the particular department, but they may spread throughout the organisation, and sometimes spread even beyond the organisation. For example, Human Resources Manager, Finance Manager and Production Manager form a negotiation group in order to settle a salary dispute of factory workers. This negotiation group is an example of task group.

(v) **Interest Group:** People with common interests like maintaining and developing working conditions, recreational facilities, providing employee services, etc., form the interest group.

(vi) **Friendship Groups:** People with common characteristics form groups. These common characteristics include hard working, work avoiding, smart working, status seeking, family orientation, risk taking, etc. For example, two employees from the production department and marketing department with a common character of work avoiding, making friendship and forming a group in order to defend each other's behaviour is called friendship group.

(vii) **Primary Groups:** If the individuals with a feeling of comradeship, loyalty and a commonsense of values form into a group. Such group is called a *primary group*. Group of family members *viz*., father, mother, brother and sister is an example of primary group.

(viii) **Coalitions:** Individuals from different groups form into an ad hoc group in order to achieve a specific task or goal. Such groups are called *coalitions*. The individuals have dual membership, *i.e.*, one in the original group and another in the coalition. The coalition gets dissolved after the goal for which it is formed is attained. The characteristics of coalition include:

(a) interacting group of individuals,

(b) deliberately constructed by the members for a specific purpose,

(c) independent of the formal organisation's structure,

(d) lacking a formal internal structure,

(e) mutual perception of membership,

(f) issue-oriented to advance the purposes of the members,

(g) external forms, and

(h) concerted member action, act as a group.[6]

These different types of groups form and are developed through various stages. Now we shall discuss the stages of group formation and development.

(D) STAGES OF GROUP FORMATION AND DEVELOPMENT

Groups are formed and developed through various stages. Bruce Tuckman has developed five stage model of group process.These stages are forming, storming, norming, performing and adjourning. Figure 17.1 presents Tuckman's five stage model.

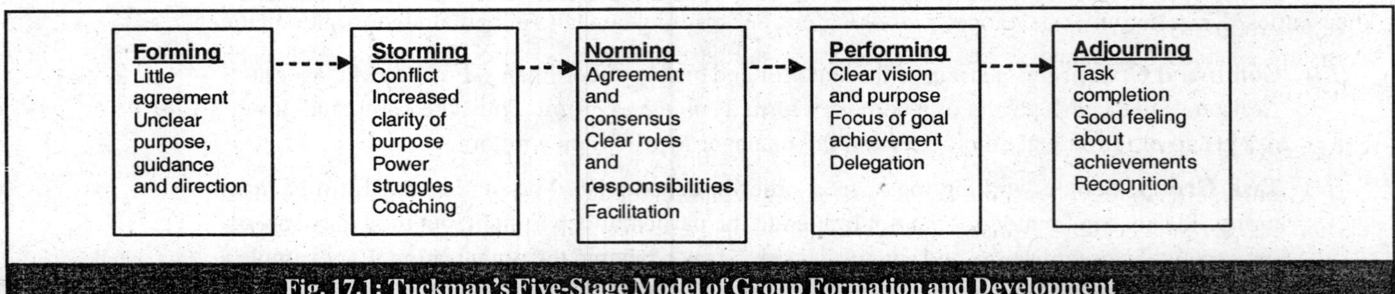

Fig. 17.1: Tuckman's Five-Stage Model of Group Formation and Development

Stage 1: Forming

Stages of group formation include: forming, storming, norming, performing and adjourning.

Individuals during the initial stage are not clear of the purpose for which they would like to form into groups, other members, structure of the group, group tasks, leadership and group process. This stage is characterised by uncertainty and confusion. Members observe others, various events and issues and decide what type of behaviour is acceptable. Thus, members 'test-the-waters' during this stage and decide within themselves as part of a group. This stage is the potential source for intra-group conflicts as individuals feel that individual interests and preferences are shadowed by those of the group as well as other members of the group. In addition, members are confused of the hierarchy and the control points. Once, members cross this stage, they are clear of the hierarchy and relationships.

Mr. Chandra of Reliance could not join with other employees, interact with them openly during his early days of employment as he did not know the characteristics, traits, views and behaviour of others in the company. This is because Mr. Chandra was not clear of human relations structure and group hierarchy of Reliance during that period.

Stage 2: Storming

Storming stage is characterized by conflict and confrontation among the group members due to confusion over relationship, hierarchy, purpose and direction. In addition, people resist the imposition of others' interests over their interests. During this stage, members accept the group, but there would be conflict over the leadership, objectives as well as relationship. Thus, this stage is also a source of intra-group conflict. Members know the hierarchy and chain of command when the leader within the group is determined. This stage is complete when the members are clear about the leader, purpose and the hierarchy.

Mr. Prakash joined the Finance department of TELCO in 2009. The Chief Finance Manager asked him to work with the other three Assistant Finance Managers of the department. The other Assistant Finance Managers imposed various limitations on the work activities and interests of Mr. Prakash. This stage created a conflict between Mr. Prakash and others for two months. This process of confusing and confronting stage is called storming. Later, Mr. Prakash was made clear that Mr. Chandra one of the Assistant Finance Managers supervises the work of all the Assistant Finance Managers.

Stage 3: Norming

During this stage members are clear of their leader, group hierarchy, purpose of the group and group relationships. So, members settle, start cooperating and collaborating with each other, develop close relationship among them, exhibit cohesiveness and prefer to identify themselves with the group during the norming stage. Members formulate common goals and expectations of the group.

Mr. Chandra explained the work activities, rules and regulations of work to Mr. Prakash and other Assistant Finance Managers. He started guiding and counselling all the group members in carrying out their duties. These activities developed close relations and a strong bondage of belongingness among the Assistant Finance Managers of TELCO. Members started cooperating and collaborating with each other.

Stage 4: Performing

Group members develop the relationships among themselves in the previous stage as explained earlier. Group members during this stage exert all their energies towards functioning and performing the tasks in order to attain the group goals. They share their ideas, skills, knowledge and competence in order to excel in the organizational activities forgetting their individual preferences and differences.

All Assistant Finance Managers of TELCO after developing close relations among themselves diverted all their energies towards achieving high performance and group goals by forgetting their egos and personal differences. This group achieved the targets with regard to the lowest ratio of debtors to sales.

Permanent groups continue to work as achieving orgnaisational objectives is never ending task until the organizations exist. But, temporary groups cease to exist, one their time-bounding activity or project-oriented purpose is accomplished. For example, the group formed to construct a hospital building ceases to exist, once the building construction is over and the building is handed over for running the hospital. Such groups are adjourned. Similarly, committees that are formed with a specific task are adjourned, once the task is achieved.

Stage 5: Adjourning

The Chief Finance Manager of TELCO appointed a two-member committee with Mr. Chandra and Mr. Prakash as its members to suggest the measures to reduce the amount of cash on hand. This Committee studied the issue and suggested the measures within two months of its formation. This group has been disbanded and adjourned immediately after its task was over.

Temporary groups like committees, taskforces, commissions and teams reach this stage after completing their task which is purely a temporary setup. This disbandment cause worry to some members due to loss of friendship and effective leaders. But the permanent or relatively long-run groups like formal groups in the organisations and informal groups either reach this stage rarely and that too in the long-run.

Punctuated Equilibrium Model

Though the five stage model of group formation is widely accepted and quoted, it is argued that this model is unrealistic in many situations. It is also established that conflicts take place in all the stages of group formation. Connie Gersick proposes that groups do not necessarily progress linearly from one step to another in a predetermined sequence as proposed by Tcckman, but alternate between periods of inertia with little visible progress toward goal achievement punctuated by bursts of energy as work groups develop. It is in these periods of energy where the majority of a group's work is accomplished.[7]

Stage of Group Formation and Performance

Normally, it is felt that group performance is highest during performing stage. But it is found that some people perform better during the stage of storming.

Normally, it is felt that group performance is highest during performing stage. But it is found that some people perform better during the stage of storming as their inner potentialities are realised due to the challenges posed by other members as well as group environment. Some argue that performance is highest even during the forming stage, provided the group norms, structure, hierarchy, rules and purpose are well written and provided to the members. A study of a group of three cockpit employees in an airline company produced highest performance in the first ten minutes of the group formation as the rules; purpose, relationships and hierarchy were written and provided to the members. It can't be concluded that the group performance would be highest during the performing stage. However, group performance may be highest during performing stage, when the rules and structures are not well defined and communicated to the members as well as members confront with each other to establish these during the storming stage.

Ad hoc Groups

Some groups are formed temporarily for a specific purposes and/or deadlines. Once that purpose is achieved, groups are dismantled or disbanded. Project teams, committees and commissions belong to ad hoc groups category. These groups formulate rules, specific purpose, relationships and structural hierarchies in the first meeting and then concentrate on the performance from the second meeting on wards. The group members will pay attention on disbanding the group structure in the third meeting.

Having studied the different stages of group formation and development, now we shall study the groups at the work place.

(E) GROUPS AT THE WORK PLACE

Groups at workplace are formal and informal groups.

Work place is more prominent for the formation and development of groups. Groups are formed both officially and unofficially at the work place. *Officially formed* groups are called *formal groups* and unofficially formed groups are called *informal groups*.

Formal Groups

Formal groups are relatively permanent. However, they get changed whenever there are changes in organisation structure, job structure, job design, etc. Formal groups are usually formed at the workplace. Management formulates the formal groups.

External Influence on Formal Groups

Various external forces influence the groups. Groups cannot function in isolation. They depend on several external factors. These external factors include:

Now we shall discuss these factors:

(i) **Line of command:** Organsations follow the superior-subordinate relationship in carrying out the organisational activities. Superiors and subordinates depend on each other. Superior commands the subordinate and the latter follows. Thus, the formal group with the superior and the subordinate is formed.

(ii) **Organisational structure:** Tall structures impose more controls and regulations. Managers in tall organizations control the activities of subordinates scrupulously. Therefore, span of management and control is narrow in tall structures, which in turn makes the small group as a viable unit. The flat structure provides freedom and autonomy to the employees. As such managers would not interfere in routine and normal activities of their subordinates. Therefore, a large number of employees interact with each other. The span of management and control is large in flat structures. Thus, flat structure makes a large group as a viable unit.

Mr. Sharma, Branch Manager of Andhra Bank says that their bank allows the formation of small groups while Mr. Kishore of ICICI Bank says their bank allows the formation of larger groups.

The tall structure of Andhra Bank is the reason for the formation of small groups and the flat structure of ICICI Bank is responsible for the formation of large groups.

(iii) **Nature of work:** Performance of routine duties enables the formation of larger and loose groups as employees need not concentrate on new and critical ideas and issues. In contrast, the strategic and critical work demands the employees to discuss various issues closely with other employees. The work requiring close interaction among colleagues and does not allow them to discuss with larger groups. Therefore, the strategic nature of work allows the formation of smaller and closely knitted groups.

Mr. Michael of the Accounting Department of Hero Honda is a member of a large group and there is no close bondage among the group members. Mr. Michael and his colleagues mostly perform routine duties. Mr. Nissar of Modi Xerox is a member of a small group as they make decisions, implement them and follow them up.

(iv) **Areas and levels of decision-making:** Managers make the decisions regarding different areas like marketing, human resources, etc. The most important areas are finance and marketing. The significant areas of decision-making require the close interaction and involvement of employees, which in turn requires the formation of small groups. In contrast, the decision-making regarding the non-significant areas allows the formation of larger groups.

Similarly, decision-making at the lower level requires a small group interaction and vice-versa is true in case of top level.

(v) **Formal regulations:** Too many formal regulations framed by the management allows the formation of larger and loose groups as the relations among the group members are mostly mechanical. In contrast, the fewer formal regulations require human judgment and intensive thinking process. As such, they allow the formation of small groups with closer bondage.

(vi) **Company's human resources:** Composition of the company's human resource in terms of attitude of the employees towards working together, their family background, regarding the degree of living together, educational background regarding the studying together, aptitude regarding meeting the challenges jointly influence the size of the group and cohesiveness of the group.

(vii) **Performance appraisal and reward system:** Groups form and develop, if the company's performance appraisal is based on group appraisal. Otherwise, employees tend to work individually. Similarly, if the company has the group reward system, groups form and develop out of necessity. Alternatively, if the company has individual reward systems, group formation and development are hindered greatly.

(viii) **Job design:** Job design of the company is the main basis for the formation and development of formal groups. If the jobs are designed tightly and structured rigidly, employees would be forced to work individually, separately and in isolation. These aspects of the job design hinder the formation and development of groups. If the jobs are designed loosely providing for interaction and involvement, employees would be encouraged to work in groups. In fact most of the organizations are designing flat structures and thereby lose jobs after liberalization and globalisation. Lose jobs enhance employee performance and thus enable the organization to perform better and meet the competition.

Mr. Anil Verma of LML views that the people in their company work in groups mostly because the individual jobs are designed loosely and structured in a more flexible way.

Most of the companies including the public sector units like BHEL, SAIL, etc., have also been encouraging group work formally after the announcement of liberalisation, privatisation and globalisation. This practice is widely prevalent in the private sector as groups provide the benefit of synergy to the company.

(ix) **Customer needs:** Customer is the end for most of the businesses after globalisation. Most of the private companies like Uninor are structuring their organisations and jobs based on customer needs. Customer needs regarding the products and services vary. Some customers need integrated product and services. Mr. Kartik of Airtel says about 30 per cent of their customers need instruments and also a full package of value based services. Employees of all units of such organizations work very closely to provide closely integrated package of instruments and services to the customers. Therefore, such areas and departments form and develop highly integrated groups.

Highly integrated groups are not necessary, if the customers need only a product like in fast moving consumer goods industry (like soaps, toothpaste and cosmetics). Thus, customer needs influence much in forming and developing groups in organisations.

(x) **Organisational crisis:** Management of Visakhapatnam Steel Plant of SAIL formally formed temporary groups during the period of its sickness during 1998-2000. In fact, these groups helped the company to turn around the plant. Similarly, A.P. Paper Mills and Rourkela Steel Plant formed the ad hoc groups in order to turn the sick units into profitable units.

Organisational crisis cannot be dealt by individual employees. In fact, they have to be dealt and managed from all angles simultaneously by a group of employees. Therefore, organisations form close-knitted and highly integrated groups to manage their crisis situations.

(xi) **Organisational strategies:** Strategy is an integrated and unified action in order to achieve organisational goals. Strategy is to be implemented by a group of employees belonging to different functional areas. Groups are formed and developed in order to implement organisational strategies. Organisational strategies like mergers and acquisitions need a larger and highly cohesive group for their successful implementation. Strategic business unit (SBU) level strategies like development of a new product need a relatively small group with 5 to 6 members with cohesiveness. The functional strategies like outsourcing need a

small group of 2 to 3 employees. Thus, groups with different sizes and with different degrees of cohesiveness are formed and developed in order to implement the organizational strategies. ITC formed a large group of executives to implement its diversification strategy of establishing hotels.

(xii) **Company resources:** Most of the organisations do not possess all kinds of resources. Such organisations develop the deficit resources through group action. Thus, organisations need to form and develop groups in order to acquire all kinds of resources.

(xiii) **Organisational culture:** Organisational culture is a system of shared meaning held by members that distinguishes the organisation from other organisations.[8] Organisational cultures are classified as dominant cultures, sub cultures, strong cultures and weak cultures. If the organisation's dominant culture is working together, the new employees would also adopt to such culture and start working along with other employees.

If the existing employees work independently, the new employees should adopt to work individually, even though they prefer to work along with others. Culture of most of the Japanese companies is group culture whereas the culture of most of the American Companies is working independently.

Japanese subsidiaries operating in India and other countries follow the same organisational culture of group working. Therefore, Indians working in Japanese subsidiaries in India adapt to the group culture. Thus, organisational culture influences the process of group formation and development formally.

Formal groups are formed and developed out of the organisational requirements. Further, formal groups are structured and nurtured by the management. They contribute to the achievement of these goals. Having studied the formal groups, now we shall study the informal groups.

Formal groups are formed and developed out of the organisational requirements.

Informal Groups

Groups formed out of social interaction, social needs and psychological factors are *informal groups*. If two or more people join together as a group because of their common social needs, attitudes, likes and dislikes, values, opinions, personality traits and other psychological factors, such a group is known as informal group. Thus, the informal group is outside the officially prescribed relationships, structures, line of authority and responsibilities of the organisations. Though the organisations form formal groups, people prefer to form informal groups.

Need for Informal Groups

People perfer to form and join informal groups due to various reasons. They include:

(i) **Social relations:** People cannot live in isolation as they are social beings. In addition, most of the people would like to work along with others. They exchange their ideas, views, problems, experiences, etc., while working with each other. In addition, people satisfy their social needs like affiliation needs, belonging needs, need for involvement, interaction and participation, need to be heard, etc.

Physical proximity of work places, common personality traits, need for dependency of one member and providing security by another member encourage the employees to form informal groups. Thus, the need for social relations is the main cause for the formation of informal groups.

Informal groups naturally arise from human being's quest for social satisfaction. Keith Davis observed that, along with men's technical imperative, there is also social imperative to work together. Mr. Dwarakanath, Assistant Marketing Manager of Mahindra and

Mahindra prefers to join Mr. Alok of the HRD department during lunch time everyday as the latter listens to the former's problems, offers solutions and shares his ideas. Further, Mr. Alok supports Mr. Dwarakanath during his distress caused due to his failures in meeting the targets. Thus, both formed into a cohesive informal group due to the social needs.

(ii) **Insignificant role in formal group:** Some employees with the need of high degree of recognition and affiliation face the confronting situation, if their roles in the formal group are insignificant. This confronting situation forces them to fulfill their need through informal groups. Therefore, such employees form and join informal groups. Most of the trade union leaders in the past formed trade unions due to their insignificant role in formal groups.

Mr. Jogesh of Ranbaxy works in its Materials Management Department as a checker. His family members work as executives in various other companies. This insignificant role in the materials management department of Ranbaxy in comparison with his family background created a deficiency of social recognition in Mr. Jogesh and made him to take initiatives for forming a social group with the Manager of the marketing department and Assistant Manager, HRD of the company.

(iii) **Recognition for achievement:** Some employees fail to get due recognition for their job achievements and contributions to the organisation. The reasons for this situation are:

- Organisational politics
- Stealing the credit by the superiors
- Non-appreciative attitude of the boss and
- Lack of interpersonal skills by the employee concerned.

If the management fails to recognise the achievements of the employee, he is attracted by informal groups where he gets the recognition and words of appreciation for his contributions to the formal job.

(iv) **Failure to abide by the formal rules:** Some employees fail to abide by the rules and regulations of the company either due to their incapabilities or due to their state of mind or frustration. Such employees receive warnings or other kinds of punishments. This category of employers joins together informally for defending themselves and to challenge the formal authority.

(v) **To release frustration:** Employees experience frustration due to various causes in the organisation. They include: inconsistency of the leadership skills with the situations, inconsistency of rules and regulations of the company, conflicting job structure, job expectations beyond the capabilities of the employees and organisational politics. Formal groups may not provide the scope for the ventilation of employee frustration. Therefore, the frustrated employees join social and other informal groups in order to release their frustration.

(vi) **Techno-structure of the jobs:** The job design and structure of certain jobs is influenced more by the technical aspects rather than social and psychological factors. The incumbents of such jobs experience monotony, boredom and alienation. Therefore, employees performing such jobs prefer to form informal groups in order to free their minds and relax from the consequences of alienation, boredom and monotony.

(vii) **Low work pressure:** Certain jobs demand less work from the employees compared to their capabilities, skills, etc. In such cases, the employees have more of leisure time and

untapped potentialities. Employees use that leisure time and those of untapped potentialities for forming and developing informal groups.

(viii) **Tall organisation structure:** Tall organisation structures are mostly bureaucratic. They are characterised by strict controls, rules and regulations. As such, these structures are mostly mechanistic and the social needs of the employees cannot be fulfilled in the formal groups. As such, employees in these organisations prefer to form informal groups in order to satisfy their social and psychological needs which hitherto could not be met in the formal groups.

Having studied the reasons for the formation of informal groups, now we shall study the types of informal groups.

Types of Informal Groups

Informal groups are classified differently by various authors. Mayo and Lambard identified three groups[9] viz.,

(i) **Natural:** They are formed out of the natural course of action without any predetermined structure.

(ii) **Family:** This group consists of the regular members. Each member influences, moulds and determines the behaviour of other members.

(iii) **Organised:** This is a highly structured group with an acknowledged leader.

Sayles identified the four types of informal groups viz:

(i) **Apathetic Group:** Unaccepted leadership, lack of cohesiveness, disunity and conflict are the features of this group.

(ii) **Erratic Group:** Absence of control, inconsistent behaviour, and autocratic leadership is the characters of this group.

(iii) **Strategic Group:** These groups are highly organised, consistent and planned. They build up continuous pressure and take up grievance activity.

(iv) **Conservative Group:** These groups are characterised by cooperation, collaboration, unity to a moderate extent. They build up pressure to a limited extent. These groups also take-up grievance activity through trade union means.

Informal groups produce both favourable and unfavourable outcomes. First, we shall study the favourable outcomes of informal groups.

Advantages of Informal Groups

Though the informal groups are formed and developed outside the scope of organisational structure, they contribute to organisational goals, employee satisfaction and welfare. As such, most of the companies recognise the informal groups and started encouraging the formation and development of informal groups. The favourable outcomes of informal groups include:

Informal groups also contribute to organisational goals, employee satisfaction and welfare.

(i) **Collaborative group:** Members of common interest, values and aptitude join together and form informal groups. These members understand each other's values, ideas, habits, aptitude etc. They mould their aptitude and values in order to accommodate others' values. Sometimes group members also sacrifice for others. Thus, all the members of the group have the same values, aptitude, attitude and as such formulate and achieve common goals. Thus, informal groups develop collaboration among the group members. Formal groups can achieve cooperation but they can rarely achieve collaboration. Efforts of the informal group would result in synergy benefiting the total organisation.

(ii) **Employee satisfaction:** As indicated earlier, employees who cannot have status, significant role and recognition in formal groups, join informal groups. This is because informal groups provide status, significant role and recognise employees' achievements. In addition, informal groups provide wide scope for interaction to the employees across the organisational hierarchical levels and across the departments. In simple terms, an assistant finance manager can interact with the General Manager of his company, share his ideas, discuss his family and career issues, etc. Thus employee experiences social satisfaction.

In addition, the informal groups at the work place reduce boredom, monotony and the feeling of alienation. They provide conducive environment for social interaction. The enhanced socialisation process improves the employee job satisfaction. Thus, informal groups contribute to employee satisfaction.

(iii) **Efficient employee performance:** The informal groups exert the employee skills, knowledge, abilities, etc., and direct them towards the job performance. Further, reduced boredom, monotony and alienation also pave the way for directing employee resources towards job performance. In addition, these groups provide favourable social and psychological environment and enable the employees to come up with creative and innovative ideas. All these aspects of informal groups enhance employee performance on the job.

(iv) **Norms of behaviour:** Informal groups also formulate and maintain norms, mostly unwritten. In fact, the members follow the norms willingly and effectively. These norms provide the guidelines for good conduct, and acceptable activities to the majority of the members of the group. In addition, the informal group specifies other norms such as honesty, loyalty, sacrifice for the group, cooperation, collaboration, etc.

Though the informal groups formulate norms for their conduct, they do also mould and shape the employee behaviour in tune with the organisational requirements regarding employee behaviour. In fact, informality with the formal group certainly enables the members to follow the norms more willingly and behave in the manner of organisational expectations.

(v) **Protection to members:** Members of the informal groups interact very intensively with each other, share their resources and talents. This process enhances group cohesiveness. The group with a high degree of cohesiveness achieves high degree of unity and strength. Such informal groups protect members from social uncertainties, economic fluctuations, psychological problems and physically unsafe conditions. Informal organisations also protect the members from the top management's autocratic and bureaucratic decisions.

(vi) **Effective communication:** Communication in formal groups flow through official channels of authority and mostly from the top to bottom. The parent ego of the superiors mostly does not allow the free flow of communication from bottom to top.

In contrast, communication flows freely through all directions in informal groups. In addition members in informal groups send and receive communication with an open mind. Members receive the information that is actually sent by the sender. Further, they understand the message in the same meaning and sense of the sender of the message. The purpose of the communication is served mostly in the informal groups. Thus, the communication would be effective in informal groups.

(vii) **Effective human resources management:** Line managers can manage the employees effectively, when the former understand the traits, skills and qualities of the latter. Informal groups allow the managers to interact with their employees closely and understand them. In other words, managers understand the skills, qualities, characteristics, needs and desires

of the members of the informal groups. Having understood the subordinates, the line managers manage the human resources effectively. Thus, informal groups enable managers to manage the human resources of the organisations more effectively.

(viii) **Improved productivity:** Informal groups improve employee commitment, loyalty and understanding. In addition, informal group members contribute their human resources to the maximum extent, which in turn maximizes employee productivity.

Most of the global companies experienced these favourable outcomes and realised that the informal groups provide maximum contribution to the organisational goals when they are interwoven with the formal groups. As such, these companies allowed the formation of informal groups within the formal groups, work in coordination with them which result in collaboration between both these groups. However, the proverb, "every coin has two sides" indicates that the informal groups can create hindrances to the organisational process.

Global companies allowed the formation of informal groups within the formal groups, work in coordination with them which result in collaboration between both these groups.

Now, we shall discuss the hindrances caused due to informal groups.

Disadvantages of Informal Groups

As indicated earlier, informal groups are not only functional but also dysfunctional. The dysfunctional aspects of informal groups create hindrances in the organisational process. They include:

(i) **Challenge the formal authority:** Employees derive power from the informal groups. They challenge the formal authority of their superior with the help of power they derive from the informal groups. This may result in insubordination.

(ii) **Challenge the formal leadership:** Formal leaders direct and influence their subordinates. They also lead and motivate the members of the formal group. The same members also belong to the informal group and the informal leader also leads them. Thus, the same employees are led by both the formal leader and informal leader. Both of them may lead differently. In most of such cases, the employees prefer the informal leader rather than the formal leader. Thus, the informal leader challenges the formal leader. For example, trade union leaders challenge the authority of the General Manager.

(iii) **Role conflict:** Members of the informal group are also the members of the formal group and they may play conflicting roles in these two groups. Formal groups require adherence to rules, hierarchy and regulations whereas informal groups require more of adherence to relationships and interests. The conflicting norms of these two groups sometimes result in conflicts. Thus, informal groups may result in role conflict.

Mr. Subrahmanyam works as Research Analyst in the General Manager's office of Kakatiya Cements Ltd. Thus, he attends to various needs of the General Manager as he is the subordinate of the latter. But as leader of an informal group Mr. Subrahmanyam teaches Palmistry to a number of people including the General Manager. Mr. Subrahmanyam faces the problems of conflicting roles of subordinate in the formal group and leader in the informal group.

(iv) **Miscommunication:** Informal groups sometimes create rumours and may fail to communicate the correct message.

(v) **Resistance to change:** Formal organisations plan to introduce changes for growth and development. But the informal groups prefer to continue the status quo. Therefore, informal groups resist the changes.

(vi) **Confirmity:** Leader and members of the informal group influence and exert pressures for conformity. They disobey the formal commands and controls, once the group activities are confirmed.

Most of the managements discourage the formation and avoid the informal groups in view of the hindrances caused by them. But the modern managements prefer to modulate and rationalise the informal groups as there are clear benefits of these groups.

Having studied the formal and informal groups, now we shall study the structure of the groups.

(F) GROUP STRUCTURE

Formal groups are structured while informal groups are mostly unstructured.

Formal groups are structured while informal groups are mostly unstructured. Formal groups are structured according to several variables, which determine the behaviour of individual members within the group and the overall group behaviour. The group structured variables include:

Group Norms

'Technical Personnel do not speak much.' Marketing people do not speak close to reality. 'Administrative personnel mostly confirm to the precedents.' 'Bureaucrats strictly follow rules.' These are some of the common behaviours of groups. Groups of people behave in a similar pattern. This type of similar behaviour of groups is called the *normative function* of groups. Normative function enables the managers why and how the group members behave as per the group norms. Now, we shall study what is a norm and what is meant by group norms.

According to Stephen P. Robbins, norms are, "acceptable standards of behaviour within a group that are shared by the group's members."[10] Norms specify the group members 'Dos' and 'Don'ts'. They also indicate the expectations of the group from its members'. Thus, norms influence and shape the individual behaviour in accordance with the group expectations.

Norms vary from group to group, but certain norms are common for groups. All the work groups have the common norms of achieving high performance, improving productivity, doing the job in the right time, working smart, etc.[11] Other common norms include appearance norms including dress, facial expressions, body language, social norms like treating the guests, friends, respecting the elders and superiors, salary levels, job family, etc.

Individuals' values and behaviour vary from that of the group's norms. But the group influences the individuals to modify their behaviour in accordance with the group's norms.[12] Adjustment of employee's behaviour to align with the norms of the group is called *conformity*.[13] Employees sometimes modify their attitude and behaviour willingly to conform with the expectations of the group as the employee is aware of other members of the group. Such groups are called '*reference groups*.'

Thus, employees modify their values, attitudes and behaviour in accordance with the group norms.

Roles

Mr. Tirumalacharya is in-charge of the Cigarette design in VST Industries and also an honorary Priest in the temple of the colony where many employees of the company live. He is very serious with his subordinates while at work and shares love and affection with the same employees while performing his duties in the temple. Similarly, he respects and obeys the orders of his boss in the company and feels embarrassed when his boss bends his head before him while he is in the temple. He occasionally experiences conflicting situations while making innovative decisions regarding the inputs for the cigarettes. These conflicting situations are regarding customer taste versus ethics. Mr. Tirumalacharya, thus plays a variety of roles in addition to the roles in his family in different dimensions.

Definition

Role is defined as a "set of expected behaviour patterns attributed to someone occupying a given position in a social unit."[14] Each role expects a specified behaviour pattern from the employee. Now we recall the previous example. Product design — job requires innovative skills, skills of being serious at work and also with the colleagues, exploit the unsatisfied want of the customer by infusing a new input into the cigeratte, etc.

Role Shift

But different roles expect different kinds of behaviour. The role of the Priest in a temple requires counselling, preaching, sympathetic, compassionate, accommodative and stress releasing skills. Mr. Tirumalacharya is able to shift his role quickly and perform both the duties efficiently. People normally have the abilities to shift roles and meet the expectations of the jobs and/or roles. The teachers who were student leaders earlier had different attitudes compared to their present attitude towards college administration and education system. Thus, they have the ability to shift the roles when the situation and its demands require new and changing attitudes.

Role Perception

Individual employees play different roles based on their own assumptions and views of their performance in the organisation. Thus, individuals perform the role based on his/her own perception of the role functions. This is known as role perception. In addition, individual employees play their role depending up on the expectations of others.

Role Expectations

Now we recall the example of VST industries. Other employees expect Mr. Tirumalacharya to be ethical while designing a cigarette as he is also a priest in a temple.

The belief of others regarding the role performance by the role incumbent is called role expectation.

Role Ambuiguity

The example of VST Industries indicates that the colleagues of Mr. Tirumalacharya expect him to be ethical while deciding the inputs whereas the management of the company expects him to design the product based on the customers' tastes. These divergent expectations result in ambiguity and such an ambiguity is called role ambiguity. When an individual is confronted with contradicting expectations from the role, the result is ambiguity of the role. The individual has to balance the expectations and reduce or eliminate the ambiguity.

Role Conflict

Mr. Tirumalacharya is expected to be at the workplace on an auspicious day and time and also be present at the temple at the same time, and offer prayers to the deily by the visitors of the temple. Mr.Tirumalacharya is confronted by the divergent expectations of the two roles resulting in conflict. Such a conflict is called role conflict. Role conflict results when an individual experiences that compliance with one role requirement may make more difficult the compliance with another role requirement.[15]

Group Cohesiveness

Information technology revolution along with liberalisation, privatization and globalisation (LPG) brought significant changes in the management of various businesses. The important among them are

Group cohesiveness is the degree to which group members are attracted to each other and are inspired and motivated to stay in the group.

Enterprise Resource Planning (ERP), Business Process Reengineering (BPRE) and Supply Chain Management (SCM). All these three concepts require the employees to work very closely through the groups. Group members are attracted to work closely and continue in the group when they perform innovative and challenging work. This is known as a high degree of cohesiveness.

Group cohesiveness is the degree to which group members are attracted to each other and are inspired and motivated to stay in the group.[16]

Group cohesiveness is high when:

- the employees spend more time for working together
- the group size is small
- group members interact with each other closely and frequently
- the group members have common threats
- members agree with the common goals
- the members aim at increase in the group status
- there is competition with other groups
- when they physically isolate the group.[17]

Exhibit 17.1 presents the effects of group cohesiveness and Exhibit 17.2 presents the factors that increase or decrease group cohesiveness.

Exhibit 17.1 Effects of Cohesiveness

Effects of Cohesiveness: Cohesiveness influences productivity. Cohesiveness alongwith induction and performance norms influences productivity.

- High cohesiveness along with positive induction of the employee to the work, company, colleagues, etc. leads to high productivity
- Low cohesiveness along with negative induction leads to low productivity
- High cohesiveness along with high performance norms result in high productivity
- High cohesiveness along with low performance norms leads to low productivity
- Low cohesiveness along with high performance norms results in moderate productivity
- High cohesiveness along with negative induction results in low productivity.

Exhibit 17.2 Factors that Increase and Decrease Group Cohesiveness

Factors that Increase Group Cohesiveness	*Factors that Decrease Group Cohesiveness*
• Group members spend more time with each other	• Spend less time with each other
• Small size of the group	• Large size of the group
• Frequent interaction among members	• Infrequent interaction among members
• Group members have common threats	• No Threats
• Agreement on Common Goals	• Disagreement on Common Goals
• High competition with other groups	• No competition with other groups
• Personal attractiveness	• Unpleasant experiences
• Favourable Evaluation	• Domination by one or more members

(**Source:** *Modified version from Andrew D.Szilagyi et al.,* "Organisational Behaviour and Performance," *1990, pp. 282-283.*

Social Loafing

Some members have the tendency of not contributing or reduce the contribution whenever possible in the group environment and rely on the efforts of others for achievement of group goals. This situation is referred to as social loafing. Thus, social loafing occurs when, "one or more members of the group rely on the efforts of others members of the group and fail to contribute their own time, effort, thoughts, or other resources to a group."[18] Social loafing or free riding results in reduction in group output though it is the normal character of some of the people. Some argue that social loafing is a rational behaviour of some people in response to inequity or when the individual efforts can't be measured. However, members may not resort to social loafing when the individual roles and tasks are clearly assigned and individual performance is measured categorically.

Social loafing results in reduction in group output though it is the normal character of some of the people.

Loss of Individuality

Intensive group activity with no clear-cut direction and purpose coupled with excitement and emotional imbalance would result in loss of individuality of members. Thus, loss of individuality is a 'social process in which individual group members lose self-awareness and its accompanying sense of accountability, inhibition and responsibility for individual behaviour.'[19] People engage in social loafing resort to violent and immoral acts as there won't be any direction and responsibility for individual as well as group acts. People resort to violent acts when they act in a mob during strikes and attacks. For example, attacks on Reliance businesses in Andhra Pradesh, India and on all government properties during separate *Telengana* state movement within Andhra Pradesh, India are examples for violent behaviour consequent upon loss of individuality. (See Box 17.1).

Box 17.1: Statewide Attacks on Reliance Stores

Congress activists on Thursday attacked Reliance outlets in many places in the state after private TV news channels aired a report allegedly filed by a Russian website that named Mr Mukesh Ambani in relation with the death of Y.S. Rajasekhar Reddy.

The report reportedly appeared in theeXile.ru, a Russian lifestyle magazine, on September 6 last year, four days after the death of the then Chief Minister in a helicopter crash. The report alleged that the crash was the result of a conspiracy.theeXile.ru was banned in Russia in 2008 and shifted to the United States where it is facing restrictions.

The report surfaced in local TV channels on Thursday evening, and triggered attacks on the outlets belonging to the company. Police promptly posted personnel to guard the outlets.

Employees and guards of Reliance Fresh in the city downed shutters and in some cases abandoned their stores after they came under attack by Congress activists. Two Reliance offices in Brodipet and Lakshmipuram were attacked and local activists staged a dharna, a report from Guntur said. In Vijayawada, company officials closed their outlets as a precautionary measure.

In Gandhi Chowk, Nellore, activists attacked a Reliance Web World showroom and damaged glasses and furniture. They burnt computers and fled before the police reached the spot with their forces.

In Tirupati, Congress activists led by the Tirupati Urban Development Authority (TUDA) chairman, Mr C. Bhaskar Reddy, stormed Reliance outlets.

In Visakhapatnam, petrol and retail outlets belonging to Reliance were damaged.

Activists in Khammam called for a district bandh on Friday as a fallout of the report. Two closed Reliance petrol bunks were burnt in the district.

When asked whether any action would be initiated against TV channels for triggering such attacks, Hyderabad police commissioner B. Prasada Rao said, "We will look into the matter after verification."

http://www.deccanchronicle.com/hyderabad/state-wide-attacks-reliance-stores-330 (Accessed on 22/01/2010).

Group Leadership

Leaders make significant impression on the group members in exerting their human resources towards organisational goals. Similarly, the inefficient leaders mar the group activities. Therefore, the management has to appoint an efficient employee as the leader of the group. The leader is expected to balance the expectations of the group members, management and the informal group. He has to follow different types of leadership styles depending upon the situational requirements.

Group Status

During the initial days of industrialisation, production group in the industries was treated on a priority basis compared to that of the marketing group, finance group and human resources group. This priority has been shifted to other groups over the period. This is because of the social requirements. In other words, when a variety of products were not available, the society used to give top priority to the production group. This type of priority or position given by the society to groups and group members is referred to as *status*.

Status is "a socially defined position or rank given to groups or group members by others."[20] Group members get high status or low status in the group based on their authority and performance. High-status members of the group have more freedom to deviate from the norms. This facility enables them to have the discriminatory powers in decision-making. Low-status members of the group should not have freedom to deviate from the norms as it leads to status inequality. Similarly, high-status groups should also have freedom to deviate from norms as it enables high organisational performance. In such cases, group members believe that there is status equality. Otherwise it results in status disequilibrium, which needs corrective behaviour.[21]

Group Size

Group size plays an important role in group behaviour. Certain activities like problem solving, investigation and inquiry need to be performed by larger groups. In fact, larger groups perform these activities efficiently. However, certain activities like decision-making can be efficiently performed by small groups. Smaller groups complete the tasks quickly and also work productively than the larger groups.

Research findings indicate that groups with odd numbers are preferable. Groups with five to seven members are efficient.[22] However, the size of the group needs to be large when there is social loafing among the group members. *Social loafing* is the tendency among the group members to extend less effort when working collectively than when working individually.[23]

Group Composition

Group members belonging to the same demography can do the non-creative jobs more efficientlv.

Groups are formed with a number of people, may be with the diversified skills and characteristics or with unified skills and characteristics. The modern and global organisation prefers diversified groups because diversified groups have members with varied skills, cultures and heterogeneous background which bring a variety of information to the company. Such information is useful to the company for making organisational strategies. Further, diversified composition of the group in terms of skills, knowledge, age, education, experience, gender, functional specialisation, personality traits, culture, etc., make creative decisions and perform creativity-demanding tasks.[24]

Group members belonging to the same demography can do the non-creative jobs more efficiently. Group demography is the degree to which group members "share a common demographic attributes such as age, sex, race, educational level or length of service in an organisation."[25]

The appropriate group structure should result in efficient group performance and sound group decision-making.

(G) COMMUNICATION NETWORK IN GROUPS

Communication is a process by which all forms of information are transferred from one person to the other. So, for the communication to take place there must be some information to be conveyed and there must be two or more persons — one to deliver the message and the other to receive it. Communication is said to be perfect only when the receiver understands it in the sense the sender expected him to understand.

According to McFarland communication is, 'a process of meaningful interaction among human beings. More specifically it is the process by which meanings are perceived and understandings are reached among human beings.'

Communication is said to be complete when the receiver has understood it in the same sense the sender has conveyed it. It is up to the sender to find out whether the receiver has understood the true meaning of the message. So a constant feedback becomes an essential component of the communication process.

Communication is said to be perfect only when the receiver understands it in the sense the sender expected him to understand.

Communication Channel and Network

Downward Communication

Downward communication flows from higher level to lower level in the organizational hierarchy. This type of flow is an essential character of an authoritarian atmosphere. Thus, downward flow of information is from superior to subordinate.

Upward Communication

Upward communication flows from lower level to upper level in organizational hierarchy. This flow is often hindered by managers in the chain particularly in case of unfavourable information.

Upward communication is necessary to offer suggestions, to lodge complaints, ventilate grievances, to response to the counselling, opinion survey, exit interviews, to discuss in meetings and participate in decision-making.

Methods of Improving the Effectiveness of Upward Communication

Group members initiate and encourage upward communication for the operational and organizational efficiency. Managements use the following methods to improve the effectiveness of upward communication.

1. Managing by Walking Around;
2. The Open-door/ Open-mind Policy;
3. The Ombudsman Position;
4. An Empowerment Strategy;
5. Participative Management;
6. Counselling, Attitude Surveys and Exit Interviews;
7. The Grievance Procedure; and
8. E-mail.

Communication Network

Groups establish communication flows with others in different patterns in order to facilitate the flow of information from one point (or source) to all other points. These patterns of flow of information are called communication network. There are innumerable ways or patterns of communication. There are a few frequently used networks.

Communication networks reduce the channels by which information flows. These networks are classified into two, viz., formal networks and informal networks.

Formal networks are typically vertical, follow the authority chain and are limited to task-related communications. In contrast, the informal network usually known as grapevine- is free to move in any direction, skip authority-responsibility relationship levels- The likely purpose of informal network is to satisfy social needs of the group members with a view to motivate the members of task accomplishment.

Formal Networks

There are three common small-group networks. These are chain, wheel, and star. The chain rigidly follows the formal chain of command. In the wheel network, communication flow depends on the superior to act as the central point for all group communications. The star or all-channel network all group members actively communicate with each other. This type of network is essential for teamwork.

The effectiveness of each network depends on the dependent variables. For example, speed of communication is fast in wheel and star. Accuracy of information is high in chain and wheel networks. Dependency on leader is high in wheel network. Members are highly satisfied in star network. Distortion is high in chain network and low in star network. Work overload is moderate in chain and star networks and very high in wheel network. All chain/star network is best for team work, which satisfies members as well as produces qualitative work. It is also clear that no single network will be the best for all occasions.

Informal Network

The informal network is widely used in informal groups and has three main characteristics, viz.,

- It is not controlled by management;
- Most employees perceive that they get reliable information through this technique; and
- It is largely used to serve the self interests of the members. There are no clear patterns of flow of information in informal network. Information can flow in any direction in this network.

Group Communication Networks

Group communication networks are mostly as follows:

Decentralised Communication Network: Groups that need to interact intensely for sharing information, skills and competency and need to work cooperatively and collaboratively resort to interactive communication networks. Members of this network have the facility of decentralized communication network. Members in decentralized networks work interdependently and in close coordination.

Centralised Communication Networks: Formal groups in tall organizations resort to centralized communication as the entire management and control is normally centralized in tall organizations. Communication flows from the manager to his/her subordinates who in turn pass the information to their subordinates.

(H) TEAM WORK — AN INTRODUCTION

Most of us normally assume that groups and teams are the same and group is synonymous to team. There are clear distinctions between the two concepts. First we discuss the meaning of the term team and then discuss the distinctions between the two terms.

Meaning

Team is two or more people with complementary skills join together to work interactively as a single unit and achieve a common purpose for which all of them held collective accountability. Complementary skills mean that the two members of the same team are not strong in the same skill. All members possess diversified skills that are necessary to achieve the common purpose of the team. Cricket team is the best example at this juncture. *Indian students might draw the example of 'Lagaan' movie wherein the members of the Indian cricket team are drawn based on complimentary skills that are necessary to achieve the common purpose of 'winning the game' against that of the British team.*

Team is two or more people with complementary skills join together to work interactively as a single unit and achieve a common purpose for which all of them held collective accountability.

Team members work interactively and collaboratively does mean that the members not only share data and information, but carryout the entire work without delineating the boundaries of roles and jobs. It does mean that everyone will not only carry their work, but also carry-out the work of others who are either unable to rise to the occasion or unable to attend to the work. Thus, the training manager is ready to do the work of recruitment manager and vice versa in times of need in human resource team.

Team members work as a single unit does mean that they work like a single individual with full coordination and collaboration without any room for overlapping and missing links/piece of an activity. Everyone in the team attend to any piece of activity that seems to be. Team members held collective accountability does mean that every one works from the end/final result in mind rather than escaping from the final result. Having discussed the meaning of teams, now we discuss the differences between groups and teams.

Groups versus Teams

We have discussed widely about groups in the previous section of this Chapter. As discussed earlier, group is a combination of two or more people formed with a purpose of achieving their common and shared goals through their interactive effort. Group is also a combination of two or more people as in case of a team. But, the group members need not have complementary skills as well as may not be held common accountability. Similarly, group members may not work as a single unit. Thus, group members come together to share information and work together, but not as a single unit. Exhibit 17.3 presents the distinctions between groups and teams.

Exhibit 17.3 Distinctions between groups and teams

Base	Group	Team
Skills	No stipulation	Complementary
Contribution and Performance and work as a single unit	Individual contributions	Collective contributions
Accountability	Individual	Collective
Purpose and Commitment commitment	Common purpose, but individual commitment	Common purpose and
Responsive to	Management's demands	Self-imposed demands
Interaction to achieve Goal achieve goal	Sharing information	Collective performance to
Impact of Synergy	Mostly no impact	Mostly positive impact

Skills: Groups are structured naturally with the people who join together voluntarily without any specific selection procedure. Therefore, group members may possess the same skills and ultimately groups used to heave duplicate skills. Teams are structured with a purpose and therefore team members are selected based on the skill requirements of the purpose or the project. Hence team members have complementary skills.

Contribution and performance: Group activity is divided into roles and tasks. These roles and tasks are delineated and entrusted to each member. Therefore, members contribute individually and these contributions are coordinated with a planned structure. Teamwork is entrusted to all members without categorically delineating the roles and tasks. Team members contribute collectively like a single individual performing the total task. Hence, coordination of activities in teams is done naturally without any pre-structured activity.

Accountability: As explained earlier, group activity is delineated into roles and activities and each of them are delegated to each member. Therefore, each member performs his/her role and task and assumes accountability to the role and task delegated to him/her. Team members are not delegated with clear-cut individual task and responsibility. As such team members perform tasks in an automatic coordinated approach. Therefore, team members assume joint responsibility and accountability for the end result.

Purpose and commitment: Group members as well as team members have common purpose. Group members commit individually to their respective roles and tasks. But, team members work in collaboration and commit to the final results as well as to the process of the project jointly.

Responsive to demands: Group members are lose in structure and therefore, await management's instructions and guidelines from time to time. As such members in a group respond to management's demands. Members in teams are structured tightly leaving no room for confusion and planned coordination. Therefore, coordination is achieved naturally and automatically. As such team members respond to self-imposed demands.

Interaction to achieve goals: Group members mostly interact with each other to share information. They work individually after sharing information. Team members not only share information, skills and experiences, but work jointly from the begging to the end of teamwork or the project.

Impact of synergy: Synergy results in teams as the sum of team output is more than the total output of all individual members. Synergy takes place in teams as a positive force is stimulated by the interactive and collaborative effort of the team members. Group activity normally does not produce any synergy as the group members don't work in collaborative approach where as team activity results in synergy. So team activity results in higher rate of performance than that of group activity.

Now, the differences between teams and groups are clear to us. Now, we will discuss types of teams.

(I) TYPES OF TEAMS

Types of teams include:work teams, project teams, high performance teams, improvement teams, self managed teams, semiautonomous teams and virtual teams.

There are several types of teams. They can be grouped as work teams, project teams, high performance teams, improvement teams, self managed teams, semiautonomous teams and virtual teams.

Work teams: Work teams are concerned with the primary organizational activities and organizational goals. These teams use organisation's resources to achieve organisation's goals and strategies within the activity/project assigned to the team. However, the basic orientation of these teams has been changed significantly over the period. Work teams during 1980s were to enhance good feelings of the members and now are to enhance productivity. They used to have one formal leader during 1980s and now have more than one leader depending upon the project. Exhibit 17.4 presents the shifts in work teams.

Exhibit 17.4 Shifts in Work Teams

Shift Factor	Teams in 1980s	Teams in 2000s
Underlying Purpose	To enhance good feelings	To enhance productivity
Leadership	One formal Leader	More than one leader depending up on the project
Organisational Level	Upper level	All levels
Performance Appraisal	Individual accomplishments	Team accomplishments
Measure of effectiveness	Feelings of members	Attainment of team goals
Typical Training	Inter-personal skills, getting along with others.	Wide variety of job skills, and soft skills.

Source: Adapted from Jerald Greenberg and Robert A. Baron, "Organisational Behaviour", Prentice-Hall of India, New Delhi, 2007, p.293.

Purpose/Mission: Work teams are designed with a specific mission/ purpose like innovation, and development of new products, serving customers, developing new markets, and the like.

High performance teams: Members of these teams are highly committed to each others' personal development and career success.[26] These teams work beyond the normal characters, scope and level of work teams. Members of these teams show mutual care, trust and respect for each other like families in the eastern countries. The additional characteristics of high performance teams include:

- **Empowering people to make decisions:** Members are empowered to make decisions relating their area of operation without waiting for the superior or others.
- **Sharing responsibility:** All the team members share the responsibility.
- **Common sense of purpose:** All the members agree to a common purpose as well as direction and follow it.
- **Focus on the task at hand:** Teams project the end results and the efforts of the individuals are drawn towards the projected end results.[27]

Improvement teams: These teams concentrate on improvement of existing systems, organizational improvement, finance improvement, sales improvement, etc.

Semiautonomous work teams: These groups have rights to make certain decisions and implement them without referring to the top management. These groups are empowered teams.

Self-managed and directed teams: These teams are autonomous in decision-making as well as implementing them. Members of the team manage themselves as well as team activities without the interference of the top management. In addition, members of these teams direct themselves as well as other members of the team.

- **Loose teams:** These teams are almost like ad hoc teams. These teams are used in independent routine work and assembly lines.
- **Collaborative team:** These teams are used for constant creative work.
- **Short-term specific problem/task teams:** These teams are used for temporary tasks.
- **Cross-functional team:** These teams are used when different kinds of expertise is needed.

- **Executive team:** Executive team is used at the top level in order to make use of cross-functional skills and knowledge by CEO.

(J) TEAM BUILDING STRATEGIES

Purpose of team building is to enhance efficiency of strategic management in an organization.

Purpose of team building is to enhance efficiency of strategic management in an organization. Teams enhance human resources of members and thereby members' contribution as members learn from each other. Teams use members' diversity as an opportunity to win competition. Teams work in collaboration to bring innovation and manage organizational change and development. Team building strategies include:

- Select those members who can contribute to the achievement of organizational goal/strategy
- Divergence of skills required
- Balance the team structure
- Each member should have something to contribute
- Free flow of communication
- Team Structure Follows Strategy
- Decide appropriate team style for the Strategy
- Cross-functional teams
- Cross-Cultural Teams
- Cross-Demographic Teams
- Cross-Team Role Players
- Strong Bonds with other Formal/ Informal Teams

Team Roles

Team structure is critical as team members should possess complementary skills as each member of the team is expected to play a different role. Team roles include leader, critic/challenger, implementer, external contact, coordinator, idea generator, inspector, contributor, collaborator, and communicator. Activities of each of these roles include:

- **Team leader:** Team leader finds new team members and develops the team working spirit, judge the talents and personalities of members, adopt him to overcome weaknesses and communicates efficiently with superiors as well as subordinates.
- **Critic/challenger:** Team critics or challengers act as a guardian and analyst of the Team's long-term effectiveness. They are never satisfied with anything less than the best. They analyse weaknesses of the members and possible failures of the teamwork and mercilessly correct faults. They act as devil advocates. These members further, challenge the goals, methods, and even the ethics of the team. They are even willing to disagree with the leader or higher authority and eencourage the team to take well-conceived risks. As such the team members and others appreciate the value of challenger's candour and openness. People describe the challenger as honest, outspoken, principled, ethical and adventurous.
- **Implementer:** Members of this category ensure momentum and smooth running of the team's actions. These members are born time-tablers. They predict possible delays and provide information before hand to the members.

- **External contact:** These members look after the team's external relationship, judge others' needs and provide resources to meet the needs. They grasp overall system and external agencies related to the organization as well as teams. They handle confidential information.
- **Coordinator:** The member playing this role pulls together the work of all members as a whole into a cohesive plan, understands interrelationship of tasks, sense priorities, grasp several things at one time, maintains internal contacts and networks and heads of potential troubles.
- **Idea generator:** The member playing this role sustains and encourages the team's innovative vitality and energy. He/ she is enthusiastic and lively with a zest for new ideas, sees every problem as an opportunity and never at a loss for a hopeful of suggestions.
- **Inspector:** The member playing this role ensures that high standards are sought and maintained, strict/pedantic in enforcing rules, judges performance of others, brings problems to surface and praise the members for success and find fault of other members.
- **Contributor:** Members playing this role provide the team with good technical information and data by doing homework, push the team to set high performance standards and to use their resources wisely. These members may become too bogged down in the details and data and do not see the big picture or the need for positive team climate. People describe these members as responsible, authoritative, reliable, proficient and organized. People also see the contributor as dependable.
- **Collaborator:** Members playing this role sees the vision, mission, goal of the team as paramount and are flexible and open to new ideas. They are willing to pitch in and work outside his or her defined role and are able to share the limelight with other team members. People view them as a big-picture person. They may fail periodically to revisit the mission, to give enough attention to the basic team tasks, and to consider the individual needs of other team members. These members are forward-looking, goal directed, accommodating, flexible and imaginative.
- **Communicator:** The member playing this role is a process-oriented member, effective listener and facilitator of involvement, conflict resolution, consensus building, feedback, builder of an informal, relaxed climate, positive "people person". People may see him/her as process and an end in itself. This member may not confront other team members, or may not give enough emphasis to completing task.

Team Building Interventions

Team building activities, for both kinds of groups, aim at

- Diagnosing barriers to effective team performance,
- Improving task accomplishment and improving relationship between team members.
- Understanding and managing group process and culture,
- Role analysis technique for role clarification,
- Definition and role negotiation techniques is important.

Diagnostic meeting may involve the total group and several sub-groups and require only a brief time in order to identify strengths and problem areas and to conduct a general critique of the performance of the group. Actual team building requires a subsequent longer meeting ideally held away from the work place. The purpose of this meeting is to improve the team's effectiveness through better management of task demands, relationship demands and group processes.

The role analysis technique is designed to clarify role expectations and obligations of team members to improve team effectiveness. Role negotiation intervenes directly in the relationships of power, authority and influence within the group.[11] A follow-up meeting evaluates the success of the action steps.

Purpose of Team Building

The purposes of team building are:

(i) to set goals or priorities;

(ii) to analyse/allocate the way the work is performed;

(iii) to examine the way a group is working and its process;

(iv) to examine the relationships among people.

The primary goal of team is maintenance of interpersonal relationships is secondary.

(K) ESSENTIAL CONDITIONS OF TEAM BUILDING

The essential conditions for team building include:

- Every member must have a clearly assigned role;
- The team must take collective responsibility for the action of each of its members;
- Team must speak with one voice;
- No appeal from one member to another;
- Good team is small in number;
- No inordinate difference in salary of members and
- Each member should be able to handle responsibilities of other members.

Ingredients of Team Building

The major ingredients of team building are:

- Get the right people together;
- Have a large block of uninterrupted time;
- Deal with high priority problems/opportunities;
- Work on all the identified problems;
- Structure in all ways to enhance the likelihood of success;
- Develop realistic solutions and action plans;
- Implement the solutions enthusiastically; and
- Follow up to assess actual vs expected results.

Building Teams Successfully

The essential hints to the manager to build the team successfully are:

- Hold small and informal meetings for minor problems and large and long meetings for strategic issues;
- Create a climate of cooperation;

- The rule of order is to pick easy problems first;
- Keep the atmosphere casual and light;
- Compliment the participants and strengthen the spirit of cooperation and collaboration;
- Keep an open mind;
- Don't harp on a pet idea and do not let anyone else hog the floor either;
- Encourage the subordinates to formulate the goals though you are the boss;
- Workers expect something to fulfill their goals;
- Help the members when they need it;
- Protect the workers when they do something wrong;
- Provide the members all necessary material, finance, etc.;
- Follow feedforward and feedback and keep the members informed always; and
- Be aware that the democracy is almost always the best policy.

Advantages of Team Building

The main factor in the success of Japan is teamwork. Team does wonders. It can do the things what the high technology cannot do. It creates an open and participatory climate. It improves communication, problem solving and interpersonal skills of the members. It results in high level group effectiveness, mutual influences, trust, confidence and personal involvement. It enhances the power of self-reliance, trust one's own capacities and manipulate the circumstances. It minimises interpersonal and intergroup conflicts and enhances collaboration and thereby enhance organisational effectiveness. Ultimately, it results in high organisational efficiency and productivity.

KEY TERMS

- Group
- Group Size
- Nominal Group
- Role Conflict
- Synergy
- Formal Group
- Strategic Group
- Cohesiveness
- Informal Group
- Collaborative Group
- Self Esteem
- Conservative Group
- Role Shift

QUESTIONS

1. What is a group? Explain the need for formation of groups.
2. Discuss the various types of groups and their characteristics.
3. Discuss the different stages of group formation and development.
4. Differentiate formal groups from informal groups.
5. Explain the need for informal groups.
6. What are the favouralble outcomes of informal groups?
7. Discuss the group structure.
8. What is group cohesiveness? Explain the factors those affect group cohesiveness.

REFERENCES

1. Stephen P. Robbins, "*Organisational Behaviour,*" PHI (P) Ltd., New Delhi, 2001, p. 218.
2. Homans, G. C., "*The Human Group,*" Harcourt Barce and World, New York, 1959.
3. John M. Ivancevich and Michael T. Matheson, "*Organisational Behaviour and Management*," Irwin Homewood, Illinois, 1993, p. 286.
4. Debra l. Nelson and James Campbell Quick, "Organisational Behaviour", Thomson Learning Inc., New Delhi, 2008, p. 285.
5. jack Wood et al., 'Organisational Behaviour',john Wiley and Sons Australia Ltd., Milton,2003, pp. 268-269.
6. William B. Stevenson et al., "*The Concept of Coalition in Organisation Theory and Research,*" Academy of Management Review, April 1985, pp. 261-262.
7. C. J. G. Gersick,'Time and Transition in Work Teams', The Academy of Management Journal, 31, 1988, p. 9-14.
8. E. H. Schein, "*Organisational Culture and Leadership,*" Jossey-Bass, San Francisco, 1985, p. 168.
9. Robert Dubin (Ed.), "*Human Relations in Administration,*" PHI, New Delhi, 1970, pp. 467-68.
10. Stephen P. Robbins, *op.cit.*, p. 230.
11. G. Blan, "*Influence of Group Lateness on Individual Lateness*," Academy of Management Journal, October 1995, pp. 1483-1496.
12. C. A. Kiesler and S. B. Kiesler, "*Confirmity,*" Addison-Wesley, Reading, 1969.
13. Stephen P. Robbins, *op.cit.*, p. 231.
14. *Ibid.*, p. 227.
15. Peterson et al., "*Role Conflict, Ambiguity and Overload,*" Academy of Management Journal, April 1995, pp. 429-452.
16. Keyton and Springston, "*Redefining Cohesiveness in Groups*," Small Group Research, May 1990, pp. 234-254.
17. J. L. Gibson *et al.*, "*Organisations,*" Irwin, Burr Ridge, 1994, p. 323.
18. K. H. Price, 'Working Hard to get People to Loaf', Basic and Applied Social Psychology, 14, 1993, p. 979.
19. Debra L. Nelson and James Campbell Quick, 'Organisational Behaviour', Thomson, p. 286
20. Stephen P. Robbins, *op.cit.*, p. 233.
21. J. Greenberg, "*Equity and Workplace Status,*" Journal of Applied Psychology," November 1988.
22. Thomas and Fink, "*Effects of Group Size,*" October 1983, pp. 145-159.
23. D. R. Comer, "*A Model of Social Loafing in Real Work Groups,*" Human Relations, June 1995, pp. 647-657.
24. R. A. Guzzo and G. P. Shea, "*Group Performance and Intergroup Relations in Organisations,*" in M. D. Dunnette and L. M. Hough (Eds.), "*Handbook of Industrial and Organisational Psychology,*" Consulting Psychologists Press, 1992, pp. 288-290.
25. Stephen P. Robbins, *op.cit.*, p. 236.
26. Katzenbach, "Teams at the Top", Harvard Business School, Boston, 1998.
27. Herbelin, " Work team Coaching", Riverbankbooks, Chang, 1999.

CHAPTER **18**

GROUP CONFLICTS AND NEGOTIATIONS

Chapter Outline

(A) Introduction
(B) Intra-personal/Intra-Individual Conflicts
(C) Interpersonal/Intra-Group Conflicts
(D) Intergroup Conflicts
— Key Terms
— Questions
— References

Learning Objectives

After studying this Chapter, you should be able to:

✓ Know the causes of intra-personal conflicts and analyse conflicts due to frustration, goals conflicts and role conflicts;

✓ Understand the causes of inter-personal conflicts and evaluate them through Transactional Analysis, and Johari Window model;

✓ Negotiate the means and strategies by which inter-personal or intra-group conflicts can either be avoided or minimised;

✓ Discuss the reasons for and the strategies to reduce inter-group conflicts; and

✓ Suggest how team building activity negotiate to solve group conflicts and enhance organisational productivity.

(A) INTRODUCTION

We have already studied various concepts of group in the chapter on "Foundations of Group and Team Behaviour." Now, we refresh the important concepts relevant to group conflicts and negotiations.

Group dynamics describe how a group should be organized and conducted. It encompasses the dynamics of interaction patterns within the group, the subtle and not-so-subtle pressures exerted by group members, the manners in which decisions are made in the group, how work gets done and how members' needs are met. Understanding group dynamics will enable managers to strategically and completely harness the synergy of the group members. Individuals join groups for security, social relations, affiliation, leadership, etc.

There are numerous types of groups. The important among them are primary groups, secondary groups, formal groups and informal groups.

Primary groups are small groups enough for face-to-face interaction, having a feeling of commandership, loyalty and a common sense of values among its members. Coalitions are very relevant to organisations. *Coalition is group of groups.*

Formal groups are collections of employees who are made to work together by the organisation to get the job done.

On the other hand, informal groups emerge on their own due to the affinities that develop among the group members.

Norms can be described as shared beliefs among group members as to which behaviours are appropriate, if one desires to be a part of the group. Status refers to the importance and difference that people give to others. Cohesion refers to the extent of unity in the group and is reflected in the members' conformity to the norms of the group, feeling of attraction for each other and wanting to be co-members of the group.

Having refreshed our cognition, now we shall study the conflicts and negotiations.

K. W. Thomas defines the term conflict as "a process that begins when one party perceives that another party has negatively affected, or is about to negatively affect, something that the first party cares about." Conflict may be a difference between what is expected and what really happens or is going to happen. It may be disagreement or misunderstanding with others or events. Conflicts may be over expectations, roles, goals, viewpoints, etc. They also may be struggle between or among incompatible interests, needs, goals, people, ideas, etc.

Conflict may be a difference between what are expects and what are happens or going to happen.

Conflicts also arise due to competition between individuals or groups for the same resources, opportunities, positions, markets, etc.

Shift in Views on Conflict

The traditional view is that a conflict whatsoever, is bad. Conflicts were viewed equal to violence, destruction and irrationality. They are further viewed as dysfunctional. It was viewed that conflicts were undesirable and as such, they should be avoided. The human relation school view that conflict is a natural aspect in the group process in an organization and as such they should be accepted as an inevitable part of group relations and functions. Therefore, conflicts can't be totally avoided. The modern view is that conflicts result in constructive competition and they enhance individual as well as organisational competitive ability and as such they are desirable up to a certain extent.

The interactionsists view is that conflicts that contribute to enhancing functional performance of the group are desirable and those conflicts that hamper relationships as well as group functional performance are undesirable and should be avoided, if possible and otherwise should be reduced. Thus, the desirability of conflicts is to be judged based on their contribution to group functions, group process and relationships. According to this view the conflicts that enhance group thinking, sharing skills, knowledge, creating innovations and thus contributing to highest and constructive group performance are known as functional conflicts and are highly desirable. Functional conflicts are close to task conflicts that are desirable. Conflicts that are mostly based on ego states as well as self-centred of the members contributing negatively to group performance are known as dysfunctional conflicts and are quite undesirable. Relationship conflicts are mostly related to interpersonal relations and mostly are dysfunctional and undesirable. Process conflicts are concerned with the formation, structure and process of group tasks and performance. Process conflicts are therefore inevitable and desirable.

The interactionsists view is that conflicts that contribute to enhancing functional performance of the group are desirable.

Exhibit 18.1 provides the details of shift in the views on conflict. The present day organisations realised that they can increase the value to the individuals, groups and to themselves by encouraging conflicts to a moderate degree. Organisations, however, should discourage and reduce the dysfunctional conflicts as they reduce the values.

Exhibit 18.1 Shift in Views on Conflict

Traditional	*Modern*
1. Conflicts leads to loss of individual and group temperaments, energies, etc.	1. Conflicts encourage competition. They result in exhancing competency of individuals, groups and organisations.
2. Conflicts are the result of improper policies, unreasonable goals and dreams.	2. Conflicts are the result of the natural course of living of people, existance of teams and organisations. Therefore, they are the result of challenging goals which is the order of the day of global competition.
3. Conflicts impose ceiling on human potentialities as they affect the human psychology and hurt the feeling of individuals.	3. Conflicts tap the unused human potentialities. Natural resources, etc., by creating challenge.
4. Conflicts destroy assets and waste the resouces and erode the value of existing assets. This leads to decline in organisational and country's effectiveness.	4. Conflicts create the value, enhance the value and create assets. They lead to organisational and country effectiveness.
5. Conflicts are undersirable. Therefore they should be avoided.	5. Conlicts to a moderate extent are highly desirable. Therefore, they should be encouraged to a moderate extent.

Conflicts

Conflict is the difference between the perception/expectation and reality. Conflicts are of different types. They are intra-personal, inter-personal/intra-group, and inter-group/intra-organisational conflicts.

(B) INTRA-PERSONAL/INTRA-INDIVIDUAL CONFLICTS

Intra-personal or intra-individual conflicts take place within one individual and is normally there within every person. These conflicts arise due to:

- A number of competing needs and roles;
- A variety of ways that drives and roles can be expressed;
- Various barriers which can occur between the drive and the goal;
- Attachment of positive and negative aspects of desired goals.

These factors complicate the human adaptation process and result in conflict. Intra-personal conflicts can be analysed in terms of the frustration model, goals and roles.

Conflict Due to Frustration

For example, the need of a CA (Chartered Accountant) student is to have a better economic and social status after completing his CA programme. His drive is to acquire financial managerial skills, leadership skills, secure excellent score in the examinations. His goal is to get a financial manager's job in a multinational company. If he fails to get success in his CA programme due (*barriers*) to lack of time for preparation or his psychological weakness, he may get frustrated. The defence mechanisms available to a CA student are: behaving aggressively with friends or family members (*aggression*), discontinuing the course (*withdrawal*), taking the examinations again and again until the course is completed (*fixation*) and trying to join another course and another job in another organisation (*compromise*). Frustration occurs when a motivated drive is blocked before a person reaches a desired goal. The barriers which stands as an obstacle towards achieving a goal may be outward or inward. Frustration normally triggers the *defence mechanism* in a person. The defence mechanisms include: aggression, withdrawal, fixation and compromise. Fig. 18.1 presents the frustration model.

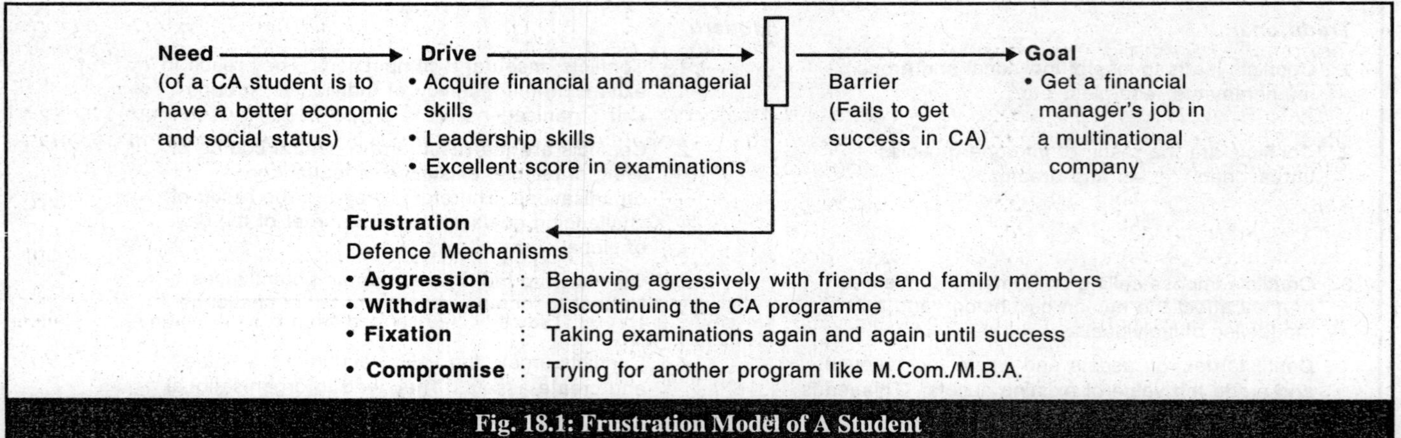

Fig. 18.1: Frustration Model of A Student

Goal Conflict

Another common source of conflict for a person is a goal which has both positive and negative features or two or more competing goals. But in the frustration model, the single motive is blocked before the goal is reached. Three separate types of goal conflicts are normally identified:

Approach-Approach=Two or more positive, but exclusive goals.

(a) Approach-Approach Conflict: A person is motivated to approach two or more positive but mutually exclusive goals. Trying for promotion from junior management position to middle level management position in the same company and trying for a middle level management position in another company is an example for this type of conflict.

Approach-Avoidance= Approach a goal and at the same time is motivated to avoid it.

(b) Approach-Avoidance Conflict: A person is motivated to approach a goal and at the same time is motivated to avoid it. The single goal contains both positive and negative features.[1] Trying for promotion and at the same time avoiding it if the promotion is accompanied by transfer to a disturbed place like Afghanistan or Iraq is an example of approach-avoidance conflict. Going to USA for higher education/ job in recent times(2009 and 2010) is also an example for approach-avoidance conflict for Indian youth. (See Box 18.1).

Box 18.1: Approach-Avoidance Conflict for American Dream: H-1B visa-holders being deported from port of landing!

Several Indians who arrived with an H-1B visa at Newark and John F Kennedy airports were deported based on a new rule, immigration attorneys and activists have reported.

The new rule stipulates that those who arrive on a work visa should 'arrive at the place of work'.

The rule could seal the fate of thousands of Indians who have applied for Green Card too.

It could bring an end to consultation, termed by some as 'body-shopping'. Airport deportations have frightened those on work visas and many have cancelled their travel plans, too.

"The airport deportations," Morley Nair, an immigration attorney based in Philadelphia, "have sent shockwaves through the H-1B community. H-1B employers, employees and their attorneys alike are flabbergasted by this brazen act of official highhandedness where individuals arriving on H-1B visas were singled out even before their primary immigration inspection, put through sham questioning, forced into making coercive statements, issued expedited removal orders, and sent back."

Their crime? They landed in the US with legitimate H-1B visas to work for genuine US employers, but at a location other than the employer's office that is, at a client site or third party site," he said.

"Fifty to 80 per cent of Indian H-1B visa holders come for a consulting company. Their companies will send them to client sites. The new rule stipulates that the petitioner of the visa should be present at the work place," according to Aman Kapoor, founder of ImmigrationVoice, an organization working for H-1B visa holders and Green Card applicants.

Kapoor said the number of airport deportations were few as the memo from Donald Neufeld, associate director, Service CenterOperations of USCIS, was issued only on January 8. But overzealous officers at airports began to use it in no time. H-1B employees working at a client site or a third party site is a practice as old as the H-1B program itself, and is not a violation of the regulations when supported by appropriate documentation, Nair said.

Source: http://business.rediff.com/slide-show/2010/jan/25/slide-show-1-h-1b-visa-holders-being-deported-from-port-of-landing.htm#content Top (Accessed n 25/01/2010).

(c) **Avoidance-Avoidance Conflict:** A person is motivated to avoid two or more negative but mutually exclusive goals. The person may not choose either of them and simply leave the situation. Motivated to avoid transfer to the branch office in Kashmir or another office in Sri Lanka is an example of this type of conflict.

Avoidance-Avoidance=Two or more negative, but exclusive goals.

Role Conflict

A variety of functions which are divided into jobs, positions and tasks should be performed by those associated with the company. They perform these functions with a view to attain objectives of the organisation as well as the individual employees. This function results in the specific behaviour of the individual.

Role is defined as the action performed by the person to indicate the occupation of this position.[2] Keith Davis viewed role as the pattern of actions expected of a person in activities involving others. Similar opinion has also been expressed by Newcomb that roles are ways of behaving towards others, which are defined for different positions. A role is dynamic. It refers to the behaviour of the occupants of a position, not all their behaviour as persons, but to what they do as an occupant of the position.[3]

Role reflects a person's position in the social system with its accompanying rights and obligations, power and responsibility.

Role reflects a person's position in the social system with its accompanying rights and obligations, power and responsibility. People need some method to anticipate others' behaviour in order to be able to interact with each other. Role performs this function in the social system.[4]

Thus, the role theory views the person as a member of the social system. Further, a person has several roles in the society like occupational role as a worker, family role as a parent, social role as a club member, religious role as a disciple, role in marketing as a consumer, etc. The role behaviour of an employee is influenced by the various sub-systems of the organisational system, the economic system, the social system, the religious system, policies, objectives, goals and programmes of the company, etc.

Role Perceptions

Activities of employees are guided by their views about their behaviour, *i.e.,* how they think about their behaviour at work. In other words, they are guided by their imagination about their own roles in reaction to the roles of others at work. This is called *perception* of employees about their own roles.

Employees must be highly adaptable to different situations in order to change from one role to the other without any delay as they perform difficult roles in dynamic situations. (See Box 18.2). Managers have to essentially change the roles quickly as they work with different levels and types of people like their superiors, subordinates, colleagues, field supervisors, technical and non-technical employees. Thus, for each manager, there are three different roles like superior, subordinate and colleague. Obviously, one cannot meet the needs of the other employees, unless one can perceive what they expect.[5]

Each manager experiences conflict of different roles as employees, managers, customers and government officials perceive and expect differently from his role and he cannot meet all his expectations without limiting/resisting others. This is mainly because a human being has limited resources and time. Thus, every employee has a role conflict.

18.2: Less than two years after Kevin Rudd took office as the Australian PM, more than half of his staff have left the Cabinet- Variations in role Perceptions.

Less than two years after Kevin Rudd took office as the Australian Prime Minister, more than half of his staff has left the cabinet.

Rudd, who had promised to rid Australia of workplace bullies, is described as "manic" by his staff, as he has emerged as a very "demanding" employer.

"He's demanding and a bit all over the place," News.com.au quoted one former staffer of the PM, as saying.

Another said: "He gives little in the way of constructive feedback. And he just doesn't listen to anybody."

At least 23 of 39 staff have left Rudd's office at a time when the next election is just one year away. Sources said more are set to follow suit.

In recent weeks, four senior advisors - including Jack Lake, a 25-year parliamentary veteran - have announced their departures, raising questions on Rudd's office management skills.

"That is a very high turnover rate. You need to look at the work environment and your recruitment (methods)," said Kathy Kostyrko, a recruitment expert.

Rudd has not apologised for the gruelling routine his staff has to undergo, and his department has already begun making replacements for the departed staffers.

A spokesman for Rudd said: "Political staff work is both rewarding and demanding - and working in the Prime Minister's Office is no exception." (ANI)

http://in.news.yahoo.com/139/20091017/900/twl-maniacal-kevin-rudd-is-a-boss-from-h.html (Accessed on 18/10/2009).

Role Ambiguity

It exists in organisations when roles are either defined inadequately or substantially unknown. In this situation, employees are not quite sure of playing their roles. Role ambiguity and role conflict reduce job satisfaction and need fulfilment.[6]

Having studied the intra-personal conflict, we shall discuss the inter-personal conflicts, i.e., conflicts between/among two or more people.

(C) INTERPERSONAL/INTRA-GROUP CONFLICTS

Interpersonal conflict arises when two or more individuals interact with one another. These conflicts are also called intra-group conflicts. Interpersonal conflict can be explained through *(i)* Transactional analysis and *(ii)* Johari window.

Transactional Analysis

This is developed and popularized by Eric Berne through his book on "*Games People Play*" and Thomas Harris through his book on "*I'm OK, You're OK*" respectively. Transactional analysis is the analysis of transactions between two or more persons. The major areas of transactional analysis can be explained through ego states, transactions and stroking.

Transactional analysis = Analysis of transactions between two or more persons.

Ego is a hypothetical construct and is used to help explain the complex dynamics of the human personality. Transactional Analysis uses three ego states, viz., Child (C) Ego; Adult (A) Ego and Parent (P) ego.

Child ego: *Child ego (C)* is the state in which the individual acts like an impulsive child. The characteristics of child ego include being submissive or subordinate, adaptive, emotional, joyful or rebellious. The child state is characterised by immature behaviour. For example, the Area Marketing Executive says to the Chief Marketing Manager, "you know better," when he is asked to offer a suggestion. The ego state of Laxmana when his mothers along with Bharat and Shatrugna came to the forest in the Ramayana may be referred to as child ego as Laxmana emotionally says to the Lord Rama " brother Bharat and Shatrugna are coming to wage war against us".

Child Ego: Submissive or subordinate, adaptive, emotional, joyful or rebellious.

Adaptive and free child egos: Child ego can be classified as adaptive child and free child. People sometimes listen to others and adapt themselves as per the requirements of others' needs as well as their own situational needs. Such state is referred to as adaptive child ego. For example, the subordinate accepts the decision of the superior and modifies his/her travel plans when the superior clarifies to the subordinate the conditions under which his/ her leave was not granted. People sometimes prefer to enjoy the life, and not to accept any responsibility. Such state is referred to as free child ego.

Adult ego (A): In the *Adult ego,* an individual acts like a matured person. The characteristics of adult ego state include 'cool-headed,' rational behaviour, calculative, objectivity, fairness, gathering and analysing information, logical choice, etc. Lord Rama collected all information from his mothers; Bharat and Satrugna when the latter came to the forest to explain the reasons led to disqualifying the former from being the king of Ayodya and request the former to accept the position of the king of Ayodya. Then Lord Rama analysed the information collected and made a decision of not accepting the position based on analysis of information, consequences of all alternative solution, etc. The ego state of Rama in this incident is referred to as '*Adult ego.*'

Adult Ego: 'Cool-headed,' rational behaviour, calculative, objectivity, fairness, gathering and analysing information, logical choice, etc.

Parent ego (P): In the *Parent ego* state, individual acts like a dominating parent. The characteristics of this state include: protective, loving, controlling, nurturing, critical, directive, commanding, etc. For example, people sometimes prefer to control others and critical of others' acts and decisions. Similarly, traditional superiors used to control and of critical of subordinates' activities as well as performance.

Parent Ego: Protective, loving, controlling, nurturing, critical, directive, commanding, etc.

Critical parent and nurturing parent egos: Parent ego is further classified as critical parent and nurturing parent. People under critical parent ego prefer to criticize others' activities, decisions as well as performance. People under nurturing parent ego prefer to be supportive of others' decisions and performance even though they fail to contribute to the achievement of organizational goals.

Transactions between ego states: A number of transactions take place between two or more individuals. They are classified as complementary, crossed and ulterior transactions.

Complementary Transactions

Transactions are complementary, if the message sent or the behaviour exhibited by one person receives the appropriate and expected response from another person's ego state. (See Fig. 18.2). Conflict does not arise between the transacting persons in complementary transactions.

P-C transaction: For example, the production supervisor tells the foreman to change the scheduling. The foreman obeyed the order. The production supervisor is in the parent ego state and the foreman is in the child ego state. This is a *parent to child transaction* {See Fig. 18.2 (a)}. The transaction between the production supervisor and the foreman is called *complementary transaction*. In this transaction, the foreman simply obeys the order of his boss without using his skills and knowledge. As such, this type of transaction does not allow the subordinates to grow. Further, the superior overestimates his competency and underutilises the human resources of his/her subordinates, which in turn leads to underutilisation of the organisation's human resources. However, this transaction is appropriate for routine decisions as well as activities where sharing of other's skills and expertise is not needed.

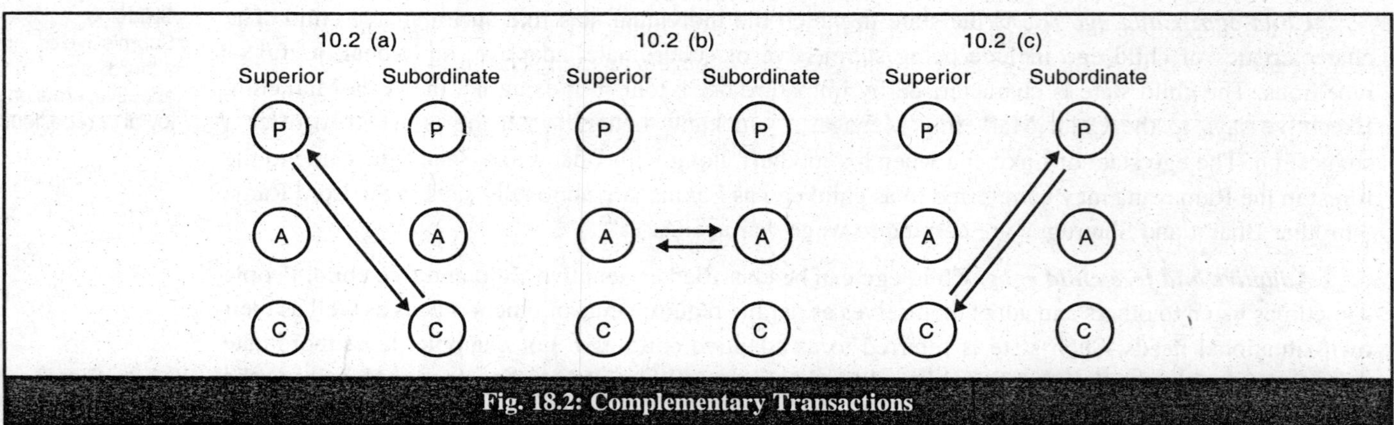

Fig. 18.2: Complementary Transactions

A-A transaction: In another incident, the Production Manager asked the Assistant Production Manager (APM) to suggest measures to reduce the cost of production. The APM analysed the data, identified the low cost sources and suggested measures to reduce the cost of production to the production manager. This transaction is *Adult to Adult transaction* {see fig 11.2(b)}, which encourages both the parties to think rationally and allows them to use their human resources. This type of transaction is useful to make strategic decisions as well as use the human resources of subordinates and to make most effective decisions. Further it enables the subordinates to satisfy the need for belongingness and other social needs. However, this transaction consumes more time and as such may not be needed for routine and less important issues.

C-P transaction: Mr.Prakash is a clerk in marketing department of Zuhari Cements, *Yerraguntla*- a faction area in Andhra Pradesh and also the Secretary of the Employees' Union of the Company. Mr. Prakash is a follower of powerful local factionist. Employees' Union resorted even to the physical threats in solving their problems in the past. One day, he ordered the marketing manager to promote the Marketing Executives as the Senior Marketing Executives. The Marketing Manager had to accept the order due to the power of the trade union. Subordinate (Mr. Prakash) assumes parent ego while superior assumes child ego due to compulsion or fear of physical threat. This is *Child-Parent transaction*

{See fig 10.2 (c)}. This transaction is also a complementary transaction, but is used by the powerful subordinates. These transactions also do not allow the employees particularly of superiors to use their human resources.

Crossed Transactions

Crossed transaction occurs when the message sent or the behaviour exhibited by one person's ego state is reacted to by an incompatible, (See Box 18.3) and/or unexpected ego state on the part of the other person[7] (see Fig. 18.3). For example, a customer came to the bank branch after business hours to encash a cheque and the branch manager ordered the officer concerned to pay the money (transaction is parent ego to child ego), but the officer replied as: withdrawals are not allowed after business hours (transaction is adult ego to adult ego). Crossed transactions are the source of much interpersonal conflict. The consequences of this type of transaction include hurt one's feelings and lead to frustration on the part of the parties and dysfunctional conflicts / consequences to the organisation. The branch manager, clerk and the customer in the previous example, experience conflict and frustration. This type of conflict is dysfunctional and damages the bank's image. Therefore, steps should be taken to avert crossed transactions by managing ego states of oneself and others.

Crossed transaction takes place between parent ego and adult ego, between parent ego and parent ego, between adult ego and child ego and child ego and child ego. These take place as one parent can't control another parent or one parent can't nurture another parent. Similarly two persons who are in child egos can't depend on each other or can't become subordinates to each other.

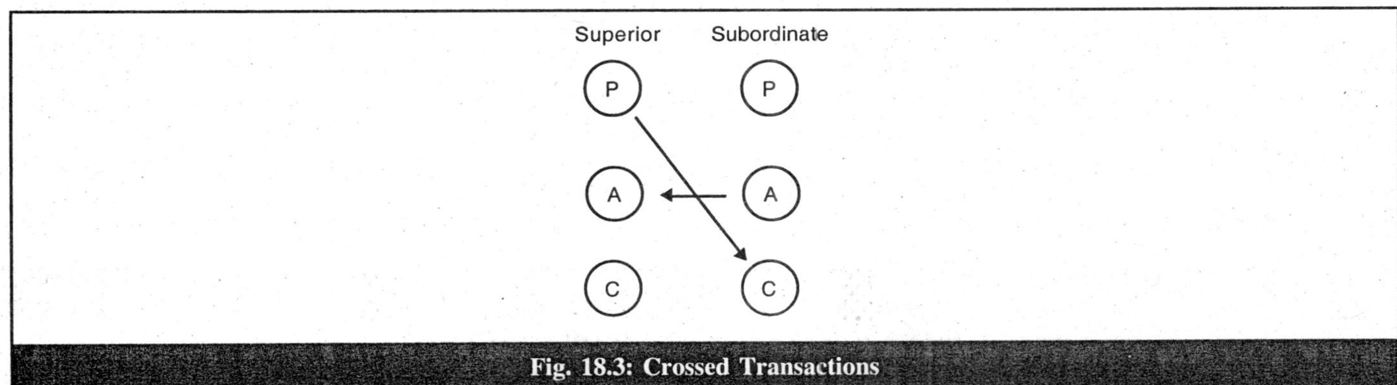

Fig. 18.3: Crossed Transactions

Box 18.3: Five Signs You May Pick up a Crossed Transaction

Here are five signs that you might be the one pushing your coworkers to the limits of their sanity:

1. You dump last-minute work on people when you could have avoided doing so. *There will always be projects that pop up at the last minute, but don't be the coworker who sits on something and doesn't assign it out until late in the game. You'll come across as inconsiderate, and maybe disorganized, too.*

2. You complain about people without telling them your beefs directly. *We've all had the frustrating feeling of discovering that a coworker is complaining to others about something we did, but won't bother to come talk to us about it directly. When you talk to someone directly, not only do you act more fairly by giving them the chance to know about your complaint and to respond to it, but you may also learn new information that makes you see things in a different light.*

3. You exude negativity. *Suggestions, new practices, the new guy down the hall-you hate them all and you make sure people know it. You may think that you're demonstrating your value by pointing out flaws all the time, but if you find fault in every suggestion, you'll lose credibility, and eventually people will start finding ways to avoid your input altogether.*

4. You bring your personal life to the office in ways that make people uncomfortable. *For instance, I used to work with someone who was constantly making personal calls that involved yelling and swearing at the person on the other end. Crying wasn't unheard of either. She never noticed that everyone around her was cringing in discomfort.*

***5. You're chronically defensive.** You bristle at the slightest hint that your work wasn't perfect — even when the hint is imagined. As a result, your coworkers spend more time trying to avoid you than talking to you because they don't want to deal with your prickliness. If you recognize yourself in any of the above habits, you may be the irritating coworker that colleagues are complaining about to me. Try a one-month moratorium on the behaviour and see if any of your relationships improve.*

Source: http://finance.yahoo.com/career-work/article/18158/signs-you-may-be-a-bad-coworker?mod=career-worklife_balance (Accessed on 13/11/2009).

How to Manage Ego States?

Crossed transactions mostly take place due to incompatibility of ego states of two or more people who are parties to a transaction.

Crossed transactions mostly take place due to incompatibility of ego states of two or more people who are parties to a transaction. Crossed transactions can be averted or avoided by avoiding the incompatible ego states of either of the parties to the transaction. Crossed transactions take place when one person is in parent (P) ego and the other person is in adult (A) ego. In other words, crossed transaction takes place when one person is either commanding or nurturing, the other person is responding or behaving rationally and logically to the situation. Either of the parties to the transaction or both the parties have to change their ego states depending up on situational requirements to avoid/ avert the crossed transaction. If the situation is routine and less important, the one in adult ego (A) can shift to child (C) ego and convert the Parent-Adult transaction to Parent- Child transaction to avoid crossed transaction and thereby its negative consequences. If the situation is more important and strategic, it needs the knowledge as well as expertise of other person. Then the person who is in parent (P) ego should shift to adult (A) ego. This would convert the Parent-Adult transaction into Adult-Adult transaction.

The issue here is who will change his/her ego state? It would be better to the subordinate or the younger one to change the ego state initially and then change ego state of the superior or the older one later through the convincing approach. For example the manager of a bank who is in parent ego orders an officer-in-charge of granting loans to a notorious customer without any security and the officer normally rejects it by being in adult ego. The officer can avert the situation by saying initially that he would grant the loan and after a span of 15 minutes can counsel the manager that this act would cause risk to both of them as well as the bank and convince the manager to think logically and rationally. If the manager then accepts the views of the officer, it is said that the manager shifted from parent ego to adult ego. Thus, the subordinates can change the transaction and avert the consequences of crossed transactions, as and when the superiors initially fail to change.

Ulterior Transactions

Ulterior transaction: The individual may say one thing but mean quite another.

The ulterior transactions involve at least two ego states on the part of a person. The individual may say one thing but mean quite another (See Fig. 18.4). For example, branch manager says to an officer: Come to me if you can't balance the day book. But the branch manager really means is: "don't come to me with your troubles. Find an answer within yourself." These transactions are very complicated and result in interpersonal conflict. They damage the psyche of the two parties and interpersonal relations. (See box 18.4). Therefore, either of the parties to the transaction should not resort to ulterior transaction.

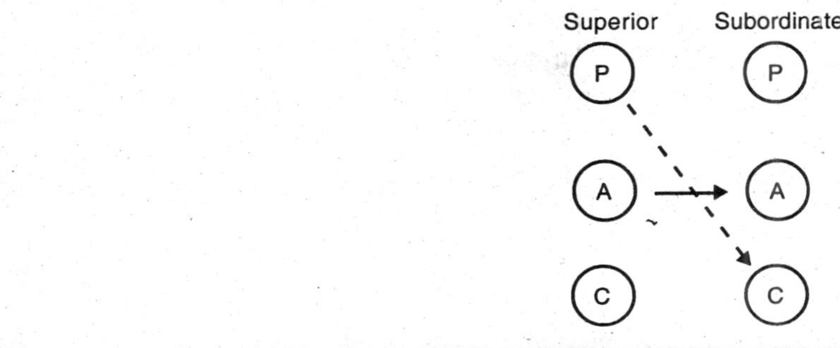

Fig. 18.4: Ulterior Transactions

Box 18.4: Example of Ulterior Transaction — Indian Railway Strike

All railway trade unions of Indian Railways formed into Joint Action Committee in 1974 in order to negotiate and settle various long pending issues like parity of salaries with those of other public sector employees and bonus. At the final stage of negotiations, one-day the Joint Action Committee negotiated with Mrs. Indira Gandhi, the then Prime Minister of the Country.

There were strong arguments and counterarguments between the Joint Action Committee and the top manager during the negotiations. Mrs. Gandhi expressed her views that the demands can't be met due to reasons obvious. Joint Action Committee has given tough time to Mrs. Gandhi and hence she realized that it would be impossible to settle the issues through fair means in the negotiation process at around 10.00 pm.

Then the Prime Minister told the Joint Action Committee "the time now is already 10.00 pm and I would like to solve the problem amicably tomorrow. Shall we meet tomorrow at 8.00 am?" (In fact, Mrs. Gandhi told to herself that I won't solve the problems of the railway employees' viz., salary hike and bonus.). The Joint Action Committee felt very happy for the change in the attitude of the top manager and replied that "we will meet tomorrow at 8.00 am."

Next day, Mr. L.N. Mishra, the then Union Railway Minister represented the top manager in the negotiations meeting and informed the same to the Joint Action Committee. The Committee said it is OK. Mr. L.N. Mishra listened the version of the Committee and coolly replied that "Neither have I had authority to solve your problems nor the top manager delegated any power to me to solve the problems."

The Joint Action Committee realized the ulterior motive of the top manager and immediately called for the May 1974 strike in Indian Railways.

Situation-Transaction Match

Normally people believe that adult (A) - adult (A) transaction is the best. But this assumption is wrong as all situations do not need the expertise and knowledge of other party to the transaction. Therefore, adult (A) - adult (A) transaction is appropriate to only those situations like strategic and important that require the expertise and knowledge of other party. The parent (A)–child (C) transaction can be used in those situations that don't require others' expertise and knowledge of others. Similarly, managers can be in the nurturing parent ego when the subordinates are in adaptive child ego state and when the situation needs counselling about performance as well as career. Managers can be in critical parent ego when the subordinate is in free child ego when the situation needs turnaround of the company or a department. Thus, transactions should be compatible to the situations to produce positive consequences in terms of relationships as well as functions.

Stroking

Stroking is recognising the presence of others. It may be positive, negative, sarcastic or mixed. Positive stroking develops interpersonal relations, whereas negative and mixed stroking damages interpersonal relations. But sarcastic stroking is highly dangerous to interpersonal relations.

The Johari Window

The other framework to explain interpersonal conflict is Johari Window developed by Joseph Loft and Henry Ingham (Johari). There are certain things that a person knows about himself and there are certain things that are unknown. This holds good for other persons also. This idea is the basis for Johari Window. Four cells are identified based on the above assumption (See Fig. 18.5). They are: open self, hidden self, blind self, and undiscovered self.

In the open self form of interaction, the person knows about himself/herself and about the other person. This situation results in openness and compatibility and a little interpersonal conflict.

In the hidden self situation, the individual only knows about himself/herself, but does not know about the other persons. The person remains hidden from the other since he does not know how the other might react. Thus, the person hides his true feelings or attitudes. This situation results in potential interpersonal conflict.

In the blind situation, the individual remains blind about himself but other people know about his behaviour. The individual may be unintentionally irritating the others and hurting the others' feelings. The situation is also prone to high interpersonal conflict. (See Box 18.5).

1 • The person knows about the others • The person knows about himself/herself **OPEN SELF**	2 • The person does not know about the others • The person knows about himself/herself **HIDDEN SELF**
3 • The person knows about the others • The person does not know about himself/herself **BLIND SELF**	4 • The person does not know about the others • The person does not know about himself/herself **UNDISCOVERED SELF**

Fig. 18.5: The Johari Window

Box 18.5: The 6 Most Annoying Coworkers — Hidden and Blind Selves

A great coworker can help you look forward to going to work each day. An annoying coworker, on the other hand, can make hide under the covers.

A large survey by the staffing firm Ranstad USA asked employees what their biggest office peeves were. It turns out they all involved coworkers. Annoying ones.

Do you recognize any of the top six most annoying coworker types?

The Psst-er: Gossipers were the number one pet peeve in the survey. While some people like to hear juicy tidbits about the boss or their colleagues, too much gossip can undermine the spirit of the workplace. Plus you're always wondering when the Psst-er will make you the topic du jour.

The Broken Clock: These coworkers stink at time management. They're routinely late for everything, including work. They tend to spend too much time on emails, take long lunches, and then scramble to get others to help them meet their deadlines, which, for some reason, they keep missing.

Mold Guy: Coworkers who mess up communal spaces were third on the list of workplace pet peeves. Their month-old leftovers sport a thick layer of fur in the company fridge. Every office seems to have at least one who stinks up shared spaces.

The Whiffy Wonder: You can smell these coworkers wafting about from the other end of the office. They just wear too much perfume or cologne. Some have an obsession with Obsession. Others feel the need to douse themselves with Old Spice. And hiding in your cubicle won't make the overpowering smell go away.

The Cracker: Crackers are loud. They crack loud jokes, they crack their knuckles, they crackle their chewing gum, they clank spoons in coffee cups like they're calling the cows to come in from the fields. People who work near crackers can find themselves ready to crack.

The Tapper: Tappers are generally quieter than Crackers. But that doesn't make them any less annoying when they're tap-tap-tapping on their personal communication devices during meetings. It's distracting, rude, and yes, just plain annoying!

The one positive aspect of these annoying coworkers is that they tend to unite the rest of us who can bond over the latest outrageous offense. Besides laughing at the insanity, here are some other ways to cope:

** Even the most annoying types may annoy you less if you love everything else about your job. Take the free career test to find a job you absolutely love.*

** If you find yourself subject to one or more of these annoying types and they're driving you batty, it may be time to find a new job that offers greater job satisfaction, with fewer obnoxious coworkers. Take the free resume test to ensure your resume is in shape.*

** If you find that all of your coworkers get under your skin, you may be better off working for yourself with the power to select your own co-workers. Take a free entrepreneur test to find out if you have what it takes to start your own business.*

Source: http://hotjobs.yahoo.com/career-articles-the_6_most_annoying_coworkers-1022 (Accessed on 17/12/2009).

In undiscovered self-situation, the person does not know about himself/herself and about the others. This situation results in much misunderstanding and interpersonal conflict. Thus, this is potentially the most explosive situation.[8]

Strategies for Interpersonal Conflict Resolution

The simple strategies for interpersonal conflict resolution include: complementary transactions (particularly Adult ego state to Adult ego state) in transactional analysis, moving towards the open self of self-disclosure and feedback in the Johari window model, emotion management and management through reason and action.

In addition to the above, there are three basic strategies for management of conflict. They are: lose-lose, win-lose and win-win.

Lose-Lose Strategy: In the first approach, both the individuals lose. In other words, the solution to the problem would be a compromise or to take a middle point in a conflict. Another approach is pay-off (mostly in the form of bribes) to the one party. Third approach is to use a third party as an arbitrator. The fourth approach is to resort to the bureaucratic rules and regulations to resolve the conflict. Both the parties are involved in this strategy.

Win-Lose Strategy: In this approach, one party wins and the other party loses. This is I win. You lose approach. This strategy is common in a competitive type of culture.

Win-Win Strategy: There was only deputy production manager position in HLL during 2010. Mr. Prakash and Mr. Santosh were trying for promotion to the deputy production manager and consequently had conflicts. Both of them worked together like a team and adopted a new product based on the advise of the production manager. The company developed another unit for the new product and created another deputy production manager position and promoted both Prakash and Santosh. This is win-win strategy to solve conflicts. In a win-win strategy, energies and creativity are aimed at solving the problem rather than beating the other party. This strategy takes the advantages of win-lose strategy and eliminates many of the dysfunctional aspects. The needs of both the parties are met and both the parties receive rewards.[9] by enhancing the resources available or output by both the parties. No one need to lose or sacrifice in this strategy.

(D) INTER-GROUP CONFLICTS

Conflict between two groups or departments in an organisation refers to intergroup conflict.

Conflict between two groups or departments in an organisation refers to intergroup conflict. Conflicts between employees and management are also due to inter-group conflicts. (See Box 18. 6). Conflict between production department and marketing department is an example of this conflict. Intergroup conflict arises due to:

- Overlapping roles;
- Absence of cooperation;
- Lack of comprehensive understanding;
- Competition for sharing the same facilities;
- Resource Crunch: when the available resources are less than the demand for the same;
- Lack of open minded approach;
- Absence of collaboration between/among groups;
- More concern for group goals rather then organisational goals; and
- Resistance either to communicate or receive communication.

Box 18-6: Management Behaviour is Meeting Employee Expectations Around 50% of the Time, Krauthammer Study Indicates

The behaviour of managers in several fundamental areas of practice is not meeting employees' expectations in 50% of cases, indicates a study published by Krauthammer International, one of Europe's leading consulting, training and coaching companies. Krauthammer surveyed people representing a variety of industry sectors in researching the behaviour employees seek from their managers and, in return, experience.

"These potentially alarming results show that in many key tasks, and basic management skills, such as guiding others, listening to ideas, securing delivery and giving feedback, managers simply fail to meet their employees' expectations", commented Ronald Meijers, Krauthammer Executive Board member. "And this lack of performance obviously has a direct impact on companies' success in business itself, so these results present company executives with interesting food for thought, to say the least. The survey offers managers some unambiguous clues to ways in which their day-to-day behaviour can contribute to improved levels of performance and trust", Meijers concluded.

In the core areas of management behaviour that were surveyed, amongst the biggest gaps between the expectations of employees and reality were the following:

- 95% would like their manager to analyse their task problems together with them, 41% experience this.
- 86% would like their manager to create the right context prior to implementing a decision, this is the case 42% of the time.
- 82% would like their manager to listen to their ideas, and encourage them to continue, 56% experience this.

On the other hand, managers seem to be closer in meeting the expectations of their employees in the following areas:

- 94% would expect their manager to spontaneously admit their mistakes, and 69% actually do this.
- 90% would like to be fully involved in the definition of thei. development goals, and this is the case 68% of the time.
- 83% would expect their manager to arbitrate conflicts, and 65% of the time this indeed happens.

Based on the results, which indicate several common pitfalls of management, a list of "golden rules" for managers has been identified alerting managers to an important series of "win areas". Here is a selection:

- In receiving an objection, use questions (rather than defending facts) to formulate your response.
- In handling dilemmas, involve employees more (rather than chewing on them in splendid isolation).
- Check your own emotions and assumptions first before giving feedback - and then deliver it without a delay (rather than either telling people off or not confronting them at all).

- When communicating change, the rationale behind it is not enough - people expect to hear both what the change means for them and to get regular updates on the progress.

The material in the Krauthammer Observatory has been organised into a "dashboard" - a model for management behaviour. Over the next five years Krauthammer observatory will fill the dashboard with ever more data concerning the behaviour employees seek and receive. Please download the complete study here www.krauthammer.com

Source: http://www.trainingpressreleases.com/newsstory.asp?NewsID=2800 (Accessed on 10/02/1010).

Strategies to Reduce Intergroup Conflict

- *Avoidance:* Keep the conflict from surfacing at all.
- *Diffusion:* Deactivate the conflict and cool off the emotions and hostilities of the groups.
- *Containment:* Allow some conflict to surface and contain it carefully by pointing out which issues are to be discussed and how they are to be resolved.
- *Confrontation:* Bring all issues out into the open and allow the conflict groups to confront directly in an attempt to reach a mutually satisfactory solution.
- *Believe in win-win situations:* The groups should have belief and advantages in Win-Win situations as they help both the groups in particular and the organisation in general. (See Box 18.7).

Box 18.7: Conflicts between AIG and US Government: AIG Chief Urges Staff to Return Bonuses

Edward Liddy, chief executive of AIG, on Wednesday tried to soothe anger against the bailed-out insurance group by urging employees to give back the $165m in bonuses that have sparked a political firestorm.

He told legislators he had asked employees of AIG Financial Products – the arm that brought the group to the brink of collapse – to "step up and do the right thing". The concession came as President Barack Obama defended Timothy Geithner, Treasury Secretary, amid criticism of the administration's handling of the controversy.

Mr. Obama said he had "complete confidence" in Mr. Geithner as the Treasury chief faced calls to quit from at least two Republican legislators. Republicans want to know why he did not challenge the bonuses before approving $30bn of fresh federal aid to AIG this month. Congressman Connie Mack said Mr Geithner "should either resign or be fired for the good of the country".

The president praised Mr Geithner for tackling the crisis with "intelligence and diligence", arguing that he faced the toughest challenge of any Treasury secretary since Alexander Hamilton after the Revolutionary War. "Nobody's working harder than this guy," said Mr Obama.

The resignation calls were echoed by protesters at a Congressional hearing into the AIG bail-out, while Republican members pressed Mr Liddy for information about Mr Geithner's role in waving through the bonuses. The Obama administration has published a timeline of events that shows Mr Geithner learning of the pay-outs on March 10, phoning Mr Liddy on March 11 and informing the White House on March 12. It stressed that Mr Geithner had no part in drafting the bonus deal.

The controversy took a new turn on Wednesday when it emerged that Fannie Mae, the US mortgage financier taken over by the government in September was planning to pay executive retention bonuses of as much as $611,000 for 2009. Fannie issued a vigorous defence of the bonuses, arguing the scheme was specifically designed to sustain mortgage agencies' ability to function.

Source: www.ft.com/cms/s/0/ca794ce4-13ce-11de-9e32-0000779fd2ac.html (Accessed on 14/12/2010).

- *Information sharing:* The departments in the company should share the information and data available with each other for the overall organisational development.
- *Free flow of communication:* The groups should allow their members to communicate with each other freely.
- *Trust and confidence:* Each group should have trust and confidence in other group.

- *Collaboration:* Teach the groups about total organisational productivity, profitability and effectiveness and encourage collaboration, among all groups and avoid organisational politicking.
- *Team building:* Build interdepartmental teams and encourage the people to work beyond their departmental boundaries.
- Realise that organisational goals are superior to group goals.

We can understand this concept most efficiently by playing "Win-As-Much As You Can" game presented in Part-6.

Having studied the group conflicts, we shall study the negotiations through building teams.

Team-building is a method of improving organisational effectiveness at the team level by diagnosing barriers to team performance and improving inter-team relationships and task accomplishment. Team building analyses the activities, resource allocations and relationships of a group or team to improve its effectiveness. This technique can be used to develop a sense of unity among members.[10] Team building is for two types of teams, viz., *(i)* an existing or permanent team comprising of a manager and his/her subordinates often called a *family group* and *(ii)* a new group made through a merger or other structural changes in the organisation or formed to solve a specific problem called the *special group*.

Teamwork needs collaboration among its members. It is said that one plus one may be three in teamwork due to the impact of synergy. The synergetic effect is evident in teamwork. Each team is a linking pin to another team and to the total organisation. Teams do wonders. They make the impossible things possible.

We can understand this concept most efficiently by playing the game on presented in Part-6.

KEY TERMS

- Group
- Intra-personal Conflicts
- Interpersonal Conflicts
- Intra-group Conflicts
- Intergroup Conflicts
- Collaboration
- Role Ambiguity
- Stroking
- Johari Window
- Goal Conflict
- Role Conflict
- Family Groups
- Special Groups
- Role Perception
- Transactional Analysis
- Child Ego
- Parent Ego
- Adult Ego
- Complementary Transactions
- Crossed Transactions
- Ulterior Transactions

QUESTIONS

1. What are the causes of intra-personal conflict? Explain the mechanism to reduce intra-personal conflicts.
2. What are the various kinds of intra-individual conflicts? Explain them in detail.
3. What is transactional analysis? Explain various kinds of transactions.
4. Why do the conflicts take place within a group? Suggest strategies to resolve them.
5. Explain interpersonal conflicts with the help of Johari Window model.
6. What are the reasons for intergroup conflicts? Suggest the strategies to resolve them.

REFERENCES

1. Fred Luthans, *Organisational Behaviour*, McGraw Hill, New York, 1998, p. 401.
2. Theodore R. Sarbin, *Role Theory*, in G. Lindzey (Ed.) "*Handbook of Social Psychology*," Adison-Wisley, Cambridge, 1954, pp. 223-258.
3. Theodore M. Newcomb, *Social Psychology*, Dryden Press, New York, 1980.
4. Keith Davis, *op.cit.*, p. 32.
5. *Ibid.*, p. 33.
6. Craig E. Schmier, *Behavioural Modification-Training the Hardcore Unemployed*, Personnel, May-June 1973, pp. 65-69.
7. Fred Luthans, *op.cit.*, p. 408.
8. *Ibid.*, p. 412.
9. *Ibid.*, p. 414.
10. James A.F.Stoner and R.Edward Freeman, *op.cit.*, p. 421.
11. Wendell L. French and Cecil H. Bell Jr., *Organisational Development*, Prentice-Hall of India (P) Ltd., New Delhi, pp. 142-148.

CHAPTER 19

COMMUNICATION

Chapter Outline

(A) Meaning
(B) Management Information System and Information Technology
(C) Methods of Communication
(D) Communication Channels
(E) Communication Networks
(F) Organisational Communication
(G) Barriers to Communication
— Key Terms
— Questions
— References

Learning Objectives

After studying this Chapter, you should be able to:

✓ Know the meaning and purpose of communication;
✓ Discuss the functions and process of communication;
✓ Find out the role of MIS and information technology in organisational communication;
✓ Appraise the oral, written and non-verbal communication in organisations;
✓ Know how effective the downward and upward communication channels are;
✓ Analyse the communication networks and their effectiveness in improving interpersonal communication;
✓ Study the role of formal communication and the significance of informal communication in team organisations; and
✓ Understand various barriers to communication and how to overcome them.

(A) MEANING

Communication is a process by which all forms of information are transferred from one person to the other. So, for communication to take place, there must be some information to be conveyed and there must be two or more persons — one to deliver the message and the other to receive it. Communication is said to be perfect only when the receiver understands it in the sense the sender expected him to understand.

Transfer and understanding of information

Dale S.Beach defines communication as "the transfer of information and understanding from person to person.[1]

According to McFarland, communication is "a process of meaningful interaction among human beings. More specifically it is the process by which meanings are perceived and understandings are reached among human beings.[2]

Scott and others define communication as "a process involving the transmission and accurate replication of ideas reinforced by feedback purporting to stimulate actions to accomplish organisational goals.[3]

Purposes of Communication

The purposes of communication in human resources management include:

- Communication is needed to exchange the ideas, opinions, information, etc., with the colleagues, superiors, subordinates, customers, public, etc.
- Communication is needed for designing jobs and human resources planning.
- Employee orientation and socialisation programmes become possible mostly through communication.
- Recruitment and selection functions are performed through communication by persuading the prospective employees to apply for a job, knowing the skills and knowledge of the prospective employees.
- Employee's performance is evaluated by getting information, opinions and ratings from the superiors, subordinates and employers.
- Almost all the process of training and executive development are carried out through the communication process. In fact, most of the training and development are done through teaching and learning processes.
- Employees ventilate their grievances to their superiors through communication. Superiors also redress the employee grievances and deal with the disciplinary cases through communication.
- Collective bargaining process is mostly carried out through communication process of exchanging the demands, offering proposals and counter proposals, etc.
- Participative management is successful through effective communication process.

Importance of Communication

Communication is important in the organisation for three reasons.

Managers manage though communication

First, all the functions of management such as planning, organising, leading and controlling involve the act of communication without which they cannot be performed at all. Secondly, managers devote a major portion of their time to the activity of communication. Third, interpersonal relations and group relations are maintained and developed only through the system of communication.

Also, communication is essential to integrate and coordinate the activities of the people in the organisation. In the absence of communication, no individual worker can appreciate the overall objectives of an organisation, and there is a possibility that people in the same organisation will work towards different goals instead of a common goal.

Communication is also significant as it performs various actions like:

(i) It acts as a basis for action;

(ii) It facilitates planning;

(iii) It helps in decision-making;

(iv) It acts as a means of coordination;

(v) It improves relationship among peers, superior and subordinate; and

(vi) It improves motivation and morale.

Fundamentals of Communication

Though all of us use the word communication quite often, none of us are precisely clear of its meaning and its nature. Since the effectiveness of a manager's strategies pertaiing to management largely depends on communication, it is important that he knows the fundamentals of communication. 'Needless to say that this knowledge helps him to improve his communication.'

Words do not have meaning in themselves. Though a word represents a thing, an action or a feeling, the meaning of words actually depends on the way they are interpreted. Words mean different things to different people. 'Different people may interpret the same word in different ways when their background, education and the culture, etc., are different. Perceptions of people may differ from the reality.' If two people experience the same phenomenon, we cannot take it for granted that they have felt or perceived it in the same way because a person's perception does not depend only on the physical and social environment but also depends on his background, attitudes, prior knowledge and experiences accumulated since birth. An optimist may say half the cup is full while a pessimist says that half the cup is empty.

Sometimes, the emotional state of a person also affects understanding. For this reason, the manager may also have to learn the emotional state of a person before he communicates. This will help the manager to express his ideas in such a way that the true meaning is understood by the receiver.

Facts must be distinguished from opinions. A careful speaker always distinguishes opinions from facts. "We must analyse, study, investigate and collect statistics to arrive at facts." While expressing opinions, one has to use the expression 'It seems to me', 'I think', 'Suppose', etc.

Communication is said to be complete when the receiver has understood it in the same sense the sender has conveyed it. It is up to the sender to find out whether the receiver has understood the true meaning of the message. So, a constant feedback becomes an essential component of the communication process.

Functions of Communication

No organisation can function without communication. It is an ever present activity among participants in the organisation. Communication in the organisation performs mainly the following functions:

(1) Information and knowledge are transmitted from one person to another;

(2) People are motivated and directed only with the help of communication;

(3) People's attitude and beliefs are moulded and their behaviour is influenced positively with the help of communication, and

(4) It also performs the function of entertainment and the maintenance of social relations among them. Scott and Mitchell summarised the functions of communication as shown in Exhibit 19.1.

Exhibit 19.1 Functions of Communication

Function	*Orientation*	*Objectives Sought*
1. Emotive	Feeling	Increasing acceptance of the organizational tasks.
2. Motivation	Influence	Seeking commitment to organizational objectives.
3. Information	Technological	Providing data necessary to rational decisions.
4. Control	Structure	Clarifying duties, authority, accountability.

Since the manager continuously interacts with other people in the organisation, his job mainly involves communication and to do this better, he is required to be skilful in speaking, listening, reading and writing.

Now, we shall study how communication takes place.

Process of Communication

To express the process of communication in the simplest manner (See Fig. 19.1).

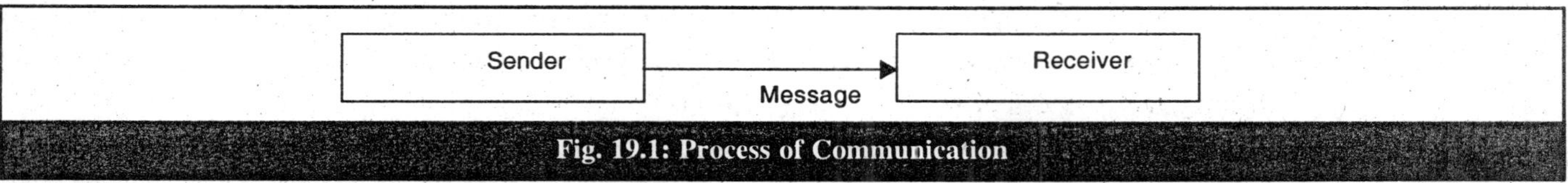

Fig. 19.1: Process of Communication

The above model is too simple and it contains only three essential elements of communication by which we mean that in the absence of these, there cannot be any communication. For the communication process to be complete, it must have the three elements.

The communication, in fact, is a more complex process that involves the following components (Fig. 19.2).

It can be seen from the above figure that there are seven basic elements of communication. Let us examine each component.

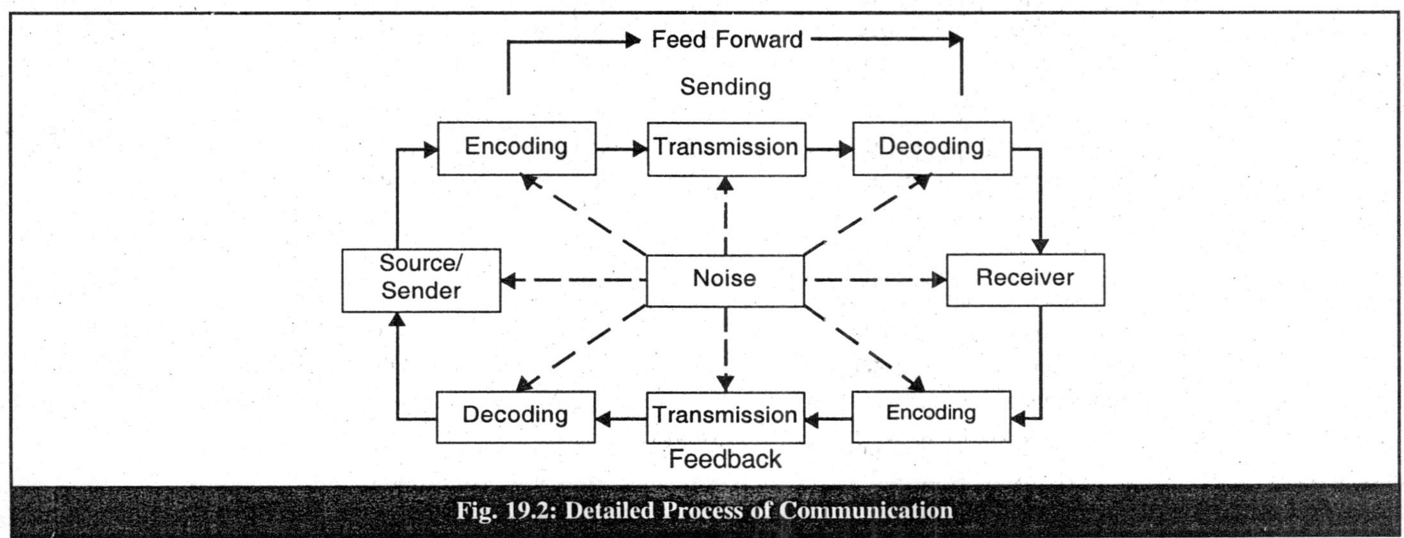

Fig. 19.2: Detailed Process of Communication

(**Source:** Modified Version from Moorhead & Griffin, *op.cit.*, p. 264.)

(i) **Sender:** Sender is a person who has something to communicate, he is the source where the idea originates, he is the one who invites or begins the process of communication.

(ii) **Encoding:** Encoding involves the translation of information into series of symbols or gestures which will carry the same meaning to the receiver.

(iii) **Message:** When the information is encoded into a physical form, it is called *message*. The form of the message should be such that it can be experienced and understood by one or more of the senses of the receiver.

(iv) **Channel:** A channel is a vehicle by which the message travels to the receiver. For spoken words, air is a channel and for written messages, paper is a channel. Efficient communication also involves the selection of appropriate channels depending on the kind of message to be conveyed.

(v) **Decoding:** When the channel brings the message to the receiver, he interprets the message and translates it into information that is meaningful to him.

(vi) **Receiver:** Receiver is a person who has to perceive the meaning of the message in its proper sense. If the receiver does not receive the message, we can say that the communication has not taken place at all.

(vii) **Feedback:** All that helps the sender to know what and how the receiver understood the message is called *feedback*. This is important for effective communication. Better feedback always results in better communication. Without feedback, the communication process is not said to be complete.

MIS and information technology created wonders in organisational communication. Now, we shall study the role of MIS and IT in organisational communication.

(B) MANAGEMENT INFORMATION SYSTEM (MIS) AND INFORMATION TECHNOLOGY

MIS makes information available for decision-making

Management information system is a formal method of making available to the management accurate and timely information necessary to facilitate the decision-making process and enable the organisation's planning, control and operational functions to be carried out effectively. Management information systems do not have to be computerised. But the number of computer based information systems has grown exponentially during the past two decades.

An information system is a set of organised procedures which when executed, provides information to support decision-making. Communication through computers and electronic media plays a vital role in management information systems. Telecommunications revolution has brought significant changes in the communication modes and channels.

Telecommunications

Telecommunications is closely related to the management information system. Computers and telecommunications closely interact with each other and make the communication fast, direct and cheap. This revolution resulted in telecommuting. Telecommuting refers to home-cum-offices. It does mean performing office work including product design at home and communicating the same to the office through local-area-network or Intranet.

The important modes of telecommunication include: e-mail, video-conferencing, local-area-network, intranet and internet (See Box 19.1). These modes resulted in efficient organisational communication.

Box 19.1: Intranet Makes Inroads

The purpose of the intranet is for employees in different parts of a company to share information. For example, at Ford Motors, an Intranet links engineering and design centres in the United States, Europe, and Asia; it was used to help design the new Taurus, which Ford introduced in 1996. At VISA International, intranets provide member banks with instant customer data, fraud alerts and information on marketing issues; previously this information had only been available in huge quarterly manuals.

The use of Intranets arose because many companies found that although project teams in various parts of the world were making progress in research, testing, product development, marketing promotions and other areas, each team seemed to be reinventing everything for itself each time it did a project. They needed a way to share their work with other divisions so they would not make the same mistakes, which was increasing development times and slowing down a company's response to the market. They are finding that a series of intranets within the company allows instant information sharing across organisational units. Use of intranet slashes development times and gives the company a chance to respond to important market segments.

In one example of intranet use, Exxon Chemical Company needed a computer software tool to help it blend typical off-the-shelf software with its custom software throughout its operations. It had spent months looking for help and expected development to take up to eighteen months. A French computer service company, CAP Gemini Sogeti, explained the problem over its intranet to its seventeen thousand software engineers. Within fortyeight hours, CAP Gemini had the solution, which they implemented in three weeks to solve Exxon's problem. CAP Gemini reports that their project time has been cut in half and that bids are presented faster because the intranet keeps designers from repeating the same work on different projects.

(**Sources:** Gail Edmondson, "One Electronic SOS Clinched the Deal," Business Week, February 26, 1996, p.83; Amy Cortese, "Updates? Just a Mouse Click Away," Business Week, February 26, 1996, p. 84; Amy Cortese, "Here Comes the Intranet," Business Week, February 26, 1996, pp. 76-84, Jenny C. McCune, "The Intranet:Beyond E-Mail," Management Review, November 1996, pp. 23.27 and Moorhead and Grifflin, p. 268).

Information technology brought revolutionary changes in the communication process and media through Electronic Mail (E-Mail). E-mail has become the common method of communication not only in the general society but also in the corporate world. Computers are connected either by telephone lines or by fibre optic cables for the purpose of e-mail and internet. E-mail provides flexibility, fastness and convenience in communicating even with a large number of employees. Many organisations find it easy to send circulars to the employees through e-mail. In fact, e-mail is used for sending applications, organising interview call letters in the employment process. But e-mail causes privacy problems (See Exhibit 19.2). Hence, companies formulate their own communication policy. Exhibit 19.2 presents a model employee communication policy.

Exhibit 19.2 A Model Employee Communication Policy

Because many organisations do not have explicit policies about communication, employees do not know what levels of privacy thay can expect. The following points represent what many experts consider the basic features of a good electronic privacy communication policy:

- Employees are entitled to reasonable expectations of personal privacy on the job.
- Employees know what electronic surveillance tools are used, and how management uses the collected data.
- Management uses electronic monitoring or searches data files, network communications, or electronic mail to the minimum extent possible. Continuous monitoring is not permitted.
- Employees participate in decisions about how and when electronic monitoring or searches take place.
- Data are gathered and used only for clearly defined work-related purposes.
- Management will not engage in secret monitoring or searches, except when credible evidence of criminal activity or other serious wrong doing comes to light.
- Monitoring data will not be the sole factor in evaluating employee performance.
- Employees can inspect, challenge and correct electronic records kept on their activities or files captured through electronic means.
- Records no longer relevant to the purposes for which they were collected will be destroyed.
- Monitoring data that identify individual employees will not be released to any third party, except to comply with legal requirements.
- Employees or prospective employees cannot waive privacy rights, and
- Managers who violate these privacy principles are subject to discipline or termination.

(**Source:** From "*Bosses with X-ray Eyes*" by Charles Piller in MACWORLD, July 1993, p. 191.)

(C) METHODS OF COMMUNICATION

People communicate through different methods like oral, written and non-verbal methods. Now, we shall study them.

Oral Communication

Oral communication is also called *verbal communication*. It is considered to be the earliest common medium of communication. Speech is a widely adapted tool in oral communication. Human relations is the fundamental element in this communication (See Box 19.2).

Box 19.2: Oral Communication in Satyam Computers

Mr.Raju, the Managing Director of Satyam Computers, communicated the routine issues of the communication orally to the first level managers. In fact, he encourages the first level managers also to communicate orally with him in order to avoid the delay in flow of information.

Principles of communication: clarity, brevity, precision, etc.

Principles of effective oral communication include: clarity of the message, brevity of the message, choosing precise and most appropriate words, sequence of the message, avoiding use of jargons, etc.

Techniques of oral communication include: maintenance of a friendly atmosphere, using personal greetings, showing appreciation and personal interest, opening of speech with a smile, making the listeners feel important, showing empathy towards listeners, using appropriate language, appropriate personal appearance, taking care to see that actions won't contradict words, use of aids, using sense of humour, etc.

Advantages of Oral Communication

Advantages of oral communication are:

- It saves time and cost;
- It is an effective media;
- Easy to understand the message due to the possibility of two-way communication;
- Effectiveness of communication can be measured immediately;
- It can be used in emergency situations;
- It involves accuracy and speed;
- Various mechanical devices can be used; and
- Proper control and supervision.

Disadvantages of Oral Communication

Despite these advantages, oral communication suffers from various disadvantages. These are:

- It can be disturbed by noise;
- Secrecy and confidentiality can't be completely maintained;
- Involvement of problem of language;
- Problem of technical and mechanical devices;
- Problem of record and evidence, and
- Sometimes it is costly.

Written Communication

The primary important category of communication is written communication. The process of communication involves sending messages by written words. It covers all kinds of subject-matters like notices, memos, minutes, prospectus, etc. (See Box 19.3).

Box 19.3: Written Communication in Super Speciality Hospitals Ltd.

The doctors and administrators of Super Speciality Hospitals Ltd. prefer reports, memos and other forms of written communication in order to have accuracy of information and data.

Essentials

The essentials of written communications include:

- Unity of writing the message. It implies a condition of being one;
- Coherence. It is most essential for good communication. Clear communication in simple sentences helps the reader to understand;
- Emphasis on a particular aspect;
- Clarity of written message is most important. The message should be correctly planned and expressed;
- Complete message with comprehensive coverage of subject matter,
- Avoiding jargons;
- Conciseness;
- Brevity;
- Accuracy; and
- Strength.

Objectives

The objectives of written communication include:

- To provide the facility for further reference;
- To have a record of evidence;
- To measure the progress;
- To provide necessary information on earlier activities and decisions;
- To reduce mistakes and errors based on the earlier records;
- To provide information for effective decision-making;
- To improve organisational efficiency; and
- To meet the legal requirements.

Advantages

The advantages of written communication are:

- Influence of self-interest and attitude is minimum;
- Written communication is more reliable and one can trust it;
- Written communication does not suffer from the danger of being destroyed;

- It is the best method of communication when the sender and the receiver of the message are located geographically far off;
- It has capacity of being stored;
- It is suitable for lengthy matters to be communicated;
- It is useful where documentary work is involved;
- It will not carry rumour or gossip; and
- This method is useful when secrecy or confidentiality of matters is involved.

Disadvantages

However, written communication suffers from some limitations. These limitations include: confusion and misinterpretation, absence of personal touch, absence of two-way communication, absence of grapevine, slow movement, absence of scope for interaction, absence of immediate feedback, etc.

Non-verbal Communication

Acts speak louder than words

"*Acts speak louder than words.*"

We summon a bearer in a restaurant with a signal of the hand. We blink our eyes when we do not understand what the other person is talking about. We raise our left eyebrow indicating our surprise and disbelief. All these actions are nothing but non-verbal communication. Communication can never be complete and effective without non-verbal communication (See Exhibit 19.3)

Even before verbal communication was established, communication was non-verbal. Communication is most effective when the non-verbal communication exists along with that of verbal. Visual aids are always considered better than audio aids.

Apart from body language, non-verbal communication also includes mode of dressing, physical distance maintained, etc. These body movements are labelled as 'kinesics,' which include gestures, facial configurations and other movements.

It is very important for the manager to observe the communication expressed through Kinesics apart from being attentive to verbal communication. For example, a good salesman can watch the spark of acceptance from the eyes of a customer, at a particular rate of product and can stick on to it.

It is also important to observe the emotional state of the other person which is expressed through facial expressions. If he is looking at his wristwatch very often, it does mean that he is in a hurry and anxious to end the meeting soon. An accountant may outwardly accept to work after office hours to meet the overlead but his impatience would be obvious in his face. In such situations, it is wise to depend upon non-verbal communication, because the person who is in a hurry cannot concentrate on what you are talking and as such communication is not effective.

Exhibit 19.3 Hand Gestures Mean Different Things in Different Countries

The A-OK Sign

In the United States, this is just a friendly Sign for "All right" or "Good going." In Australia and Islamic countries, it is equivalent to what generations of high school students know as "flipping the bird."

The "Hook'em Horns" Sign

This sign encourages University of Texas athletes, and it's a good luck gesture in Brazil and Venezuela. In parts of Africa it is a curse. In Italy, it is signalling to another that "your spouse is being unfaithful."

"V" for Victory Sign

In many parts of the world, this means "victory" or "peace." In England, if the palm and fingers face inward, it means "Up yours!" especially if executed with an upward jerk of the fingers.

Finger-Beckoning Sign

This sign means "come here" in the United States. In Malaysia, it is used only for calling animals. In Indonesia and Australia, it is used for beckoning "ladies of the night."

(**Source:** "What's A.O.K. in the U.S.A. Is Lewd and Worthless Beyond." *New York Times*, August 18, 1996, p.E7. From Roger E.Axtell, GESTURES:The Do's and Taboos of Body Language Around the World.)

Physical distance maintained is also important in assessing the other person's attitude. But this again changes from place to place depending upon their cultural norms. For example, what is 'business like' distance in some European countries would be viewed as 'intimate' in many parts of North America."

Improving Non-verbal Effectiveness

The managers who read the non-verbal cues and behave accordingly in social situations, would become efficient and successful in communicating with the people. These managers have high emotional intelligence. Non-verbal communication can be improved through the following means:

1. Look at what is happening in the situation.
2. Consider the discrepancies between the non-verbal behaviour and verbal statements. Non-verbal signals are correct rather than verbal statements when there is discrepancy between them, and
3. Watch for subtleties in the non-verbal behaviour. The real smile can be easily differentiated from a fake smile.

Cultural differences must be recognized in non-verbal communication. The cultural differences are influenced by sex, community, region, age, etc. Employees in L&T Cement Factory respect the trade union leader who is a politician rather than their boss. Employees in Bellary Steels and Alloys Ltd. never walk in front of their boss. People in Italy and Eritrea generally shake their hands with everyone. Japanese respect the elders. North Indians touch the feet of the elders as a mark of respect. Punctuality in Spain is taken seriously only when attending a bull fight.

Communication channels and network play vital role in making the communication effective. Now, we shall study them.

(D) COMMUNICATION CHANNELS

Information must flow faster than ever before in modern organisations. Even a dismal stoppage on fast-moving operation time can be very costly. What is more important is providing more, relevant and faster information. Managers need information to carry out managerial functions and activities effectively. There is no universally applicable communication system. But individual managers have to tailor their own system depending on their needs.

Communication channels include: downward, upward, horizontal, and diagonal

Communication flows through various channels. These channels include vertical, i.e., downward and upward, horizontal and diagonal or crosswise. Traditionally, downward communication was emphasised. But later, it is realized that upward communication is also equally important.

Vertical Communication

Vertical communication includes downward communication and upward communication.

Downward Communication

Downward communication flows from higher level to lower level in the organisational hierarchy. This type of flow is an essential character of an authoritarian atmosphere. Thus, downward flow of information is from superior to subordinate (See Box 19.4).

Box 19.4: Downward Communication at Dr. Reddy's Lab.

Dr. Reddy of Dr.Reddy's Laboratory prefers to communicate the company's policies, vision, mission, objectives, strategies and tactics through the downward communication method to all employees of the company.

The basic purpose of communication are:

- To provide specific task directives or instructions;
- To provide information about task relationships;
- To provide information about an organisation's missions, objectives, policies, procedures, programmes, etc.;
- To provide feedback about subordinate's performance;
- To let the people know the pride of being relatively well informed.

The advantages of downward communication are:

- It helps to inform the employees about policies; objectives, etc.;
- To execute and implement various programmes;
- It facilitates to improve quality of response.

The disadvantages of downward communication are:

- It causes delay and time consuming process;
- It is only a one way process;
- There is no provision for feedback;
- It provides for rigid communication network; and
- There is no scope for subordinates to express their views.

Media Used for Downward Communication

The organisational culture pertaining to its structure, lines of command and communication have changed dramatically after the globalisation and privatisation of business. The traditional style of downward communication has been changed significantly. The traditional downward communication includes, print and oral media. The written media include letters, manuals, handbooks, house magazines, noticeboard items, reports, posters, orders, and the like.

The oral media in downward communication include face-to-face orders, instructions, telephonic orders, speeches, meetings, closed-circuit television programmes, and the like.

The shift in organisational culture reduced the gap between or among the organisational hierarchies. Consequently, downward communication has been acquiring the characteristics of informal communication for the purpose of free flow of information. Further, the development in telecommunication increased the effectiveness of downward communication. These developments include video-conferences, Local Area Network (LAN), Wide-Area Network (WAN), fax, telephone and the like.

Upward Communication

Upward communication flows from lower level to upper level in organisational hierarchy. This flow is often hindered by managers in the chain particularly in case of unfavourable information (See Box 19.5).

Box 19.5: Upward Communication at L&T Cement Works, Tadipatri

Mr. Ramana Rao, Human Resources Manager, L&T Cement Works, Tadipatri, encourages the subordinates to ventilate their grievances and lodge their complaints through upward communication. Further, he encourages upward communication for expressing views and ideas by the employees in meetings and for decision-making.

Upward communication is necessary to offer suggestions to lodge complaints, ventilate grievances, to respond to counselling, opinion survey, exit interviews, to discuss in meetings and participate in decision-making (See Exhibit 19.4).

The techniques summarized in exhibit 19.4 are designed to improve organisational functioning by providing top management with information about the attitudes and ideas of the workforce. They are used to promote the upward flow of information.

Exhibit 19.4 Obtaining Employee Feedback: Some Useful Techniques

TECHNIQUE	*DESCRIPTION*
Employee surveys	Questionnaires assessing workers' attitudes and opinions about key areas of organisational functioning, especially when results are shared with the workforce.
Suggestion systems	Formal mechanisms through which employees can submit ideas for improving things in organisations (often by putting a note in a suggestion box); good ideas are implemented and the people who submitted them are rewarded.
Corporate hotlines	Telephone numbers — employees may call to ask questions about important organisational matters; useful in addressing workers' concerns before they become too serious.
Brown bag meetings	Session in which subordinates and superiors meet informally over breakfast or lunch to discuss organisational matters.
Skip-level meetings	Meetings between subordinates and superiors two or more levels above them in the organisational hierarchy.

(**Source:** Jerald Greenberg and Robert A.Baron, p. 359.)

Managers should encourage upward communication with a view to:

- Create receptiveness of communication;
- Create a feeling of belonging through a shared meaning;
- Evaluate communication; and
- Demonstrate a concern for the ideas and views of lower level employees.

Advantages of upward communication include:

- Scope for two-way communication;
- Possibility for immediate feedback; and
- Scope for employee satisfaction.

Methods of Improving the Effectiveness of Upward Communication

As stated earlier, the globalisation and privatisation of business brought significant changes in the communication culture due to severe competition. Top management initiates and encourages upward communication for the operational and organisational efficiency. Managements use the following methods to improve the effectiveness of upward communication.

(i) **Managing by walking around:** Managers under this style of leadership do not confine their office to their chambers. Instead, they walk around and meet all their subordinates at the workplace of the latter. They discuss various issues relating to the job, organisation and employee. The subordinates freely express views, share their ideas, offer their suggestions and ventilate their problems as the subordinate is in his place of work and the boss comes down there. Many managers started using this style as it has been improving upward communication.

(ii) **The open door policy:** The open-door policy does mean that the managers would invite and encourage the subordinates to meet them always and communicate with them on various jobs, organisational and individual related issues freely. When the managers say that 'my doors are always open to you,' they mean that others can have unlimited access to the former. This policy also improves upward communication. Managers should put this policy in practice as the adage, 'actions speak louder than words' applies.

(iii) **The ombudsman position:** The ombudsman position is largely held by the senior people in the organisation who are about to retire. These senior people offer suggestions and advice to the junior employees regarding career and personal issues. These senior people offer suggestions based on their experience and expertise. The ombudsman plays a figure-head role and a well-wisher's role. Therefore, he encourages upward communication through the open-door policy.

(iv) **An empowerment strategy:** Empowerment involves imparting power to the subordinates by providing them information, knowledge, expertise and special skills in addition to delegating authority. Managers empower their employees with a view to equip the latter with necessary power to make appropriate decisions in the right time by avoiding the unnecessary procedures and formalities. This, in turn, helps to carryout the job most efficiently. In fact, subordinates communicate upward freely in the empowerment situation as they are regarded as knowledgeable and expert employees.

(v) **Participative management:** Participative style of management involves the employees in information sharing, arguments, proposals and counter proposals, development of alternative decisions and selection of the best decision. This entire process enables and enhances upward communication. Employees in participative decision-making are more satisfied and motivated as they are allowed to communicate freely.

(vi) **Counselling, attitude surveys and exit interviews:** Human Resources Management department conducts employee and career counselling sessions to encourage the employee to communicate his feelings freely. Further, managements conduct attitude surveys through questionnaires which solicit employees' views. Similarly, exit interviews also solicit employee's reactions to the policies and practices of management. Thus, counselling, attitude surveys and exit interviews facilitate upward communication.

(vii) **The grievance procedure:** If employees are not satisfied with the action of their superiors, they can communicate their dissatisfaction beyond their immediate superior and seek redressal of the grievance. This process allows employees to communicate upward.

(viii) **E-mail:** Sending messages through e-mail to any one has become the order of communication today. Employees who were reluctant to speak to their bosses face-to-face, and to speak on phone can use e-mail freely. Therefore, use of e-mail encourages upward communication.

Problem of Upward and Downward Communication

Downward communication keeps reducing as it is modified and filtered at each level. Superiors always think of what should be passed down to subordinates and passed on only that which they feel can be passed down. Upward communication also undergoes all this as middle managers believe that it is part of their job to decide what information should go up and how much. For these reasons, vertical communication is often incomplete.

Horizontal Communication

Communication is said to be horizontal when it takes place between two employees of the same level in the organisational hierarchy. For example, communication between production and marketing managers. Horizontal communication is essential because of the fact that the departments in an organisation are interdependent and the coordination of their activities is necessary.

Horizontal communication is used to bring about task coordination among peers, to provide emotional and social support, to strengthen relationships among peers and to allow the flow of information faster.

Diagonal Communication

Diagonal or crosswise communication is between two or more persons of various departments of an organisation. Diagonal communication allows the communicator to communicate the message exactly to the person to whom it is meant. For example, the quality controller sends the message to the sales executive in order to ascertain whether a high quality product moves in a particular market or not? It is diagonal communication. The quality controller need not send the message through the production manager and marketing manager. This communication system violates the principle of unity of command. However, diagonal communication suits the conditions of competition where fastness is the order of the day.

(E) COMMUNICATION NETWORKS

Managers in organisations establish communication flows with others in different patterns in order to facilitate the flow of information from one point (or source) to all other points. These patterns of flow of information are called *communication networks*. There are innumerable ways or patterns of communication. There are a few frequently used networks.

Pattern of flows of information are called communication networks.

Communication networks define the channels by which information flows. These networks are classified into two, viz., formal networks and informal networks.

Formal networks are typically vertical (Fig. 19.3), follow the authority chain and are limited to task-related communications. In contrast, the informal network usually known as grapevine-is free to move in any direction, skip authority-responsibility relationship levels. The likely purpose of informal network is to satisfy social needs of the group members with a view to motivate the members of task accomplishment.[4]

Formal Networks

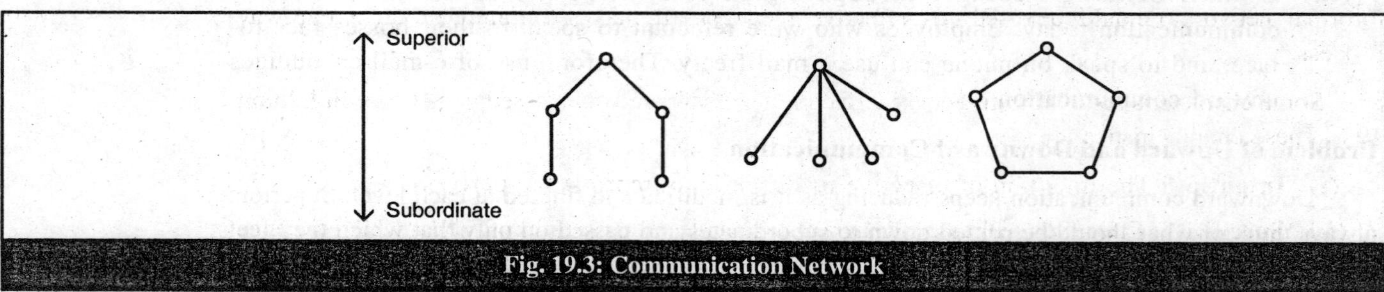

Fig. 19.3: Communication Network

There are three common small-group networks. These are chain, wheel and star (Fig. 19.3). The chain rigidly follows the formal chain of command. In the wheel network, communication flow depends on the superior to act as the central point for all group communications. In the star or all-channel network, all group members actively communicate with each other. This type of network is essential for teamwork.

The effectiveness of each network depends on the dependent variables (Exhibit 19.5). For example, speed of communication is fast in wheel and star. Accuracy of information is high in chain and wheel networks. Dependency on leader is high in the wheel network. Members are highly satisfied in the star network. Distortion is high in chain network and low in star network. Work overload is moderate in chain and star networks and very high in the wheel network. Both chain/star network is best for teamwork, which satisfies members as well as produces qualitative work. It is also clear that no single network will be the best for all occasions.

Exhibit 19.5 Effectiveness of Formal Networks

Criteria	*Chain*	*Networks Wheel*	*Star/All Chain*
Speed	Moderate	Fast	Fast
Accuracy	High	High	Moderate
Efficiency of a leader	Moderate	High	None
Member satisfaction	Moderate	Low	High
Distortion	High	Moderate	Low
Overload	Moderate	Very high	Moderate

Adapted from: Stephen P.Robbins, *op.cit.*, p.321 and Brian L.Hawkins and Paul Preston, *Managerial Communication*, Scott, Foreshman and Co.

Informal Network

The informal network has three main characteristics, viz.

- It is not controlled by the management;
- Most employees perceive that they get reliable information through this technique; and

- It is largely used to serve the self interests of the members.[5] There are no clear patterns of flow of information in informal network. Information can flow in any direction in this network.

Interpersonal Communication

Inter-personal communication is to effect behavioural change

The major emphasis in interpersonal communication is on transferring information from one person to another. The purpose of interpersonal communication is to effect behavioural change by incorporating psychological processes (perception, learning and motivation) and language. In addition, listening sensitivity and non-verbal communication are also included. Getting feedback and providing feed forward are most important in interpersonal communication. The importance of feedback cannot be overemphasised as effective interpersonal communication highly depends on it. Both formal and informal networks should be used for effective feedback. It makes communication a two-way process.[6]

Some characteristics of effective and ineffective feedback are summarised and shown in Exhibit 19.6. These characteristics are:

(i) **Intention:** The intention of effective feedback is to improve job performance.

(ii) **Specificity:** Effective feedback is designed to provide with specific information to recipients.

(iii) **Description:** Effective feedback is descriptive rather than evaluative.

(iv) **Usefulness:** Effective feedback provides employees with useful information to improve job performance.

(v) **Timeliness:** Effective feedback provides information in the right time.

(vi) **Readiness:** Employees must be ready to receive information in order to make feedback effective.

(vii) **Clarity:** The recipient must understand the information clearly and

(viii) **Validity:** The information communication must be reliable and valid.

Exhibit 19.6 Characteristics of Feedback

Effective Feedback	*Ineffective Feedback*
1. Intended to help the employee	1. Intended to belittle the employee
2. Specific	2. General
3. Descriptive	3. Evaluative
4. Useful	4. Inappropriate
5. Timely	5. Untimely
6. Employer Readiness for Feedback	6. Make the employee defensive
7. Clear	7. Not understandable
8. Valid	8. Inaccurate

(**Source**: Fred Luthans, and Mark J.Martinko, *The Practise of Supervision and Management*, McGraw Hill, New York, 1979, p. 183.)

Other Variables

In addition to feedback, other variables like trust, expectations, values, status and compatibility influence interpersonal communication greatly. If the subordinate does not trust his boss, communication will be ineffective. Similarly, the other variables also contribute for ineffective communication. Interpersonal communication is the centre of organisational communication.[7]

Listening

Listening is a very important aspect in the process of communication, but it is a very difficult task. Many people take their skills for granted and they confuse hearing with listening. Listening is different from hearing. Hearing is merely picking up sound whereas listening is making sense from what we hear. Hence, listening requires paying attention, interpreting and remembering sound stimuli.

Active and Passive Listening

Effective listening must be active but not passive. In passive listening, the receiver just records the information. Active listening gets the receiver inside the sender of the information as the receiver understands the information from the point of view of the sender. The receiver has to concentrate and fully understand the information in the process of receiving the information (See Exhibit 19.7).

Essentials of active listening: intensity, empathy, acceptance, willingness to be responsible, etc.

The four essential requirements of active listening are: *(i)* Intensity; *(ii)* Empathy; *(iii)* Acceptance; *(iv)* A willingness to take responsibility for completeness.[8] Our brain is capable of handling four times the speed of the average speaker. It leaves a lot of time for idle mind. Hence, listeners have to summarise and process the information that they receive. Empathy requires the listener to get into the shoes of the speaker. It does mean that the receiver should try to understand what the speaker wants to communicate. An active listener should demonstrate acceptance. Finally, the listener should do whatever is necessary to get the full intended meaning from the speaker's communication.

Exhibit 19.7 Principles of Effective Listening

Principle	*Good Listener*	*Bad Listener*
1. Look for areas of interest	Seeks personal enlightenment and/or information, entertains new topics as potentially interesting.	Turns out dry subjects, narrowly defines what is interesting.
2. Overlook errors of delivery	Attends to meaning and content, ignores delivery errors while being sensitive to any message in them.	Ignores if delivery is poor, misses messages because of personal attributes of the communicator.
3. Postpone judgment	Avoids quick judgments, waits until comprehension of the core message is complete.	Quickly evaluates and passes judgment, inflexible regarding contrary messages.
4. Listen for ideas	Listens for ideas and themes. Identifies the main points.	Listens for facts and details.
5. Take notes	Takes careful notes and uses a variety of note taking or recording schemes depending on the speaker.	Takes incomplete note using one system.
6. Be actively responsive	Responds frequently with nods, "uhhuhs", etc., shows active body state, works at listening.	Passive demeanour, few or no responses, little energy output.
7. Resist distractions	Resists being distracted, longer concentration span, places loaded words in perspective.	Easily distracted, focusses on loaded or emotional words, short concentration span.
8. Challenge your mind	Uses difficult material to stimulate the mind, seeks to enlarge understanding	Avoids difficult material, does not seek to broaden knowledge base.
9. Capitalise on mind speed	Uses listening time to summarise and anticipate the message, attends to implicit messages as well as explicit messages.	Daydreams with slow speakers, becomes preoccupied with other thoughts
10. Assist and encourage the speaker	Asks for clarifying information or examples, uses reflecting phrases, helps to rephrase the idea.	Interrupts, asks trivial questions, makes distracting comments.

(**Source:** David J.Cherrington, *Organisational Behaviour*, p. 577.)

Developing Effective/Active Listening Skills

The specific behaviours of effective active listener are:

(i) **Make eye contact:** The receiver should maintain eye contact with the sender during the process of receiving information.

(ii) **Exhibit affirmative head nods** and appropriate facial expressions.

(iii) **Avoid distracting actions or gestures:** When listening, don't do any other work.

(iv) **Ask questions:** Asking questions during the process of listening provides clarification, ensures understanding and assures the speaker that the receiver is listening.

(v) **Paraphrase:** Paraphrasing means restating what the speaker has said in the listener's own words.

(vi) **Avoid interrupting** the speaker.

(vii) **Don't overtalk:** Allow the speaker to talk completely and speak only to the extent necessary.

(viii) **Make smooth transitions** between the speaker and listener. Concentrate on what the speaker has to say rather than what you are going to say.

(F) ORGANISATIONAL COMMUNICATION

What all is true of interpersonal communication is also true of organisational communication. Here too the effective communication involves getting an accurate message from one person to another. However, there are certain factors that are unique to the organisation which influence the effectiveness of communication.

Raymond V. Lesikar has described four factors that influence the effectiveness of organisational communication.[9]

1. The formal channels of communication.
2. The organisation's authority structure.
3. Job specialisation and
4. Information ownership.

Formal Communication

Communication effectiveness is influenced by formal channels in two ways. First, the formal channels cover the widening distance that usually occurs when the organisations develop and grow. Second, the formal channels inhibit the free flow of information between organisational levels, particularly in upward communication. For example, a worker communicates his problems to a foreman or supervisor rather than to the Plant Manager. It has both advantages and disadvantages. The advantage is that the managers are fed with the limited important information and the disadvantage is that sometimes the manager may not receive the information he should receive.

The authority structure in the organisation also influences the effectiveness of communication. The content and accuracy of information are also affected because of the differences in authority and status. For example, there cannot take place a frank conversation between a clerk and the company managing director, since the clerk's speech is always characterized by politeness and formality.

Job specialisation also affects the effectiveness of communication. Members belonging to the same work group use the same jargon and understand each other better, while communication between highly differentiated groups is likely to be a problem for both.

Information ownership refers to the unique knowledge and information about their jobs possessed by the individuals.[10] For many individuals, such information is a sort of power that helps them function more effectively than others. Most of the persons with such scales are often reluctant to share the information with others. Hence, open communication is not always possible in the organisation.

Organisational communication can be formal or informal

Organisational communication may be formal or informal. Formal communication is an official communication having official support and sanction. Formal communication flows through the authority and responsibility channels of an organisation which exists in order to: *(i)* Measure and control outputs; *(ii)* To coordinate complex activities in the system and relate the sub systems to the total systems; *(iii)* To regulate response to external environment; *(iv)* Coordinate resource allocations and *(v)* Create a climate within which the organisation can adjust its output as it receives and process feedback.[11]

The advantages of formal communication include: *(i)* Providing correct information; *(ii)* Having official support with authority; *(iii)* Uniformity in transmission and *(iv)* Handling of message efficiently. However, formal communication suffers from the drawbacks like: (a) Delay in sending information due to official channels; (b) Absence of immediate feedback; (c) Absence of interest to send and receive and (d) Lack of ability to communicate upward.

Organisational communication takes place in a variety of ways. It may flow vertically or horizontally. The vertical communication can be either downward or upward.

Managers, today realised that informal communication is more important and useful than formal communication. Why? We, now study informal communication to answer this question.

Informal Communication or Grapevine

Communication based on social relationships is informal communication.

The communication that arises not out of formal relations between people but out of informal or social relationships is called the *grapevine* or *informal* communication. The management has no absolute control over this type of communication as they neither created nor destroyed it. Communication need not flow through authority-responsibility relationships or channels of organisation in informal communications. In informal communication, there is no formal superior-subordinate relationships.

The informal communication does both good and bad to the organisations. The advantages of informal communication are: *(i)* It acts as a driving force to unite the workforce in cases of common matters; *(ii)* It saves time and energy as the information flows at a high speed; *(iii)* It has immediate response from the receiver; *(iv)* It provides the scope for creation of new ideas; *(v)* It satisfies the communication needs of various employees and *(vi)* It provides scope for immediate feedback.

Informal communication suffers from various drawbacks. They are: *(i)* Informal communication sometimes spreads wrong information and rumours; *(ii)* It distorts information; *(iii)* Grapevine provides only inadequate information; *(iv)* Information provided through grapevine has no formal authority and *(v)* It overlooks superiors.

According to Koontz and O'Donnel, "the most effective communication results when managers utilise informal organisation to supplement the communication channels of the formal organization.[12]

It should be remembered that it is a part of the manager's job to have a little control over this informal communication so that he can take the appropriate action to minimise the adverse effect of this channel.

Organisational Climate and Communication

Organisational climate is very important in the context of communication. Organisational climate is the summary perception which people have about an organisation. It is thus a global expression of what the organisation is:

Organisational climate is more essential for communication.

Organisational climate refers to a system of shared meaning held by members that distinguishes the organisation from other organisations. The characteristics of organisational climate are:

(i) **Individual Initiative:** The degree of responsibility, freedom and independence that individuals have.

(ii) **Risk Tolerance:** The degree to which employees are encouraged to be aggressive, innovative and risk-seeking.

(iii) **Direction:** The degree to which the organisation creates clear objectives and performance expectations.

(iv) **Integration:** The degree to which units within the organisation are encouraged to operate in a coordinated manner.

(v) **Management Support:** The degree to which managers provide clear communication, assistance and support to their subordinates.

(vi) **Control:** The number of rules and regulations and the amount of direct supervision that is used to oversee and control employee behaviour.

(vii) **Identity:** The degree to which members identify with the organisation as a whole rather than with their particular work group or field of professional expertise.

(viii) **Reward system:** The degree to which reward allocations are based on employee performance.

(ix) **Conflict tolerance:** The degree to which employees are encouraged to air conflicts and criticisms openly and

(x) **Communication patterns:** The degree to which organisational communications are restricted to the formal hierarchy of authority.[13]

Thus, the dependence on formal communication denotes higher degree of organisational climate.

Communicating with the Employees

Both formal as well as informal communications channels are used to communicate with the employees. In addition to following written communication, oral and non-verbal communication should be relied upon. In addition to downward communication to communicate rules, procedures and programmes of the organisation to employees, employees should also be encouraged to communicate to their superiors.

In order to make use of teamwork, all channels of communication or star communication patterns should be encouraged. Interpersonal communication should be encouraged with a view to develop interpersonal relations. Employees should also be encouraged to develop effective and active listening skills.

Managers often fail to communicate due to the barriers involved in this process. Now, we shall study the barriers to communication.

(G) BARRIERS TO COMMUNICATION

There are certain factors that impede the proper flow of communication. All those factors that adversely affect the effectiveness of communication may be called *barriers* to communication. The barriers to communication may be classified into:

External Barriers

External Barriers are usually in the following forms:

(i) **Semantic barriers:** These barriers arise at the stage of encoding or decoding in the process of communication. These barriers are often due to linguistic capacity of the sender and receiver.

Badly expressed message: If the message is not expressed clearly and precisely and when the right word is not used at the right place, it may not convey the proper meaning that the person has in mind.

(ii) **Faulty translations:** Managers are often required to translate the messages into a form suitable to their superiors or subordinates. Unless one has good linguistic capacity, he cannot do this job well.

(iii) **Specialist language:** Technical personnel and other experts usually fall into the habit of using their own technical jargon which others outside their group fail to understand. This hinders the communication to a large extent.

Emotional or Psychological Barriers

The emotional or psychological state of a person also influences the communication. The following are some emotional or psychological barriers:

(i) **Premature evaluation:** People often jump to conclusion even before the message is completely communicated. This discourages the sender and may even give him a feeling of futility.

(ii) **Existence of preconceived notions.**

(iii) **Inattention due to lack of interest.**

(iv) **Distrust in communication:** If the receiver does not trust that sender for any reason, he does not pay the required attention to the message and he does not believe in the message received.

(v) **Fears:** *(a)* Fear of misinterpretation of message by the receiver. *(b)* Fear of distortion: sometimes the message of the sender is filtered when it reaches the receiver. This is also known as loss by transmission. *(c)* Fear of exposing oneself to criticism. *(d)* Information is held back deliberately by the sender with the feeling that some action will be taken against him if he expresses his opinion frankly. This is known as *fear of reprisal*.

(vi) **Poor retention** by the receiver because of his inability.

(vii) **Defensive behaviour:** Employees have a tendency to become defensive when they feel they are being threatened. In such circumstances, they tend to stop listening to the sender's message.

Organisational Barriers

Organisational policies, rules and regulations, status relationships also affect the effectiveness of communication. For example, a frank feedback cannot be expected from the subordinate because of the existing superior-subordinate relation.

Personal Barriers

Personal barriers can again be classified into two types: *(i)* Barriers in superiors and *(ii)* Barriers in subordinates.

(i) Barriers in Superiors (Barriers from Superiors)

(a) *Attitude of Superiors*: If the superior has an unfavourable attitude to the subordinate's act of giving message, adequate information cannot flow from the subordinate to the superior.

(b) *Lack of Confidence in Subordinates*: The information from the subordinate does not interest the superior when he lacks confidence in him.

(c) *Lack of Awareness of Importance of Communication*: The manager does not understand the communication with the subordinate if he doesn't know the importance of it.

(d) *Insistence on Proper Channel*: Superiors always insist on the subordinates giving the information through proper channel and this definitely discourages him to furnish the factual information.

(ii) Barriers in Subordinates (Barriers from Subordinates)

(a) *Unwillingness to Communicate*: Subordinates are often reluctant to provide information for the fear that a piece of information may have adverse effect on the attitudes of the superiors.

Even if they provide information, they modify it in such a manner to protect their own interest.

(b) *Lack of Proper Incentive*: If a novel suggestion made by a subordinate does not evoke any attention of the management, this experience will keep him away from conveying anything in future.

Despite these barriers, some managers communicate effectively? Hence, we shall study the measures of effective communication.

How to Make Communication Effective

The analysis of the communication process involves the following four elements: Communication can be made effective through the effective use of these elements.

(i) **The content:** It calls for clear thinking about objective (must be definite), message (frank and sensible), wording (accurate, clear, convincing and untwistable) and presentation (planned, appropriate and effective).

(ii) **The system** must be clearly defined and recognised.

(iii) **The technique:** It involves selection of the most appropriate technique. The techniques are oral, written, graphic and psychological.

(iv) **The media:** The media of communication are personal contacts, meetings, conferences, telephone talks, letters, reports, minutes, notices, handbooks, periodicals, schedules, balance sheets, organisational charts, attitude, gestures, expression, inflexion, etc.

Communication can be effective based on content, system, technique and media.

A proper regard for content, system, technique and medium will help to communicate effectively. But there is no substitute for real basic elements of good communication, viz. honesty, sincerity, clear thought and simplicity.

Further, clear thinking is necessary primarily to all successful communication and decision-making. The mental process involved in clear thinking covers (a) Collection of all relevant information; (b) Sorting out facts from opinions and inferences; (c) Checking the facts, opinions and inferences and (d) Evaluating the information and drawing conclusions from it.

Ten Commandments of Effective Communication

The American Management Association (AMA) suggested ten commandments for effective communication. They are:

(i) Clarify ideas before attempting to communicate;

(ii) Examine the process of communication;

(iii) Understand the physical and human environment when communicating;

(iv) In planning communication, consult with others to obtain their support as well as the facts;

(v) Consider the content and the overtones of the message;

(vi) Whenever possible, communicate something that helps or is valued by the receiver;

(vii) Communication to be effective requires follow-up;

(viii) Communicate messages that are of short-run and long-run importance;

(ix) Actions must be congruent with communication; and

(x) Be a good listener.

KEY TERMS

- Group
- Communication
- Inter-Personal Communication
- Downward Communication
- Communication Networks
- Formal Communication
- Communication Channels
- Non-verbal Communication
- Upward Communication
- Written Communication
- Communication Channels
- Communication Barriers
- Cohesiveness
- Grapevine
- Oral Communication
- Synergy
- Telecommunication
- Body Language

QUESTIONS

1. What is communication? Why should we study communication specially?
2. Discuss the fundamentals and process of communication.
3. Comment on the contributions of MIS and information technology to the organisational communication.
4. Write the advantages and disadvantages of oral, written and non-verbal communication.
5. "Greater significance is attributed to the upward communication in team organisation structures." Critically comment.
6. "Modern managers prefer and encourage grapevine rather than formal communication." Comment.
7. What is listening? Explain the role of effective listening in the communication process.
8. "Despite taking all possible care, mangers often fail to communicate." Why?
9. Suggest the measures to make communication effective.

REFERENCES

1. Dale S. Beach, *op.cit.*, p. 581.
2. McFariand, *Management: Principles and Practice*, p. 552.
3. Walter D. Scott *et al.*, *op.cit.*, p. 255.
4. Stephen P. Robbins, *op.cit.*, p. 320.

5. *Ibid.*, p. 321.
6. Andrew D. Szilagyi *et al.*, *Organisational Behaviour and Performance*, Scott Foreshman, 1987, p. 410.
7. Fred Luthans, *Organisational Behaviour*, McGraw Hill Book Co., New York, 1987, pp. 515-17.
8. C. P. Rogers and R. E. Farson, *Active Listening*, Industrial Relations Centre of the University of Chicago, Chicago, 1976.
9. *Ibid.*
10. *Myers, M.* T. and Myers, G. M., *Managing by Communication*, McGraw Hill International Book Co., 1982, p. 137.
11. Harold Koontz and Cyril O'Donnel, *op.cit.*, p. 137.
12. *Ibid.*
13. Stephen P. Robbins, *op.cit.*, pp. 572-573.

CHAPTER 20

LEADERSHIP AND FOLLOWERSHIP

☛ Chapter Outline

(A) Introduction
(B) Leader vs Manager
(C) Leadership Theories
(D) Leadership Styles
(E) Followership Styles- A New Approach
(F) Outstanding Leaders
(G) Leadership Skills
(H) Leadership Under Cross-Cultural Environment
(I) Women and Leadership
(J) Global Leading
— Key Terms
— Questions
— References

☛ Learning Objectives

After studying this Chapter, you should be able to:

✓ Estimate the leadership tasks;
✓ Know the meaning of leadership, power of the leader and difference between leader and manager;
✓ Analyse different types of leadership theories, viz., traditional theories, behavioural theories, contingency/ situational theories and modern theories;
✓ Understand various leadership styles and their effectiveness;
✓ Comment upon the new dimension of leadership, i.e., Followership styles;
✓ Understand the qualities and skills of a leader;
✓ Understand how the leaders perform under cross-cultural environment; and
✓ Discuss the skills of women leaders.

(A) INTRODUCTION

The concept of leadership has undergone a sea change from the concept of 'born-leader' to 'situation-leader' and to effective leader. Views, assumptions and theories of leadership have changed significantly in recent years. Business and industry have set managers more as leaders to achieve the challenges. The quality of leadership provided by the managers determines the degree of success of business. Some people are born leaders and need little training or development. But many managers are not born with qualitative leadership skills. Such managers need training and development to acquire and develop leadership skills. However, born leaders can be more efficient with training.

For example, Jamshediji Tata and Dheerubhai Ambani belong to the born leaders category whereas Vikram Singh of Hindustan Aluminium and Parthasaradhi of Hindustan Lever belong to the 'made leaders' category.

Leadership: influence on the part of the leader

Leadership involves the exercise of influence on the part of the leader over the perception, motivation, communication, personality and ultimately over the behaviour of other people (preferably followers). Leadership is, therefore, the study of leader's influence over the thoughts, feelings, opinions, beliefs, attitudes and actions of followers (See Box 20.1).

Box 20.1: Leader's Influence

There is no single, universally accepted definition of a leader. At a broad level, the common characteristic of a leader is that he should be ahead of others and have the ability to articulate his thoughts clearly.

A leader should also have the ability to effectively demonstrate confidence in his people. Respect, trust and acceptability should be gained, and not commanded. A good leader should master the art of listening to his team, being sensitive to his people's needs, and above all, to lead by example. Of course, the styles will vary.

Leaders are born, not made. Leadership cannot be taught in B-schools. Only the styles can be altered and refined. A leader moves ahead, trying new things, knowing that not all the loose ends are tied up, that not everyone is fully aboard, and that success is not assured. A leder must follow the maxim "practise what you preach". Leadership also means upholding, at all costs, the ideals, principles and credos that one considers sacrosanct.

The process of influencing others is subject to interpretation and differs with culture, age and society. However, one attribute applies to all leadership: setting the right example. The only way leaders can utilise their ability to touch the lives of those around them is to become involved themselves.

(**Source:** Adapted from *Business Today*, May 12, 2002.)

Leadership is defined as "the process whereby one individual influences other group members towards the attainment of defined group or organizational goals."[1]

Mutual Influence of Leader and Follower

The definition on leadership indicates that the leader influences the follower. However, it is viewed that the followers also influence leaders. In fact, leader and follower influence each other mutually. The followers' factors those influence leader include:

- Subordinates'/Followers' performances
- Subordinates'/Followers' characteristics
- The nature of the work itself
- Business policies and incidents.

Fig. 20.1 Presents the Mutual Influence of Follower and Leader on Each Other.

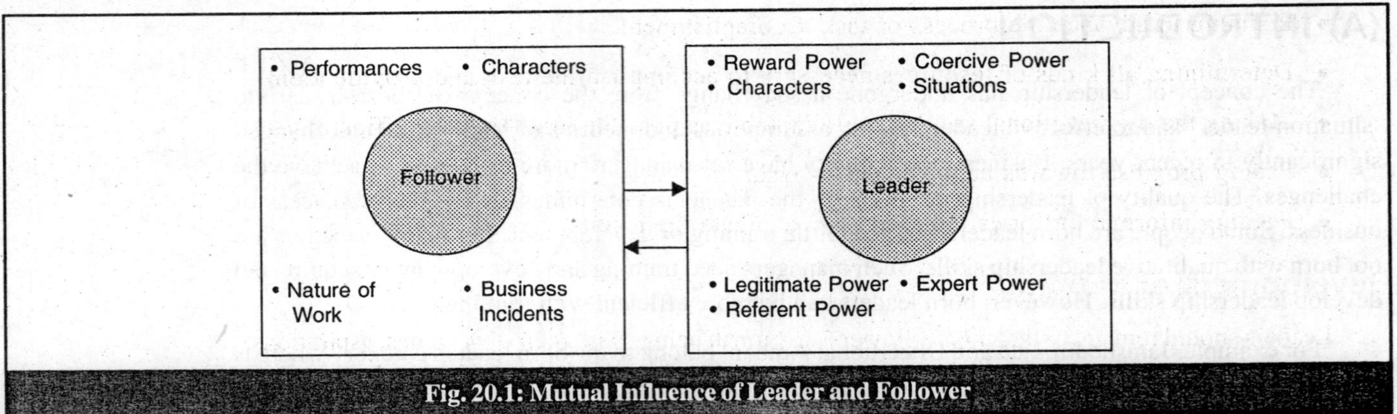

Fig. 20.1: Mutual Influence of Leader and Follower

Effectiveness of Leaders

Leaders' effectiveness depends on task accomplishment

The effectiveness of leaders depend on their ability to influence and be influenced by the followers in the task accomplishment. In essence, leaders

- Ensure that the necessary tasks are accomplished
- Build and reinforce the team and foster teamwork and team spirit and
- Develop each member of the team. (See Box 20.2).

Box 20.2: Business Leaders in India — What and Why?

Business, Economy, Entrepreneurs, Leadership, MNCs, Top Honchos, Leaders, Industry, International Business, Knowledge Economy....are some of the key words which define what India is emerging as an economic superpower. Today India is one of the biggest and the fastest growing economies in the world and is on the forefront of emerging as one of the decision-makers in the global economy.

Indian entrepreneurs and business leaders are defining the global economic scenario with some of the top companies being led by Indian breeds of businessmen and thought leaders.

Leaders In India

Leaders In India is apt and is surely entering India at the righteous time. When the global economy has taken a hit, it affected countries like India and China which are re-defining rules of the game and are changing the ways of the world. Indian entrepreneurs have created some of the most innovative success stories, which have transformed into multinational giants.

With the world knocking at the doors and the spirits high, India is poised to be a global economic superpower. A land of opportunities as has been remarked by Donald Trump Jr.

"India is one of the most dynamic markets of the world, where innovation, business, and technical acumen will contribute to grow and thrive for many years to come".

Being at the forefront of the 21st knowledge century, India's inherent knowledge resources are now being more comprehensively harnessed by and interconnected with Indian and global business.

(**Source:** http://www.leaders-india.com/)

Task Achievement

Leader's ability to contribute to the accomplishment of the given task depends on:

- Clarity of purpose, formulating it with enthusiasm and reinforcing the followers of it quite often.
- Understanding clearly the long-run as well as the short duration plans of the company and know how the task fits in the overall plans.

- Planning in advance the process of task accomplishment.
- Determining all kinds of resources necessary to accomplish the task and provide them.
- Making the organizational structure as adaptable as possible to do the task efficiently.
- Pacing progress towards achievement of task.
- Feeding information forward and back to evaluate the results.

Development of Individuals

Leaders should remember that their followers are human beings with their own values, aspirations, needs and attitudes. Therefore, the leader should respect his followers and create conducive work environment and culture so that the followers must

- have satisfaction from personal achievement in the job they do,
- have a feel that they make a worthwhile contribution to the objectives,
- have a feel that the job is challenging, demanding the best of them and give them higher responsibilities,
- be recognized adequately for their achievement,
- have control over the jobs/tasks delegated to their followers,
- have a feel that they grow, develop and advance as human beings.

Building the Teams

Most of the organizational activities are done in teams. Therefore, the leader should build teams, and understand the needs of his team. Leader should respond to the team even by leading from behind. To achieve the team effectiveness, the leader should:

- Formulate and maintain team policies, objectives and standards.
- Involve all the team members in achievement of objectives.
- Communicate and brief the team members face-to-face regarding the matters affect them at work.
- Consult and involve the team members in decision-making which affect them.

Make the Vision Tangible

Leaders have to formulate vision, mission and purpose. Followers commit to the achievement of the vision, if it is tangible and attainable. The leaders transform the vision into tangible reality, promote it and convince the followers regarding its significance. The leaders have to carry out the following steps in order to make the vision tangible and realize it.

- Formulation of vision and mission.
- Formulation of objectives and goals to be achieved for successful achievement of mission.
- Analysis of external environment for opportunities and threats.
- Appraise the organization to know the strengths, weaknesses, competitive advantages and core competencies of the company.
- Formulation of strategic alternatives to achieve the goals.
- Develop the organizational structure appropriate for the strategy.

- Create organizational climate necessary to achieve the strategy.
- Formulation of the tactics necessary to achieve the strategy.
- Development of feedforward and feedback systems to evaluate the strategic management process.
- Implement the strategy and modifying it, if necessary, based on the environmental changes.

Leader's Power

The leader's influence over followers depends on various factors like:

- the nature of the leader,
- the nature of the followers,
- the leader's behaviour,
- organizational situation,
- follower's behaviour, and
- leader's capacity to influence followers.

Among these factors, the capacity of the leader to influence his/her followers plays a significant role. The leader's influence over his followers is derived from various sources of power. The important sources of power of the leader include:

Reward Power

Reward power: salary rise, promotions, favours etc.

The superior granting a salary rise to his subordinate in order to encourage him to work better is referred to as reward power of the superior. Reward power refers to offering monetary and non-monetary rewards by the leader to his followers. Leader has the formal and informal control over organizational resources, opportunities and decisions. Leader, rewards his followers, by exercising his control over these resources. These rewards include salary increase, promotions, transfers, providing fringe benefits and perquisites.

Other types of rewards are offered by the leader to his followers based on the former's personal power, motives, dynamism and communication and appreciation skills include: praise, recognition, granting autonomy, freedom, empowerment, etc. Leader's success depends on the nature and extent of valuing these rewards by the followers.

Coercive Power

Coercive power: Ability to coerce/ punish

Leader motivates his followers not only through rewarding but also through punishing. Coercive power is the opposite to reward power. Coercive power is the ability or the capacity of the leader to coerce or punish his followers for carrying out the assigned tasks.

The sources of coercive power include both personal and position. Leaders personally have coercive power or power to punish their followers. If the followers do not do the work on their own, then the leader influences and coerces them. Leaders also have coercive power which are derived from their superior positions in the organisation. This coercive power includes deferring promotions, salary reductions, demotion, transfer to an unpleasant place or job, retrenchment, and the like.

Legitimate Power

Legitimate power: rights based on the job.

The job analysis consists of job description and job specification. Job description consists of the rights of the job incumbent. The job of the leader gives rights to the leader regarding issuing orders, work assignment, delegation of authority and responsibility to his subordinates in order to get the work done. This power of the leader to influence his followers through the rights of his job is referred to as legitimate power. Therefore, the orders, requests, direction issued by the leader based on his/her job rights are viewed by the followers as legitimate and valid.

Subordinates'/followers' job description indicate their duties and obligations. These obligations indicate that they have to comply with such requests and orders in order to carry out the organizational activities. Therefore, legitimate power is derived from the position and it has nothing to do with the leader's characteristics.

Expert Power

Expert power: Expertise, knowledge, skills, etc.

Expert power is derived from the expertise, knowledge, information, skills and abilities that the leader possesses over the jobs of his subordinates.

The subordinates expect the leader as a source of knowledge, information and skills in carrying out their duties. If the subordinates get continuous and timely support from their leader in the form of offering expertise that they do not have, then they respond very positively to their leader. Thus, the leader can influence the subordinates very much positively by possessing the expert knowledge, skills and abilities.

The leader should acquire knowledge, skill, abilities to become expert. He should also update them continuously in order to retain that expert position in order to influence the followers effectively and contribute to the organizational goals.

Referent Power

Referent power: Role model

The leader should be resourceful in terms of knowledge and skill. He should be capable of rewarding the followers properly. Further, he should discriminate the followers who avoid the work and use his coercive power to make them work.

Subordinates would like to find extraordinary characters, abilities and qualities in the leader and see him as their role model. Further, the followers would like to identify with the leader and to emulate the leader. If the followers admire the leader's abilities and qualities very much, they would like to be influenced by the leader to a greater extent. Then the leader has greater referent power over subordinates.

Leader gets the referent power to a greatest extent from his personal expertise, characteristics and knowledge rather than from his formal organizational position. Exhibit 20.1 presents the uses and outcome of power.

Exhibit 20.1 Uses and Outcomes of Power

Source of Leader Influence	*Type of Outcome*		
	Commitment	*Compliance*	*Resistance*
Legitimate Power	*Possible* If request is polite and very appropriate	*Likely* If request or order is seen as legitimate	*Possible* If arrogant demands are made or request does not appear proper
Reward Power	*Possible* If used in a Subtle, very Personal way	*Likely* If used in a mechanical, impersonal way	*Possible* If used in a manipulative, arrogant way

Coercive Power	*Very Unlikely*	*Possible* If used in a helpful, Nonpunitive way	*Likely* If used in a hostile or manipulative way
Expert Power	*Likely* If request is persuasive and Subordinates share Leader's task goals	*Possible* If request is persuasive but subordinates are apathetic about Leader's task goals	*Possible* If leader is arrogant and insulting, or subordinates oppose task goals
Referent Power	*Likely* If request is Believed to be Important to leader	*Possible* If request is perceived to be unimportant to leader	*Possible* If request is for something that will bring harm to leader

(**Source:** Table adapted by Gary A.Yukl from information in John R.P.French,Jr., and Bertram Raven, "The Bases of Social Power," in Dorwin P.Cartwright (ed.), *Studies in Social Power* (Ann Arbor, Mich.:Institute for Social Research, University of Michigan, 1959), pp.150-167.

(B) LEADER VS. MANAGER

Managers in the past like Mr.Krishna Murthy of Maruti Udyog Limited ran the business under the relatively stable environmental factors. But, the leaders in the new millennium like Mr.Bill Gates of Micro Soft, Mr. Dhirubai Ambani of Relliance Petrochemicals, won over the competitors, created the new external environment, and conquered the market.

Leaders manipulate the environment whereas managers act within the environment.

As Warren G. Bennis put it, "To survive in the twenty-first century, we are going to need a new generation of leaders — leaders not managers. The distinction is an important one. Leaders conquer the context – the volatile, turbulent, ambiguous surroundings that sometimes seem to conspire against us and will surely suffocate us if we let them — while managers surrender to it."[2]

Thus, managers surrender to the external environment, white leaders fight with the environment and create new environment. Theorists and practioners differentiate the leaders from managers only in recent years. This is more so, particularly after globalisation and liberalization of world economies. Abraham Zaleznik argues that leaders and managers are very different kinds of people. They differ in motivation, personal history, etc.

Managers tend to be impersonal towards goals while leaders take active and personal attitude towards goals.

- Managers tend to view work as an enabling process while leaders work from high task positions, seek out risk and danger when opportunity and reward appear high.
- Managers work with people while leaders relate ideas to people in more intuitive and empathic ways.[3]
- Managers cope up with change whereas leaders bring change. Leaders develop a vision and direction for the future.[4]

Bennis presents the differences between Manager and Leader as shown in Exhibit 20.2.

Exhibit 20.2 Managers vs. Leaders in the Twenty-First Century

Managers	*Leaders*
Administers	Innovates
A copy	An original
Maintains	Develops
Focusses on Systems and Structures	Focusses on People
Relies on control	Inspires trust
Short-range view	Long-range perspective
Asks how and when	Asks what and why
Eye on the bottom line	Eye on the horizon
Imitates	Originates
Accepts the Status Quo	Challenges the Status Quo
Classic good soldier	Own person
Does things right	Does the right thing

(**Source:** Warren G.Bennis, "Managing the Dream:Leadership in the 21st Century," *Journal of Organisational Change Management*, Vol.2, No.1, 1989, p.7).

(C) LEADERSHIP THEORIES

There is a lot of literature on leadership. Most of this literature is confusing and contradictory. Hence, we should draw different approaches to classify and study the leadership. Study of leadership theories is one of the best approaches to study leadership. Leadership theories are classified as shown in Fig. 20.2.

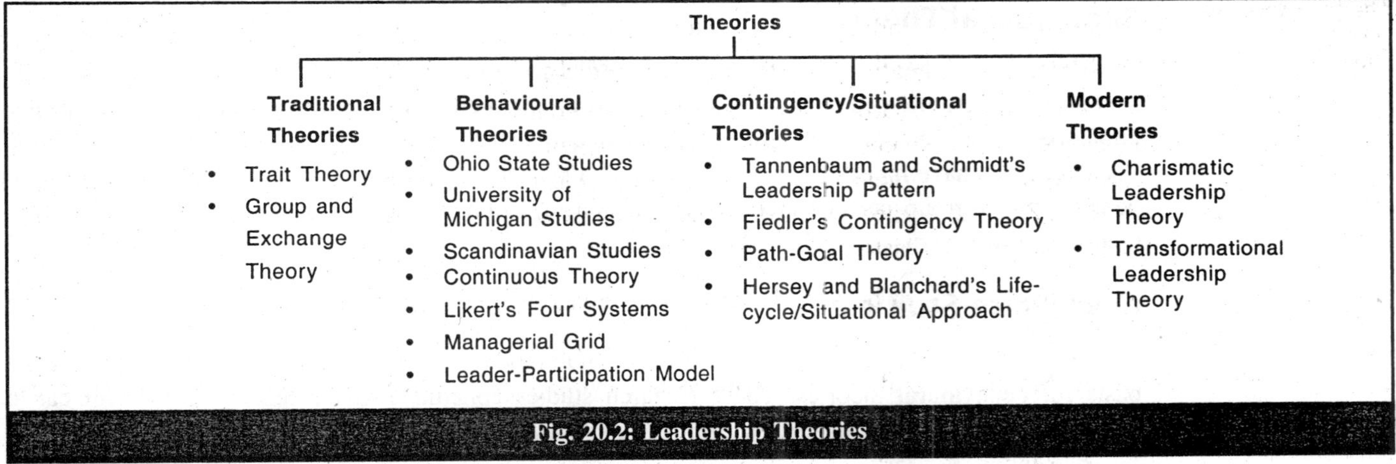

Fig. 20.2: Leadership Theories

Traditional Theories

Traditional theories of leadership include traits theory and Group and Exchange theories of leadership.

Trait Theory

Traits: personality, social, pysical and intellectual

Trait theories of leadership sought personality, social, physical or intellectual traits that differentiated leaders from non-leaders. Trait theorists refer to people like Mahatma Gandhi, Indira Gandhi, Margarat Thatcher, Nelson Mandela, N.T.Rama Rao and describe them in terms of charismatic, enthusiastic and courageous traits.

Trait theories assume that leaders are born, not made. The research studies focus on personal traits or characteristics that distinguish the leaders from the followers and a successful leader from an unsuccessful leader. A number of research studies were conducted during the last 50 years. The cumulative findings of these studies conclude that some traits increase the likelihood of success as a leader, but more of the traits guarantee success.[5]

Stodgill classified these traits into five categories, viz.,

- intelligence and scholarship,
- physical traits like age, height, weight, strength, etc.,
- personality characterized by self-confidence, honesty, integrity, creativity and imitation,
- social status and experience, and
- task-orientation.[6]

Group and Exchange Theories of Leadership

Social Psychology is the basis for group theories of leadership. Social exchange view of leadership indicates that, "exchange theories propose that group members make contributions at a cost to themselves and receive benefits at a cost to the group or other members. Interaction continue because members find the social exchange mutually rewarding."

Social exchange indicates that leadership is an exchange process between the leaders and followers. This theory indicates that there are three domains of leadership viz., leader-based domain, follower-based domain and relationship-based domain.

Behavioural Theories

Behavioural theories of leadership propose that specific behaviours differentiate leaders from non-leaders. These theories opine that leader's style is oriented either an employee-centred or a job centred emphasis. These theories attempt to explain leadership in terms of the behaviour that the leader exhibits. These theories have modest success in building consistent relationship between patterns of leadership behaviour and group performance. However, consideration of situational factors is missing in these theories. Now, we discuss behavioural theories.

Ohio State Studies

The research that was conducted at Ohio State University, USA in the late 1940s provides the basis for behavioural theories. These research studies concluded that a leader's behaviour can be categorised into two dimensions viz., initiating structure and consideration.

Initiating structure: Initiating structure refers to the extent to which a leader is likely to define and structure his/her role and those of subordinates in the search for goal attainment.[7] The leader's behaviour includes job/work design, work relationships, assigning the work groups and individual workers, establishing the work standards, performances, goals, indicate the groups and individuals to achieve the goals, meet the bench-marks/standards and deadlines.

Considerations: Trust, respect, etc.

Consideration: Consideration is the extent to which a person is likely to have job relationships that are characterised by mutual trust, respect for subordinate's ideas and regard for their feelings. He/she has concern for followers' comfort, well-being, status and satisfaction.

A leader who attempts to solve the personal problems of his subordinates and helps them is friendly and, approachable. He treats all his subordinates as equals. Such a leader is viewed as high in consideration. *Research establishes that high consideration leads to high performance of subordinates and vice versa.*

Mr. R. K.Nair of a Pune based company is high in consideration. He empowers the people and emphasises on friendliness. Mr. Nair improved the productivity of his company significantly compared to the competing firms.

University of Michigan Studies

Survey Research Centre of University of Michigan conducted leadership studies in the late 1940s. The objective of the study were to find behavioural characteristics of leaders that appeared to be related to measures of performance effectiveness.[8]

The Michigan group concluded that there are two dimensions of leadership behaviour, viz., employee-oriented and production-oriented.[9] Employee-oriented leaders emphasise inter-personal relations whereas production-oriented leaders emphasise technical or task aspects of the job. The goal of both employee-oriented and production-oriented leaders is to accomplish and get the things done by the group members.

Michigan Studies also concluded that employee-oriented leadership results in high productivity and higher job satisfaction. And *vice versa* is true in case of production-oriented leadership. Hence, the Michigan studies favoured employee-oriented leadership to achieve the goals of both higher productivity and higher job satisfaction.

Scandinavian Studies

The researchers in Finland and Sweden felt that the Ohio and Michigan Studies were conducted during 1940s and 1960s when the world economies were more or less stable. Therefore, these studies may not be applicable when the world economies are developing. According to them, the leaders should exhibit development-oriented behaviour in a developing world. These leaders value innovation or creation, seek new and challenging ideas, experimentation, generate and implement change.

In fact, Ohio studies used developmental items in their research. But they were not received any attention at that time. Hence, the Scandinavian studies were conducted by including the third dimension, i.e., development orientation – for the effective leadership. The preliminary results of the Scandinavian studies show that the leaders of 1990s support development oriented behaviour. Leaders who demonstrate development-oriented behaviour, developed more competent and satisfied subordinates.

Continuous Theory of Leadership

Lewin, Lippitt and White suggested a continuous theory of leadership which identified three basic styles of leadership, i.e., autocrat, democrat and laissez-faire. Robert McMurree suggested the benevolent autocrat between autocrat and democrat leadership. *Bank managers in India used to adopt autocratic style before 1969. But, this style proved to be ineffective after 1969 in view of new values, expectations, desires, culture, etc., inducted in banks with the massive entrance of new employees with massive branch expansion. However, the bank managers feel that even the democratic style has not proved effective, leading to indiscipline in most situations. In view of this it is suggested that the bank managers may adopt a benevolent autocratic style.*

Likert's Four Systems

Rensis Likert suggests that managers operate under four different systems. In System-I, the leader behaves like an exploitative authoritative way and exploits the subordinates. In System-2, leader takes a paternalistic approach and in System-3, he uses democratic approach, where he consults subordinates in decision-making. In System-4, the leader allows his subordinates to participate in decision-making process and the decisions are taken by the leader and subordinates (Table 20.1).

Table 20.1: Likert's Four-System Construct

System 1 Characteristic	System 2 (Exploitative Authoritative)	System 3 (Benevolent Authoritative)	System 4 (Consultative)	Participative Group
Trust in Subordinates	None	Condescending	Substantial	Complete
Motivation Accomplished by	Fear and Threats	Rewards and Punishment	Rewards, Punishment, Involvement	Group Participation Involvement
Communication	Very Limited	Limited	Fairly Widespread	Widespread
Interpersonal Interaction	Very Limited	Limited	Moderate Amount	Extensive
Decision-making	Centralised	Mostly Centralised	Broad Participation Allowed	Dispersed
Goal Setting	Centralised	Mostly Centralised	Some Participation Allowed	Participation Allowed
Control	Centralised	Mostly Centralised	Moderate Delegation	Extensive Delegation
Informal Organisation	Always Developed And in Opposition To the Organisation	Usually Developed and Partially in Opposition to the Organisation	May be Developed and May Support or Oppose the Organisation	Informal Organisation Is the Same as the Formal Organisation

Managerial Grid

Concern for production and people

Industrial psychologists Blake and Mouton developed the managerial grid basing on the Ohio State study. The managerial grid identifies a range of management behaviour based on the different ways how production/service-oriented and employee-oriented styles interact with each other. Different styles of leadership are shown in Fig. 20.3.

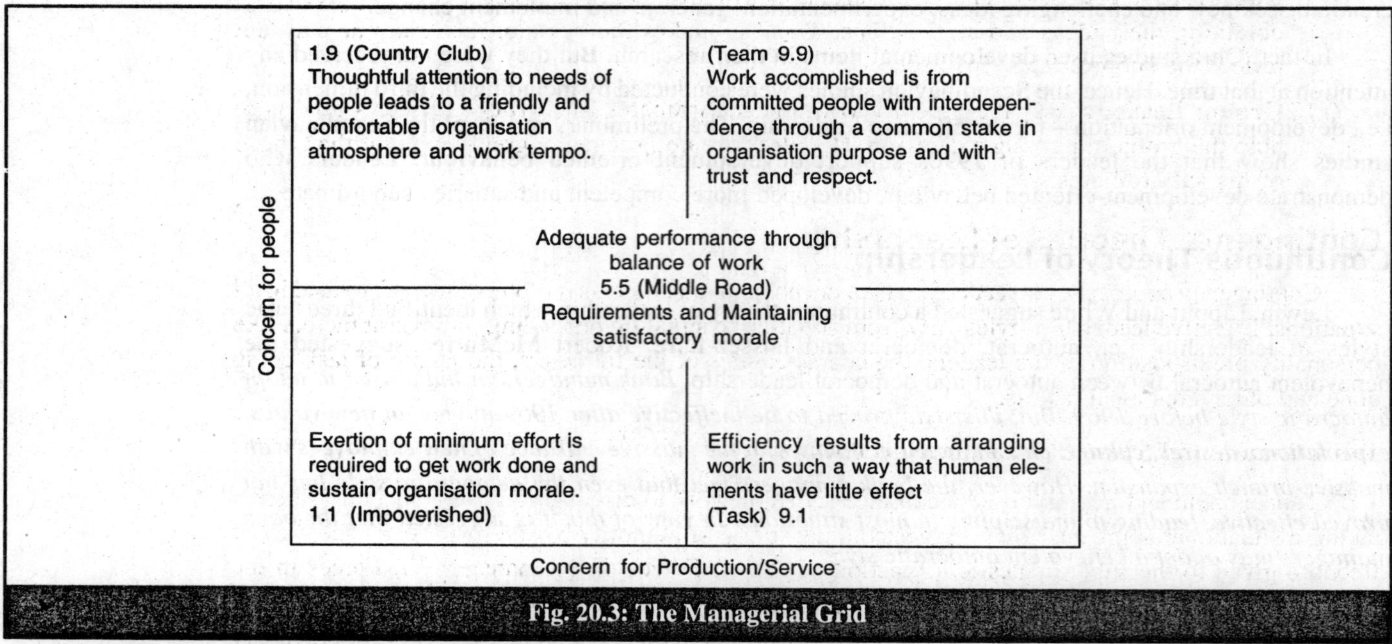

Fig. 20.3: The Managerial Grid

(**Main Source:** Adapted from R.R.Blake and J.S.Mouton, *The Managerial Grid*, Gulf Publishing Company, Houston, Texas, 1964, p. 10).

The style 1-1 is impoverished management-low concern for both people and production. This style is also called *laissez – faire* management. Style 1-9 management is country-club management-high concern for employees, but low concern for production. Style 9-1 management is task or authoritarian-oriented-high concern for production and low concern for employees. Style 5-5 is middle-of-the-road management – and intermediate amount of concern for both production and employees. Style 9-9 management is team or democratic management – a high concern for both production and employees. Blake and Mouton strongly argue that the 9-9 management style is the most effective type of leadership style. Hence, it is felt that the management may adopt 9-9 style for effective goal attainment.

Leader Participation Model

Victor Vroom and Phillip Yetton developed a leader participation model. Leader participation is a leadership theory that provides a set of rules to determine the form and amount of participative decision-making in different situations. This model is a normative and it provides a sequential set of rules that should be followed for determining the form and amount of participation desirable in a decision-making as determined by different situation.[10]

This model assumes that any of five behaviours may be feasible in a given situation. These five behaviours are:

(i) **Autocratic I:** Leader solves the problem or makes a decision by himself using whatever facts he has at hand.

(ii) **Autocratic II:** Leader obtains the necessary information from subordinates and decides on the solution to the problem by himself. He may or may not tell the subordinates about the nature of the situation. He seeks only relevant facts from them, but not their advice or counsel.

(iii) **Consultative I:** Leader shares the problem with relevant subordinates one-on-one getting their ideas and suggestions. However, leader makes the final decision.

(iv) **Consultative II:** Leader shares the problem with his subordinates as a group, collectively obtaining their ideas and suggestions. Then he makes the decision that may or may not reflect the subordinates' influence.

(v) **Group:** Leader shares the problem with his subordinates as a group. Leader's goal is to help the group in making a decision. His ideas are not given any greater weight than those of his subordinates.[11]

Contingency Theories of Leadership

Contingency approaches to leadership take the position that there is no "one best way" to lead in all situations. Effective leadership styles vary from situation to situation depending on several factors like personality predisposition of the leaders, the characteristics of the followers, the nature of task being done and other situational factors.

Tannenbaum and Schmidt's Leadership Pattern

Tannenbaum and Schmidt used a contingency framework to discuss effective leadership patterns taking a situational approach. They suggested that the use of authority by the manager or the area of freedom given to the subordinates is a function of the: (i) Forces of the manager, (ii) Forces in the subordinate; and (iii) Forces in the situation (Fig. 20.4). They concluded that a successful leader is one who can accurately assess the forces that determine what behaviours would be most appropriate in any given situation and is able to be flexible enough to adopt the most functional leadership style.[12]

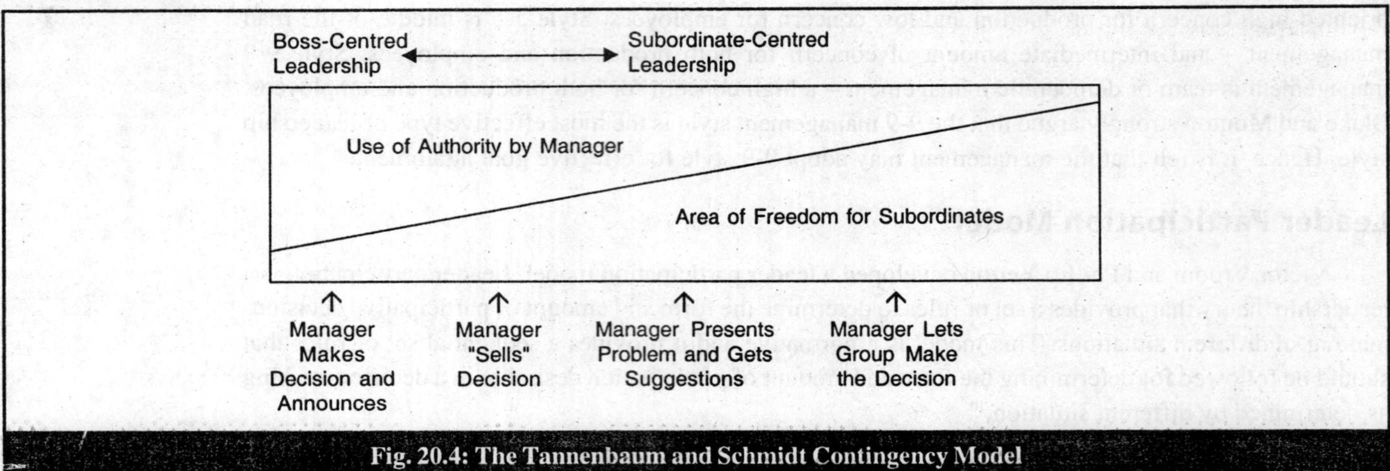

Fig. 20.4: The Tannenbaum and Schmidt Contingency Model

Fiedler's Contingency Theory

Fiedler developed a model to predict work group effectiveness by taking into consideration the 'fit' or match among-(i) The leader's style (task/relationship-oriented); (ii) The leader-member relations; (iii) Task-structure; and (iv) The position power of the leader (Fig. 20.5). Certain combinations of the last three factors are considered to be situations where the leader finds himself/herself to be in either a high degree of control or low control over the situation one finds oneself in.[13]

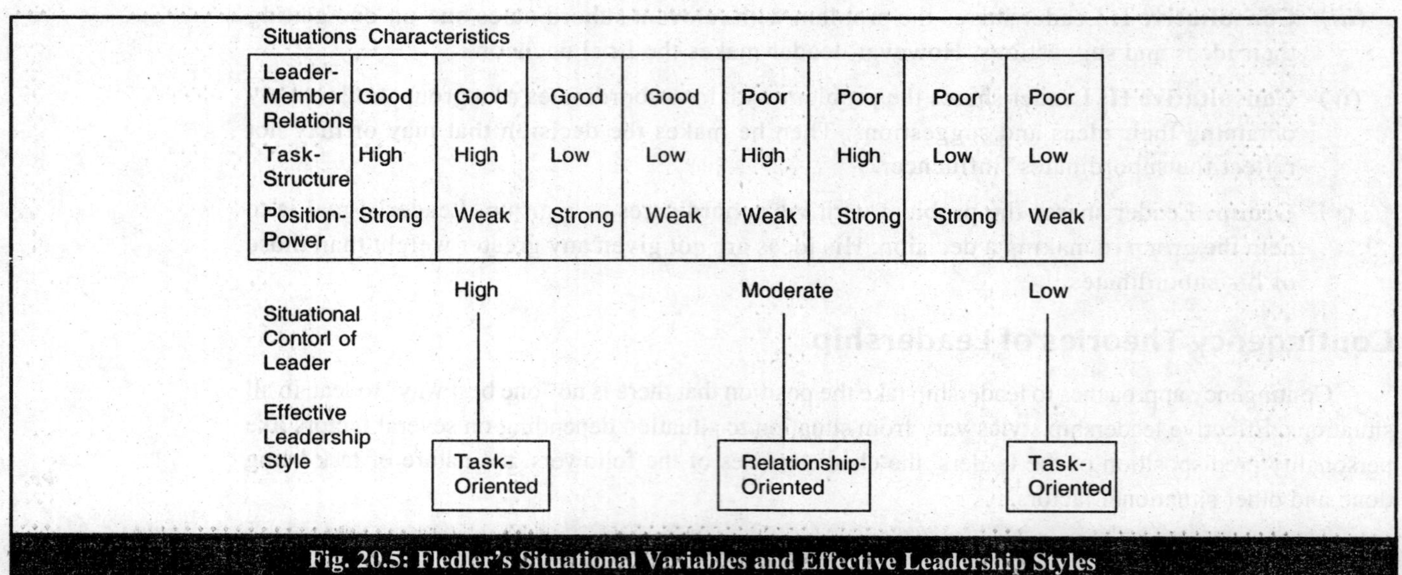

Fig. 20.5: Fiedler's Situational Variables and Effective Leadership Styles

Path Goal Theory of Leadership

This theory of leadership is developed by Martin Evans and Robert House using contingency approach based on the expectancy theory of motivation. This theory states that leaders can exercise four different kinds of styles, viz., directive (giving directions), supportive (friendly and approachable), participative and achievement-oriented (setting challenging goals) leadership. It also states that the leader can use any of these styles depending on situational factors like subordinate characteristics (ability, internal locus of control) and attributes in the work-setting (task characteristics, formal authority system and primary work groups). A good fit between leadership style and situational factors will result in job satisfaction of subordinates and they accept and value the leader as a dispenser and will engage in motivated behaviour (Fig. 20.6).

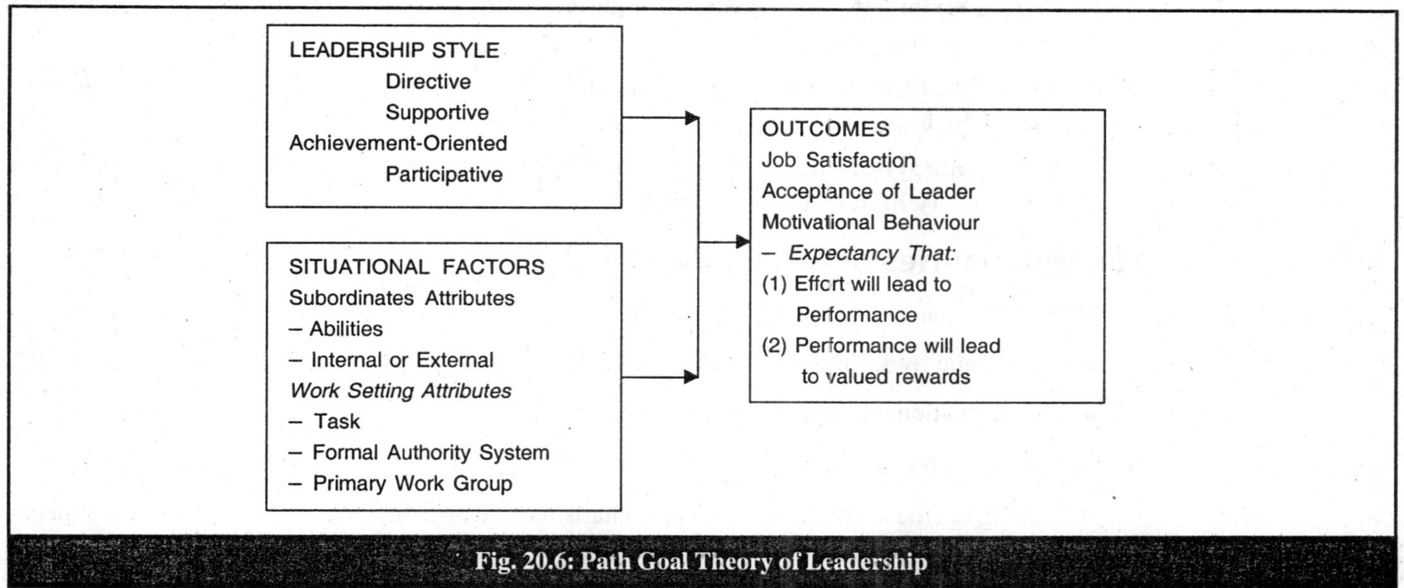

Fig. 20.6: Path Goal Theory of Leadership

Hersey and Blanchard's Life Cycle (or) Situational Approach

Relationship, task and maturity level of followers

It is an extension of the managerial grid approach. Hersey and Blanchard's approach identifies two major styles, viz., task style and relationship style. Hersey and Blanchard incorporated the maturity of the followers into their model taking the lead from some of Fiedler's work on situational variables. The level of maturity is defined by these criteria, viz., degree of achievement motivation, willingness to take on responsibility and amount of education and/or experience. The key for leadership effectiveness in this model (Fig. 20.7) is to match up the situation with the appropriate style. The four styles are:

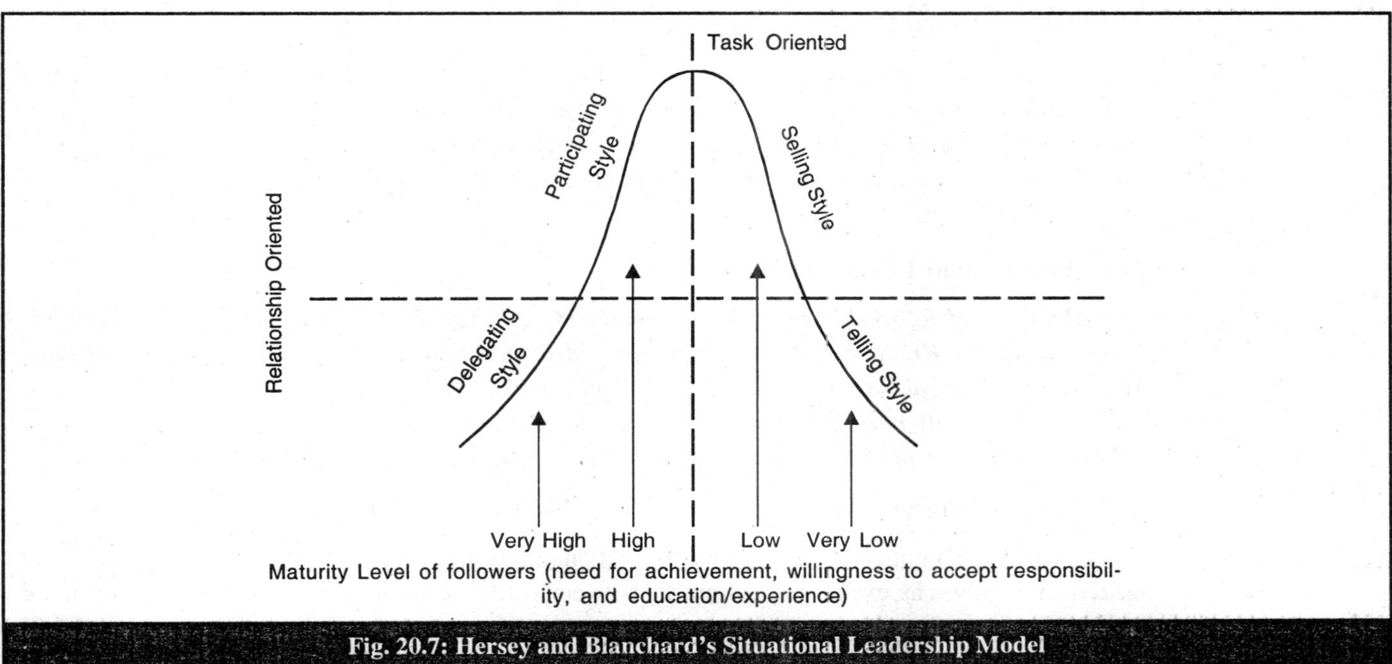

Fig. 20.7: Hersey and Blanchard's Situational Leadership Model

(**Source:** Paul Hersey and Kenneth Blanchard, *Management of Organisational Behaviour: Utilisation of Human Resources*. Prentice Hall, Englewood Cliffs N.J., 1977, p. 170).

(i) **Telling style:** This is a high task, low relationship style. It is effective when followers are at a very low level of maturity.

(ii) **Selling style:** This is a high task, high relationship style. It is effective when followers are on the low side of maturity.

(iii) **Participating style:** This is a low task, high relationship style. It is effective when followers are on the high side of maturity.

(iv) **Delegating style:** This is a low task, low relationship style. It is effective when followers are at a very high level of maturity.

Modern Theories of Leadership

The modern theories of leadership include:

- Charismatic leadership theory; and
- Transformational leadership theory.

Charismatic Leadership Theory

Charismatic leader: Self-confidence, expectations, vision etc.

According to House, the characters of the charismatic leaders include: self-confidence, confidence in subordinates, high expectations for subordinates, ideological vision, and use of personal example. The characters of the followers of the charismatic leader include: identification with the leader's mission, exhibit extreme loyalty to and confidence in leader, emulate the leader's values, behaviours and derive self-esteem from their relationship with the leader.[14]

Mahatma Gandhi's characters of self-confidence, ideological vision and personal example made him as a charismatic leader. Mr.Dheerubhai Ambani's character of self confidence, Mr.Ramalinga Raju's (of Satyam Computers) character of confidence in subordinates and high expectation for subordinates made them charismatic leaders. These characters of Ramalinga Raju resulted in performance of the followers beyond the expectations. Similarly, Mr.Kurian's ideological vision resulted in the success of 'white revolution'. Dr.N.T.Rama Rao's unconventional behaviour made him Chief Minister of Andhra Pradesh.

Charismatic leaders, thus, lure and motivate the subordinates towards performance beyond expectations, innovations, creations, and create the work culture among the followers. Charismatic leaders tend to be portrayed as wonderful heroes. However, there can also be unethical characters associated with these leaders. Behavioural components of charismatic and non-charismatic leaders are presented in Exhibit 20.3.

Transformational Leadership Theory

Mr. Nair of Roorkela Steel Plant of SAIL, Mr.G.Subba Rao of Andhra Pradesh Paper Mills Limited, and Mr. Krishna Kumar of Tata Tea and Prof.M.Rama Mohana Rao of Indian Institute of Management, Bangalore transformed their organisations from loss-making/less performed into highly profit making/highly performed companies/organisations. Mr. Anji Reddy of Dr. Reddy's Labs made his company as one of the leading Pharmaceutical companies with R&D base.

Transformational leadership theory conceptualises such developments.

Two types of political leadership viz., transactional and transformational are identified.[15] Transactional leadership involves an exchange relationship between leaders and followers. Whereas transformational leadership is based on leaders' shifting the values, beliefs and needs of the followers.[16] Exhibit 20.3 presents the characteristics of transactional and transformational leaders.

Exhibit 20.3 Behavioural Components of Charismatic and Non-charismatic Leaders

	Non-charismatic Leader	*Charismatic Leader*
Relation to Status Quo	Essentially agrees with status quo and strives to maintain it	Essentially opposed to status quo and strives to change it
Future Goal	Goal not too discrepant from status quo	Idealized vision which is highly discrepant fromstatus quo
Likableness	Shared perspective makes him/her likable	Shared perspective and idealized vision makes him/her a likable and honorable hero worthy of identification and imitation
Trustworthiness	Disinterested advocacy in persuasion attempts	Disinterested advocacy by incurring great personal risk and cost
Expertise	Expert in using available means to achieve goals within the framework of the existing order	Expert in using unconventional means to transcend the existing order
Behaviour	Conventional, conforming to existing norms	Unconventional or counternormative
Environmental Sensitivity	Low need for environmental sensitivity to maintain status quo	High need for environmental sensitivity for changing the status quo
Articulation	Weak articulation of goals and motivation to lead	Strong articulation of future vision and motivation to lead
Power Base	Position power and personal power (based on reward, expertise, and liking for a friend who is a similar other)	Personal power (based on expertise, respect, and admiration for a unique hero)
Leader-Follower	Egalitarian, consensus seeking, or directive. nudges or orders people to share his/her views	Elitist, entrepreneur, and exemplary. transforms people to the radical changes advocated

(**Source:** Richard M.Hodgetts, *Organisational Behaviour*, p. 234).

Some of the characteristics of transformational leaders are:

- Identify themselves as change agents
- Courageous
- Believe in people
- Value-driven
- Lifelong learners
- Have the ability to deal with complexity, ambiguity and uncertainty.
- Visionaries.[17]

(D) LEADERSHIP STYLES

Leadership is practised by its styles which may be positive or negative. The styles used by the military officers and traditional managers are mostly negatives whereas those of the modern and high-technology organisations are positive. The styles used by the Japanese companies like Mitsubishi, and Toyota and Korean companies such as Lucky-Goldstar(LG), Samsung, Hyundai and Daewoo are the positive and people oriented styles. The styles used by some of the Indian Public Sector Companies like Indian Railways, HCL and HMT are negative styles.

Styles Based on Traditional Theories

Different types of the leadership styles are derived from the leadership theories. These are four popularly known traditional leadership styles, viz., Free-rein, autocratic, participative and democratic.

Free-rein or Laissez-faire Style

These leaders avoid authority and responsibility. They mostly depend upon the group to establish objectives and goals, formulate policies and programmes. The group members train and motivate themselves. Contrary to the autocratic style, the leaders play minor or negligible roles and depend upon the group.

Autocratic Style

Centralise power of decision-making

Autocratic leaders centralise power of decision-making in themselves. Followers have no say either in decision-making or in implementation. They have to completely obey and follow the instructions of the leaders. The leaders take full authority and full responsibility. Autocratic leaders are classified into: (a) Strict autocrat who follows autocratic style completely where the method of influencing subordinates is thoroughly negative; (b) Benevolent autocrat who typically gives awards to the followers; and (c) Incompetent autocrat who adopts autocratic style with a view to hide his incompetency.

Democratic Style

Decentralise authority

Democratic leaders decentralise authority and encourage subordinates to express their opinion in decision-making as well as in implementing the decision. However, decisions are taken by the leaders. Thus, decisions are arrived at by consultation.

Participative Style

Follower involvement in decision-making

Participative leaders decentralise authority and encourage subordinates to participate and involve in decision-making and implementation processes. Decisions are made by the leader and his subordinates.

It is, however, concluded that there is no clear-cut leadership style which is applicable universally and in all circumstances. Therefore, the leaders have to adopt appropriate style depending upon the situational requirements.

Leadership Styles Based on Modern Theories

Leaders of the modern, high-technololgy and highly competitive organisations exhibit inspirational style with vision and perform the work effectively, i.e., do the right things.

Mr. Kulkarni of Larsen and Toubro leads the company with clear vision, emphasis on quality, comprehensive outlook and perfectness in work, creation and diversification into the related areas. He sets high goals by consulting the managers and followers of the company and employees. He encourages and inspires the employees for working efficiently.

The leadership styles based on the charismatic and transformational theories are classified into three, viz., envisioning, energising and enabling.

(i) **Envisioning:** This style includes creating a picture of the future or a desired future state with which people can identify. Envisioning generates excitement. Thus, this style emphasises on articulating a compelling vision and setting high goals and expectations.

(ii) **Energising:** The leader in this style directs the generation of energy, the motivation to act among the organizational employees. This style also includes demonstrating personal excitement and confidence, seeking, finding and using success.

(iii) **Enabling:** The leader helps the followers psychologically to act or perform in the face of challenging goals. This style includes empowering, expressing personal support and empathising.[18]

(E) FOLLOWERSHIP STYLES — A NEW APPROACH

There is a misconception that an effective leader is enough to mould and direct in group behaviour towards the attainment or organisational goals. But attainment of organisational goals more or less equally depends on the committed and effective followers. In fact no leader can be effective without effective followers. Here, the term effective follower is used in the sense that the follower should be potential and he should be in a position to willingly contribute most of his potentialities towards the organizational goal.

The followership styles are not given due recognition except mentioning them at the maturity level of followers. Various authors have failed to recognize the significance of the follower in the leader-follower interaction. In fact, the follower is as important as the leader in any situation. In view of this background an attempt is made in this paper to develop the followership styles suitable to situational requirements.

Followership Styles

We come across different types of followership styles in real life situations. They can broadly be divided into six categories, viz., No-boss, Yes-boss, Grumbling, Escapism, Intellectual Arrogant and Critical.

A brief clarification of the Followership styles is as follows:

(1) **No-boss style:** The follower in this style is a non-obliging type. He says 'No' to the leader for his instructions/orders irrespective of the nature and magnitude of the instructions.

(2) **Yes-boss style:** The follower in this style blindly says yes to leader for his instructions irrespective of the nature and magnitude of the instructions and he carries out the orders without critically evaluating them. Excessive humility in this style may be referred to as subserviant style of the followership.

(3) **Grumbling style:** Follower in this style grumbles while responding to the order of instructions of the leader only to show his reluctance for carrying out the instructions. However, he carries out the orders.

(4) **Escaping style:** The follower in this style responds positively to the instructions of the leader, but escapes himself in carrying out the orders.

(5) **Intellectual arrogance style:** Some followers may be highly qualified, more than the leader either in terms of formal educational qualifications or intelligence or knowledge. Such followers in some situations think that they can function effectively than their leaders as they are more intelligent than their leader. The followers in such styles respond arrogantly to the orders of their leaders. Such style is referred to as Intellectual Arrogance.

Analyse the pros and cons

(6) **Critical style:** Followers in this style 'do not respond either positively or negatively to the orders of their leaders. They critically appraise the instructions/orders of the leaders, consider the pros and cons of the decisions of the leader and then if the order is wise, they carry it out. If the order is unwise, they appraise the pros and cons of it to the leader and advise him to modify his order. If the leader does not positively respond to the advice of the followers, then they carry out the order of the leader. If the leader does not positively respond to the advice of the followers, then they carry out the order of the leader. If the leader changes his order, they carry out the modified orders. This style of the follower can be compared to the 'Vidhura, followership style towards Dhrithrashtra in the Mahabharata.'

All of us belong to the categories of both the follower and the leader, but we may be leaders in some situations and followers in other situations. Similarly, each follower would not limit his style to any of the above-mentioned followership styles and may go on changing his styles depending upon the situations.

Most of the writers have identified three leadership styles, viz., Exploitative Autocratic, Benevolent Autocratic, Participative or Democratic. The problem arises when there is lack of coordination between the leader's style and the follower's style. The leader-follower interaction would be effective when there is harmony between the styles of the leader and the followers, otherwise the interaction would not be effective and it may lead even to leader-follower conflict.

How to Match the Followership Style with the Leadership Style?

Matching of these two styles is most essential in management as its basic objective or getting things done by others can be effectively attained only when there is perfect match between these two styles. Conflict between these two adversely affects the management effectiveness. Hence, the leader should make himself fit for a match. The possible matches between leadership and followership styles are shown by arrow mark in the Fig. 20.8.

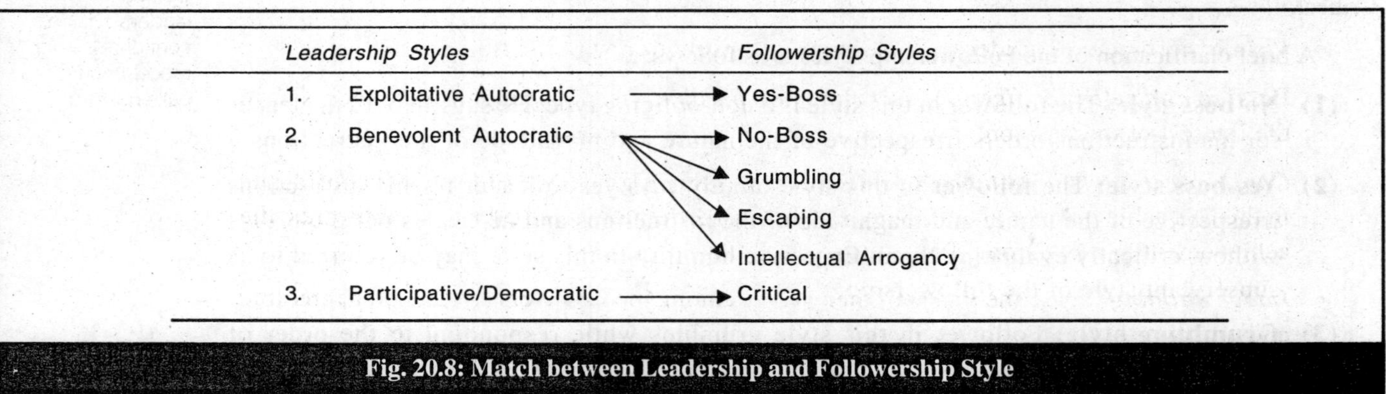

Fig. 20.8: Match between Leadership and Followership Style

Zero Level Conflict

As shown in the above figure, the level of conflict would be 'Zero' when the leader with exploitative autocratic style interacts with the follower with the 'Yes-boss' style. Similarly, the conflict would be at zero level when the leader with participative style interacts with the follower with critical style. Benevolent autocratic leader by offering monetary and non-monetary benefits and by conferring new designations on his followers with the styles of 'No-boss', 'Grumbling', 'Escaping' and 'Intellectual Arrogance' can minimize the level of conflict but he cannot bring down the conflict to 'Zero' level. Thus, the Zero level conflict matching are: (i) Exploitative autocratic style of the leader and Yes-boss of the followers; and (ii) Participative/democratic style of the leader and critical style of the follower.

Effective Match

Though it may be said that the match between participative style of the leader and critical style of the follower is effective and desirable, there is no such effective match in practice as these two styles are subjected to situational requirement.

Match of Situation-Leadership Style-Followership Style

The mere coincidence of leadership and followership styles will not produce effective results. What is more essential is the coincidence of these two styles which should meet the situational requirements to maximize the human resources contribution towards the organisational effectiveness. The emergency situations can be handled effectively if the leader is in exploitative autocratic style and the follower is in Yes-Boss style. Other styles of the leader and the follower may not suit to this situation and hence, they may be ineffective match in situations of exigency.

The leader has to insist the followers to accept his decisions in some situations like adoption of latest technology which normally is resisted by the followers. In such situations, the leader in the 'Benevolent Autocratic' style can impress upon the follower to accept the decision of adoption of technology by offering benefits.

It is clear from the anlysis that leader-follower and situations interaction should be taken into account to attain the organisational goals rather than mere leadership styles. One may agree to this but he faces the problem of integration of these three variables. There may not be specific and ready made answer to this question but the problem can be minimized when the follower and leader adopt to their style based on the situational requirements.

(F) OUTSTANDING LEADERS

Outstanding leaders': vision, confidence, role model, image building, etc.

Qualities or approaches practised by the outstanding leaders include:

- ***Vision:*** Formulation of ideological vision in consultation with the followers.
- ***Passion and self-sacrifice:*** Display a passion for their vision. They sacrifice their self in the interest of their vision.
- ***Confidence, determination and persistence:*** Display high degree of faith and confidence in them in achieving the vision. They also have determination and persistence towards the achievement of the vision.
- ***Image building:*** Build the image of themselves among the followers as competent credible and trustworthy.
- ***Role modelling:*** Act as the role models to their followers.
- ***External representation:*** Act as external representation and spokesperson for their organisation.
- ***Expectations and confidence in followers:*** Set high expectations from the followers and have strong confidence in their abilities and commitment.
- ***Frame alignment:*** Engage in frame alignment. They make followers' interests, values and beliefs congruent and complementary with those of their activities, goals and ideology.
- ***Inspirational communication:*** Often communicate their messages in an inspirational manner using vivid stories, slogans, symbols and ceremonies.
- ***Selective motive arousal:*** They identify the appropriate motivational factors to motivate the followers for the successful achievement of vision and mission.[19]

(G) LEADERSHIP SKILLS

The skills of the effective leaders include:

1. Personal Skills

Personal skills include developing awareness, managing stress and solving problems creatively.

- Developing Self-Awareness include:
  - Determining values and priorities
  - Identifying cognitive style
  - Assessing attitude towards change
- Managing Stress includes:
  - Coping with stressors
  - Managing time
  - Delegating
- Solving Problems Creatively includes:
  - Using the rational approach
  - Using the creative approach
  - Fostering innovation in others

2. Interpersonal Skills

Interpersonal skills include gaining power and influence, communicating, motivating and conflict management.

- Gaining Power and Influence comprise:
  - Gaining power
  - Exercising influence
  - Empowering others
- Communicating includes:
  - Informing and listening
  - Coaching and counselling
- Motivating includes:
  - Diagnosing poor performance
  - Creating a motivating environment
  - Rewarding accomplishments
- Conflict management includes:
  - Diagnosing the conflicts
  - Finding causes
  - Developing and selecting the best strategies
  - Resolving the confrontations.

Developing Leadership Skills

Employees have to develop their leadership skills. Guidelines to improve leadership skills include:

- Observe the great leaders and learn from their leadership skills.
- Take risks, try and learn from your mistakes.
- Read the autobiographies of leaders and learn from them.
- Do lots of practice.
- Make mistakes, learn from them and follow different approaches.
- Engage others purposefully and learn from them.
- Put yourself in positions of responsibility and learn from them by practice.
- Go to difficult areas by getting out of your comfort zone. Don't remain in easy and non-challenging situations.
- Enter, create and face situations that require change.
- Build something from nothing, fix or turn around a failing operation, take project or taskforce responsibilities, accept international assignments.
- Have exposure to positive role models.
- Work with people of diverse backgrounds.
- Confront with other people's performance problems.
- Undertake formal courses, challenging job experiences, supervise others.

(H) LEADERSHIP UNDER CROSS-CULTURAL ENVIRONMENT

Cross-cultural environment includes employees from different cultural backgrounds, beliefs, capabilities, gender, values, geographical region, religions, ethnic groups, age, veteran status, expectations, lifestyle, skill level, education level, economic status, work style, social status and position in a company. Thus, cross-cultural environment includes a variety of variant aspects of people in an organisation.

Free movement of human resources consequent upon globalisation resulted in cross-cultural environment or diversity of workforce. The diversity of workforce brings a variety of advantages like:

- Fulfilling social responsibility;
- Attracting, retaining and motivating efficient employees;
- Gaining greater knowledge and skill of diversified marketplace;
- Promoting creativity, innovation and problem solving;
- Enhancing organisational flexibility;
- Bringing gender equality; and
- Balances the power of the groups of employees.

However, managing diversity poses challenges, viz.

- Lower cohesiveness among employees of different cultural backgrounds
- Cultural differences cause communication and understanding problems, and
- Scope for mistrust and tension.

Multicultural Organisations

In order to get the maximum advantage of cross-cultural environment, leaders and organisations should understand the cultures and assumptions about various cultures and people.

Organisations may be monolithic or plural or multicultural. A monolithic organisation has a low degree of structural integration — employing a few women and other minorities. Thus, it has highly homogeneous employee population. Plural organisation has a relatively diverse employee population from various cultural backgrounds. Multicultural organisation values cultural diversity and seeks to utilise and encourage it.

Leadership Activities under Cross-Cultural Environment

Leadership activities under cross-cultural environment include:

• ***Commitment:*** The leader has to commit towards diversity and communicate the same to all employees as well as to the external stakeholders. The leader has to incorporate the organisation's attitude into the mission statement, objectives and strategies. Employee remuneration should be based on performance. Leader should participate in social and cultural programmes of all diversified groups. Leader should get feedback from all diversified groups about the company's treatment.

Table 20.2: Presents Diversity Assumptions and their Implications for Leader

Common and Misleading Assumptions
Homogeneity: We are all the same
Similarity: They are all just like me
Parochialism: Our way is the only way. We do not recognise any other way of living or working
Ethnocentrism: Our way is the best way. All other approaches are inferior versions of our way
Less Common and More Appropriate Assumptions
Heterogeneity: We are not all the same; groups within society differ across cultures
Similarity and Difference: Many people differ from me culturally. Most people exhibit both cultural similarities and differences when compared to me
Equifinality: There are many cultural distinct ways of reaching the same goal and of living one's life
Culture Contingency: There are many different and equally good ways to reach the same goal. The best way depends on the culture of the people involved.

(**Source:** Quoted in Bateman and Snell, *op.cit*., p. 384.)

Leader should get information from minority groups to monitor organisational policies, practices and attitudes and correct them wherever necessary, based on the expectations of employees.

Leader should also enable employees of different backgrounds to form small groups in order to ventilate their feelings and experiences for fair and equal treatment.

• ***Assessment:*** The leader has to assess the ongoing cultural policies and practices and their impact on recruitment, promotions, benefits and remunerations. So that the leader can initiate corrective measures, wherever necessary.

• ***Attracting employees:*** The leader can attract a diverse workforce, just based on their suitability by accommodating their work, family, social and psychological needs.

• ***Diversity training:*** Leader should initiate diversity training programmes in order to identify and reduce hidden biases and develop the skills to adjust with others and work along with others efficiently.

• ***Retaining employees:*** Leaders should take steps to retain employees by encouraging the formation of support groups, mentoring, career development and promotion, accommodating the needs of different groups of employees based on their cultural background and requirements.

• ***Styles:*** Leaders have to adopt participative and democratic leadership styles while dealing with the employees of different cultures so as to get their ideas based on background and make a decision, rather than take a decision and force the followers to follow it.

(I) WOMEN AND LEADERSHIP

Do women lead the followers differently from men? Do women behave differently from men in leadership roles? According to an article in Harvard Business Review, women tend use their charisma, interpersonal skills, hard work and personal contacts in influencing the followers.

Women leaders encourage participation, share power and information and enhance people's self worth.

It is widely felt that though there are several 'policies' against gender discrimination, managers still find all sorts of ways to keep women employees 'under'. In addition, though women are getting quick promotions, their salaries still lag behind.

Different Values?

Greg Butcher from the Netherlands says he runs several international businesses, and denies that there is any pre-selection bias for top jobs in his companies. He says that when recruiting directors they ask candidates if they are prepared to put in the long and often anti-social hours needed for the role. Many female candidates, he says, decide not to proceed or answer "unfavourably" when quizzed. "Perhaps the female (candidates) are simply more in balance with life and are following other values which downplay or balance commitment to business," he says. "The single-mind pursuit of profit is motivated by greed, which has been a peculiarly male trait from the beginning of time," she says. "Women are failing to reach the top jobs not because we don't have the talent or ability for it, but because our goals are more holistic and less selfish."[20]

Diversity

Yet women directors could bring new perspectives to the boardroom, from their diverse experiences, for example, as consumers, decision-makers and users. Whilst male managers tend to be similar thinking, decision-making types, women managers bring greater variety of thinking and personality types. They also offer different ethical, communicative and environmental values and a preference for a more androgynous leadership style. The valuing of this different voice which women directors could bring still seems a long way off in almost half of the top 100 companies.[21]

Evaluating Leader

Leaders can be evaluated based on the effectiveness and efficiency of their styles, behaviours and actions. Leader's activities include task performance and group maintenance. Checklist to evaluate the leader in these two areas is as follows (Responses are from the followers):

The following statements help in evaluating leaders.

	1	2	3	4	5
	Nil Extent				Greatest Extent

1. Leader is strict about observing regulations.
2. Leader instructs and issues orders to subordinates.
3. Leader is strict about the amount of work to be done.
4. Leader is particular in completing the work in the specified time.
5. Leader inspires the followers to do the work to the maximum capacity of the followers.
6. Leader identifies the groups in the work completed.
7. Leader seeks the followers to report about the work completed.
8. Leader plans for work to be done.
9. Leader is pleasant in performing work.
10. Leader is friendly with followers.
11. Leader accepts the followers.
12. Leader helps the followers.
13. Leader is enthusiastic.
14. Leader is relaxed even during critical incidents.
15. Leader is physically and psychologically close to the followers.
16. Leader is cooperative with the followers.
17. Leader supports the followers.
18. Leader's actions are interesting.
19. Leader maintains harmonious relations.
20. Leader is efficient in performing tasks.
21. Leader is cheerful mostly.
22. Leader is open in approach.
23. Leader is concerned with personal problems of followers.
24. Leader trusts the followers.
25. Leader seeks the suggestions and opinions of subordinates.
26. Leader is concerned of the career of followers.
27. Leader treats the followers fairly.
28. Leader nominates followers for training and development programmes.
29. Leader coaches the followers.
30. Leader counsells and mentors the followers.

Note: Add the scores of all the 30 students and evaluate the leader as indicated hereunder:

30 = Most inefficient leader.
60 = Inefficient leader.
90 = Efficient leader.
120 = Leader efficient to greater extent.
150 = Most efficient leader

(J) GLOBAL LEADING

Though there are several theories of leadership emphasizing the leadership styles and interactive behaviour of leadership and followership styles, leadership is significantly influenced by the culture and other factors, which are peculiar to a particular country. Thus, it is viewed that leadership practices vary from country to country. Now, we study the leadership practices in Japan, India, the USA and China.

Leadership in Japan

Japanese leaders: paternalistic

Leaders in Japan are like elders in the family as well as society. They adopt paternalistic leadership style and take care of the welfare of the subordinates as the leaders view the subordinates as children. Leaders become the part of the group and work along with other members of the group. Leaders set common values for the group and create conducive work and social environment to work in a collaborative environment. Leaders in Japan avoid face-to-face confrontation and prefer to solve all the problems in compromise/ give and take approach. Leaders understand the followers needs and provide various facilities to meet them, even before the followers realise them. Leaders influence the subordinates indirectly and through peer pressure rather than using autocratic approach. Leader maintains relationship with followers not only at workplace but also in the society and therefore exerts influence on a continuous basis. Thus organisational, social and private lives are integrated. Leaders provide adequate opportunity to the followers to express their opinions and ideas as and when necessary. In fact leaders use face-to-face and oral communication rather than written communication and impersonal one.

Leadership in India

Leaders in India mix the autocratic and participative styles. They prefer to follow autocratic styles, if organisational and other environmental influences are absent. They follow democratic and participative styles in social environments. So, sometimes employees prefer to present the official issues in social settings in order to force the leaders to be in participative/ democratic styles. The traditional and cultural factors in India force the leaders to follow participative styles. Leaders influenced much by social and family factors take care of the needs of employees and their family members even beyond the financial issues. In addition, leaders in bureaucratic set ups make decisions on their own and push them down for implementation and they follow collaborative approach in social set ups.

In fact, competition due to globalisation and information technology changed the leadership styles in India. Leaders today follow more of collaborative approach and team leadership rather than autocratic approach.

Leadership in USA

Leaders in USA mostly follow the impersonal approach. In other words, they don't take the followers' views into consideration. They push down their views and directions for implementation. They believe that leaders have to directive and strict in approach. In other word they have to follow autocratic approach. They follow individualistic approach. This is mostly due to the influence of western culture. Therefore, it would be rather difficult for the leaders to build teams and infuse collaborative approach at workplace. In addition leaders don't understand the followers and their needs. The relation between the leader and the follower is more of formal. Leaders don't mix the work life with social and private life. Therefore, privacy assumes top most importance in USA unlike in India and Japan. Leader makes organizational decisions as he/she has the prerogative to do so and the followers implement them, as it is their responsibility. Thus, leader-follower relation in USA is mostly formal.

Table 20.3 presents the comparisons of leadership in Japan, India, USA and China.

Table 20.3: Comparison of Leadership in Japan, India, the USA and China

Japan	India	USA	China
(1) Leader acts as a social facilitator and group member	(1) Leader acts as a boss and as a social facilitator and group member depending upon situations	(1) Leader acts as head and decision-maker	(1) Leader acts as head of the group and decision-maker
(2) Partly autocratic and partly democratic	(2) Paternalistic style	(2) Directive style	(2) Directive Style
(3) Common values	(3) Common values, when influenced by social factors	(3) Often divergent values	(3) Mostly common values
(4) Avoids face-to-face confrontation	(4) Confrontation initially and compromise at a later stage.	(4) Face-to-face confrontation is common.	(4) Avoids face-to-face confrontation
(5) Communication both ways	(5) Preferably top-down, but resorts to both ways, if necessary.	(5) Mostly top-down	(5) Mostly top down
(6) Takes care of followers development	(6) Takes care of followers development	(6) Does not take care of the followers development.	(6) Does not take care of the followers development.

Source: Adapted from Heinz Weihrich and Harold Koonz, "Management", Tata Mc Graw Hill, New Delhi, 2002, p. 566.

Leading in China

Leader in China mostly resembles that of USA, in the sense that it is formal. Leaders as the head of a unit make the decisions and the followers as subordinates in bureaucratic organization simply follow them. Leaders as administrators of a bureaucratic organization follow the rules and are responsible to their bosses rather than to customers. In other word, they don't take customer needs into consideration. However, leaders in China like their counterparts in Japan avoid face-to-face confrontations.

KEY TERMS

- Leader
- Legitimate Power
- Managerial Grid
- Manager
- Expert Power
- Autocratic Leader
- Benevolent Autocratic Leader
- Leadership
- Referent Power
- Task Achievement
- Leadership Traits
- Democratic Leader
- Building Teams
- Leadership Process
- Participative Leader
- Reward Power
- Creativity
- Coercive Power
- Flexibility

QUESTIONS

1. What is leadership? State the differences between a leader and a manager.
2. Discuss various sources of power of a leader.
3. Explain trait theories of leadership.
4. Compare and contrast different behavioural theories of leadership.

5. Discuss in detail the Path-Goal theory of leadership.
6. Explain the superiorities of The Hersey-Blanchard situational approach to leadership.
7. Discuss the relevance of charismatic and transformational theories of leadership.
8. Discuss different leadership styles.
9. What is followership? How do you match different styles of leaders with those of followers.

REFERENCES

1. G. A. Yukl, "Leadership in Organisations," Prentice-Hall, Englewood Cliffs, 1989.
2. Warren G. Bennis, "Managing the Dream:Leadership in the 21st Century," *Journal of Organisational Change Management*, Vol. 2, No.1, 1989, p. 7.
3. Abraham Zaleznik, "Excerpts from Managers and Leaders:Are they Different?" *Harvard Business Review*, May-June 1986, p. 54.
4. J. P. Kotter, "What Leaders Really Do?" *Harvard Business Review*, May-June 1990, pp. 103-111.
5. G. Yukl and D. D. Van Fleet, "Theory and Research on Leadership in Organisations," p. 150.
6. George R. Terry and Stephen G. Franklin, *op.cit.*, p. 327.
7. Kirkpatrick, S. A. and Locke, E. A., "Leadership:Do Traits Matter?" *Academy of Management Executive*, 5, 1991, pp. 48-60.
8. *Ibid.*, p. 58.
9. Stephen P. Robbins, "Organisational Behaviour," Prentice-Hall of India, 1999, p. 350.
10. *Ibid.*, p. 351.
11. R. Kahn and D. Katz, "Leadership Practices in Relation to Productivity and Morale," *Group Dynamics: Research and Theory*, New York, 1960.
12. Stephen P. Robbins, *op.cit.*, p. 363.
13. Robert J. House, "A 1976 Theory of Charismatic Leadership," in Hunt and Larson (Eds.), "*Leadership: The Cutting Edge*," pp. 189-207.
14. J. M. Burns, "*Leadership*," Harper and Row, New York, 1978.
15. Fred Luthans, *op.cit.*, p. 396.
16. Noel M. Tichy and Mary Anne Devanna, "The Transformational Leader," John Wiley, New York, 1986.
17. Fred Luthans, *op.cit.*, p. 413.
18. Robert House and Philip M. Podsakoff, "Leadership Effectiveness:Past Perspectives and Future Directions," pp. 58-64.
19. Michael Useem, "Leadership Lessons of Mount Everest," Harvard Business Review, October 2001.
20. http://news.bbc.co.uk/2/hi/business/2255362.stm (240807)
21. http://news.bbc.co.uk/2/hi/business/2191286.stm (240807)

CHAPTER **21**

POWER AND POLITICS

☛ Chapter Outline

☛ Learning Objectives

After studying this Chapter, you should be able to:

- ✓ Understand the meaning of power and sources of power;
- ✓ Understand how to measure power;
- ✓ Analyse consequences of power;
- ✓ Know the meaning of organisational politics;
- ✓ Analyse whether organistional politics are desirable or undesirable;
- ✓ Discuss the factors affecting organisational politics;
- ✓ Understand the consequences of organisational factors;
- ✓ Analyse types of organisational politics; and
- ✓ Know how to regulate organisational politics.

(A) BASICS OF POWER

Power is the capacity of a person, team, department or an organisation to influence others.

Power involves the potential to influence others. Potential to influence includes among other things rational persuasion by using logical arguments and facts, inspirational appeal, asking for participation and involvement, putting others in good moods, proposing some benefits for complying the influence, social networks, etc. Influence is a behavioural response to the exercise of power. Power is the ability to make others do the things or render service as the power-holder wants.

Meaning

J. Pfeffer defines power as "the capacity of a person, team, department or an organisation to influence others."[1] Power is the potential to change others' attitude or behaviour.

Power may be:

- An act of one person (realised potentiality) or
- Potentiality or capacity of one person

in order to influence the behaviour of the other person to act in accordance with the organisational requirements or the wishes of the person who has the power.

- People many times do not use the power they have, and
- Some people may not know that they have power.

Dependence in Power Relationship

Normally, the subordinate depends on his superior for some favours in work allotment, work schedules, job security, transfers, promotions, information, etc. Therefore, the superior can have power over his subordinate and control his behaviour.

Thus, the basic prerequisite of power is that one person believes he/she is dependent on the other for something of value.[2] As such the superiors have power over subordinates by controlling something that subordinates need to achieve their goal. Sometimes, superiors may depend on subordinates for some information, higher productivity, etc. Then subordinates have power and control the behaviour of superiors. Thus, superiors and subordinates depend on each other (See Fig. 21.1). Dependency relationships are an inherent part of organisational activities in all forms of organisational structures and companies including the sole trading firm. The owner depends on the customers and other stakeholders in the sole trading/proprietorship firm. Thus, power exists when others believe that you control facilities/resources they want.[3]

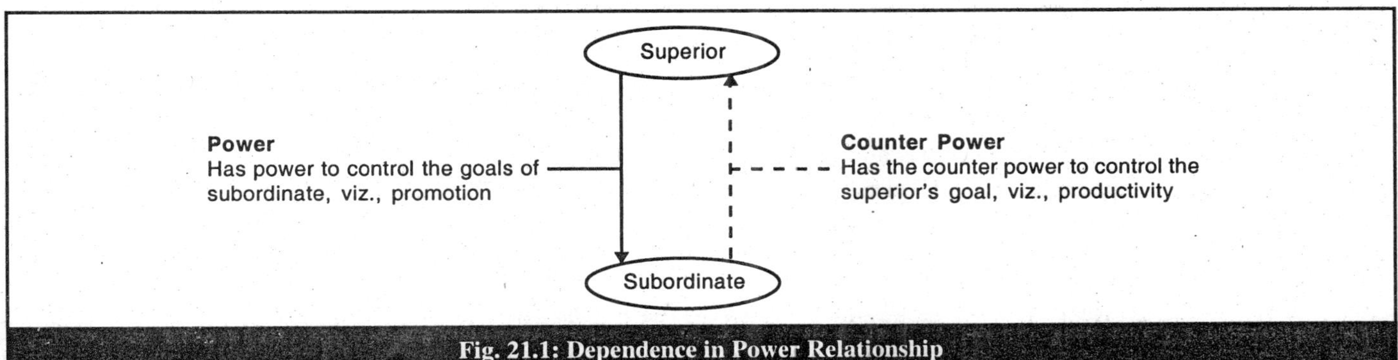

Fig. 21.1: Dependence in Power Relationship

Counter Power

Two parties depend on each other in power relationship, *i.e.*, one has the power and the other member has the counter power. For example, as indicated earlier, the superior has the power to control the subordinate's goal of promotion and the subordinate has the counter power to control the superior's goal of higher productivity. Counter power makes the superiors to use their power judiciously, carefully and maintain the relationship.

As discussed earlier, power is the capacity to influence others. Mere capacity cannot influence others. Certain factors enable or disable the capacity. These factors are called *contingencies of power*. Capacity is derived from various sources. These are called *sources of power*. Sources of power are influenced by the contingencies of power and the outcome of this influence is the power over others. First, we shall study the sources of power.

(B) SOURCES OF POWER

Sources of power *are* legitimate, reward, coercive, expert and referent.

John French and Bertran Raven suggested five sources of power, *viz.*, legitimate, reward, coercive, expert and referent.[4] The first three sources of power, *viz.*, legitimate, reward and coercive are drawn from the person's job authority and roles in an organisation and the latter two sources, *viz.*, expert and referent power are derived from the person's personal characteristics. We can add one recent source of power, *i.e.*, role model power.

Legitimate Power

Superior's right to command his/her subordinate is referred to as legitimate power.

Job description for each job specifies not only the duties and responsibilities, but also the rights of the jobholder. These rights include right to request the superior for resources and/or order the subordinates to behave in a specific way in order to perform organisational activities and contribute to the organisational goal. These rights are incorporated in job descriptions and rules of conduct. Superior's right to command his/her subordinate is referred to as legitimate power. Thus, people get legitimate power from the authority-responsibility relationship of the job. Superior can enjoy legitimate power as the subordinate has the responsibility to obey the commands of his/her superior.

The Marketing Manager of Zuhari Cements ordered the Regional Marketing Manager to sell 100 tons of cement to a non-government organisation at a price 40% lesser than the company's official price. The Regional Marketing Manager refused to accept the authority of the Marketing Manager of the company saying that this order is against the company's interest. The price reduction is allowed up to 40% of the official price when the production is in excess of demand. The Regional Marketing Manager further quoted that the demand for cement at that point of time is more than that of the production level. Thus, the Regional Marketing Manager did not follow his boss's order as he placed the company's interest above the legitimate power.

Thus, legitimate power is derived not just from the organisational position, but when it is accepted by the subordinates and is in the interest of the company. In addition, most of the subordinates in modern organisations do not comply with authority blindly, but they prefer to be consulted, allowed to participate in decision-making, empowered to carry out their activities rather than being directed or ordered or influenced by their executives.

Therefore, the legitimate power has little role to play in influencing the behaviour of subordinates in private sector. As such, the executives depend upon expert and referent power in influencing other's behaviour.

Reward Power

Reward Power: Power to reward others in the form of promotions, salary hikes, incentives and contribution to organizational goals.

People mostly prefer to be influenced by positive approach. Reward power influences the people through positive approach. People are influenced to follow instructions of the executives with a pre-assumption that they will get positive outcome by following the instructions. These rewards include increase in salary, bonus, promotion, transfer to a better job, interesting work, convenient work shifts, etc., and subordinates value these rewards much.

Executives get the reward power from their job authority to regulate and monitor the allocation of rewards, resources, and opportunities valued by subordinates. Thus, superiors derive formal authority that gives power to them over the distribution of organisational rewards[5] like promotion, leave, work allotment, bonus, and transfer to a convenient job. (See Box 21.1).

Box 21.1: Anil Ambani's Reward Power

Achievement: *Chairman of Anil Dhirubhai Ambani Group; Chosen as the 'CEO of the Year 2004' in the Platts Global Energy Awards and MTV Youth Icon of the Year' in September 2003.*

Anil Ambani is one of the foremost entrepreneurs of Independent India. He is the Chairman of Anil Dhirubhai Ambani Group. Earlier, before the split in the Reliance Group, Anil Ambani held the post of Vice Chairman and Managing Director in Reliance Industries Limited (RIL).

Born on June 4, 1959, Anil Ambani did his Bachelors in Science from the University of Bombay and Masters in Business Administration at The Wharton School at the University of Pennsylvania.

Anil Ambani joined Reliance in 1983 as Co-Chief Executive Officer. He pioneered India Inc's forays into overseas capital markets with international public offerings of global depository receipts, convertibles and bonds. Starting from 1991, he led Reliance in its efforts to raise, around US$2 billion from overseas financial markets. In January 1997, the 100-year Yankee bond issue was launched under his stewardship.

After the split in Reliance Group, Anil Ambani founded Anil Dhirubhai Ambani Group. He is the Chairman of all listed Group companies, which include: Reliance Communications, Reliance Capital, Reliance Energy and Reliance Natural Resources Limited.

Anil Ambani was elected as an independent member Rajya Sabha MP in June 2004. But he resigned voluntarily on March 25, 2006.

Anil Ambani has won several awards and honours. Major among these include: 'CEO of the Year 2004' in the Platts Global Energy Awards, 'MTV Youth Icon of the Year' in September 2003, 'The Entrepreneur of the Decade Award' by the Bombay Management Association, and 'Businessman of the Year Award' by leading Business Magazine, Business India in 1997.

Source: http://www.iloveindia.com/indian-heroes/anil-ambani.html

Subordinates also have the reward power over their superiors in the following aspects, viz.,

- **Appraisal of the superior's performance:** Superior's promotion, salary levels, other monetary and non-monetary benefits to some extent depend upon the rating by the subordinates,
- Subordinates contribute to the achievement of the targets fixed for the superiors, and
- Subordinates have power of influencing the award of rewards to their superiors by influencing the superior's superior informally.

Now, we shall discuss the third source of power derived from the formal job authority, *i.e.*, coercive power.

Coercive Power

Coercive power is the ability to apply punishment. Superiors have coercive power through their authority to reprimand, demote and retrench employees.[6] This power is dependent on fear on the part of the subordinate. Employees react to the fear of negative consequences which take place, if one fails to comply with the superior's commands. Expert employees can also have the coercive power of threatening the management of quitting during the periods of crisis.

Employees of Hughes Software Systems (HSS) were afraid of the Human Resources Manager for the pink cards consequent upon the downsizing of the company. The Human Resources Manager has the power in deciding the redundant jobs. This power is called *coercive power.*

Trade union leaders also have coercive power through their power of organising strikes, creating brinkmanship etc. Software engineers used to have coercive power over their employers as the former posed a higher risk of quitting during the software boom period of 1997 to 2000. Thus, employees also have coercive power in those sectors in which the supply of human resources is less than demand.

Team members use coercive power over other team members in order to control their contribution, attendance, etc., in team-based organisations.

The remaining two sources of power are derived from the personal characteristics of the individual. These two sources are expert power and referent power. Now we shall study the expert power.

Expert Power

Expert power is the individual's capacity to influence others by possessing expert skills and knowledge that they need.

Expert power is the individual's capacity to influence others by possessing expert skills and knowledge that they need. Thus, expert power is the influence based on special skills or knowledge.

Daewoo Motors' engineers used to be influenced by its Managing Director Mr. Kim because the latter is an expert in automobile engineering. Thus, Mr. Kim had the power to influence his employees due to his expert knowledge. Mr. Kim's power is called *expert power.*

Some people possess in-depth knowledge, understanding and talented skills in certain well defined areas. Such persons are regarded as experts in the area concerned. People would like to follow the instructions and influence of such experts. (See Box 21.2).

Box 21.2: Expert Power of Women CEO

Mallika Srinivasan

Economic Times Businesswoman of the year 2006, she is a well known entrepreneur of India. She has always strived hard to reach for skies, but has deeply rooted her foot into the ground. She is a strong headed woman, who is leading the activities of a company that is involved in macho business such as tractor manufacturing. She has been able to rise and stand out above all others and make a name for herself in the competitive business world of today. Well, we are talking about Mallika Srinivasan, director of the Rs 2500 crore Amalgamations Group Tafe. Mallika Srinivasan is one of the most successful women CEOs in India. In this article, we will present you with the biography of Mallika Srinivasan, so read on...

Life History

Born on November 19, 1959 as the eldest daughter of industrialist A Sivasailam, she is the pride of her parents. She was always brilliant in academics. She did her MA (econometrics) from Madras University. Thereafter, she went abroad to pursue further studies. She did her MBA from the Wharton School of the University of Pennsylvania. Married to Venu Srinivasan, the CMD of TVS Motor, she is living happily with their two children.

In the year 1986, she planned to join the family business. She was made the General Manager of Tafe (Tractors and Farm Equipment) Company. When she took over the responsibility of furthering the economic wealth and business, the turnover of the Company was Rs 85 cr. Under the expert guidance of her father and the whole hearted support of the team, she brought about a major transformation. She converted Tafe into a high technology-oriented company, thereby becoming the initial choice of the farmers. There was a period, when the Company had to face a tough time, however; even then, the Company invested a huge amount of over Rs. 70 crore in the designing and development of product.

At present, the Company is earning a business over Rs. 1,200 cr. It has been a long journey for the Company, which has witnessed many ups and downs. But, it was the strong determination of this courageous woman that slowly and steadily made the firm climb the ladders of success. Today, the Company has not only found a niche for itself as the leading tractor manufacturer, but also expanded its area of operations. It has also entered into other businesses like engineering plastics, panel instruments, automotive batteries, gears, hydraulic pumps, and farm implements.

The company has had a long alliance with Massey Ferguson, which is now a part of Agco. The company is looking forward to exporting fully constructed tractors to Agco. Presently, Agco has a stake of 24% in the Company and the rest lies with Simpson & Co. Presently, Mallika Srinivasan is serving as the president of premier industrial bodies like Tractor Manufacturers Association and the Madras Management Association. She is the first lady to have assumed the role of a president of the Madras Chamber of Commerce and Industry. She is also a prominent member of the governing board of the Indian School of Business, Hyderabad.

Source: http://www.iloveindia.com/indian-heroes/mallika-srinivisan.html

Who can have the expert power: All people irrespective of their level can have the expert power, by possessing skill and knowledge which is useful to other employees, departments, teams and for the organisation as a whole.

Referrent Power

Referent power also comes from within. It is the individual's ability to influence the others' behaviour through interpersonal relations, amicable, pleasing personalities and charisma. Charisma is a form of interpersonal attraction whereby followers develop a respect for and trust in the charismatic individual.[7]

Executives with referent power influence the subordinates to follow his direction and orders willingly. People with referent power motivate the subordinates easily.

The students and intellectuals were attracted by Mr. Abdul Kalam — the former President of the Republic of India. Many people particularly from Andhra Pradesh used to like and be attracted by Mr. N.T. Rama Rao – the former Chief Minister of Andhra Pradesh. Mr. Shyam Sunder of GE Electronics (India) understands the psychology, thinking and behavioural patterns, personal preferences and problems of his subordinates and deals with them accordingly. As such, his subordinates like him, identify with him, respect him and prefer to work with him according to his orders. Thus, the interpersonal skills of Mr. Shyam helped him to have power and to influence the behaviour of his subordinates. This type of power is referred to as '*referent power*.'

Often we come across with another kind of power, i.e., Role Model Power.

Role Model Power

BoSome people play their roles most efficiently. Others who are thrilled of such performance and are influenced indirectly to initiate or follow such personalities.

For example, the role of Dhirubai Ambani in managing by walking around in the office is adapted by his two sons and several managers. These managers have viewed the role of Dhirubai as a model. (See Box 21.3).

Box 21.3: Role Model Power of Kumar Mangalam Birla Profile

Born: *June 14, 1967*

Achievement: *Chairman of the Aditya Birla Group; Chosen as Ernst & Young Entrepreneur of the Year - India in 2005.*

Kumar Mangalam Birla is the Chairman of the Aditya Birla Group. The group is India's third largest business house. Major companies of Aditya Birla Group in India are Grasim, Hindalco, UltraTech Cement, Aditya Birla Nuvo and Idea Cellular. Aditya Birla Group's joint ventures include Birla Sun Life (Financial Services) and Birla NGK (Insulators). The group also has its presence in various countries such as Thailand, Indonesia, Malaysia, Philippines, Egypt, Canada, China and Australia.

Born on June 14, 1967, Kumar Mangalam Birla spent his early life in Calcutta and Mumbai. He is a Chartered Accountant and did his MBA (Masters in Business Administration) from the London Business School, London. Kumar Mangalam Birla took over as Chairman in 1995, at the age of 28, after sudden demise of his father, noted industrialist Aditya Birla, after whom the group is named.

When Kumar Mangalam Birla assumed the mantle at the Aditya Birla Group, doubts were raised about his ability to handle a giant business house with interests spanning viscose, textiles and garments on the one hand and cement, aluminium and fertilisers on the other. But Kumar Mangalam proved his sceptics wrong. He brought in radical changes, changed business strategies, professionalised the entire group and replaced internal systems. Kumar Mangalam reduced his group's dependence on the cyclic commodities sectors by entering consumer products.

Under Kumar Mangalam Birla's leadership, the Aditya Birla Group, apart from consolidating its position in existing businesses, also ventured into sunrise sectors like cellular telephony, asset management, software and BPO.

Kumar Mangalam Birla also holds several key positions on various regulatory and professional boards, including chairmanship of the advisory committee constituted by the ministry of company affairs for 2006 and 2007, membership of the prime minister of India's advisory council on trade and industry, chairmanship of the board of trade reconstituted by the union minister of commerce and industry, and membership of the Central Board of Directors of the Reserve Bank of India.

Kumar Mangalam Birla has won several honours. Major among them include The Business Leader of the Year (2003) by The Economic Times, Business Man of the Year - 2003 by Business India, and The Ernst & Young Entrepreneur of the Year - India in 2005.

Source: http://www.iloveindia.com/indian-heroes/kumar-mangalam-birla.html

Now, we shall discuss the other aspect of the power in organisations, i.e., contingencies of power.

(C) CONTINGENCIES OF POWER

Power can be realised and used under the presence of certain conditions. These conditions are also called *contingencies of power*. The contingencies of power include: substitutability, centrality, discretion and visibility.[8] Now, we shall discuss the contingencies of power. Dr. Jayasankar of Apollo Hospitals is an expert doctor, but could not influence the behaviour of others through his expert power, because the conditions in Apollo did not favour him to use his expert power. Thus, possessing power is not just enough to influence the others' behaviour.

Substitutability

Substitutability refers to the availability of alternative sources for the same resource.

Substitutability refers to the availability of alternative sources for the same resource like courier services and also the availability of substitutes for resources like e-mail for Indian Posts.

Employees of Indian Posts were strong during 1980s. Their strike in September 1985 affected a number of companies and the general community as other modes of communication particularly e-mail and courier services were not developed. But the Indian Posts during the 21st century became weak due to the significant development of e-mail and courier services. Similarly, software professionals were strong and used to dictate the terms to their employers until 2000 and became weak after 2000 due to the recession in the industry.

Thus, the power is strongest when someone's resources are in great demand. And power becomes weak when the alternative sources are developed for those resources as in the case of Indian Posts.

People increase their power through non-substitutability through the following means, while some people do not prefer to increase non-substitutability.

- **Controlling tasks:** People control others from performing the tasks they do perform. For example, the accounts of the companies are to be audited by only the Chartered Accountants and the Secretarial Services to the companies are to be provided by the qualified company secretaries from the Institute of Company Secretaries of India. (See Box 21.4).

Box 21.4: Azim Premji's Controlling Power

***Born:** July 24, 1945*

***Achievements:** Chairman of Wipro Technologies; Richest Indian for the past several years; Honoured with Padma Bhushan in 2005.*

Azim Premji is Chairman of Wipro Technologies, one of the largest software companies in India. He is an icon among Indian businessmen and his success story is a source of inspiration to a number of budding entrepreneurs.

Born on July 24, 1945, Azim Hashim Premji was studying Electrical Engineering from Stanford University, USA when due to the sudden demise of his father, he was called upon to handle the family business. Azim Premji took over the reins of family business in 1966 at the age of 21.

At the first annual general meeting of the company attended by Azim Premji, a shareholder doubted Premji's ability to handle business at such a young age and publicly advised him to sell his shareholding and give it to a more mature management. This spurred Azim Premji and made him all the more determined to make Wipro a success story. And the rest is history.

When Azim Premji occupied the hot seat Wipro dealt in hydrogenated cooking fats and later diversified to bakery fats, ethnic ingredient based toiletries, hair care soaps, baby toiletries, lighting products and hydraulic cylinders. Thereafter Premji made a focused shift from soaps to software.

Under Azim Premji's leadership Wipro has metamorphosed from a Rs.70 million company in hydrogenated cooking fats to a pioneer in providing integrated business, technology and process solutions on a global delivery platform. Today, Wipro Technologies is the largest independent R&D service provider in the world.

Azim Premji has several achievements to his credit. In 2000, Asiaweek magazine, voted Premji among the 20 most powerful men in the world. Azim Premji was among the 50 richest people in the world from 2001 to 2003 listed by Forbes. In April 2004, Times Magazine, rated him among the 100 most influential people in the world. He is also the richest Indian for the past several years. In 2005, Government of India honoured Azim Premji with Padma Bhushan.

Source: http://www.iloveindia.com/indian-heroes/azim-premji.html

- **Controlling knowledge:** Many professional organisations and educational institutions control the spread of knowledge by restricting the enrolment of membership and admissions.
- **Controlling the contribution of human resources:** Some people reduce their working hours and rendering their services in order to create artificial scarcity and gain power. Prominent doctors, software professionals, lawyers, etc., resort to this practice. Similarly, trade unions used to resort to these means before 1991 economic liberalisation.
- **Differentiation:** Some organisations and individuals claim that they only provide services which others do not provide. For example, a corporate hospital says, "we only provide full range of computer-aided tests." One consulting firm claims that their uniqueness is turning around the sick and less-profit-making organisations. They would like to increase their power by creating such differentiation or uniqueness for their services.

The second contingency of power is centrality. We shall now discuss this factor.

Centrality

Centrality is the degree and nature of interdependence between the powerholder and others.[9] The two dimensions of centrality are: (i) how many people are affected by the actions. Mrs. Syamala, the

Centrality is the degree and nature of interdependence between the power-holder and others.

Chief Personnel Manager of the Maharastra State Road Transport Corporation (MSRTC) was asked to help in turning around the Corporation. She accepted the challenging task and educated all the employees by visiting all the depots and offices. She created a sense of commitment among all the employees by saying, "I used to have only one brother before joining MSRTC, but now I have one lakh brothers (number of male employees of MSRTC). She could change the behaviour of the employees and turned around the MSRTC into a profit- making organisation within six months. Thus, Mrs. Syamala could influence almost all employees within a short span of six months.

Almost all the employees of the MSRTC are affected by the actions of Mrs. Syamala, (ii) how quickly people are affected by the actions. Employees of MSRTC were affected by the action of Mrs. Syamala within six months.

Thus, the centrality with higher degree and positive nature and enhances the strength of the power and vice versa.

Discretion

Discretion is the freedom to make decisions without referring to rules or receiving permissions from superiors.

Discretion is the freedom to make decisions without referring to rules or receiving permissions from superiors.[10] Discretion makes the power strong and absence of discretion makes the power weak. Thus, the supervisors become powerless due to absence of discretion even though they may have access to some sources of power.[11] In other words, supervisors having access to some sources of power become more powerful with discretion.

Mr. Iyer is the Production Manager of a Pune-based private sector company. Mr. Iyer is empowered and his job is autonomous. He makes all the decisions of his department without seeking permission from the General Manager. Company's rules are flexible and Mr. Iyer has to follow only one criteria while making the decision, *i.e.,* maximization of the value to the company.

In contrast, Mr. Satyanarayana, Marketing Manager of Hindustan Cables Limited (a public sector company) has no freedom in taking decisions. He has to follow a number of rules and consult his superiors even for a minor decision. Mr. Satyanarayana has no discretion even in implementing rewards and punishments.

Mr. Iyer has discretion in making decisions, and in implementing rewards and punishments whereas Mr. Satyanarayana has no discretion.

The next contingency factor is visibility. Now we shall discuss this factor.

Visibility

Visibility increases as the number of people with whom the employee interacts increases. Mr. Parasuram of SRK Pharma is an expert in biotechnology. But he does not interact with other employees of the company. As such, though Mr. Prakash has access to the source of expert power, he has become powerless. In other words, employee's power become strong when he makes others know his sources of power. (See Box 21.5).

Box 21.5: Vijay Mallya's Power

Achievements: *Chairman of the United Beverages (UB) Group; Launched a new domestic airline called Kingfisher Airline; Rajya Sabha M.P.*

Vijay Mallya is the Chairman of the United Beverages (UB) Group. He recently launched a new domestic airline called Kingfisher Airline which is making great waves. Vijay Mallya is famous for his flamboyant and flashy lifestyle.

Vijay Mallya is the son of a famous industrialist Vittal Mallya. He assumed the Chairman of the UB Group in 1983 and took the company to great heights. Under his dynamic leadership the group has grown into a multinational conglomerate of over sixty companies. During this process United Beverages acquired several companies abroad. The UB Group has diversified

business interests ranging from alcoholic beverages to life sciences, engineering, agriculture, chemicals, information technology and leisure.

In 2005, Vijay Mallya established Kingfisher Airlines. In a short span of time Kingfisher Airline has carved a niche for itself. It was the first airline in India to operate with all new aircraft. Kingfisher Airlines is also the first Indian airline to order the Airbus A380.

Vijay Mallya has other interests too apart from business. He has won trophies in professional car racing circuits and is a keen yachtsman and aviator. Vijay Mallya has also won numerous trophies in horse racing including several prestigious Derbies.

In 2000, Vijay Mallya entered politics superceded Subramaniam Swamy as the president of Janata Party. Presently, he is a Rajya Sabha M.P.

Source: http://www.iloveindia.com/indian-heroes/vijay-mallya.html

Dependability

Powerholder will get the advantage only when others do not have the same power. Whenever one has computer skills in the organisation, acquiring those skills will not give you power. As such, the companies develop multiple dealers in the same town, multiple suppliers of raw materials, etc., in order to reduce its dependency on one agency.

One day Prof. Rao suddenly became powerful as the Superintendent of Police came to his chambers and requested him to organise a training programme on 'Interpersonal Relations,' for the newly employed Circle Inspectors in July 1996. The Superintendent of Police depended on him as such training could not be provided by others in his place. Therefore, he gained power. Thus, the dependency of others on the powerholder makes him more powerful.

Enhancing dependency: Powerholder can increase the dependency of others on him when the resource he has is important, scarce and non-substitutable.

- **Importance:** Software professionals are more powerful in Satyam Computers, Infosys and Tata Consultancy, as developing software is more critical, uncertain and important in these organisations. Marketing professionals are important in Hindustan Lever Limited, Procter and Gamble, and Godrej as most uncertainty is involved in selling in these companies. Strike by the drivers halts the wheels of Indian Railways and State Road Transport Corporations as drivers perform more critical and important job in these organisations.

Software professionals in Software Companies, marketing professionals in fast moving consumer goods companies and drivers in transport organisations reduce uncertainties. As such, their resource is important to the respective organisations. Thus, the more important resource you have, the more the others depend on you.

Scarcity

A lower level employee in the salary unit of Human Resources Department is powerful during the period of filing income tax returns as he only knows the art and science of minimising tax liability within the rules and regulations. Others do not try to acquire this skill as they perceive it as difficult to learn. As such, this resource became scarce. The scarcity makes others depend on the powerholder very much. Thus, more scarcity makes more dependency and vice versa.

Non-substitutability

More the non-availability of a viable substitute for a resource, leads to the more power it controls over others. Mr. Prakash Chowla is a highly skilled negotiator in balancing and unifying the diversified corporate cultures in Bangalore. No other consultant has the skills either equal to or better than him.

Hence, he has been in high demand in the merging companies. Thus, Mr. Prakash is highly powerful in the area concerned.

Mr. Prakash has been more powerful because his resource has no viable substitute.

(D) MEASURING POWER BASES

Though it is difficult to know and measure the power bases, the questionnaire presented in the Exhibit 21.1 provides guidelines to measure the power bases of the boss.

Exhibit 21.1 Measuring Power Bases

Note: **Answer yes indicates the nature of the basis and the 1, 2, 3, 4 scale indicates the level of the power with '1' the lowest level of power and the '4' the highest level.**

For Coercive Power:

- My boss makes things difficult for me, and I want to avoid getting him or her angry. Yes/No

  If yes, indicate the level | 1 | 2 | 3 | 4 |

For Reward Power:

- My boss is able to give special benefits or rewards to me, and I find it advantageous to trade favours with my boss. Yes/No

  If yes, indicate the level | 1 | 2 | 3 | 4 |

For Legitimate Power:

- My boss has the right considering his/her position and my job responsibilities to expect me to comply with legitimate requests. Yes/No

  If yes, indicate the level | 1 | 2 | 3 | 4 |

For Expert Power:

- My Boss has the experience and knowledge to earn my respect and I defer to his/her judgment in some matters. Yes/No

  If yes, indicate the level | 1 | 2 | 3 | 4 |

For Referent Power:

- I like my boss and enjoy doing things for him/her. Yes/No

  If yes, indicate the level | 1 | 2 | 3 | 4 |

(**Source:** Modified version from G.Yukul and C.M.Falbe, "Importance of Different Power Sources in Downward and Lateral Relations," Journal of Applied Psychology, June 1991, p. 417).

So far, we have discussed the sources and contingencies of power. The interaction among the contingencies of results in the consequences of power.

The ultimate consequence or output of power is influencing others. People may be influenced in a desirable way or in an undesirable way. It does mean that the consequence of power may be positive or negative. For example, the management of Indian Railways used coercive power in its negotiations with the trade unions in May 1974. Consequently, workers organised a strike for 18 days in May 1974. Thus, the consequence of coercive power in this example was the use of counter power by trade unions. The consequences of different sources of power is as follows:

Source of the Power	*Consequences of the Power on Others*
• Coercive Power	• Resistance • Use of counter power • Reduce the trust between the parties • Increases employee dissatisfaction • Being influenced unwillingly

	• Influence is until the other party acquires balancing power
• Reward Power	• Tend to produce compliance • Works only during short run • Influence is only for a specific issue • Can't create enthusiasm
• Legitimate Power	• Tend to produce compliance with subsistence • Works in accordance with job description and organisational rules • Influence is direction-based
• Expert Power	• Employee commitment • Develops enthusiasm in subordinates
• Referent Power	• Employee commitment • Develops enthusiasm in subordinates • Self motivation • Exerts employee resources more than expected/anticipated

Power influences not only others but also affects the powerholder. The consequences of power on the powerholder include:

Type of the Powerholder	*Consequences*
• People with strong need for power	• Motivated to acquire more power • Are satisfied with the job when influence others • Commit to the job when responsibilities and authority are increased
• People with weak desire for power	• Motivated to relinquish power • Use the power only to the extent required for minimum level of job performance
• People with too much power (more than necessary for job performance)	• Abuse power for self-interest • Devalue the less powerful colleagues and subordinates • Exploit the subordinates • Reduce interpersonal associations with subordinates • Acquire still more power. According to Lord Action, "power tends to corrupt, absolute power corrupts absolutely."[12]

Power can be used for the attainment of organisational goals, group goals or individual goals at the cost of group and organisational goals. Power can be used for personal interest when the powerholder has discretionary behaviours.

Effective use of power: People should handle the power they have properly. Otherwise, it would result in wastage of the resources employed in the entire process. There are different strategies which can be adapted for proper use of power (Exhibit 21.2). Different strategies used for various sources of power as shown hereunder.

Exhibit 21.2 Uses and Outcomes of Power

Source of Power	Type of Outcomes		
	Commitment	Compliance	Resistance
Legitimate Power	*Possible* If request ispolite and very appropriate	*Likely* If request or order is seen as legitimate	*Possible* If arrogant demands are made or request does not appear proper
Reward Power	*Possible* If used in a subtle, very personal way	*Likely* If used in a mechanical, impersonal way	*Possible* If used in a manipulative, arrogant way
Coercive Power	*Very Unlikely*	*Possible* If used in a helpful, non-punitive way	*Likely* If used in a hostile or manipulative way
Expert Power	*Likely* If request is persuasive and subordinates share leader's task goals	*Possible* If request is persuasive but subordinates are apathetic about Leader's task goals	*Possible* If leader is arrogant and insulting, or subordinates oppose task goals
Referent Power	*Likely* If request is Believed to be Important to leader	*Possible* If request is perceived to be unimportant to leader	*Possible* If request is for something that will bring harm to leader

(**Source:** Table adapted by Gary A.Yukl from information in John R.P.French,Jr., and Bertram Raven, "The Bases of Social Power," in Dorwin F.Cartwright (ed.), *Studies in Social Power* (Ann Arbor, Mich.:Institute for Social Research, University of Michigan), pp. 150-167.

Coercive Power

- **Pressure:** Use demands, threats, persistent reminders.

Legitimate Power

- **Legitimating:** Seek to establish legitimacy of a request by claiming authority or by verifying consistency with policies, practices, traditions and established practices.

Reward Power

- **Exchange:** Offer salary increase, promotion, transfer, bonus, profit-sharing, incentives, etc.

Expert Power

- **Rational persuasion:** Use logical arguments and factual evidence.

Referent Power

- **Inspirational appeal:** Appeal to values, ideas, aspirations to arouse enthusiasm.
- **Consultation:** Seek participation in planning a strategy, activity or change.
- **Integration:** Attempt to create a favourable mood before making a request.
- **Personal appeal:** Appeal to feelings of loyalty or friendship.
- **Coalition:** Seek aid or support of others for some initiative or activity.

When power is used for the achievement of self/individual goals at the cost of group and organisational goals, it is referred to as *politics*. Power and politics are closely related to each other.

(E) POWER, AUTHORITY AND OBEDIENCE

Power is the capacity to influence others. In other words it is the potentiality to influence others. Authority is the right to demand others or influence others. People derive authority by virtue of their formal position in an organization. People use authority to exert their power to influence others. Thus, people with authority have the legitimacy to use their capacities or potentials to influence others. However, there is a limitation to use authority. Superiors can exercise authority only when their subordinates obey such authority. Some subordinates obey authority sincerely, mostly when superiors exercise authority without humanity, (See Box 21.6), while some subordinates disobey authority. While some subordinates disobey authority. Then the question is why some subordinates refuse to obey the orders and commands of their superiors while others obey them?

People derive authority by virtue of their formal position in an organization.

Box 21.6: McDonald's in a Pickle Over Cheese Slice Firing

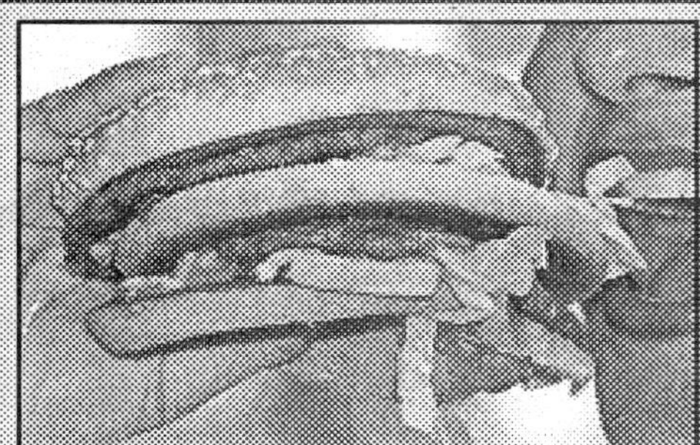

A Dutch branch of McDonald's was wrong to fire a worker for giving a colleague an extra piece of cheese on a hamburger, a court ruled.

"The dismissal was too severe a measure," the district court in Leeuwarden in the north of the Netherlands said in a written judgment.

"It is just a slice of cheese." A written warning would have been a more appropriate punishment, said the court, which ordered McDonald's to pay the worker the salary for the remaining five months of her contract — a total of 4,265.47 euros (6,006.69 dollars).

The company was also ordered to pay court costs. The worker was fired at a McDonald's branch in the northern town of Lemmer in March last year for giving a colleague on a break a more expensive cheese burger instead of the hamburger she had paid for. McDonald's maintained she had broken the rules, which prohibit any free gifts to family, friends or colleagues.

Source: http://www.google.com/hostednews/afp/article/ALeqM5i0pkHqjJ6pryrV_V4kLcd3-GXiaw (Accessed on 14/02/2010).

Why do some subordinates disobey the authority?

Some research studies found that direct defiance of authority is rare in organizational settings. However, certain subordinates under the following circumstances disobey the authority of their superiors:

- When the subordinates fail to understand the commands;
- When the subordinates don't have physical and/ or mental abilities to carry out the commands;
- When the subordinate feels that the commands of the superior are inconsistent with organizational norms, ethics and objectives;[13]
- When the subordinate feels that carrying-out of the command contributes to the personal interest of the superior, but not himself/herself either in total or disproportionately;
- When the subordinate feels that nothing will happen to him/ her by disobeying the authority;
- When the subordinate feels that he/she has more power in other areas like personal power than that of the superior;
- When the subordinate feels that his/ her contributions to the organization or more than the organization's contributions to him or her;
- When either the superior or subordinate or both are not in good moods; and
- When the superior is in parent ego state and the subordinate is either in parent ego state or in adult ego state.

How to Use Position Power/Authority to Influence?

As indicated earlier the authority sometimes may not be accepted and obeyed by the subordinates. This disobedience sometimes may be detrimental to organizational interest. So the superiors should enhance their power position. Superiors should consolidate their position and authority with the help of their personal power. They should also demonstrate that their units make significant contributions to organizational goals. In addition, superiors can enhance their power position as indicated below:

- Increase the centrality and criticality of their role in the organization;
- Increase the personal discretion and flexibility of the job rather than following routine norms;
- Build the tasks in the job that are difficult to be evaluated;
- Enhance the job performance;
- Enhance the relevance of their jobs to organizational goals;
- Do the job ethically. It does mean that don't entertain personal gains from the job;
- Enhance organizational contribution to subordinates, so that subordinates feel that they get more from the organization;[14]
- In addition, managers should enhance their personal power by acquiring critical knowledge and information, improving personal traits to attract people and enhance efforts.

Convert Power and Authority into Influence

Influence is the ultimate act that converts human efforts into desirable result. Power and authority need to be converted into influence. Power can be converted into influence by using the following strategies:[15]

- Present the facts and logical argument in communicating or commanding subordinates;
- Use of social and friendly networks in influencing the people;
- Build friendship with subordinates and use it while use power and authority;
- Offer benefits and favours to subordinates in exchange of their efforts in obeying the commands sincerely and seriously;
- Use forceful and direct approach in times of need;
- Brief higher authorities if you expect or foresee any disobedience;
- Involve the subordinates in decision-making as well as formulating various plans and schedules. Subordinates those are part of such plans and schedules accept the directives and commands based on such plans and schedules;
- Some times and particularly during the critical situations make a personal appeal for subordinate's unreserved cooperation;
- Inspire the subordinates to achieve higher order targets and do greater activities; (See Box 21.7).
- Become a role model for subordinates, so that they would like to obey the commands more willingly;
- Use of emotional intelligence tactics in commanding the subordinates;
- Use of tactics to persuade subordinates; and
- Empower the subordinates by delegating required authority, providing required skills and knowledge through training and offering autonomy in decision-making as well as in implementing decisions. Such subordinates would accept responsibility and accountability automatically.

Box 21.7: Mr. Narayana Murty Inspires People

Achievements: *One of the founders of Infosys Technologies Limited; Chosen as the World Entrepreneur of the Year - 2003 by Ernst and Young*

Narayana Murthy is the Non-Executive Chairman and Chief Mentor of Infosys Technologies Limited. He is a living legend and an epitome of the fact that honesty, transparency, and moral integrity are not at variance with business acumen. He set new standards in corporate governance and morality when he stepped down as the Executive Chairman of Infosys at the age of 60.

Born on August 20, 1946, N.R. Narayana Murthy is a B.E. Electrical from University of Mysore (1967) and M.Tech from IIT Kanpur (1969). Narayana Murthy began his career with Patni Computer Systems in Pune. In 1981, Narayana Murthy founded Infosys with six other software professionals. In 1987, Infosys opened its first international office in U.S.A.

With the liberalization of Indian economy in 1990s, Infosys grew rapidly. In 1993, the company came up with its IPO. In 1995, Infosys set up development centres across cities in India and in 1996, it set up its first office in Europe in Milton Keynes, UK. In 1999, Infosys became the first Indian company to be listed on NASDAQ. Today (in 2006), Infosys has a turnover of more than $ 2billion and has employee strength of over 50,000. In 2002, Infosys was ranked No. 1 in the "Best Employers in India 2002" survey conducted by Hewitt and in the Business World's survey of "India's Most Respected Company." Conducted in the same year.

Along with the growth of Infosys, Narayana Moorthy too has grown in stature. He has received many honours and awards. In June 2000, Asiaweek magazine featured him in a list of Asia's 50 Most Powerful People. In 2001, Narayana Murthy was named by TIME/CNN as one of the 25 most influential global executives. He was the first recipient of the Indo-French Forum Medal (2003) and was voted the World Entrepreneur of the Year - 2003 by Ernst and Young. The Economist ranked Narayana Murthy eighth on the list of the 15 most admired global leaders (2005) and Narayana Murthy also topped the Economic Times Corporate Dossier list of India's most powerful CEOs for two consecutive years - 2004 and 2005.

Source: http://www.iloveindia.com/indian-heroes/narayana-murthy.html

(F) EMPOWERMENT

Introduction

The traditional management/administration believed that lower level employees do not have managerial skills, managerial knowledge and managerial aptitude. Therefore, the manager at the top level used to take strategic decisions, managers at middle level used to take executive decisions and managers at the lower level used to take operational decisions and the workers used to carry out/implement the decisions taken by the lower level managers.

Increase in levels of formal education, increase in the contents in the educational programmes, entry of highly qualified candidates even at the lower levels of the organisations made the managements to realise that even the employees at the lower levels can take operational and executive decisions, if they are (i) provided with the required additional skills and knowledge through training and development and (ii) are delegated with the required authority and responsibility. Some of the modern managements enabled the employees to take executive and operational decisions and also implement them by providing training and development and delegating authority and responsibility.

Meaning

Empowerment refers to enabling a lower level employee to make all the decisions required/relevant for carrying out his duties or discharge his responsibilities, on his own and implement them.

Empowerment refers to enabling a lower level employee to make all the decisions required / relevant for carrying out his duties or discharge his responsibilities, on his own and implement them.

Example: The concept of empowerment can be understood better through the following example:

Premier Optics Limited, Vangalapandi, produces and sells high qualitative contact lenses through its retail outlets.

One day, a customer visited its Bangalore retail outlet along with a lens which had cracks. He enquired from the salesman behind the counter, the cost of replacement of the lens. The salesman examined these lenses and identified that the lens was produced by Premier Optics Ltd. and the cracks were developed due to the defect in the production process. He told the same to the customer and noted the telephone number of the customer. He informed the customer that the new lens will be supplied at the customer's home next day at 10.00 a.m. without any cost.

The customer felt immensely happy. Being the production manager in the Zuari Cements Ltd; the customer was confused of the decision of the salesman and asked him how could he identify the production defects, being the salesman, how could he decide to replace the product without referring the matter to the Finance Department. Then, the salesman replied that the employees in the Premier Optics Ltd., are empowered to take and implement all decisions relating to an operation based on the customer.

The customer has turned into a most loyal customer and acted as a link in the chain of advertisements.

Importance

Organisational restructuring — reorganisation — through Business Process Reengineering can be possible only with employee empowerment. The liberalisation, globalisation and privatisation resulted in severe competition. The competition forced the companies to serve and satisfy mostly the customer. Therefore, the organisations started empowering the employees to serve the customers better without any loss of time and inconvenience of going around various departments like finance, production and marketing/commercial. Empowerment enables the customer to get the better service/products without the loss of any time and at one point of contact. Thus, the satisfied customer will not only be loyal to the company but acts as a link in the chain of advertisements without any cost.

Characteristics of Empowered Organisations: Empowered organisations have the following characteristics:

- They do not have barriers between people and departments
- Formulate a vision.
- People at all levels are made champions of the vision
- Create the feeling of belongingness
- Creativity of the employees is encouraged.
- Keep the organisational strengths simple.
- Employees learn and teach the art of self-leadership.

Conditions for Effective Employee Empowerment: The following conditions are necessary for effective employee empowerment:

- Provide the information of the company to all employees.
- Employees should have multi-skills and knowledge.
- Employees should assume power to make substantive decisions.
- Employees should understand all the jobs, job specification and descriptions.
- Management should create and maintain conducive organisational culture.
- Management should delegate authority and power.
- Management should encourage the employees to take risk.
- Management should reward the employees adequately.

- The environment should be receptive to people with innovative ideas, risk taking, new methods and practice.
- Empowered employees should be accountable for the results, cost, behaviour, credibility and positive approach.

Specified Communities and Categories: According to the government directives the organisations, particularly public sector has to recruit candidates to the specified extent from the scheduled castes, scheduled tribes, backward communities and from specified classes like physically handicapped, ex-servicemen and the like.

Alternatives to Recruitment

Organisations, sometimes, may opt for alternatives to recruitment in view of the cost of recruitment as well as failure of recruitment appeals in getting right candidates. These alternatives include: work sharing/part-time employment, overtime, employees leasing and temporary employment.

Work Sharing/Part-time Employment: Organisation can employ the people working in other organisations on work-sharing basis or as part-time employees rather than on full time basis. This arrangement reduces the cost of staff, though it has its own limitations.

Overtime: Organisation, by providing additional salary and benefits ask the present employees to work overtime. This arrangement will reduce cost of staff per unit, provides additional income to employees, in addition to several other benefits to both employees and organisation. However, this arrangement suffers from its own limitations like fatigue, increased accidents and absenteeism. This facility suits to the short-term work pressures.

Employee Leasing: Employee leasing is paying a fee to an outsourcing firm or client and make use of the services of its employees, for a specified period. The client company pays salaries and benefits to such employees. This arrangement is suitable for short-term purposes/projects.

Temporary Employment: Some organisations employ the people on temporary basis which does not involve the detailed recruitment process. This arrangement helps the organisation to employ the people for short-term purposes/projects and to test the performance and provide permanent employment, if performance is satisfactory.

(G) ORGANISATIONAL POLITICS

Meaning

Influencing others by using discretionary acts to promote personal objective or interest for protecting or achieving self- interest even at the cost of others' interest or well-being is referred to as *organisational politics*. Protine Confectionary Limited, Rajkot produces different kinds of chocolates. The demand for its products is heavy in summer than in other seasons. Producing more in other two seasons, stocking it and delivering the product to the market in summer was the company's strategy until 1990. The company found that this strategy suffers from high cost of inventory. The Human Resources Manager along with the Finance Manager of the company formulated another strategy of producing twice the normal production during summer. This strategy significantly reduces the cost of working capital and inventory. However, the workers would require to work double the normal working hours. The company requested the workers and trade unions to accept this strategy along with 200% of the normal pay as overtime pay. Both the workers and the trade unions opposed the strategy and did not accept the management's request as working for 16 hours a day during summer affects their health adversely.

Influencing others by using discretionary acts to promote personal objective or interest for protecting or achieving self-interest even at the cost of others' interest or well-being is referred to as *organisational politics.*

Then, the Human Resources Manager organised a get-together of the family members of all employees and distributed *sarees(national dress of Indian women)* along with turmeric powder and *kum kum* powder (a cultural gift of the Hindu religion) to all the wives of the employees. Further, he announced a scheme of cash gift plus free life insurance policy to the wives of those employees who accept the company's strategy. This reward power of the management lured the employees' wives and ultimately influenced the employees to accept the company's strategy. Thus, the HR Manager got the credit from the top management and was promoted to the position of Chief Human Resources Manager. Consequent, upon the implementation of this strategy, the life span of most of the employees is reduced remarkably, just within five years. Then, the company was forced to withdraw this strategy.

Thus, the Human Resources Manager used his discretion and influenced the workers to promote his personal objective of securing credit even at the cost of the workers' health. This act of the HR Manager is referred to as *organisational politics.*

Organisational Politics: Desirable or Undesirable?

To a certain extent, organisational politics enables the company to achieve its goals while certain politics are dysfunctional and detrimental to the organisation.[16] The Protine Confectionary example reveals that organisational politics enabled the company to reduce the cost of inventory and achieve its objectives. As such, some executives feel that organisational politics is desirable. One of the production supervisors of Integrated Alloys and Steel Limited was practising organisational politics. His action was encouraging the workers to join the strike organised by the Trade Union in 1992. The management of the company felt that the political activity of the supervisor was undesirable as it was dysfunctional and dismissed the supervisor from the service.

(H) FACTORS CONTRIBUTING TO POLITICAL BEHAVIOUR

A number of factors are responsible for political behaviour. These factors are grouped into individual factors and organisational factors.[17]

Individual Factors

Factors contributing to the political behaviour at the individual level are:

- **High self-monitors:** Skilled in political behaviour.
- **Internal locus of control:** Proactive and prone to manipulate situation in their favour.
- **High machiavellian personality:** Will manipulate and generate a desire for power. Use politics to further self interest.
- **Investment in organisation:** Investment in terms of expectations forces the individual to use illegitimate means.
- **Perceived job alternatives:** More job opportunities an individual has results in more political behaviour.[18]

Organisational Factors

Organisational factors contributing to political behaviour include:

- **Reallocation of resources:** The reallocation of resources is necessary when the resources available either increase or decrease. These situations force the individuals to resort to politics.

- **Promotion opportunities:** Normally, the opportunities for promotion or advancement are lesser than the candidates expecting promotion. This situation leads to competition and thereby political behaviour by the competing candidates.
- **Low trust:** Low trust in organisations leads to tight control which in turn makes the subordinates to behave illegitimately.
- **Role ambiguity:** The unclear expectations from the employee makes him to act politically.
- **Unclear performance appraisal system:** Employee does not know what to do? And to what level of perfection he has to do? etc., under the unclear performance appraisal system. This situation creates ambiguity and leads to political behaviour.
- **Zero-sum reward system:** The win-lose approach in reward allocation is called zero-sum approach. People perceive that they won double if others lose. For example, if only one employee is promoted have employee's joy is immense. Therefore, this situation makes people take the chance, even through illegitimate means.
- **Democratic decisionmMaking:** The traditionally autocratic managers cannot make the decisions democratically in its true sense. Therefore, they refer the issues to committees and commissions to offer recommendations, and finally they make the decisions as they desire.
- **High performance pressures:** High performance pressures make the people to find short-cuts and politics to show superfluously high performance or through window-dressing.
- **Self-serving senior managers:** The political behaviour by the top management with rewards encourages the people at the lower level to resort to politics.

(I) CONSEQUENCES AND ETHICS OF POLITICS

Some of the organisational politics benefit the organisation. But they also:

- Consume time,
- Disrupt the work activities,
- Reduce the motivational level of the employees,
- Increase employee stress,
- Increase employee turnover, and
- Cause the loss of life of the people suspected to be involved in it. (See Box 21.8).

Box 21.8: Indian-American Professor Shot Dead in Alabama, USA — Is it Due to Organisational Politics?

Washington: An Indian-American professor hailing from Andhra Pradesh was among three people killed when a woman lecturer allegedly opened fire during a faculty meeting at a university in Alabama after learning that she had been denied tenure.

The incident, which also left three people injured, occurred at the University of Alabama at Huntsville (UAH) on Friday evening.

Huntsville police chief Henry Reyes identified the professor as Gopi Podila, who was the chairman of the biological sciences department. The other two killed, Maria Davis and Adriel Johnson, were associate professors of biology.

According to media reports, Amy Bishop, also a professor and one of the star researchers of the university, opened fire at the biology faculty meeting.

Police did not give any reason behind the incident, but local television WAFF, citing authorities, said the woman resorted to shooting after learning about her tenure.

Ms. Bishop (42) was charged with murder, which means she could face the death penalty if convicted, the media said.

College spokesman Ray Garner said two of the three people injured remained in a critical condition while a third was in a stable condition at a Huntsville Hospital.

Ms. Bishop, who joined the faculty in 2003, and her husband are credited with inventing a mobile cell incubation system touted as a replacement for the old-fashioned petri dish.

University president David Williams predicted in November 2008 that the device would "change the way biological and medical research is conducted."

(**Source:** http://www.hindu.com/2010/02/14/stories/2010021458060100.htm)

Ethical Aspects of Organisational Politics

Some political activities are ethical. The political actions become ethical under the following conditions:

- When the political activity benefits a larger number of people and harms a few,
- When the political activity provides the basic benefits like food, clothing and shelter for a less number of people even it harms a large number of people in lesser degree,
- When it provides the benefit to the generations together (through the innovations) even by harming the people,
- When it saves the customers from adulteration, etc. even by harming the employees,
- When it does not violate the moral rights and privacy of others and
- When it benefits the worse-off even by harming the well-off.

It is, however, difficult to conclude whether political activities are desirable or undesirable. Likewise it is difficult to say they are ethical or unethical. Further, it is difficult to categorise a particular activity as desirable or undesirable. In fact, certain activities labelled as political by one are labeled as an effective management activity by the other (See Exhibit 21.3). Therefore, they have to be decided or categorised based upon the situation.

Exhibit 21.3 Politics in the Eyes of the Beholder

	Political Label		*Effective Management Label*
1.	Blaming others	1.	Fixing responsibility
2.	'Kissing up'	2.	Developing working relationship
3.	Apple polishing	3.	Demonstrating loyalty
4.	Passing the buck	4.	Delegating the authority
5.	Covering your rear	5.	Documenting decisions
6.	Creating conflict	6.	Encouraging change and innovation
7.	Forming coalitions	7.	Facilitating teamwork
8.	Whistle-blowing	8.	Improving efficiency
9.	Scheming	9.	Planning ahead
10.	Overachieving	10.	Competent and capable
11.	Ambitious	11.	Career-minded
12.	Opportunistic	12.	Astute
13.	Cunning	13.	Practical-minded
14.	Arrogant	14.	Confident
15.	Perfectionist	15.	Attentive to detail

(**Main Source:** T.C.Krell, M.E. Mendenhall and J.Sendry, "Doing Research in the Conceptual Morass of Organisational Politics," Paper presented at the Western Academy of Management Conference, Hollywood, CA, April 1987 quoted in Stephen P.Robbins, op.cit., p. 364.)

Now, we shall discuss the types of organizational politics.

(J) TYPES OF ORGANISATIONAL POLITICS

Political tactics are presented in Exhibit 21.4.

Exhibit 21.4 Political Tactics Derived from Research

Tactics	*Description*
Pressure tactics	The use of demands, threats or intimidation to convince you to comply with a request or to support a proposal.
Upward appeals	Persuading you that the request is approved by higher management or appeals to higher management for assistance in gaining your compliance with the request.
Exchange tactics	Making explicit or implicit promises that you will receive rewards or tangible benefits if you comply with a request or support a proposal, or remind you of a prior favour to be reciprocated.
Coalition tactics	Seeking the aid of others to persuade you to do something or using the support of others as an argument for you to agree also.
Ingratiating tactics	Seeking to get you in a good mood or to think favourably of the influence agent before asking you to do something.
Rational persuasion	Using logical arguments and factual evidence to persuade you that a proposal or request is viable and likely to result in the attainment of task objectives.
Inspirational appeals	Making an emotional request or proposal that arouses enthusiasm by appealing to your values and ideals, or by increasing your confidence That you can do it.
Consultation tactics	Seeking your participation in making a decision or planning how to implement a proposed policy, strategy or change.

(**Source:** Adapted from Gary Yukl and Cecilia M.Falbe, "*Influence Tactics and Objectives in Upward, Downward and Lateral Influence Attempts*," Journal of Applied Psychology, vol.75, 1990, p. 133. Quoted in Fred Luthans, op.cit., p. 334).

Different organisational politics are grouped into seven types of organisational politics.[19] They are: (See Fig. 21.2).

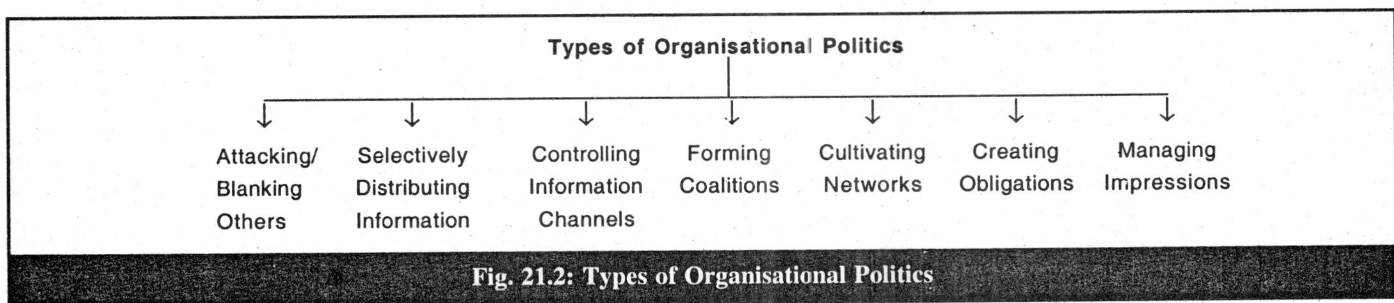

Fig. 21.2: Types of Organisational Politics

- **Attacking/blaming others:** Some people in order to cover up their inefficiencies blame others. Further, some people blame others in order to make them weak and then use the coercive power to achieve their personal goals. Many people use brinkmanship tactics in order to attack others.
- **Selectively distributing information:** Information is power. People selectively distribute information to shape perceptions of others about themselves or their departments. People resort to this strategy to limit the potential performance of rivals and enhance their power.[20] Since knowledge is power in today's organisation, people even use the strategy of 'hoarding information' in order to retain and exhibit their power.

The marketing department of SRK Pharma informed the stores department that the demand in 1999-2000 would be 240 tonnes and informed production department that it would be 440 tonnes. This divergent information created chaos in the organisation.

The Human Resources Manager of Indian Foods Ltd. supplied the incentive bonus information to the compensation unit of his department and did not provide this information to the Finance department, intentionally with a view to show low cost of staff. This selective distribution of information pulled down the image of the Finance Manager, when he failed to report the total figure to the CEO of the company.

- **Controlling information channels:** Managers prevent the employees from communicating directly to the top management and also with other employees in order to enhance and protect their power.

  Mr. Razak, the Branch Manager of A. P. Diary Development Corporation's Bhopal Branch wanted to communicate his idea to the Managing Director directly, in order to save the delay in the formal communication process. But the Regional Manager ordered him to process the information through the formal hierarchical channel only. He also warned him of the consequences of ignoring the formal channel. Consequent upon this order, Mr. Razak processed the information through the former channel. The regional manager through his political activity prevented Mr. Razak from getting the credit from the CEO for his idea.

- **Forming coalitions:** Coalition is an informal group that attempts to influence people outside the group by pooling the resources and power of its members through the synergetical impact.[21] Members of the group cannot influence the people individually, therefore, the members pool their resources, knowledge and power in order to achieve their common objective. As such coalition is a political activity. Coalitions are formed mostly with good intentions. However, coalitions influence others through pressure and monopolising the resources.

  People of Kerala relish the clove and as such the sales manager-in-charge of a toothpaste company provided this information to the employee concerned of the production department and the Assistant Finance Manager. Three of them formed into an informal group, shared their knowledge, and changed the product with the additional amount of clove after getting the approval from the CEO. Then, they released the product in the market. This action enhanced the market share in Kerala. The three members by forming an informal group could influence the CEO, other managers and the customers. This group activity is referred to as *coalition*.

- **Cultivating networks:** Some people develop social relations with others by developing the networks in order to achieve their personal goals. Networking cultivates social relationships with others to achieve one's goals through exchanging of resources, knowledge, etc.[22] Networks are one form of informal group and they are permanent in nature. Networks enhance the power of the members and influence others. Networking is a political activity as they deprive others from having benefit of information and resources from members of the networks. Men have the advantage of the networks and women are mostly excluded from the networks created by men.

- **Creating obligations:** People help the managers either in their official work or personal work and create obligations in their favour. Mr. Prakash helped the HR Manager of his company in settling the company's provident fund case. Later, he requested the HR Manager to transfer him to the job he opted. The HR Manager has the obligation to accept his request. This is creating obligations and is called the norm of reciprocity. This is political activity as people help others in order to get a more valuable favour at a future date.

- **Managing impressions:** Some people purposefully behave in a specific way like cultivating interpersonal relations, blaming others, hiding information, increasing visibility etc. in order to build up their image in the opinion of others. This practice is called '***impression management***,' which is a political activity because people influence others in order to achieve their personal goals.

Regulating Organisational Politics

Political behaviour of the employees cannot be eliminated completely. Political behaviour sometimes contributes to the achievement of organisational goals. Managements can maximise the desirable outcome of organisational politics by regulating the dysfunctional political activities.[23] Strategies to regulate dysfunctional political activities include:

Political behaviour of the employees cannot be eliminated completely, so it needs to be regulated.

- **Sufficient supply of resources:** Minimise the superior's discretion over critical resources by ensuring sufficient supply of material, financial, human and other resources.
- **Clear rules:** Formulate the clear rules regarding the distribution of critical resources when they are scarce even after taking all possible steps.
- **Open communication:** Open communication allows communication flow of freely in all directions through the establishment of intranet facility.
- **Employee involvement:** Involve the people in decision-making and implementation areas.
- **Empowerment:** Empower the people, so that their human resources are used for organisational effectiveness.
- **Flat organisational structure:** Follow the flat and team organisational structure where the people have to attend to the challenging activities and thereby do not find time for political activity.
- **Open door policy:** Follow open door policy and open-minded approach in sorting out the issues.

Implications on Behaviour and Performance

Power and politics are both functional as well as dysfunctional. In other words, they are constructive and contribute strategically for the organisational goals. Similarly, they are destructive and create hurdles for the achievement of organisational goals. However, political behaviours can be regulated and channeled towards the constructive activities. In such cases, power and politics result in moulding the employee behaviour towards the desired lines. The specific implications of power and politics on behaviour and performance include:

- **Teamwork:** Power and politics enable the individuals to form coalitions in the short run and form teams in the long run. They enable exchange of human skills, knowledge, etc. and get the advantage of synergy.
- **Motivation:** Power and politics enable the executives to use their different kinds of power and motivate the subordinates.
- **Moulding the behaviour:** Power and politics make the unwilling workers to accept the requests and orders of the superiors willingly.

- **Performance:** The referent power makes the employees to involve in organisational activities with self-commitment, motivation and discipline. Expert power makes the subordinates to enrich their skill and knowledge. The enriched employees improve their job performance.
- **Empowerment:** The referent power and expert power help employee empowerment.
- **Employee involvement and participation:** The counter power and politics provide the way for employees to involve and participate in decision-making and formulate strategies jointly with the executives.
- **Satisfaction:** Power and politics, if they are used and handled properly, lead to employee job satisfaction for the achievement of higher performance and organisational goals.

KEY TERMS

- Power
- Counter Power
- Reward Power
- Referent Power
- Dependency
- Role Ambiguity
- Empowerment
- Confirmity
- Power Relationship
- Legitimate Power
- Expert Power
- Organisational Poltics
- Cultivating Networks
- Managing Impressions

QUESTIONS

1. What is power? Explain the various sources of power.
2. How do you measure power? Explain with examples.
3. Explain the positive and negative consequences of power.
4. Discuss 'Organisational Politics'. Explain its desirability.
5. What are the factors that affect organisational politics?
6. What are the consequences of organisational politics?
7. What are the different types of organisational politics?
8. How do you regulate organisational politics?
9. Explain the influence of power and politics on behaviour.

REFERENCES

1. J. Pfeffer, *"New Dimensions in Organisational Theory,"* Oxford University Press, New York, 1997, Chapter 6.
2. R. M. Emerson, *"Power-Dependence Relations,"* American Sociological Review, 27(1962), pp. 31-41.
3. D. J. Brass and M. E. Burkhardt, *"Political Power and Power Use,"* Academy of Management Journal, 36(1993), pp. 4410-470.
4. J. R. P. French and B. Raveen, *"The Bases of Social Power,"* in D. Cartwright (ed.), *"Studies in Social Power,"* University of Michigan Press, Ann Arbor, 1959, pp. 150-167.
5. Steven L. McShane and Mary Ann Von Glinow, *"Organisational Behaviour,"* Tata McGraw Hill, New Delhi, 2001, p. 373.
6. *Ibid.*, p. 374.
7. J. D. Kudisch and M. L. Protect, *"Expert Power, Referent Power and Charisma:Towards the Resolution of a Theoritical Debate,"* Journal of Business and Psychology (Winter 1995), pp. 177-195.

8. R. M. Kanter, *"Power Failure in Management Circuits,"* Harvard Business Review, July-August 1979, pp. 65-75.
9. Brass and Burkhardt, *"Potential Power and Power Use,"* pp. 441-470.
10. Steven L. McShane and Mary Ann Von Glinow, op.cit., p. 379.
11. Kanter, "Power Failure in Management Circuits," p. 68.
12. C. E. G.Catlin, *"Systematic Politics,"* University of Toranto Press, Toranto, 1962, p. 71.
13. Chester I Bernrd, *"Functions of Executive"*, Harvard University Press, Cambridge.
14. David A. Whetten and Kim S. Cameron, *"Developing Management Skills"*, Foresman, Glenview, pp. 250-259.
15. david Kipinis et.al *"Patterns of Managerial Influence"*, Organisational Dynamics, Vol. 12,pp. 60-61.
16. Bauchanan and Badham, R., *"Power, Politics and Organisational Chance,"* Sage London, 1999, p. 64.
17. K. M. Kacmar and G. R. Ferris, *"Politics at Work:Sharpening the Focus of Political Behaviour in Organisations,"* Business Horizons, July-August, 1993, pp. 70-74.
18. Fred Luthans, op.cit., pp.365-369.
19. R. W. Allen, et al *"Organisational Politics:Tactics and Characteristics of its Actors,"* California Management Review, Fall, 1979, pp. 77-83.
20. Steven L. McShane and Mary Ann Von Glinow, op.cit., p. 385.
21. *Ibid.*, p. 386.
22. *Ibid.*
23. G. R. Ferris et al *"Perceptions of Organisational Politics,"* Human Relations, 49, 1996, pp. 233-63.

CHAPTER **22**

ORGANISATIONAL THEORY

Chapter Outline

Learning Objectives

After studying this Chapter, you should be able to:

✓ Know the meaning of organisation;

✓ Discuss the classical theory of organisation and its features;

✓ Understand why the classical theory of organisation is criticised;

✓ Discuss the neo-classical theory of organisation;

✓ Understand why the neo-classical theory was also criticised;

✓ Understand the modern organisation theory;

✓ Evaluate modern organisation theory;

✓ Analyse the contingency or situational theory; and

✓ Appreciate organisational learning theory.

(A) ORGANISATION

Organisation is a process of combining and interrelating the various organs of a system or of an institution in a sequence. These organs include tasks, jobs, responsibilities, roles, individuals, working and social groups, material, machines, services, information, computers, intranet, internet, etc. The purpose of grouping these organs/parts is to channelise all the resources towards the achievement of the strategies of the company. In other words, grouping of those organs is like building relationships among the building blocks of jobs, individuals, etc. To be specific, organisation is a consciously coordinated social entity, with a relatively identifiable boundary. It functions on a relatively continuous basis to achieve a common goal or set of goals.

Theory

Theory is a systematic grouping of interrelated principles. Principles are believed to be truths at a given point of time, explaining relationship between two variables or among more than two variables. Richard S.Rudner defines theory as "a systematically related set of statements including some law-like generalisation that is empirically testable and the sort of systematic relatedness is deductive relatedness."

Organisation Structure

Organisation structure deals with the allocation of tasks, activities, formal coordinating mechanisms and interaction patterns among members.

Organisation Design

Organisation design emphasises the management side of the organisation theory. It deals with constructing and changing an organisation's structure to achieve the organisation's goals.

Organisation Theory

Organisation theory is the study of structures

Organisation theory is the study of structure, functioning, perceived and actual performance of individuals, groups and organisation in general. Tosi defined organisation theory as, "a set of interrelated concepts, definitions and propositions that present a systematic view of behaviour of individuals, groups and subgroups interacting in some relatively patterned sequence of activity, the intent of which is goal-directed.

The concepts to be viewed as theory must be observational or experimental. The existence of the concepts must be verified through the examination of the phenomenon. They are tested in the deduction process based on certain rules. It tests the relationships between or among concepts. These tests help to draw findings, conclusions and inferences based on derivations, deductive approach and selected concepts.

Definitions provide useful guidelines for the purpose of analysis. But they can't be theories. Similarly, analysis also give broader details of an event or case and they also cannot be theories.

Need for the Study of Organisation Theory: The study of the organisation theory helps to observe, explain and anticipate the behaviour of individuals, subgroups and groups during or at the end of the work. This, in turn enables the manager to manipulate the relationships by changing the organisation design, in order to derive the desired human behaviour. In addition, discussion and study on organisation theory will develop the knowledge in the area, clarify, establish or contradict the existing knowledge as in the case of other theories. The study of organisation theory also helps in analysing and understanding of the organisation's functioning and providing solutions for the problems involved therein.

(B) CLASSICAL THEORY OF ORGANISATION

The term *classical* does mean that something traditionally accepted or long established. The beginning of classical theory can be traced back to the industrial transformation during the second half of the nineteenth century. Before the industrial revolution, production was carried on by the cottage industries. These industries were producing customised products. The changing technology and increasing population led to massive production - production of standard products. Industrial revolution led to the establishment of large-scale industries. Massive production, standard products and large-scale industrialisation created economic, social and psychological problems at the workplace. Managements of large-scale industries created organisational forms to solve the problems at the workplace. This situation changed the work structure from the individualistic approach to the organisational form of structure. Organisational structure is building the relationships among the tasks, activities, operations, people, material, machines, etc.

Building the relationships can be done based on different approaches. One such approach is building the relationships based on mechanical approach. Mechanical approach is traditionally accepted by the classical management scientists. Thus, classical theory is the first one in the line of systematic study of the organisations.

Mechanical Approach: Classical management scientists treated organisation as a machine and human resources as components or nuts and bolts of the machine. They felt that the efficiency of the organisation depended on the efficiency of human resources. Their approach is based on the input cost and output revenue. In other words, classical theory focusses on input and output mediators. As such, this theory neglected the external environmental factors which have a bearing on the work and relationships.

Features of Classical Theory

Mason Haire in his paper on, '*Philosophy of Organisation*,' observed the main features of classical organisation theory. They are:

- This theory is built on an accounting model as the input cost and output revenue is the main focus of classical theory.
- It maximizes neatness and control.
- It puts special emphasis on error and particularly on the detection of error and its correction.
- This approach to the organisation is the classical embodiment of the extra pair of hands concept.
- Classical organisation theory assumes man to be relatively homogeneous and relatively unmodifiable in designing the jobs and in picking these extra pairs of hands.
- Another feature of the classical theory is that the stability of the employee – stability in the sense of minimizing employee turnover is a goal.
- Classical organisation theory is in its essential character centralized.
- The integration of the system is achieved through the authority and control of the central mechanism.

Two Streams of Classical Theory

Some of the classical management scientists emphasised on the technological aspects of the organisation whereas others emphasised the structural aspects of the organisation. Classical theory, thus, presents two separate streams viz., (i) scientific management stream and (ii) administrative management stream.

Scientific Management

Scientific management provides the real basis for the classical theory of organisation. This also provides solutions to the engineering and organisational problems. The important contributions to scientific management include those of Robert Owen, Charles Babbage, Henry Robinson Towne, Frederick Winslow Taylor, Henry L.Gnatt, Frank B.Gilbreth and Lillian M.Gilbreth, Mary Parker Follett and Chester I.Barnard.

Administrative Management Theory

Managerial and organisational problems were not analysed by the scientific management group. This group concentrated on the operational problems at the work place. The administrative management scientists have concentrated on the managerial and organisational problems. The administrative theorists include Weber, Henry Fayol, Gulick, Sheldorn, Urwick and Mooney and Reiley.

Assumptions of Classical Theory

The classical theory of organisation is designed based on the following assumptions:

- The relationship between employee and employer, superior and subordinate and manager and workers is completely formal.
- *Worker is an Economic Man:* The worker is treated basically as a wage earner and can be motivated by money alone. He can be managed by paying economic rewards. Thus, the worker was viewed as an economic man.
- *Managers are Rational:* It was assumed that the traits of a manager include: rational approach, being kind-hearted, intelligent and honest. They possess required qualifications and they deal with the workers firmly.
- *Organisation is a Machine and Employees are its components:* The classical theory treats the organisation as a machine. The relationship among various parts is just sequential and mechanical. Workers are treated as nuts, bolts and components in the machine.
- *Emphasis on Internal Environment:* Classical theory gives emphasis on internal factors neglecting the external environmental factors.
- *Productivity centred:* Classical theory is centred around productivity. Workers perceive that their interests are best protected, if they increase the level of productivity.
- *Emphasis on Control:* This theory emphasises on the detection of the deviations after they occur and correct or control them.
- *Man is Relatively Homogeneous:* This theory assumes that man is relatively homogeneous. Therefore, it is viewed while designing the jobs that man cannot be modified.
- *Centralisation:* It is assumed that, the organization system can be integrated through the centralization of authority.

Pillars of the Theory

According to Scott and Mitchell, the classical organisation theory is based on the four pillars, *viz.* division of labour, vertical and horizontal organisations, structure and the span of control.

Division of Labour

Division of Labour: Dividing the job into sub-tasks and allotting each sub-task to individual worker.

Division of labour refers to dividing the work or job into tasks and sub-tasks and allotting each sub-task to an individual worker. Consequently, each individual worker has the narrow task and does the same work again and again. By doing the same work frequently, the worker specialises himself in doing that work. The specialisation leads to improvement in worker efficiency, quality of the work and productivity. Improvement in quality and productivity contributes to the achievement of organisation's goals, objectives and mission.

Vertical and Horizontal Organisations

The vertical organisation is also called the *scalar process*. In the scalar process, the number of supervisors is more as the management believes the assumptions of Theory X. Consequently, the number of hierarchies increase.

There would be less number of supervisors in the horizontal organisation, which is built on the basis of the assumptions of Theory Y. Management trusts the subordinates and their potentials. In fact, workers work in a free environment, use their potentialities and perform to the extent of their efficiency. Therefore, a large number of subordinates report to the single superior.

Structure

Structure implies relationship among functions, individuals, material and machine in order to perform the operations and to accomplish the goals. These relationships are divided into line relations and staff relations.

The Span of Management

Large-scale organisations need to employ the people in thousands and millions.

Span of control/management refers to the number of subordinates a supervisor can supervise/ manage/control the subordinates effectively. If the span is narrow, there would be a large number of supervisors, and a large number of hierarchies. This, in turn results in a tall organisation. If the spans are wider, there would be less number of hierarchies and it would result in a flat structure. The tall structure slows down the communication process whereas the flat structure expedites the communication process.

Criticisms of the Classical Theory

Classical organisation theory combines both psychological theory and administrative management theory. This theory was attacked from many quarters as it suffers from various limitations. Criticisms against this theory include:

Unrealistic assumptions: As stated earlier, the classical theory is based on certain assumptions. The assumptions which are unrealistic are discussed hereunder:

- **Close system:** As discussed earlier, the classical theory emphasises the internal environment. It completely ignores the impact of external environment.

This theory fails to identify external environment. Therefore, this theory is incomplete and non-practicable.

- **Static view of organisation:** Classical theorists viewed the organisation as a static one. But we have a lot of experience that the organisations are dynamic.

- **Human behaviour:** The classical theory assumed that human behaviour is rational. But human behaviour is complex, irrational and difficult to predict. Thus, the assumption regarding human behaviour is unrealistic.
- **Hierarchical structure:** Classical theory favours narrow spans of management, too many supervisors and too many hierarchies. Consequently, the organisation structure is based on authority-responsibility-accountability relationship. This, in turn, results in superior-subordinate class conflict. Finally, the outcome of hierarchical structure is a tall structure.

Excessive Reliance on the Strength of Pillars

The classical theorists excessively depend on the key pillars, *viz.*, division of labour, scalar functional process, structure and span of control. The neoclassical theorists attacked these key pillars.

But the neoclassical theorists criticise that bureaucracy kills individual initiativeness, creativity, innovativeness and voluntary contributions of the employees. In fact, bureaucracy results in red-tapism. Observation of rules, regulations, procedures and formalities become the main activities of the management rather than achieving the company objectives or goals.

(C) NEOCLASSICAL THEORY

Human behaviour is influenced by various factors.

The classical organisation theory emphasised mainly on physiological and mechanical variables in constructing the organisation structure. The objectives of the classical organisation theory are to enhance employee efficiency and productivity. But the organisations designed based on this theory could not enhance employee efficiency and productivity. In other words, organisation structures based on this theory failed to achieve their objectives effectively.

The behavioural scientists enquired into the reasons for the failure of this theory in producing results. They investigated the human behaviour at work. They found that human behaviour is influenced by various factors other than physiological factors. These research studies generated the new dimensions of human behaviour in the organisations.

These research studies are referred to as behavioural theory of organisation, human view of organisation and human relations approach in the organisation. These approaches are also termed as *neoclassical* theory of organisation.

The neoclassical approach to organisational design was developed by Mary Parker Follett, Chester I Barnard and Elton Mayo and his associates.

The neoclassical theory was developed consequently upon the criticisms and reactions against the classical theory. The neoclassical approach emphasised (i) social terms in addition to economic and technical factors and (ii) the social process of group behaviour can be understood in terms of the clinical method like the diagnosis of human organs by a medical doctor. This theory is developed to overcome the deficiencies of the classical theory.

Though this theory also supports the pillars of classical theory, it modified these factors by incorporating the informal groups, informal organisation and independent work of the employees. This theory combines both formal and informal organisations.

Facts discovered by hawthorne experiments: As mentioned earlier, Mayo and his associates discovered the following facts through their experiments:

- Social system defines individual roles and establishes norms. These roles and norms of the social system differ from those of the formal organisation.

- Workers follow the social norms rather than achieving the goals.
- Non-economic rewards and social sanctions, in addition to economic rewards play a vital role in guiding the human behaviour at work.
- Perception of the workers of the situations rather than of the management matters much.
- Workers fear retaliation for violating the group norms and therefore, they are motivated by group norms much rather than economic incentives.
- Individual worker's attitudes and performance are shaped and determined by the groups. Workers mostly react as members of groups but not as individuals. Workers prefer to change their behaviour based on the changes in group behaviour.
- Informal leader sets and enforces group norms. Official leader proves himself ineffective unless he conforms to the group norms.
- Workers have need for communication, participation and involvement in decision-making and democratic leadership. Lower level workers are informed of the decisions and the process which affects them.
- High level job satisfaction leads to high level organisational effectiveness.
- Managers should have social skills in addition to technical skills and
- Motivating the workers is possible by fulfilling not only lower level needs but also by higher level needs.

Appraisal of the Neo-Classical Theory

This theory is influenced by micro human behaviour

Neo-classical theorists interwove applied behavioural science in the organisation design and made the latter as a full-fledged one. Thus, this theory emphasized on the micro-level human behaviour. This theory developed certain important concepts like group norms, informal group, informal group leader, social and psychological rewards. This theory seems to be an improvement over the classical theory. The major improvements are recognising informal group/organisation and social and psychological factors.

Despite the positive contributions of this theory, it was criticised on certain grounds.

Criticism against Neo-classical Theory

- **Invalid assumptions:** Neo-classical theory is based on certain assumptions. One of these assumptions include availability of solutions for every problem. This assumption is not valid. Thus, neo-classical theory is also based on invalid assumptions.
- **Conflict of interests based on structure:** There are certain group conflicts which are neither social nor psychological. But they are structural. Neo-classical theory is criticised for its excessive emphasis on social and psychological factors.
- **Limited application:** Principles developed by the neo-classical theorists are not universally applicable. They have only limited application. In fact, there is no single structure applicable to all companies. Even the same structure is not applicable to the same company in all situations.
- **Ignorance of environmental factors:** It is criticised that this theory like classical theory ignored the external environmental factors in constructing this theory.
- **Absence of total approach:** The neo-classical theory does not have a unified and total approach. This theory is only a modification and improvement over the classical theory. Thus, it is criticised that neo-classical theory is not at all a theory by itself.

- **Excessive emphasis on human aspect:** Neo-classical theory gives more emphasis on the human behaviour in designing organisations. It is criticised that this theory ignores structural, mechanical and formal aspects.

Thus, the critics of the neo-classical theory feel that it is not a new theory, but only a modification or improvement over the classical theory.

(D) MODERN ORGANISATION THEORY

Modern organisation theory has its origin from the General Systems Theory. The chief architect of this theory was Bertalanffy. This theory was developed during the early 1960s. This theory suggests two approaches, viz., *systems approach* and *contingency approach*. This theory is developed consequent upon the limitations of and criticisms against the classical and neo-classical theories.

Modern organisation theory combines social and psychological issues with the classical model. As stated earlier, this theory is developed in the pattern of General Systems Theory.

Systems Approach

A system is essentially a set or assemblage of things that are interconnected or interrelated or interdependent so as to form a complex whole. Kast Rosenzweig defines the term system as "an organized unitary whole composed of two or more independent parts, components or subsystems and delicated by identifiable boundaries from its environmental suprasystem."

System is a set of things that are interconnected

Systems can also be divided not only on the basis of main operative functions of a company but also on the basis of management functions like organisation systems, planning systems, directing system, controlling system, marketing functions, human resources management functions, financial management functions, operation management functions and information management functions.

Features of a System

For the analysis of definitions of a system and its focus, we can derive the following features of a system:

- **Independent parts:** System is a composition of several parts. All the parts are independent, interdependent and interrelated to each other. Each part is dynamic, affects all other parts and is being affected by other parts.
- **A system is composed of several sub-systems:** Each system is composed of several sub-systems. Each sub-system is, in turn, composed of sub-sub-systems.
- **Every system has its own norms:** Though there are several systems and each system has several sub-systems, each system/sub-system can be distinguished from the others. They can be distinguished from others in terms of objectives, processes, roles, structures and norms of operations.
- **Systems are processors:** Systems receive inputs from the external environment and other sub-systems of the internal environment. The system processes the inputs and converts them into output and supplies the output to other sub-systems of the internal environment and to the systems in the external environment.
- **System influences and is influenced:** As indicated earlier, the systems are open. System influences other systems and sub-systems. In addition, all systems are influenced by other systems and sub-systems. For example, the sub-system of customer taste influences the product design and is influenced by the sub-system of technology upgradation sub-system.

- **System arranges the parts in a related manner:** System does not simply mean a group of parts. It is a sequence of related parts. The sequence is arranged based on the purpose.
- **Systems have boundaries:** Every system has boundaries. Physical systems have fixed boundaries whereas social and psychological systems have flexible boundaries. Organisational system is composed of physical, social and psychological systems. Therefore, part of the organisational system's boundaries are fixed while the others are variable.
- **Systems are open and close:** Systems are classified into two categories, *viz.* open system and closed system. The open systems influence and are being influenced by other systems while closed systems do not influence other systems. The differences between the open system and closed system are as follows:

Open Systems	Closed Systems
• Interact with environment and other systems freely.	• Do not interact with the environment and other systems.
• Depend on the environment.	• Self-contained and self-maintained.
• Flexible and dynamic.	• Rigid and static.
• Humanistic in character.	• Mechanical in character.
• Like negative entropy.	• Like close a loop.
• Have feedback and feedforward mechanisms.	• Do not have feedback and feedforward mechanisms.

The linking process takes place by building up relations, communication process, net-working process, authority, responsibility and accountability relationship, power, social relationship, team-building, decision-making process and goal formulation and achievement process.

Classification of Sub-Systems

Important sub-systems are: technical, social and power

As mentioned earlier, these are several sub-systems of an organisation. All these sub-systems can be grouped into three categories *viz.* technical sub-system, social sub-system and the power sub-system.

- **Technical sub-system:** Technology means application of knowledge. This sub-system is mostly concerned with formal organisational structure and deals with application of knowledge in the process of converting the inputs into output.

This sub-system deals with the designing of factory layout, selection of the appropriate technology, machinery, process, policies, procedures, rules and regulations, hierarchical levels, authority and responsibility, etc. In addition, it decides upon the job design, jobs involved in the process, selection of employees, assigning the duties, working hours, decision points, decision-making authority and responsibility, communication patterns, coordination and leadership styles.

Technical sub-system receives the inputs from the external environment, and internal environment transforms them into products and services and provides the products or services to the external environment. This process conditions the employee activities and behaviour through rules, norms, policies and procedures. The employee behaviour in the existing social system is modified by the technical sub-system.

- **Social sub-system:** Organisational system cannot exist and work only with the technical system. It is basically designed and run by the people. Man is basically a social animal. As such, he prefers to live in and work alongwith the group. Thus, the social system formed by the employees at the work place constitutes a major sub-system in the organisation.

- **Power sub-system:** Power is referred to as the ability to influence other people and events. According to White and Bednar, power "is the ability to influence people or things, usually obtained through the control of important resources." Power plays a dynamic role in the organisational system. The sources of power include expertise, knowledge, ability, charisma, coercive power and reward power.

The organisational power system influences the individual and group relations, their performance patterns and organisational performance and behaviour. In addition, the power system interacts with and interferes in the activities of technical and social systems.

The interactive and coordinated influence of technical, social and power sub-systems forms the organisational system. Rocco Carzo and John N.Yanozas have presented the characteristics of technical, social and power sub-systems as shown in Exhibit 22.1.

Exhibit 22.1 Characteristics of Technical, Social and Power Sub-systems of Formal Organisation

Characteristics	*Technical subsystem*	*Social subsystem*	*Power subsystem*
1 Origin	Deliberate employment and arrangement of men and capital to performtasks required by formal objectives.	Arises spontanecusly from social interactions and shared vlaues of men placed in contact with each other.	Arises as people use various sources of power to acquire things that are judged valuable by others and successfully implement decision.
2 Process	Decision communication and action.	Interaction, sentiments and activity.	Politics, decision implementation and maintenance of order.
3. Structure	Arrangement of jobs in relation to each other. Process and authority relations.	Differentiation based on expression of sentiment of members of each other. Friendship relations.	Differentiation based on the number of behaviour areas controlled.
4. Status	Man holds status because of his ability to meet the job requirments. Status is same as job in importance in the technical structure.	Man holds status because of sentiments of others in the system. For example, the leader is liked most in the group.	Man holds status because of degree of success attained in implementing his decisions.
5. Roles	Man plays role according to job requirements.	Man plays role according to sentiments, beliefs. attitudes and social moves.	Man plays opportunistic role.
6. Source of Authority and Power authority.	Directly related to the job and is delegated from those who have higher on sentiments.	Informal authority is derived from those who are its subjects. Based personal characteristics	Official Position, location, job importance, expertise, interest and tenure, and coalitions.
7. Norms	Job description, written policies, procedures and rules.	Values and accepted norms of behaviour. Unwritten tacit agreements.	Expediency. That behaviour which sustains power. People who are objects of power follow orders of power holder to obtain desired values.

(**Source:** Carzo and Yanouzas, Op.Cit., p. 240 [Quoted in L.M.Prasad, Op.Cit., pp. 376-377]).

Contingency/Situational Approach

The conclusions of various models of organisation theory indicates that have indicated that there is no one best way of structuring organisations. This is mostly due to the fact that the one appears to be appropriate in one situation may not be the same in other situation. For example, neither centralisation nor decentralisation is apt for all situations and companies. Organistic structures are more appropriate for growing companies while bureaucratic structures are suitable fcr shrinking companies. Tight control is appropriate in emergency, declining and routine situations whereas democratic and participative

Contingency approach considers the ever-changing environmental factors

leadership styles are suitable for innovative and fast growing situations. This is due to the influence of a number of internal and external variables on organisation structure.

It is criticised that systems theory does not take into consideration the environmental variables and their requirement for a specific organisational relationships. The conclusions of a systems approach may not be appropriate for the different situations of a specific business like initial stage, growing stage, maturity stage, declining stage, crisis situations, normal situations, competitive situations, etc., contingency approach bridges this gap by linking the situational requirements with the relationships.

According to Fremont E.Kast and James E.Rosenzweig, "the contingency view seeks to understand the interrelationships within and among systems as well as between the organisations and environment and to define patterns of relationships and configurations of variables. It emphasises the multivariate nature of organisations and attempts to understand how organisations operate under varying conditions and in specific circumstances. Contingency views are ultimately directed to suggesting organisational designs and managerial actions most appropriate for specific situations."

Systems Approach vs Contingency Approach

Systems approach deals with macro-micro-macro paradigm for the study of organisational design while contingency approach deals with more specific situations and interrelationship patterns among subsystems.

The following exhibit 22.2 presents the views of systems approach and contingency approach.

Exhibit 22.2 Systems Approach vs Contingency Approach

Systems Approach	Contingency Approach
1. Provides macro-micro-macro Padadigm for the study of organisations	1. Provides patterns of interrelationship among sub systems of an organisation.
2. Involves relatively a high degree of generalisation	2. Concentrates on more specific situations and characteristics of organisations.
3. Provides a broad model for understanding all organisations.	3. Treats each organisation as different from other organisation and each situation in an organisation is different from other situations in the same organisation.
4. Does not see the uniqueness of each environmental factor and its specific impact on each organisation.	4. Considers the uniqueness of each environmental factor and its its specific impact on each organisational situation.
5. Does not consider environment for designing organisations, leadership styles and managerial actions.	5. Sees environment as a basis for designing organisations, leadershipstyles and managerial actions.
6. Considers only universal organisational principles.	6. Balances universal organisational and management principles unique organisational situations and their requirements.
7. Does not recognise the specific problems of modern organisations.	7. Recognises the problems involved in running modern and global business and provides solutions to solve them.
8. It is easy to understand systems approach.	8. It is difficult to understand the contingencies and balance their requirements with the organisational systems. Managers should have conceptual skills to balance these two.

Organisational Learning Approach

Organisations should be proactive and learn before changes take place in the environment and consequently change in the environmental demands. Chris Argyris and his colleagues drew the attention to the double-loop learning or second order learning. Double-loop learning implies learning to learn, innovation, creativity, proactive to change rather than reactive to change, generative learning rather than adaptive learning. Adaptive learning organisations change within their existing cultural values while generative learning organisations change and learn from the change in the new cultural value environment.

Change makes the organisation to learn more and enhances learning abilities though feed forward, experimentation and feedback. The features of learning organisations are:

- Sharing information
- Innovation/creation
- Empowerment
- Encouraging new ideas
- Learning from its own mistakes
- Learning through networking issues, events, data and people
- Personal efficacy of the people
- Long-term interpersonal relations through sensitivity and a sense of empathy
- Mutual problem solving, confidence and trust.

Thus, the double-loop and generative learning view has been widely accepted as an appropriate organisational theory.

Organisations are congregation of individual employees and other humnan resources. Organisations learn and acquire the knowledge as the individual employees do. In fact, organisations learn through the learning of their employees. Organisational learning output is the synergitical outcome of individual learning of all employees working in an organisation. Organisational learning is as old as organisations. But it is signified after the globalisation.

Need for Organisational Learning

Organisational learning is highly essential due to the following reasons:

- Organisational activities like manufacturing, marketing, etc., have become more intellectual;
- Recognition and acceptance of knowledge as competitive advantage;
- Rapid change and complex nature of business environment especially after globalisation;
- Cultural unification and globalisation of culture;
- Increased customer awareness regarding his/her rights;
- Increased competitiveness of the business due to liberalisation and globalisation;
- Change in employees' attitude towards change and adaptable organisations; and
- Increased pace of innovations, creations and outcome of research and development.

Organisations learn by creating conducive environment for knowledge acquisition, knowledge sharing, knowledge creation and development through discussions, interviews, brain storming, etc. Learning organisations are open systems. They allow the multi-way flow of information and knowledge. They encourage the employees to apply the knowledge and improve the products, existing systems, serve the customer better and achieve the organisational goals.

Evaluation of Modern Organisational Theory

The analysis of systems approach and contingency or situational approach of modern organisational theory shows that they have made significant contribution to the organisational design and structure. The evaluation concludes that:

- This theory has empirical and analytical base.
- Treats the organisation as a single and total system.
- Seeks interrelationships and interconnections among various sub-systems of the organisation.

- It clarifies or answers the questions relating to interconnections and interdependence.
- This theory presents a holistic view. In other words, it presents the whole rather than the sum of the points.
- It presents the interdependency of each sub-system on the other sub-systems.
- It presents a realistic view of the organisation.
- This theory suggests open and humanistic or organic organisational system, and
- This theory analyses the micro sub-system of a macro system for the effective functioning of the latter. Thus, it follows the macro-micro-macro approach.

Criticism: Despite these contributions of the modern theory, it is criticised for its shortcomings. These criticisms include:

- It is criticised that this theory is not lived up to its expectations it made at the initial stages;
- This theory failed in providing adequate and comprehensive explanation of an organisation;
- The initial enthusiasm could not live for long;
- Attempts made in this direction were just isolated but not integrative; and
- This theory is still in the formative stage and not developed completely yet.

KEY TERMS

- Organisation
- Scientific Management
- Mechanistic Structure
- Division of Labour
- Open System
- Contingency Approach
- Classical Organisation Theory
- Neo-classical Organisation Theory
- Modern Organisation Theory
- Situational Approach
- Systems Approach
- Span of Management
- Organisational Learning
- Organic Structure
- Close System
- Behavioural Approach

QUESTIONS

1. What is organisation? How do you structure it?
2. Discuss the classical theory of organisation.
3. Examine the assumptions of and criticism against the classical theory of organisation.
4. Comment on the neo-classical theory of organisation. Explain the assumptions of and criticisms against neo-classical theory.
5. Give a detailed account on the modern theory of organisation.
6. Evaluate the modern theory of organisation.
7. Discuss the contingency or situational theory of organisation.
8. Explain the organisational learning theory of organisation.

REFERENCES

1. Stephen P. Robbins, "*Organsiation Theory,*" Prentice Hall of India, New Delhi, 1998, p. 4.
2. Richard S. Rudner, "*Philosophy of Social Science,*" Prentice Hall, Englewood Cliffs, 1966, p. 30.
3. Henry L. Tosi, "*Theories of Organisations,*" St.Clair Press, Chicago, 1975, p. 7.
4. Mason Haire, "*Philosophy of Organisation,*" in Donald M.Browman and Francis M. Fillerup (Eds), "*Management, Organisation and Planning,*" McGraw-Hill, New York, 1974, pp. 4-5.
5. Harold Koontz, Cyril O'Donnel and Heirz Weihrich, *op.cit.*, p. 9.

CHAPTER 23

ORGANISATIONAL DESIGN AND STRUCTURE

Chapter Outline

(A) Introduction
(B) Organisational Design
(C) Nature of Organising
(D) Structuring Organisation
(E) Approaches to Organisational Structure
(F) Line and Staff Organisation
(G) Responsive Organisations
(H) Global Organising
— Key Terms
— Questions
— References

Learning Objectives

After studying this Chapter, you should be able to:

- ✓ Know the meaning of organisational design and method of designing an organisation;
- ✓ Understand why the organisations are structured and the steps in organisational structure;
- ✓ Differentiate the flat structure from that of all other structures;
- ✓ Discuss the functional, geographical and product organisation structures and their relative advantages and disadvantages;
- ✓ Analyse the relative merits and demerits of divisionalised structures and strategic business unit structures;
- ✓ Explain the specific situations when the matrix organisational structures are used;
- ✓ Appreciate the recent approaches to organisational structures, viz., team structures and virtual structures; and
- ✓ Analyse line and staff organisational structures.

(A) INTRODUCTION

Public sector companies attracted the tabulated human resources of the country during 1950s to 1980s by paying high salaries and by providing better benefits companies did not allow their employees to use their talents and skills to the full as they were organised based on the bureaucratic principles.

Private sector companies, on the other hand, provide the freedom to the employees as they are organisations based on the humanistic structure. These companies performed better than the public sector companies during 1950s and 1980s even though they had less talented workers talented to public sector due to their organisational structure.

Thus, the organisational structures make or mar performance. As such, it is interesting for us to study how the organisations are designed and structured for efficient performance of the business firms

(B) ORGANISATIONAL DESIGN

Organisations are economic and social entities in which a number of persons perform multifarious tasks in order to attain common goals. Organisations are effective instruments in that they help individuals accomplish personal objectives that they (persons) cannot achieve alone. According to Argyris, organisations are usually formed to satisfy objectives, "that can best be met collectively."[1]

Organisation is only a means to an end. It takes certain inputs from the environment and converts them into specified outputs desired by the society. Organisational design deals with structural aspects of organisations. It aims at analysing roles and relationships so that collective effort can be explicitly organised to achieve specific ends. The design process leads to the development of an organisation structure consisting of units and positions. There are relationships involving exercise of authority and exchange of information between these units and positions. Thus, organisational design may lead to the definition and description of a more or less formal structure.

Organisational design is "the process of systematic and logical grouping of activities, delegation of authority and responsibility and establishing working relationships that will enable both the company and employee to realise their mutual objectives."[2]

Organisational Structure

Organisational structure is an established pattern of relationships

Organisational structure is an established pattern of relationships among the component parts of an organisation. Structure is made up of three component parts, *viz.,* complexity, formalisation and centralisation.

Complexity refers to horizontal differentiation, vertical differentiation and locational differentiation. *Horizontal differentiation* is horizontal separation between units based on occupations and specialisations. *Vertical differentiation* is the potential for communication distortion. Locational differentiation refers to the degree to which the location of an organisation's offices, plants and personnel are geographically spread.

Formalisation refers to the degree to which the jobs within the organisation are standardised. High standardisation of jobs results in less freedom and discretion. *Centralisation* refers to the degree to which decision-making is concentrated at a single point in an organisation.

Initially, firms adopt a structure. As it grows, in size, spread into new businesses, new geographical regions, it will change the structure and adopt new type of organisational structures. Many companies change their structures as and when there is a change in their strategies and/or size.[3]

Efficient strategy implementation largely depends on appropriate organisational structure Structuring an appropriate organisation should be a top priority for the management.

Organisational structures based on high complexity, more formality and centralisation result in tall structures. While organisational structures based on low complexity, less formality and decentralisation result in flat structures. Now, we shall study tall structures and flat structures.

Steps in Designing Organisational Structure

The first step in organisational design is analysis of present and future circumstances and environmental factors. The next stage deals with detail planning and implementation. Organisation analysis is the basis for organisational design and is the process of defining aims, objectives, activities and structure of an enterprise. Organisation analysis includes an analysis of the following aspects:

(i) **External environment** - Social, Technical, Economic, Polictical, International and natural.

(ii) **Overall aims and purpose of the enterprise** - Survival, growth, profit maximisation, wealth maximisation, etc.

(iii) **Objectives** - specific aims or targets to be achieved.

(iv) **Activities** - assessment of work being done and what needs to be done if the company is to achieve its objectives.

(v) **Decisions** to be taken across horizontal and vertical dimensions.

(vi) **Relationships** - from the viewpoint of communications.

(vii) **Organisational structure** - includes grouping of activities, span of management, management levels, etc.

(viii) **Job structure** - job design, job analysis, job description, job specification, etc.

(ix) **Organisation climate** - working atmosphere of the enterprise. It includes team- work and co-confidence and trust.

(x) **Management style** - includes laissez-faire, benevolent-autocratic, participative and democratic.

(xi) **Human resource** - includes availability of human resources marked by skill, knowledge, commitment, aptitude, etc.

(C) NATURE OF ORGANISING

Organising is establishing relationships and networking among various parts. It is formalised intentional structure or networking among roles and positions. However, the relationships among parts can be formal and/or informal. So organisations can be formal and informal.

Formal organisation refers to intentional structure of roles in an enterprise. In fact formal structures should also be flexible in order to enable employees to contribute their resources to achieve organisational goals.

Informal organisation is a joint personal activity without a conscious joint purpose

Informal organisation, according to Chester Barnard refers to any joint personal activity without conscious joint purpose, eventhough contributing to joint results.[4] Keith Davis described informal organisation as "a network of personal and social relations not established or required by the formal organisation but arising spontaneously as people associate with one another."[5] Thus, informal relationships not necessarily appear in the organisation chart: for example, the system administrator, human resource manager and accounting assistant spontaneously establish relationship based on their personal interest in naturopathy. This relationship would help them in their formal jobs.

Organisations are designed and structured based on certain principles, viz.

- ***Principle of objective:*** The organisation is established with a specific mission, purpose and objective like constructing buildings for profit.
- ***Principle of specialisation and division of labour:*** The organisation activities are divided into departments, units and tasks and each employee may be assigned with separate task. Employees can specialise in that activity.
- ***Principle of coordination:*** All the activities, units and departments should be coordinated with the organisation's objective, purpose and mission.
- ***Principle of co-equal authority and responsibility:*** Authority and responsibility are equally delegated. Otherwise subordinate may misuse authority, if more authority than required to discharge the responsibility is delegated. Alternatively, the subordinate can't discharge responsibility, if responsibility is more than the authority.
- ***Span of control:*** Span of control is number of subordinates, that can be managed efficiently by a superior. The span should be optimum depending upon organisational requirements.
- ***Principle of continuity:*** Organisations should continue their operations. Therefore they should be flexible and responsive to the environmental changes.
- ***Principle of teamwork:*** The purpose of the organisation is to achieve its mission. Achieving mission, strategy and goal efficiently is possible through a collaborative work of a team of people, even though the organisation is departmentalised.
- ***Principle of efficiency:*** Organisations should be designed in such a way that they should perform their activities with least cost and achieve highest return. Therefore, organisations should perform most efficiently.

Organisation Levels

There are three major levels in an organisation, viz., top level, middle level and lower level. However, the recent trends state that organisations need not have three levels. The flat organisations have only two levels while the virtual organisations are not built around levels. Team structures are flexible structures and as such do not follow the levels strictly.

(D) STRUCTURING ORGANISATION

Vertical/Tall Organisations

Verticle organisation possess many levels

Vertical/Tall organisations refer to increase in the length of the organisation's hierarchical chain of command. The hierarchical chain of command represents the company's authority — accountability relationship between superiors and subordinates. Authority and responsibility flows from the top to the bottom through all the levels of hierarchy. Accountability flows from the lowest level to the highest level. Fig. 23.1 shows the vertical/tall organisation. Employees at each level should report to their superior, who in turn should report to his boss. Thus, the activities are reported to the top. Authority is more centralised in a tall organisation.

Managerial implication: The advantages of tall organisation include: effective analysis of factors and efficient decision-making are possible as a number of managers at different levels supervise and

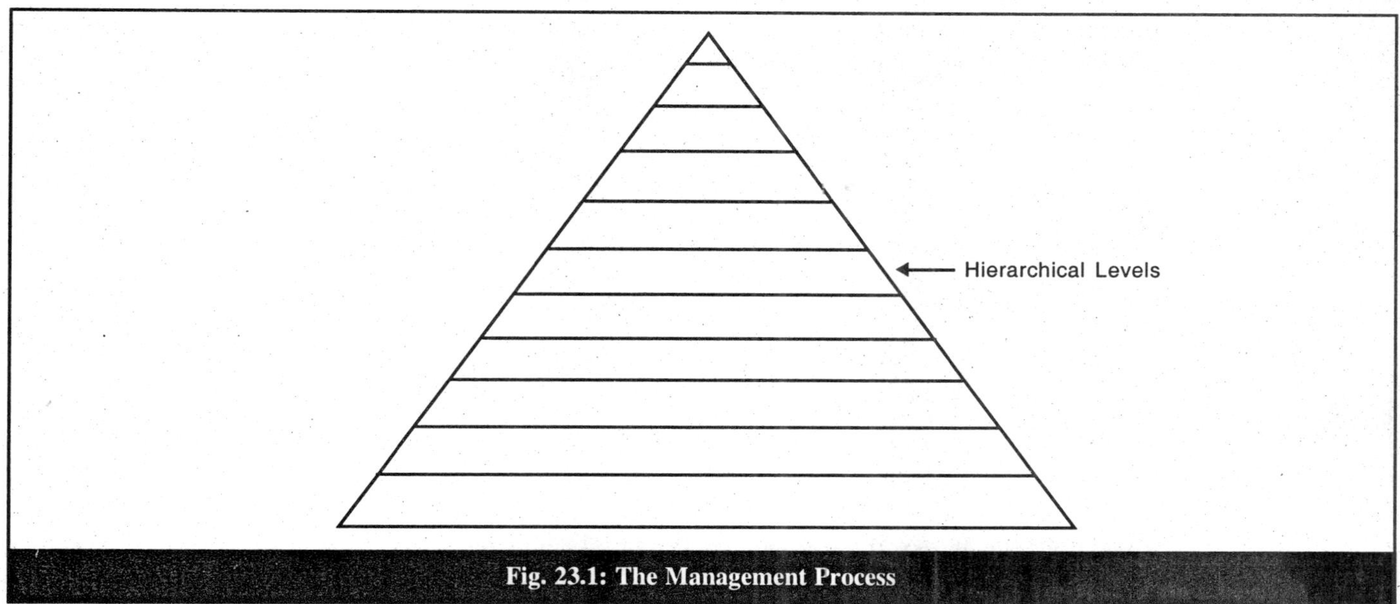

Fig. 23.1: The Management Process

check the activities. The organisation can formulate effective policies, programmes and control mechanisms. Further, it provides promotional avenues to the employees.

Tall and centralised organisations allow for better communication of company's mission, goals and objectives to all employees. It also enhances coordination of functional areas to ensure that each area will work closely with the other functions. Since, all employees are centrally directed, coordination becomes possible.

Tall organisational structure is appropriate for the firms having bleak growth opportunities, (like problem children/dogs category of Boston Consultancy Group Matrix). Further, firms with cost minimisation strategy and firms in maturity stage can adopt tall organisations. Thus, these types of structures are well suited for environments that are relatively stable and predictable.[6]

But, too many hierarchical levels result in bureaucratic characteristics rather than commercial characteristics to the business firm. Tight operational controls delay the decision-making process. This process makes the organisation incompetent.

Horizontal/Flat Organisations

Horizontal/flat organisations refer to an increase in breadth of an organisation's structure. Fig. 23.2 presents the model of horizontal/flat organisation. The number of levels in the organisational hierarchy are a few. The span of control is relatively large.

Horizontal organisations have few levels

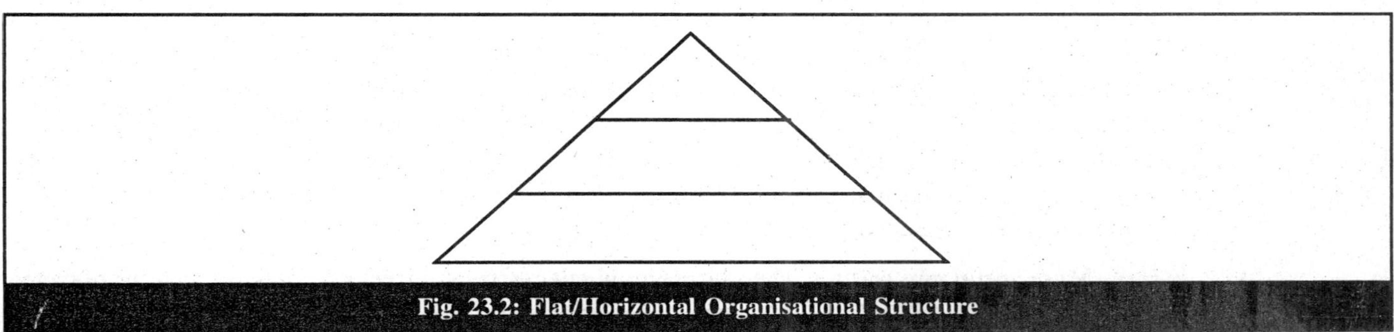

Fig. 23.2: Flat/Horizontal Organisational Structure

The increasing bio-professionalisation and multi-professionalisation and wide acceptance for empowerment allow even the large business firms to reduce the number of hierarchical levels of their organisations. Consequently, large sized firms also started adopting horizontal/flat organisation by delayering. In fact, this structure is well suited for the small size business firms.

Authority is more decentralised in relatively flat structures. Managers with broad span of control must grant more authority to his subordinates. Decisions are more likely to be made by the employees who are at the helm of affairs and more familiar with the situations and ground realities. Organisational activities are mostly performed informally. Professional managers are treated as real professionalists.

Managerial implications: The major advantage of flat structure is quick decision-making. Thus, it enables the management to take decisions in right time. Other advantages of this structure include: low administrative costs, freedom and autonomy to the managers to operate, decision-making by the managers who are at helm of affairs and empowerment of managers. These benefits motivate the managers to accept responsibility and commit themselves towards organisational objectives. Further, these characteristics enable the organisation to be duly sensitive to the environmental demands. The employees also become innovative and creative.

The horizontal/flat organisational structure are appropriate for the organisations with horizontal and vertical growth strategies, stars and cash cows (BCG Matrix). Thus, these structures are useful for competitive and dynamic business firms.

However, this structure suffers from certain disadvantages like, absences of control, effective co-ordination and proper reporting to the superiors. In addition, this structure is not suitable to the companies which are stable or which are in diclining stage in the life cycle.

(E) APPROACHES TO ORGANISATION STRUCTURE

There are nine approaches towards the structure of an organisation. They are: *(i)* Entrepreneurial structure, *(ii)* Functional organisation structure, *(iii)* Product organisation structure, *(iv)* Geographical organisation structure, *(v)* Decentralised business divisions, *(vi)* Strategic business units, *(vii)* Matrix organisational structure. *(viii)* Team structure, and *(ix)* Virtual structure.

1. Entrepreneurial Structure

This structure provides for creativity

Generally, the small businesses when they are started consist of an owner-manager – alone structure or also with a few employees. (Fig. 23.3) These types of organisations do not require an organisational chart and formal assignment of responsibilities. Organisation structure is fluid with each employee often knowing how to perform more than one task and with owner-manager involved in all aspects/areas of business.

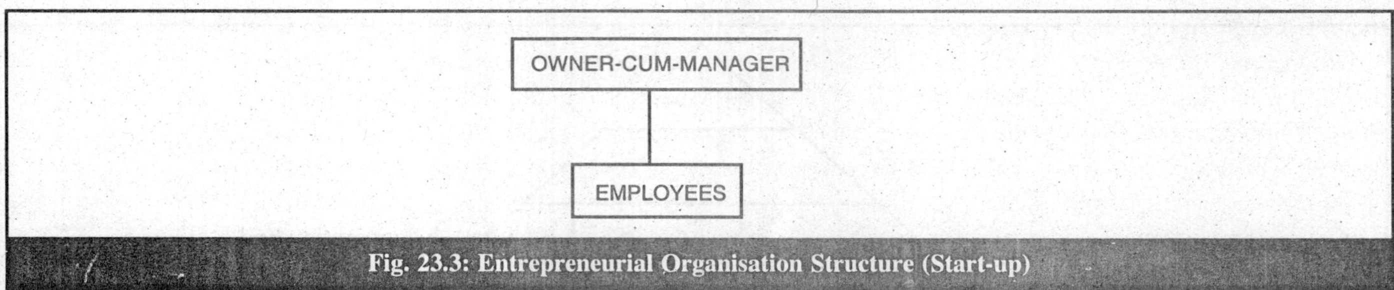

Fig. 23.3: Entrepreneurial Organisation Structure (Start-up)

The small firms, if, they are successful during the starting phase, it would be due to the increased demand for products or services. The entrepreneurs develop the business and increase the size of the firm to meet the increased demand. The business begins to evolve from fluidity to a status of more permanent division of labour due to the growth. The owner-manager, who was performing all functions in the initial stage now finds that he has to perform more managerial activities than operational activities. The growth demands the owner to employ new workers resulting into assigning specialised functions to these employees.

The business growth results in expansion of organisational structure both vertically and horizontally. The entrepreneurial organisational structure with expansion is depicted in Fig. 23.4. As can be seen from this figure, the operative functions of manufacturing are assigned to manufacturing manager and the operative functions of marketing are assigned to the marketing manager. These two managers perform the activities with the help of employees. The owner-manager performs managerial and strategic functions.

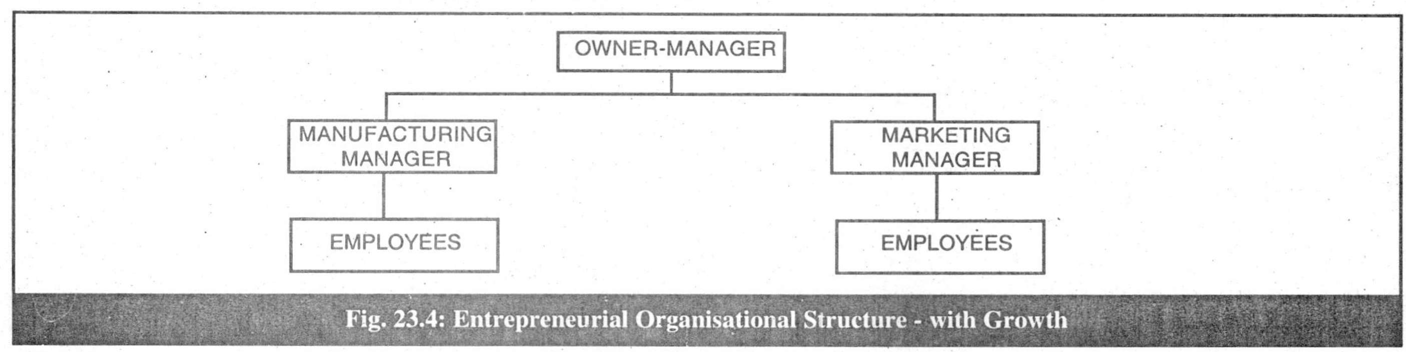

Fig. 23.4: Entrepreneurial Organisational Structure - with Growth

Managerial implication: The entrepreneurial structure is simple and it offers some advantages like: timely decision-making, sensitive to environmental demands and operational flexibility.

But, this structure results in excessive depending on owner-manager who normally is not a professional manager. This structure cannot respond to the increasing demand beyond a certain point. Thus, this structure is mostly suitable to the strategy catering to the needs of a local market by being small.

2. Functional Organisation Structure

This structure is based on functions of business firm

Functional organisation structure is the most widely used structure. Each functional department consists of those jobs in which employees perform similar jobs at different levels. The commonly used functions are: marketing, finance and accounting, human resources, manufacturing, research and development and engineering. Fig. 23.5 illustrates a typical functional structure.

Advantages: *(i)* A functional structure would be effective in single business firms where key activities revolve around well defined skills and areas of specialisation. *(ii)* Indepth specialisation and focused concentration on performing functional tasks can enhance operating efficiency and the development of core competencies.[7] *(iii)* This type of structure promotes maximum utilisation of up-to-date technical skills and enables the firm to capitalise on specialisation and efficiency. These are strategically important considerations for single business companies, dominant product companies and vertically integrated companies. *(iv)* The functional structure is most appropriate when firms compete on the basis of technical specialisation or efficiency in a relatively stable environment. *(v)* This structure promotes common values and goals among employees of the department, facilitating cooperation and collaboration within the functional department.

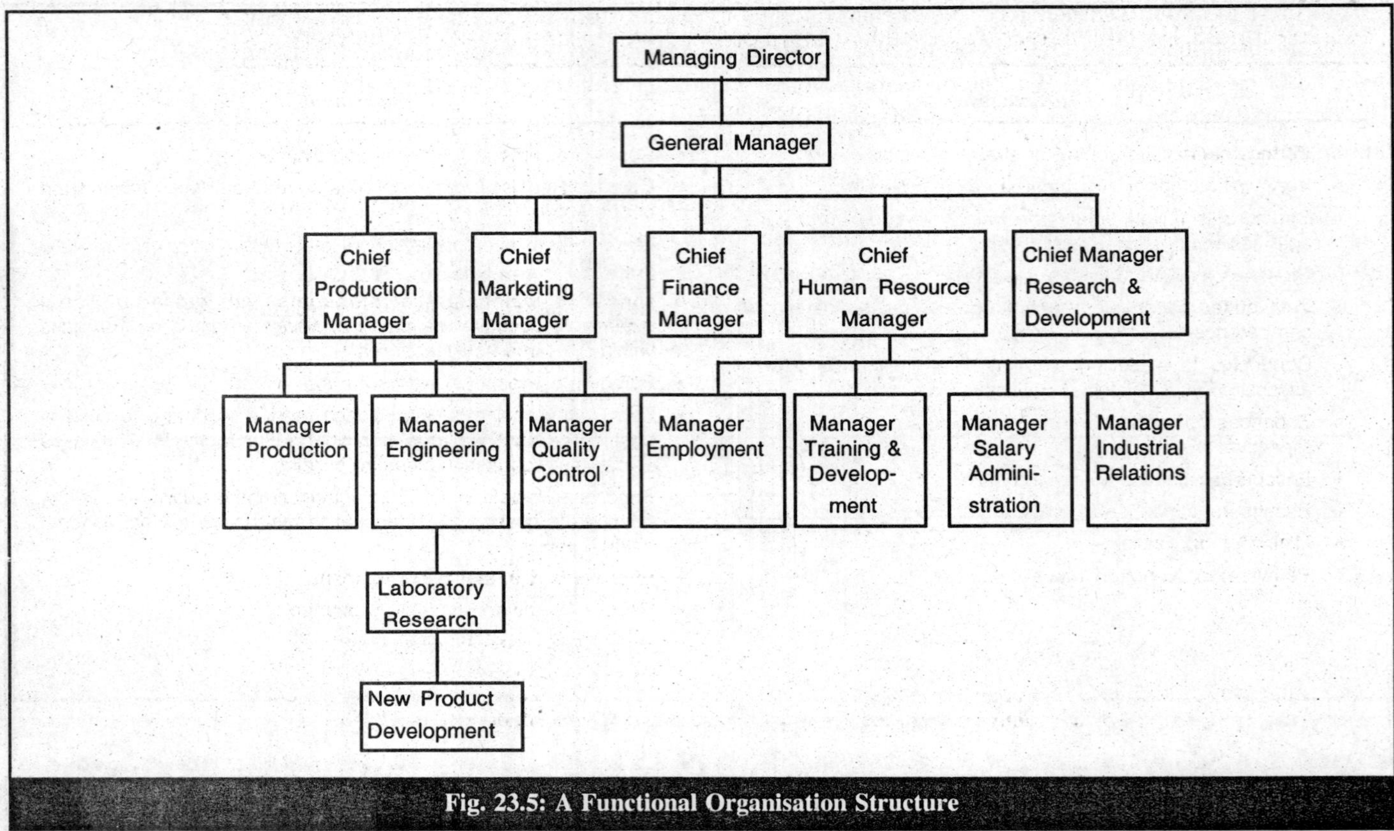

Fig. 23.5: A Functional Organisation Structure

Disadvantages: *(i)* The horizontal diversification of the business reduces the efficiency of the functional structure. *(ii)* The departmental members may see the activities from the narrow viewpoint of the department rather than the total organisation. This aspect results in absence of interdepartmental coordination and cooperation. *(iii)* Interdepartmental policies further result in conflicts. This situation leads to indecision, delay in decision-making or ineffective decision-making. *(iv)* Further, the narrow specialisations kill the initiative of entrepreneurs and the zeal of innovativeness and creativeness. Consequently, the firm may lose sensitiveness to the customer demands, technological changes and environmental demands. These limitations of functional structure may make the firm to reassess the suitability of the structure to the strategy and decide accordingly. Exhibit 23.1 presents advantages and disadvantages of functional organisation structure.

3. Product Organisation Structure

This structure is based on the products produced by the firm

Companies producing more than one products tow the time of product structure.

Activities are divided on the basis of individual products, product line, services and are grouped into departments in product organisation structure. All important functions, *viz.*, marketing, production, finance and human resource are contained within each department. This type of organisation structure overcome many of the major limitations of functional organisational structure. Fig. 23.6 presents the product organisation structure.

Exhibit 23.1 Advantages and Disadvantages of Functional Organisational Structure

Advantages	*Disadvantages*
• Permits centralised control of strategic results. • Very well suited for structuring a single business. • Structure is linked tightly to strategy by designating key activities as functional departments. • Promotes indepth functional expertise. • Well suited to developing a functional based distinctive competence. • Conducive to exploiting learning/experience curve effects associated with functional specialisation. • Enhances operating efficiency where tasks are routine and repetitive. • Encourages collaborative work. • Results in economies of scale. • Minimises duplication. • Permits congruence of goals.	• Poses problems of functional coordination. • Can lead to interfunctional rivalry and conflict, rather than cooperation. • May promote overspecialisation and narrow management view points. • Hinders development of managers with cross-functional experience because the ladder of advancement is up the ranks within the same functional area. • Forces profit responsibility to the top. • Functional specialists often attach more importance to what is best for the functional area than what is best for the total business — can lead to functional empire building. • Functional myopia often works against creative entrepreneurship, adapting to change and attempts to restructure the activity-cost chain. • Effective only in stable environment. • Results in slower response to change. • Result in poor coordination. • Result in absence of accountability.

(**Source**: Modified version: Thompson and Strickland, op. cit., p. 225.)

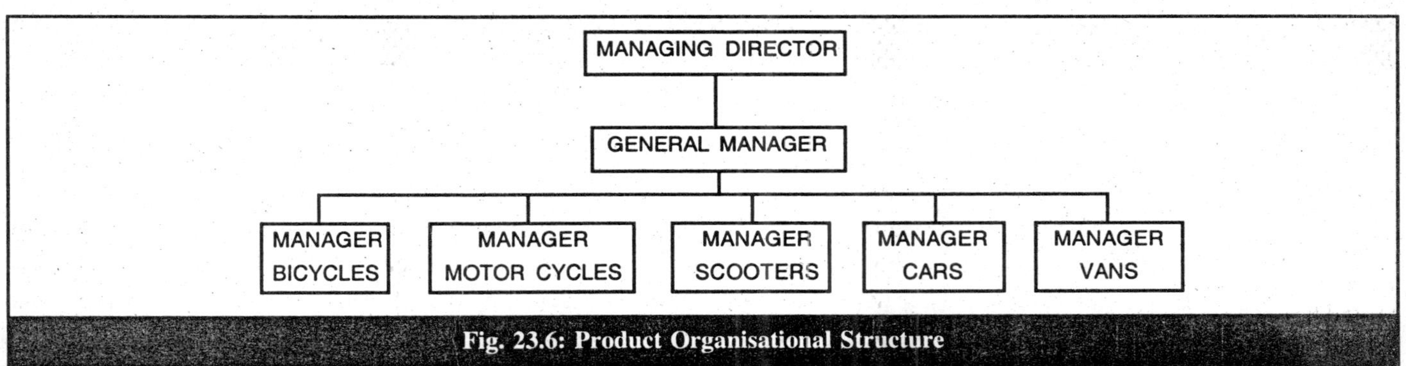

Fig. 23.6: Product Organisational Structure

Advantages: *(i)* The product organisation structure is more appropriate than the functional form of organisation for firms producing multiple products. *(ii)* Coordination among functional areas like product design, producing, distributing, marketing is effective as all functions are performed in each department. *(iii)* Since, each department is independent, most of the decisions can be made at departmental level without involving the top management in this process. It will result in fast decisions, enhancement of organisational competency to compete in rapidly changing environment. *(iv)* Responsibility and accountability for market share, sales, profit/loss is clearly fixed. Thus, either the credit for the success or blame for the failure of a product can be clearly attributed to a particular department. This advantage cannot be present in case of functional organisation structure. Exhibit 23.2 presents advantages and disadvantages.

Disadvantages: Product organisational structure is also not free from limitations: *(i)* One of the major limitations is that unnecessary duplication of equipment and personnel among various departments. This results in loss of specialisation. *(ii)* Each department will have production, marketing, human resource, finance managers, secretarial and support staff, computers and testing equipment. As such specialised personnel and equipment cannot be procured. *(iii)* Some decisions like pay, promotion, product quality, design and pricing strategy may be inconsistent between departments. *(iv)* Interdepartmental conflicts arise regarding sharing of common resources, allocation of common and overhead expenses, etc.[8]

Exhibit 23.2 Advantages and Disadvantages of Product Organisation Structure

Advantages	*Disadvantages*
• Appropriate for organisations with multiple products.	• Result in inconsistent decisions from one department to another.
• Improves coordination across functions.	• Involves difficulty in allocating overheads.
• Suited to a more dynamic environment.	• Results in duplication of equipment and personnel.
• Moves decisions close to the problem.	• Encourages dysfunctional competition for resources.
• Release Managing Director's time	• Results in loss of specialisation.
• Clarifies profit/loss accountability.	• Emphasises departmental rather than organisational goals.

(**Source:** Modified Version: Joe G. Thomas, op. cit., p. 266.)

4. Geographical Organisation Structure

This structure is based on the geographical areas of operations of the firm

Companies operating in various geographical regions of the country and/or world, structure their organisations based on geographical structure. The activities or functions are grouped into departments based on the activities performed in the geographical areas/regions. Each geographical unit includes all functions required to produce and market the products in a particular geographical area. Figure 23.7 presents a geographical organisation structure. Multinational organisations, enterprises operating in diverse geographic markets or serving an expansive geographic area are organised based on the geographic structure. This structure is also used by chain stores, power companies, restaurant chains, dairy products, banking companies, insurance companies, etc.

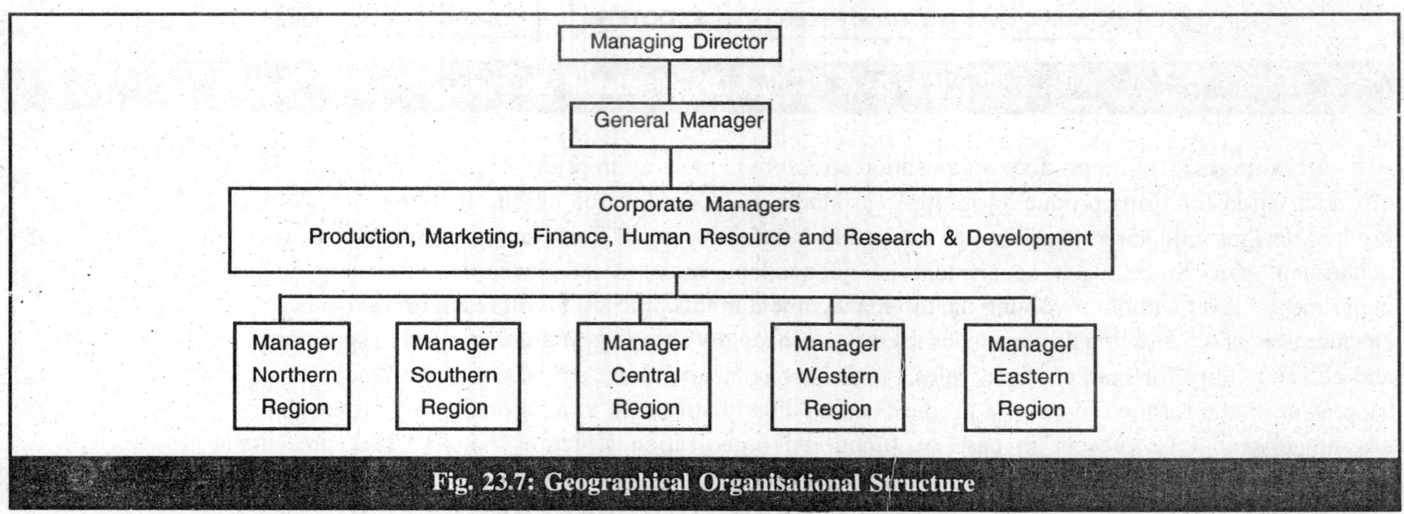

Fig. 23.7: Geographical Organisational Structure

Advantages: The advantages of this type of organisational structure are: *(i)* Products and services are better designed to the climatic and cultural needs of specific geographical regions. *(ii)* A geographical structure allows a firm to respond to the technical needs of different international area. *(iii)* Producing and distributing products in different national or global locations may empower the organisation to better serve the consumer needs of the perticular geographical area concerned. *(iv)* This structure enables a company to adapt to varying legal systems prevalent in the area region. *(v)* It also allows firms to pinpoint the responsibility for profits or losses on an individual unit basis.

Disadvantages: This organisational structure is also not free from limitations. The limitations of this structure are similar to those of product structure. *(i)* Often more functional personnel are required. The firm cannot appoint specialists unlike in functional structure due to duplication of personnel. *(ii)* There would be duplication of equipment and facilities. *(iii)* Coordination of company-wide activities would be difficult. *(iv)* There would be a problem of imposing degree of uniformity and diversity. *(v)* It is difficult to maintain consistent company image or reputation. *(vi)* This structure adds another layer of management to run the geographic units. Advantages and disadvantages are presented in Exhibit 23.3.

Exhibit 23.3 Advantages and Disadvantages of Geographical Organisation Structure

Advantages	*Disadvantages*
• Allows tailoring of strategy to needs of each geographical market. • Delegates profit/loss responsibility to lowest strategic level. • Improves functional coordination within the target market. • Takes advantages of economies of local operations. • Area units make an excellent training ground for higher level general managers. • Clarifies profit/loss accountability. • Results in good functional coordination.	• Poses a problem of how much geographic uniformity headquarters should impose versus how much geographic diversity should be allowed. • Greater difficulty in maintaining consistent company image/reputation from area to area when area managers exercise much strategic freedom. • Adds another layer of management to run the geographic units. • Can result in duplication of staff services at headquarters and regional levels, creating a relative cost disadvantage. • Results in inconsistent decisions from one region to another region. • Results in duplication of equipment and personnel. • Encourages dysfunctional competition for resources. • Results in loss of specialisation. • Emphasises regional rather than company goals.

(**Source:** Thompson and Strickland, op. cit., p. 226 and Joe. G. Thomas, op. cit., p. 267.)

5. Decentralised Business Unit Structure

Grouping activities based on product lines has been a trend among diversified companies since 1920. In a diversified firm, the basic organisational building blocks are its business units, each business is operated as a stand-alone profit centre. Fig. 23.8 depicts a skeleton of a Decentralised Business Unit Structure.

Functional structure and geographic structure are standard organisational building blocks in a single business firm. But, in multibusiness firms, the businesses are diversified.

Advantages: *(i)* Diversification is generally managed by decentralised decision-making and delegating authority and responsibility to a manager at each business unit. *(ii)* Each business unit should be managed by an entrepreneurially – oriented and capable general manager who is delegated with authority to formulate and execute business strategies. *(iii)* Each business unit operates as a stand-alone profit centre. Each business unit is structured on the basis of either functional structure or geographic structure depending upon strategy, key activities and operating requirements.[9]

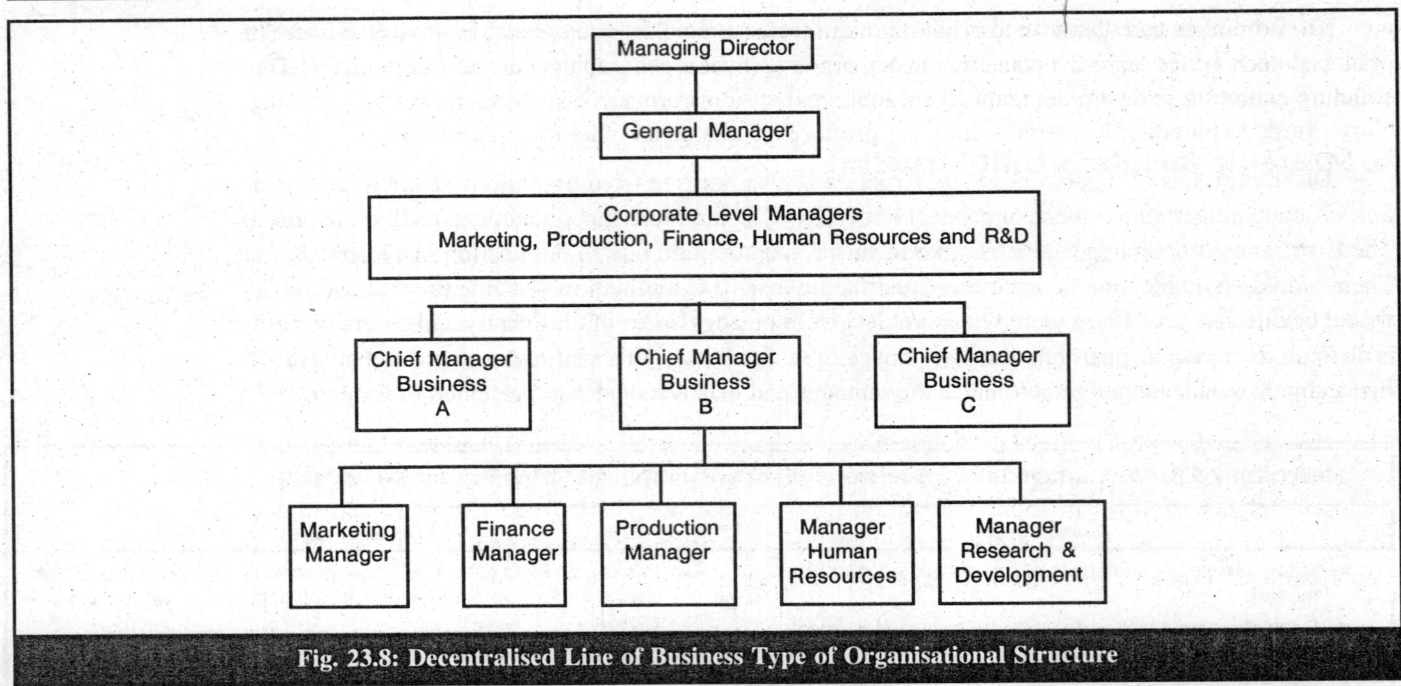

Fig. 23.8: Decentralised Line of Business Type of Organisational Structure

Disadvantages: The strategic advantages and disadvantages of a decentralised line-of-business type of organisation structure are presented in Exhibit 23.4. The disadvantages are: *(i)* The major problem of this type of organisation structure is absence of mechanism for coordinating related activities across business units. *(ii)* The general manager in charge of each business unit functions independently. It makes coordination a complicated task. Therefore, corporate headquarters must devise some internal mechanism for achieving strategic coordination and to capture benefits accordingly. Coordination can be achieved by developing corporate R&D department, corporate sales force, sales force of closely related businesses, merging the order processing and shipping functions of businesses with common customers and consolidating the production of related parts.

Exhibit 23.4 Advantages and Disadvantages of Decentralised Line of Business Type of Organisation Structure

Advantages	*Disadvantages*
• Offers a logical and workable means of decentralising responsibility and delegating authority in diversified organisations. • Puts responsibility for business strategy in close proximity to each business's unique environment. • Allows each business unit to organise around its own set of key activities and functional requirements. • Frees the managing director to handle corporate strategy issues. • Puts clear profit/loss responsibility on shoulders of business-unit managers.	• May lead to costly duplication of staff functions at corporate or business unit levels, thus raising administrative overhead costs. • Poses a problem of what decisions to centralise and what decisions to decentralise (business managers need enough authority to get the job done, but not so much that corporate management loses control of key business-level decisions). • May lead to excessive division rivalry for corporate resources and attention. • Business/division autonomy works against achieving coordination of related activities in different business units, thus blocking to some extent the capture of strategic fit benefits. • Corporate management becomes heavily dependent on business-unit managers. • Corporate managers can lose touch with business-unit situations, end-up surprised when problems arise, and not know much about how to fix such problems.

(**Source:** Thompson and Strickland, op. cit., p. 229.)

The corporate managers can also build up a suitables strategical relationship involving transfer of skill and technology across business units. Corporate office can set up interbusiness task forces, standing committees, or project teams for the purpose of transfering skills and technology.

6. Strategic Business Unit Structure

This structure is based on the strategic business units of the firm

A single chief executive cannot control a number of decentralised units of a broadly diversified company. The business can be effectively controlled, if the related businesses are grouped into strategic units and the efficient and senior executive is delegated with the authority and responsibility for its management. The senior executive will in turn report the matter to the chief executive. This arrangement will improve strategic planning and implementation, though it adds one layer in the organisational hierarchy. Top management coordinates the interests of the diversified business units.

A strategic business unit is a grouping of business subsidiaries based on some important strategic elements common to each. The common or related elements could be an overlapping set of competitors, a closely related strategic mission, a common need to compete globally, an ability to accomplish integrated strategic planning, common key success factors and technologically related growth opportunities.[10] Fig. 23.9 presents SBU type of organisation structure.

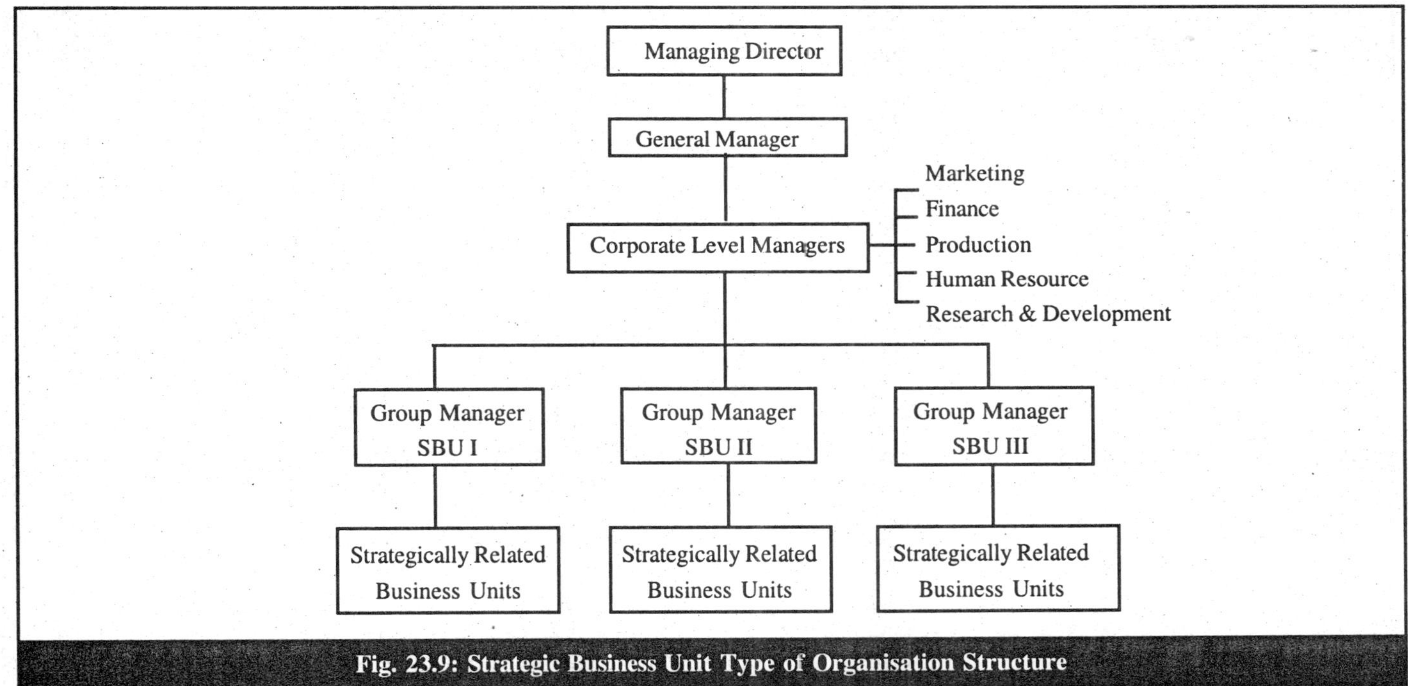

Fig. 23.9: Strategic Business Unit Type of Organisation Structure

Advantages: The advantages and disadvantages of the strategic business unit structure are presented in Exhibit 23.5. The advantages of this structure include: *(i)* reduction of the corporate headquarter's span of control. The chief executive at the corporate head- quarters has to control the general managers of the strategic business units. *(ii)* This structure permits better coordination between divisions with similar missions, products, markets and technologies. *(iii)* It allows strategic management to be done at the most relevant level within the total enterprise. *(iv)* It helps allocate corporate resources to areas with greatest growth opportunities. *(v)* Business units are organised based on the strategically relevant method.

Disadvantages: The strategic business unit structure also has certain disadvantages. *(i)* The first disadvantage is that corporate headquarters become more distinct from the division. *(ii)*

Conflicts between/among the strategic business unit managers for greater share of corporate resources can become dysfunctional. *(iii)* Corporate portfolio analysis becomes a complicated one in this structure.

Exhibit 23.5 Advantages and Disadvantages of Strategic Business Unit (SBU) Type of Organisation Structure

Advantages	Disadvantages
• Provides a strategically relevant way to organise the business-unit portfolio of a broadly diversified company. • Facilitates the coordination of related activities within an SBU, thus helping to capture the benefits of strategic fit in the SBU. • Promotes more cohesiveness among the new initiatives of separate but related businesses. • Allows strategic planning to be done at the most relevant level within the total enterprise. • Makes the task of strategic review by top executives more objective and more effective. • Helps allocate corporate resources to areas with greatest growth opportunities. • Improves coordination among businesses facing similar strategic issues.	• It is easy for the definition and grouping of business into SBUs to be so arbitrary that the SBU serves no other purpose than administrative convenience. • If the criteria for defining SBUs are rationalisations and have little to do with the nitty-gritty of strategy coordination, then the groupings lose real strategic significance. • The SBUs can still be myopic in charting their future direction. • Adds another layer to top management. • The roles and authority of the managing director, general manager, SBU level managers have to be carefully worked out. • Unless the SBU head is strong willed, very little strategy coordination is likely to occur across business units in the SBU. • Performance recognition gets blurred; credit for successful business units tend to go to corporate managing director, then to business unit head, and lastly to group manager. • Increases layers of management. • May result in SBU goals that differ from corporate goals.

(**Source:** Thompson and Strickland, op. cit., p. 231.)

7. Matrix Organisation Structure

Organisational structures discussed earlier have possessed a single chain of command. In other words, employees in those structures report to only one manager. But, the organisation structure possesses a dual chain of command. Both functional and project managers exercise authority over organisational activities, in a matrix structure. Thus, personnel in this structure have two superiors, *viz.*, a project manager and the manager of the functional department. Fig. 23.10 presents the matrix organisational structure.

A matrix organisational structure is appropriate when:[11]

(i) Management attention is focused on two or more key issues (technical issues, consumer needs, functional efficiency);

(ii) Large amounts of diverse information need to be processed;

(iii) Problem solving is complex (environmental uncertainty, interdependence among organisational units, complex products or technology); and

(iv) Economies of scale require the sharing of human resource expertise to achieve high performance.

Advantages: The matrix structure is commonly used in the firms whose technological change is rapid. The advantages of matrix structure include: *(i)* the company can have the advantages of both project type of organisational structure and functional organisation structure. *(ii)* Functional personnel are paid for their services whenever, they are used by project managers. This practice enables the management to reduce the cost. *(iii)* This structure has considerable flexibility. The personnel can be

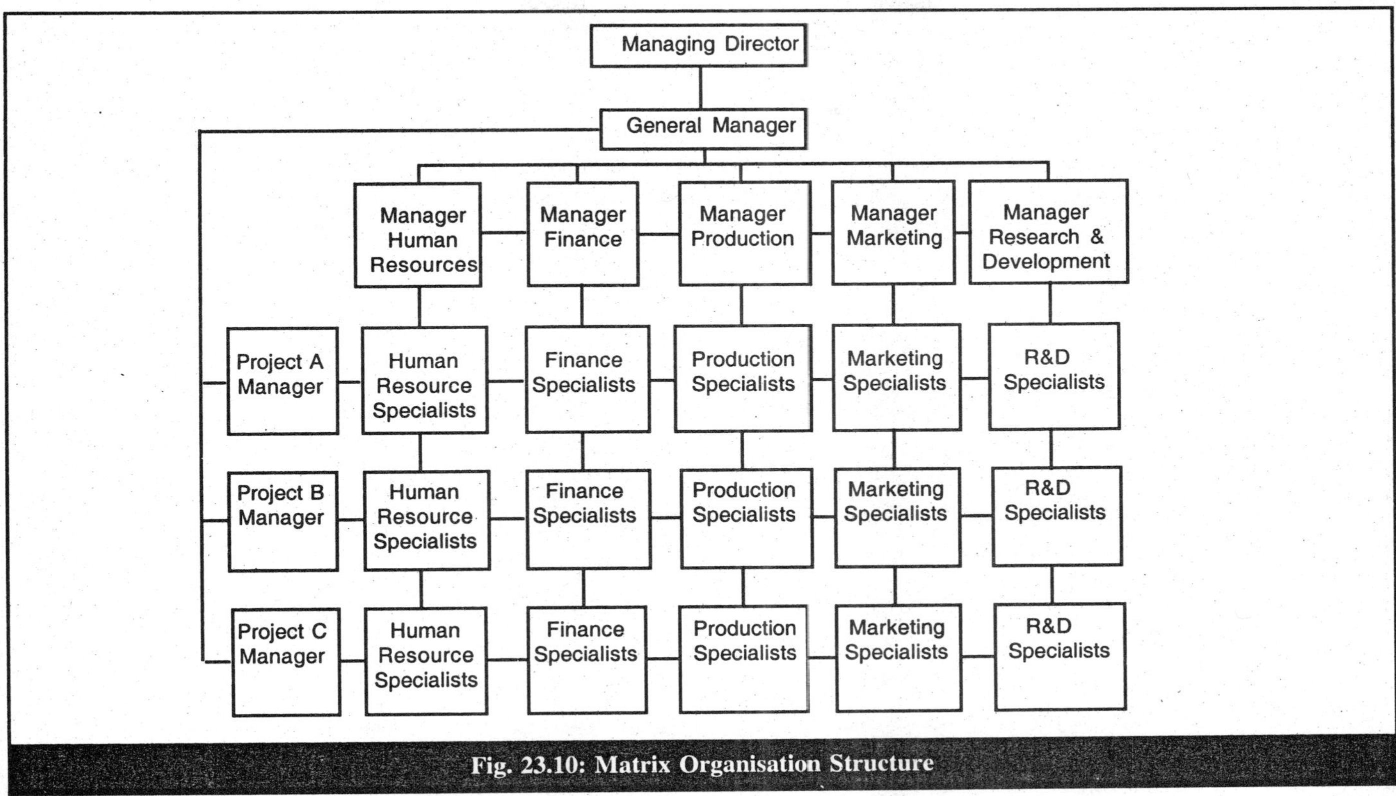

Fig. 23.10: Matrix Organisation Structure

transferred from one project to the other depending upon the need of the project. *(iv)* The lower level functional employees are highly motivated and satisfied with their job as they are involved in decision-making. *(vi)* Each project manager is in-charge of a unit. Therefore, he can be developed as a general manager through performing general managerial functions. Exhibit 23.6 presents the advantages and disadvantages of matrix organisational structure.

Exhibit 23.6 Advantages and Disadvantages of Matrix Organisation Structure

Advantages	*Disadvantages*
• Gives formal attention to each dimension of strategic priority. • Creates checks and balances among competing viewpoints. • Facilitates capture of functionality based strategic fits in diversified companies. • Promotes making trade-off decisions on the basis of, "What is best for the organisation as a whole." • Encourages cooperation, consensus-building, conflict resolution and coordination of related activities. • Permits focus of attention on more variables and encourages generation of new ideas. • Makes efficient use of functional expertise. • Facilitates operation in complex and dynamic environment. • Encourages optimisation of organisational goals. • Managers are aware of strategic issues.	• Very complex to manage • Hard to maintain balance between the two lines of authority. • So much shared authority can result in a transactions log jam and disproportionate amounts of time being spent on communications. • It is hard to move quickly and decisively without getting clearance from many other people. • Promotes an organisational bureaucracy and hamstrings creative entrepreneurship. • Violates unity of command. • Managers should have interpersonal skills. • Requires too much time for meetings and collaboration. • Requires decision-making input from many sources. • May result in conflict between functional and project managers.

(**Source:** Thompson and Strickland, op. cit., p. 232 and Joe G. Thomas op. cit., p. 269.)

Disadvantages: The significant disadvantages of matrix organisational structure include: *(i)* greater administrative costs associated with its operation. Much of the valuable time and effort of key personnel are utilised in meetings and exchanging information, ideas and thoughts to coordinate functional areas with the projects. *(ii)* In view of the two forms associated in this structure, they are characterised by conflicts. The most critical conflict is between functional managers and project managers. *(iii)* Functional employees experience stress by working in matrix structure. Reporting to two bosses, creates role ambiguity and role conflict. Some companies reverted their organisational structures back to traditional structures from matrix structures due to these problems.

8. Team Organisation Structure:[12]

This structure is based on the business teams

Strategies of business are not always static. They go on changing depending upon internal and external environmental factors. Hence, a single type of organisational structure is not suitable for all times and all situations. Blending the basic forms of organisation to match the structure to strategy in the units concerned is essential. Another option is to supplement special situation devices to the basic organisational structure. This option is Team Structure.

Team structure takes three forms *viz., (i)* Project Team, *(ii)* Taskforce Team, and *(iii)* Venture Team.

(i) **Project team:** Project teams are created to handle special kind of situations with a finite life expectancy. Project teams are self-sufficient work groups. These are created to supervise the completion of a special activity. The special activities includes setting up a new technological process, starting up a new venture, producing a new product, initiating and completion of a joint venture and the like.

(ii) **The taskforce team:** Interdisciplinary assignments necessitate the formation of a task force team. A task force team consists of top level executives and specialists in different areas from the organisation. The advantages of special task force team include: increased opportunity for creativity, open communication, cross-functional authority, effective integration of talents, quick conflict resolution, collaborative approach for problem solving.

(iii) **The venture team:** Venture team is a group of individuals. The purpose of forming this team is to bring a specific product or a new business into being. The problems of venture team are:

(i) Difficulty of deciding the manager to whom the report should be made, *(ii)* Source of funding to the venture, *i.e.,* is the source from department or business or corporation *(iii)* methods of keeping the venture clear of bureaucratic and vested interests, and *(iv)* problem of coordinating large number of different ventures.

9. Virtual Organisational Structure

These structures are not visible, but their presence is felt wherever necessary.

There is a Footwear Company. But it does not produce footwear. Small industries in Kanpur, Kharagpur, Tamil Nadu, etc., produce shoes for this company. New lane **Shoe design**: Company's executives prescribe the shoe designs, models, specifications, etc., and communicate the same to the small industries through internet. **Quality control:** Company's quality control inspectors inspect the quality of the shoes produced by the small industries and certify them.

This company does not sell the shoes to the customers. But the shoe retailing shops throughout the country sell the branded shoes of this company. Transport Corporation of India transports the shoes for this company from the manufacturing points to the retailing outlets. Commuiq Ads advertises for this company. Thus, several agencies perform various business functions relating to this shoe compny, i.e., design, production, logistics and marketing which are connected through a social network which operate in physically dispersed locations by different electronic devices like phones, mobile phones, internet, etc. This type of an organisation is called a virtual organisation.

Virtual organisation, according to Biswajeet Pattanayak, is a "social network in which all the horizontal and vertical boundaries are removed. It consists of individuals working out of physically dispersed workspaces, or even individuals working from mobile devices and not tied to any particular workspace. It is the coordination intense structure, consisting primarily of patterns and relationships, and this form needs the communication and information technology to function."[13]

Virtual organisation is a "social network in which all the horizontal and vertical boundaries are removed. It consists of individuals working out of physically dispersed workspaces, or even individuals working from mobile devices and not tied to any particular workspace. It is the coordination intense structure, consisting primarily of patterns and relationships, and this form needs the communication and information technology to function."

Virtual organization is an organization that exists in the minds of stakeholders, as a network or alliances of independent companies that collaboratively pursue a particular business.

Business Week describes virtual organization as follows:

Technology: Virtual partnerships are based on electronic network among independent companies, some times located in different places.

Excellence: Virtual partnerships draw on the core competencies of each member to create and deliver the best final product and/or service like medical services.

Opportunism: Virtual organization is based on opportunities available. Once, the opportunities disappear some or all the partners may separate from the network/ strategic alliance.

Trust: Partner companies of virtual organization build and maintain network based on mutual trust and confidence.

No borders: Partners of the virtual organization, with their complex network of relationships, make it hard to identify the boundaries among themselves.

Virtual Workplace: People/employees of various partners of virtual organization, some time may not have a common workplace. They can work from any place and coordinate their activities through internet. Telecommuting/tele-work is quite common in virtual organizations.

Characteristics of virtual organisations

The following are the characteristics of virtual organisations:

- Flexi-work, Flexitime and Flexi-workplace
- Part-time work
- Job sharing
- Home-based working
- Dependency on information technology like e-mail integration, voice-mail, mobile phone network, computer-telephony integration, etc.
- Loose organizational boundaries
- De-jobbing
- Multi-skilling

- Flexibility in power, work, etc
- Goal directed
- Customer centred.

Virtual Organisations and Behavioural Implications

Behavioural implications of virtual organisations are:

- Organisation's human resources are the loose web of people;
- Knowledgeable people are hired for short-term projects depending upon market demand;
- Employees have autonomy at work but are accountable to the targets, performance etc.;
- Employees can work from their homes (home-cum-office) or from any other place as such social and work environment do not draw much attention of HR Manager;
- Career planning and development are based on projects;
- Employees are selected based on not only technical skills but their ability to work in teams; and
- Emotional and attitudinal quotient (EAQ) is the prime factor in employee selection rather than intelligence quotient (IQ).

Employees' Features in Virtual Organisations

Employees' features in virtual organisations include:

- Self-motivation, adaptability, self-commitment, effective communication, goal/result-orientation, technical competency, multi-skills, etc.;
- Employee performance is managed based on three dimensions, viz.;

  (i) Setting performance standards/requirements;

  (ii) Facilitating performance by providing required facilities, resources, eliminating obstacle, etc.;

  (iii) Encouraging the employees to perform successfully; and
- Create a network of employees and enable them to create and share information and knowledge.

Advantages: *(i)* These structures enable for doing business with less capital, less human resources and other inputs, *(ii)* These structures provide for flexibility of operations, *(iii)* These structures react to the environment demands most efficiently, *(iv)* These structures develop the ancillary industries.

Disadvantages: *(i)* Companies do not have strong foundations or strengths in their operations, *(ii)* Organisations have to heavily depend on outsourcing, *(iii)* Failure in the network results in the failure of the entire organisation.

(F) LINE AND STAFF ORGANISATION

The relationships with which the managers in an organisation deal with one another are broadly classified into two categories, viz., line and staff. Line and staff are often used in ways that are loose and unclear. Attempts have been made in some organisations to dispense with them. Line and staff are characterised by relationships but not by departments.[14]

Line Relationship

Relationship due to command is called line

The relationship that exists between two managers due to delegation of authority and responsibility, and giving or receiving instructions or orders is called *line relationship*. Thus, line relationship generally exists between the superior and his subordinate. Line refers to those positions of an organisation which have responsibility, authority and are accountable for accomplishment of primary objectives. Managers identified as line managers are not subject to command by staff position. In case of disagreement between line and staff, the line manager has the right to make final decisions.

Line authority represents an interrupted series of authority and responsibility delegating down the management hierarchy. In other words, the board of directors delegates a part of its authority to the general manager. The general manager in turn delegates part of his authority to different departmental heads and through them, to the next level managers. However, the line managers are completely responsible and accountable for the results achieved by the employees of the respective departments and sections. This means that though the authority is delegated, responsibility for action taken by a subordinate still rests with the superior. Staff control is monitoring and reporting, which brings the results of information to the attention of the line managers for action by the line.[15]

Staff Relationship

Relationship due to offer of advice, suggestions, etc., is called staff relationship

The staff concept is probably as old as organisation itself. It is virtually impossible for the busy line managers to perform all their functions and concentrate on all the activities, including management of the people in their respective departments. This gives rise to securing advice and help from specialists. This creates staff relationships. The relationship between two managers is said to be staff relation when it is created due to giving and taking advice, guidance, counsel, information, help or assistance, etc., in the process of attaining organisational goals.

Thus, staff managers analyse problems, collect information and develop alternative suggestions and help the line managers to make the right decision quickly. They reduce the work load of the line managers and allow them to concentrate on their operative issues.

Managers identified as lines are not subjected to command by staff positions. The line managers do not have authority over staff. The decisive factor in the authority limitations of relationship is that, in case of disagreement, the line manager has a right to make the final operational decision.

Organisation can also be structured on the basis of line and staff. As discussed earlier, line and staff are viewed as relationships but not by departments. Some functional managers have line relations with other managers while some other managers have staff relations with other managers in the organization as shown in Figure 23.11. But those functional managers having staff relations may have line relations in relation to the subordinates. Thus, organisation structure is designed on the basis of line and staff relationship within the departmental structure. It is often regarded that the personnel manager has staff relation with other managers in an organisation. Now, we shall discuss the line and staff relationship and personnel management in an organisation.

As discussed earlier, the responsibility of line managers is to attain effective goals of their respective departments by the proper management of materials, machine, money and men. Thus, management of four Ms which includes management of personnel in their respective departments is the responsibility of line management. Since management is getting things done through and by the people, responsibility of management of these people rests with line managers.

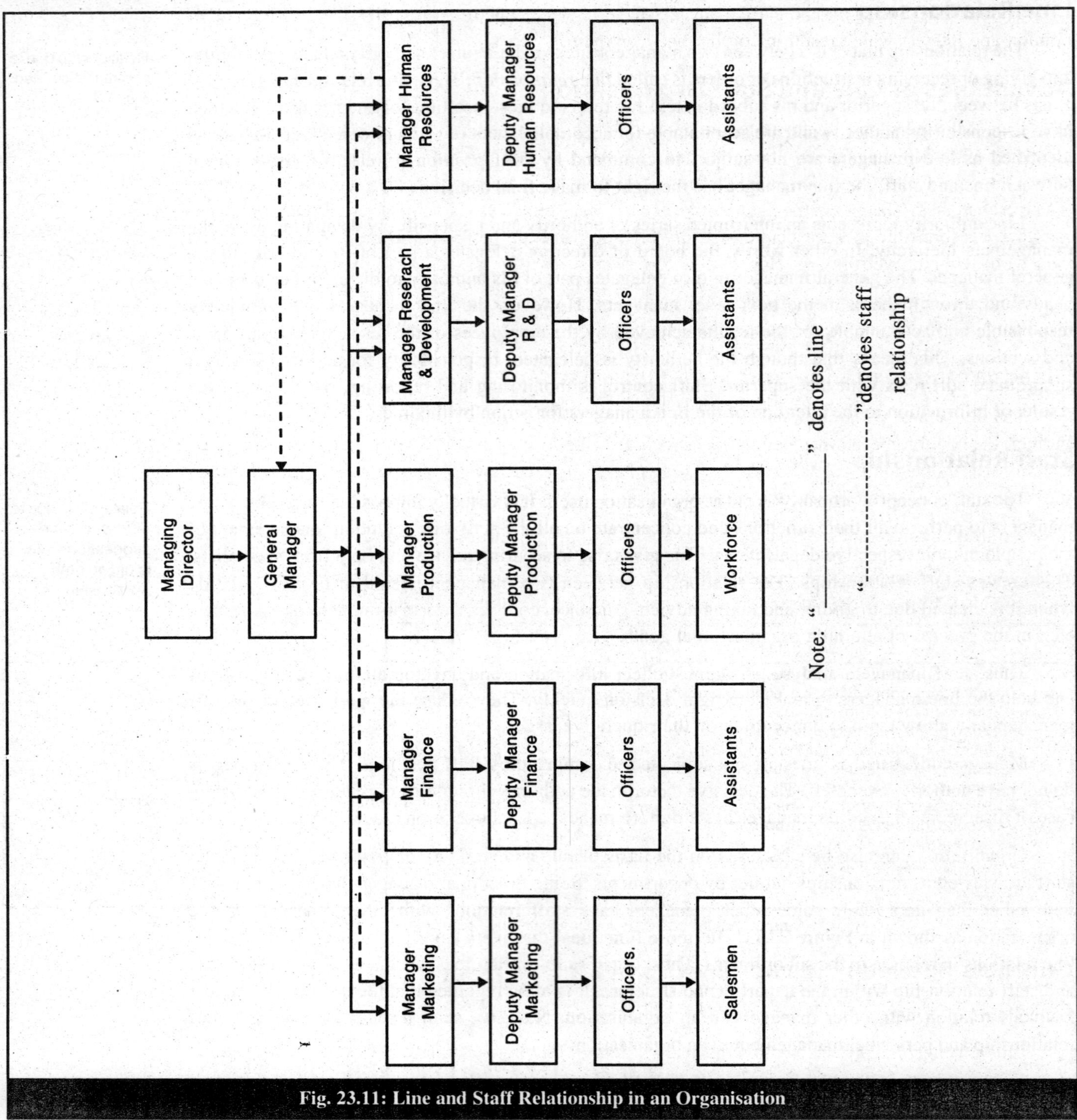

Fig. 23.11: Line and Staff Relationship in an Organisation

Line Relation in Staff Departments

The relationship between superiors and subordinates is the line relation even within the staff department. But the staff departments/managers have staff relations with other departments/managers in the organisation. Having the staff relation, these managers/departments can be of great value to the entire organisation. They are responsible for advising various line managers from top to bottom. Thus, the staff departments/managers serve as a source of assistance to the line managers.

Though line managers and staff managers have to work together, often they find difference of opinion and interest which result in conflict between them.

Advantages of Line and Staff Organisation

Line Managers can concentrate on operational issues whereas staff managers specialise in providing Valuable suggestions. It enables the employees to perform the activities at a faster rate. It allows the employees to specialise in their respective areas. The organisational human resources can be effectively utilised. Changes in the organisation can be implemented easily without resistance. Employees can accept responsible jobs. Principle of Unity of Command can be followed. Line Managers can do their work without interruptions. Hence, they can meet production schedule efficiently.

However, line and staff organisation suffers from certain disadvantages. Now, we shall study the disadvantages of line and staff organisational structure.

Disadvantages of Line and Staff Organisation

The division of Organisational Activities into line and staff creates confusion among employees. Further, the cognition of human beings allow them to think as well as do. If some employees are asked to think while others are asked to do, then it results in underutilisation of human resources. Further, staff managers may offer impracticable suggestions as they do not have operational knowledge.

Exhibit 23.7 presents the advantages and disadvantages of line and staff organisation.

Exhibit 23.7 Advantages and Disadvantages of Line and Staff Organisation

Advantages	*Disadvantages*
• Line Managers concentrate on operations and staff managers concentrate on suggestions. • Provides for division of labour and specialisation • Enables for fast performance of duties • Increases efficiency and productivity • Efficient and effective utilisation of organisational human resources. • Principle of Unity of Command is followed • Production schedules can be met • No interruption in the work • Change can be implemented without much resistance	• Leads to conflict between line and staff • Staff advises without operational experience • Creates confusion among employees • All aspects of human brain cannot be used • Line may not perform better as staff steals credit • Much of the time is wasted on conflict resolution and other disfunctions • May not fit during the era of multi-skilling • Experienced line managers do not accept staff as they would be efficient.

(**Source:** Modified version: Thompson and Strickland, op. cit., p. 225.)

Conflicts Between Line and Staff

Line Point of View

Line managers express the following reasons for conflict between them and the staff managers:

(i) **Staff assumes line authority:** Line managers are keenly aware of their responsibility and authority. Though they recognize that the staff man is necessary and valuable, they frequently resent what he does or what he thinks, because they feel the staff man encroaches upon their duties and prerogatives. Line managers also complain that personnel staff assume line authority, particularly in union-management negotiations.

(ii) **Staff does not give sound advice:** Many line managers complain that the counsel and advice offered by staff is not always fully considered, well-balanced and soundly tested. Since staff is not held accountable for the ultimate results, some staff managers show a

tendency to propose new ideas without testing them thoroughly. Sometimes, the staff man is not sufficiently acquainted with the operating conditions or processes.

(iii) **Staff steals credit:** Another common complaint is the tendency of the staff to assume credit for programmes that are successful and to lay the blame on line when they are not.

(iv) **Staff fails to see the whole picture:** Line managers frequently point out that the staff tends to operate in terms of the limited objectives of their own speciality rather than in the interest of the business a whole.

Staff Point of View

The staff managers, for the conflict between them and the line managers, feel that:

- Line does not make proper use of staff;
- Line resists new ideas; and
- Line does not give staff enough authority.

Measures to Resolve Conflict

A proper understanding and appreciation of the line and staff relationships is the only way to avoid conflicts between line and staff. The line must be made to listen to the staff and accept their suggestions in good faith. The staff must be constantly informed of the line manager's problems and also of the actual environment in which the line managers are operating. The staff should act as a source of help but not as a threat. The staff should present its recommendations as clearly as possible for consideration to the line. Both of them should recognise the essence of unity of purpose and realise that team spirit in their work is essential to attain the common end.

(G) RESPONSIVE ORGANISATIONS

Responsive organisations react to the environmental changes

Organisations cannot function in isolation as they are open systems and continuously interact with external as well as internal environment. The external environment particularly after globalisation has become more volatile. In addition, the strides in information technology and significant developments in manufacturing technology have their impact on organisations. Therefore organisations have to design their structures to be flexible and responsive to internal and external environmental factors.[16]

Organisations to be responsive to the influences of environmental factors should:

- Organise to manage information by either reducing the need for information or increase information processing capability.
- Organise for technological response.
- Organise for flexible manufacturing by adapting computer-aided manufacturing, establishing flexible factories and employing lean manufacturing technologies.
- Organising for speed in production, distribution, innovation, customer services, etc., through time-based competition, logistics management, just in time operations, etc.
- Organising for strategic response by organsing around core competencies, network organisations, strategic alliances, lean organisations and high involvement organisations.

(H) GLOBAL ORGANISING

Organising is setting structures and coordinate them within human efforts in order to enable people to maximise their contributions to organisational goals.

Organising in Japan

Organisations in Japan emphasise collective responsibility and accountability. However, individuals are implicitly held responsible for results. Therefore, individuals cannot be pointed out for their mistakes or incorrect decisions. Organisation structures are flexible and ambiguous. Organisations promote informal relations with less emphasis on formal authority and responsibility.

Japanese organisations emphazise collective responsibility

Japanese organisations place importance on culture, philosophy, values, unity and harmony. They promote corporative spirit rather than cut-throat competition with other organisations. Organisational change is comprehensive change covering the processes and parties/organisations involved in/affected by it.[17]

Thus, organising in Japan is a collaborative effort of all those parties and individuals involved in/ affected by it.

Organising in USA

Organisations in USA are structured around individual authority

USA is highly individual-oriented society. Organisations in USA are structured around individual authority, responsibility and accountability. Individual's responsibilities are clearly and explicitly determined alongwith specific job descriptions. Organisations with stability strategy adapt formal structures with specific individual responsibilities. Professionals and technical managers are more affiliated to their profession than loyal to the company. Employee mobility rate is high as people are highly mobile. As such their contribution to the creation of organisational culture is insignificant. Organisational change is not comprehensive as it is accompanied by only goals rather than processes. Companies therefore employ consultants from outside in order to focus on behavioural science orientation and interpersonal processes.

Table 23.1 presents the comparisons of organising in Japan, USA and China

Table 23.1: Comparison of Organising in Japan, USA and China

Factor	Japan	USA	China
Responsibility and Accountability	Collective	Individual	Collective and Individual
Decision Responsibility	Ambiguous	Clear & Specific	Factory Responsibility
Organisation Structure	Informal	Formal and Bureaucratic	Formal, Bureaucratic
Common Organisation Culture	Present	Absent	Absent
Employee Loyalty	To Company	To Profession	To Company

(**Source:** Adapted from Heinz Weihrich and Harold Koontz, "Management", Tata McGraw Hill, 2002, p. 348.)

Organising in China

Historically, Chinese organisations are owned by government and therefore, designed and based on bureaucratic structures. Factory managers are responsible to achieve annual plans on low scale and more or less on collective basis. Personal relationships, family networks and seniority are more important than the position in the organisation. Thus, informal relations prevail within the formal structure.

'Factory Responsibility System' introduced recently helps for delegation of responsibility and authority to lower levels. People do not change jobs as it is difficult in stationed enterprises. Therefore, employees are rather forced to be loyal to the company.[18]

KEY TERMS

- Organisation
- Functional Structure
- Matrix Structure
- Organisational Design
- Geographical Structure
- Team Structure
- Organisational Structure
- Product Structure
- Virtual Structure
- Flat Structure
- Divisional Structure
- Project Team
- Tall Structure
- SBU Structure
- Task Force Team
- Authority
- Responsibility
- Accountability
- Delegation
- Informal Delegation
- Centralisation
- Decentralisation
- Span of Management
- Formal Delegation
- Responsive Organisation
- Wide Span
- Narrow Span
- Recentralisation

QUESTIONS

1. What is organisational design? Explain how the organisations are designed.
2. What is organisational structure? State the steps in structuring an organisation.
3. Differentiate the features of tall organisations from those of flat organisations.
4. What is functional organisation struture? State its advantages and disadvantages.
5. Explain the suitability of matrix structure for the global business.
6. What is virtual organisational structure? Explain the reasons for its popularity.
7. Explain the advantages and disadvantages of line and staff organisation structure.
8. What is responsive organisation? Why should organisations be responsive to environmental factors?
9. Write short notes on:
   - Geographical structure
   - Product structure
   - Team structure
   - SBU structure

REFERENCES

1. Poter Wright, Charles D. Pringle and Mark J. Kroll, *op.cit.*, p. 149.
2. Arthur A. Thompson and A. J. Strickland, *Strategic Management*, *op.cit.*, p. 223.
3. R. Duncan, *"What is Right Organisation Structure?"*, Organisation Dynamics, Winter 1979, pp. 59-60.
4. Joe G. Thomas, *op.cit.*, pp. 265-266.
5. *Ibid.*, p.228.
6. Poter Wright, Charles D. Pringle and Mark J. Kroll, *op.cit.*, p. 160.
7. S. Davis and P. R. Lawrence, *"Matrix"*, Addison Wesley, Reading, Mass, 1977, pp. 11-12.
8. Arthur A. Thompson and A. J. Strickland, *Strategic Management*, *op.cit.*, p. 233-235.
9. P. R. Lawrence and J. W. Lorsch, *"Organisational and Environment"*, Richard D. Irwin, Homewood, 1967, p. 138.
10. Louis A. Allen, *op.cit.*, p. 116.
11. Louis A. Allen, *"Management and Organisation,"* McGraw-Hill, Auckland, 1958.
12. Edwin B. Flippo, *op.cit.*, p.99.
13. Louis A. Allen, *op.cit.*, pp. 156-171.
14. Louis A. Allen, *op.cit.*, pp. 156-171.
15. Harold Kountz, Cyril O'Donnel and Weihrich, *op.cit.*, pp. 262-269.
16. *Ibid.*
17. Lathur, G. and Lyndall, F. W. (Eds.), *op.cit.*, pp. 183-187.
18. Urwick Lyndall, F., *"Scientific Principles and Organisation,"* American Management Association, New York, 1938, p. 8.

CHAPTER **24**

ORGANISATIONAL CULTURE AND EFFECTIVENESS

☛ Chapter Outline

(A) Definition
(B) Creating Organisational Culture
(C) Approaches to Organisatioanal Culture
(D) How Employees Learn Organisational Culture
(E) How to Measure Organisational Culture?
(F) Organisational Effectiveness
(G) Nature of Organisational Effectiveness
— Key Terms
— Questions
— References

☛ Learning Objectives

After studying this Chapter, you should be able to:

✓ Understand the meaning and features of organisational culture;
✓ Differentiate organisational culture from organisational climate;
✓ Know how the organisational culture is created;
✓ Discuss the approaches to study organisational culture;
✓ Know the methods of changing organisational culture;
✓ Understand the meaning of and approaches to organisational effectiveness; and
✓ Study the nature of organisational effectiveness.

(A) DEFINITION

Organisational culture: System of shared meaning held by members

Organisational culture is a system of shared meaning held by members that distinguishes an organisation from other organisations.[1]

J. C. Spender defines organisational culture as "a belief system shared by an organisation's members."[2]

According to Kouzes, Caldwell and Posner organisational culture is "a set of shared, enduring beliefs communicated through a variety of symbolic media creating meaning in people's work lives."[3]

Organisational culture is the set of values that helps the organisation's employees understand which actions are considered acceptable and which are unacceptable.[4]

Features of Organisational Culture

The analysis of the above definitions indicate the following features of organisational culture:

- **Innovation and risk taking:** 'Innovation is the way of life in Microsoft.' 'Innovation is the key characteristic of Gillette Company.' Companies encourage the employees to be innovative and risk takers at different degrees.
- **Attention to detail:** 'Employees in the Boston Consultancy Group are expected to be precise, analytical and pay attention to even the minor details.' Thus, organisations require their employees to be precise, analytical and pay attention to the minute details at different degrees.
- **Outcome orientation:** 'Coromandal Cements expects its employees to improve their performance at least by 5% every year irrespective of the approaches they follow.' Thus, the organisations require their employees to pay attention or the results.
- **People orientation:** 'Hewlett and Packard announced one day unpaid holiday for every nine working days and avoided lay-off.' Thus, the organisations take the effect of its decisions on the employees.
- **Team orientation:** "Global Solutions repeats: "We Work." It does mean that the activities are designed around teams but not individuals. Thus, we today find team jobs rather than individual jobs.
- **Aggressiveness:** The employees of State Bank of India were not allowed to be aggressive whereas the employees of IDBI Bank are expected to be aggressive and competitive. Thus, aggressiveness is the level to which the employees are expected to be competitive rather than easygoing.
- **Stability:** Most of the Indian Universities still have the status quo strategy of maintaining the traditional values and beliefs of *'Guru and Shishya' parampara of Gurukulas.*
- **Radical change:** In contrast to the stability strategy, most of the organisations after 1991 have the growth, diversification and conglomerate diversification strategies. It is the degree at which the organisational activities emphasise growth and diversification.
- **Customer orientation:** Pizza Huts build up relationship with the customers and then adapt aggressive marketing strategies. It is the degree to which the management decisions take into consideration the effect of outcomes on customers of the organisation.

Cultural Concepts

These different cultural concepts include:

Dominant culture: Most of the employees of Videsh Sanchar Nigam Limited (VSNL) believe that the business strategies of the company are not aggressive compared to those of the private sector. This core shared belief by most of the employees is called *dominant culture*.

Dominant culture: Core values of majority of employees

Dominant culture, thus, denotes the core values which are shared by majority of the employees in the organisation. It is the macro-cultural perspective that presents the organisation's personality.[5]

Sub-cultures: HPCL started its own retail outlets. Managers and employees of these outlets have autonomy and freedom to operate. The shared value of the employees of the retail outlets is that they are allowed to be competitive. This retail outlets culture of HPCL is sub-culture.

Thus, sub-cultures are denoted by units/departments/geographic separations. They are mini-cultures within the company.

Core values: Employees in HPCL are not allowed to be competitive. It is the core value. Core values are primary or dominant values, those are accepted by the majority of the organizational members (See Box 24.1).

Box 24.1: Common Culture

There's more in common between the Tatas and the Godrejs than the fact that they share the same faith. Both are front-rankers when it comes to being good corporate citizens. So when the low-profile Pheroza Godrej, conservationist and wife of Godrej & Boyce Chairman Jamshyd Godrej, and Tata Steel's Managing Director J.J.Irani, teamed up to create a green belt in and around Mumbai, it didn't come as a surprise. What did is the scale of operations. Before the coming monsoon (just around the corner), Friends of Trees, a Mumbai-based NGO overseen by Godrej, will plant 100,000 saplings. What do the Tatas bring to the table, sorry, ground? The saplings, of course. Irani, a self-confessed environmentalist and avid gardener, will provide the saplings from Tata Steel. Says Godrej, 52, who has been involved in preservation of heritage buildings in Mumbai: "The idea is not to confine it to the elite environs of South Mumbai." Tata Steel, which planted a million trees in Jamshedpur over two years, as part of its Green Millennium project, will also lend its expertise. Adds Irani, 65, "We can provide support to other responsible organisations in cities, other than just Mumbai and Jamshedpur." Remember the old slogan that went "We also make steel"?

(**Source:** *Business Today*, June 6, 2001.)

Strong cultures: The system of the public sector organisation does not allow the potential employees to be competitive. These values are intensely held and widely spread. Thus, the organisation's core values which are intensely held and widely spread are called *strong cultures*.

Strong culture values are intensely held and widely spread

Strong cultures have great influence on the employee behaviour. As such, most of the competent employees in the public sector are highly frustrated.

Weak cultures: In a weak culture, the organisation's core values are lightly held and occasionally shared. For example, Indian Railways is more concerned towards its customers.

Mechanistic and organic cultures: The most important aspects of organisation in public sector companies include hierarchies, supervision, control, formalisation, flow of authority and communication from top to bottom, etc., rather than the results or outcome. Organisations with these characters are termed as *mechanistic organisations*. They follow status quo strategy and therefore resist innovation and aggressiveness on the part of employees. These organisations also lack customer-orientation and employee welfare.

Tata Infotech, on the other hand, is more flexible and open. Jobs and roles are not defined rigidly and employees are given freedom to adjust themselves to the environmental requirements. Concern is more towards the outcome and results, but not the procedure or hierarchy.

Communication in this company is more multi-directional. The informal communication is widely used. Decision-making is more decentralised. People with the ability to handle problems are given freedom to assume authority and responsibility. This company is a continuous learning organisation from the environment and such companies are termed as *organic structures*.[6]

The mechanic culture de-motivates the competent people and leads to negative organisational culture. Whilst the organic culture motivates the able employees to be competitive and innovative.

Authoritarian and participative cultures: Authority to make the decisions is centralised at the top management level in Nagarjuna Fertilisers Limited. Consequently, the CEO of the company makes the decisions and informs them to the lower levels in the organisation. Such culture of concentration of authority and power at the central level is called *authoritarian culture*. Such a culture kills the initiative and innovativeness of the employees at different levels.

In contrast, Cybertech Systems and Software decentralises the power and authority of decision-making. In fact, employees are involved in decision-making. Communication flows not only from the top to bottom but also from the bottom to the top. Such type of culture is called *participative culture*. Participative culture encourages the employees to be innovative, aggressive and to take risks.

Having discussed various other concepts of organisational culture, we shall now study another concept, *i.e.*, organisational climate.

Organisational Culture vs Organisational Climate

Organisational culture is based on anthropology while organisational climate is based on psychology.

With the popularisation of the term organisational culture, another concept of organisational climate has emerged. Some managers feel that these two are quite different terms while other managers feel that these two are similar concepts.

These two are similar concepts as both of them are concerned with overall work atmosphere of an organisation. In addition, both of them deal with the social context in organisations and are believed to affect employee behaviour in organisations.[7]

However, some view the following differences between organisational culture and organisational climate. According to them:

- Organisational culture is based on anthropology and sociology
- Organisational climate is based on psychology
- This climate refers to current situations in organisations and the linkage among teams, employees and performance
- Organisational culture refers to the historical context and its input on employee behaviour
- It is difficult to alter organizational culture in the short run
- People learn and communicate what is acceptable and unacceptable in an organisation (its values and norms) through organisational culture[8] and
- Organisational climate does not deal with values and norms. It is concerned with the current atmosphere in an organisation.

After studying organisational culture and other related concepts, we shall now discuss the ways of creating organisational culture.

(B) CREATING THE ORGANISATIONAL CULTURE

Mr. Prasanth Koul tells his father: "It is not the way of doing the business."

He did his MBA from the Warwick School of Business and joined his father's business recently. His father has been producing petrochemicals since 1976. He follows authoritarian style and pushes his decisions down the line.

Mr. Prasanth Koul, after joining his father's business, observed various aspects and concluded that his father's authoritarian style is the main reason for lack of creativity and slow growth of business.

He convinced his father and assumed an active role in the business. Immediately, he adopted participative style and slowly encouraged most of the employees to be creative, aggressive and to take risks.

Thus, he introduced new strategic values of participative approach and created the new culture in his organisation.

Business people normally, do not concentrate on creation of culture during the early days of their business, rather they concentrate on manufacturing and marketing. Later, they concentrate on culture creation with a view to develop the business alongwith the new strides. But, undesirable cultures are created by some employees during such period when the entrepreneur concentrates on manufacturing and marketing. An entrepreneur, at the later stage, has to spend a lot of resources to erase the undesirable cultures. As such, it would be better to concentrate on culture creation at early stage of the business in order to prevent the creation of undesirable cultures.

Thus, the culture is linked to the strategic values.[9] Culture creation is based on the strategy as 'culture follows strategy.' Culture creation is linking the strategic values to culture values as shown in Exhibit 24.1.

Culture is linked to strategic values

Exhibit 24.1 Culture Creation in an Organisation

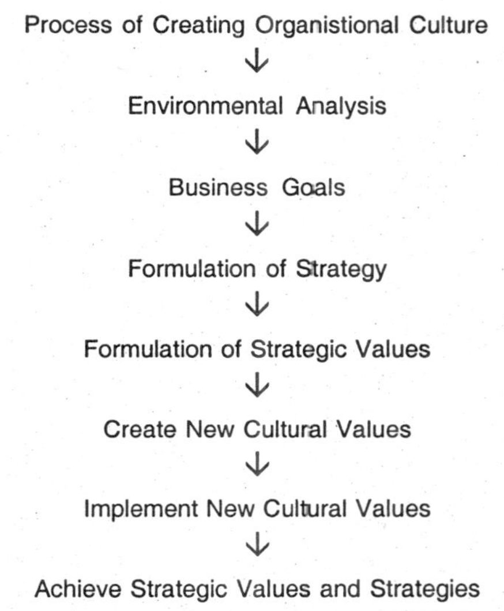

Process of Creating Organistional Culture
↓
Environmental Analysis
↓
Business Goals
↓
Formulation of Strategy
↓
Formulation of Strategic Values
↓
Create New Cultural Values
↓
Implement New Cultural Values
↓
Achieve Strategic Values and Strategies

Establish strategic values: Management determines organisation's strengths, weaknesses, opportunities and threats based on environmental analysis. Subsequently, the management formulates strategies to achieve goals. Management decides the values to achieve the strategies. These values are called *strategic values*.[10]

Strategic values are the basic beliefs about an organisation's environment those shape its strategy. For example, adopting the participative management style to grow at a faster rate. The strategic values can be acquired only when the employees acquire necessary cultural values. For example, the employees should acquire the involvement characteristic to make participative style of management successful. Thus, this characteristic is cultural value for the strategic value of participative management style.

Cultural values are the values that employees need to have and act on for the organization to act on the strategic values.[11]

Combining strategic and cultural values: The next logical step, after acquiring strategic values and cultural values is appropriately combining these two values. Management should encourage the employees to involve in the decision-making process, appreciate their ideas and considering them when the strategic values are participative styles on the part of the management. This combination makes the employees to be creative, risk taking and aggressive in order to exploit the business opportunities.

Strategy implementation: The next logical step is implementing the strategies. After the appropriate culture is created and implemented, it contributes for the proper implementation of strategy. The participative style of management and involvement character of the employees makes the employees creative. Employees with creative ideas invent new products, add now functions to the existing products, find new markets and new customers. These, in turn, enable the company to achieve its growth strategy.

Reinforce Cultural Behaviour

The next logical step is reinforcing the cultural behaviour of employees. The management has to continuously encourage the employees to involve in the decision-making process, express their feelings and ideas openly, etc. This process of reminding the employees of their cultural values is called *reinforcing cultural behaviour*.

Having discussed how culture is created, we shall now discuss how the culture is maintained.

Maintaining Organisational Culture

After the organisational culture is created and developed, the next step is to maintain it. Figure 24.1 presents the model of managing organisational culture.

Infosys Technologies India Limited believes in creating and maintaining desirable culture. Organisational culture is a part of the organisational strategy of the company. The company takes utmost care for maintaining the culture by selecting the right personnel at the entry level, placing the employees on the appropriate job, encourage employees to excel on their jobs, rewarding the employees based on their performance, adherence to the core values, reinforcing the stories and folklore and recognition and promotion. Now, we shall discuss each of these factors below:

- **Selection of entry-level personnel:** Gujarat Gas Company has special recruiters to screen the candidates at the entry level based on the organisation's norms, values and beliefs in addition to the technical knowledge and skills. They do this type of screening in order to make a match with the existing organisational culture of the company.

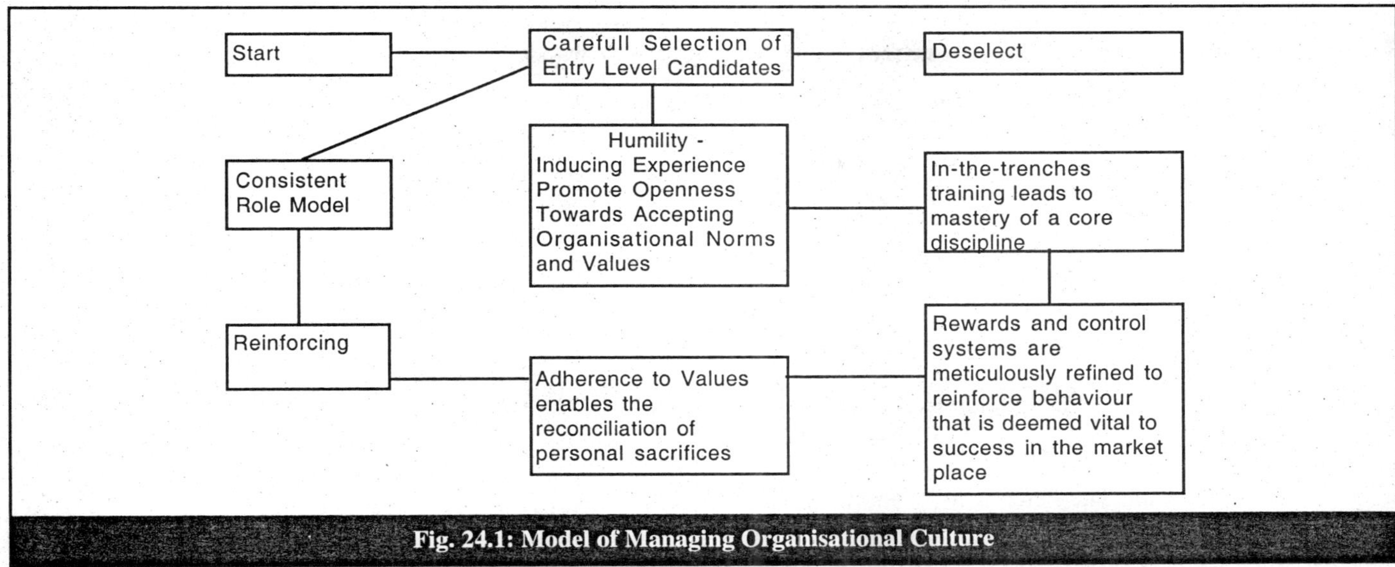

Fig. 24.1: Model of Managing Organisational Culture

(**Source:** Richard Pascale, "*The Paradox of Corporate Culture*", California Management Review, Vol. 27, No.2, Winter 1985, p.38)

- **Placement on the job:** Information Technologies Limited normally assigns the work to the new employees more than their abilities in order to judge the employee's placement on the job. The objective is to teach the employee the importance of humility in the process of maintaining the culture. This process also makes the new employees emotionally close to the colleagues and intensifies group cohesiveness.
- **Job mastery:** Most of the emerging organisations like HCL Technologies and Hughes Software Systems believe that the suitability of a candidate to an organisation should be judged based on emotional balance rather than intelligence or technical competence.

The emotionally balanced employees easily adjust and encounter the initial cultural shock and concentrate on mastery of their jobs. Superiors and trainers help the employees in this process.

- **Measuring and rewarding performance:** Hindustan Beverages Limited set three performance areas *viz.*, sales/profit, adherence to the cultural values and team building. Employee's performance is measured and rewarded based on performance. Thus, steps are taken to maintain the culture by rewarding the employees.
- **Adherence to core values:** At this stage, the employees are inspired and encouraged to adhere to the company's core values even by sacrificing their personal comforts like missing weekends, working long hours and taking up inconvenient job assignments. Employees who sacrifice their personal comforts are rewarded by connecting the costs of sacrifices to higher human values. For example, Honda Motors Company took American Technical Specialists and their families to Japan for a holiday trip.
- **Reinforcing the stories and folklore:** At this stage, companies reinforce organisational folklore. The best way of folklore is stories with morals that the company wants to reinforce in its cultural values. Procter & Gamble reinforces the cultural value that ethical claims are more important than money by spreading the story that it fixed an outstanding brand manager for overstating the features of a product.

In contrast, the weak cultural values of Indian Public Sector organisations are reinforced through the stories that the managements could not fire corrupted, unethical and insincere employees. In the lighter vein, it is said that the government employees are viewed as "sons-in-law of the government."

There are numerous stories about field employees of telecommunications industry, who had undergone physical sufferings in discharging their primary responsibility.

- **Recognition and promotion:** Management maintains culture by recognising and promoting the employees who serve as role models in implementing the cultural values. Procter and Gamble recognises the role models with motivational skills, energy and tough-mindedness while Morgan Stanley prefers energy, aggressiveness and team play as the features of role models.[12]

Having studied how the organisational culture is maintained, now we shall discuss how organisation culture is described.

(C) APPROACHES TO ORGANISATION CULTURE

Ouchi's approach: period of employment, evaluaion, career paths, decision-making and control

Basically there are two approaches to describe organisation culture viz., The Ouchi's Framework and The Peters and Waterman Approach.

The Ouchi Framework

William W.Ouchi has first analysed the cultures of a limited group of companies. He has analysed the culture of three groups of companies *viz.,* (a) typical US companies, (b) typical Japanese Companies and (c) type Z companies.

- **Period of employment:** Japanese companies provide lifetime employment. Similar culture of providing long-term employment is also adopted by theory Z companies. Typical US companies do not have the culture of providing employment commitment to its employees.
- **Evaluation:** Theory Z firms concentrate on evaluation and training and promote the employees slowly. Japanese companies also promote the employees slowly. But the typical US companies promote the employees at a faster rate.
- **Career paths:** Japanese firms follow the culture of very general careers. Employees are rotated among jobs and are encouraged to be familiar with all areas of operations. Theory Z firms also adopt similar culture. But the typical American companies adopt the culture of highly specialised jobs.
- **Decision-making:** Japanese firms and theory Z firms have participative decision-making culture whereas typical American companies have the culture of individual decision-making.
- **Control:** Japanese companies have the culture of implicit and informal control whereas the typical American companies have the culture of explicit and formal control. Theory Z firms' culture in this regard includes informal control and explicit performance appraisal.
- **Responsibility:** Typical American companies and theory Z firms share the same culture of individual responsibility. Japanese firms follow the culture of group responsibility.
- **Concern for people:** Japanese firms are concerned with the total life of the employee. Theory Z firms also follow similar culture of expanding to more aspects of the worker's total life. Typical American firms' culture is limited to worker's work life only.

According to Ouchi, the culture of Japanese firms and Theory Z firms helped them to outperform typical US companies. Toyota introduced management styles and culture of Japanese firms in North America. Investment and positive belief in human resources by Japanese companies and Theory Z firms resulted in significant improvement in long-term performance (See Box 24.2).

Box 24.2: Cultural Sensitivity

The stylish CFO of Hambrecht & Quist Asia Pacific (H&Q), one of the oldest private equity investment firms in the Asia Pacific region, likes to downplay her gender but not her Indian genes. Pretty much the successful NRI professional, Purvi Gandhi, 31, who was born in Surat but is based in San Francisco, takes her job very very seriously. As H&Q's finance chief, Gandhi has overseen investments in over 250 companies in the region, through 16 funds, comprising a managed capital of $1.6 billion. Her latest deal was in providing expansion capital to At India, the business value accelerator, kick-started by another go-getting Indian, Ramesh Vangal. Says Gandhi, a Berkeley finance graduate, who earned her stripes at a Wall Street brokerage firm, followed by a stint at consulting major Deloitte & Touche before signing on at H&Q in 1996: "I joined at a time when the Valley had started humming. So, finding the tech focus was not really difficult. But I had to learn a lot on the job." What's the secret of her success? The ability to execute a vision, a willingness to work really hard and, of course, her Gujarati roots that helps her drive a good bargain. "As an Indian, I also bring in a lot of cultural sensitivity, a factor that helps in striking deals with Valley entrepreneurs, many of whom are Indians. But some of them balk at dealing with a woman CFO," quips Gandhi. Some things never change...

(**Source:** *Business Today*, January 6, 2001.)

The Peters and Waterman Approach

Relationship between the organisational culture and performance is focussed more explicitly by Tom Peters and Robert Waterman in their book on "*In Search of Excellence*." Peter and Waterman described the management practices of highly successful US companies. They found that cultural values led to successful management practices.[13] Exhibit 24.2 presents the cultural values of excellent firms.

Exhibit 24.2 Cultural Values of Excellent Firms

- Bias for action
- Stay close to the customer
- Autonomy and entrepreneurship
- Productivity through people
- Hands-on-management
- Stick to the knitting
- Simple form, lean staff
- Simultaneously loosely and tightly organised.

Peter and Waterman approach: bias for action, stay close to customer, etc.

- **Bias for action:** According to Peters and Waterman, managers of successful firms make decision, even if all the facts are not available as delay in decision-making costs the organisation. Thus, they show bias for action. Organisations with the cultural values of bias for action out-perform the companies without such values.
- **Stay close to the customer:** Superior customer service and building relations with the customers are the cultural values of the excellently performing firms. Scandinavian Airlines with these cultural values started making money when other airlines were in financial problems in 1989. Therefore 'provide and perform what the customer needs' should be the cultural value for excellence.
- **Autonomy and entrepreneurship:** Successful firms never opt for bureaucracy. They go for small, independent and autonomous business units. Managers are expected to be entrepreneurs and intrapreneurs in order to bring creations and innovations into the business.[14]
- **Productivity through people:** The most important asset for successful organisation is its human resources. It is the core value for organisation culture. Organisations achieve higher productivity through such valuable people.
- **Hands-on-management:** Managers should not manage by sitting in their offices. Instead, they should manage by 'walking-around' or 'wandering around' the plant, the design facility, R&D etc., in order to have first hand experience in managing.

- **Stick to the knitting:** Successful business firms stick to their core and distinctive competencies. Therefore, they stick to the business portfolio in which they have core and distinctive competencies and do not opt for conglomerate diversification (or unrelated diversification).
- **Simple form, lean staff:** Excellent firms are with a flat structure with a few levels and less number of employees. This type of firms depend on the performance of the staff concerned and not on their size.
- **Simultaneously loose and tight organisation:** Peters and Waterman view that successful organisations are tight as the members share common values and the organisation is loose as the members can take their decisions.

We have discussed various approaches to organisational culture and the cultural values of the excellent firms while discussing the relationship between the culture and performance. We learnt that participative and humanistic culture leads to higher performance. Now, most of us get a nagging doubt that how employees learn such organisational culture. Therefore, shall we now discuss the methods learning culture?

(D) HOW EMPLOYEES LEARN CULTURE?

Employees learn culture through: stories, rituals, material symbols and language

Employees learn culture through different modes *viz.*, stories, rituals, material symbols and language.

- **Stories:** It is very hard to find an employee who does not know the following story in Housing Development Finance Corporation of India Limited.

One day a customer came to the Hyderabad branch of the Corporation along with his pass- book and complained to the clerk that he paid the 25th instalment of his housing loan and the bank entered only up to 24 instalments and asked the clerk to make the entry for the 25th instalment also. The clerk at the counter checked in his computer and hard copies of ledger and cash book. But the company's records failed to confirm the payment of the 25th instalment.

The branch manager was observing the incident and the facial expressions of the clerk and confirmed for himself that the customer was wrong. But he did not want the clerk to say to the customer that he is wrong.

The branch manager told the customer: "we are sorry for not making the entry for your payment of the 25th instalment and we shall do it now."

The branch manager asked the clerk to make the entry in his pass book and then come to his chamber. When the clerk met him, the branch manager said, "I am sorry, I know the customer is wrong. But I did not want to disappoint our valuable customer."

In fact, the customer after recollecting the truth that he did not pay the 25th instalment, came to the branch and tendered his apology. Since then he became a very loyal customer and also a main source for spreading of the company policy.

Such stories are circulated among the employees and customers of the organisation. Employees learn the organisational culture through such stories. These stories anchor the present in the past and provide explanations and legitimacy for current practices.[15] Normally, such stories develop spontaneously. However, some organisations have an employee in-charge of culture who records such events and stories and communicate them to the new employees.

- **Rituals:** Reliance Industries conducts company foundation day every year, where the CEO of the company rewards the employees for their best performance, best customer relations, etc. This helps to reinforce company values, goals and future benchmarks. All the family members of all employees participate in the events and interact with each other in the whole day celebrations. It is one of the important occasions for Reliance employees to learn organisational culture. Such activities are called '*rituals*.'

Rituals are repetitive sequences of activities which express and reinforce the key values of the organisation, which goals are most important and which people are important and which are expendable.[16]

- **Material Symbols:** Employees in Maruti Udyog Limited (MUL) do not have individual offices - rather they have cubicles, common areas and common eating and meeting rooms. Employees in MUL learn from this kind of office accommodation the organisational values of openness, equality, interaction, creativity and flexibility.

Some companies provide various facilities to the employees like cars, telephone, elegant furniture, executive perks, etc. These facilities are called *material symbols* which make the employees learn as to how the organisation should treat the employees and who are important to the company.

- **Language:** Language refers to the technical jargon used by the business to denote people, equipment, customers, etc. New employees know these technical jargons and their meanings. For example, the staff dealing with cash in foreign companies is called '*bursers*.' People working in the production department in foreign companies are called '*operators*.' Employees after assimilating this terminology become part of the culture. Thus, this terminology acts as a common denominator that unites members of a given culture or sub-culture.

(E) HOW TO MEASURE ORGANISATIONAL CULTURE

Though it is difficult to measure exactly the picture of the organisational culture can be obtained by measuring each of these features as given below:

- Structure a questionnaire using five or seven degree scale on a continuum from very low to very high (+2 to –2 in case of five degree scale and +3 to –3 in case of seven degree scale).
- Appraise each of the features of organisational culture (for example +2, +1, 0, -1-, -2)
- Give weightages to each of these features. The total weightage of all the features should be equal to +1 (for example 0.01, 0.15....)
- Calculate the average appraisal of each feature.
- Multiply the average appraisal of each feature with the weightage of the feature concerned and obtain the weighted score.
- Add the weighted scores of all the features and obtain the total weighted score. This total weighted score is the composite picture of the organisation's culture.

Though we can calculate the composite picture of the organisation's culture, it would not represent the beliefs or values of all the organisational members. These varied beliefs of the organisational members can be categorised into different cultural concepts.

Organisational Culture: Asset or Liability?

Culture can be an asset or a liability

Some managers argue that culture performs a number of functions and therefore, it is an asset. For example:

- Culture keeps the people together and increases the cohesiveness or bondage among its members.
- Culture performs boundary-defining role. In other words, it creates distinction between one unit and another unit of the same organisation and between one organisation and another organisation.
- It conveys a sense of commonality among organisational members.
- It conveys a sense of identity among the members.
- It creates a social system of shared values.

However, some view culture as liability in view of the following factors:

- When the organisation is operating as a dynamic environment, culture does not allow the organisation to change in accordance with the environmental demands.
- New entrants bring diversified cultures into the organisation. But the strong cultures demand new employees to conform to its values rather than modifying it through their diversified culture, whatsoever their merits may be.
- Many business alliances like mergers and acquisitions, today, are tending towards divorce due to the strong cultures of the partners to the alliance.

Thus, culture works both as an asset and as a liability. Culture should be both tight and loose in order to maximise its asset value and reduce the value of liability. Thus, change in organisational culture is necessary in order to allow the organisation to change in accordance with the environment and to act as a change agent to the environment.

Changing Organisational Culture

Organisational culture can be changed through new stories, new rituals and new language

As discussed earlier, organisational culture should be allowed to change in order to keep the organisation dynamic. Sometimes the culture has to be changed forcibly. Some of the public sector organisations in India are being privatised consequent upon economic liberalisations by means of divestment or outright sale. The culture of the public sector, *i.e.,* bureaucracy, uncaring the customer, protecting the inefficient employee, treating efficient and inefficient employees at par, should be changed along with the private sector culture like organic structure, concentrating all organisational operations around the customer, smart sizing the employees, treating the efficient and inefficient employees differently, etc.

Organisational culture can be changed through:

- Creating new stories
- Initiating the conduct of new kind of rituals
- Providing new and varied material symbols and
- Creating new language.

Having discussed various aspects of organisational culture, we shall now discuss emerging issues in organisational culture.

Emerging Issues in Organisational Culture

Cultures change gradually, picking up new ideas and dropping old ones. Therefore, new issues emerge in cultures. Now, we shall discuss these emerging issues:

- **Innovation:** According to Fortune Magazine, most innovative organisations, which pickup new values continuously are the most admired organisations.[17] Innovation is the process of creating and doing new things that are introduced into the marketplace as products, processes or services. Types of innovations include radical innovation, system innovation and incremental innovation.
- Radical innovation is a major breakthrough that changes or creates whole industries. For example, information technology industry.
- System innovation creates a new functionality by assembling parts in new ways. Combining information technology and process technology and formation of new business process (Supply Chain Management) is an example for system innovation.
- **Incremental innovation:** It continues technical improvement and extends the application of radical systems innovation.
- **Entrepreneurship:** Entrepreneur is the one who creates the total venture.
- **Intrapreneurship:** Intrapreneurship is an entrepreneurial activity that takes place within the context of a large organisation.
- **Empowerment:** Empowerment is the process of enabling workers to set their own work goals, make decisions and solve problems within their sphere of responsibility and authority.
- **Information technology:** Information technology brought significant changes in the organisational culture through adding values like teamwork, caring for the customer the most, downsizing, delaying, de-jobbing, autonomous work groups and deleting culture values like bureaucracy, authoritarian styles, treating efficient and inefficient employees differently and the like.

(F) ORGANISATIONAL EFFECTIVENESS

Chief Executives of many organisations, today claim that the goal of their organisations is to achieve excellence and effectiveness in many areas. CEOs set such goals due to the global challenges and competitiveness consequent upon globalisation. The organisations cannot live for a long time and grow steadily unless otherwise, they perform effectively in multiple areas including: customer service, employee management, maintaining close relations with the market intermediaries, input suppliers, bankers, collaborators and other stakeholders. The ineffective organisations do not exist and disappear very soon. Mafatlal, Binny, GRS Finance, Kurd Bank Limited, Global Foods are some of the non-existing companies. In fact many financial companies, merchant banking companies, mutual fund companies which were started during the finance boom of 1992-94 died before they grew. Similarly, many dot.com companies which were started during 1999-2001 also disappeared overnight.

Closure of the organisations costs a lot of national resources and hinders the economic growth of the economies. As such, the CEOs set the goal of achieving organisational effectiveness. The Manager of Hindustan Lever Limited (HLL) focused on one of the objectives of his company: "we want to run our organisation most effectively."

Having discussed why the organisations want to be effective, we shall now discuss the concept of organisational effectiveness.

Meaning

Organisational effectiveness is the degree to which organisation realizes its goals.

Though we use the term 'organisational effectiveness' more often, it is rather difficult to define the term precisely. This is because, the finance manager equates effectiveness with return on investment or market capitalization while the marketing manager equates effectiveness with increase in sales. The human resources managers prefers to mean effectiveness with employee satisfaction while Research and Development Managers mean effectiveness to innovations. However, there are certain comprehensive definitions on effectiveness.

According to Amitai Etizioni, effectiveness is "the degree to which organisation realizes its goals."[18]

Paul E.Mott defines effectiveness as, "the ability of an organisation to mobilize its centres of power for action-production and adaptation."[19]

Organisational effectiveness "is the extent to which an organisation, given certain resources and means, achieves its objectives without placing undue strain on its members."[20]

Thus, organisational effectiveness is more concerned with the achievement of organisational objectives. The term efficiency is used quite closely to effectiveness.

Effectiveness vs Efficiency

Effectiveness is studied through: goal, functional, system and behavioural approach

Efficiency is doing the things right and effectiveness is doing the right things. In other words, efficiency is the ratio between input and output. It is also termed as *productivity*. Efficiency is producing maximum output with a unit of input or reducing the input to produce the same level of output.

For example, e-business has more opportunities and fewer threats. Then, starting the e-business firm is effectiveness and performing maximum operations by the e-business firm with the minimum resources is efficiency.

The firm to be successful initially should be effective and it should be efficient to be successful in the long-run. In fact, effectiveness of the organisation also contributes for its long-run success. Thus, effectiveness refers to the achievement of organisational goals by performing functions and using resources. Therefore, organisational effectiveness can be studied through:

- Goal Approach
- Functional Approach
- Systems Resource Approach
- The Strategic Constituencies Approach
- Behavioural Approach

(1) Goal Approach

Organisational theorists believe that organisational effectiveness depends upon the degree of achievement of organisational goals. This approach is built on two assumptions, *viz.,*

- The complex organisations strive for their ultimate goal and
- Ultimate goal can be identified and progress of achievement of the goal can be measured.

Effectiveness, according to the goal approach is:

- Profit-maximisation
- Productivity maximisation
- Maximum employee morale
- Providing efficient service
- Maximisation of sales revenue
- High employee job satisfaction.

Campbell included a long list of factors to denote organisational effectiveness. Some of the factors include:

- Quality
- Profit/Return
- Utilisation of environment
- Motivation
- Productivity
- Stability
- Accidents
- Satisfaction.
- Readiness
- Turnover
- Morale

Bernad Bass suggests that an organisation should be evaluated in terms of:

- The degree to which it is productive, profitable, self maintaining, etc.;
- The degree to which it is valuable to its members; and
- The degree to which it and its members are of value to society.[21]

But, the organisations in recent times have set the goals like customer relationship, superior customer service, superior quality, superior delivery and superior guarantee, earning per share, sales and market capitalisation. The second approach to study organisational effectiveness is functional approach.

(2) Functional Approach

The organisation, under this approach, formulates its activities or functions to be performed based on the requirements of the society in which it operates. The goals of the organisation, in turn, are formulated based on the functions. This approach is expected to contribute to solve the social problems and to the attainment of organisational goals. Organisation's effectiveness is evaluated by comparing the individuals and groups with each other and the contribution of the organsiation to the values and interest of its members. Thus, under this system, the organisation's effectiveness is evaluated in terms of its contribution to others rather than for itself.

The third approach to study the organisaitonal effectiveness is *systems approach.*

(3) Systems Approach

A system is a set of interrelated but separate parts working towards a common purpose. The arrangement of elements must be orderly and there must be proper communication facilitating interaction between the elements and finally the interaction should lead to achieve a common goal.

Open system has flows of information, materials and energy. These enter the system from the environment as inputs, undergo transformation process within the system (like production and operation process) and exit the system as output (like goods and services).

The interdependence between organisation and its environment is in the form of input-output transactions. Organisation through its interaction and interdependency with the environment provides those goods and services which are needed and/or desired by the society. Further, the organisations utilise the society's resources.

The effectiveness of the organisation depends upon how exactly it selects the environmental opportunities, products, services how accurately it selects the best sources of inputs and how efficiently it transforms the inputs into output.

(4) The Strategic Constituencies Approach

With the increasing significance of strategic management, strategic constituencies approach to organisational effectiveness has emerged. Under this approach, the organisation is expected to interact and be interdependent with its relevant environment. In other words, the organisation understands the environmental opportunities, selects the appropriate product/services and provides the same to environment. In addition, the organisation draws inputs from the relevant environment. The major difference between this approach and the systems approach is that the latter deals with the total environment whereas the former deals with the relevant environment only.

Thus, under this approach, the effectiveness of the organisation depends on how best it draws the inputs, how efficiently it converts inputs into output and how appropriately it meets the needs of the relevant environment.

(5) Behavioural Approach to Organisation Effectiveness

This approach recognises the significance of human resources in an organisation and its contribution to the organisational effectiveness. In fact, the success or failure of an organisation depends upon the quality of human resources it possesses. The appropriate human behaviour makes the employee

- understand organisational goals, adjust the individual goals with the organisational goals and commits to it,
- integrate individual goals with organisational goals as latter are superior to the former,
- exert the individual resources and skills to the attainment of organisational goals.

Thus, the effectiveness of the organisation depends upon how exactly individual employees understands the organisational goals and integrate them with their personal goals in the direction of superiority of organisational goals over individual goals. The degree of effectiveness is high where organisational goals are superior to individual goals. The degree of organisational effectivenesses is moderate where the individual goals are equal to organisational goals. The degree of organisation effectiveness is low where individual goals are superior to organisational goals.

This approach indicates that organisational effectiveness leads to individual effectivenesses. We shall now discuss the nature of organisational effectiveness.

(G) NATURE OF ORGANISATIONAL EFFECTIVENESS

Different approaches to organisational effectiveness indicate that the achievement of organisational objectives efficiently is the outcome of organisational effectiveness. But it depends on the contribution of the individual employees, groups and the total organisation.

- Individual effectiveness depends upon the employee's positive attitude, commitment to and involvement in organisational activities. Individual's contribution to organisational effectiveness depends on individual's skills, abilities, aptitude, emotions, knowledge, attitude motivation and stress.

Some individuals make phenomenal contributions to organisational effectiveness. For example, contributions of Krishna Murthy to SAIL, contributions of Thomas to Hindustan Lever Limited, contributions of Kurien to Amul, contributions of Dhirubai Ambani to Reliance and Dr. Anji Reddy to Dr. Reddy's Lab are significant.

- Employees today prefer to work along with others in order to satisfy their individual needs and achieve organisational goals through the impact of synergy. Consequently, groups and employees in a group contribute much to the organisational success. For example, the success of ISRO in launching various satellites has been due to group efforts of scientists.

Group contribution to organisational effectiveness depends upon group cohesiveness, data, group structure, status, roles and norms.

- Effective contributions of individual employees and groups result in organisational effectiveness. Organisational effectiveness depends upon individual's contribution, group contribution in addition to environment, technology strategic choice, organisational structure, process and organisational culture.

Figure 24.2 presents the three levels of effectiveness:

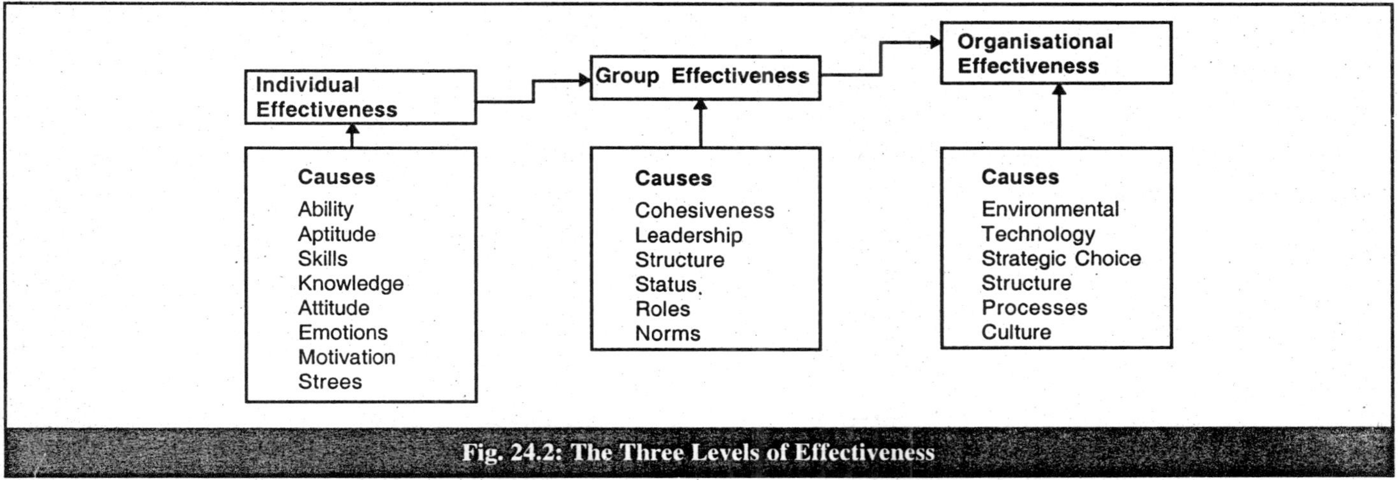

Fig. 24.2: The Three Levels of Effectiveness

(**Source:** Modified Version from James L.Gibson, *et al Organisations*, p. 28)

So far, we have discussed various approaches to and nature of organisational effectiveness. Now most of us may have the inclination to know which are the effective organisations in practice? Hence, we shall now study the effective organisations.

Effective Organisations

Organisations can be effective in terms creating an excellent climate for work. 34 Indian companies have been listed out of 2000 global effective companies for the year 2008. The top 14 companies in terms of revenue, profits, assets and market value are presented in Exhibit 24.3. The great organisational behavioural practices of these companies include: taking care of emotional well-being of its employees through counselling sessions, tracking one's own performance as the company's intranet, believing that tolerance of mistakes and an open culture help build an innovative organisation.

Exhibit 24.3 India's Top MNCs among the World's Largest 500 MNCs in 2010

Country Rank	*Company*	*Global 500 Rank*	*Revenue (in Million Dollars)*
1	Indian Oil	125	54,288
2	Reliance Industries	175	41,085
3	State Bank of India	282	28,213
4	Bharat Petroleum	307	26,596
5	Hindustan Petroleum	354	23,881
6	Tata Steel	410	21,582
7	Oil and Natural Gas	413	21,448
8	Tata Motors	442	19,501

(**Source:** http://money.cnn.com/magazines/fortune/global500/2010/countries/India.html)

KEY TERMS

- Organisational Culture
- Organisational Effectiveness
- Sub Culture
- Organisational Efficiency
- Strategic Values
- Core Culture
- Rituals
- Strong Culture
- Cultural Values
- Material Symbols
- Weak Culture
- Systems Approach

QUESTIONS

1. What is organisational culture? How do you measure it?
2. Discuss various organisational cultural concepts.
3. How do you create and maintain organisational culture?
4. Explain the different approaches to describe organisational culture.
5. How do employees learn organisational culture?
6. Discuss the emerging issues in organisational culture.
7. What is organisational effectiveness? Explain the difference between efficiency and effectiveness.
8. Discuss the nature of organisational effectiveness.

REFERENCES

1. A. S. Becker, "*Culture:A Sociological view*," Yale Review, Summer, 1982, pp. 513-527 and E. H. Schein, "*Organisational Culture and Leadership*," Jossey-Bass, San Francisco, 1985, p. 168.
2. J. C. Spender, "*Myths, Recipes and Knowledge Bases in Organisational Analysis*," 1983, p. 2.
3. J. M. Kouzes, D. F. Caldwell and B. Z. Posner, "*Organisational Culture:How it is created, maintained and changed,*" 1983.
4. George Moorhead and Ricjy W. Griffin, "*Organisational Behaviour*," AITBS Publishers and Distributors, Delhi, 1999, p. 513.
5. T. A. Timmerman, "*Do Organisations have Personalities*?" August 1996.
6. Y. Weiner, "*Forms of Value Systems:A Focus on Organisational Effectiveness and Cultural Change and Maintenance*," Academy of Management Review, October 1988, p. 536.
7. Danniel R. Denison, "*What is the Difference between Organisational Culture and Organisational Climate? A Native's point of view on a Decade of paradigm wars*,: Academy of Management Review, July 1996, pp. 619-654.
8. O. Reilly and Chatman, "*Culture as Social Control*."
9. Richard L. Osborne, "*Strategic Values:The Corporate Performance Engine*," Business Horizons, September-October 1996, pp. 41-47.
10. George Moorhead and Ricky W.Griffrin, *op.cit*., p. 518.
11. *Ibid*.
12. Richard Pascale, "*Fitting New Employees into the Company Culture*," Fortune, May 18, 1994, pp. 28-43.
13. Peters and Waterman, "*In Search of Excellence*."
14. Kenneth Labich, "*An Airline that Soars on Service*," Fortune, December 31, 1990, pp. 94-96.
15. A. M. Pettigrew, "*On Studying Organisational Cultures*," Administrative Science Quarterly, December 1979, p. 576.
16. K. Kamoche, "*Phetoric, Ritualism and Totemism in Human Resources Management*," Human Relations, April 1995, pp. 367-385.
17. Brian O. Reilly, "*Secrets of Most Admired Corporations*," Fortune, March 3, 1997,pp. 60-64.
18. Amitai Etizioni, "*Modern Organisation*," Prentice Hall, Englewood Cliffs, 1964, p. 8.
19. Paul E. Mott, "*Characteristics of Effective Organisations*," Harper, New York, 1972, p. 17.
20. Basil Georgopolous and Arnold S. Tannenbaum, "*A Study of Organisational Effectiveness*," American Sociological Review, 22, 1957, pp. 535-536.
21. Bernard Bass, "*Ultimate Criteria of Organisational Worth*," Personnel Psychology, 3, 1952, pp. 157-173.

CHAPTER **25**

ORGANISATIONAL CHANGE AND DEVELOPMENT

Chapter Outline

(A) Organisational Change: Meaning and Types
(B) Technology and Change
(C) Resistance to Change vs. Inviting Change: Reasons
(D) Approaches to Organisational Change
(E) Planning and Implementing Change
(F) Organisation Development
(G) The OD Process
(H) OD Interventions/Techniques
— Key Terms
— Questions
— References

Learning Objectives

After studying this Chapter, you should be able to:

✓ Understand the meaning and types of organisational change;
✓ Analyse the impact of technology on organisational change;
✓ Appreciate whether the change is resisted or invited?
✓ Discuss the planning and implementing stages of organisational change;
✓ Know the meaning, characteristics and values of OD;
✓ Understand the OD process; and
✓ Appreciate the role of OD techniques in moulding employee behaviour.

(A) ORGANISATIONAL CHANGE

Organisational change: Creation of imbalance in the existent pattern/ situation

The term 'Organisational Change' implies the creation of imbalances in the existent pattern or situation. Adjustment among people, technology and structural set up is established when an organisation operates for a long time. People adjust with their jobs, working conditions, colleagues, superiors, etc. Similarly, an organisation establishes relationship in the external environment. Change requires individuals and organisations to make new adjustments. Complexity and fear of adjustment give rise to resistance and problem of change. Human resource is an important factor in the adjustments among individuals as well as between the organisation and environment, as an organisation is mostly composed of people. Individual members can resist either individually or in group.

Change could be both reactive and proactive. A proactive change has necessarily to be planned to prepare for anticipated future challenges. A reactive change may be an automatic response or a planned response to change taking place in the environment.

Types of Changes

Changes can be broadly divided into: *(i)* Work change; and *(ii)* Organisational change. Work change includes changes in machinery, working hours, methods of work, job enlargement and enrichment, job-redesign or re-engineering. Change may also be in the working hours like morning shifts, evening shifts, operation of the organisation on Sundays/holidays.

Changes relating to organisation include change in employees due to transfers, promotion, retrenchment, lay-off, restructuring or organisation, introduction of new products or services, imposition of regulation, changes in organisational goals or objectives, etc.

Reasons for Change

Changes in organisations are a must, whether brought about deliberately or unwillingly. The reasons for change are categorised as follows: Changes in business conditions, changes in Managerial Personnel, Deficiency in existing Organisational Patterns, Technological and Psychological reasons, Government Policy, size of the organisation, etc.

Response to Change

Work change does not produce direct adjustment. Instead, it operates through each employee's attitude to produce a response that is conditioned by feelings towards the change.[1] People often show this attachment to the group by receiving it in some uniform response to the change, though they individually interpret the change differently. This response makes possible some illogical action like mass walk-outs when obviously only a few people actually want to. A group develops responses in response to its members' conflicting attitudes towards change. Therefore, each pressure encourages counter pressure within the group. The net result is a self-correction mechanism to restore balance wherever change threatens. Thus, people act to establish a steady state of need fulfilment and to protect themselves from disturbances of that balance.

Every change is likely to have some cost as well as bring additional benefits to the organisations. Organisations introduce change when the benefits (additional benefits derived due to change) are relatively more than the cost (additional cost incurred due to change). Cost and benefits are not only economic but also social, psychological, environmental, etc.

(B) TECHNOLOGY AND CHANGE

Change is the order of the day. 'Change, before change changes you' and 'change or decay' are the buzz phrases of the day. The factors that force the change include: nature of the workforce, technology, economic shocks, competition, social trends and world of politics.(See Exhibit 25.1)

Exhibit 25.1 Forces for Change

Force		Examples
Nature of the workforce	:	• Cultural diversity and the need for unification • Increase in professionalisation • Increased formal education • Increased level of soft skills • Positive attitude
Technology	:	• Faster and cheaper computers • Total Quality Management • Business Process Reengineering
Economic Shocks	:	• Asian real estate collapse • Russian devaluation of the ruble • Changes in oil prices (decline $22 a barrel to $13 in the late 1990s)
Competition	:	• Global Competitors • Mergers and Acquisitions • E-business • Customer Relationship Management and Quality
Social Trends:		• C102 (Career first and others second) • Increased career orientation among young ladies
World Political System:	:	• Collapse of the Soviet Union • Opening of Markets in China and China becoming a number of WTO • Black rule of South Africa

(**Source:** Modified version from Stephen P.Robbins, "*Organisational Behaviour*", Prentice Hall of India Ltd., 2001, p. 540.)

Just as necessity is the mother of invention, competition and a host of other reasons are responsible for the rapid technological changes and innovations all over the world. As a result of these changes, technical personnel, system specialists, technical workers and machine operators are increasingly required while the demand for other categories of employees has declined. But it is found that the supply of former category of employees is less compared to the demand for the same. Hence, procurement of skilled employees and maintaining them is highly essential. Further, the changes in technology continuously demands the existing employees to upgrade their skills and knowledge.

Human resources development techniques help the employees to acquire new skills and knowledge necessary to carry out the changed duties due to upgradation of technology.

Technology is the most dramatic force shaping the destiny of people all over the world. Technology is self-reinforcing and in a big way affects society. In fact, technology reaches people through business.

It increases the expectations of the customers. It brings social change and makes social system complex.

The impact of technology on human resources is significant, direct and complex. The impact of technology on HRD is through (i) jobs becoming intellectual, (ii) need for bio-professional and multi-professional managers, (iii) change in organisation structure, (iv) TQM and (v) BPRE.

Impact of Technology: Jobs became intellectual, multi-professional, structural change, BPRE

(i) Jobs become intellectual: Enhancement of the level of the technology needs high level skills and knowledge. These high level skills and knowledge should be incorporated in the job description.

Jobs handled by semi-skilled employees are now to be handled by skilled employees. Jobs handled by the clerks yesterday are now to be handled by a computer programmer. Advanced technology degrades some employees and retrenches some employees from employment unless they are trained and developed on the application of new technology and methods.

New technology demands high level skills, knowledge and values. These aspects are incorporated in the job description. Hence, jobs become intellectual. These factors demand for development of human resources.

(ii) Need for bio-professionals and multi-professionals: Recent technological advancements changed the job descriptions. These changed job descriptions require the employees with both technical skills and marketing skills. Some jobs need the employees with technical skills, marketing skills, finance skills and human resources management skills. Thus, technology demands bio-professionals and multi-professionals. But present employees are single professionals. Development of human resources of the single professional employees is necessary to make them bio-professionals and multi-professionals.

(iii) Technology and organisational structure: Technology brings changes in the span of control, delegation of authority like delegation to individual employees or groups of employees. These changes bring changes in the present organisational structure. Further, technology results in downsizing and delayering. These factors also change the organisational structure. Technology influences the organisational structure through job redesign and change in job description and demand for new skills and knowledge from the employees. These factors invariably necessitate the development of human resources.

(iv) TQM: Total Quality Management is mostly developed based on changes in technology. Further, it is influenced by changes in methods. These factors necessitate training and development of the employees in these new areas.

(v) BPRE: Business Process Reengineering basically changes the process of the business. In other words, it changes the existing patterns of production, marketing, finance and human resources functions. It brings the business process centred around a customer's needs, preferences or needs of a project or activity. Further, this process changes the existing technology and methods. These changes influence HRD.

Technology Change with Human Face

The objective of any economic institution is to provide human welfare. Technology is brought to the people through economic institutions. Therefore, technological changes should be in compatibility with the objectives of economic institutions. In other words, technological changes should result in human welfare.

Human welfare includes satisfying unsatisfied human needs, additional and untapped human needs, reducing or minimising human inconveniences or discomforts, creation of employment opportunities at least in the long run, if not in the short run. In addition, technological advancements should not cause all types of pollution in order to provide welfare to the people. Further, technology should contribute to the reduction of gaps between the rich and poor by providing sources of income to the poor. Such technology can only provide human welfare.

Technological changes with a human face means that technology should change along with the needs, preferences and well-being of the human beings. Further, technology changes should contribute to the enhancement of economic, social and psychological needs of the people.

There are several inconsistencies between technology and human face. Advances in technology reduce jobs immediately, pollute the air, water and sound. Further, they affect the natural environment and ecological balance. Further, technological changes result in the development of certain new products which harm human health like fertilizers, pesticides and even cellular phones.

Technology also changes the culture, which sometimes may be against the cultural values. For example, introduction of some TV channels which mostly transmit western culture.

It is viewed that the objective of technological change is to create additional income sources through creating additional employment opportunities. But technological changes in reality reduce even the existing jobs.

Technological changes also result in demotion of existing employees, increase in the work load, skill requirements of the existing employees, enhance boredom and monotony. Further, technological change disturbs the existing social adjustment at the workplace.

Development of human resources continuously at all the levels in the organisations and nations help in developing the human face in the technological changes, at least, to some extent.

Change agents: Change agents foresee the possible changes in technology, product and markets, plan for modifications in the company and implement the modifications. According to Robbins, change agents are, "*persons who act as catalysts and assume the responsibility for managing change activities*." Thus, change agents are responsible for managing change activities. Change agents are employees or managers or executives of a company or outside management consultants.

The activities of change agents include:

- Changing organizational structure,
- Changing technology,
- Changing the physical setting, and
- Changing people.

Changing organizational structure: Change agents introduce changes in the existing organizational structure. These changes include selecting a new approach of organization design like team structure, empowerment, open and flexible structure. In addition, change agents introduce matrix structures, flat structure and simple and dynamic structure.

Changing technology: Change agents introduce new innovative technology equipment, tools, machines, operating methods, new ideas, new knowledge, etc. Under the competitive environment, automation and information technology based techniques include Business Process Reengineering, Supply Chain Management and Enterprise Resource Planning. The change agents, in recent times, implement these new techniques.

Changing the physical setting: Change agents also introduce changes in physical lay-out of the factory, office, stores, space configurations, furniture based on ergonimics, decorations and colour.

Changing people: Change agents play a significant role in changing the attitudes, values, norms, aptitude, behaviour, leadership skills, team building skills, openness, communication abilities, problem solving abilities, etc.

Change agents foresee possible changes

(C) RESISTANCE TO CHANGE VS. INVITING CHANGE

Employees, in the past, used to resist the change

The basic problem in the management to change is the study of causes of resistance to change. Despite the fact that change is a persistent phenomenon, it is a common experience that employees resist change whether in the context of their pattern of life or in the context of their situation in the organisation. The best example is resistance of employees to computerisation. Change and type require readjustment. 'Man always fears the unknown, and a change represents the unknown.'

Reasons for Resistance

Some of the important reasons for resistance to change are as follows:

(a) Economic Reasons: Economic reasons for resistance are classified into three groups. They are:

1. Fear of Reduction in Employment: Due to the change in technology, methods of work, quantity or quality of work etc. This fear leads to resistance to change on the part of people. Opposition to automation is an example to it.

2. Fear of Demotion: Employees may fear that they may be demoted if they do not possess the new skills required for their jobs, after the introduction of change. Hence, they prefer 'status quo.'

3. Fear of Workload: Change in work technology and methods may lead to the fear that workload will be increased while there will not be any corresponding increase in their salaries and benefits. This feeling creates resistance to change.

(b) Personal Reasons: Personal reasons for resistance are also divided into three classes. They are:

1. Need for Training: If change in technology and work organisation necessitates training and re-learning on the part of employees, it may lead to resistance, as all do not like to go for refresher and retraining courses off and on.

2. Boredom and Monotony: If the proposed change is expected to lead to greater specialisation resulting in boredom and monotony, it may also be resisted by employees.

3. No Participation in Change: Some employees resist any change as they are critical of the situation and they are not being given any part in decision-making process for change. When they do not understand fully the implications of change, they resist it.

(c) Social Reasons: Social reasons for resistance are also classified into three groups. They are:

1. Need for New Social Adjustment: And organisational change requires new social adjustment with the group, work situation and new boss, etc. All individuals are not ready to accept this challenge. Some people refuse transfers and promotions for this reason only, as they will have to break their present social ties.

2. Taking Change as Imposed from Outside: Some employees take any change as imposed from outside upon them.

3. Other Considerations: Some employees may consider that every change brought about is for the benefit of the organisation only and not for them, their fellow workers or even the general public. Hence, they resist the change.

Resistance from the Side of Managers

It is not a common fact that change is always resisted by the employees only. Managers also resist change sometimes. Any change sets in new responsibilities and imposes new tension, stress and strains over them is normally resisted by managers. The feeling of uncertainty, whether they will be able to handle new circumstances successfully or not, motivates them to resist.

Inviting Change

First develop the employees, they in turn invite the change

Contrary to the classical belief that employee resists change; the management particularly the sun-rising industry invites change. This dramatic change is based on the thesis that *'first develop the employees, the developed employees invite change'*. In fact, trained and developed employees in some organizations started demanding the managements to introduce change in the form of new technology, entering into new markets, diversifying into new businesses and the like. Now, we shall discuss the conditions responsible for the dramatic change in the employees' attitudes towards change management.

Conditions Favouring Change Management

The following conditions brought paradigm shifts from resisting change to inviting the change:

- **Competition owing to globalisation:** Increased competition consequent upon globalization among multinational companies (MNCs), national companies and local companies led to the closure of most of the local companies, decline in the business volume of the national companies and business shocks to the MNCs. This competition led to the loss of jobs of some employees permanently, retrenchment of some employees, career shifts of some employees to a lower remunerative careers. Consequently, the proactive employees unlearned the attitude of resisting the change and learned that change is inevitable.
- **Information technology:** Information technology as well as computerization brought significant shifts in the manner of doing activities. Most of the jobs hither to be performed by manual labour are replaced by computers. The middle-level and coordinating jobs are now automatically performed by online, intra-net and internet facilities. Thus, information technology and computerisation have replaced certain jobs. Employees realized that the shifts in information technology and consequent changes in the jobs are more welcome as they brought most desirable changes even in their day to day life. In fact, society also started treating those employees without computer operating skills as backward. These shifts changed the employees' attitude towards change.
- **Declining role of trade unions:** The membership and activities of trade unions across the globe including India have been on declining trend after globalization. This trend is mostly due to change in the attitude of employees towards the need for membership in trade unions. Further the governments which were supporting trade unions in the process of protecting the interests of weak employees started showing deaf ear. In addition, trade union leaders also realized that organizations basically exist for their profit and they earn the profit from the customers, and as such protecting the customer's interest is the basic responsibility of every one in the company. These developments reduced the role and significance of trade unions, which were championing the cause of resisting the change introduced by managements in the past.
- **Growth in technology:** Changes in technology during 1990s and 2000s has been dramatic compared to the past. The growing competition, consequent upon globalization has been forcing the companies to adapt the latest technology. Organizations with outdated technology were being driven out of the market. So, employees realized that organizations adapt latest technologies in the best and the larger interest of the total company including the employees. So, employees started viewing the change as most desirable one even from their own long-run interest.
- **Cases of closure of companies:** Most of the local companies were closed immediately after globalization due to their inability in withstanding the stiff competition of the MNCs on the grounds of product design, product quality, and price and customer service. This

situation was mostly due to outdated technology and systems of the local companies. Consequently, employees of these companies became jobless. Employees of the remaining organizations learned from the bitter experiences of employees of closed firms and changed their attitude towards the changing situations.

- **Change in organizational attitude towards training and training expenditure:** Most of the organizations in the past used to treat training as a cost and training would not contribute to the organizational growth. They used to train the employees when it was inevitable and that too after introducing new technology or any other change. But, business organizations, after globalization realized that expenditure on training are an investment and that too as an essential investment.
- **Train employees first, then the trained employees bring change:** Business organizations, of late learnt by practice that, if the company train and develop employees, quite before the introduction of technology, systems and methods, the developed employees would be eager to apply the knowledge and skills they learnt and acquired. Therefore, such employees invite change or demand management to implement change for the better.

These factors changed the belief that employees resist change and created the view that employees invite change. In fact, information technology industry develops the employees first and then introduces the change. Therefore, this industry did not experience the employee resistance and rather enjoyed the employee cooperation for the introduction of change.

(D) APPROACHES TO ORGANISATIONAL CHANGE

Management is said to be an agent of change. It means that management has to introduce change successfully in its organisation. It has to overcome the resistance and make it a successful venture. The management must realise that resistance to change is basically a human problem, though on surface, it may appear to be related to the technical aspect of change. So, it must be tackled in a human and social manner. Management has to take the following steps to implement the change successfully.

1. Participation of employees: Before introducing any change, the employees should be fully consulted and they must be made a party to any such decision. The meaning and purpose of the change must be fully communicated to those who will be affected by it. Enough time should be allowed for discussion, and pros and cons of the change should be explained, in detail, to employees.

2. Planning for change: Before implementing any change, the management should plan for it. Employees should get an opportunity to participate both in planning the change and installing it. This will help the group of the affected employees to recognise the need for change and thus prepare them for receiving it without any fear.

3. Protecting employees' interests: Management should ensure that employees are protected from economic loss, loss in status or personal dignity. If those things are protected, the degree of resistance to change will be at the lowest ebb.

4. Group dynamics: Group dynamics refers to the everchanging interactions and adjustments in the mutual perceptions and relationships among members of the groups. Such group interactions are the most powerful instruments which facilitate or inhibit adaptation to change. Adaptation is a team activity which requires conformity to the new group norms, moves, traditions and work patterns. If these could be positivity articulated by management the results are likely to be more successful and durable.

5. Cautions and slow introduction: The management should not introduce any change suddenly and abruptly. It must be an objective for the management to build in the organisation an awareness of change and an ability to forecast it, and also to construct an attitude of welcoming change. Change must be introduced in sequential parts, if possible, the results must be reviewed, and required adjustments must be made in it.

6. Positive motion: The management should use the policy of positive motivation to counteract negative resistance. It should be the attempt of the management to make the job easier and less exerting. The management should impart proper training to its employees in new techniques and work knowledge, etc. The leadership styles should also be supportive and human oriented. This policy will also bring down the resistance to change.

7. Sharing the benefits of change: Any change whether technical, social or economic will be least resisted by the employees if the management permits the employees to share benefits which arise out of the change. So, the management must see that employees are not only assured of it, they are given due advantage of it as well.

8. Training and development: Management should plan for change. Based on the change plan, the job should be redesigned. Management should train the employees before-hand and prepare the employees to invite change. Normally, trained and developed employees will not resist change as they cannot keep quiet with enriched skill and knowledge.

9. Career planning and development: Organisation on the basis of change plans and redesigned jobs should plan for careers of employees, possibilities to move the employees to the higher levels and develop them. The developed employees for future careers demand the management to implement change.

10. Organisation Development: Organisation development aims at moulding and development of employees in the psychological and behavioural areas with a view to achieve organisational effectiveness. Employees with enriched behaviours welcome the change.

Principles of Change

Management should also follow the undermentioned principles of change:

(1) Understanding the change itself, its purpose, its benefits and then making them familiarise to the employees.

(2) Estimating the reasons for the possible resistance to change and preparing to allay their fears.

(3) Mindful of channels of authority.

(4) Preparedness for all the questions, aspersions and criticism.

(5) Listening to the suggestions and criticism of employees and incorporating them in the scheme as far as possible.

(6) Creating interest in employees, convincing them and preparing them to accept the change.

(7) Keeping in touch with the process of change.

(E) PLANNING AND IMPLEMENTING CHANGE

Management is often called a 'change agent' as its role is to initiate the change, and help make it work successfully. Employees' support is most essential in implementing the change successfully as they are at the helm of affairs, and the management is only an agent of change. Change typically involves three steps, viz., unfreezing, changing and re-freezing. Unfreezing means that old ideas and practices need to be cast aside so that new ones can be learnt. Change is the step in which the new ideas and practices are learnt so that an employee can think and perform in terms of new ways. Refreezing means that what has been learnt is integrated into actual practice.

Institutionalisation, internalisation of change

Implementation is the institutionalisation and internalisation of a change after it has been accepted by an organisation and a decision has been taken to accept and make it part of the ongoing activity. Implementation may be seen as a multidimensional process. The end result of implementation is the institutionalisation and stabilisation of change. Institutionalisation is absorbing the change permanent try and making it an integral part of organisation and internalisation means stabilisation of the change. The implementation process should start with planning. The three important stages of implementation of change process (see Fig. 25.1) are: *(i)* Monitoring the change; *(ii)* Taking action in relation to the change; and *(iii)* Making necessary adjustments in the programme accepted for implementation.[2]

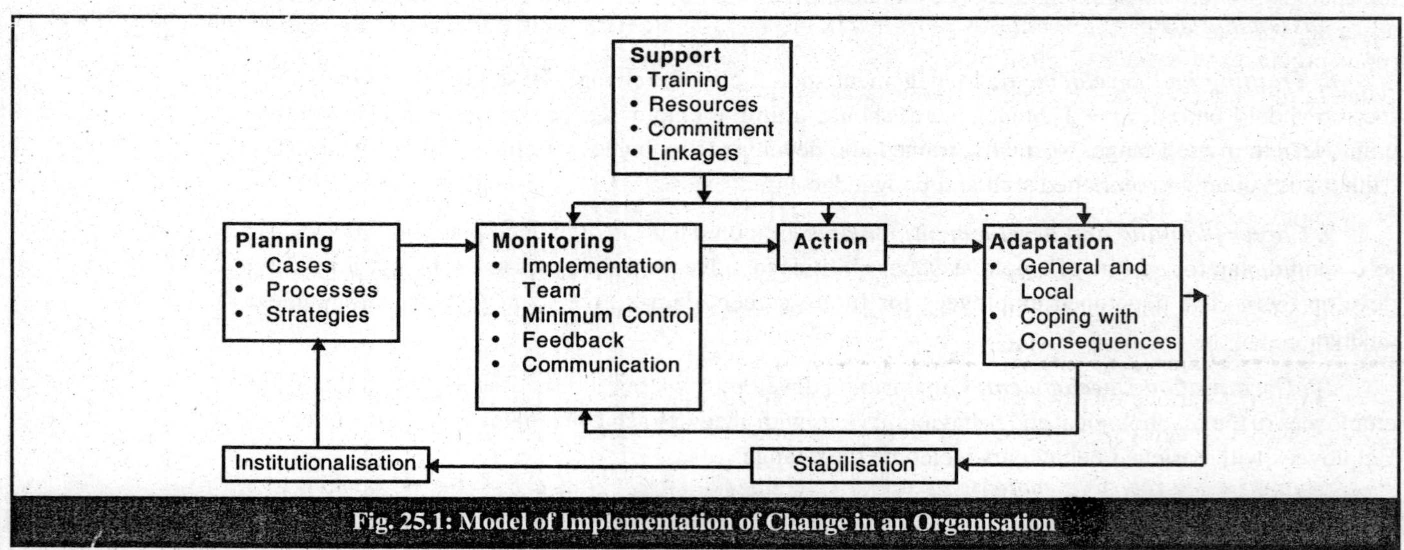

Fig. 25.1: Model of Implementation of Change in an Organisation

Planning: The main objective of planning, is to have an overall understanding of the nature of implementation. Planning process refers to determining in advance the entire process of implementation of change phasing. Planning may be focused on phasing. Phasing may be either temporal (in terms of time) or spatial (in terms of various units or the locations of the organisation).

Processes: Various processes involved in implementation should be decided in advance. Various stages of the process include: initiation, motivation, diagnosis, information collection, deliberation, action proposal, implementation and stabilisation. Attention should be paid to the process of collaboration, increasing the capability of the organisation to face the problems of change, establishing the norms and values.

Strategies: Management should formulate various strategies for implementation. These strategies should focus on taking outsider's help, change agent, designing permanent organisational structures, unit/location of the organisation to be selected for initial process, openness with the environment, etc.

Monitoring: It is the process of "routine periodic measurement of programme inputs, activities and outputs undertaken during programme implementation. Monitoring is normally concerned with the procurement, delivery and utilisation of programme resources, adherence to work schedules or progress made in the production of outputs." Monitoring is essential to make implementation effective. Monitoring/control is to ensure that a plan proceeds according to the original design. A broader group of people should be involved in monitoring function. An independent team without having interest in change may be entrusted with the task. This team may have a continuous status.

Implementation team: A broad based task group of implementation should be set-up to look after the implementation of the change programme and monitor such programme. HRD department of the organisation may be asked to take up this responsibility.

Minimum control: Controls should be minimum in order to make the monitoring effective. It is a delicate issue. On one hand, it is a control function and on the other it also attempts to develop new norms of creativity, diversity and experimentation. Key roles involved in the implementation process are task force, implementation team, chief implement or counterpart consultant and corporate management.

Review and feedback: Implementation requires reviewing various process and provide feedback. It involves getting data information and experiences and providing feedback to the people on how they are implementing compared to the design and plans.

Dissemination of information: The data, information and experiences collected in the various units/processes of the organisation may be provided to all the parties of change implementation with a view to reinforce a sense of success amongst various people.

Action: Action covers all the minute details of what is to be implemented at different stages. This process involves various phases and steps for people and various group tasks in relation to change programme.

Adaptation: Adaptation is the combination of two main criteria of effectiveness of implementation. Adaptation may be both general in the sense that some modifications may be made in the original plan and some may be developed at later stage.

Support: Various types of support from all concerned will be required for the implementation of change. Main agencies which render the necessary support are:

Human resource development: Effective implementation of change requires new and varied technical, managerial and behavioural skills and knowledge. Human Resource Development department can contribute for the enhancement of these skills through training, executive development and organisation development programmes.

Resources: Implementation requires support in the form of various fields like financial, human resources, technological etc.

Linkages: Support may also be required in terms of building linkages both with external experts, various external agencies and internal departments. Linkage among departments, implementation teams, line management and top management is essential.

To management commitment: The most important aspect of support essential for implementing change is the support and commitment of top management. Top management should involve itself in the process of change implementation, encourage the implementation team, provide all types of resources.[3]

Management has to get the support from employees through the following means: *(a)* Encouraging and using group force; *(b)* Development of leadership for change; *(c)* Encouraging participation and sharing views; *(d)* Maintenance of employees security; *(e)* Effective communication; *(f)* Participation and working with the unions; *(g)* Working with the total system of the organisation which requires adopting useful and necessary changes; *(h)* Changing by evolution but not by revolution; *(i)* Adopting the change with adequate attention to human relations; *and (j)* Identifying and taking care of post-change problems.

(F) ORGANISATION DEVELOPMENT

Change and Development

As discussed earlier change is a must. Change occurs not only in technology, marketing but also in human values, attitudes, relationships, social system, organisational climate, culture, etc. Hence, all are aware of and are concerned with change. Changes in values, etc., have tremendous impact on organisation as changes in technology and marketing. As such the management has to meet the challenges of changes. Management can effectively meet these challenges through a systematic and planned change effort. Organisation Development (OD) has emerged to help the planned change for organisational effectiveness.[4] Thus, it is said that the organisation development is the modern approach to management of change and human resource development. Organisation Development (OD) concentrates on people dimensions like norms, values, attitudes, relationships, organisational climate, etc.

History of Organisation Development

Douglas McGregor served as resource person to help Union Carbide Corporation to create an OD capability where OD department was set up in 1962. French and Bell who have done most of the work on OD feel that laboratory training and survey feedback are the main stems of OD. Sensitivity training programmes were conducted to managers under the OD movement. OD is still developing and evolving.

What is OD?

Change behaviour of employees through applied behavioural science techniques

Different managers view differently and various authors have given a variety of definitions about OD. Warren G. Bennis defines OD as "a complex educational strategy intended to change the beliefs, attitudes, values and structure of organisations so that they can better adapt to new technologies, markets and challenges and the dizzying rate of change itself."[5]

Dale S. Beach defined OD as "a complex educational strategy designed to increase organisational effectiveness and wealth through planned intervention by a consultant using theory and techniques of applied behavioural service."[6]

Wendell L. French and Cecil H. Bell Jr. defined OD as "a long-range effort to improve an organisation's problem solving and renewal processes, particularly through a more effective and collaborative management of organisation culture — with special emphasis on the culture of formal work teams — with the assistance of a change agent, or a catalyst and the use of the theory and technology of applied behaviour science, including action research."[7]

It is clear from these definitions that OD has emerged in response to needs — primarily, because of the inadequacy of training and executive development programmes and secondly, due to fast pace of change itself. It is further clear from these definitions that:

(1) OD is broader concept and includes management development and training as its sub-systems as the primary objective of OD is to change the nature of total organisation.

(2) OD is not a separate discipline but it heavily draws from other disciplines like psychology, sociology, anthropology, etc.

(3) OD is based upon theory and research.

(4) OD is concerned with people for increasing organisational effectiveness.

(5) OD is also concerned with improving organisational climate and culture.

Characteristics of OD

An indepth study of the definitions of OD indicates the following characteristics of OD. They are:

(1) OD focusses on the whole organisation to assure that all parts of the organisation are well co-ordinated.

(2) OD is concerned with the interaction and interrelation among its various sub-systems as it utilises systems model.

(3) OD used one or more change agents who stimulate and co-ordinate the change within a group. Some organisations employ the change agents while some others have their own change agents within their organisation.

(4) OD is concerned with problem-solving approach as it seeks to solve the problems rather than merely discussing them.

(5) OD emphasises learning by experience. As such participants are expected to learn by experience.

(6) OD utilises group processes like group discussions, intergroup conflicts, collaboration and cooperation.

(7) OD provides feedback data and information to the participants.

(8) OD is a long-term approach to improve the overall organisational effectiveness.

(9) OD is research based as most of its interventions are based on research findings.

Values of OD Movement

OD movement is composed of various professionals like behavioural researchers, consultants, business executives, etc. There are a number of values to these professions. The important among them are:

People are basically good

(1) People are basically good: OD movement believes the assumptions of Theory of Y of McGregor. As such it emphasises supportive and relative opportunities for growth. Self-control and personal responsibility are to be provided to the employees in an organisation rather than using controls and punishments.

(2) Need for confirmation and support: Every new employee needs confirmation and support of others. He is conditioned to believe that no 'news is good news' as he may be afraid of the negative aspects of support and security. Hence, when the new employee is appointed he is to be taken into confidence, invited to work place and into association for discussion on his personal and work related issues in private meetings.

(3) Accepting differences among people: People have different backgrounds, experiences, opinions and ideas, viewpoints and personality. Organisation is benefited by the differences in backgrounds, personality and viewpoints of employees.

(4) Expressing feelings and emotions: Allowing the people to be rational, to express their feelings, sentiments, emotion, anger or tenderness. Full range of expression of feelings result in high motivation, commitment, and creative ability. The people may be allowed to exhibit their anger, emotion and exhilaration.

(5) Authenticity, openness and directness: Most of the people exhibit duplicity, tell half-truths and mask their true motives. Such behaviour inhibits the growth of the individuals and productivity as the resources are misused in this process. Honesty and directness enable people to put their energies into the real problems and improve effectiveness.

(6) Fostering cooperation: Some executives adopt the rule of divide and manage. Thus, they believe in win-lose competition for various employee benefits. This style results in wastage of human and other resources. Hence, executives should create and develop cooperation among employees for effectiveness.

(7) Giving attention: Giving attention to process activities not only at the time of assigning activities and bringing relations among employees but also at the later stages.

(8) Confronting conflict: Some executives suppress the conflict. But it has its long-run effect on employee morale. Hence, identifying the root causes of the problem and working out a satisfactory solution rather than suppressing the conflict are needed.[8]

OD Objectives

Organisation development efforts broadly aim at improving the organisational effectiveness and job satisfaction of the employees. These aims can be attained by humanising the organisations and encouraging the personal growth of individual employees. Specifically, the OD Objectives are:

(1) To increase openness of communication among people.

(2) To increase commitment, self-direction and self-control.

(3) To encourage the people who are at the helm of affairs or close to the point of actual action to make the decisions regarding their issues through collaborative effort.

(4) To involve the members in the process of analysis and implementation.[9]

(5) To encourage confrontation regarding organisational problems with a view to arriving at effective decisions.

(6) To enhance personal enthusiasm and satisfaction levels.

(7) To increase the level of trust and support among employees.

(8) To develop strategic solutions to problems with higher frequency.

(9) To increase the level of individual and group responsibility in planning and execution.[10]

(G) THE OD PROCESS

The OD process is complicated and it takes long time to complete the process. It takes minimum of one year and sometimes continues indefinitely. There are different approaches to OD process but the typical process consists of seven steps, viz., initial diagnosis, data collection, data feedback and confrontation, action planning and problem solving, team building, intergroup development and evaluation and follow-up.[11]

(1) Initial diagnosis: If executives recognise that there are inadequacies within organisation which can be corrected by OD activities, it is necessary to find out the professional and competent people within the organisation to plan and execute OD activities. If competent people are not available within the organisation the services of the outside consultants to help in diagnosing the problem and developing OD activities are to be taken. The consultants adopt various methods including interviews, questionnaires, direct observation, analysis of documents and reports for diagnosing the problem.

(2) Data collection: Survey method is used to collect the data and information for determining organisational climate and identifying the behavioural problems.

(3) Data feedback and confrontation: Data collected are analysed and reviewed by various work groups formed from this purpose in order to mediate in the areas of disagreement or confrontation of ideas or opinions and to establish priorities.

(4) Selection and design of interventions: The interventions are the planned activities that are introduced into the system to accomplish desired changes and improvements. At this stage the suitable interventions are to be selected and designed.

(5) Implementation of intervention: The selected intervention should be implemented. Intervention may take the form of workshops, feedback of data to the participants, group discussions, written exercises, on-the-job activities, redesign of control system, etc. Interventions are to be implemented steadily as the process is not a "one-shot, quick cure" for organisational malady. But it achieves real and lasting change in the attitudes and behaviour of employees.

(6) Action planning and problem solving: Groups prepare recommendations and specific action planning to solve the specific and identified problems by using data collected.

(7) Team building: The consultants encourage the employees throughout the process to form into groups and teams by explaining the advantages of the teams in the OD process, by arranging joint meetings with the managers, subordinates, etc.

(8) Intergroup development: The consultants encourage the intergroup meetings, interaction etc., after the formation of groups/teams.

(9) Evaluation and follow-up: The organisation evaluates the OD programmes, find out their utility, develop the programmes further for correcting the deviations and/or improved results. The consultants help the organisation in this respect.

All the steps in the OD processes should be followed by the organisation in order to derive full range of OD benefits.

(H) OD INTERVENTIONS/TECHNIQUES

OD techniques aim at understanding and modifying behaviour

Organisation development intervention techniques are the methods created by OD professionals and others. Single organisation or consultant cannot use all the interventions. They use these interventions depending upon the need or requirement. The most important interventions are: Survey feedback, process consultation, sensitivity training, the managerial grid, goal setting and planning, team building and management by objectives. Other interventions are job enrichment, changes in organisational structure and participative management and quality circles.

(1) Survey feedback: This intervention provides data and information to the managers. Attitudes of employees about wage level, and structure, hours of work, working conditions and relations are collected and the results are supplied to top executive teams. These teams analyse the data, find out the problems, evaluate the results and develop the means to correct the problems identified. The teams are formed with the employees at all levels in the organisation hierarchy, i.e., from rank and file to the top level.

(2) Process consultation: Under this method, the process consultant meets the members of department in work teams, observes their interactions, problem identification skills, problem solving procedures, etc. He feeds back the team with the information collected through observation, coaches and counsels individuals and groups in moulding their behaviour.

(3) Goal setting and planning: Each division in an organisation or branch/zonal office sets the goals or formulates the plans relating to profitability, markets share, human resources productivity,

etc. These goals are sent to the top management, which in turn sends them back to the divisions/zones/ branches after modifications. A set of organisation-wide goals thus emerge thereafter.

(4) Managerial grid: Industrial psychologists Blake and Mouton developed the managerial grid on the basis of the Ohio State Study. The managerial grid identifies a range of management behaviour based on the different ways that how production/service-oriented and employee-oriented states interact with each other. Different styles of leadership are shown in the Fig. 25.2. The style 1-1 is impoverished management — low concern for both people and production. This Style is also called *laissez faire* management. Style 1-9 management is country club-management — high concern for employees, but low concern for production. Style 9-1 management is task or authoritarian-oriented high concern for production and low concern for employees, Style 5-5 is middle of the road management — an intermediate amount of concern for both production and employees. Style 9-9 management is team-oriented management — a high concern for both production and employees. Blake and Mouton strongly argue that the 9-9 management style is most effective type of leadership style. Hence, it is felt that the management may adopt 9-9 style, for effective goal attainment.

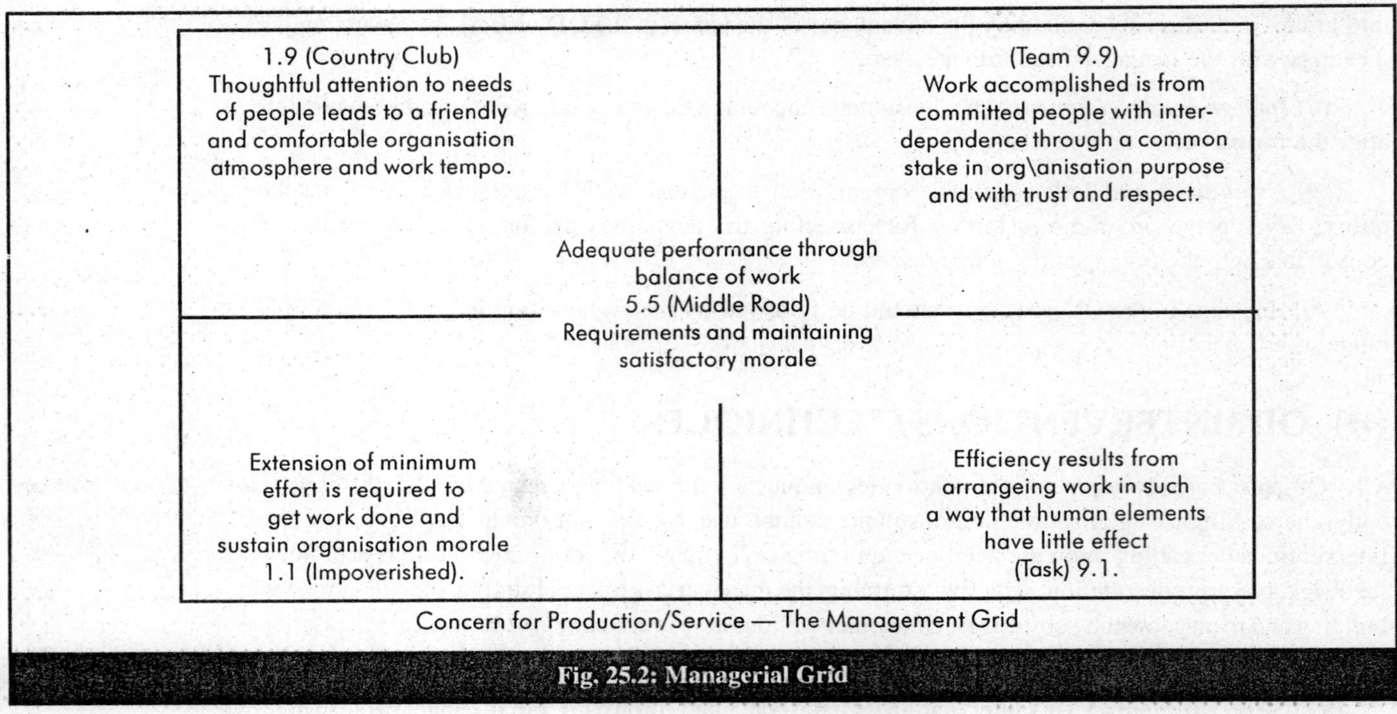

Fig. 25.2: Managerial Grid

Managerial grid is also called as instrumental laboratory training as it is a structured version of laboratory training. It consists of individual and group exercises with a view to developing awareness of individual managerial style, interpersonal competence and group effectiveness. Thus, grid training is directly related to the leadership styles. The managerial grid focuses on the observations of behaviour in exercises specifically related to work.[12] Participants in this training are encouraged and helped to appraise their own managerial style.

Management by Objectives

Management by objectives (MBO) is a successful philosophy of management. It replaces the traditional philosophy of "management by domination." It was popularised as an approach to planning by Peter F. Drucker in 1954 in his famous book *The Practice of Management.* Since that time it has acquired momentum and of late it has become a movement.

MBO: Managers and subordinates work together

There are many MBO type programmes like "management by results", "goals management", "work planning and review" "goals and controls", "appraising by results." These programmes are similar in nature[13] in spite of the difference in names.

According to Howell, the concept of MBO has passed through different stages of management development, *viz.*:

1. MBO for performance appraisal;
2. MBO for integrating the individuals with the organisation; and
3. MBO for long range planning.[14]

Management by objectives has been defined as "a result-centred, non-specialist, operational managerial process for the effective utilisation of material, physical and human resources of the organisation, by integrating the individual with the organisation and organisation with the environment.[15]

In other words, MBO is a process by which managers at different levels and their subordinates work together in identifying goals and establishing objectives consistent with the organisational goals and attaining them.[16] Thus, MBO is not only an aid to planning but also a motivating factor.

The Process of MBO

The steps in MBO process are summarised as follows:

(1) Preliminary Setting of Objectives at the Top:
(2) Clarification of Organisational Goals:
(3) Setting of Subordinate Objectives:
(4) Recycling of Objectives:
(5) Performance Appraisal:

Sensitivity Training

The most commonly used OD intervention is sensitivity training. It is also called laboratory training. It is called laboratory training as it is conducted by creating an experimental laboratory situation in which employees are brought together, in groups, to interact in an unstructured environment.[17] The members are encouraged to interact with new members and new individual behaviours.

The objectives of laboratory training are:

(i) To help people understand themselves better; *(ii)* To create better understanding of others; *(iii)* To gain insight into the group process; and *(iv)* To develop specific behavioural skills.

Some people never understand why they feel and act as they do and how the others feel about them. Some people are insensitive to the effects of their behaviour upon others and their orders upon subordinates. Laboratory training helps such people to understand the impact of their behaviour on others. Most of the people concentrate on what they are going to say rather than what the others are saying. This training develops the communication skills of the employers and develops them as good listeners. It also helps the participants to form into informal groups and teams and work more effectively.

Modus Operandi of Sensitivity Training

Sensitivity training provides face-to-face interaction. This training is carried out by largely unstructured groups without an agenda, leader and predetermined goals. The group is given complete

Sensitivity training: Face-to-face interaction

freedom in developing their own devices, interactions and ongoing process for interaction. Sometimes, the trainer introduces certain planned activities involving one or two professional trainers set in with each "T" group. The emphasis in this training is not upon learning specific facts but upon gaining understanding of feelings, gestures, attitudes and emotions, i.e., sensitivity to oneself and others.[18]

Another type of group is encounter group. These groups involve unstructured small group interaction under stress in a situation that requires people to become sensitive to one another's feelings in order to develop group activity. These groups seek to improve understanding of self and others, group process, culture and general behaviour skills.

Laboratory training may include role playing, intergroup competitive exercises, self-insight questionnaires, theory sessions with lectures, background readings, panel discussions and audio-visual aids in addition to 'T' groups.[19]

Team Building

Team is a group with complementary skills

Most of the laboratory training takes place among the employees of the same department. These employees work together as a team. Team building is nothing but application of various techniques of sensitivity training to the actual work groups in various departments. These work groups consist of peers and a supervisor. Laboratory techniques are also applied to short-term work teams. The technique, like laboratory training, aims at improving intergroup relations. This technique is designed to improve the ability of the employees to work together as teams.

Job Enrichment

Job enrichment: Vertical loading of the job responsibility and authority

Job enrichment as is currently practised all over the world, is a direct outgrowth of Herzberg's two-factor theory of motivation. It is therefore based on the assumption that in order to motivate workers, the job itself must provide opportunities for achievement, recognition, responsibility, advancement and growth. The basic idea is to restore to jobs the elements of interest that were taken away under the intensive specification. However, job enrichment is significantly different from horizontal loading, referred to earlier. Horizontal loading does not enrich the task. Washing dishes to begin with, then the silverware, and gradually switchover to pots and pans does no more to satisfy and provide an opportunity to grow. Under job enrichment, there is a conscious effort to build into jobs a higher sense of challenge and achievement. In a job enrichment programme, the worker decides how the job is performed, planned, and controlled, and makes more decisions concerning the entire process. The job enrichment approach to boring jobs is to give the individual employee more autonomy in that job. Employees decide how the job will be performed and receive less direct supervision on the job. Consequently, the employee receives a greater sense of accomplishment as well as more authority and responsibility, job satisfaction. This in turn contributes for better employee performance and higher productivity.

Changes in Organisational Structure

Various models or organisational structure, particularly matrix organisation, improves intergroup interaction and relations. Further, changes may be introduced in organisational structure to provide the scope for team work, group interaction and increased interpersonal relations.

Participative Management and Quality Circles

Participative management and quality circles are extension to team work. They provide for voluntary formation of groups/teams, association, interaction, etc. They encourage open discussion on various problems and arriving at a commonly agreed solutions and execution of the agreements by the members themselves.

Use of a Consultant

Top management engages a consultant or a change agent to help in establishing OD programmes when the qualified, competent and professional employees are not available within the organisation, OD professionals generally possess advanced qualifications in behavioural science and knowledge and experience in designing and conducting laboratory training programmes. The consultant examines the routine activities, provides information, helps the management in designing and administering the OD programme. He also helps and trains the members to become self-sufficient in problem solving. The consultant prepares the report and submits to the top management regarding OD policy and programmes on the basis of data and information collected by him from various sources of the organisation. He also helps the organisation in executing the OD programmes. The consultant helps much in developing the members to become more effective in dealing with one another.

Benefits of OD

Individual employees, groups/teams and the organisations are benefited by the OD programmes. The benefits of OD include performance improvements, job specification and self-change.

OD programmes contribute to the increase in the job performance of individual employees, groups and the organisation. Impact of OD can be measured by comparing the performance of controlled group with that of non-controlled group. Group performance will be enhanced much as OD emphasises on group activity.

OD programmes encourage teamwork, communication skills, cooperation, interpersonal relations, openness, etc. Employees with these changing behavioural dimensions feel happy and have a sense of satisfaction about the job and organisation.

OD programmes contribute to the change in behaviour, values, attitudes, perceptions, etc., by enabling the employees to understand about themselves and others in the group and organisation. This results in self-change of the employees.

KEY TERMS

- Organisational Change
- Organisation Development
- Consultant
- Job Enlargement
- Quality Circles
- Monitoring
- Team Building
- Managerial Grid
- MBO
- Sensitivity Training

QUESTIONS

1. What is organisation change? Explain the types and reasons for change.
2. Why do employees resist change? Give a detailed account of resistance to change.
3. Explain the steps to be taken by the management to overcome the resistance to change.
4. What is organisation development? Explain the various characteristics of OD.
5. Explain the values of OD movement and OD process.
6. Differentiate between *(a)* behavioural and non-behavioural interventions, *(c)* laboratory training and managerial grid training, and *(d)* individual training and organisation development.
7. What are the potential benefits of OD and problems with it?

8. In which of the following situations would OD tend to be most effective and why?
   (a) Teachers of a university,
   (b) Marketing executives of heavy plates and vessels industry,
   (c) Officers of a commercial bank.
9. Think of some organisation, where you have worked or of which you are a member. How can it benefit from OD? What specific OD intervention would you recommend and why?

REFERENCES

1. Keith Davis, *op. cit.*, p. 200.
2. Udai Pareek, *Implementing Change in Organisation*, in S. Chattopadyay and Udai Pareek (Ed.). *Managing Organisational Change*, Oxford & IBH Publishing Co. Pvt. Ltd., 1988, p. 72.
3. *Ibid.*, pp. 71-83.
4. Fred Luthans, *Organisational Behaviour*, McGraw Hill International Book Company, New York, 1981, p. 611.
5. Warren G. Bennis, *Organisational Development*, Addison Wiley, Reading Mass, 1969, p. 2. Quoted in Edwin B. Flippo, *op. cit.*, p. 219.
6. Dale S. Beach, *op. cit.*, p. 426.
7. Wendell L. French and Cecil H. Bell Jr. *Organisational Development*, Prentice Hall, Englewood Cliffs, N. J. 1978, p. 14.
8. Dale S. Beach. *op. cit.*, pp. 428-30.
9. *Ibid.*, p. 431.
10. Wendell L. French, *Organisation Development*, California Management Review, Winter, 1962, p. 24.
11. William B. Wrether Jr. and Keith David, *op. cit.*, p. 226.
12. Lawrence A. Klett, Robert G. Murdick, Frederick E. Schuster, *Human Resource Management*, Charles E. Merrill Publishing Co., Columbus, 1985, pp. 287-88.
13. Stephen J. Carroll Jr. Henry L. Tose Jr., *Management by Objectives*, Macmillan, New York, 1983, p. 3.
14. Howell R. H., *Management by Objectives*, Business Horizon, Jan.-Feb., 1970, Vol. 13, No. 1, pp. 41-45.
15. Chakrabarthy, S.K., *Management by Objectives*, The Macmillan Co., New Delhi, 1976, p. 5.
16. J. S. Chandan, *Modern Management*, Vikas Publishing House (P) Ltd., New Delhi, 1986, p. 28.
17. *Ibid.*, p. 289.
18. Dale S. Beach, *op. cit.*, 436.
19. *Ibid.*, p. 437.

CHAPTER **26**

STRESS MANAGEMENT

☛ Chapter Outline

(A) Introduction
(B) Causes of Stress
(C) Consequences of Disstress
(D) How to Manage Stress?
(E) Mild-Stress: Conducive for Organisational Effectiveness
— Key Terms
— Questions
— References

☛ Learning Objectives

After studying this Chapter, you should be able to:

✓ Know the meaning of stress and differences among various terms like distress, eustress, anxiety and tension;

✓ Understand the causes and consequences of stress;

✓ Discuss various measures to reduce stress caused by various factors; and

✓ Appreciate the need for and desirability of mild stress.

(A) INTRODUCTION

Stress is basically a pressure upon a person's psychological system which arises out of complexity or intensity of one's work life.

We come across the word 'Stress' everyday. Managers, financiers, government officials, administrators, politicians, students and also housewives experience stress. Stress has its effects on all walks of life. It is important to understand the nature and effects of stress so as to effectives stress management. Stress can be explained *basically as pressure upon a person's psychological system which arises out of complexity or intensity of one's work life.* Though stress basically affect a person's psychological set-up, it also, in turn, affects his/her physical and behavioural systems. The sources of stress can be individual, organisational and social.

According to Beehr and Newman, stress is "*a condition arising from the interaction of people and their jobs and characterised by changes within people that force them to deviate from their normal functioning*."[1]

Facial Expressions during Stressful Situations

Fred Luthans defines the stress as, "*an adaptive response to an external situation that results in physical, psychological and/or behavioural deviations for organisational participants*."[2]

Distress vs Eu-stress

More than often stress is viewed in negative terms. In fact the negative aspect, *i.e.,* distress is only one form of stress. But there is also positive aspect of stress which is called as **Eu-stress.**

Eu-stress: Stress caused due to sudden good news or positive aspects.

A minimum and desirable level of stress is called as **Mild stress.** Stress to the minimum extent helps the advancement and development of a person. Though severe stress causes many problems, a small amount of stress is always desirable for efficient and active work. With no stress, work life becomes a routine, a ritual without any enthusiasm on the part of employees. Stress is a natural word which cannot be perceived only in negative terms. It can be interpreted in different ways depending upon the situation.

A minimum and desirable level of stress is called as Mild-stress.

Fight vs. Flight Situation

Hans Selye, a Canadian psychologist, explains stress as a *survival trait.* He pioneered the concept '*fight or flight situation.*' To explain this concept, any living creature, when faced with a threat, tends to react in two ways, either the person faces and fights or runs away or flees from that situation. This type of situation causes tremendous stress on a person's psychological self. In the organisational context, where an employee is given a very complex and critical task to be done within a very short span of time, he may try to escape from the situation and later when it becomes inevitable, he works towards completing the given task. This type of situation causes stress as explained by Hans Selye.

Stress, Anxiety and Tension

According to *Fred Luthans*, stress is neither anxiety nor nervous tension. He made a clear distinction between these concepts. Anxiety has its effect only on the psychological system, whereas stress affects a person's physical, psychological and behavioural system. Nervous tension is only one of the results of stress.

(B) CAUSES OF STRESS

Performing almost all types of jobs inevitably causes stress, though the intensity may vary from job to job. As such, job performance depends upon effective management of stress in addition to the other factors which in turn depend upon identification of sources of stress. These sources are asunder:

Extra-organisational

These sources do not arise from work life but are from the outside world. Though they crop up from the outside world, they may not confine to an employee's social life. It may also tend to affect his work life. For example, an employee may not be able to cope up with the demands of the family with the limited finance that he earns. This causes stress to the employee. Consequently, he may not be able to concentrate on work. This may develop forgetfulness and fatigue. Sometimes, the employee may not be able to adjust with the change of place, culture, technology and social life as they may be entirely different from what he was used to. As such, he takes time to adjust with these conditions and cannot substantiate any work for this period. Other extra-organisational stressors include:

Extra-organisational stressors are the environmental factors that cause stress.

- Changing societies in terms of culture and relationships;
- Globalization and competition;
- Changes in organizations, jobs, practices, and relationships;
- Changing organization culture towards more commercialization and demand for efficiency from employees;
- Urbanisation and thereby complications in life;
- Burden of dependents;
- Increase in aging populations;
- Changing Gender Roles and increase in women employees; and
- Enhanced aspirations and demands of customers.

Organisational

Organisational stressors are presented in Exhibit 26.1.

Stress experienced in the work place may arise from role-related factors. A person in an organisation may have to play many roles, sometimes conflicting with each other. Thus, stress arises while dealing with these conflicting roles. Sometimes a person may be asked to perform many roles beyond his abilities due to absenteeism of other employees or understaffing. This type of situation mostly happens in the private sector. In such a condition, the stress arises and the person may not justify any one of the functions or roles assigned to him. Stress is also caused when a person is forced to take up a job which he does not like due to financial or other pressures. Employees also experience stress when they are forced to work in a place with poor physical conditions or with imperfect rules and regulations, pay structure and other policies and programmes. Other extra-organisational stressors include:

Organisational Stress: Stress caused due to conflicting organizational roles.

- Challenges of adjustments as well cultural fit at work places due to acquisition, amalgamation, absorption, and alliances (AAAA).
- Challenges of adjustments as well cultural fit at work places due to mergers;
- Coping up with the increased organizational demands due to expansion, diversification, and enhanced targets;
- Coping up with the increased organizational demands due to privatization, competition, and business-process reengineering, and structural changes;
- Need for utilization of higher order skills along with normal job skills consequent upon flat structures, job width and multi-skilling in organizations;
- People management has become more complex due to shifts in the demands and conveniences of employees;

- Understanding technology and operating it has become part of the job for all kinds of employees;
- Relocating offices, establishment of virtual offices/workplaces; and
- Increased career diversities.

Exhibit 26.1 Organisational Stressors

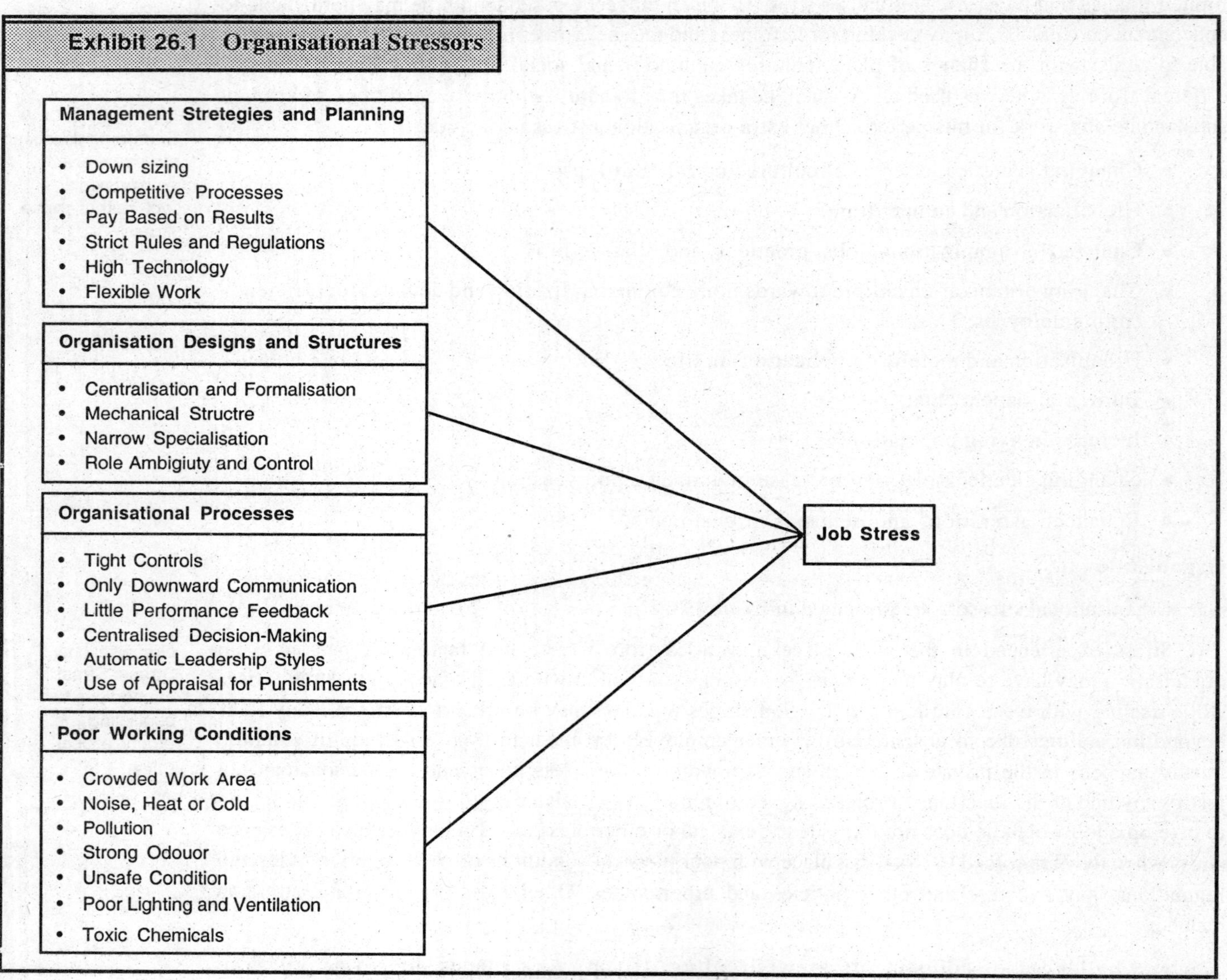

(**Source:** Modified Version from Fred Luthans, *op.cit.*, p. 333.)

Work-family imbalances: One of the important reasons for stress is excessive organizational work by leaving less time and energy to employees to concentrate on family life. Some of the highly committed employees mostly fail to give due emphasis on family life. This situation causes disturbances in the employees' family life.

Group Dynamics

Everyone in an organisation identifies himself/herself with some group or the other. Poor or unpleasant relationships with other members of this group may cause stress. Poor work relations with the superior, subordinates or peers cause stress to a person. Such relationships with the social groups outside the organisation also sometimes affect work life. Thus, group factors can be potential stressors.

Individual Factors

Individual factors like traits and characteristics widely differ from person to person. People with obesity may experience more stress than the lean persons due to its impact on brain. (See Box 26.1).

Box 26.1: Obesity Takes Big Toll on the Brain

A new study finds obese people have 8 per cent less brain tissue than normal-weight individuals. Their brains look 16 years older than the brains of lean individuals, according to researchers. Those classified as overweight have 4 per cent less brain tissue and their brains appear to have aged prematurely by 8 years. The results, based on brain scans of 94 people in their 70s, represent "severe brain degeneration," said Paul Thompson, senior author of the study and a UCLA professor of neurology.

"That's a big loss of tissue and it depletes your cognitive reserves, putting you at much greater risk of Alzheimer's and other diseases that attack the brain," said Thompson. "But you can greatly reduce your risk for Alzheimer's, if you can eat healthily and keep your weight under control." The findings are detailed in the online edition of the journal Human Brain Mapping. Obesity packs many negative health effects, including increased risk of heart disease, Type 2 diabetes, hypertension and some cancers. It's also been shown to reduce sexual activity. More than 300 million worldwide are now classified as obese, according to the World Health Organization. Another billion are overweight. The main cause, experts say: bad diet, including an increased reliance on highly processed foods.

Obese people had lost brain tissue in the frontal and temporal lobes, areas of the brain critical for planning and memory, and in the anterior cingulate gyrus (attention and executive functions), hippocampus (long-term memory) and basal ganglia (movement), the researchers said in a statement today. Overweight people showed brain loss in the basal ganglia, the corona radiata, white matter comprised of axons, and the parietal lobe (sensory lobe). "The brains of obese people looked 16 years older than the brains of those who were lean, and in overweight people looked 8 years older," Thompson said. Obesity is measured by body mass index (BMI), defined as the weight in kilograms divided by the square of the height in meters. A BMI over 25 is defined as overweight, and a BMI of over 30 as obese.

Conflict may arise between different traits of the same person. Sudden changes may occur in one's life, leaving a tremendous impact, like death of a dear person, which makes that person ineffective temporarily. Stress arises while performing complex jobs during this period. Sometimes, an employee may realize after joining a job that his personal traits, aptitude and preferences may not suit the job requirements. In addition, food, drinking and smoking habits of individuals also cause stress. All these situations cause stress.

As indicated in personality, there are Type A and Type B personalities. Type A personality profile causes stress (See Exhibit 26.2).

Exhibit 26.2 Profile of Type A and Type B Personalities

Type A Profile

- Moves always
- Walks rapidly
- Eats rapidly
- Talks rapidly
- Impatient
- Seeks results immediately
- Does two or more things simultaneously
- Can't cope with leisure
- Is obsessed with numbers
- Measures success by quantity
- Is aggressive
- Is competitive
- Never accepts #2 position and
- Constantly feels under time pressure

Type B Profile

- Never punctual
- Is patient
- Cool and calm
- Does not brag
- Plays for fun but not to win
- Relaxes without guilt
- No deadlines
- Things happen as they do
- Mild and
- Never in a hurry

(**Soruce:** Fred Luthans, *op.cit.*, p. 336.)

(C) CONSEQUENCES OF DISTRESS

Distress has great impact on the psychological system which in turn affects physical and behavioural systems.

Though mild stress makes a person attentive, active and performs better, distress always has an adverse effect on his physical, psychological and behavioural systems. Many resort to smoking, drinking, overeating and show withdrawal behaviour due to stress. As stress takes over, it begins to tell on one's age. Distress has great impact on the psychological system which in turn affects physical and behavioural systems. It is found that constant stress causes diseases like blood pressure, ulcer, heart problems, acidity and diabetes which negatively affects work performance. Distress has an impact on family, social and professional lives. Hence, there is greater need to reduce stress to the level of mild stress which is essential for effective job performance.

Stress affects individual employee, employee's family and organization. Stress affects individual's physiology, psychology and behaviour.

Thus, stress affects individual employee, employee's family and organization. Stress affects individual's physiology, psychology and behaviour. Now we shall discuss these effects:

Consequences on Individual's Physiology

- Changes in metabolism,
- Increase in breathing rates,
- High blood pressure, and heart diseases,
- Insomnia, fatigue, headache, and skin rashes,
- Increase susceptibility to upper respiratory illness,
- Poor immune system functioning,
- Digestive disorders, and ulcer,
- Dry mouth, breathlessness,
- Eyes are bloodshot and puffy,
- Backache, and arthritis,
- Cancer,
- Diabetes,
- Cirrhosis of the liver, and
- Lung disease

Consequences on Individual's Psychology include

- Unnecessarily over-emotional,
- Loss in personal appearance,
- Poor concentration/ difficulty in remembering,
- Sadness, guilt, fatigue, and apathy,
- Loss of confidence in one's own ability,
- Lack of self worth,
- Perception far from reality,
- Negative attitude,
- Uncertain mindset,
- Burnout: A Syndrome of emotional, physical and mental exhaustion coupled with feelings of low self esteem/low self efficacy,

- Depersonalization: Becoming cynical towards others, treat others as objects, and hold negative attitudes towards others,
- Feeling of low self accomplishment: Low accomplishment, feel of won't succeed in future,
- Sexual dysfunction,
- Depression, and
- Sleep disturbances.

Consequences on Individual behaviour include

- Performance/ Productivity: Low stress and high stress lead to low performance while mild stress to peak performance,
- High stress results in absence of the employee from work,
- High stress results in change of jobs,
- Distress leads to rude behaviour of the employee,
- Stressful employees resort to smoking, and consumption of alcohol/drugs,
- High stress may result in employee involvement in accidents,
- High stressful employees may resort to violence, and
- High stressful employees may lose appetite, and may resort to over eating/under-eating.

Consequences on Employee's Family include

- High stressful employees may show anger with spouse and children,
- High stress may result in family fights, and conflicts,
- High stressful employees may pass stress to spouse and children,
- High stressful employees may be sexually dysfunctional,
- High stressful employees may face health problems, and
- High stressful employees may even resort to divorce his/her spouse.

Consequences on Organisation include

- High stressful employees can't make decisions efficiently,
- High stressful employees would be highly emotional and sometimes burnout which would affect interpersonal relations at the workplace,
- High stressful employees may change the jobs and organizations frequently, and
- High stressful employees may remain absent from work frequently.

(D) HOW TO MANAGE STRESS?

Over the years, many techniques have been advocated by stress researchers to manage stress. Practising managers can use some of these techniques to prevent or reduce stress. Some of the important techniques used by individual managers are discussed hereunder:

Individual Techniques

1. **Time management:** Time management has gained momentum with industrial growth and the economy. It has become important to find ways of performing impending managerial functions efficiently within the limited time that is available. Here, time management is a useful device. All the functions are ranked according to their importance and maximum available time is divided to perform these functions, providing enough time for each function depending upon their importance. Thus, more time may be spent for important work and less time for routine and unimportant work. This predetermined schedule can reduce stress that the manager faces with the pile of work that awaits him when he enters into his office.

2. **Work home transition:** This is comparatively a new concept that advocates love and consider affection of family life as best medicine for stress. It is very relaxing to spend time with spouse and children after a day's long hectic work. Evenings should be reserved to spend at home. It is advised not to carry office work home. Nothing from office should be carried home, not even thoughts. A useful tip is to spend with light and routine work at the end of office hours and to prepare mind for total relaxation. Relaxing at home in the evening, playing favourite game at club or swimming can help in next day's work.

3. **Work-life balance:** Work-life balance is balancing the priorities of career goals and family goals. Career goals include ambitions, promotions, employment status, monetary earnings and the like. Family goals include spending more time with family members for spiritual activities, pleasure leisure, health, education and careers of family members (See Box 26.2). This concept reduces the gap between work and family in the process of balancing the demands of both.

Box 26.2: Work-Life Balance: Give Due Importance to Family–The Mayonnaise Jar

The Mayonnaise Jar

When things in your life seem, almost too much to handle,
When 24 Hours in a day is not enough,
Remember the mayonnaise jar and 2 cups of coffee.
A professor stood before his philosophy class and had some items in front of him.
When the class began, wordlessly,
He picked up a very large and empty mayonnaise jar
And proceeded to fill it with golf balls.
He then asked the students, if the jar was full.
They agreed that it was.
The professor then picked up a box of pebbles and poured them into the jar. He shook the jar lightly.
The pebbles rolled into the open Areas between the golf balls.
He then asked the students again if the jar was full. They agreed it was.
The professor next picked up a box of sand and poured it into the jar.
Of course, the sand filled up everything else.
He asked once more if the jar was full. The students responded with a unanimous 'yes.'
The professor then produced two cups of coffee from under the table and poured the entire contents into the jar, effectively filling the empty space between the sand. The students laughed.
'Now,' said the professor, as the laughter subsided,
'I want you to recognize that this jar represents your life.
The golf balls are the important things - family, children, health,
Friends, and Favourite passions
Things that if everything else was lost and only they remained, Your life would still be full.
The pebbles are the other things that matter like your job, house, and car.
The sand is everything else —The small stuff.
'If you put the sand into the jar first,' He continued, there is no room for the pebbles or the golf balls.
The same goes for life.
If you spend all your time and energy on the small stuff,
You will never have room for the things that are important to you.
So...
Pay attention to the things that are critical to your happiness.
Play With your children.
Take time to get medical checkups.
Take your partner out to dinner.
There will always be time to clean the house and fix the disposal.
'Take care of the golf balls first —
The things that really matter.
Set your priorities. The rest is just sand.'
One of the students raised her hand and inquired what the coffee represented.
The professor smiled.
'I'm glad you asked'.
It just goes to show you that no matter how full your life may seem,
There's always room for a couple of cups of coffee with a friend.'
Please share this with other "Golf Balls"
I just did......

Source: E-Mail from Dr. Nissar Ahmed

Need for Work-Life Balance

Work and life demands need to be balanced in view of the following reasons:

- Increased competition due to globalisation, liberalisation and privatisation enhanced work pressures on employees;
- Increase in stress levels of employees due to high demands of jobs in terms of targets, high productivity, high quality, customisation and better customer relationship management;
- Increase in personal ambitions for higher level salary, status and power;
- Increase in pressure of family obligations along with the accelerating pace of living standards;
- High performance culture eroded the long-term loyalty and a "sense of corporate community";
- Managements expect more and more from their employees yet offers little job security in return;
- Job targets and attractive performance-based pay results spending more than 18 hours a day on the job and neglecting the normal family life including interpersonal and sexual relationships.

Impact on Women and Men Employees

The impact of work-life balance is relatively more on women employees compared to men employees. This is because; women employees are more responsible towards taking care of children, old parents in addition to home maintenance. However, it is felt that with the breaking down of joint families even male employees need to spend more time on family responsibilities and interests.

Why Employers are Interested?

Employers are interested in bringing balance between family and personal life and work life of employees as the imbalances affect workers' health, quality and productivity. In addition the long run contribution of employees towards quality, quantity, innovation and customer care is severely affected.

Employers are interested in bringing balance between personal life and work life of employees as the imbalances affect workers' health, quality and productivity.

In addition, the employees prefer to stay with those organisations which take care of their work and family life balance. Some organizations to be a model employer prefer to invest on work life – family life balance initiatives. Without any loss of performance, employers can introduce some initiatives like flexible working arrangements in the form of part time, casual and telecommuting work.

Methods of Balancing Work and Family Life

The methods of balancing work and family life include:

- Flexible working hours and flexible working place;
- Telecommuting;
- Introduction of stress releasing measures;
- On-the job training for imparting skills to do the job in a smart way;
- Introduction of employee-assistance programmes;
- Conducting frequent surveys to understand the work-balance issues and designing appropriate measures to reduce the imbalances;
- Introduction of job-sharing mechanisms;

- Providing benefits for additional time consumed by the job;
- Encourage the employees to avail recreational leave and sick leave by designing paid leave programmes;
- Introduction of special leave programmes for women like fully paid maternity leave that provide them job security while on leave also;
- Don't encourage employees to take work home often as well as large quantities;
- Allow employees to take leave for community service, legal issues and other specific issues of employee;
- Design the programme of getting the family members including the children to work place at least on Sundays.
- Organise social and community programmes like family oriented picnics, amusement parks, fishing, religious programmes, and birthday parties;
- Conducting the work-family balance programmes throughout the year as well as during the busy workschedule seasons.

Meditating Postures by Ramdev and practioners

4. **Physical exercises:** For those who do not have time or taste for outdoor games is physical exercises for a few minutes in the morning and evening help a lot. These exercises relax the body which becomes rigid due to the day long stress in the office and prepares the body for another day.

5. **Yoga and meditation:** Physical exercises can relax only the body but yoga and meditation help both body and mind. Both are used traditionally to keep body and mind fit. Some organisations have successfully introduced yoga and meditations as a technique of stress management. (See Box 26.3).

Box 26.3: How Compassionate Meditation Can Reduce Stress

Can you train yourself to be compassionate? A new study says, yes. According to researchers at the University of Wisconsin, cultivating compassion and kindness through meditation affects brain regions that can make you more empathetic to other peoples' mental and emotional states.

According to Richard Davidson, the lead researcher, professor of psychiatry and psychology and director of the HeathEmotions Research Institute, who studied a group of Tibetan monks who were master meditators, they exhibited significant activity in the brain's insula, which is important in detecting emotions and monitoring responses such as heart rate and blood pressure. In addition the temporal parietal juncture area of the right brain, associated with processing empathy became very active. Davidson reported that these two areas of the brain, studied with an fMRI, underwent significant activation in the test subjects.

The researchers concluded that an individual's capacity to cultivate compassion which involves regulating thoughts and emotions, may be useful in preventing depression, and that self-compassion, which is a necessary first step in developing compassion for others can be developed through compassionate meditation.

In another study by researchers at Emory University's center for Collaborative and Contemplative Studies, researchers concluded that compassionate meditation improved individuals' responses to stress. They reported that the test subjects, practicing compassionate meditation, showed reductions in inflammation and distress in response to stressors. This study reflects numerous studies which show that meditation is an effective method for controlling high blood pressure.

Together these two studies demonstrate that practicing compassionate meditation can be beneficial both to the individual and in relationships with others.

Source: http://www.psychologytoday.com/blog/wired-success/201002/how-compassionate-meditation-can-reduce-stress

6. **Humour:** Humour to a large extent contributes to relaxation, reducing mental stress and tension. Stress should not continue for long to affect the body. Those who are blessed with sense of humour and take issues in a positive sense, experience less stress. Reading humour stories or jokes and watching comedy shows also help to some extent in reducing stress.

7. **Change in the food, drinking and smoking habits:** Spicy food, junk food, fat foods and meat cause stress. Therefore, people experiencing stress should avoid these foods. A well balanced diet is crucial in preserving health and helping to reduce stress. Certain foods and drinks act as powerful stimulants to the body and hence are a direct cause of stress. This stimulation, although quite pleasurable in the short-term, may be quite harmful in the long run. Consuming too much of coffee, tea, coke and chocolates causes the release of adrenaline, thus increasing the level of stress. It is suggested that there is a link between caffeine intake and high blood pressure and high cholesterol levels. When taken in moderation, coffee can increase your alertness, increased activity in the muscles, nervous system and heart. Consume more stress-free foods as presented in Box 26.4.

Like caffeine, taken in moderation, alcohol is a very useful drug. It has been shown to benefit cardiovascular system. The irony of the situation is that most people take to drinking as way to combat stress. But, in actuality, they make it worse by consuming alcohol. Alcohol and stress, in combination, are quite deadly. Alcohol stimulates the secretion of adrenaline resulting in the problems such as nervous tension, irritability and insomnia. Excess alcohol will increase the fat deposits in the heart and decrease the immune function. Alcohol also limits the ability of the liver to remove toxins from the body. During stress, the body produces several toxins such as hormones. In the absence of its filtering by the liver, these toxins continue to circulate through the body resulting in serious damage.

Box 26.4: Stress-Free Foods

Eating right isn't just about weight loss—the nutrients you take in can have a serious effect on how you think, feel, and look! Our bodies and our feelings are nothing more than reflections of the various chemicals flowing through our system on a daily basis. Make sure those chemicals are the healthy kind you get from the right mix of fruits and vegetables, proteins and fats, and you'll feel healthier, more energetic, and happier than you have in years.

In Eat This, Not That! 2010, we compiled a list of eight foods that can help keep you young. You're only as young as you feel—so add these eight nutritious powerhouses to your daily diet, and start feeling (and acting and looking) years younger!

EGGS

Benefit: Weight loss

Substitute: Egg Beaters egg substitute

When it comes to breakfast, you can't beat eggs. (That was too easy, wasn't it?) Seriously, at a cost of only 72 calories, each large egg holds 6.3 grams of high-quality protein and a powerhouse load of vital nutrients. A study published in the International Journal of Obesity found that people who replace carbs with eggs for breakfast lose weight 65 per cent quicker. Researchers in Michigan were able to determine that regular egg eaters enjoyed more vitamins and minerals in their diets than those who ate few or no eggs. By examining surveys from more than 25,000 people, the researchers found that egg eaters are about half as likely to be deficient in vitamin B12, 24 per cent less likely to be deficient in vitamin A, and 36 per cent less likely to be deficient in vitamin E. And here's something more shocking: Those who ate at least four eggs a week had significantly lower cholesterol levels than those who ate fewer than one. Turns out, the dietary cholesterol in the yolk has little impact on your serum cholesterol.

Bonus tip: Breakfast is the most important meal of the day. Choose wisely—avoid the foods on our list of 20 Worst Breakfasts in America.

GREEN TEA

Benefit: Longer life span

Substitutes: Yerba mate, white tea, oolong tea, rooibos (red) tea

Literally hundreds of studies have been carried out documenting the health benefits of catechins, the group of antioxidants concentrated in the leaves of tea plants. Among the most startling studies was one published by the American Medical Association in 2006. The study followed more than 40,000 Japanese adults for a decade, and at the 7-year follow-up, those who had been drinking five or more cups of tea per day were 26 per cent less likely to die of any cause compared with those who averaged less than a cup. Looking for more-immediate results? Another Japanese study broke participants into two groups, only one of which was put on a catechin-rich green-tea diet. At the end of 12 weeks, the green-tea group had achieved significantly smaller body weights and waistlines than those in the control group. Why? Because researchers believe that catechins are effective at boosting metabolism.

Bonus tip: The average American consumes 400 liquid calories a day. Minimize that impact—avoid the 20 Worst Drinks in America.

GARLIC

Benefit: Cardiovascular strengthening

Substitutes: Onions, chives, leeks

Allicin, an antibacterial and antifungal compound, is the steam engine pushing forward garlic's myriad health benefits. The chemical is produced by the garlic plant as a defense against pests, but inside your body, it fights cancer, strengthens your cardiovascular system, decreases fat storage, and fights acne inflammation. To activate the most allicin possible, you have to crush the garlic as finely as you can: Peel the cloves, and then use the side of a eavy chef's knife to crush the garlic before carefully mincing it. Be sure not to overcook it, as too much heat will render the compound completely useless (and your food totally bitter).

Bonus tip: Some foods keep you looking young: Others can quite literally cure what ails you. Check out these super 15 Foods That Cure.

GRAPEFRUIT

Benefit: Weight loss

Substitutes: Oranges, watermelon, tomatoes

Just call it the better-body fruit. In a study of 100 obese people at the Scripps Clinic in California, those who ate half a grapefruit with each meal lost an average of 3.6 pounds over the course of 12 weeks, and some lost as many as 10 pounds. The study's control group, in contrast, lost a paltry 1/2 pound. But here's something even better: Those who ate the grapefruit also exhibited a decrease in insulin levels, indicating that their bodies had improved their ability to metabolize sugar. If you can't stomach a grapefruit-a-day regime, try to find as many ways possible to sneak grapefruit into your diet. Even a moderate increase in grapefruit intake should yield results, not to mention earn you a massive dose of lycopene—the cancer-preventing antioxidant found most commonly in tomatoes.

Bonus tip: Eat well and you'll feel younger and more vibrant. Add exercise to the mix and you'll practically erase markers of age.

GREEK YOGURT

Benefit: Feeling fulier for longer

Substitutes: Kefir and yogurt with "live and active cultures" printed on the product label

If it's dessert you want, go with regular yogurt; but if it's protein, go Greek. What sets the two apart? Greek yogurt is separated from the watery whey that sits on top of regular yogurt, and the process removes excessive sugars, such as lactose, and increases the concentration of protein by as much as three times. That means it fills your belly more like a meal than a snack. Plus a single cup has about a quarter of your day's calcium, and studies show that dieters on calcium-rich diets have an easier time losing body fat. In one study, participants on a high-calcium dairy diet lost 70 percent more body weight than those on a calorie-restricted diet alone. If only a similar claim could be made of everything you eat.

Bonus tip: Fruit-on-the-bottom yogurt is a classic example of a food that doesn't deserve its healthy reputation—see what else makes our list of the 30 "Healthy" Foods that Aren't.

AVOCADO

Benefit: Reduced risk of heart disease

Substitutes: Olive, canola, and peanut oils; peanut butter; tahini

Here's what often gets lost in America's fat phobia: Some fats are actually good for you. More than half the calories in each creamy green fruit comes from one of the world's healthiest fats, a kind called monounsaturates. These fats differ from saturated fats in that they have one double-bonded carbon atom, but that small difference at the molecular level amounts to a dramatic improvement in your health. Numerous studies have shown that monounsaturated fats both improve you cholesterol profile and decrease the amount of triglycerides (more fats) floating around in your blood. This can lower your risk of stroke and heart disease. Worried about weight gain? Don't be. There's no causal link between monounsaturated fats and body fat.

BELL PEPPERS

Benefit: Improved immune function

Substitutes: Carrots, sweet potatoes, watermelon

All peppers are loaded with antioxidants, but none so much as the brightly colored reds, yellows, and oranges. These colours result from carotenoids concentrated in the flesh of the peppers, and it's these same carotenoids that give tomatoes, *carrots, and grapefruits their healthy hues. The range of benefits provided by these colorful pigments include improved immune function, better communication between cells, protection against sun damage, and a diminished risk of several types of cancer. And if you can take the heat, try cooking with chili peppers. The bell pepper cousins are still loaded with carotenoids and vitamin C, but have the added benefit of capsaicins, temperature-raising phytochemicals that have been shown to fight headache and arthritis pain as well as boost metabolism.*

ALMONDS

Benefit: Improved memory

Substitutes: Walnuts, pecans, peanuts, sesame seeds, flaxseeds

An ounce of almonds—or about 23 nuts—a day provides nearly 9 grams of heart-healthy oleic acid; that's more than the amounts found in peanuts, walnuts, or cashews. This monounsaturated fat is known to be responsible for a flurry of health benefits, the most recently discovered of which is improved memory. Rats in California were better able to navigate a maze the second time around if they'd been fed oleic acid, and there's no reason to assume that the same treatment won't help you navigate your day-to-day life. If nothing else, snacking on the brittle nuts will take your mind off your hunger. Nearly a quarter of an almond's calories come from belly-filling fiber and protein. That's why, when researchers at Purdue fed study participants nuts or rice cakes, those who ate the nuts felt full for an hour and a half longer than the rice cake group did.

Bonus Tip: Before you go out to eat, grab a handful of almonds; it could help keep your hunger at bay.

Source: http://health.yahoo.com/experts/eatthis/38834/8-perfect-stay-young-foods/

8. **Playing with kids:** Playing with kids is really a pleasant situation to those who experience stress. In fact, the former Prime Minister of India Mrs. Indira Gandhi used to play with her grand children Rahul and Priyanka when they were kids particularly when she faced critical situations during the emergency period. The Human Resources Manager of TELCO used to play with his grandsons when there were strikes during 1986-87 led by Mr. Nair. The pure and creative minds of kids work as a great stress reliever.

9. **Hobbies:** Practising favourite hobbies in leisur times help in relaxing the mind, which in turn reduces stress. Many forget their hobbies after joining their professional careers. Hobbies can pull us out from the materialistic world. A good painting or a beautiful handicraft can give a person great satisfaction and keeps his spirits high. Depression and frustration that result from stress can be reduced through hobbies.

10. **Take measures to shift personality from 'A' to 'B':** Individual employees possessing personality 'A' traits should shift to personality 'B' type in order to reduce the effects of stress.

11. **Acquire emotional balance skills:** Handling relationships effectively under awkward circumstances makes you emotionally intelligent. By delaying the gratification of reacting to the situation instantaneously, you may come out a winner.

12. **Be philosophical:** Listen to philosophical lectures and discourses (See Exhibit 26.3).

Exhibit 26.3 Golden Principles of Stress-Free Living

- Stress is a messenger - listen to it.
- Consider your pressures a challenge. Your coping ability will increase.
- Meet, greet and beat your stress successfully.
- There is always benefit hidden behind every event in life.
- Don't compare yourself with others. You are unique.
- Do not repeat your past mistakes; Past is a cancelled cheque.
- Do not worry about the future. Future is a promissory note.
- Don't be jealous, be content.
- Don't feel superior, give up your ego.
- The world is a huge drama. Don't get upset by scenes of sorrow and tragedy.

- Spare time to help others, and your worries will soon be forgotten.
- When you are ill or facing problems, be happy, you are simply paying off past debts.
- Your critics are instruments to carry you forward, so consider them as well-wishers.
- Don't criticize others behind their back.
- Don't think of taking revenge. Forgive and forget.
- Give happiness to others, never think of giving sorrow.
- Observe your mind, control your mental traffic, and you won't have irrelevant thoughts.
- Laughter is an antidote to stress. Laugh at your mistakes but not at others.
- Surrender all your worries to God and relax.
- Practise meditation for 15 minutes daily. It will bring peace, bliss and relaxation of mind and body.

(**Source:** Eswareeya Viswavidyalaya)

The above explained techniques more or less work towards reducing the impact of stress than prevent it in toto except for time management. Time management can be used to prevent stress. Stress management is not only managing stress after it has occurred, but also for prevention of stress. This can be best achieved through organisational means rather than by an individual. This is because, individuals are either reluctant or find no time to follow the above explained devices to cope up with stress.

Other individual stress coping strategies include:

- Stress is messenger — Listen to it,
- Pressures are challenges — increase copings,
- Meet, greet and beat your stress successfully,
- Don't worry of the future,
- Don't feel ego,
- Don't think of revenge,
- Life is short—Try to Enjoy,
- Manage your time properly,
- Think positively = positive attitudes,
- Think from others' point of view,
- Develop 'Can do attitude',
- Change/shift your attitudes,
- Discuss/share with others,
- Use open/free communication,
- Use detailed communication,
- Communicate to all concerned,
- Develop ability/willingness to communicate,
- Update communication,
- Negotiations/face-to-face discussions,
- Hand-shake,
- Wash your eyes and face with cold water,
- Comb your hair with fingers,
- See beautiful pictures,

- See attractive sceneries,
- Drink at least three litres of water a day,
- Divert your attention on to other topic/issue, and
- Develop hobbies like painting, dancing, and singing.

Organisations also started employing various strategies to help their employees in reducing their stress.

Organisational Strategies

The organisations are in fact the worst affected, due to stress experienced by their employees. This realisation paved the way for organisations to take steps to prevent stress.

The organisations are in fact the worst affected due to stress experienced by their employees.

These measures include:

- Establishment of health clubs in the organisations itself, where all the employees are supposed to be checked up regularly. Different health plans are devised by experts for different people depending upon their needs which are to be followed strictly. The employees have to undergo light exercise everyday before actually entering into work as physical exercises are the best means of sweating out stress and prepare for day's work.
- Organisations are also taking steps to create supportive organizational climate so that employees can feel secure and show their abilities.
- Efforts are also being made to make working conditions pleasant, as bad physical conditions could be potential sources of stress.
- Many organisations are providing with counselling facilities to support its employees psychologically and morally.
- They also devise career plans to remove any ambiguity as to their career development.

Other organizational coping strategies include:

- Employee assistance programmes,
- Wellness programmes,
- Less controls,
- Flat structures,
- Employee empowerment, and
- Stress management training.

(E) MILD STRESS:CONDUCIVE FOR ORGANISATIONAL EFFECTIVENESS

There is always the other side of the coin and so is stress *i.e.,* the positive aspects of stress, which is called mild stress. Mild stress is very essential for effective and efficient working. The concept of mild stress holds good especially in the Indian context, where mostly government employees at clerical grades are employed in routine jobs which do not pose any stress. In due course, the employee becomes a lazy day-dreamer.

Mild stress is very essential for effective and efficient working.

A clerk's job is only making entries or some simple calculations. The employee however starts his job with great zeal and works with enthusiasm and care. But this behaviour lasts only for a few months. As the employee realises that there is no stress accompanying the work, develops disinterest towards work and spends his time otherwise.

Stress need not be caused by assigning heavy work to be done within a short time. If done so, it may again lead to fatigue and depression in the employees. But moderate and desirable level of stress *i.e.,* mild stress can always be caused through the following methods:

- **Time frame:** Determining the fixed time for each task results in mild stress. But care should be taken to provide sufficient time to get work done efficiently.
- **Time and motion studies:** Time and motion studies are very important devices that can be employed to find out the required time to perform each job. Time specification can pose some stress which will yield positive results.
- **Job rotation:** By rotating the employees among various jobs, they are made to undergo mild stress, apart from other benefits. Learning a new job and putting it into practise also result in mild stress.
- **Variations in job methods:** Change in methods of doing the job from time to time leads to mild stress to the job holders. But it helps the employees to adapt to any kind of changes comfortably in the future.
- **Incentives:** They are the best means of achieving mild stress. To avail of the incentives, the employees are under stress to perform the jobs in time and efficiently.
- **Proper channel of authority, clear cut powers and duties:** These should be established. The superiors should be made responsible to get things done from his/her subordinates and he/she should be delegated with proper authority, so that the boss may put his subordinates under stress. The boss should plan the work, co-ordinate employees and control them.

Resistance can be expected from employees initially for all these changes. But after some time, they come out of monotony in work and start enjoying their jobs. Human resources cannot be kept idle especially in developing countries like ours whose major asset is human resource. But to one's distress, this type of problem appears mostly in developing countries.

Below optimum level of stress is mostly experienced by middle level managers with paper work. The lower level workers with physical effort experience mild stress and top level managers experience distress with their pressing mental activities. The human resources of employees who do not experience any stress at all can be better utilised by causing mild stress, with the help of the above measures.

Two extremes of stress need to be balanced and an optimum level is to be arrived at. Organisations today are becoming more and more stress conscious. With the co-operation of employees, the organisations can effectively manage stress.

KEY TERMS

- Stress
- Group Dynamics
- Meditation
- Mild Stress
- Eustress
- Yoga
- Disstress
- Job Rotation
- Incentives
- Anxiety
- Type 'B' Profile
- Organisational Stressors
- Tension
- Type 'A' Profile
- Philosophical
- Environmental Stressors

QUESTIONS

1. What is stress? Differentiate Distress from Eu-stress.
2. Discuss the causes and consequences of stress.
3. What are the various individual and organisational strategies to manage stress?
4. "Mild stress is desirable and essential for individual and organisational performance." Discuss.
5. What is distress? How do you reduce it?

REFERENCES

1. T. A. Beehr and J. E. Newman, *Job Stress, Employee Health and Organisational Effectiveness*, *Personnel Psychology*, 1978, pp. 665-699.
2. Fred Luthans, *op.cit.*, p. 330.

CHAPTER 27

CASE METHOD AND CASES

Chapter Outline

(A) Case Method

- Introduction
- How to Analysis to Case?
- Participating in a Class Discussion
- Methods of Case Discussion
- Format of the Written Case Analysis Report

(B) Cases

- Consequences of Different Perceptions
- Same Act: Perceived Differently
- Personality: Viewed Differently
- Flexibility in Values: Affect Employees
- Motivated Beyond Money

Learning Objectives

After studying this Chapter, you should be able to:

- ✓ To know the meaning of case and need for case method of teaching in management education;
- ✓ To understand the method of case analysis;
- ✓ To participate in classroom discussion of case analysis; and
- ✓ To write the case analysis.

(A) CASE METHOD

(a) INTRODUCTION

Almost all business schools across the globe use the case method as the prime teaching technique for the course on Business Policy and Strategic Management. Students of strategic management practice business policy and strategic management through case analysis.

What is a Case?

A case is a description of management problem or situation as viewed or presented to a decision maker. It is a pedagogical tool which involves a discussion centered on the case. It sets a situation with all the ancillary facts, figures, emotions, opinions, views, grapevine and the like. A case presents facts, the events and organisational circumstances surrounding a particular managerial situation. It puts the readers at the scene of the action and familiarises them with all the relevant circumstances.[1] The case method includes the special type of instructional material that is developed for the purpose and the special technique of using that material in the instructional process.[2]

Need for Case Method

Professor Charles Gragg[3] observed that managerial skills and expertise cannot be acquired through mere listening to lectures and reading books. He suggested that readymade answers about the practice of management cannot be found in text books. This is because of the fact that each managerial situation is different from others with unique aspects, requiring its own diagnosis and judgment. Cases provide the tomorrow's managers with a valuable way to practice wrestling with the actual problems of actual managers in actual companies.[4]

Most of the management students have no or limited knowledge about the practical aspects of management. Cases bridge this gap to some extent and help the students to substitute for practical knowledge by: *(i)* giving broader exposure to different types of situations, companies and industries, *(ii)* placing the students in different roles of case, *(iii)* providing an opportunity to apply principles,concepts and techniques of management to problem situations, and *(iv)* including the students to prepare managerial action plans and to deal with related issues.

Objectives of Case Analysis[5]

The objectives of the case analysis are:

(i) To increase the understanding of the students of what managers should and should not do in guiding a business to success.

(ii) To build the students' skills in conducting strategic analysis in a variety of situations, companies and industries.

(iii) To provide the students valuable practice in diagnosing strategic issues, evaluating strategic alternatives with the help of SWOT analysis and formulating practicable plans of action based on the ground realities.

(iv) To enhance the students sense of business judgment as opposed to accepting the opinion of the teacher or "back-of-the-book" answers.

(v) To provide the students an in-depth exposure to a variety of companies and industries, thereby gaining something close to actual business experience.

Thus, the purpose of the case method is to enhance the students' skills in sizing up situations and developing their managerial judgment about what needs to be done and how to do it. Case analysis helps the students to think actively, to offer critical analysis, to propose action plans based on ground realities, and to explain defend their assessments.

(b) HOW TO ANALYSE A CASE?[6]

Students who are habituated to lecture method of teaching are required to re-orient their study habits. A case assignment unlike lecture method of teaching, requires conscientious preparation before class. Student cannot get any benefit from case discussion or he/she can't contribute to the discussion unless, he/she prepares himself/herself thoroughly for the case discussion. The student has to prepare to reflect carefully on the situation presented, develop reasonable thoughts, write well supported analysis of the situation and a sound, defensible set of suggestions and recommendations about the strategic actions need to be taken. The students can follow the approach discussed below.

1. ***Read the case material quickly to get familiarity:*** The first time reading of the case provide the students an initial understanding of the situations, issues involved in the case etc.
2. ***Read the case a second time:*** This step provides a full command of the facts, information, opinions, views, company culture, values etc.
3. ***Read the exhibits, appendices etc., carefully:*** This step provides full information about the case.
4. ***Study the case:*** The student should recall the difference between reading and studying. Read in-between the lines as the problems may not be apparent in the case material itself. Students have to prepare notes about facts, important situations, information, less important information, situations etc.
5. ***Identify the strategic issues:*** Students have to identify the strategic issues in the case. It helps to identify the tools and techniques of analysis and process. As mentioned in step 4, Some times the students are required to identify the strategic issues and problems by reading in-between the lines or by digging the information given.
6. ***Diagnose the key issues:*** The students should use their creative or innovative skills, analytical skills and application skills to diagnose the key issue or key problem in the case. This is the crucial step in the case analysis.
7. ***Check the diagnosis:*** Students have to check the diagnosis made with the help of questions given at the end of the case. The students should think repeatedly even, if the diagnosis matches with the questions. Students may move to the next step after confirming the diagnosis.
8. ***Support diagnosis and opinions with reasons and evidence:*** Students have to support their diagnosis and opinions with reasons and evidence.
9. ***Checkout conflicting opinions and make some judgments about the validity of all the data and information provided:*** Case material may provide contradicting opinions, views and information. Students have to evaluate the opinions, views, data and information provided with the help of their skills of inferences and judgment.
10. ***Start analysis of the issues:*** After diagnosing the basic issues all other issues relate to the basic issue should be analysed. These issues include calculation of financial ratios, production figures, sales figures, human resource costs and benefits etc.
11. ***Identify and make notes of data and information required to solve the problem diagnosed:*** The students have to use the conceptual knowledge and skills of management in identifying the data and information required to develop solutions.

12. ***Compare the data and information available in the case with the data required to offer recommendations:*** If both these two do not match with each other and data available are not sufficient to solve the problem, the student has to identify the gaps in information available.

13. ***Fill-in the gaps:*** The student has to fill-in the gaps through inferences and assumptions with the help of information available, conceptual knowledge and by reading in between the lines of the case material.

14. ***Re-check the diagnosis:*** In view of the step (13), the student has to re-check the diagnosis and re-diagnose the basic problem, if necessary.

15. ***Use tools and techniques of strategic analysis:*** Strategic analysis is not just a collection of opinions and views. It has powerful tools and techniques as presented in the text. The students have to use these tools and techniques.

16. ***Analyse the case:*** Students have to analyse the case thoroughly with the help of strategic management tools, techniques, their opinions, judgment etc.

17. ***Generate alternative solutions:*** The detailed case analysis normally pave the way to generate alternative solutions or recommendations to solve the basic problem diagnosed. The strategic management concepts should be inter-weaved with the issues identified, in developing alternative solutions.

18. ***Evaluate the alternative solutions:*** Student should evaluate each of the alternative solutions in terms of their strengths to implement, weaknesses, opportunities provided by the external environment for implementation and threats posed by the external environment in the process of implementation. Further, the possible outcome of each solution should also be considered in the process of evaluation.

19. ***Rank of Solutions:*** The student has to rank the solutions on the basis of their score in SWOT analysis.

20. ***Select the best solution:*** The student should recognise that there is no single best solution for all situations. It varies from individual to individual and from situation to situation and based on judgment. However, the student can select the best solution based on the ranking of alternative solutions.

21. ***Prepare an action plan:*** The students have to prepare a detailed plan for executing the best solution. The possible hindrances should also be pointed out along with the means to overcome them in the plan of action.

22. ***Communicate the results to parties concerned:*** The student should prepare detailed communications and address them to the parties regarding the plan of action.

(c) PARTICIPATING IN A CLASS DISCUSSION

Participating in a class room discussion of a case is different from participating in a lecture class. The students have to take active role in case discussion. The role of the instructor includes: initiation of discussion, solicit student participation, keep the discussion on track, moderate the discussion, offer alternative views and ideas, inter-weaving the concepts and strategic management techniques in to the problem situations, play the devil's advocate (*i.e.*, if not students play active role jump into the discussion and offer opposing views), lead the discussion and the like.

The role of the students include: Analysing the situations, offering comments on reading in between the lines, identifying the strategic issues, diagnose the key issues, using the strategic tools and techniques, identifying the gaps in data and information, fill-in the gaps, developing alternative solutions, preparing and presenting the recommendations and defending them etc. Students have to broaden their views and thinking when the fellow students offer criticism or suggestions or modifications to their ideas, as the old adage goes, "two heads are better than one." In view of the different views and lines of thinking and analysis, the class will do a more penetrating and searching work of case analysis than an individual student. Normally, group effort is effective and efficient than individual effort.[7] Exhibit -1 presents the expectations from the student in a class room of case analysis.

Exhibit 27.1 Expectations from the Student in the Class-room of Case Analysis

1. Expect students to dominate the discussion and do most of the talking. The case method enlists a maximum of individual participation in class discussion. It is not enough to be present as a silent observer, if every student took this approach, there would be no discussion.
2. Expect the instructor to assume the role of extensive questioner and listener.
3. Be prepared for the instructor to probe for reasons and supporting analysis.
4. Expect and tolerate challenges to the views expressed. All students have to be willing to submit their conclusions for scrutiny and rebuttal. Each student needs to learn to state his or her views without fear of disapproval and to overcome the hesitation of speaking out. Learning respect for the views and approaches of others is an integral part of case analysis exercises. But there are times when it is OK to swim against the tide of majority opinion. In the practice of management, there is always room for originality and unorthodox approaches. So while discussion of a case is a group process, there is no compulsion for you or anyone else to cave in and conform to group opinions and consensus.
5. Don't be surprised if you change your mind about some things as the discussion unfolds. Be alert to how these changes affect your analysis and recommendations (in the event you get called on).
6. Expect to learn a lot from each case discussion; use what you learn to be better prepared for the next case discussion.

(**Source:** Modified version from: Arthur A. Thompson and A.J. Strickland, op. cit., pp. 286-287.)

Exhibit-2 presents the activities that a student should do, to be an active participant in the class discussion.

Exhibit 27.2 Activities to be done by Students to be Active Participates

- Although you should do your own independent work and independent thinking, don't hesitate before (and after) class to discuss the case with other students. In real life, managers often discuss the company's problems and situation with other people to refine their own thinking.
- In participating in the discussion, make a conscious effort to contribute, rather than just talk. There is a big difference between saying something that builds the discussions and offering a long wondering what the point was.
- Avoid the us of "I think," "I believe," I feel"; instead say, "My analysis shows.." and "The sampan should do... because.. " Always give supporting reasons and evidence for your views; then your instructor won't have to ask you "Why?" every time you make a comment.
- In making your points, assume that everyone has read the case and knows what it says; avoid reciting and rehashing information in the case instead, use the data and information to explain your assessment of the situation and to support your position.
- Always prepare good notes (usually two or three pages' worth) for each case and use them extensively when you speak. There's no way you can remember everything off the top of your head — especially the results of your number crunching. To reel off the numbers or to present all five reasons why, instead of one, you will need good notes. When you have prepared good notes to the study questions and use them as the basis for your comments, everybody in the room will know you are well prepared, and your contribution to the case discussion will stand out.

(***Source:*** Arthur A. Thompson, Jr., & A.J. Strickland III, *op. cit.*, p. 287.)

(d) METHODS OF CASE DISCUSSION

1. Individual and Syndicate Methods: Oral Discussion

There are two methods of case discussion *viz., (i)* individual method and *(ii)* syndicate or group method. In case of individual method, the instructor opens the discussion in the class, all the students participate in the discussion. The instructor moderates and coordinates the discussion. In case of syndicate or group method, students are formed into syndicates or groups in one session of the class and each group analyses, discusses the case and prepares the written report and presents the same to the class in the next session for comments and further discussion. Then all the students listen to the reports of all groups and then further discuss the case based on the reports. Finally, the class will offer recommendations and plan of action.

2. Preparing a Written Case Analysis

A written case analysis is more or less similar to the class discussion of case analysis. As there is no role of instructor and classmates, the student has to think and analyse the case from all directions, criticise his own ideas and views, modify them. Student has to follow all the guidelines of case analysis presented earlier.[8] Exhibit -3 presents the guidelines for written case analysis.

Exhibit 27.3 Guidlines for Written Case Analysis

1. Provide a sharply focused diagnosis of strategic issues and key problems.
2. Offer analysis and evidence to back-up your conclusions. Do not rely on unsupported opinions and over generalizations. Present logical arguments backed up with facts and figures.
3. Use tables and charts to present the calculations clearly and efficiently, if analysis involves important qualitative calculations. Though, you present exhibits and annexure at the end of the report, cite important figures and calculations in the text of the report. Highlight the conclusions to be drawn from the exhibits.
4. Use the conceptual knowledge, inter-weave it with problem situations. Thus demonstrate that you have the command on the strategic concepts and analytical tools you have been exposed.
5. Your interpretation of the evidence should be reasonable and objective. Don't prepare one-sided argument. Don't try to exaggerate or over-dramatise. Inject balance into our analysis avoid emotional rhetoric. Write as "My analysis shows ... "Don't write," "I think...," "I feel..." or "I believe...".
6. Avoid recommending any thing you would not yourself be willing to do if you were in management's shoes.
7. State your recommendations in sufficient detail to be meaningful.
8. Be sure the company is financially able to implement you recommendations.
9. Your recommendations should be practically viable and feasible to implement.
10. Your report should be well organized and well written.

(*Source:* Modified Version From: Arthur A. Thompson and A.J. Strickland *op. cit.*, pp. 288-289.)

(e) FORMAT OF THE WRITTEN CASE ANALYSIS REPORT

The first paper will be individual case analysis. The student's written report must be turned in during the class period in which it is presented. The package will begin with an executive summary that is at least half a page long, but no longer than one page. It will have three basic components.

1. Statement of the problem;
2. Brief discussion of the main considerations; and
3. Recommended action.

The purpose of the executive summary is to brief a busy upper-level decision maker. It must stand alone, so that it could be used independently of the detailed analysis which follows in the package. It must give a clear picture of the problem in a nutshell, with a recommendation. A recommendation of some kind must be made. Waffling will not be acceptable. If you cannot *Method of Case Analysis* 505 decide what to do, at least describe the additional information you would need in order to make a recommendation.

Next in the package will be a five-page case analysis which builds on the executive summary with a more thorough discussion. This portion is aimed at the decision-makers' aides. It should explain the logic of your recommendations, and fill in background on the points made in the executive summary. Since the audience of executive aides would not all be familiar with them, avoid using business jargon and technical business terms unless you give a plain language explanation along with them. In other words, you must convince the decision maker and his/her aides in plain English that you have gotten to the root of a problem that requires their attention and that your recommendation is the best alternative for solving it.

Each case analysis will be examined and presented based on the following format:

1. Brief resume of significant events
2. External analysis
3. Industry analysis
4. Internal analysis
5. Statement of the problem
6. Goals
7. Assumptions
8. For *each* of the alternatives:
   (a) Compare advantages/disadvantages or strength and weaknesses
   (b) Time factors — short-range considerations versus long-range factors — timing
   (c) Resources
   (d) Opportunities and threats.
9. Decision
10. Implementation
11. Feedback (control)
12. Communication to the parties concerned.

As you write the executive summary and case analysis, remember that the intended audience works for the company you are advising. They will already be familiar with the basic facts about the company. Instead, give them new insights into the situation, without simply repeating what they already know. Make it a point to get to the point.

REFERENCES

1. Arthur A. Thompson and A.J. Strickland, *op. cit.*, p. 280.
2. S. Venkatesh and Nina Jacob, "Case Method: An Effective Training tool," Management Review, April-June 1996, p. 54.
3. Charles I. Gragg, "Because Wisdom Can't be Told," in M.P. McNair (ed.) "Case Method at the Harvard Business School," New York, 194, p. 11.
4. Arthur A. Thompson and A.J. Strickland, *op. cit.*, p. 281.
5. Charles I. Gragg, *op. cit.*, pp. 12-14 and D.R. Schoen and Phillip A. Sprague, "What is the Case Method?" in M.P. Nair (ed.), "The Case Method at the Harvard Business School," pp. 78-79.
6. Arthur A. Thompson and A.J. Strickland, *op. cit.*, pp. 282-283.
7. *Ibid.*, p. 286.
8. *Ibid.*, pp. 287-288.

(B) CASES

(1) Consequences of Different Perceptions

The workshop of a small urea factory functions in two shifts-'A' and 'B'. Mr. Ramu, a mechanical engineer, has recently been promoted as manager of shift 'A'. He has trained his workers in the theoretical aspects of their job, resulting in abandoning of rule of thumb practices and increase in the productivity. Mr. Ramu has become popular among workers.

The increase in efficiency has resulted in extra work being given to shift 'A'. While workers resent it, Mr. Ramu deems it recognition of the efficiency of shift. Some workers have also sought transfer to other shift.

But the workers working in shift "A" perceived that the increased efficiency is due to their loyalty and commitment and Mr. Ramu has been stealing the credit. As such they decided to teach a lesson to Mr.Ramu.

Recently, one morning, shift supervisor informed Mr. Ramu that all his workers desired to attend the funeral of the father of a colleague and the management should provide conveyance for this purpose as has been the past practice in such cases. Mr. Ramu not only refused to provide conveyance but objected to all his workers abstaining from work. The workers did not relent and Mr. Ramu arranged gate-passes for all those who wanted to go to the funeral.

Next day, Mr. Ramu came to know that 75 per cent had gone to a cinema instead of the funeral. He issued memos to some of them. The workers were angered by this and approached the union for intervention. The news of the event caused protest in almost all sections in the factory.

Different perception of the employees resulted in this incident.

Questions

1. Can you suggest measures to avert this situation by correcting the perception of employees?
2. Why do workers and Mr. Ramu have different perceptions of the performance of shift 'A'?
3. Can you identify the factors responsible for different kinds of perceptions by the top management and employees?

(2) Same Act : Perceived Differently

Ramesh is an employee of Ind-Chem Limited. He has been working in this organisation for the last 20 years. For several years he has been a supervisor in the human resource management section. He is very loyal to the organisation and tries sincerely to follow the company's policies and the orders of the higher-level management. Higher-level managers think/perceive highly of him and he is well liked by them.

On the other hand, his subordinates have the opposite opinion/perception of Ramesh. They feel that he is excessively concerned with pleasing the higher-ups and not very much concerned about the needs and concerns of his subordinates. They perceive that they are underpaid and over-worked relative to people in the other departments. Whenever one of them goes with a new idea or a suggestion to him, he always seems to have five reasons why it cannot be done. There is considerable dissatisfaction in the department. Performance of the department began to suffer. Higher-ups seem to be oblivious to the problem. Ramesh viewed that he has been performing his duties in order to achieve the organisational goals.

The same act of Ramesh has been viewed in two totally opposite manners by the higher management and the subordinates.

The higher-ups perceive that the hard work done by Ramesh is due to his commitment to the organisation while his subordinates perceive that it is his way of pleasing the higher management.

Questions

1. Can you identify the factors responsible for different kinds of perceptions by the top management and employees?
2. What is the role played by Mr. Ramesh for providing enabling factors for a diversified perception?

(3) Personality: Viewed Differently

Pratyusha is in the last semester of the final year MBA at Andhra University. Pratyusha's friends had frequently teased her about her choice of an Accounting and Finance specialisation. The standard line was, "Pratyusha you just don't strike me as an accountant." Pratyusha seemed different in her attitude from most of her peers. She was active in her social circle and had at least two hundred best friends. Her mother frequently described her as having the "metabolism of a humming bird." Her friends stereotyped her as being in a sales or personnel job (based on her attitude) rather than sitting quietly in some isolated office preparing accounting reports.

About six weeks prior to her graduation, the job offers began to crystallize. Pratyusha narrowed her choices to a trainee position with a Hyderabad mortgage company, and a staff accounting job in Secunderabad with a prestigious national hotel chain. She accepted the accounting position, excited about opportunity to work in the hotel business.

After six months on the job, Pratyusha looked back on her experience. "I really enjoy my job. I am involved with accounts payable, preparing monthly financial statements, and doing special projects as and when the need arose. I think I am doing a good job; at least everything John (Her boss) has told me is positive. Yet, I can't ignore the contrast comments by the people I work with in accounting and some of my friends in other areas of the hotel, that I'd be happier and have better career opportunities if I was in marketing or human resources. I think that's nonsense! Sure, I'd be interested in getting into human resources. It would be a real challenge when i would be running my own hotel one day if it so happens. But the job vacancy was in accounting and that's what I studied in the Business Management Department."

She says: We should be adaptable to the needs of the business and the opportunities available rather than having static personality traits or aptitude. Gone are those days!"

Questions

1. Do you think that the comments of Ms. Pratyusha hold good?
2. Do you think that Ms. Pratyusha would have done better had she be in marketing or human resource area?

(4) Flexibility in Values: Affect Employees

Biswajit, an engineer with a private airline company, had always wanted to work at the firm's headquarters office located in city on the west coast. That city was near his native town in which Biswajit had spent his childhood days. He still remembers his childhood days and would like to spend as much time as possible in his native place.

Each year, the company offered the opportunity to move to the headquarters city to a large number of its top flight engineers. Biswajit had hoped to be on the list, but it finally became apparent to him that he would never have the opportunity to move to the headquarters city.

He waited for several years to have an opportunity to be posted the headquarters.

Over a cup of coffee, one day Biswajit was heard saying: "Even if they offered me the chance to move to headquarters city, I would not take it. It is too close to my old home. I like things just like they are. I hope they never make the offer to me. I would not want to say no to the company."

Mr. Biswajit overheard the discussions of the two senior managers regarding the "change in the company values that people would work effectively when they are placed far from their native towns and as such the company should not encourage its employees to think of a transfer near to their native towns."

Biswajit was frustrated regarding the change in the company's values. Thus, the frequent change in values upset employees and other stakeholders.

Questions

1. Do you think that the changes in company values help the company in achieving its mission?
2. Do you think that the employees should also change their personal values as and when there is a change in the company values?
3. Why does Mr. Biswajit feel different from that of the company's values?

(5) Motivated Beyond Money

Mr. Murthy- Human Resource Manager of Coca Cola (India) introduced a programme — 'Beyond 100%' — in order to exploit human potentialities with a view to enhance productivity and sales. Salary range for employees has been higher than their counterparts in other comparable organisations. The programme includes job rotation, recognition, employee growth along with his/her performance, providing challenging and achievement-oriented work.

Ms. Kiranmayi – a newly joined Industrial Relations Executive has been identified as a potential candidate for sales in a critical geographical area. She accepted the job change and assumed the responsibilities of the new job. She could increase the sales in the that particular area beyond 100% during 2007-08 and 2008-09. The Assistant Sales Manager (ASM) concerned was very much impressed with the techniques. ASM observed her work approach and performance particularly dealing with the dealers, providing additional reading material to them and so on and so forth.

ASM then had detailed discussions with Ms. Kiranmayi regarding her ideas. He designed a new and challenging job, i.e., Dealer-Relationship Manager and got the approval for this job from the central office of the company.

He arranged a meeting of the sales executives in September 2009 and appraised the new approaches adopted by them including those of Ms.Kiranmayi. Most of the sales executives were impressed of the innovative approaches of Ms. Kiranmayi. ASM announced in the meeting that Ms. Kiranmayi will be the Dealer–Relationship Manager of Andhra Pradesh region from November 2009 onwards. Ms. Kiranmayi did not expect this reward and recognition, and was very much thrilled.

She took up the new job with greater inducement and introduced several innovative approaches in motivating the dealers in turn to induce the customers and to explore new markets and new customers with various inducements and recognition based rewards, etc.

The company could achieve high sales beyond expectations in 2010 summer. "Motivation technique beyond money motivated Ms. Kiranmayi beyond 100%", ASM quoted in his inaugural speech of 2010 Sales Executives Meet, Further, he added, "Let us do it for everyone in our company".

Questions

1. Apply motivation theories you have studied to this case and analyse the theories further.
2. How can you create new jobs using motivation concepts?

QUESTIONS

1. Can you suggest measures to avert this situation by correcting the perception of employees?
2. Why do workers and Mr. Ramu have different perceptions of the performance of shift 'A'?
3. Can you identify the factors responsible for different kinds of perceptions by the top management and employees?
4. What is the role played by Mr. Ramesh for providing enabling factors for a diversified perception?
5. Do you think that the comments of Ms. Pratyusha hold good?
6. Do you think that Ms. Pratyusha would have done better had she be in marketing or human resource area?
7. Do you think that the changes in company values help the company in achieving its mission?
8. Do you think that the employees should also change their personal values as and when there is a change in the company values?
9. Why does Mr. Biswajit feel different from that of the company's values?
10. Apply motivation theories you have studied to this case and analyse the theories further.
11. How can you create new jobs using motivation concepts?

REFERENCES

1. Arthur A. Thompson and A.J. Strickland, *op. cit.*, p. 280.
2. S. Venkatesh and Nina Jacob, "Case Method: An Effective Training tool," Management Review, April-June 1996, p. 54.
3. Charles I. Gragg, "Because Wisdom Can't be Told," in M.P. McNair (ed.) "Case Method at the Harvard Business School," New York, 194, p. 11.
4. Arthur A. Thompson and A.J. Strickland, *op. cit.*, p. 281.
5. Charles I. Gragg, *op. cit.*, pp. 12-14 and D.R. Schoen and Phillip A. Sprague, "What is the Case Method?" in M.P. Nair (ed.), "The Case Method at the Harvard Business School," pp. 78-79.
6. Arthur A. Thompson and A.J. Strickland, *op. cit.*, pp. 282-283.
7. *Ibid.*, p. 286.
8. *Ibid.*, pp. 287-288.